Wiltshire Record Society

(formerly the Records Branch of the Wiltshire Archaeological and Natural History Society)

VOLUME 59

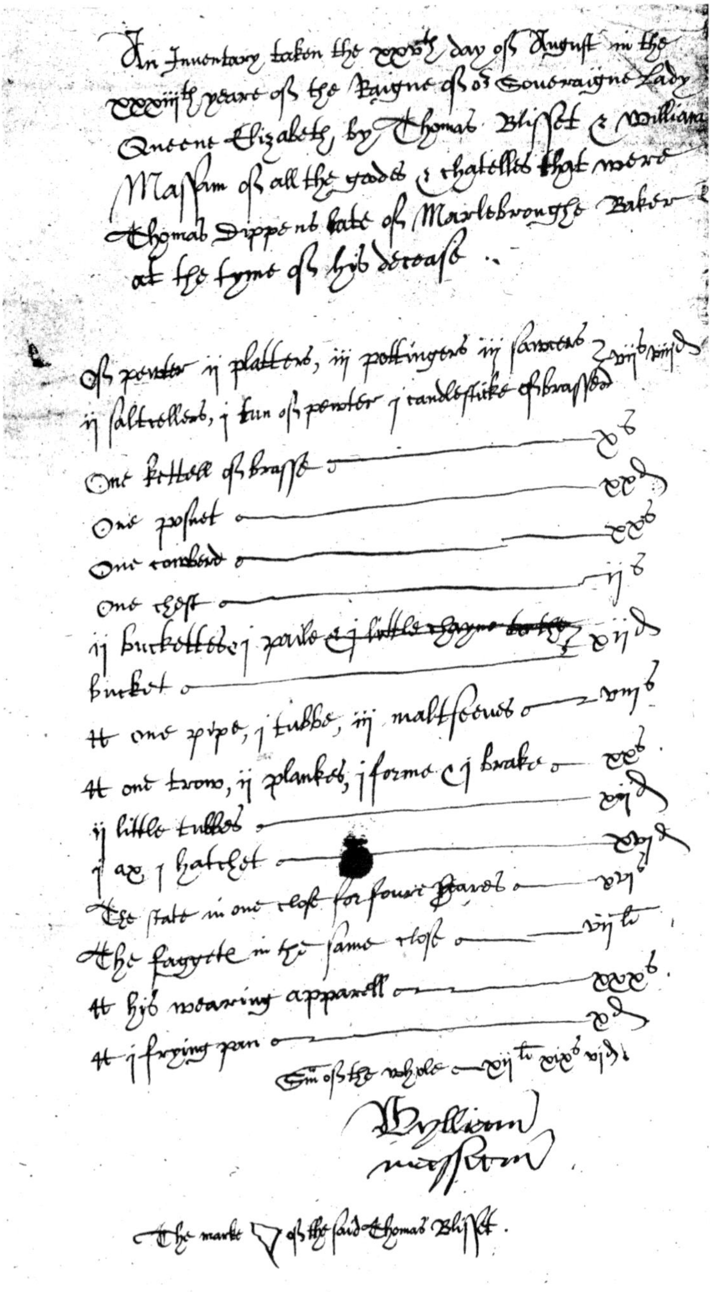

The inventory of Thomas Dippens, a Marlborough baker, proved in 1591, and the earliest document included in this edition

MARLBOROUGH PROBATE INVENTORIES 1591 – 1775

EDITED BY

LORELEI WILLIAMS

AND

SALLY THOMSON

CHIPPENHAM

2007

c/o Wiltshire and Swindon History Centre,
Cocklebury Road, Chippenham SN15 3QN

ISBN-13 978-0-901333-36-0

Typeset by John Chandler
Produced for the Society by
Salisbury Printing Company Ltd, Salisbury
Printed in Great Britain

CONTENTS

ACKNOWLEDGEMENTS

The Wiltshire Record Society acknowledges the permission of the Bishop of Salisbury to publish these documents from the diocesan archives. Due thanks are also made to Steve Hobbs and John d'Arcy of the Wiltshire and Swindon Record Office for their help and encouragement, and for making the documents available for copying and research. The help of John Chandler must also be acknowledged in the production of this volume. His advice and expertise have been unparalleled, and without his assistance, in so many fields, the volume would still be struggling to the surface. The help given by Michael Gray and his colleagues in The Merchant's House Trust, Marlborough, is also gratefully acknowledged, as is the Marc Fitch Fund. Many other people have been involved in the attempt to identify all the archaic terms used in these inventories and I am most grateful to them all – curators of museums and secretaries of the livery companies alike.

The extraction and transcription of the 454 probate inventories of Marlborough were the brainchild of the late Iris Lorelei Williams, whose interest in them formed the basis of her MA dissertation. Having obtained a grant from the Marc Fitch Fund to cover the cost of photocopying all the inventories and some of the wills, Lorelei then spent many, many hours, firstly transcribing each document with great care and accuracy, and secondly, compiling the huge glossary which forms such an important part of this work. It was while endeavouring to find out the meanings of hundreds of archaic words, that her work was cut short by her untimely death.

Sally Thomson

IRIS LORELEI WILLIAMS 1938-2004

Continuing the work of someone who has passed on to higher things is slightly unnerving. I have often sensed Lorelei at my shoulder, tutting at my obtuseness, pointing out that a mistake is mine and not hers. She was so thorough in all she did that I feel humbled by the experience of completing this volume for her.

Lorelei and I were friends, as well as colleagues. We met as early members of the Anglo-German Family History Society, when she lived on the Isle of Wight and I lived in London. We met three or four times a year at Cookham for committee meetings and I realised very quickly what a hard-working and diligent woman she was. Towards the end of 1992, I gave up my membership of the Anglo German FHS, as I believe did Lorelei. We lost touch and it was not until my family and I were settled in Wiltshire and I was once more involved in family - and house - history that I bumped into her again. I forget the circumstances, but I suspect it was in the locker-passage at the WSRO. We always seemed to meet there and would spend a long lunch-hour discussing all things historical. By then she had moved to Devizes and our friendship was renewed.

In sifting through the many files which were handed to me after Lorelei's demise, I realised just how much she was involved in. I know that her own family history was a passion close to her heart; but she also read widely around every subject and was in correspondence with many academics on a variety of topics. Her interests covered not only Marlborough, but the wider picture of Wiltshire, parts of Hampshire and Sussex, and much on Ongar, in Essex, and its Academy, about which she had an article published. She gave presentations to various societies and her files contain the core, or at least the start, of many new topics, on which she had obviously planned to work.

For an engineer, she was an admirable historian, full of enthusiasm and good sense. People still say they can recall her voice and her laugh; they always made one smile. And with her wry sense of humour, it was not really a surprise to learn that she had elected to continue as the eternal student after her death – spending the next three years at Southampton University, to whom she had given her body for medical science.

It was through Lorelei's recommendation that I enrolled with Bath Spa University College (now Bath Spa University) to read for an MA in Local and Regional History and we often met for coffee or lunch, in Trowbridge or at the College, to discuss my progress and her own work on the Marlborough inventories. Little did I know that one day it would be my sad but honoured privilege to complete that work for her. I hope I have done her credit.

Sally Thomson

INTRODUCTION

. . . *it shall be inventoried, and every particle and utensil labelled to my will* . . . [1]

MARLBOROUGH, THE TOWN

Marlborough was first referred to as a borough in 1086, when a third of its revenues was paid to the Crown. It had originally been founded as a royal estate centred on the River Kennet and extending into the downland north and south. Being a downland settlement, its main occupation was with the farming of sheep. The siting of the settlement, on the crossing of two main thoroughfares and with the Kennet as a valuable source of both water and transport, led to its development as a town; in 1204, the burgesses were granted markets for Wednesdays and Saturdays. The oldest recorded commodity in the town was corn, in 1203; weaving and fulling are known from 1215 and leather working (tanners, skinners, curriers, leather sellers and shoe makers) from 1378. A wooden castle was built in the town in the 11th century, to be replaced later by a stone-built structure. This increased the defences of the town and in its shadow trade prospered.

By the mid 17th century the High Street was lined with jettied houses, the homes of affluent merchants. For this reason the fire which broke out at the tannery at the west end of the town in 1653 caused extensive damage and many houses were destroyed, though more have survived than was once thought. The Merchant's House, for example, rose phoenix-like from the ashes of that fire and is now being restored to its former glory. It is from these middle years of prosperity, the 16th to the 18th centuries, that the probate inventories, the subject of this volume, were drawn.

At the beginning of the 19th century major roads were widened for coach transport and in 1812 New Road was created. Marlborough became an important staging post on the London to Bath route, with all the subsidiary services which that carried with it. The site of the old castle was used in 1688 for the building of a private house, but in time this became the Castle Inn, serving many of the stagecoaches passing through the town. In 1843, the building was incorporated into the newly opened Marlborough College, which has made the town well known both nationally and internationally.

[1] William Shakespeare, *Twelfth Night, or What You Will*, Act I, Scene 5.

PROBATE INVENTORIES

In the most basic terms, a probate inventory is a list of the possessions of a person who has recently died, and whose heirs have made a formal legal request to acquire those possessions. Many thousands of probate inventories have been deposited in record offices throughout England and Wales, and they are particularly useful in illustrating the lifestyles of people of lesser importance, who usually appear in the historical record only as names in a parish register or tax list, 'that sad passport to immortality', if at all.[2] One of the objectives of the probate inventory was to safeguard the executors from claims which the estate could not meet, since the acceptance by the probate court of the inventory value limited the liability of the executor to that amount.[3] The inventory also served to prevent the beneficiaries from being defrauded by unscrupulous executors, and to enable the probate court to determine its fees, which depended on the value of the estate.[4] Before the government took control of probate matters in 1858, these had always been dealt with by the ecclesiastical authorities.

The hierarchy of the Church of England was divided into several tiers, each with its own court, which dealt *inter alia* with probate and the administration of estates. Small numbers of parishes formed deaneries, but these did not normally exercise any probate jurisdiction. Deaneries were grouped into archdeaconries, whose courts granted probate of the estates of those whose property lay solely within their jurisdiction. Estates lying in more than one archdeaconry in a diocese would be dealt with by the consistory court of the bishop. When the estate lay in more than one diocese, the probate or letters of administration had to be granted by the provincial Prerogative Courts of Canterbury or York, with Canterbury exercising superior jurisdiction. The P.C.C. also dealt with the estates of those dying at sea. Many executors, particularly from the upper social classes, sought probate at the Prerogative Courts even when they were not legally obliged to do so, simply because of their prestige as the superior courts.[5] There were, in addition, a number of peculiar jurisdictions, which were exempt from the attentions of both bishops and archbishops and had autonomy under the sovereign, though sometimes with an intermediate supervisor.[6] Between 1649 and 1660 the church courts were suppressed and probate matters were administered by the Court of Civil Commission in London. Many people, particularly in the north and west

[2] W.G. Hoskins, *Provincial England: Essays in Social and Economic History* (London, 1964), p.76.
[3] E. & S. George, *A Guide to the Probate Inventories of the Bristol Deanery of the Diocese of Bristol* (Gloucester, 1988), p.xii.
[4] M. Overton, 'Probate inventories and the reconstruction of agricultural landscapes', in M. Read (ed.), *Discovering Past Landscapes* (London, 1984), p.168.
[5] D.G. Vaisey, 'Probate inventories of Lichfield and district 1568-1680', *Collections for a History of Staffordshire* 4th series, 5 (1969), p.1.
[6] A.J. Camp, *Wills and their Whereabouts*, (London, 1974), pp.xxv, xxvi.

of the country, ignored this court, and delayed probate until the church courts were reconvened at the Restoration.[7] Richard Rumsey was buried at St. Mary's church in Marlborough on 25 December 1658, but his inventory was not taken until 14 March 1660/1 [**143**]. Probate was granted to his executrix, his wife Edith, on 16 April 1661. There were in all more than 600 courts dealing with probate and administration within England and Wales until 1858.

Wiltshire lies within the Diocese of Sarum and is divided into the Archdeaconry of Sarum, which covered the south of the county, and the Archdeaconry of Wiltshire covering the north. Parts of the county were, however, subject to no fewer than 26 peculiar jurisdictions. Some of these, like the peculiar of Castle Combe, covered just one parish, but many were more extensive. The Dean of Salisbury had sole jurisdiction over more than 40 parishes in Wiltshire, Berkshire and Dorset, as well as supervisory jurisdiction over many others, including such distant places as the parish of Uffculme in Devon.[8] The two Marlborough parishes lay within the peculiar jurisdiction of the Bishop of Sarum. Their probate files, together with most of the other records of the Diocese of Sarum, have been deposited in the Wiltshire and Swindon Record Office, which acts alao as the Diocesan Record Office. Marlborough inventories deposited in the records of the Prerogative Court of Canterbury are not referred to in this edition, but it does include those from three files where probate was granted in error in the court of the Archdeaconry of Wiltshire. Mary Hill [**359**] left goods in Malmesbury, which lies in that Archdeaconry, as well as in Marlborough. In the case of Walter Jefferies [**125**] and Jone Jones [**126**], however, both of whose wills were proved on 25 October 1641, there were no such grounds for confusion. Possibly the Bishop's and the Archdeacon's Surrogates were both hearing cases in the town on the same day, and these two probates were issued unnoticed by the wrong court.

During the period covered by this survey the making of probate inventories was regulated by an Act of Parliament passed in 1529, called 'An Act concerning fines and sums of money to be taken by the ministers or Bishops and other ordinaries of Holy church for the probate of testaments'.[9] The Act is considerably more complex than its title suggests, and deals with many considerations in the processes of probate and administration. The Act demands that the executors or administrators of every deceased person's estate should have an inventory of their goods drawn up, but it is obvious that, despite the large numbers which have survived, this was not always done. Not only are there burial records for many more deceased persons than probate files in the records of the church courts, but there are also many files which do not contain inventories. In most cases there is no way of knowing whether this is because the inventories were never made, or because they have not been preserved by the relevant

[7] G.H. Williams, 'Probate inventories, a source for folk life studies', *Folk Life* vol.20 (1982), p.8.
[8] P. Stewart, *Guide to the Records of the Bishop, the Archdeacons of Salisbury and Wiltshire, and other Archdiaconal and Peculiar Jurisdictions, and to the Records from the Bishop of Bristol's Sub-Registry for Dorset,* (Salisbury, 1973), p.xiii.
[9] 21 Henry VIII, cap. 5.

ecclesiastical registries.[10] The Bishop of London's Commissary Court in Essex and Hertfordshire exercised probate jurisdiction over almost all of Essex but, though the wills proved in the court have survived in their thousands, all the inventories have disappeared.[11] In a few cases the losses are more recent. All the probate files from large parts of Devon and Somerset which had been deposited in the Exeter Diocesan Registry were lost when the building was destroyed by fire in an air raid on Exeter in 1942.[12] Many authors give the impression that inventories were not required if the estate of the deceased was valued at less than £5. In reality there is no such exemption allowed in the Act. The only reference to low value inventories is that the fees required for probate or letters of administration shall not exceed 6*d.* to the Scribe and 6*d.* for the Commission, where the value of the estate does not exceed one hundred shillings.[13] Such a low fee would not encourage the ecclesiastical authorities to pursue those disposing of the estates of the indigent.[14] There are in fact considerable numbers of low value inventories in the Marlborough collection, though the proportion of these was reduced over time as a result of inflation. Since the richest people tended to have their probates dealt with at the Prerogative Court of Canterbury, and the poorest people often avoided the probate courts altogether, it is inevitable that the records of the Archdeaconry and Diocesan Courts dealt mainly with the affairs of the 'middling sort'.

It is usually impossible to know why an estate of low value was taken to the probate court to be dealt with, but in one case it is clear, though not from the inventory itself. When John Glide **[75]** died in 1628 he did not leave a will, and the total value of his effects was £3 0s. 10*d.*, which included a 'bedsteed of bordes' valued at one shilling, and his 'wearinge apparrell' worth only eight shillings. His probate file includes a letter from Thomas Bennett, a member of one of Marlborough's leading families, to his friend Thomas Sadler, who was an official at the Consistory Court in Salisbury:

> This is the poore widow I spake of unto you when I saw you last at Marlborough. She is urged to take an Administration by an unmercifull sonne in law who lyeth in good fashion and is of a good estate. The woman hath no means to lyve but is fayne to goe to service, her husband beinge a very old man, and sick so longe that they spent and sold all for their relief in his sickness but onely this small porcion; more worthe than this have many time our Almesfolk, and yet the gready fellow hath saide he will have a share.

The letter goes on to beg Thomas Sadler to charge as small a fee as he can. Letters of Administration were granted at the Sarum court on 13 June 1628 to Mary Glide,

[10] M.A. Havinden, 'Household and farm inventories on Oxfordshire 1550-1590', *Oxfordshire Record Society* vol.44 (1965), p.3.
[11] F.G. Emmison, *Guide to the Essex Record Office, Part II, Estate, Ecclesiastical and other Deposited Archives*, (Chelmsford, Essex, 1948), p.93.
[12] M. Cash, 'Devon inventories of the sixteenth and seventeenth centuries', *Devon and Cornwall Record Society* new series vol. 11 (1966), p.vii.
[13] 21 Henry VIII cap. 5, clause 2.
[14] J.P.P. Horn, 'The distribution of wealth in the Vale of Berkeley, Gloucestershire, 1660-1700', *Southern History* 3 (1981), p.87.

widow, and the 'unmercifull' Thomas Benger, a farmer of the nearby village of Overton.

The number of surviving Marlborough inventories varies greatly over time. This is not unusual. In the dioceses of Lincoln and Canterbury, for example, there are many dating from the decades following the Act of 1529, whereas in Peterborough and Rochester there are very few before the Restoration period.[15] The earliest Marlborough inventories date from the 1590s, though they are particularly numerous in the period from 1660 to the end of the seventeenth century. Many towns and cities have a similar concentration, the city of Chichester being exceptional in that its probate courts seem never to have recovered fully after the Commonwealth period. There are few probate files from the decades before 1600 in the records of the Consistory Court of the Bishop of Sarum. This is a comparatively late start: Banbury in the diocese of Oxford has 48 inventories earlier than this, while Uttoxeter (diocese of Lichfield) has 114 dating from 1531 to 1590.[16] The Marlborough inventories, although much reduced in numbers after about 1720, continue in the main to be as detailed as those appraised before that date, and do not degenerate into the 'brief summaries . . . of little historical value' which are found in Oxfordshire.[17]

Clause 4 of the Act of 1529 is headed, 'How the Inventory shall be made by the Executor or Administrator', and sets out the qualifications of the appraisors, and the required contents of the inventory. Two appraisors at least are called for, but many Marlborough inventories from the 1590s to the 1660s were appraised by three people. It is not uncommon to find four or five appraisors in this period, and William Gunter's inventory [**104**] had no fewer than six. From the last quarter of the seventeenth century, however, it became much more unusual for more than two appraisors to be involved. Only four inventories were produced by an appraisor acting alone: Arthur Deane [**48**], Margaret Evans [**228**], Susannah Hill [**306**] and Francis Hancock [**392**]. The appraisors were to be creditors or beneficiaries of the deceased, their next of kin or, failing these, 'two other honest persons'. It is impossible to tell from the inventories if any of the appraisors were creditors or beneficiaries, and very few of the appraisors had the same surname as the deceased, as would be expected if next of kin were regularly appraising inventories in Marlborough. One exception to this is the Greenaway family. All four members whose inventories survive had others of the same surname among their appraisors. It seems likely, therefore, that the majority of the appraisors were friends and neighbours of the executors and administrators, though these were just the kinds of people who were also likely to have been debtors or creditors. Some men were appraising regularly. The name of Richard Cornwall appears on five inventories between 1593 and 1608, and Noah and Joseph Webb, who were probably cousins, signed thirteen inventories, together or separately, between 1682 and 1696. The most prolific appraisor was

[15] A. Everitt, *Ways and Means in Local History*, (London, 1971), p.40.
[16] Havinden, 'Oxfordshire', (1965), *passim*; P. Woolley, *Seven Studies in the Economic and Social History of Uttoxeter and its Adjacent Rural Parishes 1530-1830*, (Kingstone, Staffs., 1995), p.4.
[17] Havinden, 'Oxfordshire', (1965), p.3.

Bartholomew Benger, who drew up no fewer than seventeen inventories between 1661 and 1684.

There is nothing in the Act of 1529 to say how quickly after death the inventory should be produced, but since by implication it should include all the deceased person's goods and chattels at the time of death, this would become more difficult the longer after death the appraisal took place. This was particularly true of farming inventories, where the situation could change radically as crops were harvested or animals died or were sold. There is one Marlborough inventory, that of Francis Gregory [**448**], where his widow, acting as executrix, carefully listed and priced those goods which she had sold since her husband's death. In Derbyshire it was noted that the inventories were sometimes drawn up on the day of death, though there were other cases when they were not appraised until several weeks had passed.[18] A sample of 125 inventories from several different counties, where the date of death is known, has shown that almost half were made within seven days, and nearly three-quarters within two weeks.[19] In Marlborough the situation was somewhat different. There are many gaps in the burial registers, and a significant number of the inventories are undated, or have lost their dates through damage. Of the 292 inventories for which both dates are known, over half were made in the first two weeks after burial (including those drawn up between death and burial), but one third were delayed for more than one month after death. These include the inventory of Roger Davis *alias* Morris [**162**], who was buried on 7 September 1656, but whose probate was not granted until 11 May 1665, the inventory being taken one week later. Even more extreme is the case of Richard Hawkins [**374**], who was buried on 1 November 1682. His inventory was not taken until 13 July 1706, probate being granted on 24 July. Hawkins left the bulk of his estate to be divided between three of his daughters, but to the use of his wife during her lifetime. It may be that probate was delayed until her death.

The 'honest persons' were required by the Act to produce a 'true and perfect inventory', and there has been much debate both about the care and the honesty which the appraisors brought to their work.[20] The concern with which they carried out their task seems unrelated to the value of the deceased person's goods. The inventory of Thomas Whetebreade [**19**] totalled only £3 6*s*.9*d*., yet his appraisors carefully listed such minor items as six spoons worth 2*d*., a chafing dish and a skimmer worth 6*d*. and a chair valued at 3*d*. By contrast, the appraisors of George Dobson [**384**] listed only his 'household goods and shop goods' worth £8 5*s*.0*d*. with no other detail at all, in an inventory totalling £150 0*s*.6*d*., and in the case of Roger Blagden [**210**], whose inventory totalled £1,036, the appraisors merely remarked that his 'bed and other furniture' was worth £10. As there can be no independent checks on the valuations given by the

[18] J.M. Bestall & D.V. Fowkes (eds.), 'Chesterfield Wills and Inventories 1521-1603', *Derbyshire Record Society*, 1 (1977), p.xi.

[19] S. Porter, 'The making of probate inventories', *Local Historian*, 12 (1976), pp.36-7.

[20] R. Machin, *Probate Inventories and Manorial Excepts from Chetnole, Leigh and Yetminster*, (Bristol, 1976), p.3.

appraisors, this is another area where doubts have arisen as to their skill and accuracy. Steer regarded some valuations as 'ridiculously low', while West's judgement is that goods were undervalued 'quite recklessly'.[21] Swinburne, however, in his legal commentary, states that the goods should be valued at the sum which they 'may be sold for at that time', and the courts accepted that the executors would sometimes need to sell goods to finance the debts and pay the monetary bequests of a testator.[22] In the case of household goods it is their second-hand value rather than their replacement cost which is implied, so that the fact that one man's chairs were valued at 6*d.* each and another man's at 5*s.* each reveals more about the lifestyle of the two men than about the conscientiousness of their appraisors.[23]

There were in any case two independent checks on the appraisors. One was the presence of the heirs, executors and creditors of the deceased, any of whom could have complained to the ecclesiastical courts if they thought that the appraisors were not carrying out their duties correctly. In fact, disputes over the contents or value of inventories are not often to be found in the Cause papers.[24] Some disputes concerning inventories did arise, though these were usually concerned with allegations that the plaintiff had not received a fair share of the deceased person's goods when the value of the estate was less than the total value of the bequests.[25] The inventory of Mary Gillmore [**451**] refers to 'diverse goods appropriated by Joseph Gillmore, the party promoting this suit', which the appraisors were unable to value. There was a second check on the probity of the appraisors. As Laslett has written: 'All of our ancestors were literal Christian believers all of the time ... their world was a Christian world and their religious activity was spontaneous, not forced on them from above.'[26]

It is therefore unlikely that the appraisors, working under a solemn oath, would have committed deliberate fraud.[27] More recent work has judged that they valued a person's goods 'realistically', while Machin found that, at least in his Dorset parishes, the average values of inventories in each decade followed reasonably closely upon the fluctuations in the price index.[28] This is not entirely true of Marlborough, where there is an apparent lag between the rises and falls in the price index and those in the median values of the probate inventories. This is not surprising. Household goods were intended

[21] F.W. Steer, *Farm and Cottage Inventories of Mid-Essex 1635-1749*, (Colchester, 1950), p.5; J. West, *Village Records*, (London, 1962), p.92.
[22] H. Swinburne, *A Brief Treatise of Testaments and Last Wills*, (London, 1611 edn.), p.256; George '*Bristol Inventories*', (1988), p.xiii.
[23] Williams, 'Probate inventories', (1982), p.9.
[24] J.S. Moore, 'Probate inventories – problems and prospects', in P. Riden (ed.), *Probate inventories and the Local Community*, (Gloucester, 1985), pp.15-16.
[25] Cash, 'Devon inventories', (1966), p.ix.
[26] P. Laslett, *The World We Have Lost*, (London, 1965), p.74.
[27] M. Overton, 'English probate inventories and the measurement of agricultural change', *A.A.G. Bijdragen*, 23 (1980), p.61.
[28] J. & N. Cox, 'Valuations in probate inventories, Part I', *Local Historian*, 16 (1985), p.467; Machin, *Probate Inventories*, (1976), p.4.

to last a lifetime, and with care two or three (as seen in the bequests of such goods made to younger relatives of the testator), so the possessions of an old man could have been purchased at any time during the years when he was a householder, including years of higher or lower prices than the year in which he died.

Not all the possessions of the deceased appeared in the inventory. The Act required the appraisors to list 'all the Goods, Chattels, Wares, Merchandizes, as well moveable as not moveable whatsoever'. According to Burn's interpretation, the list of goods was to include: 'all the testator's cattle, as bulls, cows, oxen, sheep, horses, swine, and all poultry, household stuff, money, plate, jewels, corn, hay, wood severed from the ground, and such like moveables.'[29]

Chattels personal consisted of the clothing, money and plate of the deceased, while chattels real included leases and bonds.[30] The most important omission from the inventories, as far as the historian is concerned, is that of freehold or copyhold land and buildings. This means that the total wealth of the deceased cannot be measured from his inventory alone. For a farmer, even his potential income from the land cannot be calculated, since the fallow, uncut hay, standing timber and fruit on the trees were all regarded as part of the freehold.[31] Until the passage of the 'Act for the better settling of intestate estates' in 1670, which gave the courts powers to award an equitable distribution of the estate to the deceased's wife and children, a man's inventory did not include his wife's *bona paraphernalia*, defined as her apparel, providing it was 'agreeable to her degree', her bed and her 'jewels and ornaments for her person'.[32] Despite this, the appraisors of the goods of Thomas Patie [**129**] included his wife's apparel and her Bible, valued at £4. Undoubtedly some goods were omitted because the appraisors thought them to be of trivial monetary value.[33] It is also possible that, where probate or administration was granted to the principal creditor, he valued only enough of the deceased's goods to cover the amount of the debt owed to him, thus making the person seem to be far poorer than they in fact were.[34] Anything regarded as an heirloom would not be included in the inventory, that is, an item of particular significance to the family, which was intended to remain in their ownership for posterity.[35] The inventory of Deborah Prior [**150**] was followed by a 'Scedule of what things Remayne in the howse to be left standing', which were listed but not given a value.

As for leases, the practice seems to have varied. Leases for years should have been included, though this does not always seem to have happened.[36] Leases for lives

[29] R.S. Burn, *Ecclesiastical Law* vol. 4, (3rd edn., London, 1775), p.238.
[30] Burn, *ibid.*, p.238-9.
[31] Overton, 'English probate inventories' (1980), p.206.
[32] 22&3 Car.II c.10; Swinburne, *Brief Treatise* (1611), p.254.
[33] D.G.Vaisey, 'Probate inventories and provincial retailers in the seventeenth century', in P. Riden (ed.), *Probate Records and the Local Community*, (Gloucester, 1985), p.100-1.
[34] Vaisey, 'Lichfield inventories', (1969), p.4.
[35] V. Chinnery, *A Glossary of Terms 1500-1750* (forthcoming), section H.
[36] R.P. Garrard, 'English probate inventories and their use in studying the domestic interior', *A.A.G. Bijdragen* 23 (1980), p.61.

should have been omitted before 1676, but they were sometimes considered as leases for 99 years, and so were included.[37] Only a few are to be found in the Marlborough inventories, the first in 1672. Many of the leases listed in the inventories are for the remainder of the term on the house which was occupied by the deceased. Debts were another area of confusion for the appraisors. Money owing to the testator was included in many inventories, but it is often impossible to tell whether these were personal loans or trade debts, though 'shop debts' or 'book debts' are occasionally specified. Other forms of indebtedness included bonds, bills, specialities (which were sealed bonds), rents, mortgages and annuities. In reality, debts do not become assets until they have been collected, but despite this even desperate debts were included.[38] This term may have been used by some executors merely to indicate debts which they had not yet tried to settle, to avoid their being accused of not trying hard enough to collect them.[39] It is also possible, of course, that the debts truly were desperate. Even as late as the nineteenth century England did not sustain a fully cash economy. Many transactions were by barter or the exchange of labour and services, which worked very well during the lifetime of the individual. On his death, however, when the executors or administrators tried to turn these debts in kind into cash, the debtors were quite unable to honour them.[40] Debts which the deceased themselves owed are found in a few inventories, but should not have been included, since they did not belong to the estate.[41] The total value of the assets listed could be considerably reduced by offsetting the debts owed by the deceased. However, there is a point of view that the amount of money a man owed was a measure of his credit-worthiness, and that his economic status could be better adjudged by adding his debts to the value of his goods rather than taking them away.[42] Some inventories list the debts owing to and by the deceased in considerable detail, including the residence of the debtor or creditor. These can be used to determine the area over which the deceased was trading, or at least those places where there were people living of whom he had personal knowledge.[43]

Although a good number of the appraisors showed considerable expertise, many of them were unable to sign their names, and there is nothing in the Act to demand that they should be literate. One study estimated that about 70% of men and over 80% of women were totally illiterate in the seventeenth century, in that they were unable even to write their names. This evidence, however, seems to conflict with Comenius's

[37] D.G. Hey, *An English Rural Community: Myddle under the Tudors and Stuarts*, (Leicester, 1974), p.73.
[38] Burn, *Ecclesiastical Law*, (1775), pp.239.
[39] N. & J. Cox, 'Probate inventories: the legal background', *Local Historian*, 16 (1984), p.225.
[40] M. Reed, 'The peasantry of nineteenth-century England: a neglected class?', in B. Stapleton (ed.) *Conflict and Community in Southern England: essays in the social history of rural and urban labour from medieval to modern times* (Stroud, Glos., 1992), p.221.
[41] Overton, 'English probate inventories', (1980), p.206.
[42] Moore, 'Probate inventories', (1985), p.12.
[43] J.S. Moore, *The Goods and Chattels of our Forefathers: Frampton Cotterell and District Probate Inventories 1539-1804* (Chichester, 1976), pp. 37-8.

perception that 'bookes are growne so common in all Languages and Nations, that even common countrey people, and women themselves are familiarly acquainted with them'.[44] Although the proportion of Marlborough appraisors signing the inventories rather than making their mark increased during the seventeenth century, even in the eighteenth there were some appraisors who were unable to sign their names. It is also noticeable that the proportion of inventories in which the appraisors' names are merely listed, and in which they neither signed nor made their mark, falls considerably after the Commonwealth period. In a Staffordshire village it was found that the proportion of testators, witnesses and appraisors able to sign rose from 9.7% in the period 1590–1611 to 49.6% during the last decade of the seventeenth century.[45] Since Marlborough had a flourishing Grammar School throughout the period it is surprising that so many men were unable even to sign their names.[46]

Another measure of literacy is the proportion of individuals who owned books. In Marlborough this rose significantly in the period after the Restoration, and compares well with other areas. Two of the largest collections of books belonged, not surprisingly, to the two masters of the Grammar School whose inventories have survived, John Martin [**114**], who was also an ordained minister, and Abraham Power [**200**]. The largest library of all, however, valued at £10, belonged to Roger Blagden [**210**], who called himself a mercer in his will, but whose appraisors designated him a gentleman. He left all his property to his wife Elizabeth, and she appears to have kept his library intact, for when she died four years later her inventory included 'Item in her Clossett 107 bookes £10.00.00' [**226**]. The Bible was probably the one book which even a semi-literate appraisor could recognise, and very few other books were named.[47] William Woodes [**50**] had an 'old service book 1*s*.6*d*.' and Hester Clifford [**454**] had a Book of Common Prayer, also valued at 1*s*.6*d*. Other collections of books may well have been similar to the mixture of devotional and legal works owned by a Norfolk farmer, which included John Foxe's *Book of Martyrs* of 1571 and a collection of Statutes printed by William Rastell, who died in 1565.[48]

Although it is even more difficult to find evidence relating to number skills in the seventeenth century, a certain amount can be deduced from the inventories concerning the spread of numeracy. The ability to perform simple mental arithmetic may have been even more widespread in the seventeenth century than literacy.[49] Anyone concerned with trade would at least have needed to be able to add and subtract with

[44] D. Cressy, *Literacy and the Social Order: Reading and Writing in Tudor and Stuart England* (Cambridge, 1980), p.59; J.A. Comenius, *A Reformation of Schooles* (London, 1642), p.3.

[45] D. Stuart, 'Witnesses and appraisors in estimates of literacy in Yoxall 1590–1700', *Local Historian* 21 (1991), p.17.

[46] A. Stedman, *A History of Marlborough Grammar School* (Marlborough, 1946), *passim*.

[47] Vaisey, 'Lichfield inventories', (1969), p.36.

[48] J.H. Wilson (ed.) 'Wymondham inventories', *Creative History from East Anglian Sources* 1 (1983) p.10.

[49] M. Spufford, *Contrasting Communities: English Villages in the Sixteenth and Seventeenth Centuries* (London, 1974), p.213.

reasonable facility, and the use of tables and ready-reckoners was widespread.[50] John Aubrey declared that 'a Barre-boy at an Alehouse will reckon better and readier than a Master of Arts in the University'.[51] Aubrey appears to have been right: Dr. Busby, who was headmaster of Westminster School in the seventeenth century, was unable to add up correctly, while Samuel Pepys had to learn his multiplication tables at the age of 29 from a one-eyed ship's mate.[52] At the start of the period covered by the Marlborough inventories, almost all of the amounts given in them were written in Roman numerals, whereas by the end of the seventeenth century this had almost entirely been superseded by Arabic notation. The change-over occurred mainly in the period after the Restoration, rather later than in Bristol, where 90% of the inventories were written using Arabic numerals by 1650.[53] Given the difficulty of making arithmetical calculations using Roman figures, it is not surprising that many of the inventories in the early period had been totalled incorrectly, though the lack of competence in addition did not entirely disappear as Arabic notation took over. However, in most cases the mistakes were small.

In the inventory of William Woodes [**50**], even though the appraisors 'names are not given, one of them had totalled the list of values with great care. The values of the items are given in Roman numerals, but the appraisor has inserted his totals and sub-totals in Arabic notation. He started at the bottom, totalled a few lines, then put in a sub-total. Finally he added the sub-totals. Even though the four sub-totals are correct, the appraisor has still made an error in his final addition, and his grand total is £1 too low. There was only one case in which the amount of the addition showed a serious discrepancy with the actual total. Dorothy Winde [**201**] was a widow whose inventory is virtually identical to that of her husband Edward, who had died two years previously. The appraisors in both cases were the same three men, of whom Bartholomew Benger was almost certainly the scribe. When he copied out Edward's inventory [**187**] with Dorothy's name and the new date in the preamble he inadvertently omitted the line 'Item In Debts Due uppon the shopp Booke lj^{li} x^{s}' [£51 10*s*.0*d*.], thus making the total of Dorothy's inventory wrong by that amount.

The principal disadvantages of using probate inventories in local history have already been noted: the omission of real property and debts owing by the deceased, which make it impossible to determine a person's true wealth, together with the omission of *bona paraphernalia* and other goods legally ignored by the appraisors. However, these difficulties are far outweighed by the advantages to social and economic historians of using the information which the inventories do contain about items in ordinary household use by people of middling or lower rank. The fact that the appraisors

[50] D. Murray, *Chapters in the History of Bookkeeping, Accountancy and Commercial Arithmetic* (Glasgow, 1930), pp.296-308.
[51] Oxford, Bodleian Library, MS Aubrey 10, f.29.
[52] G.F. R. Barker, *Memoir of Richard Busby, D.D., 1606-1695* (London, 1895), p.125.; R. Latham & W. Matthews (eds.), *The Diary of Samuel Pepys* (London, 1970-83), vol. 3, pp.131,134,135.
[53] George, '*Bristol Inventories*' (1988), p.xxii.

were people who could compare the values of such goods with those in their own households makes it all the more likely that the values given to the goods were reasonable. The lists of goods are often highly detailed, though in Marlborough the appraisal of shop goods was sometimes not as meticulous as is seen elsewhere.[54] The greatest importance of probate inventories, however, must be found in the enormous numbers of them which survive in repositories throughout England and Wales, making comparisons possible over different periods of time as well as between contrasting and similar (or apparently similar) communities.

EDITORIAL NOTE

The inventories are arranged chronologically and each is numbered. The number is followed by the name of the deceased; his or her trade, occupation or status; the date of the inventory, where this is known; and the WSRO reference number.

The preamble of each inventory has been omitted, as have the words *Imprimis* and *Item,* which occur frequently in the originals, but which are unnecessary repetitions in a work of this size. Where individual rooms are mentioned, these have been included, in their original spelling, using italics. All values have been given in £ *s. d.*, and Arabic numerals have replaced the Roman variety. The total value of each inventory is given at the end of each entry; some totals have been found to be inaccurate and rectified sums have been added. The total is followed by the names of the appraisors, where these are known.

At the very end of each entry notes may be found, indicating where wills and burial registers have been used to obtain dates and even names, which could not be deduced from the inventories. Other notes may include where Roman numerals have been used, discrepancies between wills and inventories, inclusion of debts and any damage to the original document.

ILLUSTRATIONS OF INVENTORIES AND CONTEMPORARY FURNITURE

On the following pages are reproduced copies of inventories and parts of inventories, selected to illustrate the range of handwriting styles and physical conditions encountered by anyone working on this class of document. These are followed by illustrations of items of furniture and household utensils of broadly contemporary date, from the collection being assembled at The Merchant's House, Marlborough.

[54] T.S. Willan, *The Inland Trade* (Manchester, 1976), p.59; R.G. Griffiths (ed.) 'An inventory of the goods and chattels of Thomas Cowcher, mercer of Worcester, dated 14th November, 1643', *Transactions of the Worcestershire Archaeological Society* 14 (1937), pp.45-60.

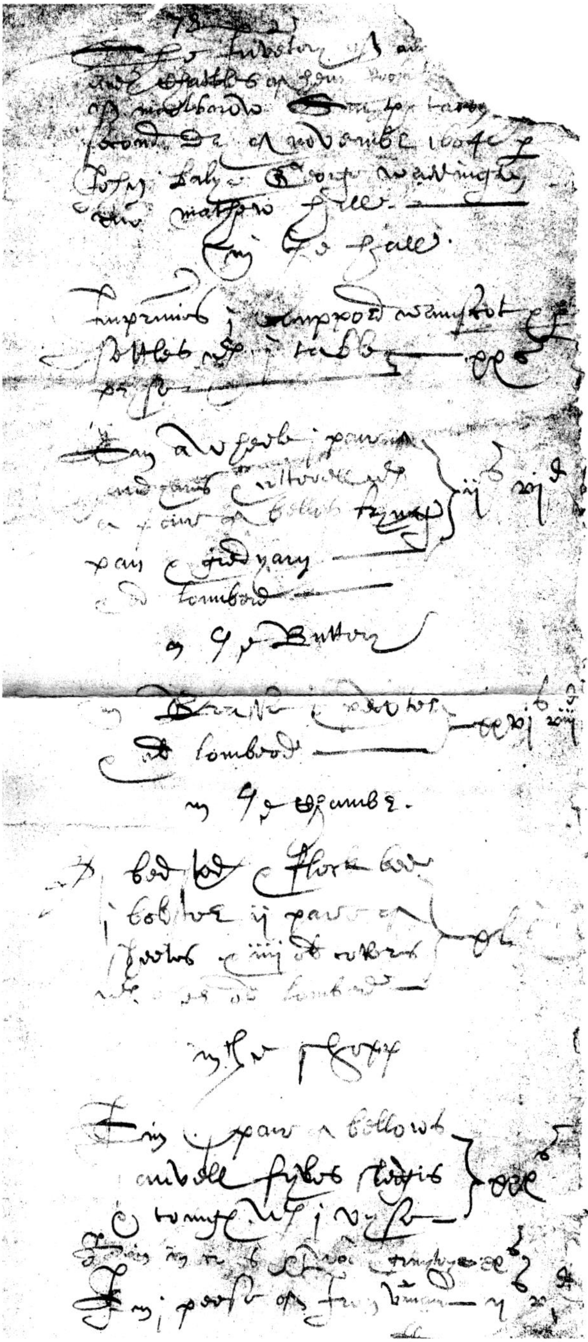

*Henry Roosell, smith, 1604 (**25**)*

*Anne Weare, alias Browne, widow, 1607 (**29**): detail*

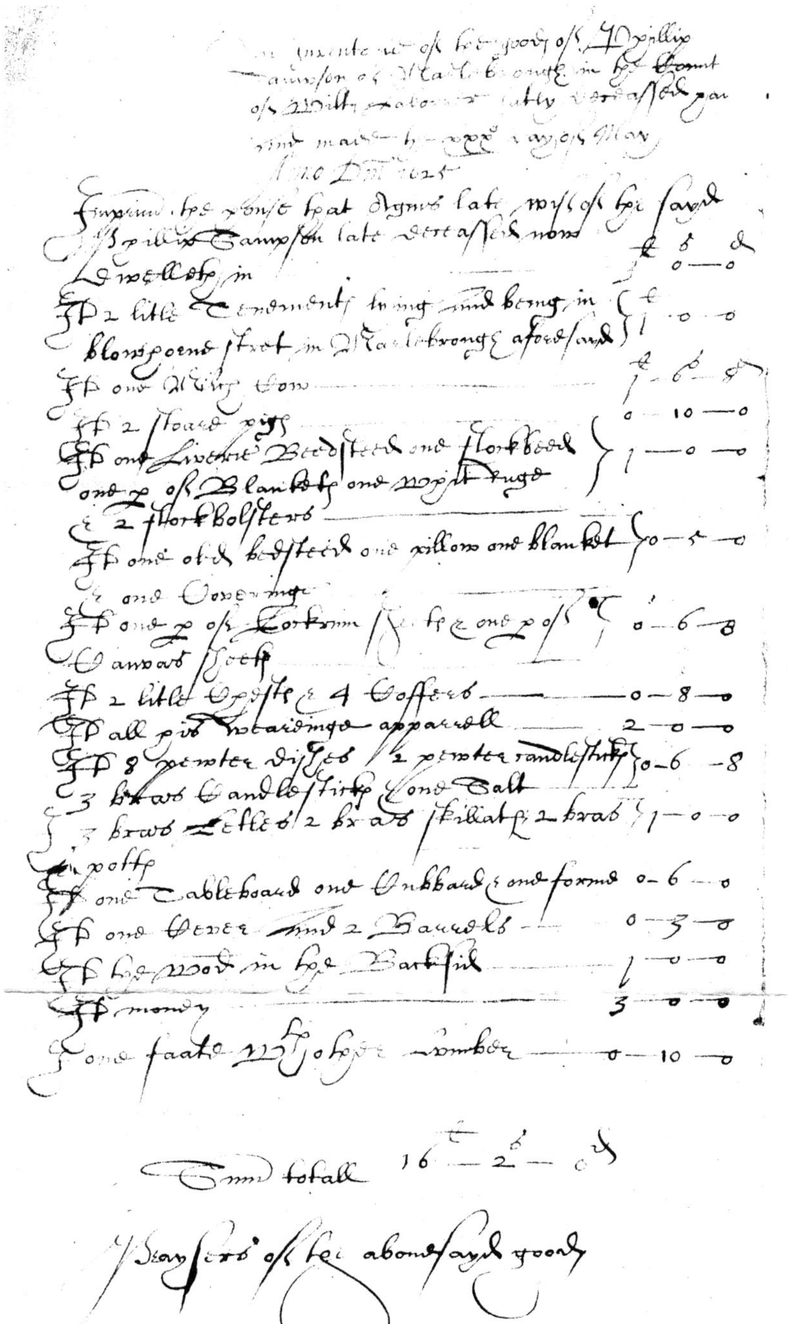

An Inventory of the goods of Phillip Samson of Marlebroughe in the County of Wilts labourer lately deceased and made the xxx dayes of May Anno Dni 1625

Imprimis the house that Agnes late wyffe of the sayde Phillip Sampson late deceased now dwelleth in	£5 0 0
It 2 litle tenements lying and being in blowhorne street in Marlebroughe aforesaid	£1 0 0
It one milch cow	£1 6 8
It 2 store pigs	0 10 0
It one livery bedsteed one flockbed one pr of blankets one white rugge & 2 flockbolsters	1 0 0
It one old bedsteed one pillow one blanket & one coveringe	0 5 0
It one pr of cotton sheets & one pr of canvas sheets	0 6 8
It 2 litle chests & 4 coffers	0 8 0
It all his wearinge apparell	2 0 0
It 8 pewter dishes 2 pewter candlesticks 3 brass candlesticks & one salt	0 6 8
It 3 brass kettles 2 brass skillets & 2 brass potts	1 0 0
It one tableboard one cubbard & one forme	0 6 0
It one cover and 2 barrels	0 3 0
It the wood in the backside	1 0 0
It money	3 0 0
It one faate with other lumber	0 10 0

Sum totall 16li 2s 0d

Praysers of the abovesayd goods

Philip Samson, labourer, 1625 (***69***)

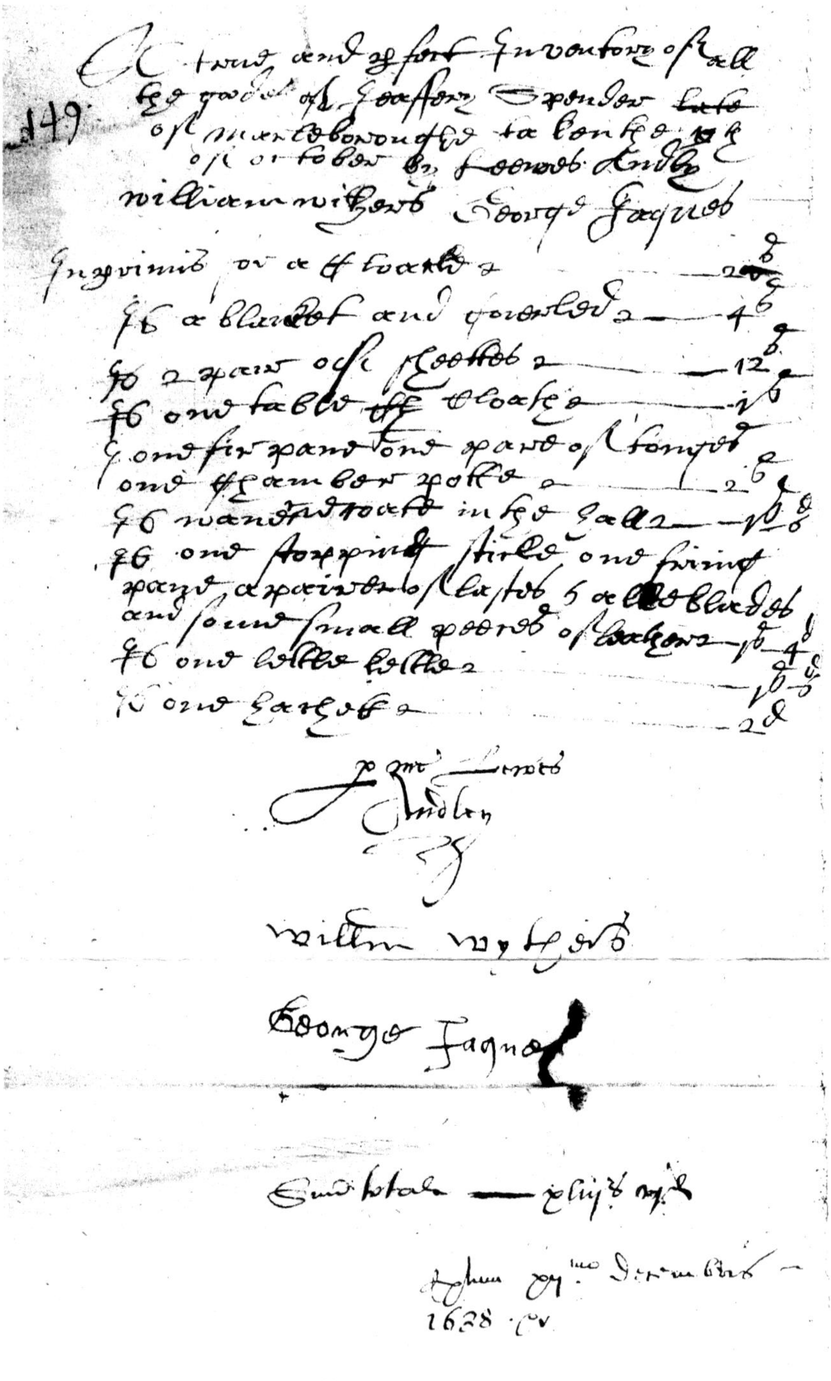

149

A true and perfect Inventory of all the goods of Jeaffery Spender late of Marlborough taken the [illegible] of October by Edward Andley William withers George Jaques

Inprimis one [illegible] — 20d

It a blanket and coverlet — 4s

It 2 pair of sheets — 12d

It one table [illegible] — 1s

It one fire pan and one pair of tongs one chamber pot — 2s

It wanscott in the hall — 10s

It one [illegible] kettle one frying pan a pair of [illegible] and some small peeces of [illegible] — 10s 4d

It one little kettle — 10s

It one hatchet — 2d

Edward Andley

William withers

George Jaques

Sum totalis — [illegible]

Exhibitum [illegible] Decembris 1638 [illegible]

Jeaffery Spender, 1638 (115)

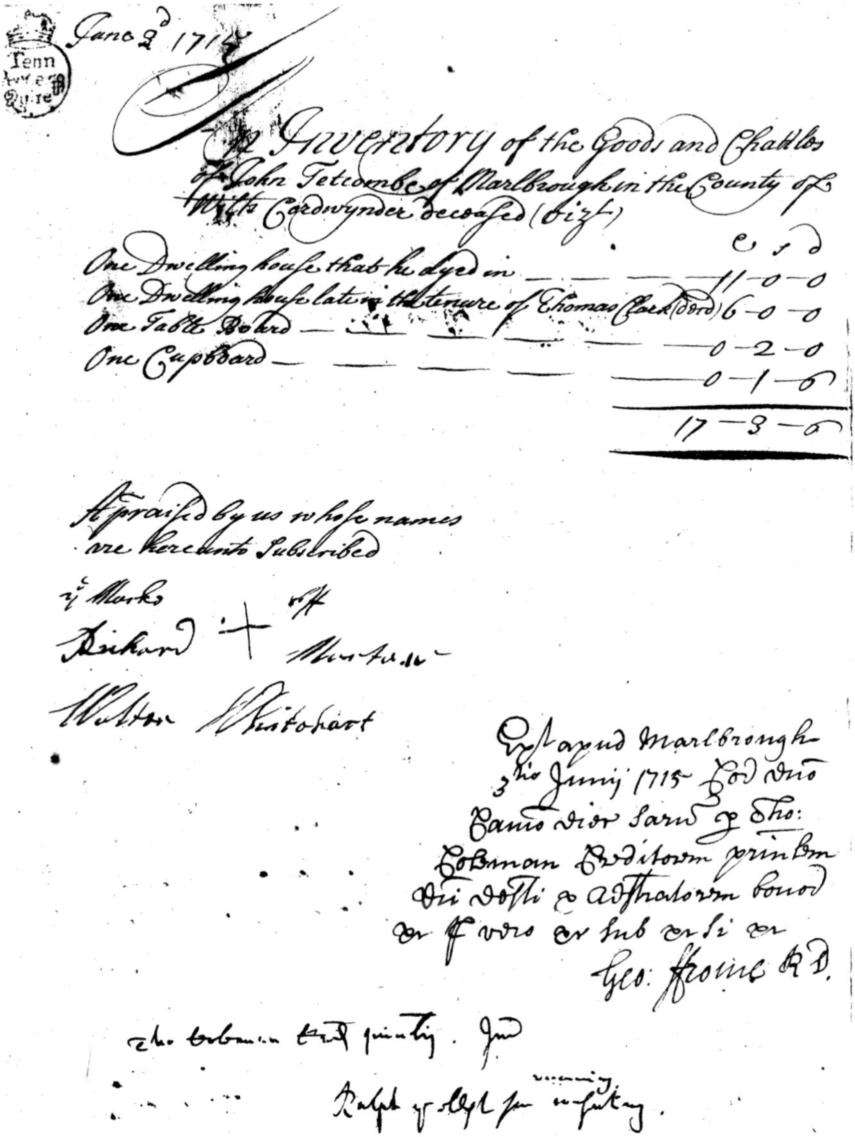

June 2d 1715
An Inventory of the Goods and Chattles of John Tetcombe of Marlbrough in the County of Wilts Cordwynder deceased (vizt)
£ s d
One Dwelling house that he dyed in 11-0-0
One Dwelling house late in the tenure of Thomas Clark (dec'd) 6-0-0
One Table Board 0-2-0
One Cupboard 0-1-6
17-3-6
Apraised by us whose names are hereunto Subscribed
Richard + Martin
Walter Whitehart
Ext apud Marlbrough 3tio Junij 1715
Geo: Frome RD.

John Tetcombe, cordwainer, 1715 (**405**)

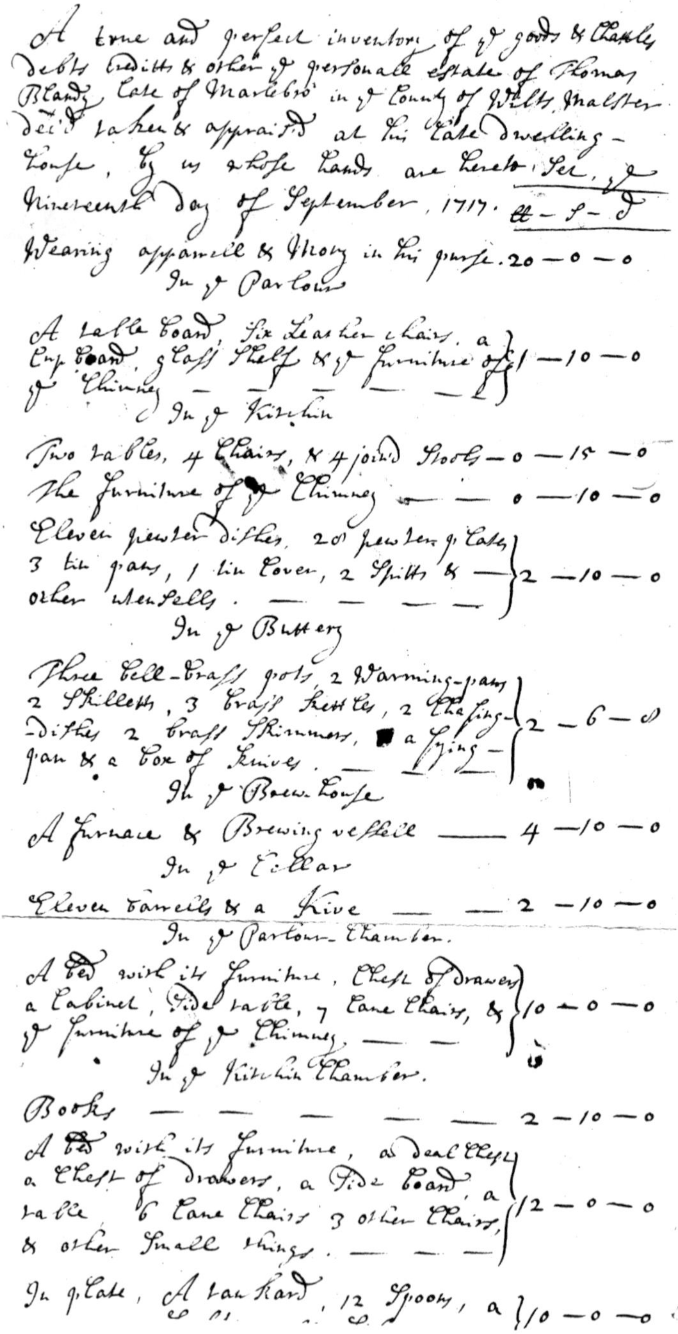

A true and perfect inventory of ye goods & Chattles debts creditts & other ye personall estate of Thomas Blandy late of Marlebro' in ye County of Wilts, Maltster dec'd taken & appraised at his late dwelling-house, by us whose hands are hereto set, ye Nineteenth day of September, 1717. li – s – d

Wearing apparell & Mony in his purse. 20 – 0 – 0

In ye Parlour

A table board, six Leather chairs, a Cup board, glass shelf & ye furniture of ye Chimney — 1 – 10 – 0

In ye Kitchin

Two tables, 4 Chairs, & 4 joind Stools – 0 – 15 – 0

The furniture of ye Chimney — 0 – 10 – 0

Eleven pewter dishes, 20 pewter plates 3 tin pans, 1 tin Cover, 2 Spitts & other utensills. — 2 – 10 – 0

In ye Buttery

Three bell-brass pots, 2 Warming-pans 2 Skilletts, 3 brass kettles, 2 Chafing-dishes 2 brass Skimmers, a frying-pan & a box of knives. — 2 – 6 – 0

In ye Brew-house

A furnace & Brewing vessell — 4 – 10 – 0

In ye Cellar

Eleven barrells & a Kive — 2 – 10 – 0

In ye Parlour-Chamber.

A bed with its furniture, Chest of drawers a Cabinet, side table, 7 Cane Chairs, & ye furniture of ye Chimney — 10 – 0 – 0

In ye Kitchin Chamber.

Books — 2 – 10 – 0

A bed with its furniture, a deal Chest a Chest of drawers, a side board, a table 6 Cane Chairs 3 other Chairs, & other small things. — 12 – 0 – 0

In plate, A tankard, 12 spoons, a ... 10 – 0 – 0

Thomas Blandy, maltster, 1717 (**412**)

Chairs, from The Merchant's House collection

(clockwise from top) Bed, Turkeywork chair, leather bottle, wooden bucket and cradle, from The Merchant's House collection

Sideboards, chests, fireplace utensils and a spinning wheel, from The Merchant's House collection

Chest, dairy mould and miscellaneous small items, from The Merchant's House collection

CALENDAR

1 THOMAS DIPPEN

baker 25 August 1591[1] P1/D/2

Of pewter: 2 platters, 3 pottingers, 3 sawcers, 2 saltcellers, 1 tun of pewter, 1 candlesticke of brasse 7*s.* 8*d.*[2]
One kettell of brasse 10*s.*
One posnet 1*s.* 8*d.*
One cawberd £1.
One chest 2*s.*
2 buckettes and 1 paile and 1 little chayne to the bucket 1*s.*
One pipe, 1 tubbe, 3 maltseenes 8*s.*
One trow, 2 plankes, 1 forme and 1 brake £1.
2 little tubbes 1*s.*
1 ax, 1 hatchet 1*s.* 4*d.*
The state in one close for four yeares 16*s.*
The faggetes in the same close £7.
His wearing apparell £1 10*s.*
1 frying pan 10*d.*

Total £12 19*s.* 6*d.*

William Massam and Thomas Blisset, appraisors.

Burial not recorded [registers not extant].
Will[3] 21 August 1591; probate and exhibition dates not recorded

1. Given as regnal year.
2. Roman numerals throughout.
3. With list of testator's debtors.

2 WILLIAM FRYBENS

28 September 1591[1] P1/F/3

In the Hall
One cubberd 4*s.*[2]
One table bord, 2 formes, 2 tressels, 1 chaire 4*s.*
Six platters, 6 pottyngers, 5 sawcers, 1 saltceller, 1 pewter cuppe 12*s.*
Foure candelsticks, 1 little morter and a pestel 1*s.* 8*d.*
2 andirons, 1 broche, 2 pothangers 2*s.*

In the Kychin
3 pottes wherof 2 are of brasse and 1 of iron 10*s.*
3 kettels and 1 skillet 4*s.*
1 dripping pan, 1 fryingpan, 1 paire of pothokes, 1 grydiron 2*s.*
4 cowles, 2 barrels, 2 kyvers, 2 bucketes 3*s.*
2 turnes 1*s.* 4*d.*
1 dussen of spones and 1 dussen of trenchers, half a dussen of treen dishes 1*s.*
1 browne bill 8*d.*
1 hedging bill, 1 hatchet, 1 mattocke, 3 iron wedges 2*s.*
1 butter churne 10*d.*
4 sackes 2*s.*
1 lyne 6*d.*
Weightes of led coming to 15 lbs. in all 1*s.* 3*d.*
1 horselocke, 1 paire of fetters 1*s.*
1 wellbucket with the chayne and rope 1*s.* 4*d.*

In the Chambers
2 bedstedes with the painted clothes over them
2 flockebeddes, 3 b[ols]ters, 2 fether pillowes £1 6*s.* 8*d.*
4 coverleddes, 2 pair of blankettes £1.
4 paire of sheetes, 2 pillowbears £1 2*s.*
1 chest, 1 cofer 5*s.*
His apparell 13*s.* 4*d.*

His gyrdell and his purse with 8*d.* in him 1*s.*
Wood in the backeside 14*s.*
1 score of sheepe £4.
The lease of the house £2.

Total £14 9*s.* 7*d.* [*recte* £14 6*s.* 1*d.*]

Thomas Clerke, Richard Harper and Thomas Toothe, appraisors.

Burial not recorded [no registers extant].
No other documents; exhibition date not recorded.

1. Given as regnal year.
2. Roman numerals throughout.

3 THOMAS BURGIES

yeoman [will] 30 January 1591/2

P1/B/1

In the Haule
A table borde with a frame, one benche, one fourme, 2 yeined stooles and a lyttill cubborde 6*s.* 8*d.*[1]
A brasse pan, a kettill, a posset, a [brasse *added*] pott, a chaffine dyche and 3 candill styckes 8*s.*
Fyve platters, one peuter dyche, 2 peuter candillstickes, 2 saltes and a [*illegible deletion*] [freing pan *added*] 6*s.* 8*d.*
A grydyre, pothangles, a fyre shovill, a pare of tonges and broche 1*s.* 8*d.*
A woode pale, a weshinge bowle, a tubb and a kever 1*s.* 4*d.*
A turne, a pare of bellowes and a glasse wyndowe 1s 10*d.*

In the Chamber
A leverye bedsteade, a flocke bed, a flocke bolster, a pillowe, a pare of blanketes and 2 keverlydes £1.
Three pare of sheetes and 3 chestes 10*s.*
A table borde with a frame 1*s.* 6*d.*
Flaxe and 3 buchils of mault 7*s.* 3*d.*
11 sheepe £1 10*s.*

Apparell
Thre dublets, 2 fryse fyrbines, cloke, a pare of bretchies and twoo chistes and a pare of sheooes £1.
Debtes due to the testator as apearethe more partycularly in the will[2] £9 3*s.* 4*d.*

Total £14 18*s.* 2*d.* [*recte* £14 18*s.* 3*d.*]

Thomas Whitfield, John New, Humpthreye Wiat and John Burgies, appraisors.

Burial not recorded [no registers extant].
Will 13 December 1591; probate 23 March 1591/2 to executrix [Mauld Burgies, testator's widow].

1. Roman numerals throughout.
2. Debtors and creditors listed:
Debtes due to the testator
Philip Reves of Marleborough £1.
Noye Stevens of Barton £1.
John Collingborne £1.
John Browne of Kynnet 12*s.*
Phillip Wickwaire of Calne 16*s.*
Thomas Brian of Brystowe 5*s.*
Bydow servant to Mr. Goddearde of Clatforde 2*s.* 8*d.*
Edward Allen of Marlebroughe 11*s.* 8*d.*
Robert Thompson of Marlebroughe 5*s.*
John Pudsey of Marlebroughe 10*d.*
The wyfe of John Grigg 1*s.*
Thomas Whitfield of Marlebroughe £1 10*s.*
Roger Hytchcocockes of Marlebroughe 5*s.*
William Hardforde of Bradforde 6*s.* 10*d.*
Mr. Weebes of Glocestershyre 1*s.* 4*d.*
Thomas Jeffereis of Bayne Asheten 2*s.* 10*d.*
William Sullygrove of Hownse Dytche beyond London £1 6*s.*

Debtes which the testator dyd ougye [these should not form part of the inventory]
To Richard Grenefield of Marlebroughe 10*s.*

To Robert Thompson of Marlebroughe 1s.
To Thomas Dyppinge of Marlebroughe 3s.

4 THOMAS COCKYE

tailor 8 February 1591/2 P1/C/1

In the haule

A table borde with a frame, a dowsand joined stooles, 2 benches, a leverye table borde £1 4s.[1]

A paynted clothe, a glasse wyndowe, a pare of andyrons, a pare of tonges, a fyre sheovill and pott hangles 8s.

2 lytill panes 1s.

In the Kytchinge

Foure brasse pottes, a posnet, 3 skylletes, one brasse pan, 3 kettilles, 2 chafinn dyshes, 2 dripinge pannes and 2 brochies £2.

A spyce morter, a turne, 2 tubes, 2 kevers, 2 cooles, 2 barrelles and 2 lytill plankes 6s.

In the Butterye

A cubborde, an old table and a chare 6s 8*d*.

3 great candilstickes and 2 lytill candilstickes 10s.

A dowsand pewter platters, a dowsand pottingers, a dowsand sawsers, a basson, 6 pewter dyshes, 2 chamber pottes, 6 floure pottes and 2 salts £1 15s. 4*d*.

In the Chamber

2 standinge bedsteades, 2 truckle bedsteades, 2 coffers, a chest, a table borde, a pare of andyrons and pott hangles £1 7s. 2*d*.

One feyther bed, 3 feyther bolsters, 4 feyther pyllowes, four flocke beddes and one flocke bolster £4 6s. 8*d*.

4 whyte rugges, 2 rede keverlydes and 2 quyltes £1 10s.

Eight pare of sheetes, a table borde clothe and 2 pare of pyllowe beares £2 13s.4*d*.

Curtaines for one bed 6s. 8*d*.

In the Shoppe

2 great chestes £1 13s. 4*d*.

2 shope bords, 3 pare of sheares, 2 yrons and a shelfe 15s. 2*d*.

Apparell

2 dubletes, 2 pare of hose, a cloke, a felt hatt, a pare of shooes and a jirkin £1.

Total £20 3s. 4*d*.

Thomas Whitfield, Myghell Coles and Jefferey Coleman, appraisors.

Burial not recorded [no registers extant]. Memorandum of administration 23 March 1591/2, administration to Martha Cockie, intestate's widow.

1. Roman numerals throughout.

5 JHON MERCHANT

28 March 1592 P1/M/1

In the Haule

2 table bordes, 2 fermes, 2 benches and old paynted clothes 2s. 6*d*.[1]

3 pott hangles, 2 pare of pott hookes, 2 broches, 2 brasse pottes and 2 tryvetts [and fyre pan *added*] 10s.

2 brasse panns, fyve kettills and a skyllett and a furnace £1.

2 chayffin dyshes, a lytill skyllett, a skyrne, eight candillstykes and a brasse floure pott 5s.

13 platters, fyve peuter dyshes, 3 sawsers, 2 floure pottes, 2 pynte pottes, 4 quart pottes and 3 saltes 16s.

In the Chamber

A table borde, a ferme, one benche, a backe borde 2s.

3 upstandes, 2 kevers, an old brubboule and a cowle 4s.

Eight flocke beds, ten bolsters where of 2 be fether bolsters, eight old keverlydes and fyve pare of old shetes £2.
[Fyve *deleted*] eight coffers, an old borde, 2 sawes, a lytill vergies barrell and eight bedsteades 8*s.*
2 old table bordes, a forme, old paynted cloathes and an old chare 2*s.*

Apparell
2 olde clokes, an old cote, a pare of hose, 2 shertes and a dublet 4*s.*
20 tegges, 30 hewes and 2 bullockes £8.
2 leacies £1.
A mault myll 2*s.*

In the Backsyde
In woode 2*s.*

Total £14 17*s.* 6*d.*

Debtes which the testator dyd oughe[2]
To Jhon Boye £4 6*d.*
To William Goffe 2*s.*
To William Francklin £1 12*s.*
To Richard Purses £1.
To Joan Hencocke 13*s.* 4*d.*

Total £7 13*s.* 4*d.*

Thomas White, Jhon Hiller and Jhon Boyce with others, appraisors.

Burial not recorded [no registers extant]. No other documents; exhibition date not recorded.

1. Roman numerals throughout.
2. Debts owed by the deceased should not form part of the inventory.

6 AGNES PAULE

22 April 1592 P1/P/4

In the Haule
One table borde with a frame and one joine forme 10*s.*[1]
A table borde with a cuberd in the same, 2 benches, halfe a backe of wainescote and 2 chaires 11*s.*
A cubard 2*s.* 6*d.*
2 pothangels, one andyer, a bar of iron 5*s.* 4*d.*
Room total £1 8*s.* 10*d.*

In the Kitching
A furnece of brasse £1.
8 brasse panes £1 7*s.*
[*from here in a different hand*]
Fyve brasse pottes £1 10*s.*
A mault myll 10*s.*
4 kyttles and a skyllet 13*s.* 4*d.* [xiij^{s} 4^{d}]
2 fryinge pannes, 1 drippinge pann 3*s.* 2*d.*
2 gridiorons, 1 brandiron and a flesh hocke and one iron bar 3*s.* 8*d.* [iij^{s} 8^{d}]
[*reverts to first hand*]
A welbucket with a chaine 3*s.*
2 mesingfates, one poudringe tub 7*s.* 6*d.*
6 tubes, one payle, two pothokes 2*s.* 6*d.*
[*reverts to second hand*]
On yoron hope at the mouth of the fornace, a bench, a chelfe, 3 stoles, a washe tubb, a dry vatte and a payre of byllowes 2*s.* 2*d.*
2 yoron wedges, a glyve and a locke 1*s.* 10*d.*
An olde chayer, a soword, 2 daggers, a jacke and a scull 7*s.*
6 olde tubbes, a trenhill and a verges barle 3*s.*
A tange and a chese racke with cordes 8*d.*
Room total £6 14*s.* 4*d.* [*recte* £16 14*s.* 10*d.*]

In the Buttery
2 upstands, 2 barrelles, a coffer, a pecke, a bushill, shelves, one trenhill and a clenseve and a coule 8*s.* 2*d.* [8^{s} ij^{d}]
A bill, a well, snyppers 1*s.* 6*d.*
Eight silver spones £1 6*s.* 8*d.* [xxvj^{s} 8^{d}]
14 platters, a pewter basson, fyve

pottengers, eight sawcers, six pewter dishes and an olde basson £1 4s. 8d.

One pewter cupp, 2 quart pottes, 3 pynte pottes, 3 sault sellers, 2 chafinge dishes, 3 candelstickes, 3 chamber pottes and a puddringe tubb 11s. 10d.

Room total £3 6s. 10d. [*recte* £3 12s. 10d.]

In the Parlour

A table borde with a frame and benches 3s. 4d. [iij^{s} 4^{d}]

One bedsteede, paynted clothes, a fether bede, a fether boulster, three fether pyllowes, one kyverlet and one quilt £1 12s. 6d. [xxxij^{s} 6^{d}]

Total £1 15s. 10d.

In the First Chamber

2 bedstedes, 2 flocke bedes, one boulster, a quilt and one keverlet 12s.

5 coffers, 3 paynted clothes 7s.

2 fether pillowes and 3 pilloperes 7s. 6d.

Six payre of sheetes £1 13s. 4d.

Room total £3 0s. 4d. [*recte* £2 19s. 10d.]

In the Second Chamber

5 bedstedes, 2 paynted testurnes 15s.

[*reverts to first hand*]

3 blankets, 5 flokebedes, 4 flokebolsters, 3 keverkeds, [2 quelts *added*] £3 9s. 4d.

One fether bolster and one old borde 5s. 7d.

Room total £4 10s. 4d. [*recte* £4 9s. 11d.]

Apparell

One olde cloke, a gowne, 2 peticotes 10s.

In the Bakeside

One sowe, 3 piges sowlde £1.

A dosen of hurdles, 3 laders, 2 hens, a coke 3s. 10d.

A cowe soweld £2 8s.

2 ewes, 2 lomes, one young shepe sowlde £1 4s.

2 piges 4s. 9d.

Sub-total £7 17s. 10d. [*recte* £5 10s. 7d.]

Debtes which she did owe[2]

Thomas Patie of Marleboroucht £3 8s.

Richard Baninge 10s.

John Boye £1 12s.

Robert Perce £1.

Toe Witt of Brinkeworth 8s. 8d.

Thomas Fletcher of the same towen 2s. 4d.

Gabrel Bayly 2s. 3d.

Walter Clines 5s.

Margeret Tipper 2s. 8d.

The good wyfe Dimer 2s. 8d.

Thes beinge presses of the goodes.

Thomas Whitfield, Robert Hitchcocke, Gabryell Bayly, Thomas Patie, John Boye and John Hiller, appraisors.

Burial not recorded [no registers extant].

No other documents; exhibition date not recorded.

1. Roman numerals throughout except as shown.
2. Debts owed by the deceased should not form part of the inventory.

7 THOMAS TYPPER

tanner 17 May 1592 P1/T/2

In the Haule

One longe table and one rownd table, a fuorme, benches, 3 cushinges and painted clothes [and a cubbarde *added*] 10s.[1]

One brasse pott, 3 lytill kettils, 2 skilletes and a skymmer 11s. 8d.

A fryinge panne, a broche, a pare of pott hookes, 2 chopinge knyfes and 2 potthangles 1s. 6d.

3 treene platters and six woodden dyshes 8d.

6 platters, 3 pottengers, 4 saucers, 2 purridge dyshes of pewter, 2 saultes, 6

sponnes, 3 brasse candilstickes, a spice morter and a latten bason 17*s.*

In the Butterie
An olde chest, a woollen tourne and a lynninge tourne 2*s.*
One kever, 2 ale tubbes and an ale bowle 1*s.* 6*d.*

In the Chamber
One flocke bed, 2 flocke boulsters, 2 fether pyllowes, a keverlyd, one pare of blankettes, one pare of sheetes, a pare of pyllowbeeres and one bedstead 13*s.* 4*d.*
3 cofers 5*s.*

In the Loft overheade
Three quarters of mault £1 8*s.*
2 olde tubbes, a bushill, a powderinge tubb, a fourme and one renseve 2*s.* 8*d.*

In the Parler
Twoo stanlles of beer 3*s.* 4*d.*

Debts owinge to the said Thomas Typpor
Nycholas Mylls of Marleborroughe £1 3*s.* 4*d.*
Henrie Baggett of Heothe in Hampshier £1.
Jhon Boye of Marleborroughe £1.

Total £8 [6*s.* 3*d. added*] [*recte* £8.]

Debtes wich he dyd owghe when he dyed[2]
To Mr Lovell of Marlbrough £1.
To Hen[ry]e Cruce of Rood £3.
To Marguret Cruce of Carlne £2.

Total £6 and so all the goods and debts which the testator was possessed of at the tyme of his death doth amount but unto the sume of [£2 3*s. deleted*] £2 0*s* 6*d.* [*recte* £2.]

Thomas Wynchecome, William Goffe and Richard Morce, appraisors.

Burial not recorded [no registers extant].
Bond 29 May 1592, administration to Margaret Tipper, intestate's widow.

1. Roman numerals throughout.
2. Debts owed by the deceased should not form part of the inventory.

8 WILLIAM SYMMES
shoemaker [will] 5 December 1592[1]
P1/S/11

In the Haule
One ioyned bedsteed, 1 truckle bedstede, 1 cubberd, 2 cofers, 1 forme 19*s.*[2]
1 flockebed, 2 flockebolsters, 2 pillowes, 3 coverlettes, 2 blanketes £1 14*s.* 4*d.*
2 paire of sheetes, 2 pillowberrs, 1 cradle, 1 cruse 9*s.*

In the Buttery
Foure platters, 3 pottingers, 3 sawcers, 1 candelsticke, 1 saltceller 8*s.*
1 lanterne, 2 covelles, 3 kyvers, 3 little barrels, 1 reele, 1 paire of pincers, 1 clenseeve, 1 bill, 1 serche 9*s.*
1 powdring tubbe, 1 stoole, 1 bushell, 1 paire of tresselles, 1 sacke, 1 bag 3*s.* 2*d.*
6 disshes, 6 spones, 1 dussen of trenchers 7*d.*

In the Welhouse
1 yoting vate, 1 bucket with the chaine and ropes to the same, 3 tubbes, 1 bowle, 1 ladell 10*s.* 6*d.*
1 cauldron [of brasse *added*], 3 brasse pottes, 2 skillettes, 1 skymer, 1 pothangers, 2 pothookes 14*s.* 10*d.*
1 east heare, [one broche *deleted*] 1 gridiron, 1 frying pan 3*s.*

In the Backeside
The wood and 1 hatchet [and 1 paire of tressels *added*] 10*s.*

Of mault tenne quarters £5.
One weight of wooll 16s.
One chest, 1 pair of hampers, 1 shovell 5s.

In the Shoppe
Leasses for shomakers trade, railes and seales and 2 reephookes 2s.

Total £12 4s. 5d.

Rychard Harpe, Daniell Hall and Nicholas Tree, appraisors.

Burial not recorded [no registers extant].
Will 20 December 1591; probate 15 November 1593 to [unnamed].

1. Given as regnal year.
2. Roman numerals throughout.

9 ROGER ELSON

?saddler [inventory goods] 6 January 1592/3 P1/E/1

In the Haule
A cubbord, a frame and one benche 4s. 8d.[1]
An andyron, 2 pott hangles and a pare of tonges 1s. 4d.
Six yeards of olde paynted clothes 1s.
17 pole of pewter 8s. 6d.
3 candlestickes and one chaffing dyshe 2s.
A chamber pott and one salt 6d.
Room total 18s.

In the Kytchinge
2 cauldrons, 2 brasse pottes and a skyllet 12s.
5 barrells, 3 tubbes and one trenchild 5s.
2 broches, a grydyron and a fryeing pan 1s. 6d.
Room total 18s. 6d.

In the Bed chamber
2 bedsteades 10s.
One flock bed, one bolster and coverlydd, 3 blankettes, one quilt and 3 pare of sheetes 13s. 4d.
Room total £1 3s. 4d.

In the Shoppe
25 head stalls and raynes 4s. 4d.
Ten cruppers and 9 dowsan of straps 4s. 8d.
Ten pare of gyrses and eight sussingles 3s. 8d.
Seven pare of sturryp leythers 2s. 8d.
4 male pyllyons and 10 snuffles 3s. 6d.
9 byttes and 3 pare of sturryps 7s. 4d.
3 pare of pasterns, 5 sussingles straps 1s.
2 dowsan of scottis trees, dennis trees and parte trees £1 1s. 4d.
One leyther hunger hyde 12s.
One dowsan of basins and 2 caulfe skinns 3s.
13 saddils £3 5s.
One case of boxis, one baye and one presse 6s.
Woorkinge tooles and heere 2s.
Room total £6 16s. 6d.

In the Back Syde
A well buckett with a chayne 6d.

Total £9 16s. [*recte* £9 16s. 10d.]

Thomas Wynde, Robert Clemence and Thomas Burland, appraisors.

Burial not recorded [no registers extant].
Bond 7 August 1593, administration to Alice Elston, intestate's widow.

1. Roman numerals throughout.

10 JOHN LYDDORL[1]

[*undated*, c. 1592/3] P1/L/1

1 table borde, 1 rounde table borde and a

cubberde and a chayre, 1 forme, 1 turne 3*s.* 4*d.*[2]
3 brase poots 6*s.* 8*d.*
1 brasse pan 2*s.*
6 kyttles, 2 posnats and 2 skymers 6*s.* 8*d.*
4 platters, 5 potingers, 5 sasers, 3 souttes 4*s.* 8*d.*
6 candlestyks 2*s.*
A peare of tongs, a fyre shovle, 1 byllys 6*d.*
1 gardyer, 1 broche, 1 peare of pothoks, a fryn pan, a drypingpan, 1 ayndyer, 1 fleshoks and a slyce, 3 choping knyffs 2*s.*
8 tubs, 1 kyfer 3*s.*
9 wegis, 6 aksys, 1 mattake, 4 hamers, 5 boryers, 3 chessels, 1 drafte, 1 hone, 1 pynsers and 3 sawes, 1 iren parr 10*s.*
3 beds, 5 pyllos, 2 poustars, 3 coverlyds, 3 blankats, 2 peare of sheats £1.
2 coffers 2*s.*
19 quarters of moulte £6.
2 fattes, 1 bushell, 1 kyffe, 2 east heares 4*s.*
3 ladders, a maulte myle 10*s.*
3 dussen of loke stoks 1*s.* 4*d.*
1 gryndstone, 1 syffe 1*s.* 4*d.*
2 hudrith of bordes 7*s.*
The woode pyle £5.
2 tres, 1 pece of tymber which lyeth abrode 16*s.*
Halfe a wayte 8*s.*

Total £16 10*s.* 6*d.*

John Hiller, Richerd Purrser, Edmond Barington and William Haskins, appraisors.

Burial not recorded [no registers extant].
Will 17 October 1592; probate 23 March 1592/3 to [unnamed] Lyddall, testator's daughter.

1. 'Lyddall' on will.
2. Roman numerals throughout.

11 JOHN SQUIRE

17 April 1593 P1/S/10

In the Hall
1 table bord, 1 forme, 2 benches, the painted clothes and the lettis 6*s.*[1]
1 chaire, 1 cubberd 4*s.*
1 paire of andirons, 1 fire shovell, 1 plate, 2 pothangers, 1 iron barre 6*s.*
1 peele of iron, 1 pair of billowes 6*d.*
Pewter: fyve platters, two pottingers, six sawcers, 4 pewter dishes, 4 saltcellers, 1 quart pot, 2 pynte pottes 11*s.* 6*d.*
1 little pewter cuppe, 1 little measure for aqua vite, 4 candelstickes, 1 chafyn dishe 2*s.* 6*d.*
1 brushe, 1 tosting iron, 1 pair of sheeres, 1 furnaise 9*s.*

In the Shop
Three pottes, 1 brasse pan, 2 caldrons, 2 posnettes, 2 skillittes, 2 pair of of pot hookes, skymmers, 1 clever £1 1*s.*
1 myncing knife, 1 chopping knife, 2 fleshookes, 2 bordes, 3 formes, 1 stoole, 4 upstands, 2 little tubbes, 1 covle, 2 pikes, 2 meashing cowles, 4 kyvers, 1 turne for woollen, 1 turne for lynnen £1.
1 kyve, 1 powdring tubbe, 1 pecke, 1 gallon, 2 little tubbes 4*s.*
2 lidging barrell, 1 lanterne 1*s.* 6*d.*
2 broches, 2 dripping pannes, 1 frying pan, 1 gridire 5*s.* 4*d.*

In the Lower Chamber
1 bord, 2 formes, 1 chest 11*s.*
1 bedsteed with the painted clothes 2*s.* 6*d.*
1 box 6*d.*
2 pailes, 1 ax, 1 basket, 1 handbasket, 3 maltseeves, 1 renseeve, 1 reele, 1 cradle 4*s.*
2 yoting vates and the thole or settle which they stand upon 10*s.*
6 tubbes 4*s.*
1 dow kyver, 1 querne 7*s.*

3 plankes, 1 litle forme 1*s.* 8*d.*
2 litle tubbes 8*d.*
3 tallettes and the wood £1 13*s.* 4*d.*
3 ladders 2*s.*
1 welbucket with the chaine and rope 2*s.*
1 colerake, 1 hogtrow 6*d.*

In the Buttery
1 standing bedsteed with a painted clothe, 3 other bedsteedes, 2 cofers, 1 settle which the barrels stand upon, 1 planke, 1 forme, 1 tunning bowle, 3 treen platters, 1 trey 10*s.* 8*d.*
6 stoning pottes, 1 pair of brasen skales 1*s.* 6*d.*
1 litle kyver, 1 dussen of woodden dishes, 1 dussen of trenchers, 1 dussen of spones 1*s.* 2*d.*
2 beames and skales, 8lbs of lead 1*s.*
1 bilhooke, 1 trewell, 1 augur, 1 settle for a round table 1*s.* 1*d.*
4 little bordes, 1 hobend, 1 woodden candelsticke, 3 bottels 2*s.*
3 flockebeddes, 4 flockebolsters, 2 fetherbolsters, 3 fetherpillowes £2.
6 coverleddes, 3 paire of blankettes £1 15*s.*
10 pair of sheetes, 5 tableclothes, 1 pair of pillowbees, 8 table napkins whereof 2 are of diaper, 1 diaper towell £2 6*s.* 8*d.*
1 cow, 1 calfe £1 13*s.* 4*d.*
1 sow 8*s.*
Twenty quarters of mault £10.

Total £29 11*s.* [*recte* £27 10*s.* 11*d.*]

Richard Cornewall, William White, Robert Buy and Henry Tooth, appraisors.

Burial not recorded [no registers extant].
Will 2 September 1592; bond 19 April 1593 and probate 19 April 1593 to Edith Squire, testator's widow.

1. Roman numerals throughout.

12 [WALTER HARRYS][1]

[*date lost*, c.1593] P1/H/10

[*unknown number of lines lost*]
Half a hundred of boardes 2*s.*[2]
Woodd and tymber £20.
Sub-total £25 16*s.*

Plate
One silver boale and a mazar cupp tipped and fotid with silver £2 10*s.*
Sub-total £2 10*s.*

The Testators Apparell
One frise gown 3*s.* 4*d.*
One black cloake 6*s.* 8*d.*
One black coate 3*s.*
Sub-total 13*s.*

Total £56 3*s.*

[*Appraisors' names lost*]

Burial not recorded [no registers extant].
Will 7 September 1592; probate 14 June 1593 to [unnamed].

1. Name lost, obtained from will.
2. Surviving amounts in Roman numerals.

13 JOHN PURLYN

barber [will] 3 August 1593 P1/P/5

In the Hall
One table borde, forme and benches 13*s.* 4*d.*[1]
One cobard 6*s.* 8*d.*
Certayne paynted clothes in the hall 2*s.*
The glasse of the wyndowes 3*s.*
Room total £1 5*s.*

In the Chamber within the Hall
A ioyned bedstede 10*s.*
A fether bede and a flock bede with 2 boulsters £2.
One cofer 1*s.*

A payre of blanckettes 4*s.*
A coverlett 10*s.*
Room total £3 5*s.*

In the Chamber over the Hall
A ioyned bedstede 5*s.*
A fetherbede and a flocke bed with 2 bolsters £2.
A coverlett 10*s.*
Six pillowes 12*s.*
A payre of blanckettes 3*s.*
[. . .] table borde and a frame 3*s.* 4*d.*
[*Room total lost, by addition* £3 13*s.* 4*d.*]

In the K[. . .]
A queren 10*s.*
A maltinge vatte 2*s.* 6*d.*
A hen cobe 6*d.*
Fyve brasse pottes £1 5*s.*
Fower brasse panns £1 10*s.*
2 great caldrons 8*s.* 8*d.* [viij^{s} 8^{d}]
3 posnettes 3*s.* 8*d.*
A litle kytle and one chaffinge dish 1*s.*
Fower candelstickes 5*s.*
One brassen spice morter 1*s.*
2 saltsellers 10*s.*
Thre dozen of pewter £2 1*s.*
3 silver spones £1.
Six payre of shetes £2.
3 payre of pillowbers 4*s.*
3 table clothes 6*s.* 8*d.* [vj^{s} 8^{d}]
One dozen of table naptkings 6*s.* 8*d.* [vj^{s} 8^{d}]
Room total £9 12*s.* [*recte* £10 15*s.* 8*d.*]

In the Utter House
3 broches, one dripinge, one fryinge pann and one gridiorun 2*s.* 8*d.* [ij^{s} 8^{d}]
Two payre of potthockes 1*s.*
2 payre of potthanngells 1*s.*
One payre of andirons 6*s.* 8*d.* [vj^{s} 8^{d}]
One [payre *deleted*] brandiron 6*d.*
One iron bar 1*s.* 8*d.*
2 wedges 10*d.*
Room total 16*s.* 2*d.* [*recte* 14*s.* 4*d.*]

In the Backeside
Certen wood £1 6*s.* 8*d.* [xxvj^{s} 8^{d}]
Eight quarters of malte £4 6*s.* 8*d.* [iiij^{li} vj^{s} 8^{d}]
Three halfes of barley in the field 16*s.*
In redie mony £2.
His wearinge aparell £2 10*s.*
Certayne packthrede and nett 16*s.*
Sub-total £11 15*s.* 4*d.*

Two carpettes 10*s.*
Sub-total 10*s.*

Total £32 5*s.* 4*d.* [*recte* £31 18*s.* 8*d.*]

Thomas Whittfield, clerke, William Francklyn, Roger Hitchcocke and James Hall, appraisors.

Burial not recorded [no registers extant].
Will 30 April 1593; probate not recorded; bond 7 Aug 1593, administration to Margaret Purlin, testator's widow.

1. Roman numerals throughout except where shown.

14 JHON CLERKE

carpenter 15 December 1593 P1/C/9[1]

In the Haule
A table boarde, a frame and a cubboard 3*s.* 4*d.*
One dowsand of pewter great and smaule, 2 brasse pottes, one kettill, 2 candilstickes and one pewter potte 12*s.* 4*d.*
One pott hangle,[2] a pare of pott hookes, one broche, a fyer panne, a pare of tonges and a fryeing panne 2*s.* 2*d.*
One puldrynge tubb, a kever, one lydgeinge barrell and one upstand 2*s.* 6*d.*
In the Chamber
One flocke bed,[3] 2 bolsters, 2 keverlydes, one pyllowe, 2 pare of sheetes 13*s.* 4*d.*
2 olde coffers and a forme 2*s.* 4*d.*

In the Backesyde
An olde mylle to grynde crabbes and one lode of wood 4*s.* 4*d.*
Apparell 13*s.* 4*d.*

Total £2 13*s.* 8*d.*

Richard Purser, John Mushe and Thomas Whitfield, appraisors.

Burial not recorded [no registers extant].
No further documents; inventory exhibited 20 December 1593.

1. Two almost identical versions exist of this inventory, the appraisors' names appear only in the second.
2. 'a pare of pothangles' in the second version.
3. 'one olde flocke bed' in the second version.

15 JOHN STUMPE

shoemaker 21 December 1593 P1/S/12

In the Hall
The wainskott and the benches 6*s.*[1]
One table with a frame, 2 stoles and a forme 6*s.* 8*d.*
One chaire and a cubborde 8*s.*
One calyver, sword, dagger and black bill 6*s.* 8*d.*
Twoo cusshions 1*s.*
Room total £1 8*s.* 4*d.*

In the New Shopp
One table with a frame and a paire of tables 5*s.*
One paire of skales and certen nayles 12*s.*
2 dossen of newe leases for shewmakers 2*s.* 6*d.*
A beame, skales and certen waytes 6*s.* 8*d.*
Shop total £1 6*s.* 2*d.*

In the Chamber over the Hall
Twoo joyned bedsteeds £1 6*s.* 8*d.*
One cubborde 2*s.*
Twoo coffers and twoo chestes 7*s.*
2 fetherbeds, 2 flockbeds and 3 bolsters £2.
4 curtaynes 2*s.* 6*d.*
3 coverledds, 2 blankettes and a quilte £1.
4 pillowes 4*s.* 6*d.*
Certen cheeses £1.
Certen pewter vessell £1.
His wearinge apparell £2.
Foure payre of sheetes £1.
Room total £10 2*s.* 8*d.*

In the Kitchin
4 lidginge barrells 2*s.* 8*d.*
The glasse there and in the chamber 2*s.* 6*d.*
One table, a benche and a forme 3*s.*
One olde cubborde 8*d.*
Fyve brasse pottes £1 13*s.* 4*d.*
One porsnett and a skyllett 2*s.*
3 kettells 10*s.*
Fyve candlestickes, 3 skymmers, one friengpan 5*s.* 8*d.*
3 broches, 2 potthangelles and a gridiron 3*s.* 4*d.*
Room total £3 3*s.* 2*d.*

In the Chamber over the Kitchin
The servants lodginges or beddinges £1.
Certen olde tubbes and barrelles 4*s.*

In the Well House
2 yotinge stones 13*s.* 4*d.*
Sub-total £1 17*s.* 4*d.*

In the Mouldinge Howse
One querne 5*s.*
For bords 6*s.* 8*d.*
Sixe quarters of maulte £1 16*s.*
A vann 1*s.*
One grindinge stone 2*s.*
The standing stuffe and haie 12*s.*
Room total £3 2*s.* 3*d.* [*recte* £3 2*s.* 8*d.*]

In the Workinge Shopp
Shewes and leather £7 13*s.* 4*d.*
The workinge tooles 10*s.*
Shop total £8 3*s.* 4*d.*

In the Backside
3 pigges 15*s.*
One horse and saddell and furniture £1.
The wood and tymber £5.
One olde furnice and an olde pann 8*s.*
One payre of andirons, one payre of tongs, a drippinge pan and a fyer shovell 4*s.*
Sub-total £7 7*s.*

Total £36 10*s.* 3*d.* [*recte* £36 10*s.* 8*d.*]

Thomas Wynde, John Aprise and John Rumsey, appraisors.

Burial not recorded [no registers extant][2].
Will 26 September 1592; probate not recorded; bond 20 April 1593, administration to Johan Stump, testator's widow.

1. Roman numerals throughout.
2. 'my body to be buried in … St Peters being the parishe church where I dwell' [will].

16 ELLEN ANDROS

20 January 1593/4[1] P1/A/4

In the Hall
One table, twoo formes, the back of joyned work and the benches about the hall 10*s.*[2]
One cupbord, one cupbord clothe, a brasse morter with a pestell, fyve candelstickes 12*s.*
17 platters, 2 pottingers, 4 sawcers and three pewter dishes, fyve pewter pottes, twoo saltsellers and 3 flower pottes £1 11*s.* 6*d.*
Sixe cusshions and two brnches 4*s.*
A payre of andirons, a fire shovell, a pair of fyer tonges, an iron barr, 2 pott hangers, a paire of billowes, twoo stooles, a fryeng pan, a gridiron, a paire of potthookes 10*s.* 2*d.*

In the Chamber over the Hall
One standing bedsteed and a testor 8*s.*
4 coffers and a chayer 7*s.*
One flockbed, 2 coverleds, a payre of blankettes and a carpett £1 13*s.* 4*d.*
Fyve payre of sheetes and 3 paire of pillowbers £1 15*s.*
Tenne kercheefes and partlettes, 7 canvas aprons and a worsted apron £1 2*s.*
3 table clothes and 6 table napkins 10s
6 smockes 12*s.*
One fetherbed, one fether bolster, 3 fether pillowes, one flock bolster and a flock pillowes £2.
One medly gowne, one frise gowne, a hatt and a petticote £2.
3 pottes, a porsenett, a littell skylett £1.
4 kyttells, one fornace and 2 small pannes £2.
One old chest, a littell table boord, a beame and skales, forty pound of lead and a broche 9*s.*
The wood, a querne, a yotinge stone, a well buckett, a chaine and a rope £2.
15 lb of woll 13*s.* 4*d.*

In the other Chamber
One standinge bedsted, one truckell bedsteed, one table boord [and the benches *added*] 10*s.*
3 upstandes, one lydginge barrell, twoo kevers, twoo payles, two twornes, a payre of cards, a beatinge hurdell, 2 maltseeves, twoo raynsyves, one bushell, one peck, a reele, a colerake and a peele 11*s.* 8*d.*
One chaffing dishe, one dossen of cruses, twoo dossen of trenchers, one dossen of spones, halfe a dossen of dishes and a hatchett 4*s.* 8*d.*

Total £21 3*s.* 8*d.*

Richarde Cornewall, Richard Franklyn, Thomas Christopher and Henry Tothe etc., appraisors.

Burial not recorded [no registers extant].
Will 3 April 1593; probate 1 Feb 1593/4 to Robert Boye, testator's son; bond 1

Feb 1593/4, administration to Alice Boye, testator's daughter [mother named as Ellen Androes alias Boye].

1. Given as regnal year.
2. Roman numerals throughout.

17 JOHN ROMSEY[1]

hosier [will] 3 October 1595 P1/R/4

In the Hall

One litle table board and frame 2*s*.,[2] one formm, one little stole and a shelf 6*d*., one paier of andirons, one old paier of bellowes, twoo paier of pothookes, twoo paier of pothangers, one flesh hooke, one spitt, a chopping knyffe and a gridiron 3*s*. 6*d*., fower brasse pottes, one brazen porcenett 13*s*. 4*d*., one brasse kettle, twoo brasse panns and one litle skyllett 10*s*., 13 pece of pewter vizt five platters, fower pottingers, three sawcers and one porridg dishe 8*s*., fower brasen candlestickes 1*s*. 6*d*., a wodden ladle, 10 trenchers, a hammer, five spoones, five wodden dishes, a brush and a salt seller 6*d*., painted cloaths and a quisshion 10*d*. £2 0*s*. 2*d*.

In the Entrie

One vate, three tubbes, one pale, one buckett, a tun boale, a clensingsive, a mault sive and an old planke 7*s*.

In the Shopp

Three chestes 10*s*., twoo barrells and a kive 2*s*., twoo plankes, one old doore and one paier of pincers 8*d*., a pressing iron and three paier of sheeres 4*d*., one fether bedd, a bolster and twoo pillowes £1 6*s*. 8*d*., one coverlett 8*s*., [the testators wearing apparrell *added*] twoo cloakes 8*s*., twoo paier of breaches 4*s*., one doblett and coate 3*s*. £3 2*s*. 8*d*.

In the Chamber over the Shopp

One longe table board with a frame 6*s*. 8*d*., twoo kivers 8*d*. 7*s*. 4*d*.

In the Chamber over the Hall

Twoo bedsteeds 13*s*. 4*d*., twoo flockbeddes and twoo flock bollsters, one paier of old blanckettes and twoo old coverlettes 6*s*. 8*d*., twoo coffers and an old wicker chaier 3*s*., old iron 1*s*. 6*d*., a paier of old bootes 4*d*., an old tubb 2*d*., one paier of sheetes and twoo pillowbeers 6*s*. £1 11*s*.

Total £7 8*s*. 2*d*.

Thomas Foxe, Nicholas Kember and John Buckland, appraisors.

Burial not recorded [no registers extant][3].
Will 3 August 1595; probate date not recorded; accounts submitted [*undated*] by Richard Strech, overseer of the will.

1. 'Rumsey' on accounts.
2. Roman numerals throughout.
3. 'who deceased in the yeare of our Lord god 1595 the third of August' [accounts].

18 RICHARD FRANCKELYN

sawyer 7 June 1598[1] P1/F/6

In the Haule

The weynscot there and 1 backebord and a benche 5*s*.[2]
One table bord with a frame and 5 ioyned stooles and 2 litle formes and 1 chaire £1.
1 cubberd 3*s*. 4*d*.
2 pothangers, 3 pothookes, 2 broches, 1 pair of andyrons, 1 fire shovell, 1 pair of tongues, 1 fleshehooke and 1 pair of billowes 7*s*.
1 clever, 1 mincing knife, 2 gridirons, 1 tosting iron 2*s*.
Of pewter 19 platters, sixteen pottingers £1 16*s*.
19 saucers 5*s*.
Foure alequartes, 2 wynequartes, 1

thyrdendale, one other alequart, 3 alypyntes, 1 half thirdendale, 4 saltcellers, 1 litle drinking cup 10*s.* 6*d.*
3 candelstickes 2*s.*
Of brasse: 12 candelstickes, 2 chafingdisshes 8*s.*
1 basyn, 1 skymer, 1 ladell 2*s.* 6*d.*

In the Kichin
3 brasse pottes 16*s.*
2 brasse pannes 12*s.*
Eight caldrons £1.
3 posnettes 2*s.*
2 chamberpottes of pewter 1*s.*
1 querne 6*s.* 8*d.*
1 wellbucket with the chayne and rope to the same 2*s.*
1 iron peele, 1 cole rake, 1 spade 1*s.*
6 tubbes, 3 pailes, 1 trey 6*s.*
6 barrels, 4 kivers, one powdring tub, 1 bushell and 1 pecke, 1 gallon and 1 serche and 1 old welbucket 11*s.*
2 turnes, 2 bottelles, 1 otemeale measure and 1 basket 2*s.*
1 old cofer, 1 old save, 2 shylfes and 1 benche 2*s.*
2 maltseeves, 3 renseeve, 1 clenseeve and 1 other old seeve 1*s.*
1 prong, 1 reele 6*d.*
1 frying pan 8*d.*
2 dussen of trenchers, 1 dussen of dishes, 1 dussen of spones, 1 ladell 1*s.*

In the Celler
Five barrels, 2 shylfes, two settles to set barrels upon and 2 small tubbes and 1 old paile 8*s.*
3 floure cuppes 6*d.*
Six stone cuppes 2*s.*

In the Chamber over the Entry
1 standing bedsted 6*s.* 8*d.*
1 other bedstede 1*s.*
1 table bord with a frame 10*s.*
1 benche with a backe of weynscot and 2 chaires 5*s.*
2 fetherbeddes, 6 fetherbolsters, 3 pillowes £2.
5 flockebeddes, 9 flockebolsters £2 11*s.* 4*d.*
5 coverleddes £2.
8 other coverleddes and 2 blankettes £1.
12 pair of sheetes £3.
2 pillowbees, two dussen of table napkyns 10*s.*
3 tableclothes 7*s.* 6*d.*

In the Chamber over the Kichin
1 standing bedsted, 1 other bedsted, 2 testers over them 5*s.*
2 old cofers, 2 old tubbes and 1 frame 2*s.* 2*d.*

In the Chamber over the Hall
2 bedsteedes, 1 bord and a frame 8*s.*
10 cofers 10*s.*
1 blackebill, 1 other bill 1*s.*
3 shylfes, 1 cheeseracke 1*s.* 4*d.*
36 cheeses 18*s.*
His apparell £1 10*s.*
1 prong, 1 hatchet, 1 tub and 1 flasket 1*s.*
The tooles belonging to his occupation of a sawyer £1.
1 beame and skales 1*s.*
1 tod stone 2*s.*
Hey 5*s.*
Wood, timber and postes and lugges to the same whereuppon wood lyeth £5.
2 ladders and other implementes in the entry 5*s.*
1 cow £2.

Total £34 17*s.* 8*d.*

Richard Cornewall, Thomas Wylde, Robert Ingles and William Cowper, appraisors.

Burial not recorded [no registers extant].
Letter of administration 10 May 1598 to Christian Francklyn and Joane Francklyn, intestate's widow and daughter; inventory exhibited 31 July 1598.

1. Given as regnal year.
2. Roman numerals throughout.

19 THOMAS WHETEBREADE[1]

1 May 1601 P1/W/11

In the Hall

One table bord with a frame 4*s.*[2]
One cubberd and 1 bench 5*s.*
Three formes 1*s.*
Pewter: three platters, 5 pottingers and 7 sawcers 7*s.*
Two flowre cuppes and thre saltcellers 6*d.*
Brasse 6 candlestickes 2*s.* 6*d.*
One chafindishe, 1 skymmer 6*d.*
One pan, 1 kettell, 1 pot, 1 skillet 8*s.*
More of pewter: 1 quart pot, 2 dishes, 3 pottengers, 1 basen, 6 sawcers, 1 flowre cup 4*s.*4*d.*
Six spoones 2*d.*
Iron stuffe: 1 hatchet, 1 broche, 1 frying pan, 1 tosting iron, 2 andirons 2*s.* 4*d.*
Two pothangers, 2 pothookes, one pressing ire, 1 pair of taylers sleeves, 1 pair of other sleeves, 1 iron shohorne 2*s.* 4*d.*
One lanterne 2*d.*
Two cannes, 6 woodden dishes, 1 dussen of trenchers 1*s.*
One chayre 3*d.*
Two bedstedes 1*s.* 4*d.*
Two beddes stuffed with shreedes 2*s.*
Foure bolsters, three of them stuffed with flockes and 1 with shreedes 3*s.*
Three coverledes 6*s.*
Three blanketes 2*s.*
2 sheetes 5*s.*
Three cofers 2*s.* 8*d.*
1 kyver, 1 woollen turne, 1 linnen turne and 1 chaire 3*s.* 6*d.*
One halfe bushell 6*d.*
One prong and 1 forme, 1 tub, 1 serche 1*s.*
Two tubbes and 1 bucket 1*s.* 4*d.*

Total £3 6*s.* 9*d.* [*recte* £3 7*s.* 5*d.*]

William Turley, Roger Dicke and Richard Johnson, appraisors.
Burial not recorded [no registers extant].
No other documents.

1. 'of the parishe of St. Mary in Marlebroughe'.
2. Roman numerals throughout.

20 SAMUEL BROWNE

18 August 1601 P1/B/12

First 10*s.* in money which his brother Thomas Browne of Commerford Marshe confesseth to pay [for one bullock which he *deleted*] unto him of money which he owed unto his said brother deceassed at the time of his decease 10*s.*[1]

One brasse pot 6*s.* 8*d.*
1 dublet and one jurkyn 6*s.* 8*d.*
1 cofer and box 1*s.* 8*d.*
1 pair of shoes 1*s.* 4*d.*
1 cloke 4*s.*
1 pair of breeches, 1 pair of drawers, 1 wastcote 2*s.* 2*d.*
1 other dublet 2*s.* 6*d.*
1 hat 8*d.*
2 pair of old stockins 6*d.*
2 shirtes 2*s.*
3 bandes and a cap 1*s.*
More 1 hamer and 1 trewell 6*d.*

Total £1 19*s.* 8*d.*

Thomas Toothe, Thomas Smith and Thomas Tayler, appraisors.

Burial not recorded [no registers extant].
No other documents; inventory exhibition not recorded.

1. Roman numerals throughout.

21 JOHN EIORS[1]

1 March 1601/2 P1/E/2

In the Haule

A cubboard, a table board with a pare of tressells 10*s.*[2]

One forme, a benche, one chaire and one keiver 2*s.* 6*d.*
2 chests, a powdringe tubb and one barrell 6*s.* 4*d.*
One old tubb and a lyttill chaire 6*d.*
Twentie pound of wooll 6*s.* 8*d.*
One bushill, one peck, one galland 2*s.* 6*d.*
One brasse pott, one cauldron, a fryinge pann, a skyllett and a kettill 10*s.*
A payre of pott hookes and pott hangles 1*s.*
7 platters, 5 pottingers, 7 sawcers, 2 salt sellers, a pewter cuppe 15*s.*
Room total £2 14*s.* 6*d.*

In the Chamber
One feyther bedd, one feyther boldster, one keyverlyd, 2 pare of blankettes, 2 flocke pillowes and 3 bedsteedes £2 3*s.* 4*d.*
One old tester over the bedd and a seeve 1*s.* 6*d.*
A pare of peore potts 1*s.* 4*d.*
A mault seeve, a meele seve, a flaskett and a baskett 1*s.*
Room total £2 7*s.* 2*d.*

Apparell
2 rousett cotes, 2 pare of brytchies, 2 dublettes, 3 shertes, 2 pare of steckins, one hatt, 2 pare of shewes and 4 bandes £1 13*s.* 4*d.*

In the Shoppe
All the smaule waires in the shoppe generallye valued and solde for £7.

Total £16 15*s.* [*recte* £13 15*s.*]

John Hencock, Richard Graften and Roger Whitfield, appraisors.

Burial not recorded [no registers extant].
Bond 16 March 1601/2, administration to Joane Eyers.

1. 'of the parishe of S[t] peters in Marleboroughe'; 'Eyers' on bond.
2. Roman numerals throughout.

22 WILLI[AM WHITE

[husband]man[1] 13 August 1603

P1/W/14

In the Hall
One litle table boord with a litle frme, a bench and two back boordes 1*s.* 4*d.*[2]
One cubbord 3*s.* 4*d.*
Three brasse potts and one posnett 12*s.*
Five old brasse ketles 8*s.*
One litle brasse pann containing 3 quarts, one brasse chafingdishe, the head of a skimmer with a litle brasse papperon 1*s.* 8*d.*
Two brass candlesticks 8*d.*
Fower platters, 6 pottingers, 3 sawcers and two salt sellers 7*s.* 4*d.*
One paire of potthookes, a pair of potthangers and one fleshooke 1*s.*
Two treen platters 2*d.*
A beating herdle 4*d.*
One spade and one hatchett 8*d.*
A paire of andirons 1*s.*

In a Litle Chamber within the Hall
One tubb, one barrell and a bushell 1*s.* 8*d.*
On old bedsteid, one old coffer with two litle shelfes 2*s.* 6*d.*

In the Entrie
One powdring tubb, one old kiver and one other old tubb 2*d.*

In the Lofte
One old flockbedd, a flock boulster, a flock pillow, a pillow case, a pair of course canvas sheetes, one old redd coverlett and one old towell wrough with black work 10*s.*
One kever 4*d.*
A coffer 1*s.*

One kitle, one pott and one litle skillett 5*s.*
Two platters, one pottenger, one saucer, one candlestick and a salt seller 2*s.* 4*d.*
One litle vate and 3 old tubbs 2*s.* 6*d.*
A way beame and a paire of skales and one leaden wate containing 4lbs 1*s.*
Two old bills, one old sithe and one spitt 1*s.*
One reele, one paire of iron combes and one cheeserack 1*s.*

In a Little Chamber within the Lofte
One standing ioyned bedsteed 10*s.*
One old flock bedd, one fether boulster and one flock boulster 6*s.* 8*d.*
One chest, one coffer and one stoole 5*s.*
Fower pair of old sheetes 8*s.*
Three pair of old blancketts 3*s.*
Two coverletts 10*s.*

In the Backside
Three old ladders and one old turne 2*s.*
Goods total £5 12*s.* 10*d.* [*recte* £5 10*s.* 8*d.*]

Debts due to the deceased at the tyme of his death as followeth
Due by bonde by John Woodroffe of Coate in the parishe of Bishops Cannings £11 6*s.* 8*d.*
By Richard Woodroffe of Puck Shipton in the parishe of Stoake by bond £18.
By Jeames Simson of Wilcot 6*s.* 8*d.*
By John Goddard of Ogburne by bonde £3.
By John Tughill of Goataker in the parishe of Helmarton £1.
By John Dyme of Fifeild [. . .]
By Henry Peasy of Marlburgh
By [*blank*] Painter of Ogborne 20[. . .]
By John Yonge of Manton by bond £4.
In ready money £1 10*s.*
By Elizabeth Woodroffe wife of John Woodroffe aforesaid 10*s.*
[Debts] total £41 8*s.* 8*d.*

Total £47 1*s.* 6*d.*

Richard Waldron and Thomas Christopher, appraisors.
Edward Johnson, witness.

Buried St. Mary 6 March 1602/3.
Will 6 February 1601/2; bond and probate 21 August 1603 to William White, testator's kinsman and godson.

1. Heading damaged, name and occupation from will.
2. Roman numerals throughout.

23 ROBERT COLE

tanner [will] 19 September 1603
P1/C/18

His apperrell £2.[1]

Debtes due to the deceased at the time of his death as followeth:
Due by William Bayley of Potterne in the Countey of Wiltes Esq £88.
By John Cole of Marlborough in the Countey of Wiltes £20.
By Edmond Mathen of Leddington in the Countey of Wiltes £10.
By William Cole of Medburne in the parish of Leddington £3.
By Martyn Lovelake of Wanborough in the Countey of Wiltes £3.

Total £126.

[*Appraisors' names omitted*].

Burial not recorded [St. Peter register not extant].
Will [nuncupative] 13 June 1603; bond 19 September 1603, administration to Isaac Cole, testator's brother.

1. Roman numerals throughout.

24 [. . .] BUCKE
tanner 27 Sep [c.1603][1] P1/B/24

In the Hall
1 table boord with [. . .] and forme and one liverye boorde 8[. . .][2]

In the Butterye
One cubberd and 1 barrell 2s 6*d.*

In the Kitchin
One table boorde with a frame 2*s.* 6*d.*
5 platters pewter, 1 chardger, 4 pottingers, 5 saucers 6*s.* 8*d.*
2 brasse candlestickes, 1 pewter candlestick 2*s.*
1 pewter salt, [1 pewter cupp, 1 salt *added*], 6 pewter spoons 1*s.*
3 brasse kettles 10*s.*
One brasse pott 5*s.*
One fryeinge pan, one skillett 2*s.*
2 broaches 8*d.*
2 skimmers 8*d.*
1 paire of andirons 3s 4*d.*
1 paire of tonges 6*d.*
1 paire of pott hookes, 2 paire of pothangles, 1 fier shovle, 1 paire of billowes, 2 stooles 18*s.*
1 washinge bowle, 1 tun bowle, 1 bushell 2*s.*
1 old cowle 6*d.*
1 maltsive, 2 little sives 6*d.*
1 kiver, 1 drye tubb 1*s.*
2 old fates, 1 meashinge cowle 13*s.* 4*d.*
2 little tubbs, 1 paile, 1 bucket 1*s.*
1 earthen pott, 1 earthen pann and dishe 4*d.*
1 choppinge boorde, 6 wodden dishes, 1 ladle, 6 trencheres 8*d.*

In the Chamber
1 featherbed, 1 flockbed, 1 feather bowlester, 1 flocke bowlester, 1 feather pillowe £1 13*s.* 4*d.*
3 coverledes, 3 blanckettes 16*s.*
3 paire of canvas sheetes, 1 hollands sheete, 3 table cloathes, 2 pillowe beeres £2.
His wearinge apparrell £2.
2 coffers, 1 boxe 3*s.* 4*d.*
1 joyned bedstead with a buckiram tester 6s 8*d.*
1 serche 6*d.*
1 cheese racke 3*d.*
3 table napkins 10*d.*
1 rapier 1*s.*
2 loose bedsteades 2*s.*

Fier woode in the wood and in the backside 13s 4*d.*
2 peeces of timber 5*s.*
[. . .]er 3*s.* 4*d.*
[. . .]arcke mill £1 10*s.*
[. . .] furnace £1.
[. . .] 2 [. . .] east haires 3*s.* 4*d.*
[. . .] an iron barr, a paire of spincers [. . .]d sawe and a chicell [. . .] crosebowe lathe 2*s.*
A wege of lead and 2 iron weges 1*s.*
A stone cupp 2*d.*
A silver spoone 5*s.*
A bushell of mault 2*s.*
2 [closes *deleted*] a lease of two closes for 12 yeares £6 13*s.* 4*d.*

Total £21 18s 8*d.*

Silvester Cooke, Richard Tapping, Simon Dringe and William Hillier, appraisors.

Burial not recorded [St. Peter register not extant].
No other documents.

1. The year that this inventory was made is not known: part of the heading has been torn away, and the date of exhibition is not given. The year 1603 has been assigned because the inventory arrived at the Record Office within the bundle for that year.
2. Roman numerals throughout.

25 HENRY ROOSELL
smith 2 November 1604 P1/R/8

In the Hall

1 cuppord, wainscot and 2 settles with 1 table £1.[1]

A wheele, 1 pair of andyarns and cotterell with a pair of bellis, frying pan and gredyarn [and od lomberd *added*] 2*s.* 6*d.*

In the Buttery

Brasse and pewter and ould lomberd £1 6*s.* 8*d.*

In the Chamber

1 bedsted and flock bed, 1 bolster, 2 paire of sheetes and 4 old cuvers with other old lumber £2

In the Shopp

1 pair of bellows, 1 anvell, fyles, sledgis and tounges with 1 vyse £1 10*s.*

6 [. . .] wod and [*illegible*] £1.

1 peese of iron unmaid 2*s.* 6*d.*

Total £7 1*s.* 8*d.*

George Waddingt[o]n, [Jo]hn Bayly junior and Mathew Hill, appraisors.

Burial not recorded [St. Peter register not extant].

Bond 14 November 1604, administration to Agnes Russell, intestate's widow.

1. Roman numerals throughout.

26 JOHN FELPS

tucker 20 July 1605 P1/F/13

In the Hall

One bord, one cubbord, one forme, one chayre and other ymplements there 8*s.*

In the Kitchen

4 brasse kettelles, 2 brasse pottes, one porsnett, one skillett, a skymmer, a broche, 2 peare of potthookes, 1 peare of potthangers, 2 peare of andiers with other ymplementes £1 10*s.*

In the Buttry

One dozen of pewter, 2 candlestickes, 2 saltes and halfe a dozen of sawcers with [o]ther ymplementes £1.

2 barrelles, 3 cowles, one kever, one payle, one powdringe tubb, halfe a dozen of dishes, 1 dozen trenchers 10*s.*

In the Chamber

One bed furnished, one chest, 3 coffers, one littell table £3 2*s.*

All his wearinge apparrell £2 10*s.*

4 peare of sheetes, one table clothe, halfe a dozen of napkins £2 6*s.* 8*d.*

2 beds more furnished £2.

One flitch of bacon with other ymplementes 8*s.*

In the Shopp

Fyve peare of sheares, one sherbord, one cutting bord, four course of handels with other thinges £2.

One tuckers rack with the ymplementes £3.

In the Backside

2 ladders, his wood with other ymplementes there 10*s.*

One dozen and a halfe of hurdels 3*s* 4*d.*

The welbuckett and rope 5*s.*

One hogg 6*s.* 8*d.*

2 horsebeastes £3 10*s.*

Total £22 14*s.* 8*d.* [*recte* £23 9*s.* 8*d.*]

Edmond Wythers, William Cowley and William Bowshere, appraisors.

Burial not recorded [St. Peter register not extant].

Will 24 June 1604; probate and inventory exhibition not recorded.

1. Roman numerals throughout.

27 JOHN LOVE
innholder [will] 10 May 1606 P1/L/11

Within the Crown Chamber
One standing bedstede with greene curtens, furnished with one fetherbed, with it a flockbed, one coverlet, twoo blankets, 2 fether boulsters [and one quilt *added*] £8.[1]
One truckle bedsteed furnished with a fether bed, one blancket and a coverlet £3.
One table bourd, 7 cooshens, one cheirstoole, 6 joyned stooles and one litle chairstoole and one carpet, one presse with a presse cloth, one basen and a yewer £2 6*s.* 8*d.*
2 dogges in the chimney 1*s.*
The wainscot and benches £3.
One close stoole 6*d.*

In the Drawing Chamber within the Crown Chamber
One fether bed, one fether bowlster, twoo white rugges, one joyned stoole and one skrine £1.

In the Fenix Chamber
One standing bed furnished with greene curtens, one fether bed, one flockbed, 2 fether bowlsters, one greene rugg, one blancket £5.
One trouckle bedsteed furnished with a fether bed, one fether bowlster, one peolow, coverlet and a blancket of red £3.
One fether bed, one flockbed, twoo bolster, one off fether and one off flockes, one coverlid off orres and one coverlet off white, one quilte with greene cushens to the same £3.
One table boorde, one liverie table boorde with a carpet, 3 joyned fourmes, 4 cooshens, one peir off smale doggs and peinted clothes with the wainskot £3.

In the Pellican Chamber
2 standing bedsteedes, 2 fetherbeds with 4 fether bowlsters, 2 coverletes, 2 blanckets with the curtens to both beds, one quilt £3.
One table bowrde, one fowrme, one cheirstoole, the peinted clothes, one iron dogg in the chimney, one bench and twoo backbowrdes £1.

In the Flower de Luce Chamber
One standing bedsted with red and yeolow curtens, one fether bed and one flockbed, 2 fether bowlsters, one orres coverlet and one blancket £2 10*s.*
One trowckle bedsteed and a flockbed [and a white rugge *added*] 10*s.*
One square table bourd with a arres carpet, 2 joyned stooles and one fourme, one iron dog in the chimney with the wainskot [and one fourme *deleted*] £1.

In the Rose Chamber
2 standing bedsteedes, 2 flockbedes, one fether bowlster and one flock bowlster and 2 coverlets and one blancket, one trouckle bedsted £2.
One litle quare table bourd with a carpet, 2 benches, one iron dogg in the chamber 6*s.* 8*d.*

In the Star Chamber
One standing bedsteed with greene and red curtens and fether bed and a flock bed, 2 bowlsters, one of fethers and the other off flockes, one coverlet and one blancket £2.
One trouckle bedsted, one fether bed, one coverlet £1.
One square table bourd, 2 fourmes, 2 benches with the painted clothes and one iron dogg in the chimney 10*s.*

In the Halfe Moone Chamber
One standing bedsteed with greene curtens, one fether bed and a flock bed, 2 fether bowlsters, one blancket, one

danix coverlet and one quilte £4.

One trouckle bedsteed with a fether bed, a flock bowlster and one white rugg £1 10*s.*

2 square table bowrdes and a liverie bowrde, one fowrme, one stoole, 2 carpets and fyve green cooshens, one peire off iron dogges in the chimney, the waineskot and painted clothes £2 6*s.*

In the Lion Chamber

One standing bedsteed with a fether bed, a fether bolster and a flock boulster, one coverlet and a blancket £3.

One trouckle bedsteed with a fether bed and a flockbed, one fether bolster, one coverlet and a blancket £1.

One table bowrde with a [carpet *deleted*], 2 fourmes, 2 cooshens, 2 iron dogges in the chimney, one peir off tables, the wainskot with the peinted clothes, one bench £1.

In the Sellers

Barrels and wooddn stuff with a small peece of wainskot £1.

In the Hall

One table bowrd, one old cowbbert and wainskot £1.

Off plate one salt, off sylver and gilt 2 sylver goblets £6.

In the Chamber within the Kitchin

One standing bedsteed and fether bed, a fether bowlster, one yeolow coverlet, one flock bowlster, one peir of blanckets £1.

More 3 chestes and one coffer [and one coubbert *added*] £1.

More tenne pillowes £1.

In the Maidens Chamber

One standing bedsteed, twoo flock beds, 2 flock bowlsters, 2 coverletes, one syde sadle with the furniture, one limbeecke, one coffor £1.

In the Kitchin

6 dossen of pewter £2.

5 brasse pottes £1 10*s.*

4 calderens of brasse £1.

2 brasse pannes £1.

1 brasse chaffer 3*s.* 4*d.*

1 brasen yewer 2*s.*

2 posnets of brasse 2*s.* 8*d.*

2 chafen dishes off brass 2*s.* 6*d.*

1 spice morter 1*s.*

2 drippen pannes 4*s.*

2 friying pannes 3*s.*

6 broaches or spites 6*s.*

2 gridyrons 2*s.*

2 skimmers 2*s.*

6 brass candestickes 4*s.*

3 pewter candlestickes 2*s.*

3 pewter pinte pots 1*s.* 6*d.*

3 pewter quart pots 3*s.*

1 peir of reckes in the chimney 3*s.*

2 peir of pot [hangers *deleted*] hookes 10*d.*

A fier shovell and tonges 1*s.* 6*d.*

One low stoole 3*d.*

One square bourd and shelfes and the dresser bowrds 6*s.* 8*d.*

One furnase with a plate 6s 8*d.*

4 peir off pot hangers and iron barr 6*s.* 8*d.*

6 pewter saltes 2*s.*

10 chamber pots 5*s.*

One warming pann 2*s.*

In the Long Stable

Reckes and maningers 13*s.* 4*d.*

One which and twoo coffers and one drye fate 2*s.*

In the Litle Stable

The reckes and maningers 2*s.*

Lynnen

28 peir off sheetes £7.

6 dosen [and a halfe *added*] off table clothes £2.

6 dosen off napkens 13*s.* 4*d.*
1 dosen and halfe of pilstowes 10*s.*
8 hand towels 1*s.* 6*d.*
One colliver and hed peese with the furniture 10*s.*
2 holbertes 4*s.*
1 burding peece being decaied 1*s.*
One byble 2*s.*
All the glasse about the house £4.
His wearing apparrell £2.

Total £97 3*s.* 7*d.* [*recte* £99 1*s.* 7*d.*]

John Fricker and John Browne, appraisors.

Burial not recorded [St. Peter register not extant].
Will 6 October 1603; bond 22 May 1606, administration to Henry Keepe, husband of Anne Love, formerly the testator's widow.

1. Roman numerals throughout.

28. [ANTONY][1] STEVENS alias H[AW]KS[2]

16 March 1606/7 P1/H/54

In the new Chamber
One bedsteade, one chest, two boxes £1 4*s.*
One fetherbed, one flockbed, two fetherbolsters, two fetherpillowes, one payre of blanckoates, two coverleds, two payre of sheetes, one matt and a bedcord £4.
Three yards of new medly cloth £1.
One warming panne, one chayre stoole, one bench with a matt 7*s.*

His Wearing Apparrell
3 shirts, 2 dublets, 2 jerkins, one coate, 2 payre of breeches, a hose cloth, 3 payre of stockins, 2 payre of shoes, 2 hats, 6 bands and one cloke £5.

In the Hall
One Bible, one maserd, one payre of andyrons, one broache, 2 table clothes, one dozen of diper naptkins, one yron shoe horne, one chayrestoole, 2 old stooles, one brush £2 4*s.*

In the Lower Chamber
One coffer, 2 lodging barrells, one looking glasse, 4 platters, 5 pottengers, 5 fruit dishes, 6 sacers, 2 saltsellers, one candlestick £1.

In the Kitching
3 kettles, one posnet, one skillet, one pewter basen, 1 dripping panne, one gruddier, one pancakeslice, a payre of pothookes, one beame and scales, 3 wayght stones £1 4*s.*

In the Backside
2 hundred of bords and one plank 12*s.*

In an other Old Howse
2 upstanders, one powdring tubb, 3 cowles, one payle, one clenseave, one search and one bottle 5*s.*
Three [. . .] quarters of mo[. . .] £42.
3 moltseaves, one bushell, 3 moltshovels, one neasthayre, one winning sheet, 3 raying seaves [. . .] willow-baskets, one flasket [. . .] sack, two yron wedges, on mattock, a gardening rake, 2 pikes, one tourne and a pair of cardes £1.
One hovell house, one dozen of [. . .] pales, two ladders [. . .]*s.*
One woodpile with other clefts £30.
A payre of bootes, a payre of gloves, a payre of garters 5*s.*

Total £92 1*s.*

Thomas Millington, John Withers, Walter Joames, Thomas Trebret and Anthony Gunter, appraisors.

Buried St Mary 1 March 1606/7.

Will 26 February 1606/7; probate 19 May 1607 to [unnamed].

1. Forename lost, obtained from will.
2. 'Hawkes als Stephans' on will.

29 ANNE WEARE alias BROWNE

widow 12 May 1607 P1/W/30

In the Hall
One longe table borde with the frame 10*s.*[1]
6 joyned stooles 6*s.*
The wainscott in the hall with the twoo benches 16*s.*
A litle square table with the frame 2*s.* 6*d.*
A lowe ioyned frame 1*s.* 4*d.*
One paire of andirons, a paire of doggs, a fier shovell, a paire of tonges and a plate of iron to sett behind the fire 6*s.*
The curtynrodd and curtyns to the hall window 2*s.*
One lookinge glasse 6*d.*

In the Chamber within the Hall
One lowe bedsteed and one truckle bedsteed 8*s.*
One feather bedd and one feather bowlster 12*s.*
One flock bedd and one flock bowlster 5*s.*
Three matts for bedds 2*s.*
Two coverliddes and twoo old blanckettes [. . .]
One old coffer [. . .]
One Bible and twoo shelves 10*s.*

In the Chamber over the Hall
One standinge bedsteed with the tester [. . .]
One cubbard with a [. . .] 12*s.*
One coverlidd, one [. . .] one p[. . .] of blankettes 1*s.* 8*d.*
Three curtyns and three curtynrodds [. . .] 3*s.* 4*d.*
A paire of [. . .] 1*s.*
Sixe [. . .] 10*s.*
A carpett and a [. . .] 3*s.* 4*d.*
A [. . .] 3*s.* 4*d.*
An olde paire of holland sheetes [. . .]aire and one [. . .] 13*s.*
Twoo paire [. . .]
One diaper cloth [. . .]
Three large [. . .]
Three square [. . .]
Fower dozen of [. . .]
One [. . .]
Two holland aprons [. . .]
[. . .]
[. . .] curtyns for a bedd [. . .]
[. . .] wearing lynnen £3.
[. . .] 3*s.* 7*d.*
One [. . .]
[. . .]

In the [. . .] Chamber
[. . .] bedd a [. . .]
Twoo coffers, a little [. . .]
One brasse [. . .]

In the Chamber[. . .]
One bedstead [. . .]
One table borde with [. . .]
One willowe and a flaskett 2*s.* 6*d.*
Pott of brasse [. . .]

In the [. . .]
One [. . .] brasse and a brasse chafing dishe [. . .]
Twoo litle brasse skilletts [. . .]
Twoo brazen candlestickes 2*s.*
Fowre brazen [. . .] 3*s.*
A spice morter 2*s.* 6*d.*
A fryinge pann, a gridiron, twoo tosting irons, a chafingdishe, a paire of fleshookes and a paire of pothookes 2*s.*
A trevett and twoo minsinge knyves 1*s.* 4*d.*
A grater for bread and twoo stone jugges 8*d.*
One safe 2*s.*

In the Celler
Twoo brasse kettelles and a litle kittle 6*s.* 8*d.*
A paire of iron rackes, fyve broaches, 2 drippinge pannes and an iron [. . .] 13*s.* 4*d.*
A fate, three barrelles, 3 kyvers, a bushell, a pecke and twoo powdringe tubbes 13*s.*
Pewter: 18 platters, 16 pottengers, 16 sauce dishes, 4 plates, 4 fruite dishes, one porridge dishe, a butter dishe, a bason and a chamber pott £2 5*s.*

In the Backside
One woodpile £8.
One chest 5*s.*
A well buckett with a rope and chaine 2*s.* 6*d.*
Plate: one silver salt celler, one silver [. . .] and sixe silver spoones £3 13*s.* 4*d.*
One goblett of silver guilt geven to her sonne Thomas Browne £5.
Sixe silver spoones geven to the said Thomas £2 10*s.*
One litle salt of silver guilt geven to the said Thomas 13*s.* [. . .]
A paire of bracelettes of golde geven to her twoo younger daughters £8.
A stone cupp with a cover and a sute of sil[. . .] to her daughter Elizabeth 10*s.*
One golde ringe geven to the said Elizabeth [. . .] £1.
Fyve holland sheetes £2.
6 elles of newe holland £1 10*s.*
One bigger trunke and one lesser trunke 10*s.*

Debtes owinge to the said Anne Browne
Owinge by Robert Pinckney Clerk £40.
Owinge by Giles Davys £10.

Total £121 13*s.* 6*d.*

Thomas Sclatter, Richard Cornwall, Hughe Whitear and Robert Harrison, appraisors.

Burial not recorded [St Peter register not extant].
Will 2 May 1607; probate not recorded, will endorsed 19 May 1607.

1. Roman numerals throughout.

30 FRANCIS PARKER
20 October 1607 P1/P/32

His part of 130 sheepe £17 10*s.*[1]
His part of 59 beastes £60.
One mare, one colt and 1 horse £8.
His part in hay £6 10*s.*
His parte in the afterleaze of grounds £6.
His estate in a lease of a howse and a shambles in Marlebroughe £20.
His tymber £10.
His apparell £4.
Debts owinge him and ready money in the howse £38.

Total £170.
[*in a different hand*] Whereof he owed at the tyme of his death in toto £40.[2]

[*Appraisors' names omitted*]

Burial not recorded [St. Peter register not extant].
No other documents; inventory exhibition undated.

1. Roman numerals throughout.
2. Debts owed by the deceased should not form part of the inventory.

31. [ROBERT JOHNSON][1]
leather dresser 11 April 1608 P1/IJ/12

In the Parlour
One standinge bedsteed, one fetherbed, one flockbed, twoo fether bolsters, two fether pillowes, one paire of blankettes, one rugg [. . .] curtens and roddes £4

10*s.*[2]

One truckle bedsteed, a fl[. . .] bedd, a flock bolster, one paire of blankettes and [. . .]erlett 10*s.*

One cupbord with one cloth [. . .]stry and another of nettwork, one bason and kiver and one towell £2.

Twoo joyned chestes 8*s.*

One table bord with a frame, some ioyned stooles, 2 ioyned chayers, one spleeten chayer, one little stoole and a benche 15*s.*

Half a dozen of cushions and one carpett 12*s.*

One paire of andirons, one plate, 2 iron barres, one fyer shovell, one paire of tonges and 1 potthanger 10*s.*

Eleven paire of sheetes, 1 windowe curten and rodd £2 10*s.*

Twoo dyaper table clothes, 1 flexen table cloth, 3 canvas table clothes, one dozen and a half of diaper table napkins, 2 dozen and a half of flexen table napkins, 3 odd napkins and 3 flexen towelles £2 13*s.* 4*d.*

3 paire of holland pillow beares and 3 paire of lokeram pillowe beares 13*s.* 4*d.*

One little drinckinge clothe 8*d.*

One silver bowle, one other silver bowle guilt, one dooble silver salt guilt and eight silver spoones £9.

All the testators apparell of wollen and lynnen £7.

Room total £31 7*s.* 4*d.* [*recte* £31 2*s.* 4*d.*]

In the Hall

One table bord with a frame, 5 stooles, one fourme, 2 wainscott benches, one litte plate, one curten and rodd, 2 Bibles and a brushe £1 16*s.* 8*d.*[xxxvj^{s} 8^{d}].

In the Chamber over the Parlour

One standinge bedsteed, 1 lyvery bedsteed, one truckle bedsteed, one fetherbed, 2 flockbeddes, twoo pillowes, 2 paire of blankettes, 3 coverlettes with curtens and roddes for one bedd £7.

One joyned chest, 1 chayer, 2 boxes, 1 square table bord, 2 little ioyned stooles, 2 cushions, a little carpett, 2 wyndowe curtens and roddes, 1 pair of andirons, 1 warminge panne and 2 lookinge glasses £2.

Room total £9.

In the Chamber over the Hall

One coffer and a stoole, 2 kyvers, 1 tubb and 1 tack 3*s.* 4*d.*

In the Celler

One frame with 7 barrells, 1 kyve, 1 powdring tubb, a tunbowle and a tack £1.

In the Chamber behind the Shopp

One bedsteed, 1 flock bedd with thappurtances 10*s.*

In the Kytchen

One table with a standerd and benche, 2 tackes, a dresser bord, a choppinge bord, 2 cowles, 1 bowle, a dozen of woodden dishes, 1 woodden ladle, 1 clen syve, 2 trayes, 2 payles, 1 dry tubb and 1 pair of byllowes 13*s.* 4*d.*

Foure brasse pottes, 2 posnettes, 4 skillettes, 4 kettles, 1 brasse panne, 2 skymers, 2 ladles, a paire of flesh hookes, 1 chafinge dishe, 3 broches, 1 iron drippinge panne, 2 fryinge pannes, 2 choppinge knyves, 1 gridiron, 1 paire of andirons, 1 fyer panne and tonges £7.

Twoo chargers, one dozen of pewter platters, one dozen of pottengers, one dozen of sawcers, half a dozen of frute dishes, 2 basons, one cullender, 4 pewter candlestickes, 6 pewter cuppes, 3 saltes and one little spice morter £3.

Two tynnen drippinge pannes, a dozen and a half of spoones, one tun dishe, 3 dozen of trenchers and five chamber pottes 5*s.*

Room total £10 18s. 4d.

In the Romthe behinde the Kitchin

One querne, one great allumminge kyver, 3 cowles, 2 tubbes and 2 hogsheddes £1 10s.

In the Stable

Two fates, one kyver, one rack and manger, one hencoobe and one shovell £1.

One horse with the saddle, bridle and furniture £3.

Room total £4.

In the Chamber over the Shopp

Three score quarters of mault, one quarter of barly, 3 bushelles of wheat and one neast haire £60.

One bushell, 1 peck, 1 galon, 1 skryne, 6 mault seeves, 3 seeves, 4 sacks, 2 garners, 4 boordes and a tack £1.

Room total £61.

In the Wooll Loft

One paire of scales, 6 leaden weightes, sixe weightes of middle wooll and 6 weightes of course wooll £4 5s.

One pewter still with a fornace, one cheese rack, 4 wooll baskettes, 4 hand baskettes, 2 paire of forcinge shears and a little paire of brasse scales 10s.

Room total £4 15s.

In the Shopp

One bord, 4 tackes, 2 scales, 1 lynen tourne and 2 iron withes 6s.

In dressed leather of buckskins, calf skynnes, sheepe skynes and sixe leather hunger hydes £17.

Shop total £17 0s. 6d.

In the Backside

One yotinge stone, one well buckett with a little chayne and rope £1.

Leather in the pitts: 13 bull hides, one hundred of calveskyns, fower hundred of peltes, 2 dozen of doe skyns and 6 dozen of wooll felles £24 10s.

The woodd and pales and two ladders £20.

Certen lyme, lugges, tresselles and glue peeces 10s.

One stack of haye and strawe £1.

Twoo leases for yeares of 2 severall closes £2.

Sub-total £49.

Total £192 6s. 8d. [*recte* £192 1s. 4d.]

Thomas Millington, Richard Cornwall, John Baylie the younger, Anthony Gunter and Walter Jones, appraisors.

Buried St. Mary 26 March 1608.

Will 20 July 1604; probate not recorded; court papers [*undated, in Latin*] refer to dispute between Anne Johnson, testator's widow and Edmund Johnson, testator's son; sentence 5 July 1608 [*in Latin*], confirming validity of will.

1. Heading damaged, testator's name from will.
2. Roman numerals throughout except as shown.

32 THOMAS BROWNE

gentleman 7 May 1608 P1/B/64

In his Dwellinge House at Marlebroughe

In the Kitchin

Fyve brasse pottes, two kettelles, foure cast skillettes, one other skillet, one brasse pan and one chaferne £2 12s. 8d.[1]

3 broches, 2 dripping pans, 1 paire of rackes, 2 paire of andires, one fryenge pan, 2 paire of pott hangels, pott hookes, grediron, fyerpan and tonge and other thinges of suche sort £1 4s.

One cubberd, one dresser, one forme, one chayer, one settle and other thinges 16s.

All the vessell and pewter £1 13s. 4d.

In the Hall
One tablebord with a frame, 3 formes, one settle and one lyvery cubberd £1 10s.

In the Buttry
One safe, one bynn, one littell table and three brasse candlestickes 15s 4*d*.

In the Parlor
One tablebord with a frame, one littell table, one lyverie table, sixe stooles, 2 formes and sixe cusshions £3 10s.
One ymbrodered chayer, two stooles, one playne chayer, two stooles and two littell joyned chayers £2 13*s*. 4*d*.

In the Parlor Chamber
One bedsteed with valence and curteynes £4.
One fetherbed and bolster, two pillowes, 2 blanketes and one rugg £4
One lyverie cubberd, 1 square table, one littell chayre, 1 desk and a chest £1 5*s*.

In the Littell Chamber
One littell bedsteed, one flockbed and bolster, one payre of blankettes and one coverled £1 3*s*. 4*d*.

In the Hall Chamber
One bedsteed with a canopy, one fetherbed and 2 bolsters, one paire of blankettes and one coverled £4 10*s*.
One truckle bedsteed, a fetherbed and a boulster, a paire of blankettes, 1 quilt, one coverled £2 3*s*. 4*d*. [xliij^s^ 4^d^]
One trunck and three chestes 16*s*.

In the Inner Chamber
One bedsteed with a flockbed and boulster, 2 pillowes and a coverlett £1 6*s*. 8*d*.
One olde presse 6*s*. 8*d*.
His plate £12.
All his lynnen £3 10*s*.
His apparrell £5.
Ready money £2 6*s*.
The furnace and the rest of the brewinge vesselles and stuffe £2.
One yotinge stone £2.

Goods and Chattelles at Polton in the parishe of Myldenhall in the County of Wiltesh.
Twenty yewes and lambes £7.
17 acars of wheat, forty acars of barly, tenne acars of pease, fatches and oates £80.
His parte of fyve plow horses, harnesse, earth plowes and harrowes £10.
Fyve nagges and coltes £10.
One cowe £2.
Wheat in the barne £6.
Fyve pigges £1 13*s*. 4*d*.
His part of fatches and hay £2.

Total £179 15*s*. [*recte* £180 1*s*.]

Stephen Lawrence, Thomas Browne, Thomas Smyth and Nicholas Edwards, appraisors.

Burial not recorded [St. Peter register not extant].
Will 23 December 1607; probate 16 July 1608 to Robert Shaw, testator's brother-in-law.

1. Roman numerals throughout except as shown.

33 [ROBERT CHAPMAN alias **HITCHCOCK]**
?weaver [inventory goods] [*date lost* c.1609][1] P1/C/40

[. . .] at 12*s*.[2]
[. . .] 5s 4*d*.
[. . .] 2 skimbers 13*s*. 6*d*.

[. . .]r over the Entry
[. . .] vessels and 2 formes 2*s*. 5*d*.
[. . .] 2 coverlits very old 10*s*.

[. . .]hambere over the Hawle
[. . .] old blanketes, 2 old coverletes and [. . .] 13*s.* 4*d.*
More 1 old flocke beed, 2 old blankettes, 2 coverlites, 1 boulster with an old bed [. . .] 8*s.*
1 old coverlit 12*s.*
Mor 2 other coffers at 2*s.*
Mor 1 old borde to lay clothes uppon and frame at 8*d.*
Mor for all his apparrell at 13*s.* 4*d.*

In the Chamber over the Shopp
2 payer of sheettes, [1 bord cloth *added*], one paire of old wole [. . .] 5*s.*
1 warpinge barr with a scarme, 1 beame and scales of wood 3*s.* 4*d.*
1 old coffer with 2 or 3 peece of ?leell 1*s.*

In the Lower Chamber
2 keevers, 2 tubbs, 2 old byshill, 1 peck at 4*s.*
Mor 2 seves, 2 irone brooches, 1 paier of smale andirons, 1 grediron, 1 payer of pott hooks, 1 flesh hooke, 2 old chopinge knyves, 1 trewell, 1 bill hooke, 1 old lanterne with 9 treen dyshes, 1 ladle and 2 shelves or bordes at 4*s.*

In the Ynner Chamber
1 forme, 2 shelves, 1 old frieing pann, 3 trene platters, 2 earth panns and 1 serch at 1*s.* 8*d.*

In the Shopp
1 ossett [lome *deleted*] laome, 1 olde spullingtorn, 1 spinning torne, 1 washinge stockes and bittle, 1 reele, 2 stooles, 1 hatchett, 1 axe, 1 iron scoope, 1 old spade, 1 wood bittle, 3 iron wegges with certayne ymplements apertayninge to the said ossett loome, 3 iron haninges, 1 iron chayne with one longe pronge at 6*s.* 8*d.*

In the Siller
1 old fatt, 2 ronnd stands, 1 barrell, 2 litle pailes, 2 old tankerdes, 2 [standing *deleted*] stone crasses at 1*s.* 4*d.*
More 1 helevling bord 4*d.*

In the Backsyde
1 loode of woode, 1 ladder, 1 old buckett and roope and certen old bordes at 5*s.* 2*d.*
The lease of the dwellinge howse at £2.
The lease of a litle gardine ground at £1.

Total £9 18*s.* 6*d.*

Robert Wayte, William Addlington, James Paine, Richard Hayward senior and Robert Webb, appraisors.

Buried St. Mary 14 July 1607.
Inventory exhibited 30 May 1607[3]; court copy of nuncupative will 11 July 1607; allegations, responses and sentence relating to the will; bond 14 June 1609, administration to John Chapman alias Hitchcock of Brinkworth.

1. Heading lost, name from will.
2. Roman numerals throughout.
3. This year is incorrect, perhaps 1609 was intended.

34 JOHN SCLATTER
tanner 17 December 1610 P1/S/48

In the Hall
One longe table bord and a ioyned frame, fower ioyned stooles and one ioyne chayer and six cusshions £1 6*s.* 8*d.*[1]
2 paire of andirons, three potthangers, two broches, one iron barre, one iron plate, one paire of tonges and one fire shovell 13*s.* 4*d.*

In the Kitchin
One table bord and a ioyned frame, one little furme and a stoole 10*s.*
Six brasse kettles, three brasse pottes, two

posnettes and three skillettes £3.
One brasse ladle, two brasse skymmers, two brandirons, two paire of potthookes, one gridiron, one little andiron and two lanthornes 5*s.*
Two yoting fates, one upstand, one brewing cowle, fower kyvers, one bushell, fower pailes, one kive, two powdring tubbes and one leatherne buckett £1 6*s.* 8*d.*
One iron barre, one little table bord and a frame, two little cowles, one flaskett and 5 maultseives 9*s.*
Two shelves, one furme, two dowles and other lumber 2*s.* 6*d.*

In the Buttery
8 barrells, one powdring tubb and 6 treene platters 12*s.*
One cupbord and two furmes 4*s.*
One fryeing pann and one warming pan 4*s.*

In the Chamber over the Hall
2 livery bedsteeds, one chest, fower coffers and fower boxes £1 12*s.*
One feather bedd, two feather bolsters and five feather pillows £3.
Two flockbedds and two flockbolsters £1.
Two coverledds, two paire of blankettes and six paire of canvas sheetes £3.
One whicker chaier 2*s.*

In the Chamber over the Kitchin
One livery bedsteed, one truckle bedsteed and one chest 13*s.* 4*d.*
4 coverledds £1.
2 flockbedds and two flockbolsters 13*s.* 4*d.*
3 shettes and 3 blanketts 13*s.* 4*d.*
The testators wearing apparell £6 13*s.* 4*d.*
One pewter charger, one pewter bason, 9 platters, 10 poringers, 18 sawsers, two pewter candlestickes, 2 pinte pottes, 3 pewter saltes, one pewter tunnell and 12 pewter spoones, two porridge dishes and one [little *added*] turne £1 10*s.*
One brass morter and a pestle and three brasse candlestickes 5*s.*
27 quarters of barley and mault £17.
Fower table clothes, one dozen of dyaper napkins, 6 other napkins, two large towells, two other towells and fower paire of pillow cases £1.
In stagers and wood £1.
The unthreshed barley £1.
Three loads of hay £2.
One cowe, one calfe and one earling bullock £4.
In debts owing to the testator £1.
12 dickers of leather and hides £84.
12 loads of barke £15.
One barkemill £1.
In ready money £14.
One lease of a close in the Marsheward £5.
3 fates, 3 quarters of lyme, three beame knyves and a beame £1.
3 willeys, 2 skuttles, 3 shovells, one spade, one mattocke, one collrake and two shaves and a hewer 10*s.*
2 shootes, one little fate, one cowle, 3 bords and one pair of tressles 7*s.*

Total £176 12*s.* 6*d.*

Robert Lyme, Thomas Randoll, William Sclatter and Thomas Sclatter the younger, appraisors.

Buried St. Mary 14 December 1610 'Slatter'.
Will 9 December 1610; probate 29 January 1610/11 to Susanna Sclatter, testator's wife.

1. Roman numerals throughout.

35 ROBERT LYME
tanner 22 March 1610/1 P1/L/20

In the Hall
One tablebord with a ioyned frame and

five ioyned stooles 13*s.* 4*d.*[1]
One cupbord and a ioyned chayer 13*s.* 4*d.*
3 brasse pottes, 2 little posnettes, two brasse kittles, 2 panns and one little furnace £2.
10 platters, 2 pewter pottes, 5 sawsers and fower candlestickes 10*s.*
One paire of andirons, 2 ironbarres, one fire shovell, one paire of tonges, two paire of potthangers, two broches and two salts 6*s.* 8*d.*

In the Chamber over the Hall
One livery bedsteed, one truckle bedsteed, two flockbeddes, two flockbolsters, one coverlett, one blankett and one sheete, two chestes, one chaire and 6 cushions £1 13*s.* 4*d.*
In mault and barley 20 bushells £1 13*s.* 4*d.*

In the Chamber next to the Hall
Two bedsteedes, one featherbedd, one flockbed, two bolsters, 2 pillowes, 4 coverlettes, five sheetes, one carpett, two blankettes and two table clothes £4.
2 little bordes, 2 kyvers, one upstand, fower beere barrells, two powdring tubbes and one coffer 13*s.* 4*d.*

In the Loft over the Lower Chamber
One powdringe tubb, two kyvers, two bushells, one beame and skales, two searches and other lumber 5*s.*
The testators wearinge apparell £4.
One brandiron, two turnes, one coverlett and one remnant of russet woollen cloth 12*s.*
8 dickers of leather £2.
13 loades of barke £15.
One barke mill £1.
2 standinges fates and one upstand 5*s.*
3 ladders, 3 shootes, one cowle, one scoope and one colerake 3*s.* 4*d.*
One nagge with his fourtiture £1 10*s.*
One lode of wood, one grindstone, one beame and stagers 10*s.*
In ready money £4.
In debtes oweing to the testator £2.

Total £61 8*s.* 8*d.*

Anthony Sclatter, Thomas Rymell and Phillipp Clifford, appraisors.

Burial not recorded [St. Peter register not extant].
Will 5 January 1610/1, probate 11 April 1611 to [unnamed].

1. Roman numerals throughout.

36 JOHN FLEMING
glover [*undated*, c.1612][1] P1/F/30

On ould chest 1*s.* 4*d.*[2]
On coffer 1*s.* 2*d.*
On bed and bolster of flockes, on pair of blanketes and on coverled 13*s.* 4*d.*
9 small peices of pewter 6*s.* 8*d.*
3 pouncing jerones 6*d.*
On short table clothe 1*s.* 3*d.*
9 pair of gloves 1*s.* 6*d.*
In money which hee laft 1*s.*
[A paire of potthookes 4*d.* *added*]

Total £1 7*s.* [*recte including added item* £1 7*s.* 1*d.*]

John Dodson, Henry Abbott and Christopher Lipyeatt, appraisors.

Burial not recorded.
No other documents; note at foot of inventory 'Elizabeth Flemminge relict Johannis Fleming. Obligator cum Jacobo Legg de Hackleston parochie de Fittleton, taylor'.

1. The year 1612 has been assigned to the inventory because it arrived at the Record Office within the bundle for that year.

2. Roman numerals throughout.

37 HENRY TARRANT

yeoman [will] 21 September 1613
P1/T/35

His wearing clothes and one horsse £2 10s.[1]

His Chamber

One joyne beadsteed, two flockbeads, two boulsters, five pillowes, two kyverledes, one blanckett £3.

One great wenskott chest and three cofferes 10s.

Three payre of canvas sheetes 6s.

Two shelvfes and one fosser 6d.

One livery beadstead 4s.

In the Halle

One cubbard 2s. 6d.

Halfe a dosen of pewter 6s.

Two dosen of trentchers, one earthen platter, one earthen panne, one stone poote, one pewter salte, one pewter candlesticke, one smale skymer, one earthen chaffendishe 2s.

Fowre kyttles, one skyllett, one potte, one frying panne £1 4s.

One payre of andyeres, three payre of poothangers, one payre of poothoockes, one spitt, one choppinge knyfe, two payre of bellowes 5s.

One tablebord, two formes, one chayre, fowre stowles, one side bentch under the wyndow 5s.

In the Buttry

Fowre leadging barrells, one powdring tubb 5s.

Three cowles, one paylle, one buckkett, three kyfforres, one bowle 10s.

Two rayingseves, two moult seves, fowre sacks, two basketts, one smalle whelle, one lanthorne, one turnne and one payre of bellowes 6s.

One bushell of wheat, three peckes of barley and fowre quarters and three bushelles of moulte £3 10s. 6d.

In the other Chamber

Two straw beads, one beadstead, two boulsters, one blanckett, one kyforlead and a payre of tressells 6s.

Gardneres 10s.

One curveing sawe, one handsawe, one axxe, one hatchette, one headging bill, one spade, one wedgge 5s.

One bushell and one gowne 1s. 2d.

In the Moulting Howse

Tree vattes, two syves and a sneed 1s.

A skaffould 3s. 4d.

Two hovells and the palles £2.

The woode and hay 10s.

One lease of the howse £3.

Total £20 3s.

John Tarrant and William Nottinggam, appraisors.

Buried St. Peter 6 September 1613.

Will 2 September 1613; probate 4 June 1614 to Katherine Tarrant, testator's widow.

1. Roman numerals throughout.

38 ROBERT LOCAR[1]

blacksmith [will] 26 January 1613/4
P1/L/30

In the Seller

On brasse pan 10s.

More 3[2] brasse chitles £1.

More for 3 brasse pottes 13s. 4d.

More for ould skillates and chafindish 8d.

More for 1 frine pan, 2 dripen pans, 2 litle skimers and ladles 5s.

More 3 paire of pothangelles, 1 grediron, 2 tostinge irones, 3 paye of pothockes, one spitt, a paire of andiornes, a fire shovle and a paire of tonges and to little

hockes 10*s.*
More for a table bord and frame and a little bench and 4 stolles 4*s.*
More for cowles, 2 upstandes and 3 kiveres, a pece, a clanser and payle and a littele barrell and chopenbord 10*s.*
More for 2 weshinge barrelles, a well bocket, leyne and rope, 2 trene platers, 2 little pottleds, 3 dishes 5*s.*
Room total £3 18*s.*

In the Butrey
3 barelles 6*s.*
3 juges, 10 tunelles, 2 batelles and poudringe tube and a salte box 2*s.*

In the Backe sid
For coules 12*s.*
More for wood and lader and grindston 13*s.* 4*d.*
More withe out house, 1 maltemell 10*s.*

[*In the Ante House* deleted]
1 bushell, 2 shovles, 2 hachetes and a pronge 5*s.* 6*d.*[3]
More ould bedsted 2*s.* 6*d.*

In the Chamber
2 flockebedes and 3 kiverlides and fether boulster, 2 flocke boulster, 2 flock pillowes £2.
One standingebedsted, 1 trucklebedsted, 1 mat and too cordes 16*s.*
More his werring apprell £1 10*s.*
One joynd couberde 8*s.*
1 tablebord and forme, 1 bench 10*s.*
More for 3 coffers, 1 boxe and chayer 6*s.*
One mouleseve, 1 serch, 3 seaves, 1 roalingpin, [1 boytle *added*] 2*s.*
More for 6 pewter platers, 4 pottingers, 12 sacers, 2 brasse candlestickes, 1 dosen of spones, 2 pouter dishes, one ton, to stoles £1.
One brush, a lente, an earthen pott, an earthen pann 1*s.*
To paire of canmassheates and a bordcloth 12*s.*

In the Cokloft
1 bedsted, 1 flockebed, a civerlid and a sheate £1.

In the Shopp
To vices 12*s.*
One bickforme 4*s.*
One andfeld 6*s.*
6 payer of tonges 6*s.*
More for 3 sledges and 3 hembers 10*s.*
14 [. . .] showes and ould iron 6*s.*
A [pa]re of skealles and beames of w[. . .]d weytes 10*s.*
More for worckinge tolles, spincers and bilis 4*s.*
For the billowes and trowe 12*s.*
For 2 coffers and a houlter 3*s.*
And 3 blockes 5*s.*
The lease of the howse at £5.

Total £23 9*s.* 4*d.* [*recte* £23 12*s.* 4*d.*]

Robert Hitchcocke and John Doodsone, appraisors.

Buried St. Peter 29 December 1613 'Looker'.
Will 13 April 1613; 6 June 1614 to [unnamed] Lokar, testator's widow.

1. 'Loker' on will.
2. Most numbers within the text are in Roman numerals.
3. v^{s} 6*d.*

39 WILLIAM APPLEGATE
victualler [will] 12 June 1615 P1/A/29

In the Halle
One long table, one forme, one litle cupbard 6*s.* 8*d.*[1]

In the Parlore
One standing beadsteead, one truckell bead steead, one bead of featheres and flockes, two flockboulsters, one

coverlead, one flockbead, one flockboulster, one flockpillow, two mattes, one smale table, one forme and a bentch £2 10*s.*

In the Lofte over the Parlore
Two standing beadsteeads, two flocke beads, three flockboulsters, two coverleads, one litle stolle £1 6*s.* 8*d.*

In the Loft over the Hall
One beadsteead, one flockbead, one flockboulster, one coverlead 8*s.*

In the Loft over the Sellor
One standingbeadstead, one truckell beadsteead, one flockbead, two payre of blanckkettes, one flockboulster, two coverleads, one chest, three cofferes, two boxes, nyne payre of sheetes, fower towells, one pillowbeere, one feather pillow, six napkines, one clocke £4 6*s.* 4*d.*

In the Rome over the Sellor
Three brasse potts, two skylletts, fower kyttles, one chaffingdishe, five platters, three pottengers, six sawesseres, two saltes, one gridiron, one frying panne, one spitt, three potthangeres, two wooden platteres, one pitchforke, one seeve, one powdring tubb, one bowle, one kyfor, one ould cubbard, one doshen of pewter sponnes, two quarte pewter pottes, two jugges, one payre of tonges, one fire showell, one payre of andiers, one payre of ould bellowes £2 18*s.*

In the Sellor
Two stands to sett beere one, two ould bowles 3*s.* 4*d.*

In the Backside
One sowe, one smale pyle of wood 16*s.*

Total £11 15*s.* [*recte* £12 15*s.*]

Swiffin Hayes and Robert Daunce, appraisors

Buried St. Peter 15 March 1614/5.
Will 8 February 1614/5; probate [undated] to Catharine Applegate, testator's widow.

1. Roman numerals throughout.

40 WILLIAM HILLER

?swordsmith [inventory goods] 9 November [c.1615] P1/H/114

In the Hall
One table with a joyned frame, one joyned forme, one back of waynscott and two benches 8*s.*[1]
Two joyned cubberdes and two chayres, fower shelves and one pew of waynscott 16*s.*
One payer of andires, one pott hanger, one fire shovle, one payer of tonges, one chafingdishe and one salte boxe 4*s.*

In the Kitchin
One table with two tressles, one forme, fyve board, one bench, one shelfe, one washing stock and one stoole 8*s.*
Three fattes, one chyve, two tubes, fower barreles, thre cevers and one poudringe tubb 10*s.*
One well throck with buckett and rope, two thoules, one klenser, one serch, one mault seve, two other seves, one sack and one bagg 3*s.*
One pott hanger, one payre of andires, two spittes, two payr of pott hookes, two flesh hookes, one gridiron, one fryinge pann and one grater 6*s.* 8*d.*
Thre brasse pottes, thre kettles, one brass pann, thre skillettes, one skimmer, one basting ladle, one brass spoone and two earthen pottes £1 6*s.* 8*d.*
Two dossen and a halfe of pewter, two pewter dishes, one pewter candlsticke, one dossen of spoones and fyve

woodden candlstickes, sixe woodden dishes, one woodden platter and one tunbowle 13*s.* 4*d.*

In the Inner Chamber

One table with a joyned frame, sixe joyned stooles, two formes, one back of waynscott and two benches, one joyned cubberd, thre other parcels of waynscott and one joyned bedsteed £2 13*s.* 4*d.*

Page total £7 9*s.* [*recte* £6 9*s.*]

One fether bedd, one fether bolster, two fether pillowes, one green rugge, one payre of blankettes, one mattris, one bedd coard, one warming pann, one flaskett and [one *added*] litle chayre £1 10*s.*

His wearring apparell £3.

In the Utter Chamber

One joyned bedd steed corded, two chestes, one truckle bedsteed, one joyned boxe, two trunkes £1.

One flockbedd, one bolster, one matt, one tapstry coverlid, one cushin, one brushe and one pynt pott 13*s.* 4*d.*

Sixe payre of sheetes, thre tablclothes, thre pillowbeers and thre napkins, thre paynted clothes £1.

One graner with two qr four lb of mault £2 3*s.* 4*d.*

In the Cockloft

One joyned bedd steed corded, one hayrbed, one strawbedd, one blankett, two coverlides, two boxes, one fram to make frenge, one bushell, one linnen wheele and one reele 10*s.*

The Forge House with thinges that are in it

The forge house being sett upon postes £1 6*s.* 8*d.*

Two ladders, one doare, two plankes, sixe boardes, six hurdeles and one fann 6*s.* 8*d.*

One payre of bellowes, one anvill, thre vises, two sledges with all the rest of his working tooles and two grynd stones £5.

Page total £16 10*s.*

In the Shoppe

Two cofers, two joyned stooles, one deske, one press, one shelf, one dossen of boxes, one frame to sett knyves 6*s.* 8*d.*

Thre dossen of swordes and rapyers, two dossen and a halfe of daggers £5.

Two muskettes and eight other peeces, sixe sword hiltes, thre pistales, one dossen of sicers, two corslettes, fower flaskes and tutch boxes, forty lb of old irne, two dossen of beltes and two dossen of stringes of flaskes and six armes for pykes, one dossen of scaberdes £2 6*s.* 8*d.*

One brass pann, one brass morter and pestle, two saltsellers, one steel plate, two plankes 3*s.*

33 dossen of knyves £5.

14 dossen of knyfe blades 14*s.*

20 dossen of sheathes for knyves 10*s.*

For one dossen of gleme and 20 lb imbry 10*s.*

One Byble with other bookes 10*s.*

In the Backsyd

Wood, seacole and charcole £3.

Pales, postes and rayles £1.

Page total £19 0*s.* 4*d.*

Total £42 19s 4*d.* [*recte* £41 19*s.* 4*d.*]

Thomas Newcombe and Robert Hitchcocke, appraisors.

Buried St. Mary 3 November 1615.

Will [*day and month omitted*] 1613; probate 16 July 1616 to Jane Hiller, testator's widow.

1. Roman numerals throughout except page totals and sum total.

41 EDITH BRUNSDON
widow [burial register] 8 [J]anu[ary c.1615/6] P1/B/127

In the Hall
A backe wainescott, a table boarde, a forme, a tressell 10*s.*[1]

In the Chamber
2 coffers, a little side board, 2 stooles, a chaier, a forme 5*s.*

In the Chamber over the Haulle
A beedsteede 4*s.*
The pillowes, the feathers, the coverlead and other olde stuffes 16*s.*
Her weareinge apparell 10*s.*
Of pans brasse: fower skoore and sixteene pound and a halfe £3 16s 6*d.*
Pott brasse: twentie five pounds 10*s.* 6*d.*
Pewter: thirtye fower pounds £1 2*s.*
The porthall 2*s.* 6*d.*
Olde iron 4*s.*

In the Out House
Treene vessell with a freestone troughe 2*s.*

Debts owed unto her
Off Edward Carter of Poulton £1.
Of John Redford £2.

[*Total omitted, by addition* £11 2*s.* 6*d.*]

Walter Jones, Phillip Clifford, Thomas Rendoll and Edward Lyme, appraisors.

Buried St. Mary 8 January 1615/6.
No other documents; inventory exhibited 22 February 1615/6.

1. Roman numerals throughout.

42 JONE BOWWLINGE[1]
widow 1 April 1616 P1/B/130

In the Best Chamber
One tablebord and frame, one flockbead and feather boulster, one rugge, one coverlead, one ould flockbead and boulster £1 3*s.*[2]

In the Outter Chamber
One ould flockbead and boulster, two ould rugges, one chest and two coffers, one litle box, two feather pillowes, three payre of canvas sheetes, one boulster case and stayned clothes handging about the howse £1 7*s.*

In the Kytchen
Two brasse pannes and a litle skyllett, one brasse pott contayns 1 gallone, one temser, one iron platter to stand before the fyre, one chayre and one litle forme, one litle iron pott, two brasse kyttles, one skyllett, one skymmer, on gridiron, one payre of pott hockes, one boule and one wooden platter, one payre of pott hangers, one spitt and one litle iron dogg 18*s.* 5*d.*

In the Hall
Two joynestolles, one cubbard, one candlesticke, one saltseller, five pewter platters, six sponnes, two pewter platters, one pint pott, two iron crocks, one wooden dishe, one litle wooden drincking dishe, three payles, two wooden candlestickes, one andiorne and payre of bellowes 16*s.*

In the Backside
One lood of wood 8*s.*
One plocke of wood 3*s.* 4*d.*
One table cloth 6*d.*

Total £4 16*s.* 3*d.*

William Parrott and Walter Jeffryes, appraisors.

Buried St. Mary 18 August 1615, 'Jone Bolon'.

Will 12 July 1615; probate [undated] to Catherine Evans, testator's daughter-in-law.

1. 'Bowlinge' on will.
2. Roman numerals throughout.

43 ROBERT LYME

tanner 10 July 1616 P1/T/40

In the Hall
One table bord with the frame, three ioyned stooles and twoo chaires £1.
In the hall one brasse pott, one posnett and one brasse candle stick [and one kittle *added*] 13*s*.
Fower platters, one bason, one chamber pott, twoo sawcers, one pewter candlestick and one salt 10*s*.

In the Chamber where he lodged
One livery bedsteed, one truckle bedsteed, one chest and one coffer 15*s*.
In the same chamber one flockbedd, twoo flock bolsters, one paire of blankettes, one paire of sheets, one feather bolster and one feather pillowe and three coverlidds £3.
Twoo cushions 2*s*. 6*d*.
Twoo bookes 5*s*.
One [paire of *deleted*] hangills, one andiron, one iron barre, one flesh hooke and one fyer pan 3*s*.
One gridiron and one brooch 1*s*. 6*d*.
One leather buckett 2*s*. 6*d*.
One barrell, one kyver and one cowle 3*s*.
One dozen of trenchardes, three dishes and three spoones and twoo stone iuggs 1*s*. 6*d*.
One powdringe tubb 2*s*. 6*d*.
His wearinge apparell £3.
One bark mill £1 6*s*. 8*d*.
Twoo water shootes, one beame and three beame knyfes 6*s*.
One gryndstone 2*s*. 6*d*.

Total £11 14*s*. 8*d*.

Thomas Randall and Anthonie Wake, appraisors.

Buried St. Mary 16 May 1616.
Will [nuncupative] 15 May 1616, probate 16 July 1616 to [unnamed].

44 WILLIAM NORTH

tanner [*undated*, c.1616] P1/N/24

38 hiddes and 2 deson and a halfe of callfe skines £22.[1]
For barke £7.
For all his tanners toulls and for his parell £2.
For a safe and for lime 5*s*.

Total £31 5*s*. [*written by court clerk*]

[*Appraisor's names omitted*]

Buried St. Peter 29 August 1616.
Bond 4 September 1616, administration to Bridget North, intestate's sister; inventory exhibited 7 September 1616.

1. Roman numerals throughout.

45 ROBERT MICHELL

?goldsmith [inventory goods] 27 November 1616 P1/M/82

Gould ware readie made: 14 ounces, quarterne and 2 pennywayte at £3 the ounce £43.[1]
Guilt plate: 38 ounces at 5*s*. 8*d*. per ounce £12 16*s*. 4*d*.
White plate: 22 ounces and a halfe at 5*s*. 6*d*. per ounce £6 1*s*.
Guilt small ware: 34 ounces and a quarter at 6*s*. 8*d*. per ounce £11 8*s*. 4*d*.
Garnished currall : 14 ounces and halfe at

6*s.* 8*d.* per ounce £4 16*s.* 8*d.*
White silver ware: 29 ounces and a quarter at 6*s.* per ounce £8 16*s.* 6*d.*
Playne get rings: 9 dosen at 6*d.* per dosen 4*s.* 6*d.*
Lyneed get ringes: 4 dosen at 2*s.* per dosen 8*s.*
5 braslets of currall 5*s.*
White bone ringes: 10 4*s.*
Guilt spones: 9 ounces at 6*s.* 8*d.* per ounce £3.
White silver spones: 35ounces 3 quarters at 5*s.* 6*d.* per ounce £9 12*s.* 6*d.*
Broken silver: 5 ounces and a halfe at 4*s.* 8*d.* per ounce £1 5*s.* 8*d.*
Currall branches 6*s.*
Pearll and stones 10*s.*
The swepe of the shop and the tooles £8.
A desk, ballands and waytes 10*s.*
Column total £111 1*s.* 6*d.* [*recte* £111 4*s.* 6*d.*]

Pewter
One bason and eure 9*s.*
One dubble salt 1*s.*
3 candle stick 3*s.*
8 porridg dishes 2*s.* 6*d.*
A little pott with a keiver 6*d.*
Platters and sawsers: 37 lbs at 10*d.* per pound £1 10*s.* 10*d.*
One aquavite bottle 6*d.*
Chamber pott and spones 1*s.*

Brass
One skimmer 6*d.*
One warming pann 4*s.*
Pott brasse: 51 lbs at 8*d.* per lb £1 14*s.*
Copper kittles: 38 lbs at 10*d.* per lb £1 11*s.* 8*d.*
A brass skillet 3*s.*
A brass kittle 7 lbs 6*s.*
Two brass candellstickes 3*s.* 4*d.*
One iron drippinge pann 2*s.*
One broch 10*d.*
4 paire of cotterells, one paire of andeers, one paire of dogges, a fire pike 8*s.*
2 paire of pott hockes, one flesh houck, one gridiron 2*s.*
One frying pann 10*d.*
One bastinge ladle 4*d.*
A leather bucket 2*s.*
A dosen twenchers 2*d.*
A lether jack 4*d.*
One well bucket, two cowles, 2 keivers, 2 bowles, payles, 4 beare barrels, 1 keiver, 2 little tubbs, one tray, one clansseve £1 4*s.*
2 mault seves 8*d.*
One searsh 8*d.*
2 rayinge seves 4*d.*
One heare [for a neast *added*] 10*d.*
[*Column total torn away; by addition* £8 9*s.* 10*d.*]

2 yeoutinge stones £2.
1 henn cubb 2*s.*
Mault: 20 bushells £2.
A lynnen whele 1*s.* 6*d.*
One liverie board 2*s.*
One bushell 2*s.*

In one of the Chambers
One bedd steed, one table board, one forme and a bench £4.
2 feether bedds, one boulster, 2 pillowes £4 10*s.*
One paire of blanketes, one keiverled, one rugg £1 10*s.*
2 chests and a box 13*s.* 4*d.*
4 curtains 10*s.*
One pece of a cope 6*s.* 8*d.*
One greate Bible 10*s.*

Lynnen
6 paire of sheetes, 5 pillowbers, 5 table clothes, 2 cubberd clothes, 3 toueells, one dozen table napkins £5 3*s.* 8*d.*
In wareing parrell £4.
Flaxen yearne 5*s.*

In ane other Chamber
One bed stede 5*s.*
One fether bed, one flock bed, one

boulster, 2 pillowes £2.
2 keiverleds £1.
One flock bed, 2 keiverleds £1.
Two chestes, one cheier, 2 boxes, two truncks £1 6*s.* 8*d.*
A flasket 8*d.*
A truckel bed steed 3*s.*
Ane ould chest 1*s.*
Bords of 2 ould bed steeds 2*s.*
A heare lyne 8*d.*
A tub with fethers 1*s.*
Column total £31 16*s.* 6*d.* [*recte* £31 14*s.* 6*d.*]

One chaffinge dish 1*s.*
Painted clothes £1.
The glass about the house £1.
Waynscot: 11 yeards demi 17*s.*
A table borde and frame and forme 8*s.*
Cheiers and low stoles 9*s.*
One cubbert [and cloth *added*] £1.
Soards and pistoule 10*s.*
Plancks and tressells and a keiver 2*s.* 6*d.*
Boards: 221 fote 13*s.*
Pale: 2 dosen 5*s.*
Haye and two tallets £1 10*s.*
Stable planckes 1*s.*
Pentess bords 1*s.* 6*d.*
Cole: 2 quartes demi 6*s.*
Tressells, forkes and lugges 1*s.*
Gardenn pales and others: 14 dosen, 2 dores and an arbor £1 13*s.* 4*d.*
A woodpile of clefftes £16.
Ane ould geldinge and saddle £2 10*s.*
A joule of hewed clefts 5*s.*
2 pronges, one rake and 2 ladders 4*s.* 6*d.*
A chopping board and knyfe and stock 6*d.*
A steele plate and poteinge stick 1*s.*
Column total £29 0*s.* 4*d.* [*recte* £28 19*s.* 4*d.*]

Total £181 1*s.* 4*d.* [*recte* £180 9*s.* 2*d.*]

Nathaniel Winter, goldsmith, William Gough, goldsmith and Morris Shakerlye, joiner, appraisors.

Buried St. Peter 17 January 1615/6.
Will 22 December 1615; probate not recorded; inventory exhibited 27 March 1617.

1. Roman numerals throughout.

46 ALCE MOORE

widow 21 March 1616/7 P1/M/81

Her old [parll *deleted*] parrell 3*s.*[1]
Twoe payre of sheetes 4*s.*
Three old smockes 8*d.*
Twoe pillow tyes 8*d.*
Three pillowes 1*s.* 6*d.*
Three coverleddes 3*s.*
Two aprons and twoe kerchers 1*s.*
One sylver rynge 1*s.*
Seaven platters, one sault and a saucer 5*s.*
Fower candle stickes 1*s.*
Twoe brasse pottes, one brasse panne, twoe brasse kittles and a brasse chafeingdish 7*s.* 6*d.*
[One paire of *deleted*] three angers, one payre of pothangeinges, a payre of potthookes and a choppeing knife 1*s.*
One bedsteed, one coffer, one covell and twoe mault seeves 3*s.*
Three tackes and one turne 1*s.* 4*d.*
One halfe pecke and halfe a dozen of trenchers 2*d.*
One old kyver 4*d.*
Total £1 14*s.* 2*d.*

In money £6.

[*Total omitted, by addition* £5 14*s.* 2*d.*]

Henry A[b]bott, yeoman, John Browne, yeoman and William Patchett shoemaker, appraisors.

Buried St. Mary 20 January 1616/7.
Will undated; probate 26 [*lost*]; inventory exhibited 26 Mar 1617.

1. Roman numerals throughout.

47 ANTHONEY LYNSEY[1]
goldsmith 28 March 1617 P1/L/45

In the Haulle
1 tabell borde with a frame 6s 8*d*.[2]
1 forme 1*s*.
2 lowe joyned stooulles 1*s*.
6 cowshinges 2s 6*d*.
1 joyned chayer 2*s*.
1 joyned cubberd 10*s*.
1 church Bibell, ould 3*s*.
The wainscote and glasse about the howsse 10*s*.
Room total £1 16*s*. 2*d*.

In the Chamber over the Shope
1 standing bedsted and 1 truckell bedsted £1 6*s*. 8*d*.
2 fether beddes £2 10*s*.
2 fether boulster and 1 flocke boulster 13s 4*d*.
2 fusten pellowes, ould 3*s*. 4*d*.
1 coverled, 1 rouge, 3 blancketes 16*s*.
2 coffers 4*s*.
6 paier of ould chanvas shetes £1.
2 tabell clothes and 10 napkinges 6*s*.
His wearinge apparell £3 6*s*. 8*d*.
Room total £10 6*s*.

In the Chamber over the Hawlle
1 bedsted with a stayned cloth 4*s*.
1 ould fether bede and 3 boulsters 13*s*. 4*d*.
1 bage of fethers 1*s*.
1 coveringe, 1 blancket, 1 straughbed 3*s*. 4*d*.
3 ould coffers
Room total £1 4*s*. 8*d*.

In the Chamber over the Entery
1 bedsted corded and matte £1.
1 joyned cheste 6*s*. 8*d*.
2 brushes 4*d*.
Room total £1 7*s*.

In the Butterey
2 beare barelles 8*s*.
1 hoorse to carry beare 6*d*.
1 ould staff 2*s*.
1 ould bourd 4*d*.
1 ould cubberd 1*s*.
Room total 11*s*. 10*d*.

In the Brewhouse
2 dossen and 7 pooll of pewter £1 3*s*. 4*d*.
2 littell tinnes, 1 pinte poot, 2 pewter dishes, 3 saultes, 3 spounes, 1 brasse candell stick 2*s*.
3 brase pootes 16*s*.
2 brase posnetes 2*s*. 6*d*.
4 brase kettelles £1 6*s*. 8*d*.
1 warninge pane, 1 skemer, 2 pootwhockes 4*s*.
1 drippinge pane, 4 brouches, 1 frying pane 5*s*.
1 poothangell 8*d*.
1 paier of andiers 1*s*. 8*d*.
1 gredier 4*d*.
1 chaffinge dishes 6*d*.
1 paier of fier tonges 8*d*.
1 fier peicke 1*s*.
1 kettell 2*s*. 6*d*.
1 meashinge veate 3*s*. 4*d*.
1 keive 2*s*.
2 kevers 8*d*.
2 coulle 8*d*.
1 bushell, 1 paille 1*s*. 4*d*.
1 brandier 2*s*.
Room total £4 16*s*. 10*d*.

In the Ketchinge
2 square tabelles 4*s*.
Room total 4*s*.

In the Chamber over the Buttery
1 powdringe tube, 1 dowe kever, 1 barell 2*s*. 6*d*.
1 gardner 1*s*.
Room total 3*s*. 6*d*.

In the Backsid
2 yeotinge stones £1 10*s*.
1 chaine, 1 well bucket, 1 spendell for a

well 1s.
Sub-total £1 11s.

In the Steabell
1 mault querne, 1 manger, 1 hene coobe 10s.
Sub-total 10s.

In the Cooll Howsse
3 mault gardners 16s.
Sub-total 16s.

In the Over Backsid
1 wood pille and 1 hovell and lousse woule in the backsid and the garden palles £3.
Sub-total £3.

Money 10*d.*
Sub-total 10*d.*

Depte owinge to him by Thomas Humpheries of Alborne £1 13*s.* 6*d.*
Sub-total 13*s.* 6*d.*

Money owinge by Robert Michell 12*s.*
Sub-total 12*s.*

Total £28 12*s.* 4*d.* [*recte* £28 13*s.* 4*d.*]

Lewes Andley, Richard Tappinge, John Dodson, Richard Grinffild and Walter Jefferes, appraisors.

Buried St. Peter 25 March 1617 'Linsye'
Will 2 January 1614/5, probate 8 May 1617 to [unnamed].

1. 'Linsy' on will.
2. Roman numerals throughout, except room totals.

48 ARTER[1] DEANE

9 October 1617 P1/D/35

Money upon a band [£20 *deleted*] £1 2*s.*[2]
Money upon a band £4 8*s.*
Money £1.
In the hands of John Partrich 7*s.*
His wearing apparrell £1 10*s.*
A koffer and an old hamper 1*s.* 4*d.*
In money more £1 13*s.*

[*Total omitted, by addition* £10 1*s.* 4*d.*]

John Lawrence, appraisor.

Burial not recorded.[3]
Will 15 July 1617; probate 21 October 1617 to [unnamed].

1. 'Arthur' on will.
2. Roman numerals throughout.
3. Possibly the burial of 'Anthony Deane' recorded in the register of St. Peter, Marlborough on 19 July 1617.

49 JOANE GODDERD

[spinster] [*undated* c.1618] P1/G/65

For waring apparell 10*s.*[1]
One lease £20.

[*Total omitted, by addition* £20 10*s.*]

Buried St. Peter 12 June 1618 'daughter of Matthew'.
Bond 17 June 1618, administration to Matthew Goddard, intestate's father.

1. Roman numerals throughout.

50 WILLIAM WOODES

joiner [will] 12 August 1619 P1/W/82

His waringe apparell £2 6*s.* 8*d.*[1]
4 beds, 4 coverleds, 3 pyllows and 2 per of shetts £3 10*s.*
2 pots, 3 kytles, 1 posnat and a chafingdishe £1 10*s.*
7 platters 7*s.*

All the copery stuffe 10s.
2 broches, 1 dripping pan, 1 frying pan 3s.
4 standing bedsteds £10.
3 levery bedsteds, 2 coberds and 1 table borde £3.
2 chests and a chayre 13s. 4d.
All his workinge tolls £1.
All the tymber £10.
The wood £4.
A yoting fate 10s.
1 seive, 6 sucinge pyggs and 1 yett £1.
1 plate, a per of aunders, 1 hangell and a fyre pan, a per of tongs 7s.
A bandoro and 2 sytherns 16s.
A ould irne clokk 5s.
Mony due by band £2 12s.
A table, 5 joyne stolls and a old chayre 10s.
The lease of the howse £10.
2 drums 10s.
1 crashion 3s. 4d.
1 old servise boke 1s. 6d.
2 weges, 1 axe 1s.
1 old burdinge pece and other lumber about the howse 5s.
2 bushell of moult and a pece of bacon 5s.
30 pound of butter with the barell 8s.

Total £53 13s. 10d. [*recte* £54 13s. 10d.]

[*Appraisors' names omitted*].

Buried St. Peter 11 August 1619.
Will 3 August 1619; probate 1 September 1619 to executrix [Ruth Engles, testator's servant].

1. Roman numerals throughout except total.

51 AGNES BORDMAN[1]

spinster [*undated*, c.1619] P1/B/161

Tow olld gouns 6s. 6d.[2]
To petticots 5s.
Thre olld patticots 1s. 6d.
Thre olld wastcots 1s.
Thre olld smokes 3s.
4 dobbell kerchers 2s.
8 singell kearchers 2s.
Thre olld tabellnackens 6d.
5 ollde partlats 1s. 8d.
One fustine wastcote 1s.
2 collored aperns 1s. 2d.
3 linning aperns 1s. 6d.
A payer of sheets 3s. 4d.
On keverled 5s.
On bolster, on pellow 1s. 6d.
On olld blanket 6d.
On olld hate 8d.
On kettell overworn 3s.
On letell skellet and a letell kettell 1s. 4d.
On coffer 1s.
On pound of pickt wolle 8d.
On covl, on barell and a kever 2s. [2s]
3 baskets 1s.
2 olld payer of shous 8d.
2 olld disshes, a odden platter and a slekston 4d.
A torne and cover 8d.
Total £2 11s. 8d. [*recte* £2 8s. 6d.]

[*Added in a different hand*] In money dewe the deceased from William Smithe of Overton £5.

[*Total omitted, by addition* £7 8s. 6d.]

Thomas Newe, Henry Abete, Steven Knight and Thomas Sloper, appraisors.

Buried St. Mary 20 May 1619.
Bond 2 November 1619, administration to Christopher Barker of Marlborough.

1. 'of St Maries in Marlburgh'.
2. Roman numerals throughout except as shown.

52 BALDINE LEE

labourer 17 December 1619 P1/L/55

His wearing apparrel 10s.[1]

In the Chamber

One bedsteed, one flockbedd, two coverlids, one paire of blancketts, three canvas sheets, one bolster of flocks, a painted cloth, one flocke pillowe, on feather pillowe £1 10s.

One cubbard, one coffer, 8 platters of pewter, tw pewter salts, one pewter tune, two brasse candlstickes, fower sawcers, one brasse chaffinge dish, one table clothe, two pillow cases, one of holland the other o lockeram £1.

Fower barrelles, one settele, one brish, one gallon of wood, one littil bole of wood, three stone juggs, one morte snagg, one drinking bowle 5s.

In the Halle

One table bord, two tressels, one fourme, foure shelves, two stooles, one paire of billowes, one lanthorne, one handsawe, one cowle, one little kive, one latchet, on axe, one auger, twe littl hatchetts, three bytells, three wedges 6s.

Two brasse kittels, two brasst skillets, one brasse pot, on pewtar quart pot, one chopping knife, on gridyron, one frying pan, one littl paile, one skimer, one wooden ladell, twe paire of pothangles, two yron crookes, one old paire of cheirs £1 3s. 4d.

In the Lofte

One press, one coffer, two kivorse, one bushell, two fourmes, two boords, one wollene turne, two sarches, two sithes, two sneads, three vessells, three bords, one lether bottl, one plainer, one cowle 10s.

In the Backhouse and Backsid

Ladders, wood and other lumber £1.

A firepan, two iron wedges, two handbaskets, a little bucket, a chaire, two earthen pans, on old bedsted 2s.

The lease of [his *deleted*] the house £5.

Total £11 6s. 4d.

William Blisset the younger and Henry Cowse, appraisors.

Buried St. Peter 16 December 1619, 'Baldwyne Lea'.

Bond 11 January 1619/20, administration to Thomas Bourne; accounts submitted 25 September 1621 by Thomas Bourne.

1. Roman numerals throughout.

53 JOHN DODSHON

21 February 1619/20 P1/D/39

In the Hall

One tablebord with a [. . .]
One forme, a littell [. . .]
2 stooles, one cr[. . .]
1 per of [. . .]
1 fier shove[. . .]
1 plate behn[. . .]
16 pe[. . .]
[. . .]mers [. . .]
Five pewt[. . .]
3 pewter ca[. . .]
Candlestickes, 2 [. . .]
[. . .] woodden [. . .]
Earthen dyshes [. . .]
7 spoones [. . .]
Nyne brasse [. . .]
[. . .]one littell pors[. . .]
4 kettelles [. . .]
One brasse p[. . .]
One drippi[. . .]
1 warmi[. . .]
1 skymer [. . .]
1 per of pothooks [. . .]
and one gridir[. . .]
1 clever [. . .]
2 payles 1 [. . .]

In [. . .]

One beds[. . .]
3 chestes [. . .]
1 bench of [. . .]scott, 1 c[. . .]
1 coffer, 1 [. . .]
2 fetherbeds, 1 flockbedd, 2 fetherbosters, 3 pillowes, 3 flockbosters 3*s.*[1]
1 kever, 1 flascot, 1 screne, to seves 2*s.* 6[d.]

In the [. . .]er Chamber
One old bedsteed, 1 [. . .]ffer 10[. . .]
2 flockbeds, 1 [. . .]
[. . .]2 bolsters, 3 pillo[. . .]
3 c[. . .]
1 carpett, 4 [. . .]
2 old [. . .]
1 [. . .]

[*unknown number of lines missing*]

4 par and 1 sheet of dowlas, canvas and holland, one drinkinge clothe £1 6*s.* 8*d.*
2 table clothes 13*s.* 4*d.*
[. . .] 2 towells, 2 dossen of table [. . .] fyve pillowbers £1 6*s.* 8*d.*
[. . .]ll £2.

[. . .]le
[. . .] 1 kyve [. . .]ashine boule 10*s.*
[. . .]de [. . .]s. 3*d.*

[. . .]10[. . .]
[. . .] £1.
[. . .]h[. . .] 2[. . .]

[. . .]pp[. . .] 10s[. . .] .
[. . .]es

[. . .]p
[. . .] 6*s.*
[. . .] £1.
[. . .] 3*d.*

Total £44 18*s.* 8*d.*

Thomas Bennett, Simon Dringe and John Fowler, appraisors.

Buried St. Peter 19 September 1619
Will [date lost]; probate [date lost] to ['Prudence my wife' named in will]; commission [date lost] to [testator's widow].

1. All surviving amounts are in Roman numerals, except total.

54 AGNES WEEB[1]

widow [commission] [*undated*, c.1619/20] P1/W/81

On lettell feather bead and on letell flockebead 10*s.*[2]
Tow bowelsters 2*s.*
On ould rouge, on blaynket, on ould covering 9*s.*
On beadsteed, on matt 8*s.*
On boulster and tow pellowes and on covering 5*s.*
There gownes 16*s.*
To pety cootes 14*s.*
On chock and safgard 6*s.* 8*d.*
On ould gowne, on ould pety coote, to ould goorgetes 3*s.*
To hattes and on black appern 3*s.*
On caulyco sheet 5*s.*
A payer of lockerum sheetes 6*s.* 8*d.*
On bordcloth and on letell sheet 2*s.*
To pelowbeares 2*s.*
There canvass sheetes 2*s.* 6*d.*
There smokes 4*s.*
Five singel kerchefes 1*s.* 3*d.*
Five penners 1*s.*
Four natkenes 9*d.*
Six partletes 1*s.* 4*d.*
On cheast 5*s.*
To cofferes and on box 3*s.* 4*d.*
To letell ferkens 2*s.*
On saddell and ould brydell [. . .]
On chayer and on ould tube 4*d.*
There platters, to pottengers 3*s.* 4*d.*
5 saser dishes 1*s.* 4*d.*

To letell kettelles and on lettell pane 2*s.* 6*d.*
On lettell brasse pot 3*s.*
On broche 1*s.*
On ould andier 6*d.*
On littell kever 10*d.*
Tow table boardes and a cubbard 5*s.*
Waynscot and binches 1*s.* 6*d.*
And ould bedsted and a tubb 1*s.*
An ould trough 1*s.*
To doores and window leades 1*s.* 6*d.*

Total £6 18*s.* 2*d.*

Robert Carver, Richard Browne and Thomas Smyth the younger of Shalborne, appraisors.

Burial not recorded.
Will 29 May 1617; commission 22 February 1619/20, oath administered to Margerie Webb, testator's daughter; probate 7 Mar 1619/20 to Margerie Webb.

1. 'Webb' on will.
2. Roman numerals throughout.

55 WILLIAM NOBELL

4 October 1620 P1/N/30

For his wearinge apparell 5[1][. . .]
Tow small brasse pannes [. . .]
Three old small kittels [. . .]
One old brasse basen [. . .]
Three old skilletes [. . .]
One brasse pott [. . .]
One little iron pot [. . .]
Six small pewter dishes and sawsers [. . .]
Fyve littell pewter potes and botells 10[. . .]
Three littell brasse candellstickes 15[. . .]
Some old bordes that do serve to make a bedsteed 1*s.*
One bedsteed and the bedding belonging to it 15*s.*
Tow old coffers 1*s.*
One old chest which is three shillinges lont one it 3*s.*
One tabell bord with the frame and the old stooles 5*s.*
One old cubbord neyled together made of old bordes and other old tubes and some other timber trumpery 4*s.*
For wood 15*s.* 6*d.*
One peare of billis and a p[ot] hangins 1*s.*
More for iron ware and some neyles 5*s.*
More one old standing [be]d steed 5*s.*

Total £3 10*s.*

Wryten by John Luxton the day and yeare above writen
William C[. . .]p[. . .] and George Basen, appraisors.

Burial not recorded.
No other documents; inventory exhibited 9 October 1621[2].

1. Roman numerals throughout.
2. Accounts [*undated*] 'laied out for my husbands funerall' listed after inventory.

56 THOMAS SHEATE

mercer 10 July 1621 P1/S/143

In the Haall
One tableboard with tresles, one benche, tuo ould formes with painted clothes, one ould chaire 5*s.*[1]
In the haall thre brasse ketles, one brasse pott, tuo skilletes, one skimmer and one spice morter with a pessell of irron £2 10*s.*
In the haall the fire pan, the fire tonges, the andirons, the drippinge pan, the grediron, the spitt, [the flesh hookes *added*] 7*s.*[vij^{s}]

In the next Rome called the Litle Haall
Fowerteene platters and pottengers and five saucers, 3 ould salt sellers, one tun

dish, one brass candlesticke £1.[xx^{s}]

In the same rome one ould cupbord, tuo litle tables with benches, one painted clothe 5*s.*

In the Best Chamber

One bedsted, one table bord with a frame, one greate chest, thre formes, thre coffers, one close stole £2.[xl^{s}]

In the same one flock bed and flock boulster, tuo pillowes, one straw bed and boulster, one white rugge, one coveringe £2.[xl^{s}]

In the samme rome 2 pair of ould canvasse sheetes, one holland sheete, tuo ould table clothes, tuo pillou beres with other ould lynnen 14*s.*

In the nexte Chamber

One flock bed and boulster with 5 flock pillowes, one white rugge, one ould blanquett, one canvasse sheete, tuo ould coffers, [one ould rugge *added*] £1 5*s.*[xxv^{s}]

In the Butrie

8 peuter [*illegible deletion*] potes, thre stone iuges, thre ale cups, tuo dozen of trenchers, one hoggesheade, seven barels, 3 bordes for shelves with the lumber in the rome £1 8*s.*[xxviij^{s}]

In the Back House

A kieve, one meshfatt, seven kievers, tuo coules, two pailes with the lumber in the rome £1.[xx^{s}]

In the Back Side

In wood 10*s.*[x^{s}]

The pales about the garden 10*s.*[x^{s}]

Tuo leases for time yett unexspired £6 13*s.* 4*d.*[vi^{li} 13^{s} 4^{d}]

One horse with ould stuff in the stable £4.

His waringe apparell £2.

[*Total omitted, by addition* £26 7*s.* 4*d.*]

William Blissett junior, Richard Cornwall junior and Thomas Sheat of Hodson, appraisors.

Buried St. Mary 6 July 1621.

Bond 20 July 1621, administration to Roberte Sheate, clerk; inventory exhibited 23 July 1621.

1. Roman numerals where shown.

57 HUMFFRYE WYATT

buttonmaker [will] 8 October 1621

P1/W/90

His waring apparrell £2.[1]

2 [. . .], 3 boulsters, 2 per of sheats, 2 blan [. . .],2 cov[er]leds and 1 quilte £2.

[. . .] £1 10*s.*

The [. . .] 6*s.* 8*d.*

1 [. . .], a v[. . .]s, [. . .] broches, 1 drypinge pan, [. . .]roks and a frynpan 4*s.*

2 bedsteds, [. . .], 4 coffers, 1 joyne [. . .], a table bord and a frame to him £1.

Monye £2.

Coppery [. . .] 2*s.*

The wood [. . .] baksyd 10*s.*

1 coberd, [. . .] bukat and chayne with other thi[. . .] in lumber 2*s.* 6*d.*

Total £9 15*s.* 2*d.*

John Hiller and Robert Chivers, appraisors.

Buried St. Peter 19 September 1621.

Will [nuncupative] 20 September 1621[2]; probate 5 February 1621/2 to [*lost*]; commission 5 February 16211/2, oath administered to Alice Wyatt, testator's widow.

1. Roman numerals throughout.
2. This date does not agree with that of the burial.

58 ELIZABETH LANE
widow 23 May 1622 P1/L/64

102 lb of pott bras at 4*d.* the lb £1 14*s.*
47 lb of pewter at 6*d.* the lb £1 3*s.* 6*d.*
Kettle bras 31 lb at 10*d.* the lb £1 5*s.* 10*d.*
Pales and old boardes £1.
One truncke, one chest and 5 coffers £1 4*s.*
2 anders, 2 pothoockes, 2 pothanges 4*s.*
2 pare of sheetes, 2 pillabers, one fine sheet £1.
All her wearinge clothes, linnine and wollen £2.
Lumber about the house £1.
Money £3.
2 smalle tenements £6.
One [...], one bolster and on[e] coveringe £1.

Total [*£20 by addition*] 11*s.* 4*d.*

William Withers, brewer and Morris Shackerley, joiner, appraisors.

Burial not recorded.
Bond 4 October 1622, administration to Agnes Wild, intestate's relict; accounts submitted 16 April 1624 by Agnes Wilde.

59 WILLIAM WYAT[1]
weaver 8 January 1622/3 P1/W/96

In the Hall
A table boord and frame 10*s.*[2]
Sixe joyned stooles 4*s.*
A paire of playeinge tables 1*s.*

In the Chamber over the Hall
A table boord and frame 8*s.*
A joyned forme 1*s.*
A liverye beedsted and a truckle beedsted 10*s.*
A flookbed, a cyverled, a bolster, two blanckettes £1.
Fowre paire of sheetes, three table cloathes, six napkines £1 5*s.*
Two cushions 1*s.*

In the Gatehouse Chamber
A bedsted 2*s.* 6*d.*
A table boord and frame 2*s.*
Foure old coffers 8*s.*
A flook bedd and bolster, two blanckettes 10*s.*
A bedstedd and a gallon and a kiffer 2*s.* 6*d.*
Fowre iron wedges 2*s.*
Two hatchettes 8*d.*
Scales, beame and waightes 3*s.* 4*d.*
A lanthorne, a search and a flaskett 2*s.*

In the Chamber next the Shopp
A table boord, two tressells and a forme 1*s.* 6*d.*
A bedstedd 6*s.* 8*d.*
A flookbed, bolster and coverled 10*s.*

In the Little Rome next the Shopp
A table boord and frame 2*s.*

In the Shopp
A weavers loome with the appurtenannces 13*s.* 4*d.*

In the Kitchin
Fower kettles and a skillet 10*s.*
A brasse pott 3*s.*
Eight platters 7*s.*
Fower candlesticks and two saltes 3*s.*
Three quart potts and a pinte pott, one bason and one chamber pott 4*s.*
Two doggs, a broche, two pothangers, one paire of pot hookes, a skimmer, a bastinge ladle and a paire of fleshookes 4*s.*
Three cowles and a bowle 3*s.* 6*d.*
A buckett 4*d.*
An old cubberd 2*s.*
Wood £1.
His wearinge apparrell £2.
A pigge 10*s.*

Total £13 3*s.* 2*d.* [*recte* £12 13*s.* 4*d.*]

Owed uppon bond by the said deceased William Wyate £5.[3]

John Eaton, Walter Geffreys and William Withers, appraisors.

Buried St. Mary 20 December 1622 'Wiat'.
Will 20 December 1622; probate 19 February 1622/3 to [unnamed].

1. 'of the parishe of St. Maryes in Marlebrough'.
2. Roman numerals throughout.
3. Debts owed by the deceased should not form part of the inventory.

60 PHILLIP INGEROM

servant[1] 3 March 1622/3 P1/IJ/33

Her woollen apparrell
One gowne 13*s.* 4*d.*[2]
Fowre wearing pettycoates 6*s.* 8*d.*
Two wearing wascottes 1*s.* 6*d.*

Lynnen
Seaven smockes 10*s.*
Seaven partlottes 7*s.*
Seaven aprons 4*s.*
Eight kerchers 4*s.*
One wearing hatte 1*s.*
Three girdles and a purse with 4*d.* in yt 1*s.* 8*d.*
One peece of shooe leather 1*s.*
Hosen and shooes 1*s.*
Two coffers 2*s.*
Two old kytles 2*s.*
One [pewter *added*] platter 1*s.* 4*d.*
One pewter potten[g]er 8*d.*
One ring silver and guilt 1*s.* 6*d.*

Debts owinge unto her
Robert Paynter of Ogborne St George £1 10*s.*
John Stapler her executor 10*s.*
[In money due to her £8 *added*]

Total £12 10*s.* 10*d.*

William Paggett and John Blake, appraisers.
William Elliott and Agnes Stapler, witnesses.

Buried St. Mary 12 February 1622/3.
Will [nuncupative] 17 January 1622/3; probate 4 March 1622/3 to [*illegible*].

1. 'unto one Thomas Snowe of Derrington'.
2. Roman numerals throughout.

61 AMBROSE PONTIN

tailor 10 April 1623 P1/P/100

In readie money £10.[1]
His wearing apparrell £1.
One hundred and four yards of ordinary woollen cloth £13.
Three hundred 57 yards of course woollen cloth £26 5*s.*
Twenty sale dubletts £5.
Twelve paire of sale breeches £3.
Six sale jurkins 17*s.*
More in little remnants of woollen cloth 4*s.*
Two skins 4*d.*
Thirteene yards of fustin 13*s.*
Forty yeards of broade list 2*s.*
Three flock beds £2.
Foure coverleds £1 10*s.*
Foure blancots 10*s.*
5 paire and a halfe of old sheets £1 10*s.*
One fether bolster 5*s.*
Two little feather pillowes 4*s.*
2 flock bolsters and 2 flock pillowes 5*s.*
One standing bedsteeds and 2 truckle bedsteeds 15*s.*
One great cheast in his chamber 10*s.*
One table bord and six stooles 15*s.*
Nine coffers 10*s.*
2 table clothes, 3 pillowbers and 6 napkins 5*s.*

10 dossen and 10 falling sale bands £3 5*s.*
More 2 dossen and halfe of smale made w[ar]e 8*s.*
Five yards of linnen cloth 6*s.*
2 dossen of smale ware unfinisht 8*s.*
Loome worke lase 6*d.*
Girdles, laces, gartering and pinnes [5*s.*] 8*d.*
11 yards of loome worke 4*s.*
Corne left in the house £1.
Painted clothes 3*s.* 4*d.*
One dossen of platters 15*s.*
Three brasse candlesticks 2*d.*
Four sawcers 2*s.* 4*d.*
One quart pott and tin bottle 1*s.* 6*d.*
Three little brasse potts 10*s.*
2 little skillets and kettle 5*s.*
A broach, a frying pan and 2 beefe prickers 1*s.* 4*d.*
A paire of doggs, a fire shovell and a pare of tongs 3*s.* 4*d.*
One gridyer, cotterells and pott hangells 8*d.*
A paire of billowes, salt box and drinking cups 6*d.*
Halfe a dossen of spoones, 2 dossen of trenchers and pewter cupp 6*d.*
A prong, a bill and a tosting yre 1*s.*
One cubard in the hall 5*s.*
One table bord and 4 stooles there 5*s.*
Wanscott and benches there 3*s.* 4*d.*
Two cheeses 2*s.*
A little cubard, curten and curten rod 1*s.*
A treene platter, a salt seller and 3 glasses 6*d.*
An old presse and paire of spencers 2*s.*
One skimmer, a dripping pan and ladle 1*s.*
4 ledging barrells and upstands 4*s.*
2 cowles, a powdring tubb and trendle 3*s.* 4*d.*
One chamber pot, a skillet and dowkeever 2*s.*
One brandier, two sives, a bushell and peck 2*s.*
One chest, a shopbord, 2 yrons and 3 paire of sheres 7*s.*
Silke lase and remnants of taffety 5*s.*
An other little box, a remnant of cotton, 1 paire of stokins and 4 yards to measure cloth 1*s.*
One horse beast £1 10*s.*
In lasts £2.
All the wood £5.
Bords, pales and planks £1.
2 pack sadles and a rode sadle 6*s.* 8*d.*
Haye 5*s.*
Due in despret debts and otherwise £1 2*s.*
The welbucket, chaine and other lomber 6*s.* 4*d.*

Total £90 18*s.* 2*d.* [*recte* £90 13*s.* 4*d.*]

Debts which I did owe at my decease[2]
First due unto my daughter Joane £8.
Due unto my daughter Anne £3.
To be paid for cloth bought at Sarum £3 10*s.*
Due to an other for cloth there £2 14*s.*
To John Paine £1.
To Restle 15*s.*

Total £18 19*s.*

Thomas Trebret and Simon Hurle, appraisors.
Jhone Payne and Ulisses Pettie, witnesses.

Buried St. Peter 2 April 1623 'Ambrose Ponting'.
Will 11 March 1622/3; probate 13 June 1623 to [unnamed].

1. Roman numerals throughout.
2. Debts owed by the deceased should not form part of the inventory.

62 [ALICE WYATT][1]
widow [will] [*date lost*, c.1623]
P1/W/97

Two best gownes and 2 [. . .] pettycoats

£2 13s. 4d.[2]
6 partletts [. . .] 10s.
3 wastcots and [. . .] 10s.
3 hollond aperns and a hatt 10s.
3 smocks and other male linine 6s. 8d.
One ould flocke bed, a boulster, a pillow, 3 sheets and 2 ould blanketts 16s.
One ould bedstead with 4 bounds and an ould coffer 4s.
One ould brasse pott, a ould kettle, a ould spitt and very ould skillett with a hole in it 6s.
One platter and 2 pottingers 2s.
For timber 10s.
One canvis flocke bedd, 2 feather blousters and 2 feather pillows £1.
One coverlett, one quilt, one ould blankett 10s.
Two per of sheets, 3 pillowbeares and a napkins 10s.
One borded bedsteed 3s.
4 ould petty coats and a cloake with a hatt 10s.
2 ould gownes 5s.
17 peeces of pewter smale and greate 10s.
4 kettles, one skillett, one brass pott, one warming pann, one brasen morter with an ireone pestle, one brasen candlestyke, one brasen [*illegible deleteion*] yewer, a brassen cupp and one skimmer £1 6s. 8d.
One per of large aneyens with a spitt, 3 per of potthookes, one per of hangers and long crooke with other poore lumber 5s.
One little table bourd with a frame, 2 long formes and a chayre, a paire of wainskott 5s.
One chest and 2 little coffers 5s.
2 ould bords 4s.
One ould cubberd, 4 tubs and a poudringe tubbe 3s.
A ould handle and well buckett with chayne and wood in the backesyde 8s.

[*Total omitted, by addition* £12 12s. 8d.]

Anthony Feild, Thomas Vokins and Richard Greaffton, appraisers.

Buried St. Peter 2 May 1623.
Will 22 January 1622/3; probate 13 June 1623 to [unnamed].

1. Heading damaged, name from will.
2. Roman numerals throughout.

63 WILLIAM HASKINS

?cooper [inventory goods] [*undated*, c.1623/4] P1/H/158

3 bedsteds, 2 coffers, boultnge whiche 13s. 4d.[1]
1 chest, a table bord with a frame, 1 coberd and a chayre 13s. 4d.
2 bedsteads 4s.
4 beds, 11 sheets £3.
1 bed, 2 boulsters, 2 blankats, 1 coferled, 1 pyllow £1 6s. 8d
His waring aparell £2.
The brasse and pewter, 1 fyre shovle, 1 par of andyers, 1 par of pothocks, 1 grydyer, 1 broche, a par of byllows, 1 friing pan £1 13s. 4d.
The coperye stufe and a fate, a well bokat with a chayne [*illegible deletion*] 18s.
1 pyge, 3 oute howses [that ar movable *added*] with the wood £3.
6 paynted clotes 1s. 8d.
4 iron weges with other iron lumber 1s.

Total £13 [ix[s] *deleted*] 10s.

Gregory Tytcum, Swythin Haies and Thomas Coxe, appraisors.

Buried St Peter 23 October 1623.
Will 18 September 1622; probate 5 January 1623/4 to Robert Haskins, testator's son.

1. Roman numerals throughout.

64 ANTHONIE GUNTER
glover 13 April 1624 P1/G/88

His wearing apparell £2 0s. 6*d.*
One standinge beadsteed and one trundle beasted £1.

In the Loft over the Hale
One fetherbead and two flockbeedes, four fether bolsters, six fether pillowes, one flock bolster £4.
Three par of sheetes £1.
Two coverledes, one par of blanketes £1 13*s.* 4*d.*
Four tableclothes, nineteen tablenapkins and towells £1 10*s.*
One large tableboard £1.
One great chest 8*s.*
One litle chest, one litle coffer, two boxes and two formes 10*s.* 6*d.*
All the wenscott and binches in the chamber over the hale £2 10*s.*
One painted cloth 1*s.* 4*d.*
One splet chayer 1*s.*

In the Hale
One large tableboard and frame, portall and all the binches £2 10*s.*
The litle walnut table in the hale 10*s.*
One great cubard with a settl standing over the same £1.
Two chayers, two formes, three joynstooles, two tressels and on board 11*s.*
Nine cushens, one old carpet cloth and one cubard cloth 8*s.*
One window leafe, one window curtaine and rod of iron and a bord behind the binch 2*s.*
One sword and one rapier 2*s.*
[. . .] one cutting knife and beame knife 2*s.*

In the Chamber behind the Shoop
[One standing bedstead 6*s.* 8*d.* *deleted*]
Two old coffers and one litle box and one chest 2*s.*

In the Citchin
One table, one forme, all the wenscot with the shelfe 6*s.* 8*d.*
One joyne chaire and stoole with one painted cloth 2*s.*
One bason and yore, twelve pewter platters, six poringers, two sasers, two salts, one pewter candlesticke, one botle, one pint pott, one tunne, one halfe pint pott, two flower pottes with other small peces of pewter with one quart pott £2.
One great braspann 18*s.*
One litle braspann 10*s.*
One litle braspann 10*s.*
Great bras pott 16*s.*
Litle bras pott 6*s.* 8*d.*
One pras furnas 16*s.*
One pras pott 13*s.* 4*d.*
One bras cettle 8*s.*
One bell posnet and morter 6*s.* 8*d.*
One bras warming pann, one colender, two chaffindishes, one skimer, one old pece of bras 10*s.* 4*d.*
One par of anders, two spits, one par of pothanges, one fire shovle, one par of tongs, one ireon dripping pan, one gridiron, one bras ladle, one bras potled, on choping knife, one prandire, one old skillet, one par of pothookes 16*s.* 8*d.*
One tenent saw, three wegges, one hatch 4*s.*
One hand basket, one search, one lantren with other implements 2*s.* 6*d.*
Fifty-four harowes to make parchment £3.

In the Workhouse
Three vates and cever £1.
Glovers beamels and one spininge whele 1*s.*
Two knives to mak marshment [?*recte* parchment] 2*s.*
One waybeames and waites 3*s.* 4*d.*
Peltes and parchment £1 13*s.* 4*d.*

In the Stable
One reckes and manger, on enstcoop, one

wattell, six hurdles 2*s.* 6*d.*
Sadle, one pad, one bridle, one pillion 6*s.* 8*d.*
One chespres 2*s.*
Five barells, one cever, one covld, one bushell and strech and other lumber 6*s.* 8*d.*
The lease of one tenement now in the tenure Robert Princ in the Marsh Ward in Marlebrough in the countie of Wiltes £13 6*s.* 8*d.*
The lease of the tenement now in tenure of Agnis Gunter wife of Anthonie Gunter deceased being in the Marsh Ward in Marlebrough in Wiltes with the barne next adioyning £20.
In corne and woll £13 6*s.* 8*d.*
All the lether and dere skins £3 6*s.* 8*d.*
One lime coob and a watle over the head 2*s.*
One shoop board and two stakes in the shoop one with one coffer one iron barr and mathooke 5*s.*
Nine lbs of yearne corse stuf and six lbs of fine yearne 6*s.*
One old bedsteed, four pounds of black wole and twenty pounds of corse leg wole 6*s.* 8*d.*
Ten dozen of pale mouding Thomas Taylers garden which he holdeth from Agnis Gunter late wif of Anthonie Gunter deceased and one hedg mounding Thomas Custer his garden which he houldeth of the forsaid Agnis 13*s.* 4*d.*
Sacks, one bushell bagg and ost heare 4*s.*

Total £89 2*s.* 6*d.*

William Guy and William Coster, appraisors.

Buried St. Mary 7 April 1624.
Will 1 April 1624; probate 30 May 1625 to Agnes Gunter, testator's widow.

65 JOHN GRUNDIE senior
tanner 24 April 1624 P1/G/81

[. . .] his wearing apparell £1 6*s.* 8*d.*
[. . .]dsteed one flockbead, 2 bolsters, one fether pillow, 2 blanketes, one coverlet £1.
[. . .] coffers 2*s.*
[. . .]eve hare, one watchbill, one reell, one waybeame of iron 3*s.*
[. . .]teene peces of pewter 14*s.*
[. . .] bras pott and pothockes, two calthrones, one bras skillat, 2 bras candlestickes, [. . .] skimmer 13*s.* 4*d.*
[. . .] frying pan, one pare of anders, one spitt, one potthanges, one pare of billowes, [. . .] pare of shers, one hatchet 4*s.*
A cubbard, one table board and one forme, one chayer stools and one litle stoole £1.
One coule, 2 cevers, one payle, one boule, one cive 3*s.* 4*d.*
One chaving dish, one fire showell, one pewter chamberpott and one stone jugg, one powdring tubb, three barrells and other small implement 4*s.* 4*d.*
The lease of the house £6 13*s.* 4*d.*
One barke mile £1.
Barke 4*s.*
One presse [and one ?pinstooke *deleted*] 4*s.*
8 hides and half £2 1*s.* 6*d.*
15 calfes skins 8*s.*
6 tanvats 6*s.*
200½ of turnes 1*s.* 8*d.*
3 lime pites 1*s.*
One beame and grindstone 4*d.*
One bushell and hare 4*d.*
One barrow, [colrake *deleted*] one draftshave and one barke hewer 6*d.*
Two ladders 1*s.* 6*d.*

Total £16 18*s.* 10*d.* [*recte* £16 12*s.* 10*d.*]

William Gunter, John Fowler and William Gostard, appraisors.

Buried St. Mary 22 April 1624.
Will 22 April 1624; probate 29 May 1624 to John Grundy, testator's son.

66 JOHN REDFORD

husbandman [will] 4 May 1624
P1/R/49

In the Hall
A table bord, on forme, 2 coberdes 10*s.*[1]
3 brase potes, 2 brass ketteles and to brase skellutes £1 13*s.* 4*d.*
2 brase panes, a brase chafindish and a [skelat *deleted*] skemer 11*s.*
6 platters, 6 pottengers and 9 saseres 13*s.* 4*d.*
On brase candelstek, 2 powter candelstekes, thre powter potes and thre satselleres 6*s.* 8*d.*
On per of rakes and on dripping pan 8*s.*
3 spetes, on per of andiares and per of doges, to eyern bares and on plat and to per of pothokes 7*s.*
3 per of pothangeles, on fiare panne and a per of tonges and a per of belusses 3*s.* 4*d.*
On tack, on stole, on dossen of dishes, 3 dossen of erthen vessell and 3 guges and 3 glasses and 2 dossen of trencheres 4*s.* 10*d.*

In the Parler
On tablebord and frame, 2 formes and 7 stoles and on chaior 10*s.*
A chest of coffer, 2 bedstedes £1 6*s.* 8*d.*
On fether bed and fether boulster, on floke bed and floke boulster £2.
3 coverledes and on blanket 15*s.*
Hes waring apparell £1 6*s.* 8*d.*

In the Seller
6 bariles, 2 upstandes, on coule, 2 kiveres, 3 payles and on bockut, on bushell and gane 12*s.*
On trow, 2 takes, 3 thoules and 2 formes 2*s.* 4*d.*

In the Shope
On tabelbord, on forme and on torne 2*s.* 6*d.*

In the [*Litel* added] *Chambor*
On tabelbord and fram, on levery bedsted and 2 formes 8*s.* 4*d.*
On floke bed, on floke boulster and 2 coverledes 3*s.* 4*d.*

In the Chambor over the Parler
On gine bedsted, 4 cofferes, on trunke and on boxe and on round tabelbord 18*s.*
On floke bed and boulster, 6 perlowes and a quilt and [. . .]es coverled £2 6*s.* 8*d.*
On livery bed sted, on floke pelow and an ould coverled and a winuing shet and 2 sawes and to iren weges 7*s.*
4 per of cannvase shetes and 6 tabell cloes, 4 peloberes, 6 napkenes, a cobercloth £2 6*s.* 8*d.*
On ould serch, on temser and ould iren 2*s.*
12 bushelles of barlye £1 4*s.*

[*unknown number of lines lost*]

In the Iner Loft
9 quarteres of mault £8 [. . .].

In the Loft over the Enterny
20 busheles of mault £2.
2 fleches of bakon 8*s.*
On bedsted, on floke boulster, 2 blanketes, to coverledes, on wach bell, on pekestafe, on moulseve 5*s.*

In the Kechen
On ould furnes, on cive, on ould querne, on trow, on forme 6*s.* 8*d.*
On yotting vate, on wishtub, on chespres, on renseve, on spad, on ruder 6*s.*

In the Stabell
Rakes, mangeres and tallutes and plankes £1.

In the Baksid
To kine £3.
To piges 13*s.* 4*d.*
Postes and pales and pigtrow and other lumbermentes £20.
On welbukut and rope and grin stone with a spendell 5*s.*

Total £36 12s 8*d.*

Robert Hitchcock, James Ellyott, William Blissett and Thomas Hitchcock, appraisors.

Buried St. Mary 27 April 1624.
Will 25 April 1624; probate 29 May 1624 to executrix [Christian Redford, testator's widow].

1. Roman numerals throughout.

67 GREGORY TYTCUMB[1]

28 May 1624 P1/T/68

[His wearing apparell *deleted*]
3 bedes, 2 boulsters, 2 pyllows 12*s.*[2]
2 coverledes, 2 per of shets and 1 pyllowbe with a table cloth 12*s.*
1 bedsted, 1 chest, 3 [cof]fers and a chayre 10*s.*
3 kyttles, 3 brasse potts, 3 brassen candlestiks, 3 skyllates and 1 brasse pan 16*s.*
1 platter, 1 potinger, 2 sawsers with a pewter pott 2*s.*
1 per of andyers, 1 broche, 1 drypen pan and a per of pothocks with a per of hangells 2*s.* 6*d.*
1 table borde with a frame, 1 forme, 1 coberd, 2 kyevers, 2 barells 6*s.*
A moult myll 2*s.*
The lease of the dwellinge howse £1 10*s.*

Total £3 12*s.* 6*d.* [*recte* £4 12*s.* 6*d.*]

[*Appraisors' names omitted*]

Buried St. Peter 22 December 1623 'Titcomb'
Bond 29 May 1624, administration to Joane Titcombe, intestate's widow.

1. 'of St. Peters in marlburgh'.
2. Roman numerals throughout.

68 ALICE PAGETT

widow 1 November 1624 P1/P/109

In the Hall
One cupbord 5*s.*[1]
One tablebord and frame 2*s.*
2 chaires and two little stooles 1*s.* 4*d.*

In the Parlor
One tablebord and frame, 2 formes and twoo stooles and a coffer 6*s.* 8*d.*

In the Kitchen
Twoo yoateing fates, 3 barrells and twoo cowles and twoo tubbs, one torne, one buckett and payle and other lumber £1.

In an Outhouse
One garner and a tallett with other lumber there 10*s.*

In the Chamber over the Hall
One standing bedsteed and one truckle bedsteed with a matt and cord, one fether bed, one flocke bedd and one fether boulster and three fether pillows with a flocke boulster £2 16*s.* 8*d.*
4 coverledds, one paire of blanckettes £1.
2 holand pillowbers, one fustian pillowber, 3 paire of canvas sheetes [and three table clothes and halfe a dozen of napkins *added*] £1.
One coffer, twoo boxes, a cheeseracke and other lumber 2*s.* 6*d.*
The testatrix her wearing apparrell £6.

In ready money £13 10*s.*
3 weight of wooll £2 10*s.*
7 quarters and fyve bushells of barley att 15*s.* the quarter £5 14*s.*
14 poude of pewter 10*d.*
One brasse pan, 3 brasse kettles, one brasse pott and two brasse skyllettes and a posnett and fower candlestickes £1 16*s.* 8*d.*
2 frying panns and one gridiron and a dripping pan, 3 broaches and one paire of andirons, 2 paire of potthookes, a fleshhooke and a scemler and 2 paire of potthangells 6*s.* 8*d.*
One bushell of wheat 4*s.*
A paire of beames and skales and weights 2*s.* 6*d.*
One bushell, one halfe pecke, twoo malt seeves and 3 other seeves with a temser 7*s.* 8*d.*
A debt owing by William Pagett £8.
The wood in the backside £5. [6*s.* *deleted*]
The lease of her house £12.
A ladder 6*d.*
3 yards of red cloth, one gold ring and two silver spoones £1 2*s.* 2*d.*

Total £64 8*s.* 4*d.*

Stephen Lawrence, Henry Abbott and John Browne, appraisors.

Burial not recorded.
Will 29 October 1624; probate 30 May 1625 to [unnamed].

1. Roman numerals throughout.

69 PHILLIP SAMPSON

labourer 30 May 1625 P1/S/162

The house that Agnis late wife of the said Phillip Sampson late deceassed now dwelleth in £3.
2 litle tenementes lying and being in Blowhorne Stret in Marlebrough aforesaid £1.
One milch cow £1 6*s.* 8*d.*
2 stoare piges 10*s.*
One liverie beedsteed, one flockbeed, one per of blanketes, one whit ruge and 2 flockbolsters £1.
One old bedsteed, one pillow, one blanket and one coveringe 5*s.*
One per of lockrum sheetes, one per of canvas sheetes 6*s.* 8*d.*
2 litle chestes and 4 coffers 8*s.*
All his weareinge apparrell £2.
8 pewter dishes, 2 pewter candlestickes, 3 bras candlestickes and one salt 6*s.* 8*d.*
3 bras ketles, 2 bras skillates, 2 bras pottes £1.
One tableboard, one cubbard and one forme 6*s.*
One cever and 2 barrels 3*s.*
The wod in the backsid £1.
Money £3.
One faate with other lumber 10*s.*

Total £16 2*s.*

William Coster and William Lyme, appraisors.

Buried St. Mary 18 September 1624 'Samsonn'.
Will 15 September 1624, probate 30 May 1625 to [unnamed].

70 RICHARD DEANCE

husbandman 10 August 1625 P1/D/44

In the Heale
Onne teabeall boearde and freame and forme and onne chiste 4*s.*[1]
Onne cobarde, thre brasen cansteckes, 10 peasses of peytear 7*s.*
To potes and thre keatteales and one scilleate 13*s.*
In luombear with it 2*s.*

In the Cambear
To beades and that doth belonge to them £1.
His wearringe apearreall 16*s.*
Monie he heade £10.
Thre coffeares 4*s.*

In the Loeafte with in the Chambear
In moealte 6 quearteares £4.

In the Rome within the Healle
Onne busheal 1*s.*
Thre barreales, 6 tobes, 3 sax, 3 bages 10*s.*

In the Weal Houes
Onne youtteane stoune 10*s.*

In the Bacside
The wode £4.
3 peges, onne soue 10*s.*
To leaddeares 3*s.*
For boeardes and lumbear a byoute the house 8*s.*
The lease of the house £2.
And for all thinges for gotene 1*s.*

Total £24 8*s.* [*recte* £25 9*s.*]

John Brone, John Huleate and William Pageate, appraisors.

Burial not recorded.
Will [undated]; probate 16 December 1625 to Joane Deance, testator's widow.

1. Roman numerals throughout.

71 ANNE BIGGES[1]

widow 19 April 1626 P1/B/205

In the Parlor
Her wearing aparell £15 10*s.*[2]
One feele bedsteed with curtaines, curtayne rodes and teaster £1 6*s.* 8*d.*
Five fether pillowes and thre fether bolsters, tow fether bedes, on flocke bed, on strawbed, tow paire of blanketes, tow ruges, one coverlid and on carpet £13 4*s.*
On livery bedsted and tow coardes 5*s.*
On paire of holland sheetes, on paire of locrum sheetes, thre [paire *deleted*] canvis sheetes, on pair of holland pillow tiese, a paire of canvis pillow tiese £2 4*s.*
On diaper table cloth, on dussen of diaper napkines, on holland table cloth, tow canvis table clothes, tenne napkines of an other sort and on towell £2 13*s.*
Her childbed linene and her wearing linene £5.
On sillver bolle, eight sillver spoones and other broken golde and silver £7 10*s.*
On brasse pott, on brasse ketle, on possnet and a skelet £2.
Sixteene dishes of pewter, five sausers, three poredg dishes, on salt, on candle-sticke and tow chamber pots £1 6*s.* 8*d.*
Tow spits, on paire of andiers, a paire of potthookes, a fier-pan and tonges 10*s.*
On chest, tow coffers, on chaire, on flasket, a scutle and basket, earthern vesselles, glasses and other lumber about house £1
On band £31 4*s.*
A stock of bees 1*s.*
Mony remaininge in Francis Freemans handes £5 18*s.* 7*d.*

Total £89 11*s.* 11*d.*

Christopher Lipyeate, Swithine Haiese and Francis Freeman, appraisors

Buried St. Peter 13 April 1626 'Anne Biggs'.
Will 24 February 1625/6; inventory exhibited 8 June 1626; bond 9 June 1626, administration to John Fluell alias Fluellin of Wroughton, miller, father of Ann, during her minority; probate 9 August 1626 to Ann Fluell alias Fluellin, testator's neice.

1. 'Byges' on will.
2. Roman numerals throughout.

72 [JOHN COLE

tanner][1] [*date lost*, c.1626] P1/C/164

[*unknown number of lines lost*]
[. . .] one cubbord £1 6*s.* 8*d.*[2]

One wainscott buttry, one back of waynscott, one scutchion £1.
One peare of a[. . .]res, 2 iron barres, 2 peare of pott hanginges, 1 iron grate, 1 fier pann, 1 peare of tongs, 1 littell lanterne 6*s.* 8*d.*
2 cusshions 1*s.*

In the Buttry
1 powdring tubb, 1 kever, 4 shelfes, 1 peare of billowes 3*s.*
Fyve barrelles, 2 kyves, 1 powdring tubb, 2 kevers, 1 stande, one shelfe 13*s* 4*d.*

In the Kitchen
1 tablebord and frame, 2 broches, 1 fryeng pann, 1 payle, 1 cowle, 1 buckett, 1 hencubb, 4 shelves, 12 trenchers 10*s.*

In the Backside
7 standinges furnished 17*s.*
2 hovelles, a ladder, 8 plankes and other lomber £7.
In leather of all sortes £3 11*s.* [6*d.* *deleted*]
1 mare, 1 colt, 1 barkmill, one loade of hay £5.
Stuffe to make turfes £1.
2 pigges £1.
His barke £29.
His apparell £2.
In hurdelles 7*s.*
2 old fates, one well buckett and chayne 13*s.* 4*d.*[xiij^{s} 4^{d}]
2 working beames, 3 beame knives 4*s.*
2 willowes 3*s.*
Pales of the inner bounds 5*s.*
1 woodden beame and scales, 1 vattestocke, 1 pronge, 1 chayne, 2 daggers, 1 sword, 1 bow, 1 old addes 3*s.*

Total £143 10s 4*d.*

[*Appraisors' name somitted*]

Burial not recorded.
Will 11 March 1615/6; probate 8 June 1626 to Phillip Francklyn, Thomas Bennett and Stephen Lawrence, testator's 'beloved friends' [will].

1. Heading damaged; name and occupation from will.
2. Roman numerals throughout, except as shown.

73 WILLYAM PATCHET

16 June 1626 P1/P/113

One tabell boarde with a frame and forme 8*s.*[1]
One cubbord 10*s.*
Three stooles 2*s.*
Two chaires and one cradell 2*s.* 6*d.*
Two broches, a peare of [an]dirons, two peare of pot hanginges, one iron to set before the [?fire], one peare of tonges 2*s.*
A bread grater and fower peeces of old bordes 1*s.* 6*d.*
All the brasse in the chamber with one brasse pot £1.
One skimer and one flesh-hooke 6*d.*
A littell peale, one boole with some trenchers 1*s.*
Three lettell judges 6*d.*
Two barrels 1*s* 4*d.*
Two cowles 2*s.*
Two littell old kyvers 1*s.*
For the wood and certayne old lumber in the backesyde £1.
For two store pigges 13*s.* 4*d.*

For a spice morter and a pessell 1*s.*
For two chestes 10*s.*
For two old cofers and a littell box 1*s.* 6*d.*
All the pewter £1.
One lyvery bedsteed and one old trokell bedsteed 5*s.*
Three old beddes £1.
Three old coverletes, two blanketes and two bolsters £1.
All his wearing cloathes £2.
One leather bucket 1*s.*
His working stuffe 1*s.*
For two akers of barley growing in Porte field £2 13*s.* 4*d.*
For two peare of old sheetes with some other old linnine 6*s.* 8*d.*
For some old hurdels in the barne and other lumber 3*s.* 4*d.*

Total £13 7*s.* 6*d.* [*recte* £13 9*s.* 6*d.*]

Henry Abbot, Richard Cornwall and John Hulet, appraisors.

Buried St. Mary 15 June 1626 'William Patchett'.
Bond 7 August 1626, administration to Margery Patchet, intestate's widow.

1. Roman numerals throughout.

74 THOMAS TREBRET

10 March 1626/7[1] P1/T/96

One flock bed 12*s.*[2]
One livery bedsteed 3*s.*
One rug 10*s.*
Two sheets 3*s.*
One bolster 4*s.*
One pillow 1*s.* 6*d.*
One liste coverled 1*s.*
One pressing ire and sheers 6*d.*
One chattle lease £2.
His apparrell £1.

Total £4 12*s.* [*recte* £4 15*s.*]

William Parrarat and John Heath, appraisors.

Buried St. Mary 23 March 1626/7.
Will [nuncupative] 18 March 1626/7; probate 13 April 1638 to executor [Thomas Trebret, testator's son].

1. This date does not agree with that of the will.
2. Roman numerals throughout.

75 JOHN GLIDE

28 April 1628 P1/G/103

In the Hall
One cubberd one shelfe 3*s.*[1]

In the Chamber
One bedsteed of bordes 1*s.*
His wood £1.
3 littell iron wedges, one mattock, one spade 2*s.*
One littell brasse pott, 2 littell old kittelles, 3 pewter dishes, one skymmer 10*s.*
His beddinge and one coffer 13*s.* 4*d.*
One littell brasse candlestick, one salt, 3 spones, 3 woodden dishes, one woodden platter, one woodden candlestick 1*s.*
Two kevers, two littell barrelles, one powdring tubb 2*s.* 6*d.*
His wearinge apparrell 8*s.*

Total £3 0*s.* 10*d.*

In the hands of Richard Glide of the testators goodes: one cloke, foure peece of pewter, one coffer, one pronge, one hatchet, one great powdring tubb [*value omitted*].

William Blisset and Thomas Rymell, appraisors.

Burial not recorded.

Bond 13 June 1628, administration to Mary Glide, testator's widow; letter 12 June 1628 concerning the administration from Thomas Bennett of Marlborough to Thomas Sadler of the Close, Salisbury.

1. Roman numerals throughout.

76 JOHN CLARE

gentleman 4 June 1628 P1/C/135

Ready money in his purse £42 10*s.* 4*d.*
One sorrell nagg, bridle and saddle £4.
His wearing apparell £1 10*s.*

Total £48 0*s.* 4*d.*

Steeven Lawrence, Barnabas Romsey and Samuell Young, appraisors.

Buried St. Peter 5 June 1628, died 'at the White Hart the 4 of June in his Travell from the Bath … 42^{li} x^{s} 4^{d} in his purse'.
Will [nuncupative, made at Bath] 2 June 1628; bond 4 June 1628, administration to John Linn of Norwich 'my man now wayting upon me' [will]; letter 16 Jun 1628 from Oliver Chiver, curate of SS. Peter and Paul, Bath [Bath Abbey] commending one of the bondsmen to the Bishop of Sarum's registrar.

77 RALPHE HARROLD

butcher 28 May 1629 P1/H/180

His wearinge apparrell £7 6*s.* 8*d.*[vij^{li} 6^{s} $viij^{d}$][1]
For a carpitt and curtaine 2*s.*
Three paire of sheetes 12*s.*
One paire of pillowbeers 1*s.* 6*d.*[j^{s} 6^{d}]
Two towelles 1*s.*
One littell flockbed, two little flockbolsters and one pillow 10*s.*
Three old blanckettes 3*s.* 4*d.*
One coverled £1.
Sixe old cushions 2*s.* 6*d.*
One livery bedsteed and a cord 4*s.*
One littell table bord 5*s.*
Two old chamberpottes 2*s.*
One flagon, one broken candlestick and a saltseller 3*s.*
Two small pottingers 2*s.*
Two pewter dishes, 6 spones and a littell tunn 2*s.*
One brode grater, 6 trenchers, a gridiron, a little candlestick 1*s.*
One paire of billowes and a littell saw 2*s.*
Iron and lidden waights 8*s.* 6*d.*
Beame and scales 3*s.*
One paire of dogges and one dripping pan 3*s.*
One axe, one clever, one wedgge, old knives, one hatchat and one old rope 6*s.*
Lumber stuff 3*s.*
Two prongs, one spade, one paddle 2*s.*
4 hookes, a tostinge ire, a paire of snuffers and hangelles 1*s.* 6*d.*[j^{s} 6^{d}]
For a saddle, bridle, mayle pillon and such other things 8*s.*
One Bible 3*s.* 4*d.*[iij^{s} 4^{d}]
Bords and lumber stuff 7*s.*
One wellbuckat and rope 1*s.* 6*d.*
Earthen vesselles 6*d.*
One geldinge, bridle and saddle in the custody of John Eaton £3.
More lumber 2*s.*
Owinge by William Morcroft £3 6*s.* 8*d.*[iij^{li} 6^{s} 8^{d}]
Left in the handes of John Dismer 6*s.* 6*d.*
Owinge by Edward Jones £1 10*s.*

Total £21 13*s.* 6*d.* [*recte* £21 12*s.* 6*d.*]

John Fowler, Robert Harrold, Francis Waker, Richard Webb and Richard Bollyn, appraisors.

Buried St. Mary 10 May 1629 'Radolf Haroll'.
Renunciation 7 June 1629 by Prudence Harrold, intestate's widow in favour of

John Harrold, intestate's son; bond 16 June 1629, administration to John Harrold; accounts submitted 16 June 1629 by John Harrold.

1. Roman numerals throughout except as shown.

78 JOHN BROWNE

husbandman [will] 31 July 1629

P1/B/221

In the Hall

One tablebord and frame, three ioyned stooles and one cubberd 13*s.* 4*d.*[1]

One dozen of pewter platters, three pottengers, 3 pewter candlestickes, 2 pewter saltcellars, one pewter cupp £1.

One brasse spice morter, 3 cauldrones, 2 saltcellars, one brasse pott, 2 brass skillettes, one brasse ladell, one skymmer, 11 spoones, one sawcer £1 3*s.*

One frying pan, 2 broches, 2 paire of potthookes, 2 paire of potthangells, 2 paire of iron dogges, one fire shovell, one paire of tonges, one dripping pan, one gridiron, one paire of billowes 6s 8*d.*

In the Buttery

3 barrells, 4 kyvers, 2 payles, one powdring tubb with other lumber 13*s.* 4*d.*

3 bushells of oatmeale, 3 bushells of salt 15*s.*

In the Chamber

2 bedsteeds, one flockbedd, 2 boulsters, 3 pillowes, 3 pillow cases, 2 coverlidds, 2 blancketts, 2 bedd matts £2 10*s.*

2 paire of canvas sheetes, 6 napkins, one tablecloth, one spleten chaier, one flaskett, 5 coffers £1 6*s.*

His wearing apparell £4 10*s.*

In the Backsid

One pile of cliftes, one pile of faggottes, one pile of lugges and rodds with other lumber £20.

One gelding, one cow £3 10*s.*

Two pigges 4*s.*

One cocke of hay £2.

The lease of his house £6 13*s.* 4*d.*

Total £45 4*s.* 8*d.*

Anthony Sclatter, George Baston and Richard Cornwall, appraisors.

Buried St. Mary 23 July 1629

Will 19 July 1629; probate 5 October 1629 to executrix [Ann Browne, testator's widow].

1. Roman numerals throughout except total.

79 RICHARD CORNWALL

13 November 1629 P1/C/136

In the Hall

One tablebord, one sidbord, one cubbord, one joyned forme, one joyned stoole and one littell chayre 15*s.*[1]

One joyned bedsted, one trucklebed, one presse, two chestes, three coffers, one side borde £2 5*s.*

In the Chamber over the Hall

One fether bed, two flock bedes, three feather boulsters, thre feather pillowes, fower paire of blancotes, six coverlides, two cortains £7.

Fyfe pair of shetes, fowr pair of pillowes, fowre bord cloathes, one dozen of napkins, two handtowels, one cobberd cloathes £3.

Fower quarters of malte £4.

In the Kitching

Two brasse pans, three pottes, one furnace, fowre caldrons, one posnat and two skilletes £5.

One dozen of platters, one dozen of

pottengers, two saucers, on bason, tow pewter dishes £1 8*s.*

Two brasse candelstickes, salte sillers, one morter and pessell, one peawter chamber pote, one dozen and halfe of spoones, one brazen chafing dish 11s 6*d.*

Two pair of andiers, one fire shovel, two pair of hanggels, two broaches, one drippinge pan, one paire of tounges, one griddier, two paire of pot hockes, one flesh hooke, one skimer, one bastinge ladle, two iron barres, fower wedges, one estplate £1 2*s.*

One beame and scales and waightes 10*s.*

One littel cobberd, fower kivers, one maltmill, fyfe barrels and pouldringe tub, one greate bowle, one kive, one tunbowlle and clanseve, one upstond £1 10*s.*

Three woodden platters, three bowles, six dishes, two wooden candellstickes, two dozen of trenchers and one potlid, tw jugges 2s 6*d.*

One flasscot, a grindstone and lanthorne and other lumber 10*s.*

In the Well House

Two yeotinge fates, two cowles, two buckets, two maultseves and two other seves, one tennant sawe, one pick, one winowing shete, one est heare, one [to *deleted*] spade, one chaine and lock £1 6*s.* 8*d.*

The woode £1 6*s.* 8*d.*

The wearinge cloathes £4.

One bushell 1*s.*

Two old watch billes 1*s.*

One old sack and bagge 1*s.*

Tenn quarters of barly £10.

Total £43 9*s.* 8*d.* [*recte* £44 0*s.* 4*d.*]

Thoms Togwell, Thomas Randall and Thomas Crapon, appraisors.

Buried St. Mary 5 November 1629 'Richard Cornewall senior'.

Will 17 December 1622; probate 12 April 1630 to [unnamed].

1. Roman numerals throughout.

80 JOHN EATON

barber 27 January 1629/30 P1/E/37

In the Hall

One table board, one frame, one bench, five [. . .] one joyned stooles [. . .] 14*s.*[1]

[. . .] cubbord [. . .]

A benche and wainscott and (?)clevyemantle 3*s.* [. . .]d

The painted cloaths 4*s.*

Two leaves for a window and a casement of glasse 2*s.*

A paire of small andirons, a fir pan, a paire of tonges, two pott hangers, a paire of pott hookes, a fire plate 7*s.*

A paire of billows 2*s.*

Room total £2 0*s.* 8*d.*

In the Chamber within the Hall

Two feather bolsters, two feather pillowes and one flock bedd £2 6s 8*d.*

A pair of blanckettes and a coverled 18*s.*

A joyned bed and curtaines £1 10*s.*

A flock bedd, a flock pillow, a flock bolster and a blanckett £1 3*s.* 4*d.*

Two coffers 5*s.*

A carpett and two yards of cloathe 5*s.*

A painted tester 2*s.*

His wearing apparell £3.

Room total £9 10*s.*

In the Seller

Five kettles and a pan £2 6*s.* 8*d.* [*repeated in Arabic numerals*]

Two pottes, a posenett and two skillettes £1.

A brasse chavingdish, a brass candlestick and a pewter candlestick 4*s.*

A fryeinge pan, a gridiron and one flesh hooke 3*s.*

A broah and drippinge pan 1*s.* 6*d.*
Sixe beere barrells 13*s.* 4*d.*
A powderinge tubb, a kive and a kever 6*s.* 8*d.*
A serch, one hair seive, two meale seeves, two little maut seeves 2*s.* 6*d.*
Two old chestes, two tressells and one boord 3*s.*
A cubberd, three old formes, two shelves, two benches 6*s.*
Sub-total £5 6s 8*d.*

Two dow kevers, two little dry tubbs, two beere horses, a vatt stocke, a mouse surtch 7*s.*
A warminge pan 5*s.*
Pewter £1.
Sub-total £1 12*s.*

In the Chamber over the Hall
A joyned bedsteed £2.
A truckle bedsteed 6*s.* 8*d.*
A flock bed and bolster, one coverled, one blanckett and one matt £2.
One table board, two formes, a frame and benches and shelves £1 6*s.* 8*d.*
Room total £5 13*s.* 4*d.*

In the Broad Rome
A bedsted, a bed, a coverled, a bolster, a blanckett, a matt and bed cord £1 10*s.*
A joyned chest 10*s.*
Fower coffers and two boxes 10*s.*
A livery boord and frame 3*s.* 4*d.*
Fower tressells and three boordes 4*s.*
One tubb and one old bowle 2*s.*
A coffer 1*s.*
Three short boordes, two tressells, two old tubbs, a spininge turne 4*s.*
Room total £3 4*s.* 4*d.*

In the Kitchin
Three cowles, a well buckett, rope and chaine with the appurtenances, a pail, a washing bowle and a flaskett 10*s.*
A malt mill 13*s.* 4*d.*
One planck and a horse to beare him and three old stooles, a pecke, a gallon, a choppinge boord 7*s.*
A buetle and fower wedges, a spade, an iron peele and an axe 4*s.*
Room total £1 14*s.* 4*d.*

In the Stable
The moudes, two ladders, a hurdle and a lugg £1 10*s.*
The wood in the backside £2 10*s.*
Room total £3 10*s.* [*recte* £4]

In the Chamber over the Shopp
A beame, skales and waightes 4*s.*
Five boordes and a doore 4*s.*
Two ladders and a trough, a pale, two luggs and a flage 5*s.*
Thirtie one pound of thrumbes 10*s.* 4*d.*
Fifteene dozen of graye cunny skinnes and three of black £2 5*s.*
Fower paire of chestes £1 12*s.*
Two table cloathes and five napkins 5*s.*
Fower pillow beeres 4*s.*
Room total £5 9*s.* 4*d.*

In the Shopp
Two dozen of shopp linnen £1 4*s.*
Seven hangeinge basons 6*s.*
Three washinge basons 8*s.*
Two pottes 4*s.*
One paire of crisping irons 1*s.* 6*d.*
A warminge and frame 2*s.* 6*d.*
One broken bason 8*d.*
Sissers and a combe, two rasors, a punch, two flemes 1*s.*
Fower brinshes 1*s.* 8*d.*
A hone 8*d.*
An eleven knittinge needles 1*s.*
A looking glasse 4*d.*
Three chaires 4*s.*
Two formes and a swift 1*s.*
A candlesticke 1*s.* 6*d.*
A wodden candlesticke 2*d.*
A bench and wainscott 5*s.*
Wainscott windows with glasse 13*s.* 4*d.*
A trammell and other small nettes £1.
A wall candlestick and two little shelves

1s.
Thred 19s. 3*d.*
A chafer 1s. 4*d.*
Half a dozen of spoones and half a dozen of dishes and a dozen and a half of trenchers 1s. 6*d.*
Three drinkeinge dishes 1s.
A iron bar and a pike 1s. 4*d.*
Room total £6 2s. 5*d.* [*recte* £6 1s. 9*d.*]

Debts owed by him[2]
To Richard Eaton £2.
To Helene Eaton 10s.
To Richard Simmes 8s.
To Robert Hitchcock 19s. 9*d.*
Sub-total £3 17s. 9*d.*

Debts owed to him
John Gilbert oweth him £1 10s.
Richard Kempe 11s.
John Palmer £1 2s.
Nicholas Dobson 3s. 4*d.*
Edward Everett 3s.
John Cooke 8s.
Left in money £3 10s.
Sub-total £7 7s. 4*d.*

Total £52 10s. 5*d.*[1]

Robert Crapon, John Ingles and Silvester Cooke, appraisors.

Buried St. Peter 26 January 1629/30.
Will 11 January 1629/30; probate 17 March 1629/30 to Margaret Leyland, testator's daughter.

1. Roman numerals throughout except final total.
2. Debts owed by the deceased should not form part of the inventory.

81 WILLIAM STOCKWELL
haberdasher [will] 5 February 1629/30
P1/S/191

In pewter 10s.[1]
In brasse 5s.
In iron 8s. 6*d.*
In lumber 2s.
1 per of hampers, 1 tilte and backreeg and frame £1 10s.
1 particion [of bords *added*] with 2 leafe windowes 10s.
1 warmingpan, 1 cullender, 1 gridiron 5s.
4 joyned stooles, 1 tablebord 7s. 10*d.*
1 livery cupbord 6s.
1 bedsteed, 2 coffers, 2 [boxes *added*] 7s.
1 flaskett, 1 search, 1 basket 2s.
1 chayre, 1 per of bellowes, 1 matt 1s.
1 bed, 1 bolster, 1 pillow, 1 coverlett, matt and corde £2 10s.
Weareing lynine £2 4s.
1 brush, 1 looking glasse, 5 bowstrings, 3 bookes 9s. 6*d.*
His weareinge aparrell £3 10s.
1 mare 13s. 4*d.*
In money £4.
[*the remainder in a different hand*]
Sub-total £18 1s. 2*d.*

In wares in the shop £42 17s. 4*d.*

[Item in the hands of his brother in law William Blandy being part of a legacy bequeathed unto Agnes wife of the said William Stokwell and is due the 11th may 1631 the some of £12 13s. 4*d. deleted*]
[Item in the hands of the said William Blandy a great chest, tablebord and brass pan worth at the least £2. *deleted*]

[*in a third hand*] *Total* £60 18s. 4*d.*
[*Total* £75 11s. 8*d. deleted*]

Out of which there is owing at the tyme of his death with the chardges of his buriall £48 12s. 6*d.*[2]

Thomas Keinton, William Gough, appraisers.

Burial not recorded.

Will 28 December 1629; probate 18 May 1630 to [unnamed].

1. Roman numerals throughout except sub-total.
2. Debts owed by the deceased and executor's expenses should not form part of the inventory.

82 JOHN HITCHCOCKE

?baker [inventory goods] 22 June 1630 P1/H/181

In the Chamber next the Street
A bedd, [an old rugg *added*], a bowlster, three little pillowes [. . .]
A bedsteed, [a coffer *added*], a coverled 4*s.*
A little table [and frame *added*] 1*s.* 8*d.*

In the Baker [House deleted*] Roome*
Sixteene pales and old readle and old boxe and a frame of a stoole, a few flockes 2*s.* 6*d.*
3 old boxes and a handbasket 8*d.*
And old coffer 6*d.*
The mare, bridle and saddle £2.

In the Hall
A little cupbord and a dowtrogh covered, a ioynd forme and ioyne stooles 10*s.*
2 little barrells and 2 chaires 2*s.*
2 doggs, a fryingpan, a little broach and hangles, a payre of pothookes 2*s.*
2 skilletts and a brasse pott 4*s.*
4 peuter dishes 3*s.* 4*d.*
2 stooles 2*d.*
An old tunboll, 2 dishes, an earthen pann 3*d.*
An old frame of a boord and a washvate and a horse 2*s.*
2 buckets and a washtubb 8*d.*
2 little piggs 14*s.*
A pigtrow 6*d.*
For wood bought of Henry Crooke 10*s.*
For to planks and a stele pleat and a hachet 2*s.*
Sub-total £5 14*s.* 3*d.*

6 planke, 1[1] little manger and one flale 3*s.*[1]
Mor 8*s.*[1]

Total £6 2*s.* 3*d.*

John Fowler and Robert Jeffrye, appraisors.

Burial not recorded.
Bond 29 July 1630, administration to William Francklin and Leonard Hammell.

1. Roman numerals as indicated.

83 WILLIAM TURLY

baker 22 February 1630/1 P1/T/76

In his Bed Chamber over the Bakehouse
His wearinge apparell £5.[1]
One fether bed £3.
3 fether bolsters and 5 fether pillowes £2 10*s.*
4 flockbeds and 4 flock bolsters £3.
2 rugges, 3 coverlettes and 3 paire of blankettes £2 10*s.*
One joyne bedsteed and one livery bedsteed £1.
9 paire of sheetes and 4 pillibers £2 5*s.*
4 table clothes and one dozen and halfe of napkins 15*s.*
23 yards of course medly cloth £2.
2 chestes and 4 coffers £1 6*s.* 8*d.*
3 bushelles of barly 10*s.*

In the Chamber over the Buttery
One long keever, one bolting hutch 5*s.*
One spleeten cheire and 5 sacks with other lumber 15*s.*

In the Buttery
2 brasse panns, one furnace and 5 kettles

£4 10s.
3 brasse pottes, 4 skillettes, one [posnett *deleted*] pestle and morter and one chafendish £2.
One dozen of platters, one dozen of pottengers, one dozen and halfe of sawsers, halfe a dozen of pewter dishes, one dozen of spoones, 7 brasse candlestickes, 2 pewter candlestickes, one quart pott, one salt, one pewter cupp, 4 skimmers and 2 basting ladles £2 10s.
10 barrelles, one powdring tubb, one cubbard, one trunke, 2 livery bords and one save £1 5s.

In the Hall
2 little table bordes, 2 chayres and 6 stooles 15s.

In the Loft over the Hall
3 weight of wooll and halfe a weight of yearne £2 3s.

In the Bakehouse
3 moulding bords, one hutch, 2 keevers and 1 brake £1 10s.
2 paire of andiers, 3 paire of hangelles, 4 spitts, one driping pan, 3 neast plates, one yron barr and 2 paire of pot hookes £1.
A winnow sheete and a neast haire 4s.
One bushe and 4 payles with other lumber £1.

In the Backside
7 hundred of faggottes £2 9s.
Timber, wood, hurdles and 3 ladders £4 10s.
One horse beast and 3 pigges £2.
Two acres of wheate £5.
Hay and straw £1.
His land for his exectrixses life and lease upon the same £10.
Lastly due upon scores £2.

Total £68 13s 8*d*. [*recte* £68 12*s*. 8*d*.]

Edward Lyme and Thomas Rymill, appraisors.

Buried St. Mary 18 February 1630/1.
Will 11 February 1630/1; probate 4 April 1631 to [unnamed].

1. Roman numerals throughout except total.

84 PHILLIPP MARTYNE

yeoman 19 March 1630/1 P1/M/115

In the Hall
One table board with stooles, benches and waynscott there unto be longinge £1 6*s*. 8*d*.[1]
One presse and one cubbert £1 6*s*. 8*d*.
One payre off andirons, pott hangers and other implements about the fyre 5*s*. 4*d*.

In the Parlour
One table bourd and forme with waynscott and stooles there to belonginge £1 5*s*.
One highbedd and one trucklebed with other thinges there to belonginge £4 10*s*.
2 coffers and one boxe 6*s*.
The pewter in the howse £1 4*s*.
The brasse in the howse £3 10*s*.
The lynninge in the howse £1 10*s*.
The trenynge vessells in the howse 15*s*.
One dripping panne, 2 iron spitts and other iron stuffe 8*s*.

In the Kitching
One table board with other old stuffe there unto belonginge £1 4*s*. 4*d*.
In mault stones in the gardner, wood and standinge stuffe for the market with the appurtenances thereunto belonginge £15.
Old iron in the howse with other old stuffe 15*s*.
In mault, the neast hayre and three sacks

£2 10s.
The tymber at the old howse 15s.
Two small pigges 16s.
8 cushions 6s. 8d.
The lease of the howse yet to come £8.
His wearinge apparrell £4.

Total £49 13s. 8d.

Robert Kingsman and Robert Freevens, appraisors.

Buried St. Peter 23 December 1630.
Bond 11 [*lost*] 1631, administration to Elizabeth Martyn, intestate's widow; inventory exhibited 9 Oct 1631.

1. Roman numerals throughout, except total.

Five pare of sheares noe better then old iron 5s.
An old racke in the backe side, an old shearebord and a few handles, two sheave waigtes and other lumber 10s.

Total £4 15s. [*recte* £4 17s.]

Thomas Boorne, Phillep Fowler and Robert Colman, appraisors.

Buried St. Mary 9 August 1631.
No other documents; inventory exhibited 7 March 1631/2, with note of administration to Agnes Dowse, intestate's widow.

1. Written 13^{s} vi^{d}.

85 WILLIAM DOWSE
?shearman [inventory goods] 5 March 1631/2 P1/D/59

His wear[. . .]parrell 13s. 4d.
One feather [. . .]feather bolster, [2 coverleds *added*] two feather p[. . .] and the bedstede 19s.
[. . .]edstede, two cov[. . .]ers 6s 8d.
Tw[. . .], two stoccards, beame [. . .] 7s.
The table bord and frame and two ioyned stooles a cubbert and two other stooles 13s 6d.[1]
Two [old *added*] kettles, an old pott, an old dreppinge pan, an old warminge pan, one skillett 13s. 4d.
A pare of andiers, 2 hangels, one broch, a stele plate and slikstone, 2 platters, 2 pottengers, 2 sasers, one bason, a candlesticke, a salt seller, three spoones 6s. 8d.
Two benches, 2 lettle peces of wanskott, five wadden dishes, one ladle, five trenchers, one griste bag, one pecke 1s. 6d.
One old cowle, one old barrell, an old buckett and an old reele 1s.

86 [THOMAS BUCKINGHAM][1]
[*date lost*, c.1631/2] P1/B/240

[. . .] paire of [. . .]ketes [. . .]
[. . .]m three paire [of] sheets 13s. 4d.
Twoo chests and one coffer 13s. 4d.

In the Malting Roomes
Half a hundred of cheese 12s.
28 quarters of malt £26 13s. 4d.

In the Hall
One table bord and frame, one fourme and chaire, one stoole, one cubberd £1 6s. 8d.
In pewter £1.

In the Kitchin
Twoo brasse pottes, two kittles, twoo skilletts, one skimmer, one brasse basting ladle £1.
One driping pan 1s.
Twoo kiffers, foure barrells, one powdring tub, one paile, twoo bowles 13s. 4d.
One fryeing pan, eight woodden dishes, a tunbou 2s.
One cradle with other lumber 2s.

In the Backside
In wood £5.
One welbucket and cheyne 2s. 6d.
Twoo flitches of bacon £1.
The lease of his house £10.
In debts owing £4 5s.
In money £2.

Total £63 9s 6d.

[*Appraisors' names lost*]

Buried St. Mary 19 December 1631.
Bond 7 March 1631/2, administration to Eleanor Buckingham, intestate's widow.

1. Heading lost, name from bond.

87. [MAUD PATIE
widow][1] [*date lost*, c. 1631/2] P1/P/124

Her wearing apparell £9.[2]
Twoo old coverliddes and twoo old blankettes 12s.
One fether bedd, twoo fether bolsters and twoo fether pillowes £3.
One strawe bedd 1s.
Three paire of sheetes and one odd sheete £1 6s.
Twoo table clothes 4s.
Five pillowtyes 16s.
Five diaper napkins 3s. 4d.
7 canvas napkins 2s.
One old sheete and a towell 3s. 4d.
One chest 5s.
One trunck 4s.
One coffer and a box 3s.
Twoo ioyned stooles 2s.
One ioyned chaire and one splitten chaire 2s.
One brasse pott, one brasse posnett, one brasse skillett, one brasse chafinge dish, one brasse pestle and morter and one warminge pann £1.
4 pewter platters, 7 small pewter pottingers, 4 pewter sawcers, one aqua vite bottle of pewter, one pewter bowle to drinke in, one chamber pott of pewter 16s.
One syde cupboard 4s.
In redy money £5 13s.
One little coffer 1s.
[*added in another hand* On fat 3s.]

Debtes owinge unto the testatrix uppon specialties
Owinge by Timothy Hiller £10 8s.
Owinge by Mr John Hitchcock £20 16s.

Total £55 4s. 8d.

Debtes owinge by the testatrix[3]
To Nathaniell Winter uppon specialty and without specialty £8 6s. 8d.

Walter Jefferyes and Lewis Andley, appraisors.

Buried St. Peter 20 February 1631/2 'Mrs. Patie, widow'.
Will 30 January 16311/2; probate 7 March 1631/2 to executrix [Katherin Smart, testator's niece, daughter of Elianor].

1. Heading damaged, name and status from will.
2. Roman numerals throughout.
3. Debts owed by the deceased should not appear on the inventory.

88 EELISEBETH WINSOR
widow [will] 7 March 1631/2
P1/W/140

Mouny £5.
3[1] brase panes £1 10s.
4[1] brase pots £1 13s. 4d.
5 brase cettels £1 [5s. *deleted*] 1s.
2 dozen pauyter wessell 16s.
2 brase candelstecks 1s.
[2 *deleted*] 1 vlocke beds and a vether bed £1.

2 boulsters and 3 pellous 8*s.*
2 couverleds and 2 blankets 8*s.*
4 sheats and one table clocke 10*s.*
A bauster case and 2 table naikpens 1*s.* 6*d.*
One chest and 3 coffers 10*s.*
One ceffer 2*s.* 6*d.*
4 ould barels 3*s.*
One yeieren bar 1*s.*
One spice morter 2*s.* 6*d.*
3 ould paire of pothocks 6*d.*
One ould broche 1*s.*
One paire of pothangels and one croke 8*d.*
All her waring barell £1.

Total £14 9*s.*

Anthony Morrice, Robert Looker and Thomas Craven, appraisors.

Buried St. Mary 25 December 1630.
Will 21 November 1627; probate 7 March 1631/2 to [unnamed].

1. Roman numerals where indicated.

89 WILLIAM DAWNCE

tailor 11 April 1632 P1/D/63

His wearinge apparrell 1*s.*[1]
One standinge bedsteed 5*s.*
One flockbedd, two bowlsters, one coverledd and one payre off blancketts 16*s.*
One payre off sheets 3*s.* 4*d.*
One chest, three coffers, one boxe and some other lumber 6s 8*d.*

In the Hall
One table board with one forme, two chayres wyth some other wooden things 6*s.* 8*d.*
One cupbert, one payle and co[w]le, one kyver and a barrell 4*s.*
One shoppe board, two shelves, a pressinge iron and a payre of sheeres 2*s.*
One brasse pott, one kyttle and other brasse things 5*s.*
In pewter 5*s.*
One iron spitt and some other iron stuffe 3*s.* 4*d.*
In meate 1*s.*
Two cheeses 1*s.*
In wood and other lumber 2*s.*
In funerall expences £1 9*s.*[2]

Total £4 2*s.* [*recte* £4 11*s.*]

Mawdett Milles, Richard Abraham and Thomas Whittye, appraisors.

Buried St. Mary 27 June 1631.
Bond 12 April 1632, administration to Ann Dawnce, intestate's widow.

1. Roman numerals throughout.
2. Administrator's expenses should not form part of the inventory.

90 ROBERT JEFFERES

20 October 1632 P1/IJ/48

His wearinge apparrell, h[. . .]
Wood and lumber stuffe [. . .]
Woodden vesselles [. . .]
[. . .] bedsteedes, 2 tab[. . .] b[. . .]ds[. . .]
2 tresselles, 2 stooles and [. . .] ches[. . .]
His brasse and pewter [. . .]
One fryeingpann, [. . .] brandier, [. . .] one choppingknife, two broches, [. . .]
One andyron, one chafingdish, one fyer panne, twoo hangles and 2 paire of pothooks 3[1] [. . .]
His beddinge £2 5*s.*
His lynn[en] 10*s.*

Total £11 6*s.* 4*d.*

John Fowle[r], [. . .] Jefferies and Nathaniel

[. . .], appraisers.

Burial not recorded.
Bond 5 [. . .] 1632, administration to [. . .] Jeffreys; inventory exhibited 5 December 1632.

1. All surviving numbers in Roman numerals.

91 [THOMA]S REDFORD[1]
18 April 1633 P1/R/70

One cow and [calfe *added*], one heyfer bullock £4.[2]
One peg 7*s.*
Five sheep £1.
[Two *deleted*] one white rug 8*s.*
One red rug 8*s.*
Five blancketes 10*s.*
Three coverings £1.
Thre peere of sheetes 15*s.*
Three coffers 3*s.*
One table bord with a frame 4*s.*
One forme 1*s.*
Three table cloths 2*s.* 6*d.*
11 naptkins 4*s.*
One flock bed 8*s.* 4*d.*
One press 10*s.*
[Flasket *deleted*] and a turn 8*d.*
One old chest 3*s.* 4*d.*
One serch and raying seif 10*d.*
One flaskat and cradle 2*s.* 6*d.*
One Bible an annother booke 8*s.*
One markin ire and gardner bords and twist 2*s.* 6*d.*
All the pewter £1 3*s.* 4*d.*
The brasse 2*s.* 6*d.*
A three fags 1*s.*
On safe and old cubberd 4*s.*
Payle and kive 1*s.* 6*d.*
His waring cloths £2.
One bedsteede 5*s.*
For his woode [with the hovill posts *added*] £2.
The pales £1.
The plankes and raks in the stables £1.
The f[3] cheese [stable *deleted*] stools 5*s.*

Total £19 7*s.* 8*d.*

Thomas Trebret, Henry Cowse and Francis Waker, appraisors.

Buried St. Mary 7 April 1633.
Bond 25 April 1633, administration to Dorothy Redford, intestate's widow.

1. Heading damaged, name from bond.
2. Roman numerals throughout except total.
3. Perhaps 'four' or 'five' was intended.

92 JOHN WILLIAMS
glazier [will] 23 April 1633 P1/W/141

In the Chamber
One bedsteed, twoe beds, thre boulsters, a paire of blankits, a coverlid and a rugg £3.
A chest, fower boxes, a table board, a coffer, a linen cupboard, a warming pan, two stooles, a lantorne, two cushions £1 10*s.*
Five paire of sheetes, 3 table cloths, one holland sheete, 3 paire of pillowbeeres, a dozen of napkins £2 7*s.*

In the Nexte Chamber
One bed for children furnished £2 9*s.*
Six cushions, [twoe *deleted*] a chaire, [twoe *added*] chests, a box, a kiever, a flaskett 14*s.* 6*d.*

In the Cockloft
One bed for servants furnished 15*s.*

In the Haall
One table, three stooles, a cupboard 13*s.* 4*d.*
Fower brasse potts, fower kettles, 3 skilletts, five brasse candlesticks, twoe skimmers, a gridiron, 3 paire of pott hookes, a paire

of andirons, one paire of tongs, twoe paire of pott hangers, a paire of dogs, a fire pan, a chaffing dish £3 4*s.* 8*d.*[1]
A dozen of pewter, 3 candlesticks, twoe salts £1 2*s.*
Twoe spitts, a brush, a paire of billowes and lumber there and in the cockloft 4*s.* 6*d.*
Glasse, a vice and led [and working tooles *added*] £2 5*s.*
A furnace, six barrels, four cowles, fower kievers, a kieve, two pouderinge tubs, a wellbuckett, fower sieves and lumber £2.

In the Backside
Wood, pales and other lumber £1.
His wearinge clothes £1.

[*Total omitted, by addition* £22 5*s.*]

Robert Sheate, William Guye and Richard Webb, appraisors.

Buried St. Mary 24 March 1632/3.
Will 14 March 1632/3; probate 24 April 1633 to [unnamed].

1. Written as iij li 4 s 8*d.*

93 RICHARD BROWNE
3 June 1633 P1/B/243

One feather beade, 2 flocke beads £2.
Thre coverings 15*s.*
One strae beade 2*s.*
Tooe blanketts 2*s.*
Five pare and one sheete £1.
Fouer pelebares 4*s.*
Tooe tabilclooths 3*s.*
Seventene napkines 3*s.*
Three shurtes 4*s.*
Five bondes 1*s.* 6*d.*
Fouer bedsteads 2 m[. . .]s and [. . .]ead cordes 12*s.*
Sixe cooffers 12*s.*
Three tabilbordes [. . .] fra[. . .] 14*s.*
His waring clo[. . .]es £1 4*s.*
Seven formes 2*s.*
Twelve stooles 10*s.*
Tooe cubbors 4*s.*
Twenty sixe pesses of puter £1.
Fower kettles £1.
One poote, one pann 10*s.*
One warming pane, one skimer, one bastin ladill 2*s.* 6*d.*
One drippin panne, tooe broches 2*s.*
One frying pane, to minsing knifes, one cleaver 1*s.* 4*d.*
One poote hocks, too hangels, one fier band 1*s.* 6*d.*
One pare of anggers, one griddier, one plate 3*s.*
Thre coules, sixe barrilles, one paile 6*s.*
For lumber 5*s.*
The wodde 8*s.*
One brase candel stike, to woodden ones 8*d.*

Total £13 12*s.* 6*d.* [*recte* £12 12*s.* 6*d.*]

William Cooper, William Wythers and Thomas Cooper, appraisors.

Buried St. Mary 23 May 1633.
Bond 14 June 1633, administration to Eleanor Browne, intestate's widow; inventory exhibited 17 June 1633.

94 HENRY [RABBINSON][1]
yeoman 24 July 1633 P1/R/69

His wearinge apparrell 10*s.*[2]
Two flocke beds [with the appurtenances *added*] £1 10*s.*
Two chests 6*s.* 8*d.*
One cupboard 10*s.*
One table board and one fourme [. . .]
One brasse pott 6*s.* 8*d.*
Two brasse kettles 13*s.* 4*d.*
[All other *deleted*] in lumbar [about the howse *added*] 11*s.*

Total £4 12*s*. 2*d*. [4^{li} 12^{s} ij^{d}]

Francis [Wa]ker, James Gibbes and Obadiah Blissett, appraisers.

Buried St. Mary 6 July 1633 'Henry Robinson'.
Will [*date lost*]; probate 4 October 1633 to [unnamed].

1. Heading damaged, name from will.
2. Roman numerals thoughout except total.

95 ANTH[. . .][1]

[. . .] August 1633 P1/A/63

In h[. . .]
and frame o[. . .]8*s*.
On coff[. . .]
In pewter [. . .]
On cuberd 8*s*.
On chaire 1*s*. 6*d*.
On iron pott 3*s*. 4*d*.
On paire of andires and a paire of dogs and two paire of pot hangings, on fier shovell and a paire of toungs and a broche 10*s*.[2]
On brass pann, tow litle ketles, on brass pot and a skellet 12*s*.
On Bible [. . .]
[. . .]

In the [C]hamber
On bedsteed, coard and matt 6*s*. [. . .]
Two flock beads, two flock bolsters, two flock pillowes £1.
Tow old rugs and on coverlid £1.
Three paire of sheetes and one paire of pillobeares 18*s*.
On joynd chest, on coffer and two boxes 8*s*.
On litle [table board *added*] and frame 4*s*.
His wearing aparrell £2.

In the Backside
In faggots 10*s*.
In lumber aboute the house 5*s*.

Total £9 2*s*. 2*d*.

Steven Larrance and Swithin Haies, appraisors.

For burial see note 1.
No other documents.

1. The head of this folio is damaged and the name is lost. It is possibly the inventory of Anthony Sclatter, who was buried at St Mary, Marlborough on 20 May 1633.
2. Roman numeral.

95A WILLIAM [FRY]

yeoman 4 Oct 1633 P1/F/526

In the halle
one tabellborde one joynde form syxe stowells one Cover[. . .]
one basen and youre and to Cussynges one couberd Cloth one to[. . .]
Wainescotte and the bynches and a payre of tabells £3

In the chamber over the hall
One tabell borde 6 jened stooles and one Joined Cheayer one Joyned presse the windscott and benches one Joyned Chest and fower boxes one joined bedsted too feather beeds and one under bed to feather boulsters to feather pillows ond orig Coverled and to owld Coverleds and one pare of Curtings and rods for a beed: oulde paire of bl[an]kets £12
For all his wearinge Aparle £8
one paire of ho[w]ll[an]d Shettes and to paire of Lockerom Shettes and 4 paire of Canmus She[t]tes and three paire of howland pillow beares and one
Canmus one and to deiaper tabell Cloths

and one dowson of deiaper tabell napkines and three Candmus hand towels £4

In the inner Chamber
to levery Bedsteds to Coff[e]rs and [ ]de s[ ]e boarde to floocke beddes and to feather boulsters one grene [. . .] Coverled one flocke boulster
one paire of blanketts £3

at the stayer head
one Coffer one joined presse one binch one dowse[n] bed staves one pade one truckell bed sted Cord and matt 20s

the roome be hinde the hall
one forme one fire bucket to baskets one shilfe 4s

In the kitchinge
one dowson pawter platters and to butter dishes and halfe a dowson of Sawsers one beason and to porridge dishes to dowson and a halfe of sponnes on
pweter Candellsticke one still one Chamber poott £2
to brason Cittells three brasse pootts one brasse posnett 3 brasse scillets to brasse leadells to brasse Cheaffinge dishes to brasse scimmers one warminge pann 3 brasse Candell stikes one paire of brasse snoffers £4
one paire of Andiers one fier pan one paire of tonuges 3 paire of hangells one <to> yeren pleate one broach to paire of poothookes one grideyrn one Cleaver one minsinge knife one eyren barr one paire of flesh howckes to stelle stickes one stell pleate one fryinge panne to eyren Candellstickes 20s
To tabell bords to freames the binches and thre Joined stooles one Joined side Cubert 3 Cheayres one powdringe tube and treay thre platters one
salt boox 5 woden dishes 3 dowson of trenckers five shilves the geardner in the Chiching 30s

in the neast lought
One neast heaire 6 quarters of malt 10 bushell bagges 3 raying seves to malt seves one bushel one strech one lader £6

in the drincke howse
7 beare barrels one Civer one Cive one shilfe one flasket one search one tunborale to short planckes one horse to carry the barrelles one torne whelle 13s 4d

in the well howse
to youghting stones one buchet with with Caine and rope and tunrelles one Cowles to pailes 3 dores £2

in the owt house
9 poundes of woull and ye[ ]ren 4s

in the backside
one hovel one lader 3s 4d

The woode in [. . .]
3 bibles and 3 other bookes
one Silver bowle
[one y]ounge bullock

The inventory appears not to have been completed; some goods not valued.

Total of goods valued: £48 14s 8d

1. The surname of the testator is lost from the will and inventory. The will mentions a wife, Alice and six unnamed children. William Fry married Alice Clemence in Marlborough St Peter church on 12 Jul 1613 They had seven baptised in Marlborough St Mary church, one of whom was buried in 1621. William Fry was buried in the same parish on 7 Jul 1632.
2. Roman numerals for money values.

96 ELIZABETH REYNES

widow 4 December 1633 P1/R/71

One old kittle, one old peire of brasse pott and two old skilletts 8*s*.[1]
One pewter quart pott, one pewter platter and five little pewter dishes 5*s*. 4*d*.
Two wooden dishes, two spoones, one kniffe and sherth 4*d*.
One old medly gowne of the best 13*s*. 4*d*.
Two old gownes more 4*s*. 4*d*.
One old red petticoate, one hatt and band, two stomager and one shooing horne 5*s*. 7*d*.
One greate chest with lock and key and one little cubbert with lock and key 7*s*. 8*d*.
A little powdered butter in a pa[. . .], one old stoo[l]e and cushion, two old petticoates, one o[. . .] a[. . .], a payre of bodice, a payre of stockinges, an aperne, a girdle and pooch 6*s*.
One rugge, a coverled and two blancketts 5*s*.
One old payre of sheets 3*s*.
Three verie old flockbeds 13*s*. 4*d*.
One good bowlster and one old bowlster 8*s*. 6*d*.
One feather pillow and case 4*s*.
One old truckle bedsteed with paynted clothes round aboutt and a matt 4*s*.
21 old pynners and ruffes 2*s*.
4 old smockes, thre apernes, one kercheiffe and one handkercheiffe 4*s*.
Two wastcoates and two old wastcoates more, one old aperne and one old woollen cloth 2*s*. 6*d*.
One coffer with locke and key and one old fryinge pan 2*s*. 8*d*.
Two yerds thre quarters off redcloth 5*s*. 6*d*.
Debt owinge unto the sayd Elizabeth by Thomas Coxe of Marlbrough without specialtye £1 10*s*.
Money in the howse £1 2*s*.
One payre of old shoes 1*s*.

Total £7 18*s*. 2*d*. [*recte* £7 18*s*. 1*d*.]

Richard Simes and Thomas Blissett, appraisors.

Buried St. Peter 2 December 1633 'Elizabeth Reeves, widow'.
Will 30 November 1633; probate 12 December 1633 to [unnamed].

1. Roman numerals throughout.

97 JOANE FURNELL

widow 10 March 1633/4 P1/F/79

Her wearinge apparell £2 10*s*.[1]
Two gold ringes and five silver spoones £1 2*s*.
Thre brasse pottes, two brasse kittles, one brasse panne, one skilett, one chaffinge dish, a warmynge pan, one old furnace and thre candlestickes £2 15*s*.
Two feather bedes, two feather bowlsters, one flocke bed, two flocke bowlsters, thre feather pillowes £4 10*s*.
Fowre coverleddes and one rugge £2.
Five payer of sheetes £1 10*s*.
8 table clothes, one dossen and a halffe of napkins, five smockes, halfe a dosson of kercheiffes, halffe a dosson of crosclothes, halffe a dosson of bands, fower coynes and fower neckclothes and one old wastcoate and eight appernes and fower pillowbers £2 4*s*.
One payer of silke garters and two old hatts 5*s*.
10 platters, one bason and two pewter butter dishes, thre salts, thre spoones, halff a dossen of sawcers, one chamber pott and one quart pott and 6 dishes £1.
Two coffers 3*s*.
One lembicke, one iron barre and one plate and another iron barre, one fyre panne and tonges 7*s*.
20 dossen of stone bottels £1 10*s*.

Two blanckettes 4*s.*
Uppon bandes £7 10*s.*
In money [in the house *deleted*] £6 8*s.* 6*d.*
One [little *added*] flitch of bacon 5*s.*

Total £34 3*s.* 6*d.*

Samuell Younge and Roger Davis alias Mawrice, appraisors.

Buried St. Peter 4 March 1633/4
Bond 8 August 1634, tuition of Elinor Clarke and Elizabeth Clarke, executrices of the [lost] will of Joane Furnell, and administration to Andrew Clarke of St. Peter Marlborough, wheeler; inventory exhibited 9 August 1634.

1. Roman numerals throughout.

98 JOHN PAINE[1]
dyer 25 June 1634 P1/P/134

In his Bed Chamber
His apparrell £3.[2]
His books 10*s.*
One standing bedsted with a tester £1 10*s.*
Two fether beds, 2 fether bolsters and 2 fether pillowes £3 6*s.* 8*d.*
One rugg and a paire of blankets £1 6*s.* 8*d.*
One truckle bedsteed 5*s.*
2 flockbeds and 2 flock bolsters 13*s.* 4*d.*
5 paire of sheets £1 5*s.*
3 paire of pillowe cases 16*s.*
Two bord clothes and 4 napkins 5*s.*
A table bord and frame, 4 joyne stooles and a joyne forme 12*s.*
One cubbard with a presse, 2 coffers and one box 15*s.*

In the Hall
One little table bord with a frame and two old chaires 1*s.* 4*d.*
3 brasse pottes and 3 brasse postnettes £1 10*s.*
Two brasse kettles 10*s.*
One brasse warming pan and 3 brasse candle sticks 8*s.*
One brass spice morter 1*s.*
7 pewter platters, 3 pottengers, 4 sawsers, one pewter dish, 2 pewter potts, one pewter flagon, one pewter bowle, one pewter salt and two pewter candlesticks and a chamber pott £1 6*s.*
One paire of andiers, a fire panne, a paire of tonges, 2 paire of hangers, two paire of potthookes, a griddier and 3 broches 16*s.*

In the Inner Chamber
One standing bedsteede 10*s.*
One flockbed and 2 flock bolsters 10*s.*
One rugg and one old coverlett £1.
One chest and two coffers 6*s.* 8*d.*

In the Chamber over the Hall
One old old livery bedsteed 5*s.*
2 old coverlettes and an old rugg 8*s.*

In the Dyhouse
Three old furnaces £10.
One dye fate £1 10*s.*
4 licker tubbs £1.
One powdring tubb, 2 cowles, 3 barrells, 2 little keevers and one payle 10*s.*
Wood and timber 10*s.*
All the lumber about the house 10*s.*
In woodwax £1.

Total [*in a different hand*] £37 17*s.* 8*d.* [*recte* £36 16*s.* 8*d.*]

Stephen Lawrance and John Inges, appraisors.
Ulisses Pettie, witness.

Buried St. Mary 19 February 1633/4, 'John Payne'.
Will 16 February 1633/4; probate not recorded; commission 23 September

1634, oath administered 4 October 1634 to Susan Payne, testator's widow.

1. 'Payne' on will.
2. Roman numerals throughout.

99 JOANE POWELL[1]

widow [will] 26 November 1634
P1/P/135

Hir wearinge apparrell £1 3s. 4d.[2]
On coverled, three blankets, two bowlsters, one pillow 10s.
One paire of sheets with other lininge 6s. 6d.
Three coffers, one table bord 6s.
Three formes 6d.
One cupbord 5s.
Two brase kittls, two skilets and one skimer 5s.
One broch, one hangels 8d.
Foure tubbs and other lumber 3s. 4d.
Two chaires 1s.
In wooll 5s.
In wood £1 4s.
In mault 1s.
Money [in the house *deleted*] her funerall discharged[3] £3 4s. 4d.

Total £7 15s. 8d.

Thomas Whittie and Mawddet Mills, appraisers.

Buried St. Mary 26 November 1634 'Jone Powel widow'.
Will [nuncupative] 'Munday' 24 November 1634; probate 2 December 1634 to executors [Thomas Hitchcock and Thomas Trebret].

1. 'of Saint Maries in Marlebrough'.
2. Roman numerals throughout.
3. Funeral expences should not form part of the inventory.

100 JOHN MAYHEW

10 December 1634 P1/M/126

In the Parlour
One tablebord with a frame and sixe stooles £1 15s.[1]
One side cubbard, a paire of tables, a low cheire and 1 forme with the andires and tonges 16s.

In the Closett there
One hogshed of metheglin £4.
Shelves and lumber there 10s.

In the Hall
1 tablebord, 1 forme, 1 side bord, 1 chayer, 2 stooles £1 6s. 8d.
1 jack with andires, fierpan and tonges with potthangles, 2 paire of billowes, 1 tosting yron £1 10s.
3 broches, 1 iron plate, 1 gridiron 5s.
3 skillettes, 2 porsnettes 10s.
2 brasse pottes, 1 warmingpan, one drippingpan, 1 fryengpan £1 10s.
3 kettelles, 2 chamberpottes, 1 kiver, 3 choppingknives £1 10s.
Dishes and trenchers 2s.
A bill and a pistoll 13s. 4d.
Candelles, oynions and lumber 6s.

Sub-total £14 14s.

In the Wainscott Chamber
1 tablebord, 3 stooles £1 10s.
1 sidebord, 1 carpett, 1 chaier, 2 low stooles £1 10s.
1 bason and yewer 6s. 8d.
1 bed steed, 1 trucklebedsteed £2.
Curteynes and valence 10s.
1 fetherbed, 1 bolster, 2 blankettes, 1 rugg £4.
Tonges, andiers and fierpann 5s.
3 pillowes, 6 cushions 13s. 4d.
1 curteyne, curteyne rodes and 1 old carpett 5s.

In the New Chamber
1 table, 1 frame, 1 sidebord and 1 chayer 13*s.* 4*d.*
2 bedsteeds, 1 trucklebedsteed and 1 cheier £2.
2 fetherbeddes, 2 bolsters, 2 blankettes, 2 rugges £5 10*s.*

Sub-total £19 3*s.* 4*d.*

In his Lodginge Chamber
1 bedsteed, 1 trucklebedsteed, 1 table bord, 1 chest, 1 trunck, 1 coffer and 1 stoole £2.
1 presse £3.
2 fetherbeddes, 2 blankettes, 1 bolster with curteynes and 2 rugges £5.
His apparrell £5.
15 paire of sheetes £8.
4 dozen of napkins and tenne table clothes £5.
12 pillowbers and 10 towelles £3.
2 cubberd clothes and 1 table cloth more £2.
1 silver salt, 1 silver boll, 3 silver spoones, 6 other spoones £5 10*s.*
4 dozen of pewter £5.
5 candelstickes, 3 chamberpottes 13*s.*
1 brasse collender, 1 pewter collender, 1 flaggen and 4 wine pottes 14*s.*
1 salt with pewter dishes, 2 basons, 1 skimer, 1 chafingdish 10*s.*

In another Chamber
1 bedsteed, 1 tablebord, 1 forme £1.
1 flockbed with the kiferled £2.
3 chayers, 2 coffers, 4 boxes, 2 chestes and a side bord £1.

Sub-total £49 7*s.*

In the Greate Chamber
2 bedsteedes, 1 table, 1 sidebord, 1 forme, 1 chayer and 2 Bibles £3.
1 fetherbed, one flockbed with their furnitures £5.
1 trucklebedsteed with a flock bed and coveringe £1.

In the Kitchin
1 furnace, 1 table with woodden vesselles there £2.

In the Seller
Woodden vesselles, a table bord and other lumber £1 6*s.* 8*d.*
14 barrelles of beare £3.

In the Backside
In wood £18.
1 yotingstone, wellbuckett and other lumber £1 10*s.*
5 pigges £4.
1 cow and a calfe £4.
In hay £2.
In herthe and ferne £1.
In standings and tiltes £3.

Sub-total £48 16*s.* 8*d.*

Total £132 2*s.* [*recte* £132 1*s.*]

William Burgis senior and Walter Jefferies, appraisors.

Buried St. Peter 30 November 1634.
Will [nuncupative] 20 November 1634, probate 29 May 1635 to [unnamed].

1. Roman numerals throughout, except sub-totals.

101 RICHARD DAWNCE

weaver 18 April 1635 P1/D/70

His wearinge apparell £2.[1]
One bedsteed, one bed and furniture £1.
One chest, too coffers 5*s.*
One bushell, one board, one gane, one haire, one bill 4*s.*
A few old bords 2*s.*
One table bord, one cobberd, one bench, one forme, to stooles, one bellowes 7*s.*

Too palatters, too candelstickes, too bettels, one pots, one skelets, one fringpan £1 14*s.*
One broch and andirons
Too joggs and small things 1*s.*
One lombe and that which be longeth to him £2 10*s.*
Some bords in a garret 5*s.* 8*d.* [v[s] 8[d]]
One oatinge stone and bowls and one old tubb £1.
In wood £1 10*s.*
One kiffer, too tubs and other things 6*s.* 6*d.*
Scales and waits 2*s.*
Malt £1 13*s.*
The lease of the house 1*s.*

Total £13 1*s.* 9*d.*

Robert Coolman, John Hewlet and George Burges, appraisors.

Burial not recorded.
Will 4 March 1635 [*recte* 1634/5]; probate 7 October 1635 to executrix [testator's mother, unnamed in will].

1. Roman numerals throughout except as shown.

102 BENIAMIN LAWRENCE
yeoman [will] 21May 1635 P1/L/97

In the Chamber over the Hall
One feather bed, 2 feather bolsters, 2 feather pillowes, one flocke bed, one paire of blanckets, one rugg, one matt and one cord £5.[1]
One table planckt, one chaire, one round table and a lowe stoole 10*s.*
2 dozen of pewter £2 8*s.*
9 small dishes and 8 sawsers 6*s.*
2 pewter candlestickes, one double salt, 5 small pewter salts, 3 pottage dishes and one bowle, one quart pott, 2 chamber potts 12*s.*
One warming pan 4*s.*

In the Little Chamber over the Midle Roome
One bedsteed, 2 flocke beds, one strawe bed and curtins and matt, one feather bolster, 3 feather pillowes, one paire of blankets, one coverlet, one rugg £4.
One truckell bedsteed, one flocke bed, one flocke bolster, one paire of blanckets, one rugg, 2 flocke pillowes, one matt and cord £1 10*s.*
3 chests with lockes and keyes unto them 16*s.*

In the Cockloft
One livery bedsteed, one flock bed, one flocke bolster, one blanket, 2 coverlets, one matt and cord £1
4 boards and 4 tressels 5*s.*
One old coffer, one dowe kever, [3 *deleted*] one bushell, one temser, one serch 8*s.*
4 bushells of wheat and 2 bagges 18*s.*
One shelfe and old waynescot 1*s.*

In the Narrow Chamber
2 table boards and frames and 3 formes £1.
11 paire of shetes £5.
One table cloth of locrum 8*s.*
6 diaper napkins, one dozen of course napkins 8*s.*
4 old table clothes 6*s.* 8*d.*
4 pillow cases 6*s.*

In the Hall
2 table boards and frames, 7 stooles, one foorme £1 10*s.*
3 cushings 1*s.* 6*d.*

In the Litle Roome by the Hall
One little table board, frame and forme 4*s.*

In the Midle Roome
One table board, tressles and forme 5*s.*

In the Seller

22 barrells, 2 kivers, one tunbowle, one paile, cupps and glasses, one bottle, one powdering tubb £2 10*s.*

In the Kitching

One table board and forme 1*s.*

One paire of dogges, one paire of andirons, 3 spitts, 2 paire of pothookes, 3 paire of hangings, one fier showle, tongs, one fender and tosting iron, one paire of billowes, one plate £1.

3 potts, 4 kittles, 3 sheets £3.

2 dripping pans, one skimmer, one flesh hooke, 3 chaffing dishes, one gridiron 12*s.*

One furnace £1.

In the Malt Howse

One table board, 3 formes and tressels 6*s.*

Tubbs, kivers and other lumber £1.

One yoating fate £1 10*s.*

In the East Loft

4 score quarters of malt £80.

One malt mill with the appurtenances £1.

The cleft wood and faggots £14.

The wearing apparell £3.

Ready money £2.

Debts oweing £14.

Total £152 6*s.* 2*d.*

Stephen Lawrence, Thomas Newby, Thomas Hunt and Richard Symmes, appraisors.

Buried St. Peter 4 May 1635, 'als Barber, the elder'.

Will 24 March 1634/5; probate 29 May 1635 to Izard Lawrence, testator's wife.

1. Roman numerals throughout.

103 THOMAS HAWKINS[1]

shoemaker 16 June 1635 P1/H/209

His wearing apparell, linnen and wollen £2 10*s.*[2]

3 bedes, 3 bolsters, 4 pillowes, 3 blankettes and 2 coverlettes £5.

Other woollen clothes and hattes £2 10*s.*

7 sheetes £1 15*s.*

3 pillow cases, a face cloth and other linnen £1 10*s.*

One standing bedsteed, one trockle bedsteed, two chestes, one coffer, a chaier £2.

2 Bibles and 4 other bookes 8*s.*

A presse, one powdringe tubb, one cowle, one cradle, a box and one joyne stoole, a flaskett, one more little box and one more little chaire 10*s.*

4 kettles, one pott, one postnett, one skillett, a spice morter and a broch £1 10*s.*

6 pewter platters, one sawser, 2 pewter dishes, one pewter pott and one salt 10*s.*

In yreware 5*s.*

3 paire of scales and waites 3*s.*

One table bord with a forme, one cubard and a bench 10*s.*

[Two *added*] cowles more, 2 little barrells, one paile and other trinnen ware 7*s.*

The wood in the backside £1 5*s.*

In leather £1.

His workinge tooles, a well buckett, rope and chayne and other lumber 15*s.*

Uppon bond £20.

In money £18 3*s.*

Total £60 11*s.*

Nicholas Knapp and Robert Plorett, appraisors.

Buried St. Mary 13 June 1635.

Will [nuncupative] 'the begininge of June' 1635; commission 11 July 1635; probate 23 July 1635 to Margaret Hawkins, testator's widow.

1. 'of the parish of St Marie in Marlebrough'.

2. Roman numerals throughout.

104 WILLIAM GUNTER[1]

23 December 1635 P1/G/131

In the Chamber over the Hall
2 bedsteeds matts and cords £1 4*s*.[j^{li} 4^{s}][2]
1 flocke bed and coverled and a bolster 6*s*.
1 feather bed, 2 feather pillows, 1 feather bolster, 1 coverlid 10*s*.[x^{s}]
1 table bord, 1 forme, 1 chaire 8*s*.
His wearing apparrell £1.[j^{li}]
All the winescote £2 3*s*.

In the Chamber over the Shoppe
3 bedstedes with the lumbar 13*s*. 4*d*.
1 table bord with the lumbar 3*s*. 4*d*.

In the Cocke Lofte
1 paire of beemes and scales with the lumbar 2*s*. 6*d*.

In the Hall
2 bedsteeds 12*s*.
1 table bord 16*s*.
1 forme, 5 joyne stoolles withe rest of the lumbar 5*s*.
The port holl dore 8*s*.

In Parler
1 bedsteed 1*s*.[j^{s}]
1 flocke bed, 1 ruge, 1 blankett, 1 bolster, 1 pilliowe 6*s*. 8*d*.
1 table bord and with the lumbar 4*s*.

In the Shopp
2 cooffers, 1 chest and 3 boxes 8*s*.
2 payre of sheetts with rest of the ould lininge 8*s*.
1 flocke bed, 2 flocke bolsters, 1 pillow, 1 coverlid and 1 bolsteres with the rest of the lumbar 8*s*.

In the Kitching
1 jake, 1 talbe bord, 1 chayre, 1 litle stolle, 2 peeces of wine scott and the binces 6*s*. 8*d*.
All the pewter 8*s*.
2 kitles, 1 iron pott, 2 brasen candle sticks 16*s*.
2 broches, three paire of hangers with a iron bar, one frying pan, 1 paire of andiers and all the rest of the lumbar 10*s*.[x^{s}]

In the Sillar
1 vate, 2 stans with the rest of the lumbar 5*s*.[v^{s}]

In the Kitching
1 kivar with the rest of the cowles 5*s*.[v^{s}]
In the out house and the wood in the backe sid 10*s*.[x^{s}]
1 heepe of stones 1*s*.[j^{s}]
The stufe in the garden 1*s*.[j^{s}]
The haves of 2 acres of wheate in the Port Feild £2.
Desperate debts owinge uppon the booke £2.
A lase of 2 litle grounds £2.
2 letell tenementes weth a letell ground which in [*recte* is] at Panne for £9[ix^{li}] and is in valeu worth £9.[ix^{li}]

Total £28 7*s*. [*recte* £28 9*s*. 6*d*.]

John Stokes, Mores Shackarley, John Medcalff, Robert New, William Wilde and Leonard Hamell, appraisors.

Buried St. Mary 23 December 1635.
Bond 21 January 1635/6, administration to Frances Gunter, intestate's widow; proclamation 22 January 1635/6 endorsed 'as proclaimed 24 January by Thomas Clerk, vicar of St. Mary'; accounts submitted 27 January 1635/6 by Frances Gunter.

1. 'of marelbrogh st mares'.
2. Roman numerals where indicated.

105 JOHN SESSIONS

carpenter 19 January 1635/6 P1/S/238

A paire of [wheeles *added*] 8*s.*[1]
Workeing tooles 18*s.*
4 apsyn boards and 2 paire of hames 1*s.* 4*d.*
[One hundred of boards 8*s.* *added*]
A malt mill 16*s.*
Lugges 7*s.*
2 ladders 4*s.*
Elming planckes and 2 elming boards 6*s.* 8*d.*
A table board 4*s.*
132 foote of timber 15*s.*
Wood and pales 11*s.*
Tooles and 2 tressles and a coffer 3*s.* 4*d.*
A dungpott 6*s.*
A cubbord, table boord and 2 joyned stooles £1 8*s.*
2 barrells a fourme and window leafe and portall, a chaire and one plancke 8*s.*
2 beddsteeds and one boulting trow 14*s.*
6 jyce 2*s.*
A paire of bellowes 4*d.*
Weareing apparell £2 3*s.* 4*d.*
A flockbedd, one boulster, one case and one blanckett, one beddmatt and one coverlett 16*s.* 8*d.*
5 sheetes, 2 napkins 17*s.*
Pewter 4*s.* 4*d.*
4 paire of stockinges [4 *deleted*] 1*s.* 6*d.*
One paire of bootes, 2 paire of shoes 2*s.*
Earthen ware and trenchers 4*d.*
Bookes 8*s.* 6*d.*
2 cushion stooles, one cushion 10*d.*
One earthen drinking pott 2*d.*
2 woodden buckettes 6*d.*
One millstone 3*s.*
2 hattes 1*s.* 6*d.*
3 boxes 1*s.*
One frying pann 1*s.*
One paire of gloves 1*s.*
One brasse pott 3*s.*
6 [wearing *added*] bands and 2 shirtes 4*s.*
One cubbord 2*s.*
Debtes [due *deleted*] oweing to the intestate £11 6*s.*

Total £25 1*s.* 4*d.* [*recte* £24 18*s.* 4*d.*]

Edward Winde, George Blanchard and Thomas Cox, appraisors.

Buried St. Peter 11 January 1635/6.
Bond 21 January 1635/6, administration to Agnes Sessions, intestate's widow.

1. Roman numerals throughout.

106 ROGER GYBBES

30 May 1636 P1/G/133

One lyverie bedsteed matt and cord 4*s.* 6*d.*[1]
One flockbed 5*s.* 6*d.*
2 peare of blanketes and one coverlett 10*s.*
2 pillowes and a pillowcase 2*s.* 6*d.*
One peare of canvas sheetes 2*s.*
One olde chest 2*s.*
4 coffers 4*s.*
A chayre and a sidebord 2*s.*
A forme 6*d.*
9 bords 5*s.*
Parte of a bedsteed 1*s.* 6*d.*
7 short peeces of joyce timber 2*s.* 4*d.*
1 peece of timber 1*s.*
1 salt box, 1 old cradle, 3 peces of wood 7*d.*
4 kettelles, 1 brasse pott, one skillet and one skymmer £1 10*s.*
One platter, 2 pottingers, 2 sawsers, one fruit dishe 4*s.* 4*d.*
One pott hanginge 6*d.*
1 kever and one powdring tubb and one barrell 2*s.* 6*d.*
His wearinge apparrell £1.
The lease of his howse £2 10*s.*
In ready money £40.
[And in one obligacion made to Simon Dringe in trust before the testators decease by William Tayler £9. *added*]

Desperate debts owinge
[By William Tayler *deleted* £9].
By Richard Abraham £6.
By Robert Wren £3.

By John Meazan £2.
By Gabriel White £1 10*s.*
By William Carter £1 1*s.*
Edward Meazan 12*s.*
Edward Faythorne 10*s.*

Total £71 3*s.* 9*d.*

Thomas Crapon, Richard Cornewall and Bartholomew Binger, appraisors.

Buried St. Mary 27 May 1636.
Will 25 April 1636; probate 21 July 1636 to Simon Dringe, executor.

1. Roman numerals throughout.

107 CHRISTIAN HITCHCOKE alias **CHAPMAN**[1]
spinster [will] 29 December 1636
P1/C/174

In monyes £17.[2]
One coffer 1*s.* 6*d.*
One Bible and two bookes 6*s.*
One boxe 1*s.*
Her waring apparell both woolen and lining £8.
Two dishes and two sasers 2*s.* 6*d.*

Total £25 11*s.*

William Wythers and Thomas Trebretes, appraisors.

Buried St. Mary 1 December 1636 'daughter of Thomas'.
Will 19 October 1636; probate 24 April 1637 to Thomas Chapman alias Hitchcock, testator's father.

1. 'daughter of Thomas Hitchcock als Chapman deceased the xxixth of November 1636'.
2. Roman numerals throughout.

108 EDWARD CARTER
yeoman 2 January 1636/7 P1/C/173

In the Hall
One table board and twoo formes 8*s.*[1]

In the Chamber over the Hall
One standing bedsteed £2.

In his Lodginge Chamber
His wearinge apparrell £2.
One standing bedsteed, twoo fetherbeddes, three coverlettes, three blankettes, foure fetherd bolsters, foure fetherd pillowes £8
In ready money, his funeralles discharged[2] 8*s.*
Dew unto him upon one bonde £10.
Three table clothes, foure paire of sheetes, halfe a dozen of napkins and sixe pillow cases £2 10*s.*
One drinking dish tipt with silver and gilt 6*s.* 8*d.*
One chest, three coffers, one box and one cheyre £1.
One paire of andires, one spice morter with other ymplements 5*s.*
One carpett 5*s.*
One flaskett, one baskett and one sack 1*s.* 4*d.*
Foure cushons 3*s.* 4d

In the next Chamber
One old bedsteed, twoo livery tables, one rounde table board £1.
One old bedd and blankett 3*s.* 4*d.*
Twoo kiffers, one bushell, one powdring tubb, one reele, one card rake and three curteyne rodds 6s 8*d.*

In the Kitchin
One posnett, twoo brass pottes, one warmingpann £1.
Twoo brasse pannes, foure old kettles £3.
Three brasse candlestickes and one skymmer 4*s.*
Pewter £1 6*s.* 8*d.*

Twoo dripping panns, one iron plate, two spittes, one tosting iron, three paire of hangells, one grediron, one paire of pothookes 13*s.* 4*d.*
One tableboard, three stooles, one forme, one joyned cubbard and one side board £1.

In the Maulthouse
One iron beame and scales with three weightes and one iron barr 8*s.*

In the Buttery
Twoo barrelles, the horse and other lumber 6*s.* 8*d.*

In the greate Mauthouse
One yoatingstone £2 10*s.*
One hundred of elme boardes 6*s.* 8*d.*
One tenant sawe, twoo lether bottelles, twoo iron wedges, twoo boytles and one hand saw 5*s.*

In the Millhowse
One querne £1.
One woodden trough with other lumber there 12*s.*

In the Backside
Twoo ladders 1*s.*
One woodden plumpe with an iron handle to the same 10*s.*

In the Garden
Twoo stalles of bees 6*s.* 8*d.*

Total £12 6s 4*d.*

John Perlinge, John Wynde and Walter Jefferies, appraisors.

Burial not recorded.
Will 20 May 1636; probate 8 March 1636/7 to William Carter, testator's son.

1. Roman numerals throughout.

2. Funeral expenses should not form part of the inventory.

109 WALTER JONES
glover 1 March 1636/7 P1/IJ/56

In his Lodginge Chamber
His wearinge apparrell £2 13*s.* 4*d.*[1]
One fetherbed, twoo pillowes, one coverled and twoo blankettes £5.
Twoo old flockbedds with the blankettes and kifferleds £1 10*s.*
Three livery bedsteeds 15*s.*
One chest, twoo coffers, one chayre, one side bord and one joyned stoole £1.
Lynnen £4.
Twoo silver spoones 10*s.*
One standing bedsteed, one truckle bedsteed with other lumber there £1.

In the other Lodging Chamber
One table board, one waynscott presse with other waynscott and benches £1 10*s.*
Foure brasse pottes, three kettles £3 10*s.*
Pewter £1 10*s.*
Iron stuffe about the howse with other implements £1.

In the Kitchin
Three andires, twoo dripping panns, twoo broches, one paire of tonges, one fyrepanne 10*s.*
One cubbard with other lumber there £2 10*s.*

In mault and barly in the howse £13 6s 4*d.*
In woodd 10*s.*

Total £40 15*s.* [*recte* £40 14*s.* 8*d.*]

William Burgies, Leonard Hammell and Symon Hurle, appraisors.

Buried St. Mary 19 February 1636/7.

Will 10 February 1636/7; probate 8 March 1636/7 to Johane Jones, testator's widow.

1. Roman numerals throughout.

110 JOHANE TITCOMBE

widow 2 April 1637 P1/T/95

In the Hall

1 kyttle, 1 brasse pott, 1 skillett and 1 skimmer 5*s*.[1]

1 per of andires, 1 hangelles for a pott, 2 paire of pothookes and 1 broach 3*s*.

In the Chamber

1 flockbedd, 2 bolsters, 2 coverledes, 1 sheete, 1 blankett 13*s*. 4*d*.

Her wearinge apparrell 10*s*.

1 standing bedsteed, 1 matt and 1 cord 9*s*.

4 coffers, 2 boxes with other lumber there 9*s*. 6*d*.

One cubbard, one table bord with a frame, one forme, one joyned stoole, one cheyre, twoo benches in the hall with other lumber 11*s*. 6*d*.

In the Backside

One well buckett with the rope and cheyne 2*s*.

Twoo chattell leases £2.

Total £5 3*s*. 4*d*.

John Hillier and John Meadcalfe, appraisors.

Buried St. Peter 15 April 1637

Will 11 April 1637, probate 24 Apr 1637 to [unnamed].

1. Roman numerals throughout.

111 JOHN HEATH

innholder 4 December 1637

P1/H/227iv

In the Haule

One table boorde with a frame, a long forme, three gine stooles, two benches, one low chayer 16*s*.[1]

One gine cubberd 14*s*.

One jack 10*s*.

A peere of andirons, three dogs, a fire pan, a peere of tongs, a plate and a barre, one tosting ire 6*s*. 8*d*.

Three shelfs, a cubberd in the wale, a rak to carry meate, two salt boxxes 4*s*.

One fire buckat, a curtayn and rod, three old cushens and and old billows 6*s*. 8*d*.

In the Parlor

One table boorde with a frame, one jine forme and two benches 10*s*.

One chest, two livery bedsteedes, one truckle bed steed with mates and coordes and two shelfes 18*s*.

In the Crowne chamber

One table boorde, six jine stools, one forme with a chayre £1 6*s*.

One side cubberd, a pere of tables with a backe waynscot and benches £1 3*s*.

Page total £6 13*s*. 4*d*.

Two high bedsteeds with curtayns and rods, one truckle bed sted with matts and coord £3.

One long cashen and six thrum cashins 13*s*. 4*d*.

One back plate, a pere of iron dogs, a fire pan and tonges, a peere billows and a shelf 6*s*. 8*d*.

In the Rose Chamber

Two table boordes with frames, five jine stooles, one forme, one chayre stoole and two benches £1 10*s*.

One bedsteede with a curtayne and vallayne with a picture boord and curtayn rods with a mat and coord £2.

In the Checquer Chamber

One table boord, three benches, two

stooles, two chayres, one presse, a tack 16*s.*
Six old chushens, one fire shovell, two dogs 5*s.*
Two [high *added*] bedsteeds with truckle bedsteeds with cordes with curtayns and rodes £2 13*s.* 4*d.*

In the Haule Chamber
One table boorde, one fourme, two binches, a side boarde, one chayre, a cloose stoole, one tack, thre old cushens 15*s.*
One hihgh bed steede with a truckle bed steede with curtayne and [vallins *deleted*] fringe and rodes, coredes and mates with doges £1 13*s.* 4*d.*
Page total £13 12*s.* 8*d.*

In the Flower de luce
One little boorde with a frame, one livery bedsteed, one old coffer, coorde and mat 13*s.* 4*d.*

In the Ostlers Chamber
One table boorde, an old bedsteede, two benches, an old coffer 12*s.*

[*In his owne Chamber* added]
One livery bedsteed, mat and corde, three chests, one coffer and thre boxes, one hangin cubberd, thre chests £2.

In the Mayds Chamber
One livery bedsteede with mat, a coorde, four chests 6*s.* 8*d.*
One flock bed, two pillowes waing forty four pound 11*s.*
One playne covering, thre blanketes 18*s.*

The Ostlers Camber
One flock bed and bolster waying threescore twelve 15*s.*
Three old blanketes 6*s.*
Page total £6 12*s.*

The Lining
Twenty one peere of sheetes £8.
Six dozen of napkins £2.
Nine table clothes £1 6*s.*
Nine pillow bees and thre cuberd cloths £1 3*s.*
Thre towels 3*s.*
Thre score and seventeene pound of pewter £3 10*s.* 7*d.*
One bason and yewer and flagon and a quart pot 12*s.*
6 camber potes, 5 saltes, foure dishes, 14 spoomes 15*s.*
Three brasse candlestiks, a chafing dish, a brasse morter 15*s.*
Six kittles waying thre score and [twelve *deleted*] eight pound £1 19*s.* 8*d.*
Four smale skillets and a warming pan 6*s.* 8*d.*
Thre potes and [silk *deleted*] skillet waying fifty 3 lb £1 6*s.* 6*d.*
One iron pot 2*s.*
Three broches, two dripping pans, one peere of raks, thre peire of hangles, thre dogs, a fire fork and two peere of pothookes £1 10*s.*
One jack in the kitchin and a frying pan £1.
Page total £24 9s 5*d.*

The bed in the Crowne Chamber
One fetherbed and bolster waying 56 lb £2 2*s.*
One other bed and bojlster with floks and fetherswaying 3 score and 14 lb £2 3*s.* 2*d.*
Two straw beds 5*s.*
One flock bed and two bolsters waying 4 scor 10 lb £1 2*s.* 6*d.*
Two fether pillows waying 12 lb 9*s.*
Three blankets and two rugs £1 12*s.*

In the Rose Chamber
One fetherbed and two bolster waying 4 score 2 lb £2 14*s.* 8*d.*
A straw bed 2*s.*
One coverled, two blanketes £1 1*s.*

In the Checkqur Chamber
Two fether bolsters and three [foure *overwritten*] fether pillowes waying fifty-six lb £1 17*s.* 4*d.*
One flock bed waying 4 score lb £1.
Page total £14 8s 6*d.*

In the same place one bed and bolster of flocks waying 3 score 13 lb 18*s.* 3*d.*
One straw bed 2*s.*
Two rugs and one blanket £1 6*s.* 8*d.*

In the Haule Chamber
One fether bed and bolster waying 3 score 6 lb £2 1*s.* 4*d.*
One flock bed and bolster waying 59 lb £1.
Two rugs and a blanket £1 10*s.*

In the Flower de Luce
On flock bed waying 56 lb 14*s.*
One coverled 4*s.*

In the Parlour
Two flockebeds and two bolsters waying 6 score 4 lb £1 11*s.*
Two bolsters and a pillow of fethers waying thirty nine lb £1 2*s.*
Two coverledes 18*s.*

In his owne Chamber
One fether bed and a pillow waying forty nine lb £1 12*s.* 8*d.*
One flock bolster waying 17 4*s.* 3*d.*
One covering two blanketes 12*s.*
Total £13 16s 2*d.*

In the Kitching
One table boorde and frame, a meale witch, a safe, a bak of planks and a binch, a dresser 13*s.* 4*d.*
Five plate candle stickes, trenchers, one sarch, a trencher, baskat, a bred grater 3*s.*
One furnace 10*s.*
One tallet with a ladder 10*s.*
One salt, five tubs, two kowles, two bucketes, buckat and tumbrill and ire geere for the well £1.

In the Seller
One table boorde, frame, four horses, a litle cuberd, one settle, a gine stoole and a binch and a rack 12*s.*

In the Stable and the Stree[t]
One tallet, one bushell, two ladders, racks and mayngers and a witch £2.
The woode and pack binch £1.
A signe in the streete 6*s.* 8*d.*
One mare £2.
For other lumber 10*s.*
His waring apparrell £6 13*s.* 4*d.*
Page total £15 18*s.* 4*d.*

Total £95 0*s.* 7*d.* [*recte* £95 0*s.* 5*d.*]

Robert Hitchcok, William Farrington, William Purryer, Thomas Trebrett and Aldam Winkworth, appraisors.

Buried St. Peter 3 December 1637.
Bond 14 December 1637, administration to Elizabeth Heath, intestate's widow.

1. All sums of money and figures within the text are in a combination of Roman and Arabic numerals.

112 KATHERINE PEIRSE alias DASTINE[1]

singlewoman [will] 27 March 1638
P1/P/144

In money £52 19*s.*[2]
Her wearinge apparrell £3.
1 per of canvis sheets 5*s.*
1 Bible of the New and Olde testament 5*s.*
1 olde coffer 1*s.*
1 pewter dish and sixe spoones 1*s.*

Total £56 11*s.*

Thomas Keene, William Burgis the elder and Thomas Blissett, tailor, appraisors.

Burial not recorded, but St. Peter register 21 March 1637/8 lists 'Katharne the dafter of [*blank*]'.
Will 19 March 1637/8; commission 29 March 1638, oath administered to [unnamed]; probate 3 April 1638 to [unnamed].

1. 'Pearse alias Dastin' on will.
2. Roman numerals throughout.

112A JOHN HILLIAR[1] the younger

27 March 1638/9 P1/H/251

The lease of the house £2 10*s*.[2]
One flocke bead, 3 coverleades, 3 blankets, 3 sheetes, 3 pillows 10*s*.[2]
One cheste, 3 boxes, 2 coffers with other lumber 10*s*.[2]
2 pots, 2 kirttels, 2 skillats 8*s*.
7 platters, 4 tunes, 3 candle stekes, 2 butter dishes, 3 sawsers, one basen, one salt 13*s*. 4*d*.
2 andyrons, 1 broche, 2 dooges, one friing pan, 2 paire of hangeles, one paire pot hockes 4*s*.
One cuberd, one table boarde, 4 joyne stooles with other lumber £1.
Bandes, hand cuffes, lace and crasse cloathes £1.
His wearing apparrell £1 13*s*. 4*d*.

Total £8 8*s*. 8*d*.[3]

John Hilliar the elder and John Basset, appraisors.

Buried St. Peter 19 December 1637.
Bond 19 November 1641; administration to Richard Tarrant.

1. 'Hellyar' on bond.
2. Roman numerals where indicated.
3. Written 'viij^{li} viij^{s} 8^{d}.'

113 ANTHONY HATT

barber 12 July 1638 P1/H/242

In the Shopp
Eight basons and 2 waterpottes of brasse and one pott of pewter £1 5*s*.[1]
3 cases with the ymplementes therein and one large lookeinglasse £2.
18 triminge clothes £1 16*s*.
3 aprons and other shopp instruments, 2 cheyres, 1 coffer, 1 warmingpann and frame £1 4*s*.
Netts, lynes and thredd £5 16*s*.
1 chafer 5*s*.

In the Hall
1 tablebord with a frame and 7 stooles and 3 benches 18*s*.
One cubbard 12*s*.
2 brasse pottes, 3 kettles, 1 chafindishe, 2 skillettes £2.
1 spice morter, 12 platters, 2 chamber pottes, 3 candlestickes and other small pewter £1.
1 still, 1 drippingpann [*blank*] dishes, ladle spoones, trenchers and other small thinges 10*s*.
3 silver spoones 12*s*.
2 Bibles with other small bookes 16*s*.
Andires, potthangers, pothookes, 1 broche, 1 iron plate, 1 fyre pan, 1 tonges, 1 par of billowes 10*s*.
1 fyre buckett, 2 wedges, 1 axe, one spade 6*s*. 8*d*.

In his Lodginge Chamber
3 bedsteeds, 1 chest, 1 coffer, 1 box £2.
1 fether bed, 1 fether bolster, 2 pillowes, 1 rugg, 1 blankett £2 10*s*.
2 flockbedds with bolsters, 2 blankettes, 3 coverlettes £1 10*s*.
1 sword, 1 warmingpann 5*s*.
3 par of canvas sheetes, 1 par of dowlas

sheetes, 3 pillow cases, 2 table clothes, 6 napkins £2 6*s.*
His apparrell £5.
5 barrelles, 2 cowles, 2 kefers, 1 bowle, 2 tornes, 1 powdringtub, 1 bushell £1 6*s.* 8*d.*
A ladder with the wood £4 7*s.*
In bordes and timber at Wilton £2.
Debts owinge him £2 10*s.*

Total £43 4s 4*d.* [*recte* £43 5*s.* 4*d.*]

Christofer Finchthwaite, Thomas Bennett and Walter Jefferies, appraisors.

Buried St. Peter 5 June 1638.
Will 1 June 1638; probate 2 November 1638 to Anne Hatt, testator's widow.

1. Roman numerals throughout.

114 JOHN MARTEN[1]

clerk 23 August 1638 P1/M/141

Certaine goods sold since the testators death the summ of £19 7*s.* 7*d.*[2]
His wearing apparell £9.
The wood £13.
In poles and vayles £3.
His bookes £8 10*s.*
In ready money payde in by Mr Danyell and Henry Bayly since the testators death £26 15*s.*
In peuter £1 10*s.* 3*d.*
A jack, a tableboord, 2 chayres, 2 chests, 1 trunck and other lumber £3 3*s.*
Silver spoones, a watch and a warming pan £2 15*s.*
Owinge by Mr Gerard Prior £2.
1 fetherbed, 1 greene rug, 1 carpert, 6 cushions, a cupboard cloth, a tablecloth, 6 napkins, 1 brass pott, 1 skillet, 1 flagon £5 10*s.*
More in mony in Mr Walter Bayly's hands £106.
2 ruggs £1.
In desperate debts £10.

Total £211 10*s.* 10*d.*

Thomas Hunt and Edward Wynde, appraisors.

Buried St. Mary 16 March 1637/8 'Mr. Martyn, schoolmaster'.
Will 6 March 1637/8, probate 18 May 1638 to [unnamed]; inventory exhibited 24 Aug 1638.

1. 'Martin' on will.
2. Roman numerals throughout.

115 JEAFFERY SPENDER

9 October [*year omitted* c.1638]
P1/S/260

For a cloake £1.
A blanket and coverled 4*s.*
2 pair of sheettes 12*s.*
One table cloathe 1*s.*
One fir pane, one pare of tonges, one chamber potte 2*s.*
Wanesecoate in the hall 1*s.* 6*d.*
One stopping sticke, one friing pane, a pairen of lastes, 6 alleblades and some small peeces of leathers 1*s.* 4*d.*
One lettle kettle 1*s.* 6*d.*
One hachett 2*d.*

Total £2 3*s.* 6*d.*[1]

Lewes Andley, William Wythers and George Jaques, appraisors.

Burial not recorded.
Bond 12 December 1638, administration to Alice Spender, intestate's widow.

1. Total in Roman numerals.

116 JOHN ROGERS

shoemaker 26 March 1639 P1/R/82

His wearinge apparell in the chamber over the shoppe £2.
One flocke bedd, bowlster and pillow with other appurtenances there unto be longinge £1.
One table board and frame, one bedd steed, two little coffers with other small ymplements and two pewter pottengers with eight spoones and one wodden candlesticke 6*s.* 8*d.*

In the Hall
One table board and frame and forme [with all the other lumber *deleted*] 7*s.*

In the Shoppe
One brasse pott, one brasse kittle and one little skillett 3*s.* 4*d.*
His workinge tooles and other lumber 6*s.* 8*d.*
Three ladders 1*s.* 6*d.*
One chattell lease of his howse £22.

Total £26 5*s.* 2*d.*[1]

Richard Glasse[2] and Lewis Chappell, appraisors.

Burial not recorded.
Will [nuncupative] 25 February 1638/9; bond 25 September 1639, administration to Thorpe Pike during the minority of Henry Pike, his son, the executor; probate not recorded.

1. Total in Roman numerals .
2. 'off woare in the parish of wilcot'.

117 JOHN BLAKE

carpenter 24 April 1639 P1/B/289

Twoo leases of certen cottages and a plott of ground in Marlebrough aforesaid £1 10*s.*[1]
Certen lumber about the house 10*s.*

Total £2.

Christopher Lipyeatt and Thomas Hunt, appraisors.

Burial not recorded.
No other documents; inventory exhibited 25 April 1639.

1. Roman numerals throughout.

118 WILLIAM DISMAR[1]

parchment maker [will] [*undated* c.1639] P1/D/85

To such of his wearing cloathes one cloake, one coate £3.
Thre beed stees 4 nobles [£1 6*s.* 8*d.*]
One cheast, tow coaffers 16*s.*
Thre beeds £3 10*s.*
Thre bolster, tow pellows £1 10*s.*
Nine blankets £2.
Tow coverleads £1 10*s.*
Tow peare of sheates £2.
The pewter £2.
The brasse £4.
One peare of andears 5*s.*
Ther peare of hangers 3*s.*
One fire shovle and tonges 2*s.*
One cobart £1.
One table board 10*s.*
Forms, stoals and chayes 10*s.*
The bruing vessels £1.
The woode £1.
5 doson of harrowes at £2.
Screwes £1 10*s.*
Peltes and parchment £1 10*s.*
The wolle £6.
For shipp skines £1 10*s.*

Total £38 17*s.* 4*d.* [*recte* £38 12*s.* 8*d.*]

Thomas Newby, Henry Abat and Joseph Canninges, appraisors.

Burial not recorded.
Will 12 April 1639; probate 14 June 1639 to Alice Dismor, testator's widow.

1. 'Dismor' on will.

119 JAMES GIBBES
tucker 19 June 1639 P1/G/139

His wearinge apparrell £2.[1]

In the Chamber over the Hall
One feather bed and bowlster, one feather pillow, two blanckettes, two rugges, two coverleeddes, one flocke bed and bowlster and one flocke pillowe £4.
Two payre off sheetes, three napkins, three pillowtyes, two table clothes, two shirtes and one boulster case of tuke £1 6*s*.
One bedsteed, courd and matt, two coffers and one joyne chest and one cubberd and presse £1 3*s*. 4*d*.
Two chayres and a flaskett with other lumber 6*s*. 8*d*.
More in the same chamber, 8 yardes off russett woollen cloth 16*s*.
17 yardes off medlie cloth and one peice of gray £3 15*s*.
22 yardes of course russett and remnantes off white cloth £2 2*s*.
Five waight of course woolle in the chamber over the shoppe £1 5*s*.
In yarne £2.
Two waight off flice woolle £2.
30 lb of medly woole and twentye poundes of middle woole £1 18*s*. 4*d*.
Sixe poundes off lambes woole, sixe poundes off brooke woolle and two poundes of yarne 9*s*. 4*d*.
One truckle bedsteed fowre baskettes and thre tubbes 6*s*.
One iron beame and scales, leaden waightes, two payre off stockcards with other lumber 10*s*.

In the Hall
One table board and frame, one forme and one joyne chayre 14*s*.
One brasse pott and one brasse posnett and one iron pott £1.
Thre brasse kittles £2 10*s*.
In pewter 14*s*.
One payre of andirons, one drippinge panne, one firepan, one gridiron, one payre of tonges and one spitt with other lumber 10*s*.

In the Seller
Two kyvers, two barrells, two tubbes, one kyve with other lumber 12*s*.
Lumber in another roombe 6*s*.

In the Shoppe
Five payre off sheares £1 10*s*.
Tuckers handles and other tooles in the same shoppe 10*s*.
In wood in rackes and one grindinge stone in the backsyde £4 10*s*.
In desperate debts oweinge £17 7*s*. 2*d*.
Money in the howse £3 10*s*.

Total £57 10*s*. 10*d*.

Richard Greene, William Gardner, John Inggs and Richard Bollen, appraisors.

Burial not recorded.
Bond and commission 20 February 1638/9, administration to Margaret Gibbes, intestate's widow; accounts submitted and inventory exhibited 21 February 1639/40 by Margaret Gibbes.

1. Roman numerals throughout.

120 JOHN SINBURY[1]
heelmaker 24 June 1639 P1/S/263

One chest 3*s*. 4*d*.[2]
One lyvery bedsteede 4*s*.
One truckle bedsteed 2*s*. 6*d*.

One round table 2*s.*
One table in the hall 5*s.*
Two barrells 3*s.*
One cowle and one kyver 3*s.* 6*d.*
Twenty one lbs. of pewter 17*s.* 6*d.*
One pott 7*s.*
One kitle and one skillett 4*s.* 4*d.*
One cradle and one standing stoole 2*s.*
One hanger, one pothangles, pothookes and one fire pan 1*s.* 3*d.*
2 dossen 9 hurdles 9*s.*
6 litle luges and 3 blocks 1*s.* 6*d.*
3 fournies 1*s.*
One litle grindstone and trowe 1*s.*
One buckett 10*d.*
One bed, one coverlett, one blankett, one rugg and one boulster 13*s.*
One shirt, 2 pillo cases 2*s.*
A doublet hose and a coate 13*s.* 4*d.*
One gownd and a pettecoate 16*s.*
The lumber about the howse 2*s.*
2 old hatts 1*s.*
One cupboard 2*s.*
His working tooles 4*s.* 6*d.*
A spitt, a basting ladle and a steele plate 1*s.* 5*d.*
The howse praysed att £9.

Total £15 3*s.*

Thomas Keynton, Robert Looker and Joseph Gilmor, appraisers.

Burial not recorded.
Inventory exhibited 20 *September* 1639; *bond* 26 *September* 1639, *administration to Simon Hurle, glover, and Robert Peirce, tanner.*

1. 'Synbury' on bond.
2. Roman numerals throughout.

121 THOMAS CHEPMAN alias HITCHCOCK

yeoman 1 December 1639 P1/C/186

In reddie money £28.[1]
Uppon bill and bond £61 13s 4*d.*
His wearing apparell £5.

In the Hall
One table bord and [3 chayres *deleted*] frame with three joyne stooles 10*s.*
Two chayres one cubard 10*s.*
A peece of wanscott and benches 6*s.*
One payre of andirons, a paire of bellowes, a pairs of tonges, a fire shovell, two pott hangles 6*s.*

In his Bedd Chamber
One field bedsteed 10*s.*
One feather bedd, one fether bolster, 2 feather pillowes and one flock bolster £3 10*s.*
2 coverletes and two blancotts £2.
One chest, two coffers 8*s.*

In the Chamber over the Hall
One ioyne tester bedsteed £1.
One flockbedd, one feather bolster, two feather pillowes, two flock bolsters, one flock pillow, 3 paire of blancottes and three coverlettes and cord and matt £5.
One cubard, thre coffers, two boxses 10*s.*
Three cusshions 2*s.*

In the Out Loft
Nyneteene joystes, fyfteene bordes and a little gardner £2.
Halfe a wayte of wooll 10*s.*

In the Buttery
One brasse panne £1.
Five kettles, two brasse pottes, two postnettes and three skillettes £5.
Two brasse candlestickes, one pewter candlestick and one chafing dish 6*s.*
One dozen of platters and another dozen of lesser pewter £1 10*s.*
One [pewter *deleted*] plate dripinge pann, one fryinge pann, two spittes, a paire of pott hookes and a griddier 5*s.*
Five paire of sheetes, five pillowbers, two

dozen and halfe of napkins, and 5 table clothes £3.
In bearly and mault £7 10*s.*

In the Well House
Two vates, two tubbes, three cowles, one mault mill, one buckett and rope £2.
One hovell, posts and pales £3.
One brandier and waightes £1.
In wood £20.
One yron beame, one wooden beame with cordes and bordes 8*s.*
Two peeces of timber 5*s.*
The lease of the house £5.
13 yardes of cloth £2.
There is due in debts £3.
In lumber £2.

Total £168 19*s.* 4*d.*

Walter Jefferis, William Wythers, Thomas Trebret, appraisors.

Buried St. Mary 2 December 1639 'Thomas Hitchcocks'
Will 5 November 1639; probate 21 February 1639/40 to Margaret Chapman als Hitchcock, testator's widow.

1. Roman numerals throughout.

122 ELIANOR BROWNE

widow 2 December 1639 P1/B/291

One fether bedd and two flockbedds £2.[1]
Three coverlidds 15*s.*
One flockbedd 5s
Two blanckettes 2*s.*
Eleaven sheetes £1.
Fower pillowbeeres 4*s.*
Two tableclothes 3*s.*
One dozen and five napkins 3*s.*
Fower bedsteeds, two mattes and bed cords 12*s.*
Six coffers 12*s.*
Three tablebords and two formes 13*s.*
Seaven formes 2*s.*
Twelve stooles 10*s.*
Two cubbereds 4*s.*
Twenty-six peeces of pewter £1.
Fower kittles 10*s.*
One pott and pann 10*s.*
One warming pann, one skymmer and one basting ladle 2*s.* 6*d.*
One dripping pann and two broches 2*s.*
One frying pann, two mynsing knyves and one cleaver 1*s.* 4*d.*
One pott hooke, two hangers and one fire shovell 1*s.* 6*d.*
One paire of andirones, one gridiron and one plate 3*s.*
Three cowles, six barrells and one paile 6*s.*
In lumber 5*s.*
In wood £1.
One brasse candlesticke, two woodden candlestickes 8*d.*
One bed steed, one bed and boulster and two coveringes £1.
Her ringe and wearing apparrell £1 10*s.*

Total £13 18*s.* 2*d.* [*recte* £13 17*s.*]

William Withers, Joseph Blake, Thomas Cooper and Thomas Taylor, appraisors.

Burial not recorded.
Will [nuncupative] 1 December 1639; probate 21 February 1639/40 to [unnamed].

1. Roman numerals throughout.

123 WILLIAM BREWTIE

innholder [will] 9 January 1639/40 P1/B/293

In the Hall and Kitchin
Twoo tablebords, one forme and thre stooles £1.[1]
One jack, one paire of rackes, twoo peare

of andires, an iron plate, fier pan and tonges £2 10s.
Foure spittes, foure dripping pans with 3 pott hangelles £2 6s. 8d.
Twoo fryenge pannes, foure chafingdishes, twoo clevers, one mynceing knife, a sconce with other small instruments of kitchin £1.
One cubbard with the shelves 6s. 8d.
Twoo brasse pottes, foure bettelles, 3 skilletes, one brasse colendar, one fornace £8
One brasse morter with a pestle 3s. 4d.
Fyve dozen of pewter, foure basons with other pewter £8
Nyne chamber potes, tenne wyne potes and 13 candlestickes £2

In the Crowne Chamber
Two tableboards with frames, one dozen of stooles, three chayers and one side cubbord £3
One bason and ewer, seven cushions and 3 carpetes £3
One bedsted and one truckle bedsted £2
The curteynes and valence £1 10s.
One downe bed, one fetherbed, three bolsters and 3 pillowes £12
3 blanketes, 2 rugges with the mattes and window curteynes £2 10s.
Andires, fierpan, tonges and dogges £1

In the Rose Chamber
2 tablebords, twoo formes, sixe stooles, 2 chayers, one side borde £3 6s 8d. [iij^{li} vj^{s} 8^{d}]
3 carpetes, 6 cushions, one bason and ewer, the windowe curteynes and rods £1 10s.
A paire of andires with the fierpan, tonges, dogges and billowes £1
2 bedsteds with the mattes, cords, curteynes and valence £2 10s.
2 fetherbeds with 3 bolsters, three pillowes and three blankettes £10

In the Phenix Chamber
One tablebord, one livery bord, 2 stooles, one forme, one carpet, 2 cushions £1 10s.
3 bedsteds with mates and cords £2
2 peare of curteynes and valence £2
2 fetherbeds, 2 flockbeds, foure fether bolsters, 1 flockbolster, 3 pillowes £13 6s. 8d.
2 rugges, one coverlid, twoo peare of blanketes £3
A peare of andiers, tonges and billowes 6s.

In the New Chamber
One tablebord, one side b[oar]de, 2 formes, one chayer, one carpet, 4 cushions £2 6s. 8d.
2 bedsteds with the cords, mates, curteynes and valence £2
One fetherbed, 2 fetherbolsters, 3 pillowes, 1 flockbed and bolster, 3 blanketes, one rugg, one coverled £8
Wainscott and benches £1 10s.

In the Kingshed Chamber
Tablebord, 1 stoole, 3 formes, one chayer, 1 carpet, 1 cushion, 1 cubbordclothe £2
4 bedsteds with mates and cord, curteynes and valence £3 6s. 8d.
3 fetherbeds, 4 fetherbolsters, one flockbolster, five pillowes, 2 rugges, 1 coverled, 1 peare of blanketes £13 6s. 8d. [$xiij^{li}$ vj^{s} 8^{d}]
1 peare of doges, fierpan and billowes 3s. 4d.

In the Servantes Chamber
2 flockbeds, 2 bedsteds with the blanketes and coverleds there £2

In his Lodginge Chamber
3 bedsteds, 1 fetherbed, 2 flockbes, one fetherbolster, 1 peare of new curteynes with valence, mates and cords, 2 flockbolsters, 3 rugges, 1 coverled, 1 pear

of blankettes £13 6*s.* 8*d.*[1]
3 great chestes, 1 coffer, 4 boxes, one presse and cubbord, 3 shelves and two close stooles £3 10*s.*
His apparrell £6
38 lb of yarne £2 10*s.*
In plate £9
In ready money £5
18 tableclothes £6 13*s.* 3*d.*
39 peare of sheetes £20
14 dozen and a halfe of table napkins £5
22 pillowbers £3
The other lynnen £2 10*s.*
One warminge pan 4*s.*
In cheese £2
6 pigges £6 13*s.* 4*d.*

In the Bell Chamber
One tablebord and frame, 2 stooles, 2 formes, 1 chayer, 1 side cubbord, 2 peare of tables £3
2 bedsteds, 2 fetherbeds, 3 bolsters, one peare of blanketes, 2 rugges, mattes and cords £10
A peare of tonges, 1 dog, 1 cushion 3*s.* 4*d.*
The benches there 6*s.* 8*d.*

In the Chappell Chamber
1 tablebord, 1 sidebord, 2 formes, 1 chayer, 1 stoole, 1 tonges, fierpan, billowes, one iron dogg, 3 cushions, 1 carpet £2
3 bedsteds, 2 fetherbeds, 3 bolsters, 4 pillowes, 2 blanketes, 2 pear of curteynes, mattes and cords and 2 rugges £13 6*s.* 8*d.*

In the Checker Chamber
1 bedsted, 1 forme 8*s.*

In the Choffe Chamber
1 table, 1 forme, 1 stoole, 2 bedsteds with mattes and cords, 2 flockbeds, 3 bolsters, 2 coverleds, 1 blankett £5

In the Backside and other Byroomes
The wood and hay £30
1 table, 2 formes in the taphouse with stands there 13*s.* 4*d.*

In the Halfemoone
1 table form and benches 13*s.* 4*d.*
Woodden vessels and other lumber £3
Slates, lathes and fethers £2

Total £279 8*s.* [*recte* £281 8*s.*]

Thomas Bennett, Robert Hitchcock, Walter Jefferies and William Wythers, appraisors.

Buried St. Peter 15 December 1639 'William Bruty'.
Will 8 May 1637; probate 21 February 1639/40 to executrix [Katherine Brewtie, testator's widow].

1. Roman numerals throughout except as shown.

124 ELIZABETH NEWMAN
22 May 1640 P1/N/52

Her wearinge apparell £1 10*s.*[1]
1 holand sheete 10*s.*
Her coffer 1*s.* 8*d.*
In money £31.

Total [£33 *by addition*] 1*s.* 8*d.*

John Prator alias Pearse and Robert Davys, appraisors.
John Potter, witness.

Buried St. Peter 29 April 1640.
Bond 18 May 1640, administration to John Prater als Peirce of Bremhill, yeoman; inventory exhibited 19 May 1640[2].

1. Roman numerals throughout.
2. This date does not agree with that of the inventory.

125 WALTER JEFFRYS[1]

baker 22 Jan 1640/1 P3/IJ/78

In the best Chamber

On staninge bed sted, on pere of greene curtaines and valiauntes, on fether bed, on fether boulster, on flocke boulster, two fether pillowes, on straw bed, one matt and cord, one greene sett rugge, on pere of blainkcettes, on trucle bed sted, on flocke bed, on fether boulster, on flocke boulster, on pillow and on straw bed, on blainkcett, on coverlid £10.

On table bord and frame, eight ioyne stolles, on ioyne chayre, on livery cubberd, on cubberd cloth, on cubberd cushion, on bason, a yewer and three other cushions, on carpett cloth, on pere of [iron *added*] doggs, on fier pann and tonges, [on pere of billowes *added*] £3.

In the middle Chamber

On standinge bed sted, on pere of curtaines, on fether bed, on fether boulster, on flocke boulster, on straw bed and cord, on pere of blainkcettes, on greene sett rugg and two fether pillows, on truckle bed sted, on flocke bed, on fether boulster, on coverlidd and blainkcett with matt and cord £8.

On other standinge bed sted, on fether bed, on fether boulster, on flocke boulster, two blainkcetts, on cover lidd, matt and cord, on fether pillow, on livery cubberd, on bason and yewer, two cubberd cushions, on cubberd cloth, on carpett cloth, on table bord and frame, one ioyne chayre, one ioyne stole, on forme, three cushions, one pere of iron doggs, fier pann and tonges, on pere of billows £4 16*s*.

Page total £25 16*s*.

In the Chamber over the Gate House

Two standinge bed stedes, three flocke beds, on fether boulster, three flocke boulsters, three cover liddes, two pere of blainkcettes, on straw bed, 3 bed mattes and 3 cords, on carpett cloth, two table bordes, on forme, on side table, on koffer and fower tressles £5 10*s*.

In the Chamber at the Stayer Head

Two livery bed stedes, two flocke beddes, three flocke boulsters, two blainkecottes, two cover lids, two bed mattes, two bed cordes, on table bord and frame, on forme, two chestes and on straw bed £3.

In the Little Chamber adioyneinge to the Hall

On livery bed sted, on fether bed, on flocke bed, on fether boulster, on flocke boulster, on fether pillow, two cover liddes, on blainkcett, on bed matt and cord, on truckle bed, on flocke bed, tw flocke boulsters, two coverliddes, on blainkecottes, on straw bed, matt and cord, three koffers, two shelves and other small lumber £5.

His wearinge apparrele: two clokes, two dublettes, two pere of hose, two jurkins, on wascott etc £6.

In the Chamber over the Kitchen

On standinge bedsted, on fether bed, on fether boulster, on flocke boulster, three blainkecottes, on coverlid, on straw bed, matt and cord, on trucle bed [and cord *added*], on press, [two *deleted*] on cheste, two koffers, on chayre and one box, on painted cloth, on curtaine £4.

In the Kitchin

On iron backe, five broches, two iren drippinge pannes, fouer pere of iron hangels, three pere of pott hookes, on pere of iron rackes, on pere of billowes £1.

Page total £24 10*s*.

More in the Kitchin

Two bordes, on forme, on pece of wainescit, two binches, on shelve 3*s.*

In the Hall

On cubberd, two chayres, on forme, three ioyne stoles, on round table, one pece of wainescit, on painted cloth, one pere of andiers, three iron doggs, fier pann and tonges, on pere of billowes £2 10*s.*

In the Parler

On [fether bed *deleted*] standinge bedsted, curtaines and valiauntes, on fether bed, on fether boulster, on flocke bed, on flocke boulster, on cover lidd, two blainkecottes, bed matt and cord, on truckle bed with matt and cord £7 10*s.*

Two table bordes, on table cloth, five ioyne stoles, on forme, on chayre, on chest and three cushions £2.

In Pewter

On dossen of greate platters, tenn pottingers, nine sawcers, six butter dishes, three basons, two halfe pinte pottes, on pinte pott, two porridge dishes, halfe a dossen of spoones, five saltes, two flower pottes, two quarte pottes, on pewter candlesticke, seaven chamber pottes and three plate candlestickes £4 8*s.*

In Brass

Fower brass candlestickes 6*s.*

Six brass pottes, three posnettes, three skillattes, [six *deleted*] seaven kittles, on morter, on chafer, two warmeinge pannes, on fryinge brass pann, two brass chafinge dishes, two skimers, two flesh hookes, on griddier £7 10*s.*

On iron fryinge pann, on iron forke, [and *deleted*] on clever [and on bastinge sticke *added*] 3*s.*

On silver salt £2.

In Linnen

Three holland sheetes, three lockrom sheetes, [nine *deleted*] tenn pere of canvas sheetes, two dossen of canvas napkins, on dossen of flaxson napkins £5.

Page total £31 10*s.*

More in Linnen

On dossen of lockrom napkins, fower holland pillow cases, two dowlas pillow cases, seaven canvas table clothes, two dowlas table clothes, two diper table clothes, fower towells £3.

In the Seller

Two staines, on table and frame, two formes, two brass cokes, six juggs, two glasses and two great juggs £1.

In the Buttery

Two coules, two kives, two kiffers, two powdringe tubbs, two plainkes and one shelve £1.

In the Backehouse

The brake, three trowes and five mouldinge boardes and other implementes in the backehouse £3.

In the Backhouse Loft

Five bushells of beanes, on bushel of oates, in wheate meale and bread and flower to the value of 14[3] bushells and other lumber £4 10*s.*

15 cheeses 15*s.*

Bacon £1.

In both Stables

The tallettes, hay and rackes £4.

The hovele adioyneinge to the lower stable and boardes and pooles in the same hovell and three ladders £3 10*s.*

On mare £4.

Cleft wood, faggottes, lugges and timber £50.

A lease of a house in the tenure of Thomas

Tayler £40.
Owinge by specialties £13.
In debts owinge £10 8*s.*
Payd for wood and fillinge an earnest £4 14*s.*
Page total £143 17*s.*

Total £225 13*s.*

Thomas Crapon, William Wythers and William Farrington, appraisors.

Buried St. Peter 21 January 1640/1, 'Geofferies'.
Will 30 April 1636; probate 25 October 1641[2] to Alice Jefferys and Walter Jefferys, testator's children.

1. 'the elder'.
2. Proved in the court of the Archdeacon of Wiltshire.
3. Written as 'xiiij[teene]'.

126 JONE JONES

widow 25 May 1641 P3/IJ/79

Her wearing apparrell £3.

In the [Chambare deleted*] Kechene*
3 bras potts £1 13*s.* 4*d.*
2 kettells and a scellat 10*s.*
A scemmar, to brasen ladels £2.
2 peare of hangells and to peare of pot hocks 2*s.*
A peare of tongs and fiarshovle 1*s.*
1 plate 5*s.*
1 broch 1*s.*
2 dreppenes pans 2*s.*
1 cobbard and chaior £1 2*s.*
[3 *deleted*]For othar lombare £1 10*s.*
2 gentes stolls 2*s.*

In the Chambare
1 fetharbede and bolstare and 3 fethar pellas £4.
3 cofarleds £1 10*s.*
1 fethar bollstar 10*s.*
2 flockbeds and 1 flocke bollstar £1.
2 lefere bedsteds 19*s.*
1 peare of hollane shets 14*s.*
3 peare of canfos shets £1 10*s.*
3 tabele clothars and a dosen of napkens 10*s.*
5 pellacases 8*s.*
1 warmene pane 5*s.*
2 selfar spones 10*s.*
8 puttar plattars 19*s.*
2 solts an on chafene dech and canstek and spise mortar, [to putar tons *added*] 10*s.*
1 cheste, to coffars and on side bord, 1 gene forme £1.
[*one illegible line deleted*]
Owed in dectes [to the testator *added*] £1 2*s.* 4*d.*

Total £23 17*s.* 8*d.* [*recte* £23 11*s.* 4*d.*]

Thomas Kinton and Symon Hurle, appraisors.

Burial not recorded.
Will 15 April 1641; probate 25 October 1641[1] to Walter Jones, testator's son.

1. Proved in the court of the Archdeacon of Wiltshire.

127 WILLIAM HAIES[1]

baker 13 September 1641 P1/H/254

In the Halle
One table board, fower joind stooles, one forme, two chaires, one sidetable and a cuburd with a Bible and [other books *added*], three cushions £2 13*s.* 4*d.*
One paire of racks, one paire of andiers, one pare of tongs, one fier shovell, two paire of potthookes, two potthangings, a toastingiron, a chopinge knife and gridiron [and the wenscott *added*] £1.

In the Buttry
Seaven brasse poots, three skellets and a porsnett, one brasse pann, three kattles and a warminge pan £6.
A duzen of pewter platters and two duzen of pottengers, one flagon, two pinte pots, sixe saucers, three sallts and two tininge cups 5*s*.
Three brasse candle stickes, two pewter candlesticks, one brasse chaffinge dishes and a pewter bason 10*s*.
One friinge pan, two spitts, one drepingpane, a skimmer and a bastinge ladle 8*s*.
Nine barrells 16*s*.
Fower pewter dishes, one duzen of spoones, two duzen [and a halfe *deleted*] of trenchers, one duzen and fower wooden dishes and two boles, three treene platters and a tray 4*s*.

In the Chamber nexte the Hall
Two fether beds and five flock beds and three fether bolsters and fower fether pillowes and two flock bollsters £8.
One greene ruge, fower cover lids, three paire of blancketts, three bed matts, three bedcords and three bedsteads £3.
Eight paire of sheets and fower paire of pillow beares, sixe tableclothes, two duzen of napken and fower towells, one chest, fower coffers, fower boxes, one chaire, a stole and a chamber pott £5.

In the Chamber over the Hall
Two table bords and a hiee bedstead and the [*illegible deletion*] wenscott 10*s*.

In the Shopp
Two dawe kivers, two cowells, two pailes, one winnowinge sheete and an east heore £1.

In the Bakehouse
Fower trowes, one flower tub, three mouldinge bords, one brake, two serches, two temsers and one paire of scales and weights £2.
Two crackmill wheeles, three peels, one coalrake, one grater, a pastie peile, one furnace and a kive, one bushell, fower malte seaves, two raiing seeves, one pare of bellowes, one pecke and a gallon £2.

In the Mill house
One malte querne, fower duzen of hurdles and one pronge 15*s*.

In the Backside
In fagetts and cleft wood [and belletts and loggs *added*] £26.
In lumber about the howse and backside £1.
The poultry and one sowe and six sheepe [and wooll *added*] £2.
For the testaters aparell £3.
A halfe share of a muskett and furniture ther unto belonginge 10*s*.
[*Illegible deletion*]

Total £66 11*s*. 4*d*.

[Francis Freeman *deleted*, Thomas Paty, John Farmer *added*] and Richard Alexander, appraisors.

Burial not recorded.
Will 31 July 1641; probate 14 September 1641 to Grace Hayes, testator's widow.

1. 'Hayes' on will.

128 THOMAS BLISSET
[*undated*, c.1641] P1/B/298

In the Hall
A table boord and frame, 4 joine stooles, five chayres, four low stooles, one cubboard, a fire pan and one payre of billowes with a payr of angers, hangells, potthookes and a spitt £1 2*s*.[1]
Four kettles, 2 skelletes, one brass pott and an iron pott with one skimer,

chaffing dish and warming pan with pewter and tynne £1 10s.

One bedsteed, truckle bed and bedding, one board cloth, five sheetes, ten pillow cases, six napkins, one chest, three coffers and a box and side boords £4 10s.

Bookes, apparrell, woode, wheat and mault [with lumber about the house *added*] £12 10s.

Debts on speciallty £10.

More other debts £2 4s. 1*d.*

The lease of the tenement hee lived in £2.

[*Total omitted, by addition* £33 16s. 1*d.*]

Thomas Blisset and Thomas Bryant, appraisors.

Buried St. Peter 9 May 1641.

Bond 14 January 1641/2, administration to Joanne Blissett, intestate's widow; commission 14 January 1641/2, oath administered 22 January 1641/2 to Joanne Blissett

1. Roman numerals throughout.

129 THOMAS PATY[1]

yeoman [will] 4 May 1642 P1/P/164

In the Parlore

On tableboard, thre formes, fower joynd stooles, thre joynd chaires, on matted chaire £1 14s.

On [great *added*] cuboard, on livery cuboard and on glasscuboard £1 4s.

On great chest 10s.

Tenn cushins, on carpet and a cuboard cloth 16s.

On paire of andires and a paire of doges, on paire of tongs and a fier showell 6s. 8*d.*

His wearing aparrell £6.

On deske, on great Bible and five other bookes 13s. 4*d.*

In the Chamber within the Parlor

On high bedsteed, on matt, on fetherbed, tow fether bolsters, tow fether pilloes, a paire of blanketes and a rugg £5 15s.

On truckle bedsted and coard and matt, on fether bed, on fetherbolster, on flockbolster, on blanket and coverled £2.

Six paire of sheetes, five pillowbeares, tow tableclothes and a duzen of napkines £6 5s. 8*d.*

On trunk, on box, on coffer and a warming pan 14s. 6*d.*

Page total £25 19s. 2*d.*

[*remainder in a different hand*]

His wiffes wearinge apparell and her Bible £4.

In the new Chamber

One standinge bedsted, matt and cord, one flocke bed, tow flocke boulsters, one fether pillow, too blanckets and too coverlets £2 3s. 4*d.*

Too chests, too coffers £1 0s. 6*d.*

Five kivers, too coules, too tubs, one bushell, one payle, fower chese fats 19s. 4*d.*

2 sackes and a winoe sheete 3s. 4*d.*

Pewter of all sortes £2 3s. 10*d.*

Fower brase candlsticke 4s.

Too drippen pans, too spits, a bastinge ladle, one skimmer and a trivet 9s. 3*d.*

Fower brase pots, one yron pott, fower possnets, three kettles, too skellets, one cheffendish, one brase morter £5 4s.

Too silver bowles £2 15s.

In the Seller

4 barrills 11s. 6*d.*

For lumber £1 13s.

Corne in the barne [6 bushells *added*] 10s. 6*d.*

[*three totals deleted*]

Page total £21 17s. 7*d.*

Sub-total £47 16s. 9*d.* [*recte* £48 16s. 9*d.*]

[For the lease of Granham Hill £250 *added*]

[*in a third hand*]
Total £297 16*s.* 9*d.* [*recte* £298 16*s.* 9*d.*]

Francis Freeman, Thomas Keene, Samuel Younge and Rogar Davies, appraisors.

Buried St. Peter 1 May 1642.
Will 17 April 1642; probate 5 May 1642 to executor [John Patie, testator's son].

1. 'Patie' on will.

130 RICHARD CORNWALL[1]

shoemaker [will] 14 February 1643/4
P1/C/197

His wearing apparell £2.[2]
One table bord with things belonging to him, too chaiers £1.
3 bedsteeds £1.
Too flock beds, too boulsters, 4 pillows £1.
Sixte coverleds £2.
One paire of blanckets 5*s.*
Five sheets, 2 pillow casses, 3 table cloathes, one dozen of napkins £2.
One press, 2 chesse, 2 coffers, one side boord £1.
One warminge pane, one paire of doges 3*s.*
14[3] platters with other small peices £2 6*s.*
3 pottes, 1 posnat, 2 skillats £1 10*s.*
3 kettles with other brasse £3.
3 broches with other yreion thinges 10*s.*
Five barrells with other wooden things £1.
One yoating stone 10*s.*
2 brasse candle sticks 2*s.*
10[4] quatter of malte £10.
7 boards 5*s.*
In wood £3.
One pewtr pot, 2 boolls 2*s.*
In brasses and other lumber 15*s.*
The lease of the housse £10.

Total £42 18*s.*

Thomas Randoll, Steven Gilmore and Steven Longe, appraisors.

Burial not recorded.
Will 4 July 1643; bond 16 February 1643/4, administration to Joshua Sadler, testator's kinsman, executrix Anne Cornwall [testator's widow] having died; inventory exhibited 1 July 1644.

1. 'of Saint Maries'.
2. Roman numerals throughout.
3. Written 'x4'.
4. Roman numeral.

131 GREGORY YEOMANS

27 July 1644 P1/Y/17

In the Hall
2 joynt stolles, 2 chayres, one cubbert, one table board 8*s.*

In the Buttery next the Hall
3 kittells, one warming pane, 2 brasse pots, 2 brase pans, two skillets, one brase chaffindish, one skimer and one cubbert £2 2*s.*

In the Chamber
21 peces of pewter littell and great 15*s.*
2 candell sticks, one spice morter 2*s.*
One chest, 3 coffers, one table board, one beadsted, one forme 13*s.* 4*d.*
5 sheats, one table cloth 15*s.*
2 flock beads, one flocke bolster, on feather bolster, 2 fether pillows, one coverlid and 3 blanketts £2.

In the Malt House
One mault mille, 4 barrills, one bushell, 2 ladders, 2 coules, 2 tubs, 2 kivers £1

10s.
For working toules 10s.
One yeoting stone 10s.
2 spitts, 1 pair of angers, 3 pair of hangells 8s.
Old iron about the house 4s. 6d.
2 juges and other earthen pans 2s. 2s.
One Bible 2s., boules and dishes 18d. 3s. 6d.
2 bottelis 2s., timber bords and other lumber £2 16s. £2 18s.
Debts oweing by severall men £4 5s.
For his wareing apparrell £1.

Total £18 6s. 4d.

John Lawrence and Richard Ringe, appraisors.

Burial not recorded.
Will 5 June 1644; commission 23 July 1644, oath administered to John Yeomans, testator's son, executor; probate 3 September 1644 to [executor].

132 RALFE TITCOMBE[1]

shoemaker 28 January 1644/5 P1/T/112

His wearinge apparell £2 10s.[2]

In the Hall
One table boord, one cubert with other lumber £1.

In the Chamber
Too beds with the apurtinances, too chests with other lumber £2.
Brasse and pewter £1.

In the Seller
3 barrells with other lumber 5s.

In the Chamber over the Hall
One bedsted, wood with other lumber 10s.

In the Shoope
Workinge tooles and leasses 2s. 6d.

In the Backside
Lumber 2s. 6d.
One cowe £1.
In debts goode and desperate £3 3s. 6d.
The lease of the howse £1.

Total £12 12s. 6d. [*recte* £11 13s. 6d.]

[*added in another hand*]
One poore hackney mare which was carryed awaie in the Army and afterwards recovered againe of which she made but £1.

John Garlicke, Thomas Phillips and Leonard Hammell, appraisors.

Buried St. Mary 11 December 1644.
Bond 16 August 1647, administration to Margerie Titcombe, intestate's widow.

1. 'of Sainte Maryes in marleaborough'.
2. Roman numerals throughout.

133. [IZARD LAWRENCE

widow][1] [*date lost*, c.1645] P1/L/115

[*unknown number of lines lost*]
One p[. . .]

In the [. . .]
Three spitts, fo[. . .]aire of pothookes, two paire of hangers and one iron plate £1.[2]
One table bord and forme, one paire of bill [. . .], one ioyned stoole with the b[. . .] garner and other lumber 13s. 4d.
Fyve chafing dishes, one brasse skymmer, one brasse ladle and one gridiron 7s. 6d.

In the Malthowse
Fower table bords, one furnace and the brewing vessells £3.
24 quarters of malt £18.
One ost haire and skreene 15s.
One garner 6s. 8d.
14 barrells and 2 stands £1 10s.

In the Backsid
One malt mill £1.
One yoting stone and garner £2.
31 couple of linges £3.
Wood and lumber about the backsid £16.
Money in the howse £1 2s.
Debts owing £1.

Total £74 3s. 4d.

[*Appraisors' names lost*]

Burial not recorded.
Will [. . .] August [. . .]; commission 12 March 1644/5, oath administered to Stephen Lawrence; probate 4 July 1645 to executor [Stephen Lawrence, testator's son].

1. Name lost, obtained from commission.
2. Roman numerals throughout.

134 ALICE WILKES
widow [will] 27 May 1646 P1/W/207

Her weareing apparell £5.
One quarter of wheate £1 9s. 4d.
3 flitches of bacon £1 10s.
1 cwt of cheese £1.
In monyes £106.

Total £114 19s. 4d.

John Elliot and John Garlicke, appraisors.

Buried St. Mary 14 April 1646, 'Weeks'.
Will 3 April 1646; commission 20 April 1646, oath administered to Alice Wilkes, testator's daughter, executrix; probate 1 June 1646 to [executrix].

135 TOBY CROCKER
husbandman [will] 5 February 1647/8
P1/C/218

In wainescoot in the hall £1.
One cubbert 8s.
One tablebord and forme 5s.
Tuo kitles and 1 pott of brass 10s.
In workinge tooles 12s.
Tongs, fyerpann and [hangier *deleted*] andyers 2s. 6d.
2 beds and bedsteed and all that belongs to yt £1 10s.
Two coffers and 2 boxes 3s.
Two barrells 2s.
One grynestone 2s. 6d.
In lumber about the house 10s.
In wareinge apperle 13s. 4d.
Sub-total £5 18s. 4d.

1 brass pott and severall peces of pewter £1 10s.
The lease of the house £3.

Total £10 8s. 4d.

There is owinge in debts the sum of £3.[1]

Thomas Crapon, Thomas Kinton, John Ploret and Barthollomew Binger, appraisers.

Buried St. Mary 31 January 1647/8 'Tobias Crocker'.
Will 27 January 1647/8; probate 8 February 1647/8 to principal executrix [Elizabeth ?Crocker, testator's daughter].

1. There is no indication whether this sum is owed to or by the testator; if the latter, the sum should not form part of the inventory. The figure is given in Roman numerals.

136 JOHN SMITH
13 December 1648 P1/S/303

Waringe apparell and other lumber £1 10s.[1]
One band £21.

Total £22 10s.

John Hurlebut and Bartholomew Binger, appraisors.

Burial not recorded.
Will [nuncupative] 25 April 1648; probate 29 December 1648 to Alse Smith, testator's widow.

1. Roman numerals except total.

137 WILLIAM COLEMAN
?carpenter [inventory goods] 28 August 1649 P1/C/227

Four pare of shetes and one pare of blankets £1.
3 rudges 13*s.* 4*d.*
4 bolsters and 4 pellowes £1.
For 3 beadsteds 13*s.* 4*d.*
To flock beads and 2 chafe beads £1.
One doson of napkins, one table cloth, four pillow bars 10*s.*
The waring cloths £1.
One cheast, one cofor, one trunke, four boxes 13*s.* 4*d.*
Bras and putar £1.
2 [one *deleted*] table bords, one cubard, 4 barels, 3 stols 10*s.*
The lease of the house £3.
2 lett of wylls and a blind horse £4.
Swine £1.
Poultrey 2*s.*
One spet, one fire shuvl, 4 dogs of ire 4*s.*
Thre chayrs 3*s.*
Carpentars toollse and lumber 10*s.*
Sume sartaine old bowls 5*s.*

Total £17 4*s.*

Anthonie Whithed and Anthony Gyreaway, appraisors.

Buried St. Mary 31 July 1649.
Bond 30 August 1649, administration to Alice Coleman, testator's widow.

138 THOMAS GRINFILD
[*undated*, c.1649/50] P1/G/167

Won fether bede, wone boulster, two pellowes, won pare of blanketes with a coverled and apare of shetes £2 10*s.*
Two chestes, fowre cofferes 10*s.*
Won flock bede, boulster, a pare of blanketes, a ruge 10*s.*
Brase and puter £1.
A pare of anderes, a pare of hangeles, a pare of tonges with other iron £1 6*s.*
Three stolles with other lumber 5*s.*
Hise wearing clothes £1.
On the shop booke of despret detes £1 16*s.* 9*d.*

Total £8 7*s.* 9*d.*

Henry Cowsey and Edmund Ducke, appraisors.

Buried St. Peter 23 October 1648 'Thomas Grenville'.
Bond 26 February 1649/50, administration to Katherine Grinfeild, intestate's widow; inventory exhibited 27 February 1649/50

139 WILLIAM ELTON
carpenter [*day and month lost*] 1657 P1/E/91

The dwelli[. . .] £50
To beeds, th[. . .] £3 10*s.*
One bed [. . .]of blanketts £1 15*s.*
For peare [. . .] £1 8*s.*
One peare [. . .] £1.

The waring [. . .] £2 10s.
One flockb[. . .] of sheets £1.
Three h[. . .]s £2.
One duss[. . .] little pot, one little flo[. . .]r pot, halfe a dussen [. . .] £1 15s.
One [. . .] 5s.
Three ba[. . .]ett 16s.
One peare [. . .] hangills, one jacke [. . .] 12s.
Fowre ap[. . .]es with other [. . .] £2.
To loade of [. . .] £1 6s. 8d.

Total £[. . .] 17s. 8d.

[. . .]mith, and [. . .]phry Yorke, appraisers.

Buried St. Peter 26 September 1657.
Bond [*date lost*], administration to Sarah Elton, intestate's widow; inventory exhibited 15 May 1666.

140 RICHARD WYAT

?beerhouse keeper [inventory goods] 2 March 1659/60 P1/W/229

His weareinge apparrell and mony in his purse £6.

In his Lodginge Chamber
A feather bed, a feather powlster, a paire of blancketts, a blew rugg, curteynes and valierne and a ioyne bedsted £6.
4 boxes and a plaine chest, a sid table, cubbord, a twigg chaire, a low ioyne chayre, two low ioyne stooles, a coffer, a paire of andierons £1 5s. 6d.
Wainscot and a setle 5s.

In the Chamber with hiss Lodging Chamber
One feather and flocke bed, a flocke boulster, a paire of blanketts, one old red rugg, one lyvery bedsted, two smale pillowes, [matt and cord *added*] £2 5s.
One trundle bedsteed, a flocke bed, a flocke boulster, a blanckett and white coverled, [matt and cord *added*] £1 10s.
One coffer 2s. 6d.

In the Cockloft
Wood cutt into billett and faggotts £1 6s. 8d.

In the Hall
Two brasse potts, one iron pott, one ketle, three skilletts, warmeing pan, a brasse skimer and brasse ladle £1 10s.
Seave pewter platters, two butter dishes, two sawcers, a porrenger, two high candle stickes, one pint tankard, one salt 14s.
One ioyne table and frame, fouer ioyne stooles, an old chest, a matted chayer, one chyner bucket, cowle, flasket and waiste bole, [*illegible deletion*] three cup dishes, two candlestickes, a lanthorne £1 7s. 10d.
A fryinge pan, a tining dripping pan, a paire of dogs, fyre shovell and tongs, two paire of cotterills, a spitt, two paire pott hookes 10s. 10d.

In the Buttery
Two [pair *deleted*] litle barrells 1s. 6d.

Lynnen
Three paire of sheets, two table cloths, two pillow beares, two boulster cases £1 4s.

In the Backeside
In blockes and faggot wood and lugges £2.
The hovell £2.
In lumber about the house togeather with the lease of the said house £1.
Due from Mrs Katherin Finchthwayte £15.
Due from Robert Jacob upon bond as by the condicion appeareth £4 4s. 9d.
Due from Anthony Popeioy uppon bond as by the condicion appeareth ten

pounds [12*s.* *added*] whereof £5 is payd £5 12*s.*
Due from Mr William and Mr John Whythers uppon bond as by the condicion of the obligacion appeareth the sume of twenty pounds twelve shillings whereof is payd tenn pounds ten shillings £10 2*s.*
Due from Ambrosse Cottrill as by [bill *added*] appeareth £2 10*s.*
Due from William Tutle of Marlebrough £1.
Due from John Biggs of Marlebrough £1 10*s.*

In the Beere Seller
Two tables, three ioyne stooles, one forme, fower basketts, one deske, a voyder, a score bord, a tubb to waish glasses, thre barrells of beere and a halfe, juggs, glasses and cans, case of kniffes £4 8*s.* 4*d.*

Total £73 9*s.* 11*d.*

William Brutey, Robert Carpenter, Henry Cowssey and Joseph Blake, appraisors.

Buried St. Mary 1 March 1659/60.
Will 21 January 1657; probate 8 July 1661 to executor [Christopher Wyate, testator's son].

141 SYMON HURLE
glover 4 March 1660/1[1] P1/H/309

His weareinge apparell £2.[2]

In the Hall
One tablebord and sid cubberd and other lumber £1.

In the Chamber over the Hale
One standinge bedsteed, fether [bed *added*] and trucklebed and all belongeinge to it, cublerd, chest, bords and trunks and other od things £5.
4 per sheets, tableclothes, napkins and other lyninge £3.

In the Chamber over the Shopp
One bedsteed and beed and press and other lumber £1.

In the Kitchin
1 dozen and halfe pewter, three kitles, two potts, one furniss and possnett, two flagons, one iron pott and andyers and doge, spits, tablebord and cubberd, stooles and forme and other lumber £5.

In the Buttery
Five barrels and other brueinge vessells 10*s.*

In the Shopp
In lether and gloves £6.
The house and grounds annexed to my [*recte* his] house £40.
In wood and other lumber in the backside £1.

Total £64 10*s.*

Francis Wakere, Barthollomew Binger and John Sweet, appraisors.

Buried St. Mary 7 January 1650/1.
Bond 6 March 1661, administration to Mary Hurle, intestate's widow.

1. Written as regnal year.
2. Roman numerals throughout.

142 WILLIAM BIGGS the elder
11 March 1660/1 P1/B/363

His weareing apparell £1.

In the lodgeing Chamber
One bed and bedsteed and other appurtenances thereunto £2 10*s.*[1]

One paire of andirons and a fire shovell 2*s.* 6*d.*
Two coffers, an old trunke, two joyned stooles, a table board and an old chayre 8*s.*

In the Cockloft
One livery bedsteed and old rugg 8*s.*

In the Hall
One table board and frame and one standing cupboard, one Bible and 2 other bookes £1.
One coffer, one paire of iron dogs and a paire of tongs 5*s.*

In the Butry
Brasse and pewter 16*s.*
One forme and all other lumber 10*s.*
One chattle leasse of the house £16.

Total £22 19*s.* 6*d.* [*recte* £21 19*s.* 6*d.*]

Henry Cowssey, Obadiah Blissett and John Hill, appraisors.

Buried St. Mary 10 March 1660/1.
Commission 18 March 1660/1, oath administered 26 March 1661 to Susan Biggs; bond 6 May 1661, administration to Susan Biggs, intestate's widow.

1. Roman numerals throughout.

143 RICHARD RUMESEY
shoemaker [will] 14 March 1660/1
P1/R/104

His weareinge apparrell £2 10*s.*[1]
One fether beed, one fether bouster, three fether pellowes, two rugs, two per blanckets, one standinge bedsted and one livery bedsteed with matt and cords and all belonginge to it £1 12*s.*
Five per sheets, three table cloathes, nyne napkins, three per bellow cases and towels etc 14*s.*
Twelve dishes of pewter 10*s.*
One furness, one brass pott and one iron pott, two kitles, three skilletts [praised at *deleted*], brasen ladle and drippinge pann and skimmer and warminge pann and andyes and spitt, [*illegible deletion*] fyer pann and tonges £1 2*s.*
Two small tablebords, three joyne stooles and one joyne chayers and two other, one chest and one coffer and two litle old boxes, 3 cooshenns 14*s.*
Five barrels, one measinge vate, two cowles, two kivers, one stand, temser and other lumber 9*s.*
[One *deleted*] two litle maltmills, one old screen, one neast heare, one iron plate and one settell, yoateing stone, two great cubberds and five gardners and other lumber £2 10*s.*
In wood in the backsid and abroad £3 10*s.*
The house he lived in £3 10*s.*
Malt in the house and barley in the house and money and debts due to him then at his decease £30.

Total £47 7*s.* [*recte* £47 1*s.*]

Bartholomew Benger, John Townsend and Thomas Stone, appraisors.

Buried St. Mary 25 December 1658.
Deed of gift 17 August 1653, Richard Rumsey assigns his entire estate to Edde his wife, he retaining use during his lifetime; deposition 8 March 1660/1 by Batholomew Benger of Marlborough, mercer[2]; deposition 8 March 1660/1 by Robert Butcher, husband of Margery Rumsey alias Butcher, testator's daughter; commission 28 March 1661, oath administered 9 April 1661 to Edith Rumsey; bond 9 April 1661, administration to Edith Rumsey, intestate's widow; inventory exhibited 16 April 1661.

1. Roman numerals throughout.
2. 'aged 54 yeares or thereabouts, borne at Clatford within the parish of Preshute'.

144 JOHN DAVIS

baker [bond] 10 April 1661 P1/D/99

Twoo brasse potts, three kittles, one skillett, one fryeing pan, one skimmer, six platters, on flaggon, one cruse, one tynnen dripping pan, one spitt, one fire pan, twoo still plates, one salt, one payre of tongs, three porringers, six spoones, one brasse candlesticke, one payre of dogges, one payre of hangles, one greate whitch and other lumber £2 3*s.*
Fower barrells and one kive 10*s.*
Fower flock bedds, fower bolsters, three pillowes, twoo coverlettes, twoo high bedsteeds, one chayre, one truckle bedsteed with mattes and cords, twoo payre of sheetes, one blanckett with other lumber £4 4*s.*
Three cowles, one table board, one furme, three coffers and the boxes, one presse, one dry fate 16*s.*
One buckett, one payle, one payre of skales, twoo searches, twoo temsers, one pump, twoo kivers £1 3*s.*
The intestates weareinge apparell £2.
In wheate and meale eight bushells £1 12*s.*
Tenn quarters of malt £10.
Money in the howse £2.
Of desperate debts £2.
The wood in the backside £4.
One geldinge and one pigge £3.
In hay 6*s.* 8*d.*

Total £33 14*s.* 8*d.*

John Bassett, John Bowshere, farmer and Joseph Wake, appraisors.

Buried St. Peter 29 March 1661.
Bond and commission 18 April 1661, administration to Lucy Davis, intestate's widow.

145 RICHARD GRINFEILD

woollendraper 19 September 1661 P1/G/174

In the Best Roome
1 bolster, 1 pillow, 1 rugg 12*s.*
1 small flock bed 2*s.* 6*d.*
1 high bedstead, valence and curtins and coverng £1 10*s.*
1 truckell besteed 1*s.* 6*d.*
For 1 side table and cobert 8*s.*
For 1 table board and frame and 5 joyne stooles 12*s.*
1 cofer, 1 chaire and 1 box 3*s.*
Room total £3 9*s.*

In the Kitchin Camber
1 feather bed, 1 bolster, 1 pillow and covering to yt £2.
1 flock bed, 1 bolster and 1 feather pillow and also 1 blanket and 1 rugg £1.
2 bedsteed, curtaines and vallens £1.
1 chest, 1 small table boord, 1 lowe chaire, 1 stoole 14*s.*
Room total £4 14*s.*

In the 2 Garretts
For 3 flock beds, 4 bolsters and 2 covering and 3 bedsteed £3.
3 paire and 1 sheet and other small linine £2.

In the Parlor
2 table boards, 1 side board and 4 stooles 15*s.*
Rooms total £5 15*s.*

In the Kittchin
1 dozen of pewter and 4 small flaggons and also 2 chamber potts £1 10*s.*
1 brase pot, 3 kittles, 1 furnass, 1 waring pann, 1 posnet and 2 skillittes £2 10*s.*
2 driping panns, 1 bastingladle, 1 pricher

6*s.*
1 paire andirans, 2 spittes and 1 jacke 15*s.*
1 fender, 2 hangells and 2 paire toungs 4*s.*
Room total £5 5*s.*

More in the Kittchin
1 cobeard, 1 old table, 1 chaire, 2 stooles 10*s.*

In the Sollar
1 hoghead of beare 15*s.*
For hogheads and barrells and bruing vessells £1 10*s.*
For lumbar aboute the house 5*s.*
For faggot wood £2 10*s.*
For his wareing apparell £3.
[*Sub-total* £8. deleted]

Total £27 13*s.* [*recte* £27 3*s.*]

Clement Smith, Walter Titcomb and Henry Stentt, appraisors.

Buried St. Mary 10 September 1661.
Bond 11 January 1661/2, administration to Anne Greenfeild, intestate's widow; commission 7 February 1661/2, oath administered 11 January 1661/2[1] to Anne Greenfeld; inventory exhibited 18 February 1661/2.

1. This date is incorrect; probably 'February' was intended.

146 DANIEL SNOW

watchmaker 29 October 1661 P1/S/321

2 great viseses 8*s.*
2 oile stones and one great stake 5*s.*
1[1] turneing lave and all the great filles and 1 wimble 8*s.*
Parte of a watch and larum and 1 deviding plate 14*s.*
1 hamer, 1 hand vise, 1 paire of great pliers 1*s.* 6*d.*
1 boileing skillett, a sett of troy waites and 1 paire of scales 2*s.* 6*d.*
1 useing file, 1 paire of compasses, 1 litle hamer, 1 scrach brush and 3 chisells, 1 paire of pincers to draw wier, 1 litle hand vise 3*s.* 6*d.*
Parte of a movement and 1 dozen of new keyes 13*s.*
3 boxes of small viles and 1 box of turneing toules 6*s.*
2 shope boockes and 1 glasse diall 1*s.* 6*d.*
1 dozen of watch strings 1*s.* 6*d.*
1 litle trier and all the small lumber 1*s.*
1 marble stone, 1 lome, a great turneing lave, 1 old bickhorne 2*s.*
2 brase potes, 1 kitle, 2 skilletts, 1 scimer, 1 basting ladle, 2 brase candlestickes, 1 litle tallow skillett, 1 paire of potthockes 14*s.*
2 jack whells and 5 horse bells 2*s.* 6*d.*
A sett of viles for springs and 1 cristall glasse 1*s.* 6*d.*
2 spittes, 1 friingpan, 1 paire of doges, 1 paire of bellowes, 1 anger, 1 firepan, 1 sifter, 1 paire of hangings and steele plate 10*s.*
1 table bord, 1 cubbord, 3 low chaires, 1 hie one, 1 forme, 2 joyne stoules, 2 other stoules £1.
1 grineing stone 2*s.* 6*d.*
1 watch and larrum 10*s.*
1 cradle, 1 planke, 1 standing stoule, 2 drawers, 1 coppie boocke, 1 parse, 3 small boxes, 1 Bible, 1 testament 5*s.*
1 feather bead, 1 flocke bead, 2 bolsters, 3 pillowes, 1 ruge, 1 civerled, 3 blanketts, 2 sheetts £4.
4 barrells, 2 coules, 1 tundish 10*s.*
1 curtaine, 1 sacke, 2 threeping pans, 2 porringgers, 1 sault, 1 saser 1*s.* 6*d.*
1 flocke bead with all that belongs unto it 10*s.*
2 sheetts, 4 pillowcases, 1 bolster case 5*s.*
1 chest of drawers, 1 great chest, 1 coffer, 2 boxes 11*s.*
All his wereing clothes £1 10*s.*
The wooden vessell and earthen vessell in the kitchen 5*s.*
1 anvell, 1 greatt hamer, 3 paire of iron

tongs, 1 paire of great bellowes and all the lumber in the seller £3.
Sub-total £17 4s. 6d.

A parsell of lining 2s.
Mr (?)Cimer oeweth 15s.
For mending Mr Fishers clocke 3s.
John Langley oeweth 7s.
For mending Brennsens watch 6d.
Beniamin Barley oeweth 6d.

Total £18 12s. 6d.

William Greenfield, William Snow and James Bartlett, appraisers.

Buried St. Peter 28 October 1661.
Bond 7 *November* 1661, *administration to Mary Snowe, intestate's widow; inventory exhibited* 23 *December* 1661.

1. Figure '1' written 'i' throughout.

147 LEWES ANDLY

innholder [bond] 9 December 1661
P1/A/196

In the Hall
1 table board, 1 forme, 4 little chayres, 1 bacon rack, 1 setle and 1 dresser board £1.
1 dozen of pewter dishes, 1 dozen of butter dishes, 6 porringers £1 10s.
4 brasse candle sticks, 3 skillets, 3 smale kittles, 1 smale brsse pot, 1 brasse morter, 2 brasse ladeles, 1 brasse skimer, 1 brasse slice, 1 old brasse cheaffen dish £1.
1 jack, 4 spitts, 1 drippinpan, 1 pair of iron andiers, 1 pair of iron doggs, 1 firepan, 2 pair of tongs, 1 gridiron, 1 triffet, 3 pair of hangells, 3 pair of pothooks, 1 clevor, 1 minsing knife, 1 oven peell, 2 steel plates, 1 fender, 1 barr, 1 iron pott £2.

In the Little Buttery in the Hall
1 warmeing pan, 1 neading trow, 3 toernes, 1 dozen of earthen weare and other lumber 10s.

In the Parlour
1 table board, 8 joyned stooles, 1 chayre, 1 setle chayre £1.
1 standing high bedsteed with curtaines, 1 trundle bedsteed, 1 fether bed, 1 flockbed, 1 fether boulster, 1 flock boulster, 2 fether pillowes, 1 rouge, 1 coverlid, 2 pair of blanckets £6.
2 chestes, 7 boxes, 2 truncks, 1 cubbord, 1 window curtaine, 5 cushions £2.
In weareing apparrell £5.

In the Parlour Chamber
3 tablebords, 10 joyned stooles, 1 livery cubbord, 1 setle chayre £1 10s.
Page total £21 10s.

1 standinge bedsteed, 1 trundle bedsteed, 1 pair of curtaines and valliens, 1 rouge, 1 pair of blanckets, 2 fether beds, 1 fether boulster, 2 pillowes, 2 stooles, 1 chayre £5.
6 cussions, 1 window curtaine, 1 fire pan, 1 pair of dogs 10s.

In the Closset
2 great Bibles and severall other books £1 10s.
16 pair of sheets, 5 pair of pillow tyes, 3 cubbard clothes, 6 table cloths, 3 dozen of napkins £6 3s. 4d.

In the Chamber over the Hall
3 litle table boards, 3 joyned stooles, 1 forme, 1 setle chayre, 1 pair of billowes 13s. 4d.
2 livery bedsteeds, 1 pair of curtaines and vallience, 1 fether bed, 1 fether boulster, 1 fether pillow, 1 coverlid, 1 blancket, 1 flock bed, 1 flock boulster, 1 coverlid £5.
4 cussions, 1 pair of dogs, 1 fire tongs 3s. 4d.

In the Chamber over the Gatehouse
1 livery bedsteed and matt, 2 table boards and 1 forme 16*s*.

In the Garret of the Parlour
1 table board, 1 forme, 1 livery bedsteed, 1 flock bed, 1 flock boulster, 1 blancket, 1 coverlid, 1 pair of iron doges £1

In the Garret over the Hall
1 table board, 2 formes, 2 joyned stooles, 1 livery bedsteed, 1 flock bed, 1 flock boulster, 1 rouge, 1 blancket, 1 truncke, 1 coffer with other lumber £1.

In the Celler
5 hogshed, 5 barreles, 1 table board, 2 formes, 2 hogsheads and 1 barrell of bear, 2 stands with other lumber £3.
Page total £24 16*s*.

In the Brewhowse
2 furnasses, 2 cives with other brueinge vessells £6.
For the wood in the backside and the pump in the stables, 1 tallet and racks £5.
Page total £11.

Total £57 6*s*.

William Smith, Matthias Fowler and John Bassett, appraisors.

Buried St. Peter 8 December 1661.
Will 10 September 1661; bond 16 December 1661, administration to Elizabeth Andley, testator's widow, during the minority of her son Lewis, the executor; probate 20 November 1674 to Lewis Andley, now come of age.

148 FRANCIS HERRIN

feltmaker 15 January 1661/2 P1/H/311

His weareing apparrell £3.[1]
In money £32 5*s*.
In brasse [and *added*] pewter, a driping pan and a jacke £2.
One tableboard, twoo joyne stooles, three chaires and a side board 10*s*.
In bedding [two bedsteeds *deleted*] £5.
In weares £20.
In twoo little fornaces £1.
In brewing vessells £1.
Twoo bedsteeds, chests and boxes and sume other lumber £1.
In workeing tooles £1.
One cow, one hogge and a little hay £3.
In wood and cole £1.
In fruite in the garden £2.
In andirons and other lumber 10*s*.
In desperate debts due to the testator £1.
His estate [*no value given*]

Total £74 5*s*.

Whereof the testator did owe to severall persons £30.[2]

John Hulett the elder, John Rabison and Phillip Garlik, appraisors.

Buried St. Mary 1 January 1661/2 'Frances Herron'.
Will [nuncupative] 12 January 1661/2[3]; commission 23 January 1661/2, oath administered 22 February 1661/2 to Joan Herrin, testator's widow and administratrix, with John Hulett and John Rabison, witnesses to the will.

1. Roman numerals throughout.
2. Debts owed by the deceased should not form part of the inventory.
3. This date does not agree with that of the burial.

149 KATEREN HORNER

widow [will] [*undated*, c.1661/2] P1/H/312

A porshon of mony thourty pound.
Her waring aparel fifty shillings.

Total £32 10*s*.

Robard Pavy and William Swendon, appraisrs.

Buried St. Mary 16 June 1661.
Will 11 June 1661; probate not recorded; commission 20 February 1661/2, oath taken 25 February 1661/2 by John Horner, testator's son; inventory exhibited 23 October 1662.

150 DEBORAH PRYOR
widow [will] 10 April 1662 P1/P/211

5 platters, 3 porringers, 1 sawcer, 1 blood dish weight 15 lb. at 10*d.* per lb. 12*s.* 6*d.*
3 litle brass pots weight 22 lb. at 6*d.* per lb. 11*s.*
2 kettles and 2 skilletts weight 20 lb. at 7*d.* per lb. 11*s.* 8*d.*
A warming pan, chaffing dish and skimer 4*s.*
One Bible 3*s.*
2 silver spoones 2 oz. 9*d.*[1] weight at 5*s.* per oz 12*s.* 3*d.*
3 diaper napkins 3*s.*
2 dozen of flaxen napkins at 8*s.* 6*d.* per dozen 17*s.*
10 napkins wrought with blue 5*s.*
[3 *altered to*] 2 fine sheets 12*s.*
[1 *altered* to] 2 old sheets 4*s.*
2 old napkins at 3*d.* per peece 6*d.*
4 tableclothes 4*s.*
8 towels 4*s.* 6*d.*
2 payre of holland pillow cases 8*s.*
2 payre of course pillow cases 3*s.*
1 cloth chayre and stoole 3*s.*
1 fetherbed, 1 fether bolster and 3 pillowes weight 75 lb. at 1*s.* per lb. £3 15*s.*
1 bedsteed, mat and cord, curtains and rods [and valens *added*] £1 12*s.*
1 carpett and window curtains 6*s.*
2 trunkes, the best 3*s.* the other 2*s.* 5*s.*
1 bolster with 26 lbs course fethers 12*s.*
1 flockbed and bolster [and pillow *added*] weight 38 lbs at 3*d.* ob. 11*s.*
1 trucklebed, mat and corde 5*s.*
2 payre of blankets and 1 lether bag 8*s.*
7 boxes 4*s.* 9*d.*
A lanthorne 1*s.*
A steele plate 1*s.*
1 brass ladle 10*d.*
1 brass frying pan 3*s.*
1 apleroster 8*d.*
2 litle tablebords and 2 joyne stooles 11*s.*
1 kiver 3*s.* 6*d.*
4 low formes 3*s.*
2 barrels and a litle wodden horse 5*s.* 6*d.*
1 fire pan and tongs 2*s.*
1 earthern candlesticke 8*d.*
1 parye of jron doggs weight 6 lb. at 2*d.* ob 1*s.* 3*d.*
1 payre of andirons weight 12 lb. at 3 ob per lb. 3*s.* 6*d.*
[4 *altered* to] 5 shelves [*illegible deleteion*] 2*s.*
3 old chayres 2*s.*
1 payre of bellowes and 1 old cushion 6*d.*
1 greene rug 7*s.*
1 parcel of waynescot being 7 yards and a half at 2*s.* per yard 15*s.*
Some few bords in the closet 1*s.*
1 per of pothookes, hangers and crooke and 8 trenchers 1*s.* 6*d.*
In rent and ready money £1 12*s.*
[*added in a different hand*] The lease of the dweling house £60.

Total £78 17*s.* 1*d.* [*recte* £78 15*s.* 1*d.*]

Richard Webb and Francis Waker, appraisors.

A scedule of what things remayne in howse to be left standing
In the chamber 1 portall, 2 cupbords [with 2 shelves *added*] with dores and one little dore.

In the hall 2 litle benches with bordes behynde them.
In the welhowse halfe the bucket and [halfe *added*] the chayne.

Buried St. Peter 9 April 1662 'Debarah Pryere widow'.
Will 10 January 1661/2; probate 30 May 1662 to executor [Thomas Taylor, testator's brother].

1. In this instance 'd' indictes 'drams'.

151. MR [THOMAS] FOWNES[1]

gentleman [will] 18 April 1662
P1/F/112

In mony £2 10*s.* 11*d.*
His begest ring £1 6*s.* 6*d.*
His stone ring 7*s.*
The seall ring 12*s.* 6*d.*
2 rapers and two beltes 10*s.*
His best sut and coate £4 5*s.*
His second sut and coate £1 5*s.*
His stuffe sut and coate 14*s.*
His riding coate and a pare off briches and a shamy waiskot £1.
A hate and mounters 3*s.* 6*d.*
A letheren bage 4*d.*
3 pare off stokinges 5*s.*
A Bibell 2*s.* 6*d.*
2 pare of shooes 2*s.* 6*d.*
A pare of gloufes 1*s.*
Lining: 2 corvets, 2 pare off halffe sleves, one shurte, 2 bands, 2 capes, 8 pare off cuffes, one handcarcher 9*s.*
A pare of butes 5*s.*
His mare £6.

Total £18 19*s.* 9*d.* [*recte* £19 19*s.* 9*d.*]

Gorge Blanchot and Robbart Carpenter, appraisors.

Buried St. Peter 16 April 1662.
Will 4 March 1661/2; probate 22 April 1662 to executor [Richard Smith, tapster].

1. Forename from will.

152 WILLIAM BRUNSDON

22 August 1662 P1/B/385

The lease of his dwelling house and other tenements £2.
In wood about the house £5.
One cow and 2 pigges £2 10*s.*
Corne growing uppon the ground £6 10*s.*
In desperate debt £10.
Howshold goods, working tooles and other lumber £18 4*s.* 8*d.*
The testators wearing apparrell £3.
In money £1.

Total £48 14*s.* 8*d.*

John Bassett, Thomas Brunsdon and Robert Millington, appraisors.

Buried St. Peter 22 June 1662 'William Bronson'.
Inventory exhibited 15 September 1662; bond 16 September 1662, administration to Margarett Brunsdon, intestate's widow.

153 JOHN BIGGS

innholder 21 January 1662/3 P1/B/387

Twentie six paire of sheetes £9 15*s.*
Nine pillowe cases 8*s.*
Five dozen of napkins and towells £1.
Six tabell cloathes 12*s.*

In the Little Chamber
One lowe bedsteed, one matt, one cord, twoe chests, one coffer, one box 10*s.*

In the Backside
Wood, luggs and one hovell, talletts, racks, manger, billetts, cole and pigge trowes £13.

In the Brewhouse
The furnace and brewinge vessell £7.
Three leaden gutters £1 10s.

In the Beare Seller
Three hogsheads of beare £3.
Three hoggsheads, eight kinderkins, fower stands and one tablebord £3 2s.
One bine, three formes 3s. 4d.
The haye £3.

In the Kitchine
Pewter £4 2s. 9d.
Brasse [potts and keetles and one chafin dishe *added*] £2 1s. 10d.
One paire of rackes, three spitts, fower doggs, one fyarpan and tongs, one fender, one gridireon, twoe drippingpans, one jacke and jacke lyne, one waite, one table, one forme, twoe dressers, one stocke, twoe benches, one bacon racke, twoe chayres, one joyned stoole, one cubberd, three shelves and other lumber, three tininge drippinge pans, six tin candlesticks, twoe wier ones, one skimmer, one beefe prickers and one ireon greate £4 0s. 2d.

In the other Seller
Lumber 10s.
One hogge of bacon £1 5s.
Seaven feather beads and seaven feather bolsters £17 5s. 10d.
Seaven flocke beads £5 19s. 9d.

In the Crowne
Twoe table boards, one side cubbert, three carpetts, eight cushins, three leather chaires, one joyned chaire, six joyned stooles, one trundle bedsteed, one matt, one cord, twoe joyned formes or benches, one paire of aindiornes, one dogge, one fyrepan and tongs, one rugge, one blanckett £3 18s. 4d.

In The Bell
One rugge, one coverlid, three blancketts, [one *added*] joyned bedsteed, curtaines, vallens and rods, one matt, one cord, one trundle bedsteed, one matt, one cord, one forme, twoe joyned stooles, one tablebord, one carpitt, twoe binches, one window curtin £3 5s.

In The Feuex
Twoe ruggs, three blancketts, one bedsteed, one matt, one cord, one sett of curtaines, vallens and curtaine rods, one trundle bedsteed, one matt, one cord, one carpett, one window curtaine and rod, one side cubbert and cubbert cloath, one rushen, twoe joyned chayres, seaven joyned stooles, one joyned forme, one bench, one firepan and tongs, one doge and one paire of billowse £5 1s.

In the Starr
Twoe blanketts, one rugge, one table bord, five joyned stooles, one forme, one close stoole, one side bord, one joyned chayer, twoe chests, one hye bedsteed, one matt, one cord, one trundle bedsteed, one matt, one cord, curtaines and vallens and rods, one carpett, twoe windowe curtaines and rods, one paire of andiarnes and firepan and tongs £3 10s.

In the George
Twoe hie bedsteeds, one trundle bedsteeds, matts and cords, one ruge, two cufferleds, three blanketts, two setts of curtaines, vallens and rods, one tablebord, one stoole and one forme £2 11s.

In the Swan
Twoe blanketts, one rugge, one coverled, one hye bedsteed and trundle bedsteed, matts and cords, one forme, one tablebord and one bench 15s.

In The Sunne
Twoe cufferleds, one rugge, three

blanketts, twoe hye bedsteeds, one trundle bedsteed, matts and cords, twoe paire of curtaines and vallens, twoe stooles, one joyned chayer, one forme, one table bord and one dogge £2 10s.

In the Rose

Two table bords, two formes [...] stooles, binches, two doggs, one firepan [...] [tongs *deleted*] bellowes £1 [...]

His weareinge apparell £5 [...]

Sub-total £105 16s. [...]

Ther is one the booke in desperatt dept and one bond £22.

Ther is in good dept as wee supose £10 18s.

Total £138 14s.

Henry Cowsey, Clement Smith, William Smith and Richard Woorill, appraisors.

Buried St. Peter [...] January 1662/3.

Commission 25 February 1662/3, oath administered to Dorothy Biggs, intestate's widow; bond 13 March 1662/3, administration to Dorothy Biggs.

154 ANDREW CLEARKE

wheeler [will] 10 March 1662/3

P1/C/263

In the Chamber over the Hale

His weareinge apparell £3.[1]

One standing bedsteed, one fether bed and one rugg and one per blankets and two fether boysters and one fether pillow with all the ingredyents belonginge to it £4.

One chest, one tablebord, one cabberd, one cheyer £1 6s.

In the Chamber over Entry

Shets, bordcloath and other lyninge £1 10s.

One livery bedsted, one fether bed and coverled and one fether boyster and two fether pillowes and all other, one pare of blancketts £2.

One chest 6s.

In the Garret

One livery bedsteed and all ingredyence to it and other lumber £1.

In the Hale

One tablebord and seven joyne stooles, one letle round table and two benches, one low stoole, two cheyers £1.

Six platters, one flaggne and one pintpott, one latten [tyn *deleted*] roster, three chamber potts, one basson 18s.

One brass pott, two brass kitles, one brass furniss and one iron pott and one waringe pann, two brass ladles, one [brass *added*] skymner, one brass candlesticke, one brass skillett £2.

Two spitts and jacke, fyer pann and tongues and one per andyers, two pare hangels and other iron inplemt 12s.

Two hogsheads and one barrell, two coules, two kivers, two powderinge tubb and one trowe and other lumber £1.

Three fletches bacon and chese in the racke 1s.

Fifty seven pare stockes for wheeles £8.

Two and twenty hundred spookes £14.

Three tunn and halfe tymber £3 10s.

56 dozen of velles £12.

80 lugs 10s.

28 axes £1 6s.

Pillow, shutlockes and axes and post £6 14s.

In lymbers, wagin pooles and wagin blades and coachepooles etc £7 8s.

In bords £3 15s.

One gryne stone 8s.

Two piggs £1 10s.

In hey and other lumber and [all *added*] other moveables £7.

Debts on booke £32 [£34 16s. *deleted*]

Two Bibels and other bookes 10*s.*
In all workinge tooles £2.

Total £121 13*s.* [*recte* £119 4*s.*]

Thomas Grenaway, Peter Furnell and Bartholomew Binger, appraisors.

Burial not recorded.
Will 24 February 1662/3; probate 28 April 1663 to Elinor Clarke, testator's widow.

1. Roman numerals throughout.

155 WILLIAM REDFORD

husbandman [will] 30 March 1663
P1/R/115

All his weareinge apparell £2.[1]

In the lower Chamber
One flock bed, one flock bolster, two pillows, two ruggs, two blancketts and two paire of sheets £2.
More in the same chamber one chest, one coffer, one cubbard, one chaire and other lumber 10*s.*

In the Hall
One table board and frame and foarme and an old stoole 4*s.*
The brasse, potthooks and two hangells and gridiron and one paire of [hangells *deleted*] andirons and one spitt £1 8*s.*
In the same roome one chaire, two tubbs, bellaces, one search, one little paire of scales, meale, one little peece of bacon and all other lumber there 10*s.*
Fower little old books 1*s.*
A little parcell of mault and one sacke 8*s.*

In the Celler
One silt, three keevers, two cowles, two barrells, one powderinge tubb and one buckett and other small lumber 10*s.*

Without Doors
Two ladders, one showle, one spade and a small parcell of wood and other lumber 10*s.*
One furnace, one pigg, one well buckett and chayne and tumbrells 12*s.*
One old bedsteed and one iron barr 3*s.*
In money oweinge upon bond and in the howse £15.

Total £23 16*s.*

Edward Purlin and William Lewis, appraisors.

Buried St. Mary 27 March 1663.
Will 6 March 1662/3; probate 18 June 1663 to executrix [Margaret Redford, testator's widow].

1. Roman numerals throughout.

156 ROBERT GLOVER

glover[will] [*undated,* c.1663] P1/G/185

His wearing clothes 10*s.*[1]
His bed cloths 10*s.*
The peuter and bras £1.
The wooll £2 10*s.*
To bonds £10 apece wherof on of them is casselty and then left in mony £1 10*s.*
[*total omitted, by addition*] £21 10*s.*
And in lumber 10*s.*

Total £26 10*s.*

Thomas Dance, Robert New and Christopher Blake, appraisors.

Buried St. Mary 17 April 1663
Will 3 February 1662/3; commission 20 May 1663, oath administered 24 May 1663 to Elizabeth Glover; probate 24 May 1663 to Elizabeth Glover, testator's widow.

1. All amounts in words except total.

157 ROBERT DAVISE

22 October 1663 P1/D/103

In the Parller

Wone tester bedsted, cord and mat, a flockbed, a boulster [of fether *added*], a ruge, wone blanket £1 10*s.*

Twoe tabellbordes, twoe forme, four joine stoles and a chaire, a pare of tonges and won ander £1 10*s.*

In the Chamber over the Parler

A staning bedsted with mat and cord with cortenes and valenes £1 6*s.* 8*d.*

A fether bed, bolster, twoe pelose, a cover led and a blanket £2 10*s.*

A trokell bedsted, mat and cord and a flock bede 11*s.*

A tabell bord, a shelf, a cofer, a forme, twoe join stoles and a chaire, [a pare of anders *deleted*] 11*s.*

The Chamber over the Hall

Won levere bedstad, mat and corde, a fether bed[sted *deleted*] and boulster, a flock boulster, cover led and blancket £2 11*s.*

A tabelbord, [a forme *deleted*] twoe join stoles, a chest, a cofer, a chaire and other lumber 8*s.*

In Hihes Chamber

A levery bedsted, mat and corde and flocke bed 13*s.* 4*d.*

In the Outer Chamber

To levery bedstedes, twoe mates and cordes with other lumber and flockbed 15*s.*

In the Halle

A tabell bord, twoe chaires, 4 stoles, a jacke with other lumber £1 10*s.*

Sex small deses of puter, three buter deshes, sex smale saseres, twoe candell stekes, twoe flagenes, [a pote *deleted*] fowr chamber potes, fowr brash deshes, a tone and a salt £1.

Twoe fir pan and tonges, a pare of anderes, a pare of doges, twoe spites, a fender, a gred iron 10*s.*

In the Chichen

A fornes with a grate and dore, three kiteles, a brase pann, a brase pot, a scellet, a ladell, a soonne £3 10*s.*

A vate, twoe cevears, a tabell bord with other lumbe 15*s.*

A malt m[il]l, a rope and bocet and lombres 10*s.*

In the Seller

Won barell of bear full of strong bear, fife emtie bareles, a horse, a kinderkin with other lumber £1.

His wearing clothe £2.

Twoe piges £1 5*s.*

Six pare of shets, three tabell cloth, two pare of pelobearis, twelve corse napkines £1 17*s.*

Twoe faget piles with other wod in the backside £15.

Total £40 1*s.* [*recte* £41 3*s.*]

Henry Cowssey, Georg Blanchard, Clement Smith and Richard Worall, appraisors.

Buried St. Mary 19 October 1663 'Robert Davis'.

Bond 23 October 1663, administration to Joane Davies, intestate's widow.

158 THOMAS GRENAWAY[1]

[*undated*, c.1663] P1/G/187

His wearinge apparrell £2.

In the Chamber over the Hall

One feather bed, [one flock bed *deleted*] one oaten dust bed, one feather boulster [thre *deleted*] 4 feather pillows, 2 rugs, one tester bedsteed, one livery bedsteed with mats and coards and other ingrediens £4 10*s*.

In the same chamber one chest, [one *deleted*] 2 table board planks, 2 coffers, 2 boxes, 2 chaires and other lumber £1 10*s*.

4 paire of [canvas *added*] sheets, one dowlis sheet, 4 canvas pillow cases, thre boulster cases, 2 doulis pillowcases, one holland, one dozen of table napkins, one peece of new cloth £1 14*s*.

In the Chamber over the Shop

One flockbed, one flock boulster, one [kiverlid *deleted*] coverlid, one tilt, a liviry bedsteed with mat and coard and other lumber £1.

In the Hall

One table board, 2 high joine stooles, 2 low joine stooles, one cubberd, one settle, one old cubberd and other lumber £1 6*s*.

12 dishes of pewter, one pewter flagon, 2 pewter drinkinge boules, one pewter pot, one salt, one saucer 18*s*.

2 brasse pots, one brasse potkittle, 4 skillets, one brass furnace with greats and dore, one brass kittle, one warming pan, one brasen fryinge pan, [one *deleted*] 2 spitts, a paire of andirons, one pair of pothangles, one trippat, 3 peeces of bakon, 6 brasse spoones, a brasse skimer, a brasse spice morter, firepan and tongs, 2 steele plates, one lattin dippin pan [and other lumber, one Bible with other books *added*] £4 12*s*.

In the Shop

In leather and made ware £17 15*s*.

5 barrells, one kiver, 2 coules, the shop board, a drench vate with fackets and luggs and other lumber £1 10*s*.

For the dwellinge house and the appurtenances thereunto belonging £15.

Money in the house £42.

Total £93 15*s*.

Anthony Grenaway and Robert Miles, appraisors.

Burial not recorded.

Will 6 July 1663; probate 23 October 1663 to executrix [Elizabeth Greenaway, testator's widow].

1. 'who disceased the 6th day of the fifth mounth called July in the year of our Lord one thousand six hundred sixty three'.

159 MERRICK SPENDER

saddler [will] 5 April 1664 P1/S/356

In the upar Roomes

13 cheyere frames, 4 livery bedsteeds with matts and cords £1 19*s*.

6 blanketts, 2 ruggs, 2 flock pillows, 1 fether boulster £1 5*s*.

1 table bord and frame, 3 joyn stooles, 1 chest 18*s*.

Fire pan, tongs, 1 paire of doggs, 1 pair billows 4*s*.

1 fether bed and 1 flocke bed and 2 fether boulsters £2.

A frinch bedsteed, cord and matt 10*s*.

3 blankets, 1 coverled 18*s*.

2 carpetts 6*s*. 8*d*.

1 chest, 1 coffer, 1 sett of boxes 10*s*.

1 pair of doggs 1*s*. 6*d*.

3 small firkins 1*s*. 6*d*.

1 small flocke bed and pillow 5*s*.

1 cheyer, 1 candlesticke 1*s*.

A sid sadle, cloth and furniture £1.

In the Hall

6 [small *added*] peuter dishes, 1 small pewter bason, 3 pewter candlesticks, 3 peuter poots, 1 flagon and sum tyn dishes with sum more old peuter £1.

2 small kittles, 3 skelletts, 3 bras potts, 3

skimers, 3 spitts, 1 jacke £1 10*s.*
1 pair of andions, 1 hangler, 1 cheffing dish, [1 fender, 1 frying pan *added*] 6*s.* 8*d.*
1 [fryin *deleted*] table bord and frame, 1 settle, 1 low stoole, 1 forme 6*s.* 8*d.*

In the Back Kitchin
2 stills with wormes and other matarels £4.
A long ceover with all other lumber about the house £2.
For his weareing clothes £4.
4 pair of sheetes, 2 table clothes, 6 napkins, 1 pair of pillow beares £1.
In debts £10.
In despereatt debts £10.
A back ketchin £10.

Total £54 3*s.*

Henry Cowssey, Richard Worill and Thomas Brunsdon, appraisrs.

Buried St. Peter 3 April 1664, 'Miric Spender'.
Will 21 March 1663/4; probate 7 April 1664 to executor [John Tomlyns, saddler].

159A JOHN BRISTOWE[1]
6 September 1664 P1/B/409

His weareinge apparell both woollen and lynnen £4.[2]

In his Chamber att Marlebrough
One feather bedd, two feather bolsters, fower feather pillowes, one paire of blancketts, one paire of holland sheetes, one paire of dowlas sheetes [two paire of canvas sheetes *added*] six holland pillowbeers, one dozen of hollan table napkins, six diaper table napkins, tow table clothes, one coffer, two boxes and one spleeten chaire £5 5*s.*
Two silver bowles, one gilt silver salt, fowerteene silver spoones and five gold rings £13.
In ready money £53 4*s.*
In money that Mr Bartlett had of him before his death £30.
In bonds and one bill from severall persons where of some is not to be recovered £175 14*s.*
Some small interest hee had in a liveinge of John Mortymers of Manton £2.

In his Howse at Manton
Two wainscott chayres and one matted chaire 4*s.*
3 spitts, 2 paire of pot hooks, 2 paire of pott hangings and old iron 15*s.*
One brasse pann, 3 kettles, 3 potts and two candlesticks £2 1*s.*
One cupboard and one iron dripinge pann 8*s.*
Fower barrells 6*s.*
Two boards, two quarters, 3 posts, one coffer, 1 paire of andirons, 1 safe, 1 chaire, 1 malt mill, 1 cheese presse 10*s.*
2 coffers, one trunck, one malt skreene and one side cupboard 10*s.*
One bedsteed, matt and cord, 1 feather bed and [two *added*] bolsters, [one pillow *added*] and 2 ruggs £2 10*s.*
One chest and one old coffer 6*s.*
One old flock bed and halfe heded bedsteed, 2 paire of old blancketts and one old coverlid [and one flock bolster *added*] 12*s.*
Tenn lb. of old pewter 10*s.*
One table board 5*s.*
Some small old lumber 1*s.*
Due from severall persons £11 12*s.*
One dozen and halfe more of table napkins [and one table cloth *added*] and one cupboard in his chamber att Marlbrough 8*s.*
Att Manton more one jack, one paire of doggs and one plate for a chimney back 10*s.*
One long silt, one warmeinge pann, one driping pan, one flaggon, one slice, one

bastinge ladle, one brass ladle and one skimmer, one powdring tubb, 2 skilletts 12*s.*

Total £315 3*s.* [*recte* £305 3*s.*]

Peter Furnell and Robert Gough, appraisors.

Buried Preshute, Wilts 23 August 1664.
Will [*lost*] November 1662; probate 12 September 1664 to [unnamed]

1. 'of Manton' [parish of Preshute].
2. Roman numerals throughout.

160 JOHN ELLIOTT

baker 7 November 1664 P1/E/89

In the Hall
One table bord, too chaires, one jack, one paire of andiers, one pair of tongs, one fier shole,
too paire of hangels, one bar, one fendor, one paire of racks, one spit £1.
In ready money £2.

In the Parlor
One table bord, 5 gyned stoolls, one forme, one cubberd, one chayer £1.

In the Parlor Chamber
One bed, one bedsteed, one rug, [one bolster, one pillow *added*] one pair of blanckets, one chest, too coffers, [one pair of dogs *added*] one side bord £5.
His wareing clothes [3 grate coates, 2 close coats, 2 sheetts, 3 half *deleted*] £5.

In the Hall Chamber
One bedsteed, one bed, one ruge, one pair of blanckets, one boulster, one chest £2 10*s.*

In the Sellor
3 barrills, one hors 10*s.*

In the Bakehouse Chamber
2 flock beds, 2 bedsteds, 3 pair of blanckets, [2 pilloes *added*] 2 boulsters, 2 rugs, 1 coffer £3 5*s.*

In the Bakehouse
4 moulding boards, one brake, 3 tubs, 4 kivers, 3 cowls, 3 sarches, 2 temsors and other lumber therto belonging £3.
In bras and puter: one furnis, 2 bras pots, 1 kittle, 2 skillet, one duzen of puter dishes, 2 chamber pots, 2 candlestiks, half a duzen of porringers, one driping pan, too bras pans £4.

For whate and meall £2 10*s.*
For too hogs £4.
One nag £5.
Four pair of harnis £1 10*s.*
Of lining: 4 pair of sheets, 5 pair of pilloe bears, 3 table clothes, one duzen and half of napkins, 2 cubberd clothes and other lining £2.
Too pills of cleft wood and thre pills of [cleft *deleted*] faggett wood in the backside and other wood that lays skattering about the backside £55.
One aishe and other o[. . .]ill wood £10.
In timber £30.
In monnys due upon bond £67.
In monnys due [upon *deleted*] by debt £30.

[*Total omitted; by addition* £234 5*s.*]

Thomas Pidding, Thomas Spackman and Peter Furnell, appraisers.

Buried St. Mary 4 November 1664.
Will 14 October 1663; probate 8 November 1664 to James Elliot, testator's son.

161 WILLIAM HUNT

husbandman [will] 22 Febru[ary c.1664/5] P1/H/364

One coffer 2*s.*
One coat, one pair of brechis 8*s.*
2 old pair of brechis, 2 old wascotts, one old c[. . .]
3 pair of stokings and 3 pair of lininges [. . .]
3 shirtts and 5 bands, 2 pair of glofes, 3 pair [. . .]
Money uppon bonds and otherwise due to him in all [. . .]

[*Total lost*]

Samuell Fowler and Peter Capelin, appraisors.

Buried St. Peter 7 December 1664.
Will 3 December 1664; probate not recorded; commission 31 January 1664/5, oath administered to executor [Thomas Powell of Overton, gentleman]; inventory exhibited 20 [. . .].

162 ROGER [DAVIS alias *added*] MORRIS[1]

blacksmith [will] 18 May 1665
P1/D/112

A bedd and beddsteed with curtaines, vallens and other appurtenances belonging to it £1.[2]
A table board, ioyned stooles, cubbard, chest and 2 cushions 10*s.*
In brasse and pewter 15*s.*
In lumber goodes 6*s.* 8*d.*
In workeing tooles £1.

Total £3 11*s.* 8*d.*

Edward Aven and William Newman, appraisors.

Buried St. Mary 7 September 1656 'Roger Davis',
Will 14 July 1656; probate 11 May 1665 to Humphrey Yorke, testator's son-in-law; inventory exhibited 1 June 1665.

1. 'Roger Davis' on will.
2. Roman numerals throughout.

163 NATHANIEL HONE[1]

shoemaker [will] [*undated*, c.1665]
P1/H/363

His wearing apparell £1 10*s.* 6*d.*
His howses, leases and tennaments £18.
His beedding £4 4*s.* 6*d.*
His beedsteeds 10*s.*
One chest, two coffers, three old boxes 14*s.*
His lining 9*s.*
Three old cushings 1*s.*
His books[2] £2.
His brasse £1 0*s.* 8*d.*
His pewtter 13*s.* 6*d.*
Two barrells 2*s.* 6*d.*
One chair 6*d.*
One stooll 6*d.*
His ireyeare 4*s.*
His lumber £1.

Total £30 10*s.* 2*d.*

John Stout, William Swenden and John Horner, appraisors.

Burial not recorded.
Will 19 July 1661; probate 2 June 1665 to Nathaniel Hone, testator's son.

1. 'in the parish of St. Maries'.
2. Books named in will.

164 NATHANYELL WINTER

goldsmith 31 July 1665 P1/W/264

In gold ware £26 7*s.* 6*d.*[1]
In all sorts of silver ware £27 18*s.* 10*d.*
His weareinge apparell £3.

In the Chamber over the Hale

One standinge bedsteed, one fether bed, two fether boisters, one coverled, two blancketts, five curtaines and vallins and matt and cord £5.

One trucklebed, one fether bedd, one fether bouster, two fether pilloes, two blancketts, coverled, matt and corde £2 10*s.*

5 par of sheets, three tablecloathes, two cubberd cloathes of diaper, two dozen of napkins, one flaxen cubberd cloath, one par of hollan pillow cases £2 10*s.*

6 worke cussions, one cubberd cusson and cubberd carpet cloath £1 5*s.*

One side cubberd, two cheyers, two stooles, one trunke, two coffers £1 6*s.*

One par andyers, fyer pann, dogs, tongs, one par of billowes and three picters 13*s.*

In the Cockloft

One standinge bedsteed, one fether bed, two fether bousters, tw fether pillowes, five curtaines, one coverleds, two blancketts, matt and cord £5.

One flockebed, one fether boister, one coverled, two blancketts 13*s.* 4*d.*

In the Hale

In pewter weighinge 54 lbs £2 14*s.*

More in pewter 9*s.*

Three brass potts, two brass kitles, one litle brass pann, two cast posnetts, one litle skillett, brass ladle and warmninge pann, two skimmers £4.

Two iron drippin panns, four spitts, three pare pothookes, o pare andyers, one pare doggs, fyer pann and tongs, one grideron and a jacke £1.

One tablebord, five joyne stooles, two cheyers, one litle tablebord, one bord and glass cubberd 18*s.*

Five drum cussions, one Bible with other bookes 16*s.*

In the Buttery

Four barrels, one powdringe tubb and stand 12*s.* 6*d.*

In the Maltinge House

One yoatinge stone, one skreene, one bushell, one pecke, three tubbs and other lumber £2 10*s.*

In the Shopp

One cubberd, one decke, one coffer and workinge tooles £2.

Wood in the backesid and in the house £12 12*s.*

Total £103 15*s.* 2*d.*

Hee owes in debts inst £17 12*s.*[2]
Total £86 3*s.* 2*d.*

William Gough, goldsmith, John Morgan and Bartholomew Benger, appraisors.

Buried St. Peter 27 July 1665.
Will 14 January 1664/5; probate 10 August 1665 to Anthony Winter, testator's son.

1. Roman numerals throughout.
2. Debts owed by the deceased should not form part of the inventory.

165 THOMAS PIDDING

shoemaker 17 August 1665 P1/P/244

Of wareing cloaths: one shute and cloke and one shute and coate £1.

One pair of bootes, to pair of shues 10*s.* 10*d.*

In The Hall

One table board, one cuberd 5*s.* 5*d.*

Five pewter dishes, one bras candlestick 5*s.* 5*d.*

One paire of andiers, one pair of dogs 3*s.*

One iron bar, one fier shovll and tongs 2*s.*

To bras kitles, to[we *deleted*] bras potts, to spits £1.
One forme, four gynd stools, to chayers 5*s.*

In the Hall Chamber
One flock bed, one blanket, one pair of sheets, one boulster and one coverlid £1.

In the Shop
Of knives and working tooles £1 10*s.*

In the Chamber over the Shop
One father bed and boulster, to pilloes, one rug, to blankets, one pair of sheets, one bedsted, a coard and matt £1 10*s.*
One chest, one coffer, to boxes 8*s.*
Of books 10*s.*
Wood in the backside 10*s.*
Of samestery ware and some smale debts £3.

Total £10 19*s.* 8*d.*

Thomas Pidding, John Gillmore and Robert Kimber, appraisors.

Burial not recorded.
Commission 8 August 1665, oath administered 14 August 1665 to Mary Pidden; bond 14 August 1665, administration to Mary Pidden, intestate's widow; inventory exhibited 17 August 1665.

166 THOMAS SHIPREEVE
mason 29 January 1665/6 P1/S/375

The lease of the howse he lived in £40.[1]
The beddinge and bedsteed £3 10*s.*
Twoo tables and fower stooles 16*s.*
One presse 6*s.*
One chest and one trunck 7*s.*
The brasse and pewter £2.
Other lumber goods 10*s.*
His weareinge apparrell £1 10*s.*

Total £48 19*s.*

Roger Glide and Walter Sagar, appraisors.

Burial not recorded.
Bond 1 February 1665/6, administration to Ann Shipreeve, intestate's widow.

1. Roman numerals throughout.

167 THOMAS HIBARDE
26 February 1665/6 P1/H/374

His wearing aparell £6.

In the Chamber
One beedsteed and beding £3.
Towe beedsteeds and beeding £3.
In lining £5.
7 tabell boards with foarmes and stoolles £3.
One cheste and a booxe 12*s.* 6*d.*
Pewter £3 2*s.* 6*d.*
One furnace with the breweing vessell £3.
Sixe hooges heads and beare £3 2*s.* 6*d.*
One jacke with spites and other nessesaryes £1 2*s.* 6*d.*
Sixe dossen of botells 12*s.*
Wood and haye £3.
Bacone in the house £2.
One chatell lease of a house £40.
In lumber goodes and nessasaryes £1.
In brassen vessell £2.

Total £79 12*s.*

John Bowshear and William Hawkes, appraisors.

Buried St. Mary 15 May 1665 'Thomas Hibbert'.
Commission 28 November 1666, oath administered 7 December 1666 to

Elizabeth Hibbert; bond 7 December 1666, administration to Elizabeth Hibberd, intestate's widow.

168 THOMAS KEYNTON

18 September 1666 P1/K/63

In the Best Chamber

One fether bed and boulster and curtins and bedstede and [all that belongs to it *added*] £5.

Toe tabell bords, a cubbord and a chest £1.

A peare of andiorns and loucking glas 15*s.*

Three carpits, five cushens and to cubbard cloths £1 8*s.*

In the other Chamber

One fether bed and boulster and one flock boulster and curtens and bedsted with all that belongs to it £4.

One flock bed and all that belong to it £1 10*s.*

Three coffers and one trunke, one table bord, a presse and baskett chayer [*illegible deletion*] £1 6*s.* 8*d.*

Tuo peare of flexon sheets and three holand sheetts £2 10*s.*

Fower table cloths and fivetene napkins £1.

One duzen of towells 6*s.*

A pare of pillow cases 2*s.* 6*d.*

For one pare of flexon and toe par of canvis sheetts £1 6*s.* 8*d.*

His waring apparill £5.

For a boule tipet with silver £1.

In the Chamber our the Kitchen

Two flock beds, ruge and boulster and bedsted and all that belong to him £2.

In the Kitchen

13 peuter platers, one bason, 4 buter dishes, 5 potengers, 3 peuter candell stickes, one flaggon, one tankard, one soult, one coup, on chamber pot £2 13*s.* 6*d.*

3 brase pots, one posnett, 3 skillits, 4 kittells, a copper pan, a warmen pan, a bras ladell and skimer [and bras sceals *added*] £4 3*s.* 6*d.*

6 stouls, a table bord 10*s.*

A pare of fier iorns and dogs, toe spits and rack, a jack, toe pare of hingls 13*s.* 4*d.*

In the Seller

A silt, a cive and powdering tube and 4 barills £1.

A screne, a bushell and pecke 10*s.* 10*d.*

A table bord and cubbard in the hall £1.

A furnis, and toe stone to wet barly £2.

Wood in the backsid £4 10*s.*

A gerner in the backside £2.

In the Shop

3 plankes and in the out house bords 18*s.*

6 ackers of corne that was in the fild £10.

26 lb of forles 12*s.* 6*d.*

For lumber goods about the house 14*s.* 4*d.*

Total £59 10*s.*

John Bousher and Thomas Ingles, appraisors.

Buried St. Mary 20 June 1666.

Bond 2 October 1666, administration to Thomas Keynton, intestate's son.

169 ROBERT LOOKER[1]

blacksmith 3 February 1666/7 P1/L/158

In the [*Best* deleted] *Inner Chamber*

One bedsteed, one feather bed and one boulster, 2 pillowes, one pair of sheets and one paire of blankets £3.

One chest and one table board and frame 6*s.*

His wearinge apparrell £2.

In the Middle Chamber
One bedsteed, one flockbed and one bolster, one paire of blankets, one pair of sheets, one coverlid £1 10s. 6d.
One table board, one chest, one coffer, one box 11s.

In the Hall
Brass pots and kittles £1 11s.
And in pewter £1.
One iron pot, one warminge pan 4s.
One cubberd, one table board, one chaire, one fourm, two join stooles and one chest 12s.
One paire of andirons, one paire of dogs, one fire shovell, one paire of tongs, one spitt and one paire of pothooks 10s.

In the Wareshop
For marketware £9.

In the Workshop
The anvill and bellows, the cold trow and 2 vices and other tooles and old iron £8 11s.

In the out house
One furnace 15s.

In the Buttery
4 barrells, 4 coules and 1 kiver £1.
The shop book £2.
The lease of the house £1 10s.

In the Backside
One grindstone and wood and posts £1.
In lumber about the house 5s.

Total £35 5s. 6d.

Paid for attendinge the familie in the time of their sicknesse and for his buryinge and for other maintenance £7 3s. 3d.[2]

John Bowsheire and Richard Buckinham, appraisors.

Buried St. Mary 1 July 1666.
Bond 3 October 1666, administration to Alice Looker, intestate's daughter; inventory exhibited 3 May 1667.

1. 'who disceased the fierst day of July in the yeare of our Lord God 1666'.
2. Administratrix's expenses should not form part of the inventory.

170 MARGRETT REDFORD
widow 8 February 1666/7 P1/R/127

In the Chamber below
Two peeces of gold £2 2s.
And in silver £1 10s. 10d.
And six brass kitles, two kitell potes and a posnett, two skilets and a brass pott and a brass paire of skeales £3.
A paire of [*illegible deletion*] hangings and a gridiron and a paire of flesh hookes 1s.
One flock bead, one fether bolster, three fether pillowes, three blankets and two rudges £2 6s. 8d.
Five sheets with other small linen £1 10s.
A livery beadsted, a matt and cord and one chest, one box, one cofer, one hanging cuberd, one stoole, one baskett and one flaskett with other wooden ware £1.
In lumber 6s. 8d.

In the Chamber over the Hall
One bead, one bolster, one blankett and one rudg £1.
One grooneing chaire, one cofer with other lumber 3s.

In the Hall
One paire of andirons, one paire of iron doges, one fire pan, one paire of tonges, two paire of hangings, one spitt, three stele plates and a tosting iron 5s. 6d.
One tablebord, one frame, [one *deleted*]

three chaires, three stooles, one litell cuberd with other lumber 13*s.* 4*d.*

In the Seler
Foure kivers, foure litell barilles, two tubes, one buckett and one paile with other lumber 12*s.*

In the Kitchen
One litell furnis, one still with other lumber 10*s.*

In the Backside
One pidg 10*s.*
[In *deleted*] wood £1.
Her weareing clothes £2.
Seaven quarters of barely £4 4*s.*

Total £22 15*s.*

Henry Cowssey and Thomas Burges, appraisors.

Buried St. Mary 7 February 1666/7 'widow Redford'.
Commission 11 February 1666/7, oath administered 14 February 1666/7 to Cicily Garlick; bond 14 February 1666/7, administration to Cicily Garlick, intestate's daughter.

171 CLEMENT SMITH
waggoner 11 February 1666/7 P1/S/382

His weareing apparrell and mony in his purse £2 10*s.*[1]
Five horse beasts with harnis to them belonging £8 10*s.*
A wagon with lyne and wraper £3 10*s.*
One acre and a halfe of wheate and fetch in grasse £1 10*s.*

In the Hall
A setle, a table bord and frame, two stoles and a forme, one chaire 16*s.*
One paire of andirons, a paire of dogs, an iron barr, a dripping pan, a broache, a gridiron, a paire of hangings, firepan and tongs, a warmeing pan with other lumber 16*s.*

In the Chamber over the Hall
One feather bed, a boulster, two pillowes, a flock bed and boulster, a paire of blankcetts, one rugg, curteynes and valianc with bedsted, cord and matt £5.
Three paire of sheets, two paire of pillow beares, a dozen of napkins, three table clothes 18*s.*
A chest, a table bord and frame, one forme, two chaires, a side cubberd, a close stoole and pan, a paire of coale irons with lumber 12*s.*

In the Chamber over the Shopp
A side bord, two stooles, a chest, a coffer 6*s.*

In the Garret
A flocke bed and boulster, a coverlett and blanckett, besteed, matt and cord 13*s.* 4*d.*

In the Buttery
A brasse pan, a brasse pott and skellet, a ketle, twelve peeces of pewter, a poudering tubb, a barrell and safe £1 10*s.*

In the Ketching
A furnace, a frying pan, a kever, a cowle with tubbs with lumber 13*s.* 4*d.*

Total £27 4*s.* 8*d.*

[*added in a different hand*
Desporat detes besides £2.]

Robert Carpenter, Henry Cowssey and Thomas Waldern, appraisors.

Buried St. Mary 6 February 1666/7.

Renunciation 13 February 1666/7 by Susanna Smith, intestate's widow, and William Smith, carrier, intestate's eldest son, in favour of Elizabeth Smith, intestate's daughter; bond 15 Feb 1666/7, administration to Elizabeth Smith.

1. Roman numerals throughout.

172 WALTER TITCOMBE[1]

?shoemaker [inventory goods] 6 March 1666/7 P1/T/147

24 sheep at 2*s*. 6*d*. a peece £3.
2 pigs £2.
One cow £1 4*s*.
His wereinge apparrell £3 10*s*.
One feather bed, 2 flock beds, one feather bolster and 3 feather pillowes, one flock bolster, one flock pillow, [one *deleted*] 5 blankets, one rugg, one coverlid £2 10*s*.
2 livery bedsteeds and one trundell bedsteed 5*s*.
4 brass kittles, one brasse pot, one iron pot, 1 small skillet, one warminge pan, a bastinge ladel £1 10*s*.
2 pair of hangells, a pair of tongs and fire pan and one fryinge pan and 2 candlesticks [one spitt *added*] 2*s*. 6*d*.
2 Bibles 1*s*.
Pewter 5*s*.
5 small barrells and two firkins 8*s*.
2 old tablebords and frames, one fourm, 2 old chaires 5*s*. 8*d*.
3 chests, 3 coffers and 2 boxes 12*s*.

[*In the Shop* added]
Nineteene dozen of shooes and 4 paire vallued at 18*s*. a dozen £15 3*s*.
Owinge upon the shopbook great part thereof desperate debt £25.
The state in the house £2.
For wooll in the house £2.
One hollond sheet, 2 hollond pillow cases, 3 canvas sheets, half a dozen of napkins, one canvas bedcase, one canvas tablecloth, 2 canvas pillowcases and 2 canvas bolstercases 14*s*.
Wood and other othe lumber in [and about *added*] the house £1 10*s*.

Total £60 0*s*. 2*d*.

Simon Boullton and John New, appraisors.

Burial not recorded.
Inventory exhibited 2 May 1667; bond 3 October 1667, administration to Dorothy Titcombe, intestate's widow.

1. 'who diseased the tenth day of August in the yeare of our Lord God one thousand six hundred sixty and six'; 'Tidcombe' on bond.

173 SUSAN[1] GUY

widow [bond] 18 April 1667 P1/G/204

One brass pott, one brass pann, two brass ketles, two brass skillets £1 8*s*.[2]
Hangell and pothookes, iron dogs and smale iron hoabes [old fyer pann *added*] 2*s*. 4*d*.
One old tablebord and joyne forme and two joyne stooles, two coffers, one broad box 9*s*.
Three cheyers, old trunke and one coffer, two letle barels, [fryen pan *added*] 5*s*.
One joyne cubberd and stand, two shelves, two letle kivers and one cowle, two low stoles, paile, sid cubbord, other lumber 5*s*.
One fether bed and flockbed, one flock boyster, one fether boyster, [three *deleted*] two fether [pillow *added*], two blancketts and one rugg and the standing bedsteed with matt and cord £3.
One pewter flagin, tw pewter dishes, one pewter sacer and brass candlesticke and one latten pann, pewter porenger and other 5*s*.

In money 17*s*., five sheets, three hollan pillabeares, three diaper napkins and [one *deleted*] twoo towell, one sid cubberd cloth £1 10*s*.
All her weareing apparell both both lyninge and woollen 12*s*.

Total £7 16*s*. 6*d*.

Myhill Bayly and [Symon *in preamble, signs* Francis] Purdue, appraisors.

Buried St. Mary 14 April 1667.
Will 11 April 1667; bond 19 April 1667, administration to Bartholomew Benger, executor; inventory exhibited 30 May 1667.

1. Susanna on will.
2. Roman numerals throughout.

174 JOHN WATERLIN

19 April 1667 P1/W/276

On fether bed and bedsted and that [that *repeated*] belongs to it £2.
On chest, on coffer 8*s*.
On lefery bedsted, on coffer 6*s*. 8*d*.
On floke bead, on fether bolster, 2 fether pellos, on flock bolster, on rougge, on pair of blankets and a standing bedsted with courtains £3.
2 chestes, on box, on sid cobberd, on litell coberd £1.
On tabell bord and fram, on carpete 10*s*.
3 rushen chaiers, 2 cushins 5*s*.
On tabell bord and frame 10*s*.
On round tabell 7*s*.
3 chaiers in the hall 5*s*.
3 stolls, on litell forme 3*s*.
On Bibell with the rest of the bookes £1.
On bras ketell, on bras pote, on posnet, on skilet, on chafendish, 2 warminpans, on kandll sticke £1 6*s*.
Eleven peces of peuter, 2 latan dripings pans and a bryler £1.
4 baralls, 2 coules, on selt, on pouldring tube, on civer, 3 tubes, on tabll and form in the seler, on which 9*s*.
3 bushlls of wheete £1 17*s*.
On bushell and a half bushell and a gallen, on screne, 6 shovles, 3 maltseves £1.
1 pece of backen 6*s*.
On paier of andiers, 2 spites, 2 pair of toungs, 2 fier shufells, 4 pair of kotrels, on pair of pothokes, on peuter chamber pote 14*s*. 6*d*.
2 gridiorns, 2 stellplats, on clever, on mincing knife, on iern bare, on spad, on mathoocke 12*s*. 6*d*.
On cow £2.
4 paier of shetes and on shete, 3 pair of holen pelibers, 2 paire of cavnas, on pair of lockeram pelibers, 3 tabell clothes, on dusen of naptikins £2 16*s*.
Wearing parill £2 10*s*.
The wood and lumber £2.
Moneyes due to the deceased £12.

Total £38 5*s*. 8*d*.

Edward Lawarance and Thomas Trinder, appraisors.

Buried St. Peter 17 April 1667 'Waterlen'.
Bond 4 May 1667, administration to Anne Waterlin, intestate's widow.

175 ALCE MAYO

widow 17 July 1667 P1/M/202

Her wearing apparell £10.[1]
In moneys £30.
One feather bed and flockbed, one rugg and 4 blanketts and feather bolstere and 4 pillowes, curtanes and vallins and carpett £5 10*s*.
In lyninge all sorts £6.
3 gold rings and other silver plate £9.
In pewter and bras and iron £1 6*s*.
3 old trunks, 2 old chayres and 2 old

stooles, two old joyne stooles and other lumber £1 10*s.*
In books 10*s.*
One looking glass and one cushon 6*s.*
Ann annuitie off foureteen yeares at £11 per anum £80.
In debts £31.

Total £175 2*s.*

William Gough, Roger Blagden and Bartholomew Benger, appraisors.

Buried St. Peter 15 July 1667 'Mrs Alice May widow'.
Will 11 July 1667; probate 22 July 1667 to executor [John Martyn, testator's son 'and only child'].

1. Roman numerals throughout.

176 WILLIAM HOBBS[1]

husbandman 22 October 1667
P1/H/380

3 beds, 3 bolsters and 4 pillowes £4.
2 rugs, 1 coverlid and 4 blankets £1.
3 bedsteds 13*s.* 4*d.*
2 trunks, 1 chest and 1 box 8*s.*
3 old tablebords and 3 chaires 10*s.*
5 bushells of wheatt 12*s.* 6*d.*
Sempstry ware, lace and other small things and linnen cloth £16.
4 kettles, 2 brass pots, 1 iron pott, 1 brass pan, 4 skilletts, 2 warming pans £2.
1 dozen of pewter dishes, 8 pottengers, 1 flagon, 1 tankard, 2 chamberpotts and other small saucers and dripin pan £1 5*s.*
4 barrells, 1 hogshead, 4 kivers and other wooden lumber in the buttry 15*s.*
1 fire pan, 1 pair tongs, 1 pair dogs, 1 pair andirons, 2 spitts, 2 pair pot hangills, 1 small furnace 15*s.*
1 old chest, 1 forme and stooles 5*s.*
Wood in the backside and garden, 1 old malt mill, 1 stone and grindstone, well bucket and chayne and other lumber in the backside £10 10*s.*
1 old tilt, tressells and lugs for 1 standing 6*s.*
1 bay nagg £2.
Bridle, saddle and hors meatt 5*s.*
Sheetes and pillowbeares and his wearing apparrell 15*s.*
1 lease of a cottage during 2 lives £10.

Total £51 19*s.* 10*d.*

Richard Baath, Samuel Fowler and Martin Lipyeatt, appraisors.

Buried St. Peter 3 September 1667.
Inventory exhibited 19 October 1667;[2] bond 22 October 1667, administration to Margaret Hobbs, intestate's widow.

1. 'of the Parish of St Peters in Marlebrough'.
2. This date does not agree with that of the inventory.

177 HENRY KYBBLE

glazier 14 January 1667/8 P1/K/69

His weareing apparrell £1 6*s.* 8*d.*
[In money at interest £13 15*s.* 4*d.* *added*]

In the Hall
One tableboard and frame and ioyned forme, [*illegible deletion*] one ioyned cupboard, one ioyned chayre, one rushen chaire, one low ioyned stoole, one bacon racke, [a bill hooke *added*] 16*s.* 6*d.*
Twoo Bibles and other old bookes 2*s.*
Twoo paire of hangells, twoo iron dogges, one andire, one spitt, one fire pan, a paire of tonges, a fryeing pan, a paire of billowes, one spade, a little low stoole 7*s.*

In the Buttery
[Two *deleted*] one brasse potte, one iron

pott, twoo kettles, one skillett, one latten drippin pan, one earthern platter, one woodden platter, twoo pottledds, one paire of pott hookes 10*s.*

In the Seller
Three barrells, twoo tubbes, one paile, one kyver 6*s.*

In the Chamber
One bedsteed, [one *added*] matt and cord, one [fether *added*] bedd, one blankett, [one *added*] rugg, a [fether *added*] boulster, twoo [fether *added*] pyllowes, one sheete and a halfe sheete, twoo pillowcases, one old dust bedd, one old dust pillow, twoo peeces of old coverledds £3.
Fower pewter platters, a pewter tankard, one pewter salt, one pewter chamber pott, twoo pewter poringers, twoo pewter sawcers, a brasse ladle, a skymer 18*s.*
Child bedd lynnen [and woollen *added*] 5*s.*
Twoo little peeces of bacon 2*s.*
One chest, one joyned stoole, one ver box, twoo old coffers 12*s.*
A childs chayre, twoo crates, a cheese racke, a wooden cupp, a search, a seeve, an old tubb, a wooden bottle and a little other [old *added*] lumber 3*s.* 4*d.*

In the Shopp
A vice, a mould, twoo soudering irons, a paire of clippers, a collering stone and pibble, twoo melting panns, an iron melting kittle with some other shopp tooles £1 10*s.*
A little souder and ragg, tyn, twoo barrs of lead and a little cast lead 5*s.*
In glasse £2.
Workeing boards, shelves and boxes 3*s.*

In the Backside
A well buckett and chaine [and tumbrill and handle *added*] and a [*illegible deletion*] mault [mill *added*] £1 2*s.*
His estate in [the *deleted*] his twoo tenements £2.

Total [illegible amount deleted] £29 3*s.* 10*d.*

John Bassett and Richard Oatredg, appraisors.

Buried St. Peter 22 December 1667 'Henry Keble'.
Will 10 October 1667; probate 8 May 1668 to John Kibble; bond 8 May 1668, administration to John Kibble, testator's brother, during minority of John Kibble, testator's son and executor.

178 GEORGE CLARKE
pinmaker 14 April 1668 P1/C/285

His bedding £2 10*s.*
His beedsteed 6*s.*
One chest, one coffer and a box 6*s.* 3*d.*
His pewter 5*s.*
His lininge 2*s.* 2*d.*
A brasse kittle and irone pott 8*s.*
An irone greate 2*s.* 6*d.*
His settle 1*s.* 6*d.*
One booke 4*s.*
Some small wares in his shop 16*s.* 8*d.*
For his house rent for five yeares £6 10*s.*
Lumber 10*s.* 3*d.*

Total £12 2*s.* 5*d.* [*recte* £12 2*s.* 4*d.*]

John Stout, John Horner and Nathaniel None [*recte* Hone], appraisors.

Buried St. Mary 6 March 1667/8.
Bond 8 May 1668, administration to Ruth Clarke, intestate's widow.

179 JOHN KNOWLES
yeoman [renunciation] 18 September 1668 P1/K/66

In mony in the house £16 15*s.*
In debts whereof many are casuall £65 6*s.* 10*d.*
Brasse and pewter £1.
One jack, 3 spitts, pot hangills, firepan and tongs and dogs 6*s.* 8*d.*
One fether bed, 2 dust beds, 3 flock bolsters, curtaines and vallence, 4 rugs, 2 high bedsteeds, 2 trundle bedsteds with matts and cords £4.
7 paire sheets and one od sheet, 2 pair of pillowberes, one table cloth and 6 napkins £2.
2 chests, 2 little coffers, 1 cubbord 6*s.* 8*d.*
1 tablebord and 6 stooles 10*s.*
A cow and 7 pigs £4.
Cleft wood, faggots and poles £7.
Lumber £1.
Wearing apparrell £2.

Total £104 5*s.* 2*d.*

Henry Cowssey and John Boosher, appraisors.

Buried St. Mary 16 September 1668.
Renunciation 24 September 1668 by Thomas, Susanna, Mary and Sarah Knowles, in favour of John Hill; bond 5 October 1668, administration to John Hill during the minority of Elizabeth, William, Nathaniel, Symon, Martha and Katherine Knowles.

180 EDWARD MILLINGTON[1]

carpenter 14 November 1668

P1/M/209

His weareing apparell 10*s.*[2]

In the Chamber over the Hale
One livery bedsted, matt and cord, to coverleds, two old blanketts, one flockebed, one paire sheetts, two flock boysters, two fether pillowes £1 10*s.*
One par of old sheets and two pillow cases 4*s.*
Two chests, two joyne cheyers, four old [two *deleted*] boxes, two low [joyn *added*] stoles and 4 litle planckes 16*s.*

In the Hale
One tablebord and frame, four joyne stooles, two formes, one side cubberd and one old cubberd, one old cheyer and other lumber 18*s.*
Three brass kitles, two brass potts, one brass posnett, one brass skillett, one skimer £1.
Two spitts, on par andyers, fierpann and tongs, iron morter and pessell, one par of potthokes, one par hangles, beif pricker, billows 5*s.*
Three dishes of pewter, one butter dish, one pewter candlesticke, one salt, two borrengers, one chamberpott and one aquavite botle 7*s.*
Two barels, two covles, four kivers and shelves in the shopp and in the buttery 10*s.*

In the Garrett
One selt, two side of a setle and other lumber 6*s.*
Four plaines, three joynters, two hand sawes, one tennt saw, one axx, one hatshett, four [aker *deleted*] augers, chessels and all the rest of twoles and a letle parcell of fagotts £1.
Rent due from Robert Millingetonn when his father dyed £1 1*s.* 10*d.*
There is due frome Robert Millingetonn for washinge his cloathes for three yeares at three shillings and four pence per the yeare and the yeare ended at midsooomer last 12*s.*
All the tooles with one great scale, beame, two paddels and spade which all are in the hands of Robert Millingeton 4*s.*
One lookeinge glass and one iron bar 4*s.*

Total £9 7*s.* 10*d.*

Bartholomew Benger and John Munday, appraisors.

Buried Preshute 11 August 1668 'of St Peter Marlborough'.
Will 1 September 1654, probate 3 October 1668 to Eleanor Millington, testator's widow; inventory exhibited 12 Dec 1668.

1. Signs 'Myllington' on will.
2. Roman numerals throughout.

181 WILLIAM STEVENS[1]

23 November 1668 P1/S/398

His weareing apparell £5.[2]
[*illegible deletion*] the lease of his howse £60.
4 smale piggs £1.
One small hogge £1 10*s*.
Six bedds with the furniture £10.
[Three *deleted*] five table boards and furmes £3 14*s*.
One hogshead £1.
One dozen of pewter and three pewter candle potts, 4 porringers £1 12*s*.
2 brasse potts, 3 kittles, 1 skillett, 3 jron drippinge panns, 5 spitts, 2 jacks, 3 chaines, hangell, fire pann, 2 racks, 2 fenders and other things in the kitchen £5.
The wood in the backside £7.
The maultmill 10*s*.
8 flaggons, 1 pewter candlesticke £1.
Three ioyned stooles, 1 chaire, 2 table boards and some od lumber 13*s*.

In the Sellar
11 barrells, old tubbs, 1 meashing fate, a flaskett and other lumber [together with one old furnace and some cole *added*] 1*s*.

In the Hall and Shop
Two table bords and frame and forme 10*s*.
In hay £6.
[*illegible line deleted*]
Debts oweing to the testator £4.

Total £110 19*s*.

William Tarrant, Richard Shipreeve and William Wicksey, appraisors.

Buried St. Mary 13 November 1668.
Bond 23 November 1668, administration to Dorothy Stevens, intestate's widow; inventory exhibited 25 November 1668.

1. 'of the parish of St Mary the Virgin in Marlebrough'.
2. Roman numerals throughout.

182 RICHARD IDNYE

?blacksmith [inventory goods] 6 December 1668 P1/IJ/88

His wearing apparel £2 10*s*.
One flock bed, 2 bolsters, one pillow, a blanket and a rug 15*s*.
Two coffers 5*s*.
A bushel of wheat 3*s*.
3 quarters of a hundred of iron 14*s*.
Five shovels and three spades 4*s*.
Five pewter platters, one flagon, one tankard, one chamberpot 7*s*.
Two kettles, one brass pot and two skillets 4*s*.
One table board and frame, four joynd stooles, two chaires and a settle 6*s*. 8*d*.
One anvil, one pair of bellows, one bikern, one vice, one coletrough, two sledges, one hand hammer and a nailing hammer and the rest of the small tooles £5.
One grind stone and trough 5*s*.
Firewood and lumber 10*s*.
One pigg 12*s*.
Two barrels and a rundlet 5*s*.
Market ware 12*s*.
[*Sum total* 12^{li} deleted]

One jack, one spit and a dripping pan 2*s*. 6*d*.

Total £12 15*s*. 2*d*.

Stephen Hide, John Phillipps and William Rose, appraisors.

Buried St. Mary 8 December 1668 'Richard Idney'.
Commission 10 December 1668, oath administered [*blank*] 1668 to Joane Idney; bond 21 December 1668, administration to Joane Idney, intestate's widow.

183 MARGARETT BRUNSDON

widow 10 December 1668 P1/B/454

One table board and frame, one old cupboard, one furme, one settle, one ioyned stoole and warming pan, two pair of hangells, two spitts, one pair of doggs, one fire pan and tongs 16*s.* 8*d.*
Her owne and other wearing apparrell £2 13*s.* 4*d.*
The bedsteeds and bedding in the severall chambers with one table cloath and two napkins and two carpetts, three table boards, two frames, two furmes, one bench and other lumber £10 16*s.* 8*d.*
Three chests, fower coffers, one box and other lumber £1 1*s.* 4*d.*
In brasse and pewter £4 10*s.* 8*d.*
One furnace and iron grate, a pair of andirons, a meshing tubb, kivers, cowles, barrells and one stand, one cupboard, a gridiron, two friing pans and other lumber £4 4*s.*
The well buckett and chayne and coale 5*s.*
In wheat £1 3*s.* 4*d.*
In wood £2.
One pigge 9*s.*
The lease of the house £2.
In desperate debt £2 10*s.*

Total £32 10*s.*

John Bassett, Robert Millington and Nicholas Greenaway, appraisors.

Buried St. Peter 11 October 1668, 'Margreat Bronson [BT Brunsen] widow'.
Will 26 September 1668; probate not recorded; commission 5 November 1668, oath administered 9 December 1668 to William Brinsdon, executor [testator's son]; inventory exhibited 15 December 1668.

184 FRANCES HEARST[1]

[*undated*, c.1668/9] P1/H/396

A porcion of fower hundred pounds alloted to have byn paid to the said Frances out of landes in Clattford att thend of one yeare next after the decease of Richard Goddard Esqr her late father together with fowerscore and sixteene poundes arrere and unpaid of one annuity of 24[2] poundes per annum payable in the meane tyme out of the said lands for the interest of the said porcion in all £496.

Buried Preshute 2 January 1664, 'the wife of Mr John Hearst of Marlborough'.
Commission 29 December 1668, oath administered 6 February 1668/9 to Mary Carter and Elizabeth Goddard; bond 6 February 1668/9, administration to Mary Carter, widow, and Elizabeth Goddard, widow, both of Old Upton, Worcs, intestate's sisters; inventory exhibited 10 March 1668/9.

1. 'the late wife of John Hearst late of Marlebrough apothecary'.
2. Written 'xxiiij^{tie}'.

185 WILLIAM BAKER[1]

gardener [*undated*, c.1669] P1/B/457

In his Lodging Chamber
His wearing cloaathes: dublet, britches and coat with some other materialls both

for woolen and lining £2.
2 old feather beds, 4 old [feather *added*] bolsters and 4 small [feather *added*] pillows and one rug, one coverled, 3 blankets £3.
In the same chamber 3 doulace sheets, one holland sheet, 2 pair of canvas sheets, one dozen of naptkins, one table cloath, a paire of pillowbees £2.
One join bedssteed and one trundle bedsteed with mats and coards 12*s.*
One small chest, one small trunk, 2 [timber *added*] boxes, 4 joinestooles 12*s.*

In the Hall
One tableboard and frame, one join fourm, 2 chaires and a small hanging cubberd 8*s.*

In a little Buttery
3 small barrells and belonging, one coule and one kiver 5*s.*

In the Hall
Of brasse: 2 kittles, 2 pots, 5 small skillets, 3 of bell mettle and 2 of brasse, one basting ladle and skimmer, one braskandlestick £1 8*s.*
Pewter: 7 platters, 2 pewter basons, 2 flagons, one tankerd, 3 butter dishes, 2 salts, 2 candlesticks, one old chamberpot, 2 saucers, 1 porringer 12*s.*
Iron: 1 pair of tongs, 1 firepan, a paire dogs, a small pair of andiers, 1 pair of hangles, one gredian and frying pan and 1 paire of pothooks and one spit 4*s.*
A nag and a cow and calf £3.
A cock of hey 15*s.*
A tenement at Wilton called Pigsmarsh £7.
Lumber about the house 5*s.*

Total £22 1*s.*

William Godfor, Richard Hawkins and Nicholas Grenaway, appraisors.

Burial not recorded.
Will 9 July 1669; probate not recorded; inventory exhibited 13 September 1669.

1. 'who disceased the 8th of August in the yeare of our Lord God one thousand six hundred sixty and nine'.

186 JOHN BUTLER[1]

collarmaker 16 May 1670 P1/B/461

In The Hall
8 pewter dishes, 2 pewter plates, one saucer, 1 pewter porringer, 1 little flagon and 1 tanckard 18*s.*
3 brasse kettles 15*s.*
Two little brasse pots, 1 little skillett, one frying pan, 3 basten ladles, 1 skimer 5*s.*
One jack, 3 spitts, 3 drippinpans 9*s.*
One tableboard, 3 joynestooles, 3 chaires 6*s.* 6*d.*
One paire of andirons, 1 peare of doggs, one paire of hangings, 1 firepan and tonges 2*s.* 6*d.*

In the Buttry
One cubboard, 1 tableboard, two joyne stooles 4*s.*

In the Best Chamber
1 silver cup £1 10*s.*
One round table and three chaires 14*s.*
One bed, 1 bolster, five pillowes £2.
One bedsted with [other *deleted*] curtaines and vallions and one carpett 12*s.* [. . .].
One looking glasse, 1 payre of doggs, a firepan and tonges, 1 rugge, 2 blanketts £1.

In the other Chamber
One chest, one box, two payre of sheetes, 2 board cloathes, halfe a dozen of napkins, two payre of pillow cases 18*s.*

In the Garrett
One bed and bedsted, one bolster, one pillow, one coverled, 1 payre of blanketts £1.

In the Shopp
Foure bull hides, 23 horse hides, ten calves skins £8.
For halters and pipes £2.
For collers, padds and pannells £2.
And for other shopp goods £1 10*s.*
The shopp booke £47 2*s.* 7*d.*
A horse, bridle and saddle £3.
A parcell of wood 10*s.*

In the Cutting
One furnace 16*s.*
For his wareing cloathes £2.

In The Celler
5 barrells, 1 cowle, one tubb and other lumber goods £1.
Two little tennements £30.

[*Total omitted*]

Waltar Sagar, William Hitchcock and Sithne [*recte* Swithin] Yong, appraisors.

Buried St. Mary 12 May 1670.
Will 29 June 1669; probate and inventory exhibition not recorded.

1. The preamble states 'deceased 19 Maij 1670'; this does not agree with the date of the burial, perhaps 9 May was intended.

187 EDWARD WIND[1]
?shoemaker [inventory goods] 16 July 1670 P1/W/294

His wearinge apparrell £2.[2]
Foure paire of sheetes 12*s.*
For other lyninge 5*s.*
One fether bed, one fether boystor, two fether pillowes, two flocke pillowes, coverled and blanketts and standinge bedsteed, curtaines and vallens £2 10*s.*
In pewter of all sorts £1 4*s.*
One warmeinge and two brass candlestickes 5*s.*
Two tablebords, joyne stooles and cheyers, chest, side cubberd, boxes, two cussions, fyerpann and tongs, one paire of dogs and other lumber £1 4*s.*
Two Bibles and other bookes 5*s.*
One flockebed, two flocke boysters, two ruggs, two blancketts with the bedsteed etc £1.

In the Hale
One tablebord and frame and press, and in the letle room by, one flockbed, coverled and blancketts and old bedsteed and other lumber in the hale £1.
One furniss, two brass potts, one kitle and one possnett and two litle skilletts £1 10*s.*
Six barrels, three tubbs and two kivers 16*s.*
One jacke, two spits, andyers and doggs 10*s.*

In the Shopp
Six dozen of mens shooes at 34*s.* a [dozen *deleted*] paire £10 4*s.*
Twenty paire of smale shoes £2 5*s.*
Six paire of other smale shooes 9*s.*
Two dozen and [eight *added*] paire of woemens with lethren heeles £3 14*s.* 8*d.*
Foure dozen and three paire of woemen wooden heeles shooes £5 10*s.* 6*d.*
Foure paire of bootes and one paire ledgt £2 6*s.*
Two dozen and two paire of children shoes £1 6*s.*
Seaven upper leather hides and four benns £8 10*s.*
Foure dozen of lasts 16*s.*
Other lumber goods in the shopp 5*s.*

Goods att Thomas Chamberlayne

One flockebed and flock boyster and two old blancketts, two old sheets, one coverleds, one chest, one box, curtaines and vallens, one bedstedd, matt and cord, one paire of dogs, tongs and fierpan and hangles, one litle cubberd, one old barrell, one tunnbowle, one cheyer and one shelfe £1 6*s.*
Debts due uppon the shopp booke £51 10*s.*

Total £101 3*s.* 2*d.*

Oweinge to divers personns by the said deceased the sum of £45 9*s.*[3]
Soe there rest £55 14*s.* 2*d.* of which a great parte is desperate

Walter Parsonns als Sagar[4], Mihill Bayly and Bartholomew Benger, appraisors.

Buried St. Mary 1 March 1669/70.
Bond 27 July 1670, administration to Dorothy Wind, intestate's widow.

1. 'Wyne' on bond.
2. Roman numerals throughout.
3. Debts owing by the deceased should not form part of the inventory.
4. Signs 'Waltar Sagar'.

188 SAMMUELL ALEXANDER

27 September 1670 P1/A/124

4 keetelle brasse and 2 brasse potes and 2 skeletes and warmen pane £3.
6 peuter dyshes and 3 flagens and to cupes and to candelle stickes 14*s.* 8*d.*

In the Halle
1 tabell borde, 2 sidbordes, 1 cuberd £1.
1 setell, 3 chaieres, 1 forme [*value not given*]
3 broches, 1 pere of andeiers, 1 bakenracke, 1 fryenpan, 1 dripenpan and sum other small thinges 6*s.* 8*d.*

In the Chamber
2 fetherbedes and 1 flockbed and the aburtonences to it £7.
1 tabelborde and 4 ginstolles 14*s.*
3 chestes, 5 letell boxes, 1 draer, 1 presse £1.
For all the linen that hee had £1 10*s.*
For sum lumbe thinges in the cokloft 2*s.* 6*d.*
For his waring aperell £3.
For 4 barells and a cive and all the rest of the woden vessell £1 6*s.* 8*d.*
For moni ouing to him upon bandes from severall peopall, the which wee have had the site of the bandes, that is 1 hundred and 3 skore and 18 pounde [£178.]

Total £197 14*s.* 6*d.*

Thomas Bathe and Robert Millington, appraisors.

Buried St. Peter 29 September 1670.
Bond 23 August 1671, administration to Ruth Alexander, intestate's widow.

189 WILLIAM BATCHELLER

husbandman 27 October 1670
P1/B/465

His wareinge apparell £1 10*s.*[1]
Money uppon specialty £146.
23lb of woole att 9*d.* [a pound *added*] 17*s.* 3*d.*
One chest and coffer 6*s.*
Sub-total £148 13*s.* 3*d.*

Other money due to the testator without bond £13.

Total £151 13*s.* 3*d.* [*recte* £161 13*s.* 3*d.*]

Mihill Bayly and John Bayly, appraisors.

Buried St. Mary 23 October 1670.
Will 13 September 1670; probate not

recorded; commission 1 November 1670, oath administered 3 November 1670 to John Batchelor and Thomas Engles, executors; inventory exhibited 9 November 1670.

1. Roman numerals throughout.

190 JOHN WYAT

yeoman 8 December 1670 P1/W/302

His wearinge apparrell £2.[1]

In the Gatehouse Chamber

Two flockebeds, two flockeboysters, one pillow, two ruggs with bedsteed, matt and cord £2.

Two coffers, one chest, two boxes and other lumber 10s.

Halfe a hundred of chese 10s.

In the Chamber over the Hale

Two flockebeds, two flockeboysters, one pillow, two ruggs, one standinge bedsteed, one trucklebed £1 10s.

One tablebord, one forme and two cheyers 8s.

In the Kitchinge Chamber

Two flockebeds, two flockeboysters, one fether pillow, one two coverleds, three old boysters, two livery bedsteeds, one truckle bedsteed £1 10s.

In the Fox [*Chamber* deleted] *and Seller*

One tablebord and two hogshead of beare, foure empty casts, three kivers, three tubbs and two peggs £4.

In the Hale

One tablebord, five joyne stoole and other lumber 8s.

In the Kitchinge

Seaven pewter platters, seaven pewter flaggins, one pewter basonn, two pewter chamber potts, two pewter salts, two pewter porringers and three sawsers £1 4s.

One furnish, one great brase kitle, one litle kitle, three brasspotts, two skilletts, brass skimer and warmeinge pann £3.

One measeinge vate and one coule and one small barrell 5s.

One old cubberd, old cheyer, one paire andyers and doggs, fierpann and tongue and two paire hangers, fryeinge pann, two spitts, one grideron and fender and other lumber 8s.

Twelve paire of sheets, one dozen napkins, two table [cloaths *added*] and four pillow cases £1 10s.

In beanes and oats, hey, wood and coales £3.

Three corse flockebeds, one blanckett, one rugg, two coverleds, three old boysters, two livery bedsteeds and one truckle bedsteed £1.

Sub-total £23 3s.

In expences for the funerall sermon and other charges £3.[2]

Total £20 3s.

Barthollomew Benger, Nicholas Rumsey, William Buckland and Walter Seager junior, appraisors.

Buried St. Mary 7 December 1670.

Will 21 November 1670; probate 15 September 1671 to executrix [testator's widow, unnamed in will].

1. Roman numerals throughout.
2. Executor's expenses should not form part of the inventory.

191 HENRY WESTELL[1]

4 February 1670/1 P1/W/305

In his Lodging Roome
His wearing apparell, lining and woolling £2 10*s.*
One hiebedsteed and too truckell beedsteeds £1 4*s.*
His beeds and furniture belonging to them £3
One chest, too coffers, one box 10*s.*
One tableboard 2*s.* 6*d.*

In his Hall
Brasse and pewter 12*s.*
Fire pan, tongs and hangels 2*s.*
Tabelbord, chaires, stools and a littell cubberd 8*s.*
Bookes 10*s.*

In his Buttery
Barrels and brwing vessels 15*s.*

In his Shope and Seller
Tobaco £7
His press, cooting knife, tubes, shevells and lumber £1
Bacon and rack 10*s.*
His maltmill 5*s.*

In his Backside
Woode £1 10*s.*
Pigs £1 10*s.*
Grindstoon and pigtrough 1*s.* 6*d.*
A quartter of malte 16*s.*
[*illegible deletion*] and lumber 5*s.*
Desperate debt 10*s.*

Total £23 1*s.*

Paid for funerall expenses £2[2]

Robert Miles and Anthony G[ree]naway, appraisors.

Buried St. Peter 29 January 1670/1 'Henry Westall'.
Will 21 January 1670/1; inventory exhibited 15 September 1671; probate 16 September 1671 to executrix [Elizabeth Westell, testator's widow].

1. 'of Marlborough In the parish of St Petters Late deseassed January 30th 1670/1' [this date does not agree with the date of the burial].
2. Executor's expenses should not form part of the inventory.

191A RICHARD DAINGERFILD

baker [will] 15 February 1670/1
P1/D/128

Three brase kittells and one brase skillett 15*s.*
One brase pott 6*s.*
One brase warmingpan and a brase candelsteke and to brase skimers 6*s.*
One jorne dripingpan 1*s.*
Three peuter dishes and one peuter flaggon 9*s.*

In the Hall
A pare of aindorans, a pare of tongs and a gridjorne and a spit and a fier showell and three hingells 6*s.* 6d
One tabell bord in the hall and [one *added*] forme and too chayers [and one joyne stole *added*] 10*s.* 6*d.*

In the Litell Rome beehind the Shop
Fower barrells and a dressor bord 15*s.*

In one of the Chambers
One trundell beedsteed and too [flock *added*] beedes and too flock bowlsters and one peare of blanketts and one peare of sheetts and fower civerlids and a flock pillow £1 18*s.* 6*d.*

In the other Chamber
One chest, one tabell bord and thre coffer [and one box *added*] 12s
His waring aparrill £1 10*s.*

In the Oute House
Three ladders and wood 10*s.*
For lumber goods 15*s.*
In monys and depts £2 19*s.* 6*d.*
[Seven ship £1 15*s. added*]
Sub-total £13 6*s.* [*recte* £13 9*s.*]

Desperate debt £10

Total £23 6*s.* [*recte* £23 9*s.*]

The sum of [money *deleted*] the legasies given to Mary Dangerfeild in goods with a house and close £25[1]

Thomas Ingles and Thomas Keinton, appraisors

Buried St. Mary 14 February 1670/1.
Will and codicil 3 August 1670; probate 15 September 1671 to [unnamed].

1. Bequests in the will should not be deducted from the inventory value.

192 RICHARD WEBB[1]

linendraper 24 April 1671 P1/W/299

His waring apparell and books £10

In his Best Chamber
1 feather bed, 1 flock bed and bedsteed, 1 sett rug, 1 blankett, 1 boulster, 1 pillow, curtains and valliens, 6 chayres, 6 cushons, 1 settle, 1 side board, 1 table board, 5 stoole and other implements £8

In the Little Chamber by the Best
1 bed steed, 1 flock bed, 1 boulster, 2 coverleeds, 3 blankets with other implements £1 10*s.*

In the Hall
2 table boards, 4 stooles, 3 chayres, 1 jack, 1 pair of dogs, 1 pair of andiers, 1 fire shovl and tongs with other implements £2

In his Bed Chamber
1 feather bed, 1 flock bed, 1 bedstead, 1 sett rug, 1 boulster, 2 pillows, 1 chest £3

In the Maids Chamber
1 bed steed, 1 flock bed, 1 boulster, 1 coverled, 3 pillows, 2 boxes, 1 close stoole and other implements £2
In linnen: 3 table board cloths, 2 dossen of table napkins, 2 pair of pillow cases, 5 pair of cheets with other small linnen £2

In the Buttery by the Hall
1 iron pott, 2 spitts, 2 candlesticks and other implements 12*s.*

In the Sellar
7 barrells, bruing vessell, 1 furnac with other lumber goods £3
All the bras and pewter in the house £3
In plate and mony in the house £6 10*s.*
In debts good and bad £10
In Silverles Street in St Mary parish in Marlbrow 1 message or tenement £60

In the Barne
3 bushells of wheate 10*s.*

In the Back Side of the Barn
Wood £3

In the Feild
3 acres of corne £5
In sheep £8
In mault £2

Total £130 2*s.*

Joseph Webb and Richard Bell, appraisors.

Buried St. Peter 10 April 1671.

Will 28 May 1669; probate 14 June 1671 to Noah Webb, testator's son.

1. 'Mr.'.

193 STEPHEN PEARCE

gardener [will] 13 June 1671 P1/P/279

His wearing parrell £4
The beding £5 5s.
The set of corting and bedsteed £1
One chest, too boxes, one tabell bord, six joyne stooles, one tronck, one cobard and the rest of the lomber heare in the chamber £3
Bras and powther £2 5s.
Fier pan and thonges, doges and all other lomber heare in the halle 14s.
The bruing vesells and barrells 10s.
The mare and saddells and pannell, other tacklen be long to the mare £2 5s.
The cow and piges £4 10s.
The cowhouse 8s.
The crap in the home garden 5s.
The garden of the east sid of the howse 5s.
The garden in Could Harbor £5 10s.

Total £29 17s.

Francis Purdue, William Jones and William Feild, appraisors.

Buried St. Mary 11 June 1671 'Stephen Pears'.
Will 30 May 1671 'Stephen Parse'; probate 10 July 1672 to Sara Peirce, testator's widow.

194 ISAACK COLE[1]

surgeon 4 September 1671 P1/C/305

In the Kitchen
3 chargers £1 16s.
Two dozen and three pewter plates £2.
Other pewter in the kitchen and about the house £3.
Glasse bottles in the kitchen with that in them 15s.
A dripingpan and fork, a rosting jack and a toasting iron 13s.
Other furniture belonginge to the kitchen of ironworke £2 10s.
One chest with that which is in it £5.
One table board and frame, two joinstooles, one settle, three chaires £1 4s.
Other lumber 5s.

In the Bruehouse
Two furnaces with the ironwork belonging [to them *added*] £5.
For the woodden vessells for bruinge or for washinge £1 10s.

In the Pantry
One still, a limbick and pot £3.
Two kittlepots and one kittle £1 10s.
One bell brasse pot and a bell-brasse skillet 10s.
Three skillets, one skimmer, a brasse scales and weights and a fryingepan 7s. 6d.
A presse 10s.
Fower small tableboards £1.
Other lumber 2s. 6d.

In the Parlour
One paire of andirons and doggs with brasen heads and a fire pan and tongs 15s.
Eight chaires and two stooles £1 5s.
One round table and a carpit 10s.
One deske 3s.

In the New Chamber
One feather bed and bolster and two pillows £3 10s.
A paire of blankets and a rugg £1.
One bedsteed with curtaines and valions £1.
Two table boards and two chairs and one stoole 11s. 8d.

A paire of andirons and doggs with other lumber £1 10s.

In the Chamber over the Kitchen

One bed, one bolster and a paire of pillows with the appurtenances belonginge to it £2 5s.

One other bed and bolster and pillows with two blankets and a rugg and curtaines £3 10s.

Two bedsteeds with matts and cords and curtaine rods £1.

One cubberd table, a paire of andirons with brazen heads, a warminge pan, one lookinge glasse with other lumber £1.

In the Garret

One feather bed and bolster with blankets and a rugg £2.

One flockbed with thappurtenances £1.

Two trundle bedsteeds with mats and cords 10s.

Nine paire of ordinary sheets £2 5s.

Three paire of pillowbees 9s.

6 table cloathes 12s.

Two dozen of napkins and other lumber 7s. 6d.

Page total £55 16s. 2d.

In the Chamber over the Parlor

One feather bed and a bolster and 2 doule pillowes £5.

One rugg and a paire of blankets £1.

One bedsteed with curtaines and vallions of sarge, three chaires and two stooles covered with sarge and two carpits of the same £6.

Two tableboards and a stand 10s.

Six [doule *deleted*] pillows £1.

In plate £16.

One chest, a cubberd and two trunkes 15s.

Two looking glasses £1.

A pair of andirons with brazen heads, a firepan and tongs and a warming pan £1.

In the Inner Chamber

One bed and bolster and 6 pillowes £3 10s.

Fower blankets 10s.

One trundle bedsteed and a chest 8s.

One paire of holland sheets £1 10s.

Seven paire of other sheets £4.

One dozen of dieper naptkins and one dozen of dammask naptkins, two dozen of flaxen and three dozen of others £2 15s.

Three paire of holland pillowcases and a paire of doulace £1.

13 tablecloathes £3 5s.

Lumber in the same chamber 10s.

In the Seller

Six hogsheads, three barrells, 3 stands, one powderinge tub and a dropper £1 5s.

Books about the house £5.

One mare and a colt £4 10s.

Two piggs £2 5s.

His wearinge apparrell £10.

The pompe and a stone £2 15s.

[*remainder in a differrent hand*]

In money and bonds £300.

Page total £375 8s.

On the other side £55 16s. 2d.

Total £431 4s. 2d.

Christopher Lipyeatt and Richard Shepprey, appraisors.

Buried St. Peter 6 July[2] 1671 'Mr Isaac Cole'.

Will 16 June 1671; renunciation 25 July 1671 by John Cole of Kingston in the parish of Ashbury, Berks, testator's brother and William Phillips of Osten in the parish of Ashbury, testator's father-in-law, joint executors; bond 16 September 1671, administration to Martha Cole, testator's widow.

1. '... who deceased the fower and Twentieth

day of July in the yeare of our Lord God one Thousand six hundred seventy and one ...'.

2. This does not agree with the date of death; perhaps 26 July was intended.

195 JOHN BROOKES

innkeeper 31 October 1671 P1/B/482

His weareinge apparell £1 10s.[1]

One fether bed and fether boyster, fether pillowes and all the furniture belonginge to it and the wainescott bedsteed £5.

Three flockebeds and bedsteeds and all the furniture belongeinge to it £7.

Twelve pewter platters and pewter poringer 14s.

Three brass potts, one brass kitle and one large brass pann £4.

Three tablebords, six joyne stooles, two joyne formes, one chest and one coffer and other lumber £1 10s.

Two halfe hogsheads, two barells, two kinderkins and other small vessels £1.

One furnish, measeinge vate, kive, kivers, tubbs and other lumber £4.

Total £24 14s.

John Rumsey and Bartholomew Benger, appraisors.

Burial not recorded.

Will [nuncupative] 'two or three dayes next before his death ... 19 March 1658/9'; commission 23 November 1671, oath administered 28 November 1671 to William Brookes, testator's son; inventory exhibited 7 December 1671.

1. Roman numerals throughout.

196 RICHARD COLLAT

husbandman [will] 31 October 1671 P1/C/302

His waring aparell £4.

1 cofer, 2 chayers, 1 chest, 2 boxes, 1 trunke £1 1s.

1 highe bedsted and father bead and rug [and bedstead *deleted*] and all as belong to it £3.

1 high bedsted and flokbead and rug and cortins and valians £2.

1 loking glase and dogs and irons 5s.

2 pare of tounges, 2 pare of beluses, on grid iron and fire pan and taiper, 1 dripen pan, jock and 2 spits 11s.

1 setll and cobord, 2 tabll bords, 4 gin stols £1.

5 barells and hors and payll 12s.

2 ketll pots, 2 skelats, 1 ketll, 1 iron pot and 1 warning pan £1.

10 dishes of peuter, 1 bosting ladll and skemor, 2 peuter candll stikes, 2 peuter chambr pots, 4 flagons, 4 poringers, 1 saltseler, 2 sasers £2 10s.

Wood in the baksid £1.

1 fier bockat, 1 temser and saich, 2 kevers and shelves and other lumber 10s.

5 pare of shets £1 10s.

In mony and depts £147.

Total £165 19s.

Robert Miles, Coristever Kepins, appraisors.

Buried St. Peter 27 October 1671.

Will 19 October 1671; inventory exhibited 6 November 1671; probate 7 November 1671 to Mary Collet and Ann Collet, testator's daughters.

1. 'of Marelbrough St. Petters'.

197 JOAN HERRING[1]

widow 8 January 1671/2 P1/H/418

Her wearinge apparrell £2.

One feather bed and feather bolster and a flockbed with thappurtenances £2 10s.

One chest and 2 old boxes 4*s.*

In the House

6 dozen of hats £7 10*s.*

One tableboard and frame, 2 joinstooles and 2 chaires 8*s.*

Three kittles, two pots and one small skillet £2.

4 small pewter platters 5*s.*

Iron goods: one jack and one spit, one paire of andirons and one paire of doggs, one dripingpan, a hangles and a fender 10*s.*

Fower small barrells with other wooden vessell 10*s.*

One hors, one pigg, one cow £5.

In the Garden

2 plots of cabidgplants £2.

One small furnace with other working tooles for a hatt maker £1.

Money in the house £45.

Wood and cole and other lumber £1.

Total £69 17*s.*

Paid for the funerall expences £2 5s[2]

Nicholas Grenaway and John Horner, appraisors.

Buried St. Mary 11 December 1671 'Jone Hering widow'.

Will 8 December 1671; probate 11 October 1672 to Francis Herring, testator's son.

1. 'who deceased the 12 December 1671' [this date does not agree with the burial date].
2. Executor's expenses should not form part of the inventory.

198 STEPHEN LONGE

gardener 11 January 1671/2 P1/L/172

His weareinge apparell £1 10*s.*[1]

In the Chamber

Two flockbeds, one fether boyster, one flocke boyster, one fether pillow, three coverleds, one livery bedsteed, one truckle bedsteed and all that doe belonge to them £2.

Two paire of sheetts, one bord-cloath, five [five *repeated*] napkins, two pillocases 10*s.*

One coffer, litle tablebord and six bords, two stoles and other lumber 5*s.*

In the Hale

Nyne pewter platters, four salts, two boules, two porrengers, two sacers £1 6*s.* 8*d.*

One pretty big kittell, two lesser ketles, one brass pan, one pott, one skillett, two brass ladles £1.10*s.*

One paire of iron dogs, a letle paire of tongs, hangers, fryinge pann, one grideron 2*s.*

One table bord, one joyne stoole, one joyne cheyer, two little barrells, two wyer candlestickes and other lumber 10*s.*

One pouderinge tubb, three coules, one whelebarrow, all his tooles, one grinestone and all the lumber in both out houses £1 6*s.*

In plan[. . .] in both gardens £1.

In specialty the sum of £13 10*s.*

The dwellinge house stated for three lives £10.

One great Bible 8*s.*

Total £33 19*s.* 8*d.* [*recte* £33 7*s.* 8*d.*]

Barthollomew Benger and William Brookes, appraisors.

Buried St. Mary 29 December 1671.

Will [nuncupative] 'two or three Dayes next before his Death he departinge this life one the Five and Twentieth Day of December beinge Munday In the yeare of our Lord God One Thousand Six Hundred Seaventy one'; probate not recorded; inventory exhibited 18 March 1671/2.

1. Roman numerals throughout.

199 BENIAMYN LAWRENCE

woollen draper 29 February 1671/2
P1/L/173

The testators wearinge apparrell £3 6*s.* 8*d.*
A chest of drawers and a trunk £1.
Tymber and wood £1.
The lease of the houses in Marlebrough now in the possession of Richard Worrell and Tymothy Mundy £250.
[Several remnants of woollen cloth £1. *added*]
In desperate debt £10.

Total £271 6*s.* 8*d.* [*recte* £266 6*s.* 8*d.*]

Thomas Lawrence and Stephen Lawrence, chandler, appraisors.

Burial not recorded.
Will 20 September 1671; commission 26 February 1671/2, oath administered 29 February 1671/2 to Philip, John and Stephen Lawrence; bond 29 February 1671/2, administration to Philip Lawrence, testator's brother, and John and Stephen Lawrence, testator's nephews.

200 ABRAHAM POWER[1]

gentleman [bond] 24 April 1672
P1/P/278

Mony in the house [twenty shillings *deleted*] five powndes £5

In the Parlour
1 dozen of leather chayres, 2 old chayres, a payer of virginalls and frame, a round table, a standing table, two litle carpitts, two fire pans and tonges, one grate and a payer of andirons with other apurtenances £3

In the [Hall deleted] Kitchen
15 small platters, 12 plates, halfe a dozen of sawcers, one bason, 2 litle flagons, a pinte, halfe pint and a quarter pinte pott, 2 litle pewter bowles, two tankerds, two salt sellers, one cupp, 2 brasse candlestickes, two brasse warmeing pannes, 3 tinneing candlestickes, 6 pottingers, two skimmers, 2 brasse ladells, 4 brasse pannes, 4 litle brasse ketles, 4 brasse potts, 2 possnets, one skillett, 2 payer of andirons, 2 drippeing pannes, 2 spitts, one jacke, one table board, 2 joynt stooles, 2 payer of hangells with other apurtinances and 4 chayres £6

In the Buttery
5 barelles, one table board, one horse, one powdring tubbe with other appurtinances 10*s.*

In a Litle Roome next the Buttery
Two pewter stills, one dough trendle with other appurtinances 10*s.*

In the Brewe House
One small furnace, 1 vate, 3 tubbs, 2 covers and a payle £1

In the Courte
A small parcell of wood £1

In the Parlour Chamber
One bedsteed, one bedd, two small table boardes, 3 chayres and apurtinances to the bedd, one grate and iron backe £4

In the Kitchen Chamber
One bedsteede, one bedd with apurtinances, one chest, one coffer, 3 trunkes, 2 chayres, 2 doggs with other

apurtinances £2
6 payer of sheets and table linning £1 10s.

In the Studdy
A table board and frame, 4 shelves, one coffer and a parcell of bookes with other apurtinances £3

In a Litle Chamber
One bedsteede and a little flocke bedd, a rodd sadle, a pilling and syde sadle with other apurtinances £1

In the Upper Chamber
One table board, 2 bedsteeds, 2 flocke beds with other apurtinances £2

In the Garrett
One table board, trucklebed steede and flocke bedd with other lumber 15s.
His weareing apparrell fower pounds £4
[*Total £35 5s. deleted*]
[*added in another hand*] Good and desperate debts £25

Total £60 5s.

Robert Carpinter, Thomas Ingles, John Horner and Thomas Chambers, appraisors.

Buried St. Mary 19 April 1672 'Mr. Abraham Power, schoolmaster'.
Bond 3 May 1672, administration to Elizabeth Power, intestate's widow.

1. 'deceased the seavententh day of Aprill 1672'.

201 DORATHY WIND[1]
widow [will] 28 May 1672 P1/W/310

Her weareinge apparell £2.[2]
Four paire of sheets 12s.
For other lyininge 5s.
One fether bed, one fether boyster, two fether pillowes, two flock pillowes, coverled and blancketts, standinge bedsteed, curtaine and vallens £2 10s.
Pewter of all sorts £1 4s.
One warmeinge[3] and two brass candlesick 5s.
Two tablebords, joynestooles, cheyer, chests, side cubberd, boxes, two cussions, fier panns and tongs, one paire of dogs and other lumber £1 4s.
Two Bibles and other bookes 5s.
One flockebed, two flock boyste, two ruggs, two blancketts with the bedsteed £1.

In the Hale
One tablebord and frame and press, and in the little roome by one flockebed and other lumber with coverled, blanckett and old bedsteed £1.
One furniss, two brasspotts, one kitle, one possnet and two litle skitles £1 10s.
Six barrels, three tubbs, two kivers 16s.
One jacke, two spitts, andiers and dogs 10s.

In the Shopp
Six dozen of shooes for men at 34s. dozen £10 4s.
Twenty paire of other smale shoes £2 5s.
Six paire of other smale shoes 9s.
Two dozen and eight paire of woemans shoes with letherne heeles £3 13s. 8d.
Four dozen and three paire of woomens wodden heele shoes £5 10s.
Four paire of boots and one paire ledgs £2 6s.
Two dozen and two paire children shoes £1 6s.
Seaven upper lether hydes and four benns £8 10s.
Four dozen of lasts 16s.
Other lumber and goods in the shopp 5s.

Goods at Thomas Chamberlyne
One flockebed, one flocke boyster, two

old blancketts, two old sheets, one coverled, one chest, one box, curtaines and vallens, bedsteed, matt and cord, one paire of dogs, tongs, fier pann, hangle, on litle cubbert and debts on the booke £1 6*s.*

Total £101 2*s.* 8*d.* [*recte* £49 11*s.* 8*d.*][4]

Debts oweing to divers personns by the deceased £45 15*s.*[5]
Soe rest £55 13*s.* 8*d.* [*recte* £3 16*s.* 8*d.*][4]

Walter Parsonns als Seager, Mihill Bayly and Bartholomew Benger, appraisers.

Buried St. Mary 12 April 1672.
Will 3 January 1671/2; probate 3 May 1672 to executor [Jonathan Austine, testatrix's son].

1. 'Winde' on will.
2. Roman numerals throughout.
3. Presumably 'warming pan'.
4. These discrepancies occur because the appraisers, rather than draw up a new inventory for Dorothy, merely copied the inventory of her late husband, Edward (no. 187). In doing so they made several errors, including omitting the line giving the debts due on the shop book, while retaining the original totals.
5. Debts owing by the deceased should not form part of the inventory.

202 THOMAS GRINFEILD[1]

innholder [will] 3 September 1672
P1/G/226

One tabel boord and frame and 3 jhoynt stooles and 1 setall £1
3 chayers and 4 spits and a jhack and wayghts, 2 smothing irones and a minsing knife 15*s.*
2 andiers, 2 dogs, fierpan and tongs, a gridiron, 2 pote hangils and a fender and a pair of bilows 12*s.*
12 pewtar dishis, 3 flagones, 6 candalsticks, 5 pewtar porengars, 6 sausars, 2 pewtar pots, 1 quart pot, 1 pint pot, 1 half pint pot and 3 chambar pots of pewtar £3.
2 kettals, 2 bras pots, 1 skellet, 1 driping pann and 2 payr of poticks £1.
5 fethar beds, 6 boulstars, 4 pelows of fethars, 3 ruggs, 3 blanckets £10.
3 bedsteds, 2 hangings, 1 trucklebedsted £1.
3 mats and 3 cords 5*s.*
6 cushings 5*s.*
7 chayres, 1 tabel bord and frame and 3 jhoyn stools and 1 cuberd £2.
3 pair of andiers with bras bosas, 3 pair of tongs, 1 fierpan, 1 looking glass, 1 houer glass, 1 payer of bilows and 2 carpitcloths £1 10*s.*
For his own waring clothes £7.
1 warming pann 2*s.* 6*d.*
4 truncks, 2 boxes, 1 chest, 1 coffer, 1 flasket £1.
1 setall, 1 bucket, 2 bowles, 4 tubbs, 1 forem, 1 lading paill, 1 clever, 1 closstall, 2 baralls, 1 kever with wothar lumbar £1 10*s.*
For wood and 1 reek of hay and 1 frying pann £8 1*s.*
14 pair of sheets, 4 tabelclothes, 2 holen pilow [cloths *added*], 3 pair of pilow bears, 4 duzen of napkins, 4 towels, 1 cuberd cloth £8
1 chefing dish, 12 butels and 1 skimar 3*s.*
1 fethar bed and 1 carpet £1 1*s.*
And in money and bonds about £390.

Total £438 04*s.* 6*d.*

John Elliott and Rogar Glide, appraisors

Burial not recorded.
Will 15 May 1672; probate 8 October 1673 to William Greinfeild, testator's brother.

1. 'Mr.'.

203 EDWARD EATTALL

husbandman 4 November 1672
P1/E/103

The testators weareing apparell 10*s.*

In the Chamber

One bed, one sheete, one coverled, one blanckett, one bolster, one pillow, one bedsteed, one chest and one coffer 10*s.*

In the Low Roomth

One kittle, one pewter dish and one skillett 10*s.*

One forme, one chaire, one candlestick and other lumber 1*s.* 6*d.*

One kiver, one tub, one barrell and horse, five wedges, one axe, one mattock, one spead, one forke, 2 rakes, one pronge and one frieing pan 4*s.*

One axe, 2 ripe hooks 1*s.* 6*d.*

The lease of a poor howse charged with a rent nere the yearely value £2.

Total £3 17*s.*

James Elliott and Peter Furnell, appraisors.

Buried St. Mary 14 June 1672 'Edward Eatwell the younger' or St. Mary 18 August 1672 'Edward Eatwell the elder'.[1]

Inventory exhibited 6 November 1672; bond 7 November 1672, administration to Joane Eattall.

1. It has proved impossible to ascertain which of these men this inventory relates to.

204 WILLIAM BLACKMORE

yeoman 1 June 1673 P1/B/488

His wareing apparell 11*s.* 8*d.*

In moneyes in the howse and moneyes oweing to him £27.

In brasse and pewter £2 7*s.*

In wooll 8*s.*

One silt and one board 4*s.*

One chaire 2*s.* 6*d.*

One table board and frame 5*s.*

Two flitches of bacon and some other peeces of bacon £1 8*s.*

Fower cheeses and other provision 5*s.*

Five sheepe £1 5*s.*

Three coffers and one chest 9*s.*

One old bedd and boulster stuffed with chaffe 1*s.* 6*d.*

One old fether bed, one old fether boulster, one old fether pillow £1 10*s.*

One old flocke bed, one flocke pillow 2*s.* 6*d.*

One paire of blanketts, two coverleds, one paire of sheetes, one pillow beare 17*s.* 6*d.*

One old paire of andirons, one paire of tongs, one spitt 2*s.*

Two old bedsteeds 4*s.*

In old lumber goods 11*s.*

Total £37 13. 8*d.*

Thomas Lawrence and John Smith, appraisors.

Buried St. Peter 2 March 1672/3.

Will 25 February 1672/3; probate 2 May 1673 to executor [Francis Bowsher of Marlborough, innholder]; inventory exhibited 21 March 1674/5.

205 ROBERT KEMBER[1]

yeoman [bond] 29 July 1673 P1/K/76

The coach and horses £40.

In the Chamber

One feather bedd, one feather bolster, tow feather pillows, 2 blainketts, 2 pair of sheetts and one rugge and one paire of curtains and valliens £3.

In the oather Chamber

Tow flocke bedds and tow bolsters and 2

blancketts and tow couffoletts and 2 bedsteeds and 2 paire of sheetts £2.

In the Chamber offer the Hall

One dosen and a halfe of knapkins and tow tabell cloaths and one paire of doullas sheets and one hollond sheets and four paire of pillow casses and 3 silver spones £2.

In the Hall

Nine pewtter platters, 2 candelsticks and one flaggon and one pewtter chamber pott and five porrgingers, 3 pewtter sawsers £1.

More 2 brass potts, 3 brass kettells, one brass panne, 2 brass skilletts and one warminge panne £2.

One furnass of brass and one jacke and one paire of doggs and one fire pann, one paire of tongs £1.

2 tabell boards, one cubbord, 2 chests, one coffer, 2 boxses with all oather lumber £2 10*s*.

His wearinge apparell and wood in the backside with his purss and his mony in itt £5.

As for debts owed as dew debts £10.

For beans leavft in the chamber £2.

Total £70 10*s*.

John Gillmore and Thomas Keynton, appraisors.

Buried St. Mary 22 June 1673 'Robert Kymber'.

Bond 29 July 1673, administration to Sarah Kimber, intestate's widow.

1. 'of Marleborrough St Maries'.

206 ANTHONY MORRIS

carpenter [renunciation] 2 August 1673 P1/M/225

One pile of clift wood standing in the garden £8.

Slab timber standing aboute the wod pile 8*s*.

Slab timber in the bake side 3*s*.

Outside plankes and borde and timber under Mr. Shperes worke £1.

Elmin bordes in the hovill £3.

Halfinch oken bordes in the hovill £1 10*s*.

Oken quarters in the hovill 15*s*.

The tallat in the hovill 5*s*.

For plankes att the street dore £1.

For [the *deleted*] a bed and bedsteed [in *deleted*] £1.

One chest and wareing clothes £1 10*s*.

A peese of wainscot 5*s*.

One brasse pot and skillet 3*s*. 6*d*.

One driping pann 6*d*.

One olde cubberd 2*s*.

3 joynt stools 3*s*.

One silte 2*s*.

Total £19 7*s*.

Jeremiah Mathewes and Robert Webb, appraisors.

Buried St. Mary 9 July 1673.

Renunciation 30 July 1673 by Margery Morris, intestate's widow, to Joseph Morris, intestate's son; bond 7 August 1673, administration to Joseph Morris; commission 7 August 1673, oath administered 7 August 1673 to Joseph Morris; inventory exhibited 16 August 1673.

207 NATHANIELL FARMER

22 September 1673 P1/F/143

His weareing apparell £3.

2 fether beds and all other things belonging to it £3.

2 bedstedds £1.

1 trunke and 2 coffers and 1 chest 16*s*.

1 paire of brass andiernes, 1 warming pan 4*s.*
All the brass and pewter £1.
1 table bord and frame with one forme 5*s.*
Barells and other woden vessells 12*s.*
All the linning £1.
2 chayers, 2 gine stolls 4*s.*
For monyes [laying *deleted*] in the howse £1.
2 horses £4.
2 kine £3.
1 cart and 1 dugpot and harniss £1.
Wod and other lumber goods 10*s.*

Total £20 11*s.*

John Farmer, Swithen Young and Simon Pike appraisers.

Buried St Peter 14 September 1673, 'of St Marys parish'.
Bond 14 October 1673, administration to Eleonar Farmer, intestate's widow.

208 MARGERY SMYTH

widow 2 October 1673 P1/S/428

Beddinge and furniture thereunto belonging £10.
In money and ringes £20.
A chest, a [*illegible deletion*] coffer, a trunck, twoo box[es *added*] and a chaire [and books *added*] £1 [12*s. added*]
The testators weareing apparell £20.
One skillett and one flaggon 5*s.*
One dozen and halfe of [*illegible deletion*] napkins 10*s.*
In pewter and brasse 10*s.*
One cushen 2*s.*

Total £52 19*s.*

Richard Worrill and Thomas Brunsdon, appraisors.

Burial not recorded.
Will 6 November 1672; probate 17 October 1673 to Mary Barnes, testator's daughter.

209 EDWARD AVEN

glover [bond] 11 May 1674 P1/A/135

Wering parill 10*s.*
On livery bedsted and that whit belong [to him *added*] £1.
Brase and peuter £1 6*s.* 8*d.*
On litell table, on cobord 8*s.*
2 spits, 3 per of hangls, on pair of smal angrs 5*s.*
For lumbr 10*s.*
[£3 19*s.* 8*d. deleted*]
Mony £3 10*s.*

Total £7 9*s.* 8*d.*

Edward Lawarance, Thomas Godard and William Aven, appraisors.

Buried St. Mary 12 May 1674.
Bond 15 May 1674, administration to Margaret Aven, [intestate's widow].

210 ROGER BLAGDEN

gentleman[1] 14 May 1674 P1/B/493

Money in his purse £20.
His wearing apparrell £20.
Debts oweing to him upon bond and other security £750.
Due to him for rent at Litleton[2] £10.
Rent due from Allington £16.
A chatle lease of the moyety of the Prebendary of Allington for 14 yeares to come £100.
A chatle lease in Marlebrough held from the Maior and Burgesses £100.
One bed and other furniture for his chamber and closett £10.
His books £10.

Total £1036.

N. Forbes and John Foster, appraisors.

Buried St. Peter 7 May 1674, 'Mr. Roger Blackden'.
Will 28 August 1669; probate 14 May 1674 to Elizabeth Blagden, [testator's widow].

1. 'Mercer' on will.
2. Possibly Little Town in the parish of Broad Town .

211 THOMAS PEARSE

?glazier [inventory goods] 9 July 1674 P1/P/295

In the Iner Chamber
One featherbed, one flockbedd, two blankets, one bolster, one pillow, one tester bedsteed with curtains and vallins and foure paire of old sheets £3.
Three paire of old sheets, three paire of old pillowcases, halfe a dozen of napkins, halfe a dozen of towels and two old table cloathes £1 1*s.* 6*d.*
One old tableboard, one old forme, one box, one chaire, three old joyne stooles and one old chest 10*s.*

In the Outer Chamber
One livery bedsteed, one featherbedd, two bolsters, one pillow, two old coverlids and two blankets 12*s.* 6*d.*

In the Low Roome
Three small brass potts, two little old kittles, two scillets, two scimers, two old warming pans, two ladels and three candelsticks 18*s.*
One dozen and a halfe of pewter dishes, one pewter flaggon, one pewter pott, three porringers, two chamberpotts and two sacers £1 10*s.*
One little old tabelboard, one iron jack, three little spitts, two old driping pans, a fryeing pan, three paire of pott hocks, a paire of andians, a paire of doggs, a paire of hangells, a paire of old billows, a firepan and tonges and two steele plats 14*s.* 4*d.*

In the Shop
A vice, a parsell of lead soder and glass and working tooles £4.

In the Buttery
Fowre little barrels, one little tubb, one kiver, the wood and other lumber about the house 13*s.* 6*d.*
In desperate debts £10.
His wearing apparrell £1 10*s.*

Total £24 9*s.* 10*d.*

William Hitchcock, Nicholas Smith and John Harding, appraisors.

Buried St. Peter 23 June 1674 'Thomas Pierce'.
Bond 8 September 1674, administration to Mary Peirce, intestate's widow.

212 THOMAS HUNT the elder

gentleman 14 July 1674 P1/H/424

His weareing apparell £5 10*s.*
In money in the howse £1 19*s.*
Money due upon bond £10 6*s.* 9*d.*
Debts oweing to him £2 12*s.* 7*d.*
Two table clothes, five sheetes, one halfe sheete, two and twenty towells and napkins £1 10*s.*
[Greene *added*] curtins and valins for a bedd, fower window curtins, two greene cupboard clothes and one striped cupboard cloth and one callico cupboard cloth £1 10*s.*
Two flocke bolsters, one yellow rugg, two pillow cases, one bolster case, [one feather pillow *added*] 15*s.*
One side cupboard with a drawer to it,

one box of drawers, one little tableboard and frame, one old white coverled, fower cushons and three rushen chaires £1.
One great chest, one warmeing pan, a close stoole & pan 15*s.*
Two leather chaires, one skillett, one [pewter *added*] chamber pott, one fire pan and tongs, one iron cheafeing dish, a paire of bellis, one gridiron, one flaskett 12*s.*
One paire of iron dogges, two little barrells, a buckett, a heth brush, two little tubbes, two pewter spoones, eighteene earthen potts and pans, two tin cupps, a little wood 10*s.*
A meale bagg, a hat brush, an old lookeing glasse, a earthen steane 2*s.*
One Bible and certen English bookes 10*s.*

Total £27 12*s.* 4*d.*

Nathaniell Bayly and Samuell Fowler, appraisors.

Buried St. Peter 13 July 1674 'senior'.
Will 3 July 1674; probate 11 August 1674 to executor [Thomas Hunt, testator's son].

213 RUTH ALLEXANDER

widow 4 September 1674 P1/A/138

Her weareing apparell and gold rings £6.
In money in the howse and at intrest £170.
Two fether bedds, one flocke bedd, fower feather boulsters, fower fether pillowes, three bedsteeds and all the rest of the bedding £7.
Fower brasse kettles, two brasse potts, two skilletts and a warmeing pan £3.
Six pewter dishes, three flaggons, two cuppes and two candlestickes 14*s.* 8*d.*

In the Hall
Two side boards and one table board £1.
Three spitts, one paire of andirons, one bacon racke, one fire pan, one drippin pan and some other small things 6*s.* 8*d.*

In the Chamber
One table board, fower ioyned stooles 14*s.*
Three chests, five boxes, one drawer, one presse £1.
All the lynnen which she had at her decease £1 10*s.*
Some lumber in the garrett 2*s.* 6*d.*
Fower barrells, a kive and other wooden vessells £1 6*s.* 8*d.*
Other lumber 10*s.*

Total £193 4*s.* 6*d.*

Nicholas Millington and Robert Millington, appraisors.

Buried St. Peter 24 January 1673/4.
Will 30 December 1673; probate 8 September 1674 to executor [Samuell Alexander, testator's son].

214 NATHANIELL CARPENTER

5 November 1675[1] P1/C/321

His weareinge apparell and lynnen £3.[2]
One particion in his shopp of boards 10*s.*
Lumber goods in his shopp £1.
Twelve chaires and two stooles 15*s.*
One chest of drawers and 1 chest £1.
One small table board and 2 stools 6*s.*
Brass and pewter £1.
One bedd, bolster and bedinge £2.
Lumber goods £1.
In debts owinge to the testator from severall persons good and badd £21 12*s.* 6*d.*

Total £32 1*s.* 6*d.* [*recte* £32 3*s.* 6*d.*]

Nathaniel Popioy, Frances Brathwaytt and John Hill, appraisors.

Burial not recorded.
Bond 21 April 1676, administration to Margaret Carpenter, intestate's widow.

1. Given as regnal year.
2. Roman numerals throughout.

215 DANIEL COXE
husbandman [will] 20 January 1675/6
P1/C/320

His wareing aparell £2.

In the Parler Chamber
A faather bead and all things belonging to it and all other fornituer tharin £6.

In the Hall Chamber
To flook beds and all things belonging to it and all other foornituer tharein £2 10*s.*

In the Parlor
A flook bead and all things belonging to it and the other fornituer tharein £2.

In the Hall
The fornituer in it £1.

In the Chichen
One fornes and other brass and pautor and the other farnituer tharin £6.
A pille of hard wood and fagats £20.
[Five *deleted*] to young [calfs *deleted*] boulloks and three caulfs £5.
Fower pidges £2 10*s.*

In the Sceller
The baere and other vesells tharin £3.
A lase of a smale tennement £5 10*s.*
In lumber £1 5*s.* 6*d.*

Total £46 15*s.* 6*d.* [*recte* £56 15*s.* 6*d.*]

John Horner and Benjamin Lawrence, appraisors.

Buried St. Mary 16 January 1675/6.
Will 10 January 1675/6; probate 20 April 1676 to Elizabeth Cox, testator's widow.

216 ANTHONY AWST
yeoman 26 April 1676 P1/A/141

The testators weareing apparell £1.
One flock bed and bolster and one paire of sheets £1 10*s.*
One paire of blancketts and one old rugge 10*s.*
One matt and cord and one livery bedsteed 6*s.*
One old cubbard and one old chest 8*s.*
One old cofer and one deske box 4*s.*
One old trunck and one box 3*s.* 6*d.*
Five pewter platters 7*s.* 10*d.*
Twoo tining candlesticks and one driping pan 2*s.*
One tining milter, one old kittle and 2 old skilletts 4*s.* 1*d.*
One iron pott, one skimer and one bason leadle 3*s.* 6*d.*
One spitt, one paire of iron dogges and one paire of tongues 3*s.* 8*d.*
One gridiron, one weshing tubb and one brewing tubb 5*s.* 6*d.*
One kiver, 4 wooden platters and 2 barells 7*s.*
Twoo old chaires, 2 steeling irons and 2 paire of pott hookes 3*s.* 4*d.*
One paire of billowes, one paire of pott hangells and 3 old wyer candlesticks 2*s.* 3*d.*
One dozen of wooden trenchers, one wooden tunells and one wooden bowle and dishes 2*s.* 6*d.*
One Bible 2*s.*
One cottage or tenement in chattell lease for lives £5.
In lumber goods 4*s.*

Total £11 8*s.* 9*d.* [*recte* £11 9*s.* 2*d.*]

William Bayly and John Barnes, appraisors.

Burial not recorded.

Bond 28 August 1675, administration to Ann, wife of William Pike, formerly intestate's widow; commission 23 March 1675/6, oath administered 25 March 1676 to Ann Pike; inventory exhibited 13 May 1676.

217 ISAAC RINGE

vintner [. . .][1] February 1676/7

P1/R/145

In the Kitchen

Two pewter dishes, 1 bason, 1 candle stick, 1 flaggon, 1 cupp, [1 chamber pott *added*] 17s. 6d.

1 cast brass pott, 1 pott kettle, 1 cast skillett, 1 small kettle, two skilletts, [one cast skillett *deleted*] 1 sauce pann, 1 culberd [and 2 iron potts *added*] £1 7s. 4d.

1 table board [2s. *overwritten*] 3s.

[2 overwritten] 4 chairs 2s.

1 side cupboard 1s.

1 jack, 1 spitt, 1 gridiron 5s.

In the Chamber

1 feather bed and bolster £2.

2 ruggs and two blanketts £1 10s.

1 sett of curtains and vallens [15s. *overwritten*] £1 10s.

5 leather chayers 5s.

1 paire of small andirons and doggs, 1 paire of tongs 6s. 8d.

3 low stooles [*illegible deletion*] 3s.

1 chest 4s.

Weareing cloathes £3 10s.

4 paire of sheets and other small linnen £2.

Total £12 4s. 6d. [*recte* £14 4s. 6d.]

[*added in another hand*
The debts are desperate and but little to be recovered.]

Thomas Hunt and James Bartlett, appraisors.

Buried St. Peter 7 January 1676/7.

Renunciation 29 January 1676/7 by Katherine Ringe, intestate's widow, in favour of James Crosse 'of the Towne and County of Southampton, Marchant' principal creditor; bond 29 January 1676/7, administration to Mr. James Crosse; accounts presented 16 July 1677 by James Crosse.

1. 'in the Month of'.

218 ELEONAR FARMER

widow [will] [*undated*, c.1677]

P1/F/150

Warin aparell £2.

And one feth bed £1.

And cortins and vallens and that be long to it £1.

And one bedsted 6s.

And 4 puter platers 10s.

And table bord and frame 6s.

Too barels 4s.

Too covles 3s.

One chaier 2s.

Too gines stoles 1s.

One cetell 5s.

One pott 4s.

One warmin pan 2s.

Too sklets 2s.

Sub-total £6 5s.

[*Added in another hand*] Money att intrest £30.

[*Total omitted, by addition* £36 5s.]

John Farmer, John Clark and Swithing Yong, appraisors.

Buried St. Peter 24 August 1677, 'widdow Farmer of St Maries parish'.

Will 21 June 1677; probate and inventory exhibition not recorded.

219 JEREMIAH SLOPER

chandler 10 September 1677 P1/S/454

The testators weareing apparell £3 10*s*.

In the Hall

One table board and frame, eight joynted stooles, fower chaires, twoo cubberds, twoo shelves, one rack, one jack, one paire of hangells, one paire of andirons, one paire of dogges, one firepan, one paire of tongues, one flaggon, one tankerd, one pewter candlesticke, twenty peeces of pewter, fower brasse potts, one kittle, three skilletts, three iron candlestickes, one spitt, twoo lanthornes with other lumber £3 13*s*.

In the Buttery

Fower barells and other lumber 10*s*.

In the Chamber

One chest of drawers, one tableboard and frame, two chests, one cuberd, twoo trunkes, one closestoole, one box, twoo paire of blanketts, one rugg, two coverleds, three paire of sheetes, twoo beds, twoo bolsters, three pillowes, three carpettes, twoo bedsteeds, one looking glasse with other lumber £6 1*s*.

Three dozen of napkins, three table cloathes and other linen £1 6*s*.

Faggots in the backside £1 10*s*.

Ware in the shopp and ware house £62 17*s*.

Debts due to the testator £70.

Total £149 7*s*.

Beniamin Lawranc[e] and Phillip Jones, appraisors.

Burial not recorded.

Will 10 July 1677; probate not recorded; commission 11 September 1677, oath administered 11 October 1677 to Elizabeth Sloper, testator's widow.

220. [WILLIAM TOOTH][1]

blacksmith [bond] 29 October 1677 P1/T/177

The billus and althinges to it £2 10*s*.

The 2 anfildes 5*s*.

The 2 fisis 15*s*.

Hammers and sleges and other shoptooles £1.

Irne and colle [and blockes *added*] 12*s*.

Grinsstone spindel 6*s*.

5 dosen of shoultrees £2.

2 dosen of prongstafes 5*s*.

3 barrils 6*s*.

Kife and kifers and tobes 5*s*.

1 sacke of barly 10*s*.

1 bullucke £1.

Bras and peuter £2.

Table bord, chayers, stooles and binche 10*s*.

For beds and all thinges belongin to it £3.

For waring clothes £2.

For cofers and trunke 10*s*.

For wood £6 10*s*.

Tilt and stannin stuf 10*s*.

1 spit 8*d*.

Fier shoule and tongs and dogs 3*d*.

10 dorelockes 10*s*.

5 horse coomes 1*s*. 8*d*.

Nurles 10*s*.

2 dosen and halfe of locks and ginniels £1.

3 chaffin disshes 2*s*.

1 dosen and halfe of ginniels 1*s*. 6*d*.

5 candelstickes 1*s*. 8*d*.

2 sad irnes and hammer 2*s*.

1 pare of ginte and turprit 1*s*. 6*d*.

Puttine and ringes and lethers 12*s*.

Volers 2*s*.

In dets £2.

In monny £7 10s.
1 [doosen of *deleted*] cradell 1s.
Forkes and sneuds and lock stockes 4s.

Total £31 17s.

[*Appraisors' names omitted.*]

Buried St. Peter 28 October 1677.
Bond 6 November 1677, administration to Judith Tooth, intestate's widow.

1. Name omitted, obtained from bond.

221 JONE LYME
widow 18 December 1677 P1/L/186

The testators weareing apparell £5.

In the Hall
Five brasse kittles, seaven brasse potts, eight brasse skilletts, one posnett, one brasse pan and one iron dripinge pan £4 10s.
Fower and twenty pewter platters, twoo pewter flaggons, twoo tankerds, twoo chamber potts, one pewter bason, one pewter candlestick, three pewter cupps, one poringer, one butter dish and one salt £2 10s.
Three wenscote settles, twoo table boards, five joynted stooles, three chaires, one jack, three spitts, one gridiron, three pott hooks, three pott hangells, one paire of andirons, one iron grate, one fire pan and tongues, one paire of billowes and one paire of iron racks £2.

In the Chamber over the Hall
Twoo feather beds, three feather pillowes, three feather bolsters, one rugg, three coverleds, one paire of blanketts, fower bedsteeds, one great chest, twoo coffers, one trunke, one box, one little table board, one paire of iron dogges, one little cubberd, eight paire of sheets and other lynen and one flock bed £10

In the Buttery
Fower barrells, twoo kivers, twoo tubbs and other lumber £1.

In the Brewhouse
One furnace and one kive £1.
Wood and lumber in the backside £1.
The lease of the house £15.
In ready money £100.

Total £142.

Samuell Fowler and Mathias Fowler, appraisors.

Buried St. Peter 4 December 1677 'Joane Lime widow'.
Will 22 April 1676; probate 3 May 1678 to John Lyme, testator's son.

222 WILLIAM GODDARD
?innholder [inventory content] 8 May 1678 P1/G/235

In the Starr
One old tableboard, one bedsteed, one chaffe-bed, one blankett and two fourms £1 2s.

In the Lion
One bedsteed, one bed matt and cord, one sett of curtains and vallions, one green rugg, one sett of curtaine rods, one lettle tableboard, two fourms, one chaire, one pare of dogs, one pare of tongs £2.

In the Rose
One green rugg, one bedsteed, 3 longe fourms, 3 chairs, one pare of dogs, one firepan and tongs, one trunke £1 15s.

In the Kitchin
17 pewter flagons, 6 porringers, 19 pewter dishes, one basson, 9 candlestickes, 6 chamber potts, 3 fire dishes £3 1s.

2 brass kittles, one porsnett, one skimer, one beeff hooke 15*s*.
One gun and scowrer, one jake, one spitt, one racke, 4 chayers, one fire pan, one pare of hangilles, one pare of bellows, one iron barr, one fourme, two dozen of trinchers £1 10*s*.

In the Siller
One meassinge vatte and horse, 7 kiveers and two tubbs and two kives, 9 barrels, one tunells £4.
Beare and sider £3.
One sow and piggs £1.
His apparell £5.
In bonds and bills and booke[1] £19.

Total £42 3*s*.

Mathias Fowler and Timothy Mundy, appraisors.

Buried St. Peter 5 May 1678.
Commission 23 May 1678, oath administered 26 May 1678 to William Goddard; bond 26 May 1665 [*clerk's error*], administration to William Goddard of Ogborne St. George, intestate's father; testator's debts paid 8 May 1678 to 3 June 1679 by William Goddard; administration accounts submitted 5 June 1679 by William Goddard.

1. Presumably book debts.

223 PHILLIPP LAWRENCE
gentleman 15 July 1678 P1/L/188

The testators weareing apparell £10.

In the Celler
One furnace, seaven barrells and other bruinge vessells £5.

In the Kitchine
One tableboard and frame, twelve chaires and stooles, twoo cubberds together with the brasse, pewter and iron in the same roomth £11.

In the Shopp
One chest, three peeces of sarge, one peece of druckett, threescore and ten pounds of woosted and one linnen cloath together with other lumber £18.

In the Dyneing Roomth
Three pictures, eight chaires, fower tables with carpetts with the roomth hunge with kettimister and one paire of dogges and andirons and one paire of billowes and one hanginge shelfe £9.

In the Chamber over the Shopp
One feather bed and bedsteed with the furniture thereunto belonginge, one chest of drawers, one dressing table and cubberd, six stooles and chaires, one paire of andirons, dogges, firepan, tongues, billows, one lookeing glasse stand and one hanginge shelfe £8.

In the Kitchine Chamber
One featherbed and bedsteed with the furniture thereunto belonginge, six chayers and stooles, one dressing table, one looking glasse together with the kettimister hangeinge to the roomth, one firepan and tongues, andirons and doggues, one hanginge shelfe and stand £10.

In the Twoo Garretts
Fower beds with the furniture thereunto belonginge one trunke full of fine lynen, one chest of ordinary lynen with other lumber £25.
One silver tankerd, six silver saults, fower silver spoones £8.
In certen English bookes £2.

In the backside
In wood and cole £5.

The worke house and all matterialls in yt and thereunto belongeinge £40.
One chattell lease of a tenement now in the possession of Tymothy Mundy in Marlebrough £100.
In good debts £20.
In desperate debts £30.

Total £300. [*recte* £301].

John Hawkins, Richard Coleman and Samuell Fowler, appraisors.

Buried St. Mary 17 June 1678 'Mr. Philip Lawrence'.
Will 2 December 1676; probate 22 July 1678 to Martha Lawrence, testator's widow.

224 ROBERT MILLINGTON
tailor 2 August 1678 P1/M/246

In the kitchen
Two tableboards, two old chaires, one old cupboard, one fourme, one old rack and shelves, two paire of hangelles, one fyre pan, tongs, andirons and pair of billows, [*blank*] woodden dishes and trenchers 16*s.*

In the Buttery
Brass and pewter, one iron pott, one spitt, one frying pan, skimer, potthookes, one cupboard, three barrelles, two kyvers, one meashing tub, two cowles, one horse for the barrelles to stand in and other small lumber £1 12*s.*

In the Chamber
One bedd of feathers and flocks, one bed of flocks, one other old bedd, two pair of blankettes, two coverliddes, seaven canmas sheets, two feather bolsters, fower pillows, one high bedsteed, curtains and valens, cord and matt, one trundle bedsteed, cord and matt, one tableboard, three ioynt stooles, one chest, one ioynt fourme, one desk, three boxes, one warmeing pan, two coffers, one old chaire, one old stoole £3 2*s.* 6*d.*
Halfe bushell of wheate and two baggs 3*s.* 6*d.*
Faggott wood £1.
This deceaseds weareing apparell £2.
A lease of three small tenements for two lives in being £5 10*s.*
Debts due to the deceased on bond of principall money £80.
Some other small lumber goods about the house 10*s.* 6*d.*

Total £94 14*s.* 6*d.*

John Horner and Beniamin Bassett, appraisors.

Buried Preshute 24 July 1678 'of St Peters in marlebrough'.
Will 20 July 1678; probate 7 August 1678 to [unnamed].

225 EDWARD LAWRENCE
parchment maker [bond] 25 November 1678 P1/L/187

His weareing apparrell £2.[1]
One glew furnace, one brasse pott and twoo brasse skilletts £6.
Six dishes of pewter, one pewter flaggon, one pewter tankard 15*s.*
One table board and frame, one settell, one chest, one coffer, one trunck, twoo boxes and one matted chaire £1.
Feather bedd, one feather bolster, twoo feather pillowes, one rugge, three blancketts, one beddsteed, curtaines and vallens £4.
Three barrells, twoo keevers, one coule, one fire pann and tonges, one spitt, one pewter chamber pott 10*s.*
Six dozen of harrowes for glew and trowes and other lumber for the glew trade

£1 4s.
The lease of the howse he lived in £15.
One cubboard, twoo joyned furrms, one frying pann, twoo stele plates 5s.
Seaven dozen of glew netts 14s.
One paire of hangelles 1s.
One cowe £2.

Total £33 9s.

Robert Butcher and Nicholas Rumsey, appraisors.

Burial not recorded [St. Mary register wanting September 1678 to April 1681].
Bond 26 November 1678, administration to Joanna Lawrence, intestate's widow; inventory exhibited 3 December 1678.

1. Roman numerals throughout.

226 ELIZABETH BLAGDEN
widow 29 January 1678 P1/B/521

In her Chamber
One bed and bedsteed with the furniture to it £5 10s.
One presse and one chest of drawers £1 5s.
One chest 4s. 6d.
3 truncks 15s.
One couch 13s.
One trundle bed steed 2s.
4 low stooles 6s.
3 chaires 7s.
One table with drawers 5s.
One little table 1s. 6d.
One table in the Clossett 1s.
One sett of drawers in the Closset 5s.
One deske there 5s.
One leather chaire 2s. 6d.
Two other chaires 2s.
2 chushiones 2s.
One stand 1s. 6d.
6 window curtaines and roddes 5s.
3 litle carpettes 1s. 6d.
One fire pann and tongs 1s. 6d.
One paire of brasse andirons, doggs and bellowes 5s.
One close stoole and pann 5s.
Two litle boxes 2s.
In her clossett 107 bookes £10.
Her wearing apparell £10.
Money in the house £2 18s. 7d.
Two gold rings £1.
One pillion 2s.

Goods total £35 8s. 7d.

Debts due on bonds and other securaties £1414 10s.
An arreare of an annuity due from the Mayor and Burgesses of Marlebrough £20.
The like from a farme at Littleton £10.

Total £1479 18s. 7d.

Samuel Fowler and Thomas Bayly, appraisors.

Buried St. Peter 28 Jan 1678/9, 'Mrs'.
Will 10 December 1678; probate undated; commission 18 February 1678/9, oath administered to Nathaniel Bayly and John Foster, executors.

227 JOHN MILLINGTON[1]
carpenter 17 March 1678/9 P1/M/247

His weareinge apparrell £2.
In ready money £3 1s. 6d.

In his Chamber over the Hall
One feather bed with the furniture £3.
Twoe boxes with 3 sheetes and small parcells of lynnen £1.
Twoe Bibles and 3 brushes 5s.

In the Kytchin Chamber
His severall tooles and implements of worke £2.

Twoe brass potts, 1 brass kittle, 1 brass skillett, 7 pewter dishes, 1 pewter chamber pott, 1 spitt and severall small kytchin utensills £2.

In the Hall
One paire of doggs, tongs, fire pann, hanginges and crooke and paire of billows 3*s.*
Fower chaires, 2 stooles 3*s.*
One table board, frame and forme 5*s.*
In pinninge timber 1*s.*
One earthen pott, one earthen platter, 1 earthen dish, 1 wooden dish, a ladle, 8 trenchers, one goddard 1*s.*
One carpitt, 2 cushions, 1 lookeinge glass, one grist bagg, 1 knife 2*s.*
A flitch of bacon 8*s.*

In the Cellar
3 barrells, 2 tubbs, 1 kiver, one ould coffer and 1 buckett and lumbar £1.

In Good Debts
One obligation of Jeffery Daniell Esqr conditioned for payment of thirty pounds and eighteen shillinges to the intestate on the 9th day of Aprill next £30 18*s.*
One chattle lease of his howse for his relicts life under covenants therein to rebuild etc £10.
Sub-total £56 7*s.* 6*d.*

In Desperate Debts
Due from his cozen George Millington £3 15*s.*
From Robert Browne of Kynnett £4.
From Mr George Hitchcocke £2 10*s.*
From Thomas Garlicke 8*s.* 6*d.*
From William Pierce 4*s.*

[*Total* £10 17*s.* 6*d.* *deleted*]
Total £67 5*s.*

Gorg Stagg and Cornelius Porter, appraisors.

Burial not recorded [St. Mary register wanting September 1678 to April 1681].
Bond 6 March 1678/9, administration to Anne Millington, intestate's widow.

1. 'of the parish of St. Peter and St. Paull ... dyed intestate the vjth day of February last'.

228 MARGARET EVANS
widow 5 June 1679 P1/E/112

Money upon bond, mortgage and otherwise £60.
Her wearing apparell £5.

Total £65.

Christopher Lipyeatt, appraisor.

Buried St. Peter 30 March 1679.
Will 5 February 1678/9; probate and inventory exhibition not recorded.

229 ELIZABETH DUCKE
widow 10 September 1679 P1/D/153

29 disheses of pewter £3.
1 pewter flagon, 3 pewter tankerd, 2 pewter candllstikes, 1 pewter bowll, 1 pewter coop with a cover, 2 pewter salt, 1 pewter colender, 1 bras candl stike, 1 pewter half paint meser, 1 pewter musterd pote, 1 laten pepurbol, 1 laten flowerpote, 1 coval glase and 2 whit erthen salt, 2 paynted dishese, 1 blew glase, 2 pewter chamber pots, snafers and severall other small things £1 10*s.*
1 brase waring pane, 1 pare of andirons and 1 pare of doges, 1 fior pane and tongues, 3 steel plats, one brase buter dish, 3 resh cheyers, 4 lather chayers, one joyn cheyer, 2 joyn stoles, one tabll bord and fram, 4 coshenes, 1 brase pot, 2 brase skelat, 1 chafen dish, 1 sid cobord, 4 glase botles, 4 viall glases and other small

things [1 pare of belose *added*] £2.
1 trunke full of lenen £2.
Waring aparell £5.
1 father bead and straw bed, 1 red rug and bwsters and pelews and bead sted and all that be long to it £5.
1 ruge and blankats and cutins £1.
A parsell of linen and 4 boxes, 1 chest, 1 chayar, 1 coshen, 1 locken glase, 1 bresh and other small things £1.
Wodes in the closat 10*s.*
2 gold ringes, 1 silver bodken, 1 silver spone, silver sealt and toth pickes £2.
In bands and mony £136.
Fagats in the woodhous 4*s.*
1 furnese and brewing varsall £1 5*s.*
[*added in a different hand* 1 settel, 1 per poothocks, 1 blower, 1 tosting iorn, 1 gridiorn, 1 buckett, 1 frying pann 9*s.*]

Total £160 18*s.*

Henery Cowsey, Beniamin Lawrenc and Robert Butcher, appraisors.

Buried St. Peter 9 September 1679.
Will 25 July 1679; probate 8 September 1680 to [unnamed].

230 JOHN MANN

roper [will] 8 April 1680 P1/M/250

His weareinge aparell £5.[1]

In the Chamber [over] the Hale
One fether bed and chaff bed, two boysters and five fether pilloes, one rugg and blancketts £5.
One bedsteed, curtaines and vallens 8*s.*
Four paire of sheets and six napkins, two table cloathes and other lyninge £2.
One chest, two boxes 6*s.*

In the Chamber over Entry
Two flocke beds, two flock boysters and one fether boysters, two per blanketts, one rugg and coverlet and all that belonge unto it £3.
One chest and forme and other lumber 4*s.*

In the Hale
One tablebord, six joyne stooles, setle and chayer with other smale things £1 6*s.*
In brass and pewter and iron £3.
Four barels and tubbs and other lumber 10*s.*

In the Workeinge House
In ware and tooles and other lumber £35.
In debts upon the booke £40.
Money in his purse £31 14*s.*
The workehouse and wood and other lumber £8.

Total £135 8*s.*

In debts which was then oweing to divers men £45.[2]

Total £90 8*s.*

Swithin Gibbens and William Pye, appraisors.
Bartholomew Benger als Berenger, witness.

Buried St. Peter 6 April 1680 'John Man'.
Will 17 March 1672/3; probate and inventory exhibition not recorded; will endorsed 'This will with inv[y] was delivered into the Bishops Office by Mr Geo. Woodford Reg[r] of the Archdeaconry of Sarum being found by him in that Office Feb '96.'

1. Roman numerals throughout.
2. Debts owed by the deceased should not form part of the inventory.

231 ANN CRIPS

widow [will] 15 April 1680 P1/C/341

One bedsted, cord and matt, bed and bolster, coverled and blankett, curtins and vallins £2.
Waring aparill £2.
One chest, 3 shetts, 8 napkins, old brase and pewter and a little box and lookeing glase £1.
One gold ring 14*s.*

[*Total omitted, by addition* £5 14*s.*]

Nathaniel Popioy and Thomas Sampson, appraisors.
Timothy Mundy, witness.

Buried St. Peter 19 February 1679/80.
Will 11 December 1679; probate 8 September 1680 to [unnamed].

232 JOHN CLERK[1] junior
pinmaker [will] 5 July 1680 P1/C/353

Twenty douzen of pins number 10 £5.
Thirty [and two *added*] douzen of pins number 11 £9 12*s.*
Three pound and half of 4 in a row 6*s.*
Half a douzen of quartern pins 4*s.* 6*d.*
One pound of number 12 1*s.* 8*d.*
Eight rings and 14 pound of wire £12.
Eight reams of large paper and one ream of packing £4 10*s.*
Three heading blocks £2.
Draweing blocks and tooles 15*s.*
For mills and wheel £1 15*s.*
Two furnaces and mettle £1 10*s.*
Fourty six pounds of orgyle 11*s.* 6*d.*
Two cutting sheares 5*s.*
Fourty pounds of pin mettle £1 3*s.*
A pump and barrell £1 10*s.*
Weareing apparrell and money in his pockett £4.
Bed, bedstead, blanketts, coverlead, [*illegible deletion*] [pillowes *added*], curtains and vallains in the chamber over the hall £4.
Chest of drawers and cupboard £1 10*s.*
Two chests, one coffer, two boxes, 3 trunks £1 5*s.*
Three chaires 1*s.* 6*d.*
Two andirons, warmeing pan and fire shovel and looking glass 10*s.*

In a Back Chamber
Three livery bedsteads with the ordinary furniture belongeing thereunto £1 10*s.*
A chaire, pannell, pillin, sadle and tableboard 12*s.*
Brass and pewter £1 10*s.*
Three pair of sheets, a dowzin and half of napkins and tablecloth 16*s.*
Fireshovel, tongues, jack, spitts, dripping pans and doggs 18*s.*
A table board and four joynt stooles 10*s.*
A horse £3.
Three barrells and other lumber 10*s.*
Raggs £1.
In good debts £4 12*s.*

Total £66 18*s.* 2*d.*

Henry Cowsey and Richard Worrell[2], appraisors.

Burial not recorded [St. Mary register wanting September 1678 to April 1681].
Will and codicil 2 June 1680; probate not recorded; renunciation 23 November 1680 by John Clarke the elder, pinmaker, and William Cornish alias Duffe, yeoman, executors; renunciation 23 November 1680 by Anne Clarke, testator's widow, refusing to take out letters of adminiatration; commission 8 December 1680, oath administered 17 December 1680 at All Hallows Bread Street, London, to Joseph Haskoll and John Bryen; bond 5 January 1680/1, administration to Joseph Haskoll and John Bryen, principal creditors and administrators during the minority of Richard Clark, testator's son and sole executor.

1. 'of St Mary in Marlburrow'.
2. 'both of the parish of St Peter in Marlburrow'.

233 MICHAJELL BAYLY

currier 22 July 1680 P1/B/543

His weareinge apparell and money in his purse £2 10s.[1]

In the Chamber over Entry

Four paire of sheetes £1.

Three table cloathes, on per pillabeares and halfe a dozen napkins, [one tablecloth mor *added*] £1.

One flockebed, a flocke boister and one fether boster and blankete and coverle, curtaines and vallens and bedsted £2.

One prest, tablebord, chest, three coffers, boxes and cheyer and other lumber 16s.

In the Chamber over the Hale

One fether bed, one fether boyster and one flocke boyster, two blanckets and one rugg, bedsted and curtaines and vallens £2.

Two tablebords, one cubberd and foure joyne stooles and on joyne cheyer, five cheyers, one coffer [one per of brass andiers and other irons *added*] £1 10s.

In the Chamber over the Kitchine

One old flockbed, one old flock boyster and one blanckett, old bedsteed, two carpetts and one lookinge glas and other lumber in the rome 16s.

In the Kitchine

Fourteen pewter platters, one pewter flagin, five pewter porengers, one pewter quart pott, two pewter plats £2.

Five brass potts, two brass kitles, one brass furness, six brass skillets, warmeinge pane, two brass ladles £3.

One per andiers, one per iron dogs, three iron spits, jacke, fender 10s.

One tablebord and frame, three joyne stooles and one low on and settle, one letle tablebord, two cheyers and other lumber £1.

In the Sellor

Five barrells, one kive, four tubbs, one selt, one kivor, one planke and other lumber £1 6s.

In the Shopp

Three plankes, press, five knives and other lumber £1.

In fier wood 10s.

Total £20 18s.

The inventary on the other side comes to in all the sum of £20 18s.

There due in debts on booke £18 19s.

[*Total including debts owed* £39 17s.]

There is owinge from Michaiell Bayly the deseased in debts £39.[2]

And to divers men one specialty 17s.

In other debts the sum of £50.

Soe there is as it doe appeare £11 to be paid more then the goods and debts will pay and this is a just accompt by us.

Thomas Ingles, Bartholomew Benger als Berenger and Thomas Keynton, appraisors.

Burial not recorded [St. Mary register wanting September 1678 to April 1681].

Inventory exhibited 7 September 1680; bond 8 September 1680, administration to Sarah Bayly, intestate's widow.

1. Roman numerals throughout.
2. Debts owed by the deceased should not form part of the inventory.

234 FRANCIS HERRINGE

feltmaker 6 January 1680/1 P1/H/459

One bedsteed, matt and cord 13*s.* 4*d.*
A parcell of dry beanes £2 10*s.*
A parcell of seeds 4*s.*
A tableboard and 4 joyned stooles and cupboard £1 5*s.*
Two chaires and rack and 3 shelves 3*s.* 4*d.*
One cive and kiver, 1 paile, 2 barrells 10*s.*
Wood and ladder and [*blank*] 9*s.*
Hampiers 1*s.* 6*d.*
Eight earthen dishes and trenchards and firepanns 2*s.*
A fire buckett and iron plate 2*s.*
One feather bedd and bolster, rugg and blankett [and one flock bedd *deleted*] £1 15*s.*
One pott and skyllett and 2 platters 6*s.*
Weareinge apparrell £2.
1 parcell of hatts and bands £18 9*s.* 7*d.*
Bonds and money £30.
A tilt for the stanninge glass £1.
A garden of plants £2.
The lumber 5*s.* 6*d.*

Total £51 16*s.* 3*d.* [*recte* £61 16*s.* 3*d.*]

John Horner and Beniamin Lawrane, appraisors.

Burial not recorded [St. Mary register wanting September 1678 to April 1681].
Will 4 December 1680; probate not recorded; commission 10 January 1680/1, oath administered 21 January 1680/1 to Henry Bloxsome, cheese factor, testator's cousin.

235 JORAMY MORTHEAS[1]

14 March 1680/1 P1/M/258

In the Seller
For 11 hogsheads of beer £6 12*s.*
Mor 6 emtey hogsheads and 8 omtey tereses and 7 emtey barelles £1 9*s.*
One teobell and stands and coubord and other lomber with gloss and eorth bottells £1.
The working tooles belonging to his tread £1 10*s.*

In the Steebell and Shoop and other letell Shoop
Of wod and other lounbe 15*s.*
6 living stoor piges £2 10*s.*

In the Bocksid
Of wod and other loumber £1.

In the Brew Hows and Butery
One brass fornis and bruing vessill and tobes and molt mill and other loimber £4.

In the Shouffull Bord Roome
One ordneorey bed and bed steet and mat and shouffall boord and frame with foorem and blanketes £2.

In the Kichen
One brass boyler and 3 brass kitells and 2 skilote and saspanes and woreming panes £3.
Of peuter: 14 flagons, 2 potes 18*s.*
13 peuter poringers 7*s.* 6*d.*
18 dishes greet and small £2 5*s.*
Peuter sasores and pleates 7*s.*
5 chambor potes [and pleattes *deleted*] 7*s.*
Mor brass and tining candellstiks and spits and joron andorions with a rack and driping panes and a teobell and foreme and stooles and skimers and leodelles and a jock and other loumber £2 10*s.*
3 sivelliur spoones 15*s.* 6*d.*
Column total £31 6*s.*

In the Kichen Chamber
One feothor bead and bolster and blanket and roog and bed sted and cortaines and valines and one trockell bed and bolster

of flockes and a bedsteede and teobell and stooles and other loumber £5.

In the best Chamber
3 teobells and 6 chayers and corpetes £2.

In the Closet
In loumber 5s.

In the Bocke Geret
One flock bead and bolster and roge and blankets and a teobell and boxes and other loumber £2.

In the Goret next the Street
One small feother bead and bolster and flock bead and bolster and flock bead and bolstor and roges and blankets and bed steeted and teobelles and to preses and boxes and other lounber £4 10s.
His weoring close £3.
The lining sheetes and teobell naptkins and other lining £4.

In the Holl
3 teobelles and stooles and binches £1.
Column total £21 15s.

In the Shambelles
Of plainkes and wod £1.

Total £54 1s.

Roger Williams and John Munday, appraisors.

Buried St. Peter 3 March 1680/1, 'Jeremiah Matthews senior'.
Bond 15 March 1680/1, administration to Genevora Matthews, intestate's widow.

1. 'Jeremiah Matthews' on bond.

236 STEPHEN GILMORE
gentleman[1] 16 September 1681
P1/G/247

His weareinge apparell £30.[2]

In the Chamber over the Kitchin
Bed and all that belonge to him, press, cheyers and stools and other goods there £6.

In the Chamber over the Hale
Bed and bedsteed and all that belonge to it, cheyers and stools and the rest of the goods £8.

In the Chamber over the Seller
Bed and bedsteed and other goods there £1 10s.
In silver plate £8.
In lynninge of all sorts £10.

In the Hale
All the furniture there £2.

In the Kitchinn
In brass and pewter and other goods £8.

In the Seller
In brewinge vessels and other ingrediente there £2.
In barke 35 lbs. £35.
In hides and skinns £120.
In debts due on shopp booke £20.
A chatell lease of a barne, garden and patche of ground £20.
In wood and lumber £2.

Total £272 10s.

John Horner, Bartholomew Benger als Berenger and John Wayte, appraisors.

Buried St. Mary 15 September 1681, 'Mr.'.
Will 1 December 1679; probate 7 October 1681 to Sarah Gilmore, testator's daughter.

1. 'tanner' on will.
2. Roman numerals throughout.

237 ANTHONY POWELL
saddler 2 February 1681/2[1] P1/P/323

His weareinge apparrell £2 10*s.*
In ready money 11*s.*

In his Dwelling House
In the Hall
14 pewter dishes £1 1*s.*
9 flaggons 10*s.* 6*s.*
7 pottingers, 3 pewter candlestickes, 4 sawcers, 3 chamber potts 8*s.*6*d.*
4 brass potts, 4 kettells, 3 skilletts, 3 brass candlesticks, 1 warminge pan, 1 skimmer and 1 bast laddle £2 2*s.* 6*d.*
1 paire of andirons and doggs, 4 spitts, 5 paire of pothookes, 2 paire of hanginges, fire pan and tonges, 1 frying pan, 1 chaffin ditch, 1 gridiron and beefe prickers 12*s.*
1 jack 4*s.* 6*d.*
2 old cupboards, 1 table board and frame, 3 stooles, 4 old small chaires, 1 rack and lumber 17*s.*

In the Chamber over the Hall
1 feather bed, bedstead with thappertenances £3 6*s.* 8*d.*
1 table board and frame, 3 joint stooles, 2 chaires, 1 old coffer, 2 boxes, 1 fire pan and tongs, doggs and billowes 11*s.* 6*d.*

In the Roomth over the Hall Chamber
2 flock beds and 1 bedsteed with thappertenances £1 15*s.*
1 table board, 1 coffer and paire of dogs 5*s.*

In the Chamber next the Streete
1 bed, bedsteed and its appertenances, 1 truckle bedsteed £1 15*s.*
2 little table boards and frames, 2 chaires, 2 stooles and 1 firepan and paire of billowes 9*s.*

In the Celler
12 barrells great and small £1 10*s.*
In strong beare £2 10*s.*
4 stands 5*s.*
2 flitches of bacon 18*s.*

In the Brewhouse
1 meashing vate, 11 small kivers, 3 payles and lumber £1 6*s.* 8*d.*

In the Backside
1 pile of faggotts £2 10*s.*
4 store piggs £1 10*s.*

Page total £27 8*s.* 10*d.*

In his Shopp att the Shambles
17 sadles £5 19*s.*
4 dozen of bridles £1 12*s.*
9 collar holsters, stirrupp leathers, whipps, spurs, pillions, port mantles, male pillions and sundry sorts of small wares belonginge to a sadler £13 14s
2 tanned hydes £1 14*s.*
In lynnen of all sorts in the howse £1 2*s.*
In good debts and in desperate debts £14 11*s.* 5*d.*
Page total £38 12*s.* 5*d.*

[In his shopp att his howse *deleted*]
Total £66 1*s.* 3*d.*

John Horner and Noah Webb, appraisors.

Buried St. Mary 26 January 1681/2
Bond 8 March 1681/2, administration to Edith Powell, intestate's widow; inventory exhibited 9 March 1681/2; letter [*undated*] from Joshua Sacheverell[2] to Theophilus Dyer of Salibury Close, referring to the bond, and requesting a supply of licences and bonds with instructions for their use.

1. 'on the Feast of the purification of the Blessed Virgin Mary'.
2. Incumbent of SS Peter and Paul, Marlborough.

238 WILLIAM TALLBOT
collarmaker 20 February 1681/2
P1/T/185

Ware in the shop and in the pitts £10 7*s*.
His wearinge aparell and houshold goods £7 2*s*. 6*d*.
In debts upon booke £14 11*s*. 5*d*.

Total £32 0*s*. 11*d*.

Robert Skent, Henry Turner and Robert Milles, appraisors.

Layd out for a coffin and grave and funerall expences £1 13*s*. 6*d*.[1]
Payd a debt to Jeffrey Perry a debt off £5 1*s*. 3*d*.
Payd John Genings for tand leather 12*s*.
Payd Mr Burgesse and bullocke for rent £3 15*s*.
His other debts amounts to at least £12.

Debts and funerall expences £23 1*s*. 9*d*.

Buried St. Peter 20 February 1681/2.
Will 25 December 1680; probate 8 March 1681/2 to Katherine Talbott, testator's widow.

1. Debts owed by the testator, and executor's expenses should not form part of the inventory.

239 PHILLIPINE GREENFIELD
widow 19 April 1682 P1/G/246

Her wheareinge apparell whollinge and lyninge and money in her purse £5.[1]
One fether bed and one flocke beed and two fether boyster and four fether pillowes, rug and blankes, curtaine and vallings and a standinge bedsted and truckle bed stedd and all belonginge to it £7.
Four flexin sheets, two table cloathes and one dozen napkins and two dammask napkins and 1 dozen of napkins, four pair of sheets with on hollin one, a per pillo cases with on hollen and other small linige £2.
Three trunks 5*s*.

In the Hale
On tablebord, tw joyne stools, three cheyes 12*s*.
Two carpetts and six turky cussions 12*s*.
In sorts of pewter 18*s*.
In brass and warmeinge pann and dogs and fierpan and tongs and other lumber £1.
One side cubbert [2*s*. *deleted*] 5*s*.
In wooden vessells and in wood and lumber £1.
Upon a morgage the sum of £70.

Sub-total £88. 12*s*.

[In desperatt debts the sum of £10 *added*]
Three silver spones and [*illegible deletion*] three small gold rings £1 10*s*.

Total £90 2*s*.

Batholomew Buckerfield and Bartholomew Benger als Berenger, appraisors.

Buried St. Mary 7 February 1681/2 'Mistress Grinfeld widow'.
Will 28 May 1681; probate 9 March 1681/2 to Mary Eatwell, testator's kinswoman.

1. Roman numerals throughout.

240 CATHERINE HAMMON
widow 14 February 1682/3 P1/H/468

Her waring aparrill and her money in her purse [£2 *altered to*] £3 10*s*.
Too rings 9*s*.
4 sheets with other linning £1 5*s*.

2 beeds and all that belong unto it £2 12*s.*
One bedsteed 8*s.*
Brase and pewter £1 15*s.*
A presse and cubbord and table bords with other lumber goods £1 17*s.*
And irons, dogs and other iron things 8*s.*

Total £11 14*s.*

Thomas Liddyard, William Lester and Thomas Garret, appraisors.

Buried St Peter 30 January 1682/3.
Bond 11 May 1683, administration to Edward Hitchcock, intestate's son-in-law, and Elizabeth Gale, intestate's daughter.

241 WILLIAM LEWIS
yeoman 14 March 1682/3 P1/L/204

In the Lodginge Chamber
His weareinge apparell £5.[1]
All the bedinge, bedstead and all [and all *repeated*] that belonge to him £2 10*s.*
Five paire of sheets, three boysters case, six napkins, three pillo cases £1 5*s.*
One chest, three boxes, on litle tablebord, one press, two cheyers, one trunke, one lookeinge glass £1 2*s.*

In the Cockloft
One flocke bed, boyster and pillow, rug, blanketts and one coat and hose of cloth, one box and lumber £1 10*s.*

In the Woolloft
In wooll there £1.
Lumber in the chamber £1.
In malt green and dry £10.
The nest heare skreene and the measures, the malt mill and two yoateinge stones £5.

In the Hale
One tablebord, one joyne forne, two joyne stoles, setle, cubbert, three cheyers, one jacke and weights, one spitt, fierpan and tongues, andiers and fendor, hangles, two grediers and pocke hooke £1 6*s.*

In the Buttery
Twelve pewter platters, three porengers, three tankerds, on flagin, one pewter candlesticke, on pewter boyle, one pint pott, one quart pott £1 1*s.*
Four Bibles and other books 10*s.*
One furness, one brass pott, four brass kitles, two brass skillets, warmeinge pann, skimer, dripping pann £1 8*s.*

In the Seller
Three barrels, two tubbs, one paile, five kivers, one hogsheads, one powderinge tubb, two tun bowles, one safe, one stand £1 2*s.*

In the Malthouse
Five old tubbs, two fier bucketts, three ladder and lumber 10*s.*
On latten lanthorne, two ladinge pailes and three cussions 4*s.*

In the Backeside
In cleft wood and faggods £10.
And two presses and all that belonge to them and one beame and other lumber 13*s.* 4*d.*
Money and debts £150.
One brass pann and iron pott, fringe pann and other lumber £1.
The woolhouse in the possession of Joseph Lewis £26.

Total £216 7*s.* 4*d.* [*recte* £222 1*s.* 4*d.*]

Bartholomew Benger als Berenger, Peter Furnell and Thomas Spackeman senior, appraisors.

Buried St. Mary 6 March 1682/3.

Will 20 December 1682; bond 17 October 1684, John Man, son-in-law and executor, having died before completing probate, Joane his wife is to administer.

1. Roman numerals throughout.

242 HENRY TURNER[1]

collarmaker [bond] 16 March 1682/3
P1/T/186

His wareinge apparrell and monny in his purse £3.
One feather bedd withall the furnutter beloning £4.
Three beddsteeds and three flocke bedds withall oather furnutter £3.
Two tabell boards and halfe a dozen of joynt stooles 16*s.*
One furnase, two kittells, two potts, one payre of andirons, one skillett, one warminge pann £2 16*s.*
6 dishes of pewter, one flaggon and a chamber pott 14*s.*
Three payr of sheets and oather linnen £2.
Two barrells, one hogshead and a cubbard 10*s.*
Wood in the backside 10*s.*

In the Shoppe
In goods £18 10*s.* 4*d.*
One civer, one allome tubb and all oather lomber £2.
The shoppe booke £80.

Total £117 16*s.* 4*d.*

John Hill and Jeremiah Burgis, appraisors.

Buried St. Mary 18 March 1682/3.
Bond 11 May 1683, administration to Hester Turner, intestate's widow.

1. 'of Marleborrough St Maryes'.

243 JOHN DALE

yeoman [will] 20 March 1682/3
P1/D/156

His wearing apparell
One new cloth cote and britches £2.
One sarge cote and britches 10*s.*
One shamey wascoot 6*s.* 8*d.*
One dooe skine paire of britches 5*s.*
One woosted camlett coot 10*s.*
One gray frise coot 6*s.* 8*d.*
One woosted camlett coot, one cloth paire of britches, one sarge wascoot 10*s.*
Two fustine wascoots, one fustine paire of trowsers 6*s.* 8*d.*
Fower paire of woosted stockens and one paire of yarning stockens 6*s.* 8*d.*
Fower blew aprons 1*s.* 4*d.*
Three dowlas shurts 7*s.* 6*d.*
One new hatt and tw ould hatts 15*s.*
Ten cravatts, six handcerchevs, three paire of holland sleeves, two night caps £1.
Fower paire of gloves 1*s.* 6*d.*
One paire of new shoos, two paire of ould shoos 5*s.*
One Bible 5*s.*
One paire of silver buckells and one silver sale 4*s.*
One paire of ould boots and spurs 3*s.*
One pewter flaggon 2*s.*
One cane 6*d.*
Two boxes 3*s.*
Lumber goods 5*s.*
Ten quarters of malt £10.
Bands good and bad £77.
Two gould rings 8*s.*
In money £79 12*s.*
Book debts good and bad £21 9*s.* 8*d.*
Sub-total £197 4*s.* 2*d.*

Debts more 12*s.*

Total £197 16*s.*

Thomas Keynton and Francis Smith, appraisors.

Buried St. Peter 16 March 1682/3.
Will 12 March 1682/3; probate 11 May 1683 to John Sadler, innholder, and John Smith, grocer, joint executors.

244 PHILIP FRANCKLYN
gentleman 25 April 1683 P1/F/161

In his Lodging Chamber
His weareing apparell £3.
In ready money £23 10s.
In the same chamber two standing beddsteads, bedding, bolsters, pillowes, blancketts and coverings belonging £5.
In the same chamber two side boards, 4 coffers, two chaires and other lumber £1.

In the Chamber next adjoyning
Two old bedsteads 10s.
In the same chamber one feather bedd, bolster, pillows, blancketts and covering thereunto belonging £2.
In table lynen and other lynen £2.

In the Hall
In brass and pewter £3.
One jack, 1 pair of andjrons, spitts, fire shovell and tongs 10s.
One table board and frame, 1 chest, 1 cupboard with some old chaires, stooles and other lumber £1.

In the Kitchen
1 old furnace 5s.

In the Cellar
4 barrels, 1 kever and other old lumber £1 10s.
In malt £20.
Money due upon bonds £118.

Total £181 5s.

John Farmer, Robert Miles senior and John Richardson, appraisors.

Buried St. Peter 22 April 1683 'Mr'.
Will 23 March 1682/3; renunciation 11 May 1683 by John Franklyn of Woodborough and John Durnford of Grafton, overseers, in favour of Thomas Hunt 'a relacion of the deceased' during the minority of Philip Francklyn (son of John), the testator's grandson; bond 12 May 1683, administration to Thomas Hunt.

245 JOHN MANN
roper 11 June 1683 P1/M/264

In the Chamber over the Hale
His weareinge apparell £5.[1]
One fether bed, one flocke bedd, one rugg, one blanckerd, one fether boyster, three pillowes of fethers, one flocke pillow, one bedsteed, curtain and vallins £4 10s.
One chest of drawers, one other chest, two trunkes, two boxes, four cheyers, two stoles, one warminge pann and two paire of iron doggs £1 10s.

In the next Chamber
6 paire of sheetes and one, 8 pare of pillow casses and one diaper tablecloth, six napkins, four tablecloaths and sixteene napkins, one diaper cubberd cloth and one plaine on, three boysters casses, one dozen and a halfe of corse towells £2 13s. 8*d*.

In the Backer Chamber
One fether bedd, one flocke boyster, two fether pillowes, one rugg, two blancketts, one coverled, one boyster, [all paire *deleted*] curtains [and vallens *added*], one flockebed, two blancketts, a bedsteed £2 8s.

In the next Chamber
One flockbed and fether boyster, one rugg, one paire of blancketts, one truckle

bedsteed, matt and cord, two table bords, five letle cheyers, one coffer and three litle boxes, one chest and one cheyer £1 17*s.*

In the Hale and Buttery
One tablebord, one cubberd, one joyne cheyer, one setle and five joyne stooles, one letle cubbert £1.
Sixteene pewter disses, tenn plates, 8 pewter porrengers, one flagon and two tanketts £1 12*s.*
One jacke and two spitts, andiers and doggs, one paire of hangers, fender and steeleplate 13*s.* 4*d.*

In the Brewhouse
Two brass furnesses, three brass potts, one iron pott, three litle kitles, three skillits, two skimmers and two bastinge ladles, two candlestickes £4 8*s.*

In the Seller
One hogshead, five barrels, two kivers, one measeinge coule, three tubbs, one bowderinge tubb and one buckett 16*s.*
In bookes 13*s.*
Hempe and in wares £64 6*s.* 6*d.*
One horse, hey and wood £5.
In workeing tooles and lumber £1.
In money and debts £104 4*s.*
The dwellinge house £18.

Total £218 17*s.* 2*d.* [*recte* £219 11*s.* 6*d.*]

Inn debts £50.[2]

Total £168 17*s.* 2*d.*

Thomas Spackman senior, Peter Furnell, William Pye and Bartholomew Benger, appraisors.

Buried St. Peter 24 May 1683 'John Man'.
Will 22 May 1683; probate and inventory exhibition not recorded.

1. Roman numerals throughout.
2. Debts owed by the deceased should not form part of the inventory.

246 JOHN SHIPPREE[1]

journeyman shoemaker [*undated*, c.1683]
P1/S/499

His wearing apparrell £1 10*s.*
A coffer 1*s.*
A bond £2 10*s.*

Total £4 1*s.* 6*d.*

Depts to be paid out of this £1 18*s.* 6*d.*[2]

Swithin Gibbons and William Pye, appraisors.

Buried St. Mary 17 July 1683 'Shipry'.
Bond 11 September 1683, administration to Thomas Shippree, intestate's brother.

1. 'of the parish of St Maryes in the Burrow of Marlebrough, who dyed the 8th July 1683'.
2. Debts owed by the deceased should not form part of the inventory.

247 CHARITY FREMAN[1]

widow [bond] 2 October 1683
P1/F/170

Waring apparell linnen and woollen £2.
One bed and bolster £1.
One sett of curtins and vallense 10*s.*
One paire of andiers, one firepann and tongs 4*s.*
Two coverlids 4*s.*
Three leathring chaires and five cooshens 7*s.*
Four goynt stooles 3*s.*
A tablebord and carpit 7*s.*
A tablebord and settle 7*s.*
One bedsted, one litle tablebord and press 12*s.*

One bed and bolster £1.
A plate for an east 2*s.*
Therty pound weight of peuter £1.
One iron dripping pan, two spitts, two paire of pot hooks, one basting ladle, one flesh forke, one paire of tongs 5*s.*
Three lid waits and other small brass waits 10*s.*
Six small peices of brass 14*s.*
One small old furness 10*s.*
One neast of boxes and one old counter 10*s.*
Three barrels and three tubbs 10*s.*
One old warmeing pann 2*s.*
A dwelling house £160.
A leas at the Shambles £10.
Old iron and lumber goods £1.

Total £181 17*s.*

Phillip Chivers, Thomas Godfor and Thomas Grenaway, appraisors.

Burial not recorded.
Bond 18 October 1684, administration to Christopher Freeman, maltster, intestate's eldest son.

1. 'Mrs.'.

248 MARY HURLE

widow [will] 11 October 1683
P1/H/485

In the Shope
6 dozen of great leather at 8*s.* the dozen £2 8*s.*
8 dozen and halfe of mens and womens gloves at 8*s.* per dozen £3 8*s.*
2 hundred and 1 dozen of small leather at 40*s.* per hundred £4 4*s.*
5 dozen and ½ of boys and girles gloves £1 2*s.*
2 dozen and ½ of mittins 4*s.*
2 dozen and ½ of plaine gloves at 6*s.* per dozen 15*s.*
11 peare of boys lether bretches 16*s.* 6*d.*
8 peare of mens lether bretches £1.
22 peare of boys lineings £1 2*s.*
18 peare of mens lineings £1 7*s.*
2 dozen and ½ of calves leather £1 15*s.*
3 swatchells and peeces of leather about the shope 5*s.*

In the Hall
One table bord and frame, 3 joyne stooles, one side cubbord, one joyne chaire, one settle, one glass cubbord, one trencher racke, one bacon racke, one loocking glass, one cobbard cloth, one brass morter, 3 spitts, one per of bellows and tongues, 3 brass potts, 2 dozen and ½ of trenchers, one chaffeing dish, one per of honigers, one brass candlestick, one hower glass, one wooden tray, one per doggs, one fier pan, one salt box, two brass ladles, 2 flesh hoocks, one pewter bowle, one side table, one earthen salt £3 6*s.*
One dripping pan, one iron greate, 10 boocks and 3 earthen dishes 10*s.*

In the Buttery
4 barrells 10*s.*
4 pewter dishes, 2 sacers, one poringer 10*s.*
3 brass kettles, 3 skelletts, one basting ladle, one frying pan, 1 per pothoocks and other lumber £1 10*s.*
For sheeres, pareing knives and other implyments belonging to the trade[1] 5*s.*

In a Neighbours Kitchin
9 pewter dishes, 2 pewter candlesticks £1.

In the Chamber over the Hall
One bedstead, matt and cord, one trundle beadstead, one flock bed, one fether bolster, one fether pillow, one old coverlid, one yallow rugg £1 10*s.*
One great chest, one side cubbord, five joynestooles, 2 cushen stooles, one lether chaire, one basket chaire, one box, one

Bible, one cushen, one carpett, three fether pillows £2.
Herr wareing apparell £4.

In the Chamber over the Shopp
One bedstead, matt and cord, one fether bed, one coverlid, 2 blanckets, one flockebed, one coverlid, 2 blanckets, one shute of curtaines and vallands, 2 fether bolsters, 2 fether pillows, one other flockbed and bolster, one coverlid and one blancket £1 4*s.*
6 peare of canvis sheetes £1 4*s.*
One dozen of napkins, 4 canvis bolster cases, 10 pillow beeres, 2 coffers, one truncke, one search, one temser, one side board £1 6*s.*

In the Garrett
One old bedstead, one old table board, some wood and other lumber 10*s.*
Wood in the backside £2.
One furnis and brewing vessells, one brass pott, one skellett £1 10*s.*
The tilt and standing 5*s.*
Two leases £60.
Mony and depts £62 10*s.*
6 pewter dishes, 2 porengers, 2 plates, one brass pan 16*s.*
3 small silver spoons 18*s.*
4 old curtins 4*s.*
A warmeing pan 1*s.* 6*d.*
A per of doggs 1*s.*

Total £160 17*s.* [*recte* £165 17*s.*]

Tobias Chandler and Robert Butcher, appraisors.

Buried St. Mary 4 October 1683 'Mary Hurle widow'.
Will 15 September 1683; renunciation 23 October by Sarah Hunt, testator's daughter, in favour of Martha Hurle, her sister and joint executrix; probate 25 October 1683 to Martha Hurle, testator's daughter.

1. Mary Hurle's late husband, Simon (no. 141), had been a glover.

249 CHRISTOPHER ELLIS glazier and **ELIZABETH** his wife
18 October 1683[1] P1/E/117

The testators wearing apparell £1 15*s.*

In the Hall
One bedsteed, curtens and vallians, coard and matt 18*s.*
One feather bolster and pillow, one flock bed and twoo rugges £1 6*s.*
One bedsteed, coard and matt, twenty lockerum napkins, twoo pillowbeers, one paire of dowlas sheetes and course linnen £1 1*s.* 2*d.*
One paile, one powdring tubb, one buckett, one childs chayer, one little cowle, one paire of hangells and other lumber 5*s.* 6*d.*

In the Kitchine
One tableboard and frame, fower joynted stooles, one leatherne chayer, one childs chayer, one small rush chayer, one jack, one well buckett and rope, one iron kittle £4 16*s.* 2*d.*

In the Best chamber
Twoo table boards and frames, twoo rush chayers, one iron grate and one leatherne chayer 15*s.* 6*d.*

In the Clossett
34 peeces of pewter waying 62lbs att 8*d.* per pound £2 1*s.* 4*d.*
One warming pan, twoo skilletts, one copper pott, one cheffine dish, one skimer ladle and brass candlestick 12*s.*
Twoo old chamber potts, one paire of brasse [scales *added*], one paire of iron dogges with brasse [heds *added*], one paire of iron andirons, one paire of fire shovells and tongues, one fire shovell and

forke 13*s.*
One cast-brasse pott, one pott hooke, one brasse kittle, one iron frieing pan, one gridiron, one spitt, one iron dogg, three trunkes, one coffer, twoo boxes, one looking glasse, old bookes, one bedtick, one paire of billowes £1 4*s.* 4*d.*

In the Kitchine Chamber
One paire of great scales and beame, one box of tooles, the sowdring irons and other tooles and soder £3 4*s.*

In the Brew House
One furnace and grate £1 4*s.*

In the Worke House
The [*illegible*] casting frame, leade, ashes and sand 15*s.*

In the Celler
Twoo stands, fower barrells, one tun bowle, 2 dozen of glasse bottells 17*s.*

In the Shopp
His shoppboard, one iron toole, old leade, one stand, other lumber and glasse, one [kettle *deleted*] kiver and one iron spade 18*s.* 10*d.*

Total £21 2*s.* 4*d.* [*recte* £22 6*s.* 10*d.*]

Thomas Cotton and John Horner, appraisors.

Neither burial recorded.
Bond 13 October 1683, administration to Thomas Bayly, mercer, and Noah Webb, linen draper, principal creditors; commission 13 October 1683, Elizabeth Ellis having died without administering her husband's goods, oath administered to Thomas Bayly and Noah Webb.

1. 'Thursday'.

250 EDWARD CARTER

saddler 31 March 1684 P1/C/368

His wearing apparell £3.

In his Lodgeing Chamber
One bedstead, 1 feather bed, 1 bolster, 3 pillowes with coverletts, blanketts, old curtins and vallians thereunto belonging £4.
One old truckle bedstead, one small flockbed with 1 old coverlett and blankett thereto belonging 10*s.*
1 old chest, 1 coffer, 1 small tableboard, 3 small boxes and 2 small old truncks 10*s.*
6 old silver spoones £1 8*s.*
1 small looking glass, window curtaine, rod and 1 old brush 2*s.* 6*d.*
One old firepan, tongs and old doggs 1*s.* 6*d.*
One pair old holland sheetes, 2 pillowcases and cupboard cloath £1.
6 pair of old canvas sheetes 18*s.*
3 old table cloathes and one dozen and a halfe of old napkins £1.

In the Chamber over the Parlour
One bedstead, 1 feather bedd, 1 bolster, 2 pillowes, 1 blankett, 1 rugg with 1 pair old curtains and vallians thereto belonging £3.
2 little table boards, 1 old cupboard, 7 joynt stooles, 1 old close stoole with other lumber £1.

In the Chamber over the Kitchin
One old bedstead, 1 old feather bedd, 1 bolster, 1 pillow, 1 rugg, 3 blankets with old curtains belonging £3.
In the same chamber one old tableboard, 1 joynt fourme, 5 old stooles and 1 chaire 14*s.*

In the Garrett over the Parlour Chamber
1 bedstead and other old lumber 10*s.*

In the Garret over the Pelican Chamber
Old lumber 5*s.*

In the Parlour
2 old table boards and frames, 1 settle, 4 joyned stooles and 1 old chaire £1 4*s.*
1 pair old dowlis sheetes 8*s.*

In the Kitchin
16 old pewter platters, 2 small candlestickes, 5 plates, 4 poringers, 3 little salts and 3 small sawcers £1 10*s.*
8 old flagon potts and 6 old chamber potts 12*s.*
3 old brass kettles, 3 old skellets, 1 warming pan, 1 stew cover, 2 brass ladles, 2 old skimmers and 2 little fire dishes £1 2*s.*
3 small bellbrass potts, 1 skellett and 1 morter 14*s.*
2 old tableboards, 1 cupboard, 2 joynt stooles with other lumber 10*s.*
1 jack, 1 iron rack, 1 ironback, 1 firepan, 1 pair tongs, 1 paire fire dogges, 2 pair of hangells, 1 cleaver, 1 frying pan, 2 iron dripping pans, 2 spitts, 3 paire pothookes, 2 old grid irons, 3 steele plates, 1 fender, jack, weights and chaine £1 5*s.*
One old Bible 3*s.*

In the Brewhouse
1 brass furnace with brewing vessell and other lumber £2.

In the Cellar
Halfe a hogshead of beere, 4 empty hogsheads and other lumber £2.

In the Backside
1 cowe, 1 sowe and pigges, 1 barrowe pigge with a little wood and hay £4.
His goods in the shopp £15 15*s.*
Goods total £52 2*s.*

Debts owing hopeful £6 3*s.* 7*d.*
Debts desperate £22 8*s.* 7*d.*

Total £80 14*s.* 2*d.*

Richard Worrell, and John Rutt, appraisers.

Buried St. Peter 19 March 1683/4
Inventory exhibited 10 April 1684; bond 11 April 1684, administration to Anne Carter, intestate's widow.

251 EDWARD LAWRENCE

3 April 1684 P1/L/201

His waring apparell and books £4.

In the Hall
1 table bord, 3 joynt stools, 4 chayrs, 1 jack, 2 spitts, 2 driping pans, 1 payr of dogs, 1 payr of andirons, 1 fyre pan and tongs, 1 chefing dish, 1 grid iron, 2 payr of hangells, 2 steel plates, £1 14*s.*
In bras and pewter £2 10*s.*

In the Buttery
3 barrells, 1 kive, 2 covers, 1 kowl, 1 tubb 13*s.*

In his Lodging Chamber
2 flock beds, 2 rugs, 4 blanketts, 1 payr of curtains, 2 bed steeds, 1 boulster, 3 pillows, 1 chest of drawers, 2 chests, 2 boxes, 1 cofer, 1 close stool, 1 bed pan and other implements £5 17*s.*
All his linon £1 15*s.* 6*d.*

In the Garrett
1 fether bed, 1 bolster, 3 pillows, 1 rug, 1 payr of blanketts £2 16*s.*
2 bed steeds 7*s.*
Debts good and bad £22 14*s.*
Mony in the house £1 12*s.*
In wood 4*s.*

[*Total omitted, by addition* £44 2*s.* 6*d.*]

Joseph Webb and Noah Webb, appraisors.

Buried St. Mary 30 March 1684.
Will 6 April 1680; probate 10 April 1684 to [unnamed].

252 THOMAS HANCOCK
10 April 1684 P1/H/487

Cloths 15*s.*

In his Bed Chamber
2 bedsteeds, 2 flocke beds, 2 ruggs, 2 blankets and 1 pare of sheets, 1 pair of curtains and valens £1 10*s.*
1 old coffer, 1 box, 1 chest [1 trunke *deleted*] and a little old trunke and a little old table bord, 2 bolsters with other small things 10*s.*
2 old bed steeds, 2 flocke beds, 2 rugges, 2 sheets, 2 blankets, 2 bolsters £1.

In the Celler
4 barrells, 3 tubes, 2 chivers and other lumber £1 5*s.*
1 furnace, 3 kettles, 3 pots and a warming pan £2 10*s.*
1 table board, 1 cubboord, 4 joyne stools 8*s.*
9 pewter dishes with other pewter 12*s.* 6*d.*
2 pigges £2 9*s.* 6*d.*
Wood: 2 hundred halfe of faggots and other hard wood £2.
Lumber, small things 5*s.* [4*d. added*]

Total £13 15*s.* [4*d. added, recte* £13 5*s.* 4*d.*]

Buried St. Mary 25 October 1683.
Bond dated 10 April 1684, administration to Ann Hancock, intestate's widow.

253 GILES LIMOR[1]
yeoman [will] 14 May 1684 P1/L/203

In the Kechen
2 brass kettells, 2 ketill potts, 1 bras pott, 3 skillets, 1 bras chefing dishe, 1 jornpott, 1 fornes £3.
7 pewter platters, 4 poringers, 2 flagons, 1 pewter condillstik, 2 platts, 4 sasers, 10 pewter bottlls, 1 salte sellr, 1 chamber pott £1 7*s.* 6*d.*
3 tubbs, 4 kivers, 2 bocketts, 4 barells, 2 stondes, 1 lad paile, 1 basting ladle and skimer, fier pan and tongs and dogs, andiorn and friaing pan and 1 [pot hangels *added*], 1 washe bowle, 5 old chayers, earthen potts and pottes, pans and other lumbar £1 10*s.*

In the Halle
1 tabell bord, 5 stoles, 1 wanscot settell, 3 fire pans, 2 spitts, 4 still plats and other lumber £1 10*s.*

In the Chamber
2 standing bedstids, 1 trundell bed sted, 1 litell tabell, a sid bord, 1 couberd, 2 chests, 1 trunke, 1 warmingpan, 4 litell boxes, 1 firbookett, 2 coffers £2.
2 feather beads, 1 flocke bead, 3 old rugs, 5 blanketts, 4 pilows, 3 bowlsters £4.
2 sett of linse curttens and valliens £1
Savttine peces of simestrie ware and bone lace £5.
1 yuine frame, 1 sadell, 1 jorne jacke, 1 axe and hathet, 1 yornbar, 3 zas and weges, wood and other lumbar £1 10*s.*

Total £20 17*s.* 6*d.*

Samuell Fowler and Richard Bronsdon, appraisors.

Buried St. Peter 6 May 1684 'Limer'.
Will 1 November 1675; probate 16 October 1684 to [unnamed].

1. 'Lymer' on will.

254 ALICE SCORY
spinster 21 August 1684 P1/S/508

One feather bed, 2 feather bolsters, 2 feather pillows, 3 blancketts, two coverlids, one cradle rugge, one

bedstead, cord and matt £4.
One cupboard 5s.
One pewter chamber pott, 8 pewterdishes, 1 pewter bason, 1 brass warming pan, 2 brass pans, 1 brass kettle and skimer, 1 brass pott and skillett, 1 frying pan £2.
1 brass mortar and iron pestle, 3 pewter dishes, 1 pewter cupp 3s.
One trunck, 1 little trunck, 1 box of drawers, 1 coffer, 1 box, 1 stoole, 1 resh chaire, 3 barrells, 2 wooden platters, 1 pair of bellows, 1 old buckett, 1 steel plate, 1 pair of hangells, 2 wooden dishes and strayner, 12 trenchers, 1 cushen, 1 hatchett, 1 temser, 1 brass candlestick, 7 quart bottles, gally potts, earthen dishes and other old things £1.
One Bible and 4 small bookes 2*s.* 6*d.*
Two bolster cases, 3 sheetes, 2 table cloathes, 7 pillow cases and 12 napkins £1 2*s.*
3 brushes 1*s.*
Her wearing apparell £2 10*s.*
Due upon bill £7.
One looking glass 5*s.*
28 quarters of mault £27.

Total £45 8*s.* 6*d.*

Robert Butcher and Tobias Chandler, appraisors.

Burial not recorded.
Will 22 July 1684; probate 17 October 1684 to [unnamed].

255 JOHN OSGOOD[1]

wheelwright 16 September 1684 P1/O/45

Att the howse of John Farmer
Vellyes and other tooles 13*s.* 6*d.*

Att Winkworth's Howse
Tooles, velleyes and lumber and his chest £1 14*s.* 6*d.*

Att William Farmer's howse
His coat and breeches 14*s.*

Att Axford
Vellyes, spokes and stocks £3 0*s.* 6*d.*
Received in money of one Pyke of Chisbury 5*s.*

Total £6 7*s.* 6*d.*

John Clarke and John Bowshire, appraisors.

Burial not recorded.
Inventory exhibited and accounts submitted 11 May 1685 by Robert Bowshire, principal creditor.

1. 'of St. Peters in Marlebrough'.

256 JOHN SWEET

glover 10 October 1684 P1/S/507

His wearinge apparell and money in his purse £1.[1]
Four pewter platters and 1 pewter candlestick and one brass spoone, one pewter diss, one pewter saltseller, one pewter plate 8*s.*
One pewter pint pott 6*d.*
One brass pott 4*s.*
One cubberd, one trunke, one coffer and three napkins, [all *deleted*] one lookeinge glass 5*s.*
One fether bed, one bedsteed and two boulsters with all the appurtemses belonginge to itt £2.
One paire of hangles, one skillett with other sall lumber 3*s.*
Money in the house £21 10*s.*
One bond £5.

Total £30 10*s.* 6*d.*

Bartholomew Benger als Berenger and John Reeve, appraisors.

Buried St. Mary 4 May 1684.

Will 25 February 1683/4; probate not recorded; inventory exhibited 16 March 1684/5; commission 9 May 1694, oath administered to Edward Dangerfield, executor.

1. Roman numerals throughout.

257 TIMOTHY PIDDING[1]

26 January 1684/5[2] P1/B/574

Linnen close and woolling £2 14*s.*
3 knifs, a chesell, a gouge, two hamers, a pare of shears, saw and hachet 8*s.* 6*d.*
2 hats and eoirn 1*s.* 8*d.*
2 boxes 1*s.*6*d.*
In monny £8
In depts £5 10*s.*

Total £16 15*s.* 8*d.*

Thomas Glyde and Timothy Bowshear, appraisors.

Buried St. Mary 26 January 1684/5 'Piddin'.

Will [undated]; letter 27 January 1684/5 to Mr. Dyer from Cornelius Yate, incumbent of St. Mary Marlborough, refering to the will as 'a very infirm one, being without either date or Wittness'; bond 28 January 1684/5, administration to John Pidding, tailor of 'Ste Marice', testator's brother.

1. 'Bidding' on will.
2. Photocopy of original, filmed as part of DW/PC/5/1698 before deposit at the London County Council Record Office (now London Metropolitan Archives), presumably deposited in London in error, when the provincial documents were dispersed from Somerset House.

258 AN HANCOCK

widow 17 March 1684/5 P1/H/489

Wearing aparrell £2 10*s.*
A chest, trunk and box 8*s.*
A table, 2 stooles, 2 chayres and a cupboarde 6*s.*
A parcell linnen 10*s.*
A coffer and boxes 1*s.* 6*d.*
A table boarde without a frame 1*s.* 6*d.*
A table boarde and 4 stooles 7*s.*
3 chayres 1*s.* 6*d.*
A jack 3*s.*
2 payre little andirones, fire pan and tonges 2*s.*
Wooden vessell in celler and backside 14*s.*
Wood in backside and celler 16*s.*
A pig 6*s.*
For other od things 2*s.* 6*d.*
In ready money £13.

Total £19 9*s.*

Edward Hopkins and John Blissett senior, appraisors.

Buried St. Mary 9 February 1684/5 'widow Hancock'.

Will 4 February 1684/5; probate 18 March 1684/5 to executrix [Elizabeth Hancock, testator's daughter].

259 WILLIAM CORNISH alias DUFFE[1]

tailor [will] [*undated*, c.1685] P1/C/372

His wareinge apparrell £2.
In monnyes in his purss £1.
The pewtter in the kitchin £1.
6 brass potts £2 10*s.*
4 kettells, one brass pann, one warminge pann, 3 skilletts £2.
One candelsticke, pesell and morter and skimer and bastinge ladle 4*s.*
One jacke and drippinge pann and lattinge pann 8*s.*

One pott hookes and tounges, 3 hangells, one paire of doggs, grate and fender 15*s.*
One irone backe, one tabell board, one cobbord and oather lomber £1.
3 fliches baican and peece £2.

In the Chamber over the Hall
One feather bedd, 3 blanckitts, 2 bowlsters and pillow and rugge £2.
2 chests and andirons, one truncke and other lomber £1.

In the Garratt Chamber
[In *deleted*] lomber £1.
In mault in the house £4.
5 barrells, one dow trow, one saltinge trow and cowle with one yeatinge stone and lomber £3.
One furnass £1 10*s.*
5 horss beasts, one cow and boards with all harness £10.
For wood £5.
One waggon, cart and dunge pott £5.
Harrows and plows £1.
Wheate and sackes £3.
In timber £3.
One rike, stavell and boards, skreene and carte £2.
Debts dew £2.
Corne upon the ground £31.

Total £87 7*s.*

Joseph Webb and John Gillmore, appraisors.

Buried St. Mary 23 April 1685
Will 17 April 1685; renunciation 25 April 1685 by Stephen Cornish alias Duffe of Brainford, Middx., testator's son and joint executor; probate 11 May 1685 to Joseph Cornish alias Duffe, testator's son.

1. 'of marleborrough St maryes'.

260 WILLIAM KYTE
tapster 13 October 1685 P1/K/95

His wearing apparell £7.

In his Lodging Chamber
[One deleted] 2 standing bedsteads, 1 table, 1 chest, 1 trunk, 2 boxes and 7 old chaires £2 5*s.*
1 fetherbed, 1 flockbed, 3 bolsters, 4 pillows, 4 pair of sheets, 2 pair of blanketts, 1 rugg, 1 coverlett with 1 pair of curtains and vallians £5 10*s.*
Table linen 10*s.*

In the Hall
2 tables, 1 cupboard, 1 settle and 3 joyned stooles £1 14*s.* 8*d.*
In pewter 13 platters, 11 poringers, 6 flagons, 6 pint potts, 2 double flagons, 1 chamber pott, 1 bason, 3 candlesticks and 2 salts £2 18*s.* 6*d.*
In brass 2 kettlebrass potts, 2 little kettles, 1 bellbrass pott, 3 skillets, 1 warming pan, 2 scimers, 2 basting ladles and 1 pestle and mortar £2 10*s.* 6*d.*
In iron 1 jack, 2 spitts, 1 pair of andirons, 1 pair fire doggs, 2 pair of hangells, 1 fender, 2 gridirons, 1 fire pan and tongs, 1 lattin dripping pan and 1 pasty pan and a lanthorne 18*s.* 8*d.*

In the Buttery
4 dozen of trenchers 4*s.*
2 little barrells, 1 kever, 1 powdering tubb with other lumber 12*s.*

In John Sadler's Cellar
2 tables with frames, 1 cupboard, 1 coffer, 1 box and other things £1 15*s.*
Wood in the backside and street £10.
Debts on the booke £10.
Desperate debts £40.

Total £85 18*s.* 4*d.*

Robert Miles, Thomas Horne and John Richardson, appraisors.

Buried St. Peter 16 September 1685 'William Kite'.
Will 10 September 1685; bond 31 October 1685, administration to Anne Kite, testator's widow, during minority of William Kite, testator's son and executor.

261 JAMES CRABB[1]

?barber [inventory goods] [*undated*, c.1685] P1/C/374

His weareing apparill and mony in his purss £5.

In his Lodging Chamber
One feather bed and bedsteed with the appurtenances £5.
Funerall exspencis[2] £10.
One press, one table board, one bedsteed, two chests, two boxis, two trunks, one paire of hand irons, five chaires, two lookeing glassis with other lumber in the same rome £1 2*s.* 6*d.*

In the Long Rome
Two table bords, three joynt stooles, fower chaires, one cobbart, one forme, one bench 18*s.*

1st Chamber
One flock beed, two beedsteeds with the appurtenance thereunto belonging £2.
Two table boards, fower chaires 5*s.*

2nd Chamber
Two flock beeds, two beedsteeds with the appurtenances thereto belonging and other lumber £1 10*s.*

3rd Chamber
One feather beed, one flock beed, one beed steed with the appurtenances thereto belonging, one table board, one chaire, one coffer £2.
Lumber in a clossett 1*s.*

In the Chitchen
Twelve putter dishis, twlve plates, fower chamber potts, eleven porrengers, nyne flaggons, six potts, one baker, one tankord, one quartern pott, three candlesticks, one basson, one flaggon £2 10*s.*
Three brass potts, three brass kettles, two posnitts, fower brass skillitts, one warming pan, one sace pan, two basteing ladles, one skimmer £1 10s
One jack, three spitts, two driping panns, one cullender, one dredging box 5*s.*
Three paire of hand irons, two fire shevills, one paire of tonngs, two paire of bellissis, one fender, one frying pann, one fork with other lumber 8*s.*
One table bord, two dressing bords, one settle, fower chaires, one joynt stoole 5*s.*

Brew House
One copper [furnis *added*] £2 10*s.*
Two mash vates, nyne covers, two tubbs, one strayner and other lumber £1 10*s.*

Backside
One cow and calfe £2 10*s.*
Heay 1*s.*
Wood £3.
Dunng 1*s.* 6*d.*
Other lumber 1*s.* 6*d.*

Sellor
Fifteen vessells, one tunn bole, one draper, one kive £2 10*s.*
Beare and ale in the sellor £3.
Five paire of canvis sheetts 15*s.*
One dosen and half of naptins 7*s.* 6*d.*
Five table cloths 5*s.*
Two cobbord cloths, [one paire of sheets *added*] 7*s.* 6*d.*
One silver spoone 7*s.* 6*d.*

In the Shopp
One chare, one basson, two cassis with razors and sissers 5*s.*
One chattll lease £20.
Monies dew on bands £50.
Despratt debts £30.

Total £150 6*s.*

Charles Bligh, Tharp Sims and John Reeves, appraisors.

Buried St. Mary 29 May 1685.
Bond 21 October 1685, administration to Edith Crabb, intestate's widow.

1. 'of Marlborough St Mary'.
2. Administrator's expenses should not form part of the inventory.

262 LUCY WEBB
widow 30 October 1685 P1/W/265

Her weareing apparrell £3 10.
In ready money £20.
In lease, chattell £25.

In the Kitchin
Six pewter dishes 12*s.*
A little table and lumber 10*s.*

In the Buttery
A barr and lumber 8*s.* 6*d.*
A yoating stone and tubb 14*s.*

In the Great Chamber
A bed and furniture £5.
A truckle bed and bedsteed £1.
A table board and chest 10*s.*
Two joint stooles, two chaires and lumber 10*s.*
A warmeing pan 2*s.* 6*d.*

In the Little Chamber
Fower boxes and lumber 10*s.*

Total £58 7*s.*

Thomas Spackman and Henry Cully, appraisors.

Buried St. Mary 31 July 1685, 'Lucy Weeb'.
Bond 31 October 1685, administration to Elizabeth Pike, intestate's 'only' daughter.

263 THOMAS HORNE
shearman 14 December 1685 P1/H/495

His weareing apparrell £3.
In ready money £17.

In his Bedchamber
One flock bed, bedsteed, curtains, valens, rugg, blanketts, sheets and other appurtenances £3.
One greate Bible, one little Bible 6*s.*
Two cupboards, fower chaires, one colegrate and forke, one table and frame £2.

In the Garrett
One old trundle bedsteed, rugg, blankett and matt 10*s.*
One chest, one little kiver, twoe boxes, 1 joint stoole, 2 old chaires and 1 trunk 7*s.*
Fower cheeses 8*s.*
One cloath mantle laced with silver £1.
One silke mantle 15*s.*
2 dozen of diaper napkins, 1 dozen of flax napkins, three table cloaths, 1 fustian mantle and other small lynnen £2 10*s.*
4 yards of white cloath 6*s.*
In fleece wooll and lambswooll £3 12*s.*
3 parcells of yarne 10*s.*
One sett of curtains and valens 5*s.*

In the Hall
1 table board and frame and 4 joint stooles £1.
1 cupboard, 2 chaires, 1 rack, one paire of billowes 8*s.*
2 spitts, 1 dripping pan, 1 jack, 1 chafin

dish, 1 gridiron, 1 paire of andirons, 1 paire of doggs, 1 pot, 1 paire of tongs, hangells and fire pan and 1 tankard £1.
2 table cloaths, 1 towell, 2 diaper napkins 5s.

In the Buttery
6 pewter platters, 2 tin pans, 1 cullender, 15 plates, 6 pottingers, 1 flaggon, 1 tankard, 1 salt, 1 pewter candlesticke and silver spoone £2.
One little brass pott, 1 little brass kittle, 1 bast ladle and 1 dozen of trenchers 6s. 6d.

In the Shopp
5 paire of shears and other work tooles £2.

In the Celler
4 small barrells, one kiver, one powdring tubb, 1 [dripping *deleted*] frying pan and stands 10s.

In the Brewhouse
One fornace, 1 mash vate, 1 cowle, 1 [ladbe *deleted*] lade payle, 1 buckett and 1 bowle £1 6s.

In the Backside
2 paire of racks £1.
In wood and cole £1.

In the Great Chamber
1 tableboard and frame and flaskett 5s.
5 sheets, 8 napkins, 2 bolster cases, 2 pillow cases £2.
His chattells in leases £110.

In Edward Younge's Chamber
One flock bed, bolster and paire of sheets £1 10s.
One chamber pott 2s.
In lumber £1.
Two little geldings £2 10s.
In good debts £218 10s. 11d.
In desperate debts £20.
Seaven and thirty sheepe £6 5s.

Total £408 5s. 5d.[1]

Edward Hancock, clothier and Nathaniell Hone, shearman, appraisors.

Buried St. Peter 28 November 1685.
Bond 4 May 1686, administration to Edward Young and Katharine his wife.

1. Roman numerals.

264 ANN LONGMAN
widow [*undated*, c.1685/6] P1/L/206

A tenniment of chatel lase on life £9.
In mony the feuneral exspens a lowed 10s.[1]
1 flock badd, on bolster, on rugg, fower pellows, on blancket £1.
On chast and on cofer 6s.
3 old boxis 3s. 2d.
2 chayors 1s. 6d.
2 table bords and on frame 4s.
On cobert 3s.
3 kettils 9s.
On iorn pott, on brass pott 5s.
To skellots 3s.
12 pesis of peuter 9s.
Sum od lumber 3s.
3 barrils and on tubb 4s.
Wareing apparril 10s.

Total £13 10s. 8d.

Richard Sutton and John Kenton, appraisors.

Buried St. Mary 17 January 1685/6.
Will [nuncupative] 'about the 17th day of January' 1685/6; probate and inventory exhibition not recorded.

1. Executor's expenses should not form part of the inventory.

265 MARGARET BOWLES
widow 10 March 1685/6 P1/B/582

In the Chamber
Her purse and aparrell £5.
2 feather beds, 3 feather boulsters and [3 *added*] feather pillows with bedsteed, 1 pair of blanketts and rugg £4.
2 paire of sheets, 3 table cloths £1.
1 paire of blanketts, 1 rugg and 1 chaffe bed 10*s*.
One chest, one coffer, one side cupbord, 1 truckle bedsteed 12*s*.
One trunk, one coat 5*s*.
1 paire of brass andirons, 1 fire shovel, 1 paire of tongs, 1 paire of billice, 1 plate 8*s*.
1 sadle, 1 padd, 1 bridle 5*s*.
2 easts haires, 1 screen, 5 sacks, 1 honey bagg £1 10*s*.

In the Kitchen
4 brass kittles, 1 brass warming pan, 1 brass pan, 1 brass charger £1 5*s*.
1 bell brass pot and posnet and 1 low bell 8*s*.
10 pewter dishes, 4 pottingers, 4 candle sticks, 15 measures, 1 salt, 1 flagon, 1 bason £2.
1 cold still and biscake moulds 10*s*.
1 fowling [pice *added*] and halbertt 8*s*.
1 jack, 2 spitts, 2 fire tongs, 1 fire shovel, 1 paire of dogs, one greidiron, 1 plate, 2 paire of hangings, 1 paire of billice 18*s*.
1 table boord, 2 joynt stooles, 3 chaires 7*s*.

In the Shop
1 hot still and worme £2.
1 stan, 1 barrel and rundletts, tubbs with lumber and a board to cutt tobacco on 10*s*.
Hops 5*s*.

In the Malt House
[2 hogsheads, 2 pipes *deleted*]
1 malt mill and 1 press 7*s*. 6*d*.
[2 bushels *deleted*] lumber £2.

In the Backside
2 stones and lumber £2.
All other necessary things about the house 5*s*.
The dwelling house and malt house with the backside, garden and orchard £80.

Total £106 13*s*. 6*d*.

John Gillmore, gentleman and Edward Dangerfeild, appraisors.

Burial not recorded.
Will 14 January 1685/6; probate 9 March 1685/6 to Thomas Perkins, husbandman, executor; commission 16 March 1685/6, oath administered 17 March 1685/6 to Thomas Perkins; inventory exhibited 4 May 1686.

266 THOMAS GARLICK
victualler 15 April 1686 P1/G/261

In his Bed Chamber
One flock bed, one feather bed, one bolster, two pillowes, one paire of blainketts, one rugg, one tester bedsted, curtains and vallans £4.
Wearing apparrell and bookes £6.
One chest, one trunck, two coffers, one table board with other implements 15*s*.

The Roome over the Penthouse
One feather bed, one flock bed, one rugg, two coverleds, two paire of blainketts, two bolsters, two [*illegible deletion*] pillowes, two bedsteds with other implements £4.

In the Hall
One table board, [one *added*] settle, [fower *added*] 4 stooles, eight chaires, fire pann, two paire tonges, one spitt, jack, a dripping pann, a paire of andiorns, a paire of dogges £1 10*s*.

In the Parler

Two table boards, ten chaires, 6 stooles, one cubbard with other implements £2.

In the Buttery

Brass and pewter £2.

Six barells, one brewing vessell and other trining ware £1.

In lining £1 and wood £1 £2.

Fiffty [two *added*] quarters of mallt [and malt mill *added*] £47.

In money and debts £32.

And desprate debts £10.

Total £112 5*s*.

Joseph Webb and Nicholas Proffet[1], appraisors.

Buried St. Mary 12 April 1686.

Will 7 March 1685/6; probate 3 May to Elizabeth Garlick, testator's widow; inventory exhibited 4 May 1686.

1. Incumbent of St. Peter.

267 RICHARD NEW

husbandman[1] 28 April 1686 P1/N/97

One flockbed and one chaffbed and old coveringe belonginge, three old sheets and two old boystors and boystore cases and on old flocke pillow and pill case and a livery bedsted and on truckle bedsted 12*s*. 6*d*.[2]

Thre pewter platters, eight pewter porenges, two pewter candlesticke, two old saltsellers, a pewter chamberpott, one flagon, thre [of *deleted*] old candlestick of tinnen and three litle drippen pans, [*illegible deletion*] three pewter sasers, two pewter potts 13*s*.

One brass pott, on old kitle and on litle on, on old skillett and a waringe bane and a ladle and a skmmer and other brass 10*s*.

One pare of andiers and fier pan and tongues and two spitts and three pare of pothookes, two par hander and a crooke and 5*s*.

One tablebord, three joynt stolles, two old coffers, on old cubberd, two old barell, one old chest 3*s*. 6*d*.

One washinge, two old tubbs besides and other lumber 2*s*.

One old house which she pay rent for it haveinge some interest in as longe as she pay £2.

Total £4 6*s*.

Roger Glide and Richard Sutton, appraisors.

Buried St. Mary 25 October 1685.

Will [nuncupative] 'about the latter end of October in the year 1685'; probate 28 October 1686; bond 28 October 1686, administration to John Greene, testator's father-in-law, during the minority of John New, testator's son.

1. 'parchment maker' on will.
2. Roman numerals throughout.

268 JONE GODFOR[1]

3 May 1686 P1/G/266

All her wearing apparrel both woollen and linnen £8.

Two platters and two peuter porrengers 6*s*.

A legacy left her by her uncle £30.

Due from her brother Samuel[2] £2 10*s*.

Total £40 16*s*.

Benjamin Basset and Thomas Edne, appraisors.

Buried St. Peter 9 March 1865/6.

Bond 7 July 1687, administration to Joane

Godfer, widow, intestate's mother.

1. 'daughter of Jone Godfor Widdow of the Parish of S[t] Peters Marlbro'.
2. Samuel Godfer, incumbent of Huish.

269 EDITH CRABB

widow [will] 4 June 1686[1] P1/C/375

Her weareing apparell and monies in her purse £2 10s.

In her Lodging Chamber

Two beeds, two beed steeds, two cover leeds, two paire of blankitts, one press, two table boards, two chests, two boxsis, two trunks, one paire of hand irons, five chaires, two lookeing glassis with other lumber in the same roome £6.

Three rings and one spoone £2 6s. 6d.

In the Long Room

Two table boards, three joynt stooles, fower chaires, one cubbard, one forme, one bench, one screene £1.

First Chamber

One flock beed, two beedsteeds with the appurtenances and one table board £2 5s.

Second Chamber

Two flock beeds, two beedsteeds with the appurtenances and other lumber £1.

Third Chamber

One feather beed, one beedsteed with the appurtenances theireto belonging, one table board, one chaire, one coffer £1 5s.

Lumber in a clossett 1s.

In the Chitchen

Eleaven dishes, eleaven plates, fower chamber potts, eight porrengers, twelve flaggons, three potts, one baker, two tankords, one duble flaggon, one quartern pott, two candlestickes, one basson, one salt, one suck bottle all of pewter £2 10s.

Three brass potts, three brass kettles, two brass posnetts, three brass skillitts, one warming pan, one sace pan, two basteing ladles, one skimmer all of brass £1 10s.

One jack, three spitts, one driping pan, one cullender, one dredging box 8s.

Three paire of handirons, two fire shevels, one paire of tonngs, two paire of bellissis, one fender, one fryeing pan, two forks 5s.

One table board, two dressing boards, fower chaires, one joynt stoole, one grate, one gridiron, seven iron candlesticks 5s.

In the Brew House

One coper furnis with the grate £2 10s.

Two mashvates, nyne covers, two tubbs, one strainer with other lumber £1 10s.

Backside

One calfe and six store piggs £3.

Dunng in the back side 1s.

In the Seller

Fifteen vessells, one tunn bole, one kive £2 10s.

Fower paire of canvis sheets 12s.

One hollon sheete, one callowque sheete, two cubbart cloths, fower table cloths, twelve napttings, five pillowbeares 15s.

One chattle lease house £22.

Monies dew on bands £13.

Good debts £5.

Total £72 3s. 6d.

Despratt debts £16 13s. 6½d.

[*Total with debts* £88 17s. 0½d.]

Joseph Webb, John Smith and John Reeve, appraisors.

Buried St. Mary 22 December 1685
Will 1 December 1685; renunciation 20 February 1685/6 by Thorp Simms of Midgam, Berks, yeoman, testator's brother, and Thomas Crabb of St. Peter, Marlborough, clothier, testator's brother-in-law, in favour of Charles Bligh of Marlborough, gentleman, principal creditor; bond 8 March 1685/6, administration to Charles Bligh; inventory exhibited 14 September 1686.

1. '... and of the Goods, chattles and Creditts of James Crabb, her late Husband, deceased, unadministered by the said Edith his Relict and Administratrix'.

270 LUCE CHURCH[1]

widow [*undated*, c.1686] P1/C/380

Her wareing apparell £2.
A bedsteed and beding in the parler chamber £2 10*s*.
A table board and 3 chaires same chamber 5*s*.
Bedsteeds and beding in the inner chamber £2 10*s*.
2 chests, 2 boxes and a coffer 5*s*.
4 paire sheets, a duzen napkins, a board cloth and other lennen £1 17*s*. 6*d*.
1 table board, 1 chaire in same room 4*s*. 6*d*.
2 bedsteeds, 2 flocke beds, 2 feather boulsters and a flocke boulster and 2 cover lids in the kitchen chamber £1 10*s*.
In the same chamber 1 table board, 4 joyne stooles, 3 chaires 15*s*.

In the Kitchen
1 table board, 1 forme setle and a jacke, 3 spits and 1 paire of andiers £1.
Brass and pewter in the buttry £1 10*s*.

In the Seller
1 furness, 1 ketle, 2 hoggs heads, 4 barrells and other bruen vessels £3 15*s*.
For lumber goods 10*s*.

Total £18 12*s*.

William Pye and Richard Man, appraisors.

Buried St. Mary 28 May 1686.
Will 8 March 1685/6; probate 15 June 1686 to executrix [Sarah Church, testator's daughter].

1. 'of st marys in the Burrow of Marlebough ... who deceassed the 26th of May 1686'.

271 RIC WILLIAMS

30 July 1686 P1/W/368

His wareing apparrell 11*s*.
Two beds, two bedsteeds, one rugg and other appurtinances belong to it £3 10*s*.

In the Hall
1 tableboard, 1 chest, 1 foorme and other lumber £1.
In pewter 10*s*.

Total £5 11*s*.

Joseph Webb and Robert Cowssey, appraisors.

Buried St. Mary 20 May 1686, 'Rice Williams'.
Bond 8 June 1686, administration to William Roath, yeoman, principal creditor; inventory exhibited 14 September 1686.

272 TIMOTHY CHEEVERS

currier 10 March 1686/7 P1/C/388

His purse and apparrell £3.

In his Lodging Roome
One fether bed and bedsteed with a rug, curtaines, valliance and blanketts £2 10s.
In the same roome one truckle of flocks with bedsteed, blanketts and coverlett, one boulster £1.
More in the same roome 1 cheest, 1 coffer, 1 trunck, 2 boxes, 1 chaire and 1 joynstole 10s.

In the Outer Chamber
1 round table, 2 little trunks 4s.
More in the same room 4 paire of sheets, 2 table [colth *deleted*] cloths, 4 pillow cases with other linnen 16s.

In the Hall
One table board, one fourm, one joynt stoole, one [joynt *deleted*] setle, 2 chaires 5s.
More in the same roome 16 small dishes of pewter, one flagon, one chamber pott, one tankerd £1.
More one brass ketle, 2 brass pots, 2 skilletts, one skimer, one furnace and one warming pan £1 10s.
More one jack, 2 spitts, one fire shovell and tongs, one paire of dogs 6s.
More 2 Bibles and other small books 10s. 6d.

In the Buttery
3 barrills, one maishing vate with other brewing vessell 12s.

In the Oyle House
12 gallons of oyle 12s.

In the Shop
Workeing tooles, 2 workeing boards, [2 *altered to*] 1 press £1.
Lumber and wood £1.
Debts £15.
Desperate debts £5.

Total £34 15s. 6d.

His debts £9 15s. 9d.[1]

John Bowshier senior, Phillip Chivers and William Pye, appraisors.

Buried St. Mary 20 February 1686/7, 'Timothy Chivers senior'.
Will 20 April 1686; probate 19 July 1687 to Jane Chivers, testator's widow; inventory exhibited 13 July 1687.

1. If this refers to debts owing *by* the deceased, they should not form part of the inventory.

273 HENRY PIKE

maltster 14 April 1687 P1/P/357

His wareing apparell and books £1 10s

In the Kiching
1 table bord, 1 side bord, 4 joynt stools, 3 rush chayres, 1 ould settle, 2 payr hangells, 1 payr dogs, fyre shoul and tongs, cuberd and little other lumber £1 1s.
3 pewter dishes, 3 potingers, 1 salt and sawcer 7s.

In the Buttery
2 copper potts, 2 kittells, 1 skillett, 6 barrells and other lumber £2 2s.

In his Lodging Chamber
1 sett of drawers, 4 chayres, 4 low stools, 1 truckle bed steed, 1 flock bed, fyre pan and tongs and other implements £2.

In the Chamber over the Buttery
1 bed and bedsteed, 1 payr of blanketts, 1 rug, 1 coffer, 1 rush chayr, 2 boxes with other implements £2 8s.

Att Stayr Head
In lumber 3s.
3 payr ould sheets, 2 table cloths and 4 towells 12s. 6d.

In the Stable and Malt House
In lumber 10s.
1 furnace and grate £1.
2 store pigs £1 6s.
3 geldings and 3 mares with theyr harness £12.
1 waggon and 2 dung potts £6.
1 cart, 1 plough and other lumber £2.
Corn in the feild £4.
In wood £5.
In bakon 10s.
In good debts £4.
Corn in St Margaretts[1] and lumber ther in the stable £4.

Total £50 9s. 6d.

Beside desperat debts £5.

Joseph Webb and Noah Webb, appraisors.

Buried St. Peter 12 April 1687.
Bond 15 April 1687, administration to Elizabeth Pike, intestate's widow; accounts submitted 7 July 1687 by Elizabeth Pike; inventory exhibited 9 July 1687.

1. A suburb of Marlborough, in the parish of Preshute.

274 JOHN PHILLIPPS the younger blacksmith 5 May 1687 P1/P/359

His weareing apparrell £2.
In ready money 10s.
In good debts £1 10s.
In desperate debts £2.

In the Hall
2 brass kittells, 4 brass kittell pots, 1 brass cast pot, 3 brass skilletts £1 5s.
In pewter of all sorts 108 lbs weight £3 8s.
1 jack, 2 iron dripping panns, 1 spitte, 2 hangells, 1 fire shovell, tongs, fender, barr, doggs, steele plate, 5 iron candlesticks, 2 frying pans, chaffing dish, 1 paire of pothookes and iron grate 17s. 6d.
1 table board, frame, forme, settle, trencher rack and 12 trenchers, case of knives, wooden bowle 8s.

In the Chamber over the Hall
A chest for a bed, 1 little [feather *deleted*] bed, bolster, 2 blanketts, 1 rugg £1 10s.
2 table boards and frames, 1 forme, 4 rush chaires, 3 joint stooles, 1 paire of brass andirons, fire pan, tongs and bellows and doggs £1.

In his Bed Chamber
1 feather bed, 1 flock bed, 1 rugg, [2 blanketts *deleted*] 2 paire of curtains and valens, 2 paire of blanketts, 1 bolster, 4 feather pillowes, 2 small pillowes £3.
2 chests, 1 truncke, 1 close stoole and pan, 3 boxes, 1 looking glass, 1 hanging shelfe, 1 table board and frame, forme, chaire and stoole and 1 truncke £1.

In the Outward Garrett
1 standing bedsteed, 2 trundle bedsteeds, 1 feather bed, 1 f[l]ock bed, 1 chaff bed, 2 ruggs, 3 blanketts, 1 little table board £2 17s. 6d.

In the Inward Garrett
A bed, bedsteed, coverlid and blanketts 9s. 6d.
6 paire of sheets and other old lynnen £2.

Page total £23 15s. 6d.

In the Shopp
1 grindstone, 8 dozen of horse shoes and old iron £1 5s.

In the Brewhouse
1 copper fornace and brewing vessells of all sorts £3 2s. 6d.

In the Buttery
13 barrells, 3 stands and strong beere, 1 powdring tubb £6 5*s.*
One mare, 1 nagg, 6 store piggs £7 10*s.*
In oates and hey £1 15*s.*
In hard and faggott wood £4.
In lumber of all sorts 7*s.* 6*d.*

In Corne upon the Ground
1 acre of wheate, another of barley £2.

Page total £26 5*s.*

Total £50 0*s.* 6*d.*[1]

Thomas Cotton, John Horner and Samuell Fowler, appraisers.

Buried St. Mary 2 May 1687 'John Philips junior'.
Will 16 June 1685; probate 7 July 1687 to executrix [Joane Phillips, testator's widow].

1. Roman numerals.

275 ROBERT MILES the elder
joiner 19 October 1687 P1/M/281

His wearing apparel £2.

In the upper Chamber
Two bedds, two bedsteads, two pair of sheets with coverings and other things belonging £2.
2 chests and 1 coffer 10*s.*
1 chest of drawers, 1 old press and 2 boxes 10*s.*
2 old tableboards, 1 old cupboard, 1 little table board, 4 stooles and 1 fourme 12*s.*

In the Buttery
Old barrels and tubbs with other lumber £1 2*s.* 6*d.*
In brass and pewter 10*s.*

In the Shop
9 bedsteads made and unmade £2 10*s.*
Six chests, 3 boxes and 1 coffer £2.
1 tableboard and 5 joyned stooles 12*s.*
In timber 5*s.*
1 bedstead, 1 old cupboard and 1 settle 10*s.*
A lease of 2 old houses and a shop £5.
Money in his purse 18*s.*

Total £18 19*s.* 6*d.*

Desparate debts £1 10*s.*
Debts owing by the testator £11 2*s.* 11½*d.*[1]

John Farmer, William Lester and Thomas Greenaway, appraisors.

Buried St. Peter 16 October 1687.
Will 14 October 1687, probate 20 October 1687 to Ann Miles, testator's widow.

1. Debts owed by the deceased should not form part of the inventory.

276 GEORGE NORRIS[1]
23 January 1687/8 P1/N/99

In the Chambor
In moneyes £50 6*s.* 3*d.*
His waring aparill £2 5*s.*
One flockbeed and bowlster, 2 fether pillows, 2 cuferlids, a pair of blankets, 2 pair of sheets £2.
2 bedsteed, 2 chests, 2 barills with other lumbor £1 1*s.*

In the Kitchin
4 pewter dishes, 1 tankard, 1 drinking pot, 1 chambor pot, 1 candollstik 11*s.*
3 kittells, 1 pott, 1 skillet, a worming pan, a skimor, a ladell of brass £2 6*s.*
2 tubs, 2 covers, 1 powdring tub 7*s.* 6*d.*
2 cort cubards with other lumbor 6*s.*

Total £59 2*s.* 9*d.*

Christopher Lipyeatt and James Priest, appraisors.

Buried St. Peter 20 January 1687/8.
Bond dated 10 May 1688, administration to Jane Norris, intestate's widow.

1. 'of St Peters Marlburgh'.

277 EDWARD CREW
?parchment maker [inventory goods] 9 May 1688 P1/C/392

The wearing clothers and books £2.

Above Staior
2 bedstedes, 2 bedes and 2 bowllesters, 2 ruges, 1 peare of blanckettes, 2 trunckes and a chest of drares and some lumber £6 2*s.* 6*d.*
2 peare of shettes and the tabell lenen £1.

In the Buttery
2 pottes and lumber £1.
1 furnes and gratt £1 5*s.*

In the Hall
2 tabelles and 3 stolles and 2 chaiers 12*s.*
1 jacke and spett, 2 peare of ainders and feier pane and tonges £1.
1 warming pane 5*s.*
5 dises of putter, 1 flagen and tankerd £1.
2 peare of skelles and lumber 7*s.* 6*d.*

Withoutte Dore
3 hundered of pelltes £6.
2 dosen of calfe skenes £1.
And for wooll, skenes and skrowes £9.
And for the howelles and harowes and working knives £8.
And 4 rowll of parchmente £4.

Total £42 12*s.*

Henry Cully and Jeremiah Fowller, appraisors.

Burial not recorded.
Bond 10 May 1688, administration to Ann Crew, intestate's widow.

278 DORITHY TITCOM
widow 15 October 1688 P1/T/575

On father bad and bolster 15*s.*
On flock bead and bolster 8*s.*
A gound, petty coat and a petty coat and wastcoat £1 2*s.*
A [*illegible deletion*] petty coat more 5*s.*
2 coverledes 13*s.* 6*d.*
On warmeing pann 2*s.* 6*d.*
3 kettels of brass 11*s.*
3 peuter dishes 2*s.*
On bedsted and on chast 6*s.*
On barril and to tubbs 3*s.*
On cobert 2*s.* 6*d.*
On tabel bord and chaier 3*s.*
A torne, cardes and rell 2*s.* 6*d.*
Old iorn and wod and other lumber 3*s.* 6*d.*
In mony £7.
Wareing apperil £1.

[*Total omitted, by addition* £12 19*s.* 6*d.*]

The hoole funeral expens is paid amounts to £8 13*s.*[1]

Thomas Sampson and Richard Sutton, appraisors.

Burial not recorded.
Will 7 October 1688; probate 26 October 1688 to Thomas New and Margaret Deacon, executors.

1. Executors' expenses should not form part of the inventory.

279 ANN GRAMUT[1]

widow [burial register] [*undated*, c.1688] P1/G/775

Her wareing apparill woollen and linnin £2.
Her munney £20.
Her bras and pewter £1 5*s*.
A cubberd and tablebord with a kiver and barrill and meall trow, joyn stooll and forme and other lumbur 15*s*.
Her bed and all things belonging to it £1.
A chayer and cofer and other lumbering things 2*s*.
A littell wood 5*s*.

Total £25 7*s*.

Nicholas Rumsey and Richard Buckingham, appraisors.

Buried St. Mary 4 July 1688.
Will [nuncupative] 26 June 1688; probate 26 October 1688 to Richard Heall, testator's brother; inventory exhibited 27 October 1688.

1. 'Late of Marlbrough St maryes ... who dyed June y[e] 26th in the yeare 1688'.

280 THOMAS CRIPPS

16 April 1689 P1/C/401

In reddey money £26 17*s*. 9*d*.
Waring aparell £2.
1 cofer 3*s*.

Total £29 0*s*. 9*d*.

John Stokes and Noah Crook, appraisors.

Buried St. Mary 11 March 1688/9 'Thomas Crepps'.
Bond 16 April 1689, administration to Ann Cripps, widow, intestate's mother.

281 RICHARD LUFFE

yeoman 4 June 1689 P1/L/213

His wearing clothes £1 18*s*. 6*d*.

In the Chamber
One bed, a boulster, 2 pillows and one paire of blanketts £1 10*s*.
One bedsteed, mat and cord 6*s*. 6*d*.
Two chests, one coffer and 2 boxes 15*s*.
Three paire of sheetes and one table cloth, more twelve napkins 10*s*.
Lumber there 3*s*.

In the Kitchen
Pewter there 15*s*.
Fower brass pots £1.
Two kettles and 2 skilletts 15*s*.
One warmeing pan and two skimers 2*s*. 6*d*.
One table board and frame 2*s*.
Lumber there 10*s*.
Lumber in the back house 5*s*.
In moneys £30.
In desperate debts £1 17*s*. 8*d*.

Total £40 10*s*. 2*d*.

The deceased in debt £8 2*s*. 10½*d*.[1]

John Smith and George Ayliffe, appraisors.

Buried St. Mary 17 May 1689 'Richard Luffe the elder'.
Bond 17 September 1689, administration to Anne Luffe, intestate's widow.

1. Debts owing by the deceased should not form part of the inventory.

282 THOMAS SAMPSON the elder

cooper 20 August 1689 P1/S/540

In the Chamber
One high bedsteed, bedd and all belonging to it £2.

One livery bedsteed and a trundell bedsteed and all belonging to it £1.
One table board, one chest and one box of linnen £1 10s.

Kitchin
One cupboard, one warming pan, old stooles and chaires 5s.

In the Sellar
For barrells and brewing vessells 10s.

In the Backside
For wood and lumber £3.

In the Work House and Shop in the Highstreete and in the Backside
In coopery ware and coopery timber [of all sorts *added*] £103. 8s. 3d.
In workeing tooles and stocks £2 5s.
The deceased's wearing apparell £1 10s.
Debts uppon the shop booke £14.

Total £129 8s. 3d.

John Rumsey senior and John Bowshire junior, appraisors.

Buried St. Mary 16 August 1689 'the elder'.
Will 14 April 1687; probate and inventory exhibition not recorded.

283 ROBERT PAGE

farrier[will] [*undated*, c.1689] P1/P/368

One bead and all furnetuer belongen thare unto £1 10s.
Another bead and beaden thear be longen to 5s.
One chust and to cofers and one chair 5s.
One pasel of wooll 10s.
Waringe close £1.
Ten peuter platers 10s.
Other peuter 3s.
To bras potes, to ceteles, one warmen pan, one skelet and skemer £1.
One pare of anders and a par of doges, a pare of tonges and a spet and a fier forke, a fier pan, one par of hangeles, a chafen dish and chopen knife 5s.
One drepen pan and a fryinge pan 1s.
Three chaires [and a lade paile *added*] 2s.
One tabel bord and one forme, one joyen stoole 3s.
To cobrdes 4s.
Fife cushens 1s.
Backen 8s. 6d.
To tobes, one selt trow 3s.
To cowes and a hors £3.
Three peges 15s.
Woode in the bacessyd £1.
One sadel and bridel and one panel 2s.
One showel and a pronge 1s.
To peg trowes 1s.
One bead and bead sted 5s.
One pote of oyntement 1s. 6d.
One well bocket and chain 2s.
Halfe a dosen of nappins and a tabel cloth 7s. 6d.
A hamer and to par of pencers and butres 1s.
One sulling 6d.
[Total £12 7s. *deleted*]
[The house he leved in £5 *added*]

Total £17 7s.

Richard Edney and John Jones, appraisors.

Buried St Mary 21 August 1689.
Will [nuncupative] 27 August 1689[1]; probate and inventory exhibition not recorded.

1. The will date is presumed incorrect.

284 THOMAS HAVE[1]

tailor [will] 10 September 1689 P1/H/519

Waring close and mony in pocket £2 10s.

1 fether bed, 2 flockbeds, thre bedstids with rugs and blankots and shets £6.
1 chestt, 1 truncke, cofer and four boxes 10*s.*
2 tabels, 2 joynted stools 10*s.*
Bras and poter £1 2*s.* 6*d.*
2 barils and other lumbery goods £1 5*s.*
2 Bibiels and other books 10*s.*
Shopbrd and other lumbery goods 10*s.*
The furniture of the fier hearth 15*s.*
4 chayers 6*s.*

Total £13 18*s.* 6*d.*

Jeremiah Burgis and William Biggs, appraisors.

Burial not recorded.
Will 25 July 1689; probate and inventory exhibition not recorded.

1. 'Haw' on will.

285 HENERY RUS[1]

yeoman [will] 25 April 1690 P1/R/176

For money in hous and waring clothes £15 15*s.*

In the Back Chamber
On bed and bedsted and all that belong to yet £3 10*s.*
On letell bead and bedsted and all that belong to yet £2 10*s.*
Too tabels, 7 stools, on form, too chayers £2 10*s.*
Too bras andeirs, fier shovll and tongs and bles 10*s.*

For the Keichen Chamber
Bed and bedsted and all that belonge to him £2 10*s.*
A trockell bed and bedsted 10*s.*
On chest, too boxes, on tronck, on tabell, on seid cooberd, on warming pan £1 8*s.*

The Parler Chamber
Best bed and all that belong £3 10*s.*
Trockell bedsted and bead and all that belong 15*s.*
Too tabels, 4 stools, too jeyn chayers, on form £1 15*s.*
Lomber in thes 3 chambers at 1s 5*s.*

In the Garet Chamber
All that is ther, bead and bedsted and lomber with yet £2.

Brew Hous Chamber
Bed and lomber things ther 10*s.*

Parler
On tabell, on coberd, on form, too joynn chayers, too andeirs £1 4*s.*

Keicheing
On tabell, on setell, 3 stools, too chayers 15*s.*
[On *added*] bras pan, on grait keitell, on keitell pot, 4 letell keitels, 3 skeilets £3 13*s.*
Peuter platers, 12 pleates, 16 pots and 8 flageins, on bed pan, 12 sasers £3 2*s.*
For lomber in that keicheing 18*s.*
3 deyper tabell clothes, too dezen of naptkeins and other leineing £2 4*s.*

Breue Hous
On forneis, on masheing fat, 3 toobes, 3 keifers and other lumber £3 18*s.*

Boutery
6 dobell barels, on keife and other lomber things £3 2*s.*
For beear in hous: 3 hogsheads £3 15*s.*
For colle and wood £8 5*s.*
On coow, on boolock £3.
Too pigs £2 5*s.*
Hay then in poseshen £2 10*s.*
Deptes despreat £50.

Total £125 19*s.*

Edward Dangerfield, Henery Cowlly and Richeard Healle, appraisors.

Buried St. Mary 10 October 1689 'Henry Russe the elder'.
Will 18 September 1689; commission 15 October 1689, oath administered 17 October to Mary Russe; probate 23 October 1689 to executrix [Mary Russe, testator's widow]; inventory exhibited 22 May 1690.

1. 'Henry Russe' on will.

286 RICHARD TARRANT

cordwainer 20 May 1690 P11/T/208

His wearing apparrell £4.
The house £3.

In the Chamber
One bed and bedsteed, one chest, two coffers, one box, one chaire and linen £4.

In the Low Rome
Two potts, two skilletts 10*s.*
Pewter 5*s.*
One cupboard 6*s.*
One table and fower stooles 5*s.*
Two chaires 6*d.*
A jack and two spitts, one paire of andirons, a paire of dogs, fire shovell and tongs with pot hooks and hangills 12*s.*
Two barrills, one tubb and one kiver 5*s.*
Wood and lumber 10*s.*

Total £13 13*s.* 6*d.*

Richard Edney and Benjamin Bassett, appraisors.

Buried St. Peter 15 May 1690.
Will 22 April 1690; probate 22 May 1690 to Judith and Elizabeth Walter, executrices.

287 WILLIAM BAYLY

innholder 21 August 1690 P1/B/606

The testators wearing apparell £3.
In money £82.

In the Inner Garrett
One feather bed and bedsteed, matt and cord, one flock bed and bedsteed, matt and cord with the furniture thereunto belonginge £4.
Two table boards, one carpett, one window curtaine, fower stooles, two chaires, one paire of dogges and benches 12*s.*

In the other Streete Garrett
One feather bed and bedsteed, coard and matt with the furniture thereunto belonginge £2 10*s.*
One chest, one tableboard, one window curtaine, three joynted stooles, one chaire and one little bench 10*s.*

In the Starr Garrett
One flock bed and bedsteed, coard and matt with other furniture thereunto belonging with other lumber things £1.

In the Narrow Chamber
Two table boards, fower joynted stooles, three leather chaires, one paire of andirons, doggs and benches, eight pictures, one curtaine rodd and curtaine £1 15*s.*

In the Best Chamber
One feather bed and prest bedsteed with the furniture thereunto belonging, three table boards, six leather chaires, six joynted stooles, two window curtaines and one rodd and benches, nyne pictures, one pair of andirons and dogges, one candlestick against the wall, fire pann, tongues and billoweses £8 10*s.*

In the Middle Chamber
Two old tables, three joynted stooles, one paire of dogges and benches 8*s.*

In the Kitchine Chamber
One flock bed and bedsteed, coard and matt with all the furniture thereunto belonging, one flockbed, one truckle bedsteed, coard and matt with other furniture, one livery cubberd, one trunk, one looking glasse, one paire of tongues, paire of billowes and dogges, 2 chaires and one bench £3 16*s.*

In the Kitchen
One table board, brasse and pewter with other goods, one jack, spitts and doggs £5 10*s.*

In the Middle Roomth
One table board, two joynted stooles, two chaires, one paire of dogges, benches and wanscutt 12*s.*

In the Celler
Six[teene *added*] barrells, one tubb, three stands, fower dozen of bottles and beare £6 10*s.*

In the Brewhouse
Two furnaces and the brewing vessells £5.
In wood and pigges £9.
One silver tankerd £5.
In lynnen of all sorts £5 10*s.*
In lumber goods £1 10*s.*

Total £146 13*s.*

Samuell Fowler and Thomas Brunsdon, appraisors.

Buried St Peter 11 July 1690.
Will 27 June 1690; probate 14 October 1690 to Joane Bayly, testator's widow; inventory exhibited 15 October 1690.

288 JOHN STOUT

shoemaker 17 September 1690
P1/S/556

His weareing apparrell £3.

In the Chamber
A feather bed and bedsteed with the furniture, 2 chest, 1 trunck, 2 chaires and lumbar £5 1*s.* 6*d.*

In the Garrett
A bedsteed and flock bed, 2 bolsters, coverlid and lumbar £1.

In the Hall
1 table board, 1 cupboard, 4 stooles, 2 chaires, 1 jack, 1 paire of doggs, one paire of andirons, fire pan and tongs, 1 rack, 1 paire of hangells and lumbar £2 5*s.*

In the Buttery
2 kettles, 2 potts, 5 skelletts, 5 dishes of pewter, 1chafing dish, 2 brass candlesticks, 1 brass pan, 3 flaggons, 1 chamber pott, 1 pewter tankard, 1 bason, 4 barrells, 2 kivers, 3 tubbs, 1 powder tubb, 1 buckett and other od things £3 14*s.*

In the Backside
Faggotts and lumbar £1 10*s.*
In ready money £30.
The lease of the house £15.
In good debts £1.
In desparate debts £2.

Total £64 10*s.*

Nathanuel Hone and Thomas Bartlett, appraisors.

Buried St. Peter 10 June 1690 'Stowtts'.
Will 25 April 1690; probate 14 October 1690 to Ruth Stout, testator's widow.

289 EDWARD YOUNG[1]

maulster 30 September 1690 P1/Y/26

In his Bed Chamber

A feather bed, feather bolster and 2 feather pillowes, 1 rug, 2 blanketts, a covering, curtains, valens and bedsteed £6.

3 paire of fine sheets, 3 paire of canvas sheets, 6 paire of pillow beares, 3 paire of bolster cases, 2 dozen of napkins and 2 window curtains £6.

9 leather chaires, a chest of drawers and small od things £2 6*s.*

In the Back Chamber

2 flock beds, 2 bolsters, 2 ruggs, 4 blanketts, curtains and vallins, 2 bedsteeds, 2 chests, 1 trunck, 2 boxes and one close stoole £3.

[Window curtains, andirons, dogs and bellowes, warming pan, tonges and shovells £1 5*s. added*]

In the Lower Roomths

3 table boards, 6 stooles, 5 chaires and a cupboard £1 10*s.* 6*d.*

One yoateing stone 15*s.*

A skreene, shovell, bushell and peck 18*s.*

2 fatts, 6 kivers, 4 tubs, 8 barrells, a tunboule, a cupboard, a trough, 2 horses and lumbar £3 15*s.*

In the Maulthouse

22 quarters of barley £12 12*s.*

Without Doores

In cleft and faggott wood £13.

The maultmill £1.

In chattell leases £40.

His weareing apparrell £5.

In the Kitchin

In brass, pewter and lumbar £6 10*s.*

In plate £7.

In good debts £150.

In desperate debts £138 11*s.*

Total £399 2*s.* 6*d.*

John Richens and Nathanuel Hone, appraisors.

Buried St. Peter 9 August 1690

Bond 14 October 1690, administration to Katherine Young, intestate's widow.

1. 'in the parish of St Peter and St Paull Thappostles in Marlebrough'.

290 JAMES TOWER[1]

5 October 1690 P1/T/209

3 kittells and a bras pan and a bras poot and a bras dish £1 6*s.*

2 flaggins and a candellstick and a soltsellar and 2 sasars and 9 dishes of peutar £1 2*s.* 6*d.*

2 skillatts 3*s.*

1 tabell bord and 1 joynt stoll and 1 joynt chaior 10*s.*

1 cobard, 1 chest, 1 pouderingtub, 2 barells, 1 trinchar rak, 1 paill 10*s.*

1 speet, 1 drepenpan, 1 gredirn, 1 pare of hangells, pare of tungs 3*s.* 6*d.*

1 letell chaier and a bras cock 1*s.* 6*d.*

3 cofars, 1 furom 3*s.*

4 tubs 3*s.*

1 letell barell and 1 setell and 1 tronk 3*s.*

1 bead, 1 bolstar, 1 pillo, 1 pare of blankets, 1 pare of sheets, 1 ruge, 1 mat, 1 cord, 1 beadsteed £2 3*s.*

For waring aparell £1.

For hurdells £6.

Total £13 8*s.* 8*d.*

George Hull and John Bousher, appraisors.

Buried St. Mary 20 August 1690.

Bond 14 October 1690, administration to Jane Clarke, wife of Thomas Clarke, intestate's grand-daughter.

1. 'of Marlb: St Mary'.

291 RICHARD STAPLER
husbandman [will] [*undated*, c.1690]
P1/S/555

The waring clothes £1.
On ketell pot 16*s.* 6*d.*
On box, on kofer 4*s.* 6*d.*
On bedsted, on chayer 5*s.*
On bed, on shet, on pelow, on rug 10*s.*
On pot, on posnet, skelet 12*s.*
All lumber goods 8*s.*
Money in hous £3.
Depts desprat £21.

Total £27 15*s.* 6*d.* [*recte* £27 16*s.*]

Edward Dangerfield and John Tanner, appraisors.

Buried St. Mary 26 October 1690
Will 2 October 1690; probate and inventory exhibition not recorded.

292 JOANE DUFFE[1]
widow 13 December 1690 P1/D/174

Her wareinge apparell and monyes in her purss £1.

In the Chamber
One bedsteed and one bedd and all that belonges to itt £1 12*s.*
One press, two coffirs, tow boxes with other lombers 10*s.*

In the Hall
Twelfe pewtter dishes greate and smale and one flagon, one salt seller, one old bason, two old pottengers 16*s.* 6*d.*
One litell old forness and one litell old kitell with one old kitell pott, one old skillett and skimer, one bastinge ladele 8*s.* 10*d.*
One old tabellbord, one old cubbard with two civres and other lomber 6*s.*
One fire penn, one grediron and dripeinge pann and two steele platts 2*s.*
One payre of doggs, one payre of tonges and one payre of andirons 3*s.*
In woodd within doors and without 6*s.*
Two litell old barrills and another litell one 2*s.*
One chattell lease £3.

[*Total omitted, by addition* £8 6*s.* 4*d.*]

Henry Cully and Joseph [?Dast], appraisors.

Buried St. Mary 27 November 1690.
Bond 13 January 1690/1, administration to William Eaylesford, intestate's son-in-law[2] and creditor.

1. 'of Marlborrough St Maryes'; 'formerly called Joane Eaylesford' [bond].
2. Possibly 'step-son'.

293 DANIELL PIDDING[1]
14 April 1691 P1/P/377

Booke depts £3 5*s.* 5d
In raw hides £3
In backen 15*s.*
His waring apparell £5.
One fether bead [and the appurtnes *added*] £4
One flock bead and the appurtnances £1
For linen £1
For soules, lethers and ringes £6.
A bage of hopes £1.
For bras £2.
For peuter £1.
For his shop toules £1.
For too grindstones 4*s.*
For lumber goods £1 10*s.*

Total £30 14*s.* 5*d.*

[*Appraisors' names omitted*]

Buried St. Mary 2 April 1691.
Will 26 July 1689; probate 4 June 1691 to

Margarett Piddin, testator's widow; inventory exhibited 4 January 1691/2.

1. 'hew departed this Life the Forst of this instant Aprill 91'.

294 JOSEPH HOCKLEY
wheelwright 21 April 1691 P1/H/537

His wearing aparel and mony in the house £5.

In the Taret
In cheess 12*s.*
And 6 flitches of backen £2 11*s.*

In the Inward Chamber
One flock bed, boulster and bedsted, a rugg and blanket £1 2*s.* 6*d.*
A littel table and mealtrow, 2 old cofers and 2 tubs 6*s.*

In the Second Chamber
A flock bed and fether bolster and pillow, a pear of blankets and rugg and curtains and valiens, bedsted and bed matt, one sheet, one pillow cass and boulster cass £2 18*s.* 6*d.*

In the Third Chamber
A cheyer and chest and one box 5*s.* 6*d.*
A fether bed and boulster and 2 pillows, 2 pear of blankets, one rugg, curtaines and valiens, one bedsted, cord and mat, a sheet, a boulster case and pillow case £5 11*s.*
A flock bed and boulster and one pear of blankets, a coverlid and sheet and side bedsted £1.
A chest of drawers and table, 3 cheyers, 5 stools and 2 trunks £1 5*s.*
2 pear of dogs, fier pan and tongs 6*s.*
5 pear of sheets and 2 dozen of napkins, 6 table cloths and 6 pillow cases and 6 boulster cases £2 15*s.*
A hanging shelf, a looking glass and a silver tankerd and smal cups £6 6*s.*

In the Fourth Chamber
A fether bed and flock bolster and pillow, a pear of blankets, a rugg, sheet, bedsted, cord and mat and curtaines and valens £2 10*s.*
[A table 2 boxes and a stool 6*s.* *added*]

In the Littel Parler
A table and 4 cheyers 8*s.*

In the Celler
4 larg barels, 5 lesser barels, one meashfate, 7 tubs and coolers, one littel table, a powdring tub, other lumber and stands £3 12*s.*

In the Brewhouse
A furness and great £2.

In the Hall
10 candlesticks, 3 spits, a jack, 2 brass candlesticks, 3 dripen pans, steel plats and several other smal things £1 3*s.*
One pear of andirons, one pear of dogs, fier pan and tongs and 2 pear of hangels, a back, a fender and bars 12*s.*
A table and 4 joyntstools, 4 rush cheyers, a cubard, a rack, a warming pan and bellose £1 2*s.*
In good and bad debts on the book £197.

In the Buttery
11 pewter dishes, 8 porengers, 10 pleats and sawser, 2 flagons and a tankerd £1 19*s.* 2*d.*
2 cast pots, 2 kittels, bras pots, 2 skelets and a kitel £1 14*s.*
A musket and sord and pistols £1 15*s.*
A horse and cow £4.
8 qarters of malt £4 16*s.*
A beem, scale and wayts 15*s.*
The dweling house with what is receved from the next house joyning £24.

In the Out Houseing
4 score and 11 dozen and 4 felies £22 16*s.* 8*d.*
3 dozen and 8 cotch felies 10*s.*
6 dozen of bases £1.
Rath stanes £2.
4 score and 8 pear of wagon stocks £13 4*s.*
8 pear of cotch stocks 16*s.*
8 hundred and a half of spokes £8 10*s.*
5 dozen and 2 axis £6 4*s.*
19 pear of hounss £1 7*s.* 6*d.*
5 dozen and 7 paril posts 5*s.* 7*d.*
52 pear of limbers £6.
5 dozen of speals 10*s.*
107 raths £3 6*s.*
40 pear of blads £12.
28 sumers £1 8*s.*
7 cotch pols 14*s.*
26 pilos £1 10*s.*
15 shetlocks 10*s.*
4 pear of wheels £6.
37 wagon poles £3 14*s.*
9 pear of forchels 18*s.*
5 perches £1.
200 of oaken bords £1 8*s.*
2 dungpot blads 6*s.* 6*d.*

In the Green
6 tuns and 11 foot of aish £12 11*s.*
A tune and 26 foot of elme £2 4*s.*
Five foot of oake 5*s.*
A percel of tember and wood as came from Wooten Rivers £6.
A percel of elm lying at Bushen[1] £7 3*s.*
A percel of elm bought of Georg Mils £1 9*s.* 8*d.*
A percel of elm bought at Brod Town £4 10*s.*
A percel of tember and wood at Sha[2] £9 9*s.*
The hurst and the careg £3.
A percel of wood and tember £1 17*s.*
5 pear of cotch wheels £2 10*s.*
His working tools £1 10*s.*
12 ft of elm 9*s.*

In the Uper Celer
The new iron £20 13*s.*
The old iron £1 2*s.* 9*d.*
The boxes £1 11*s.* 6*d.*
The tacks and grace 15*s.* 5*d.*

Total £450 8*s.* 9*d.* [*recte* £450 9*s.* 3*d.*]

More in bad debts £20.

[*Total omitted, by addition* £470 9*s.* 3*d.*]

Edward Hopkins, Richard Edney and Isaac Martin, appraisors.

Buried St. Mary 17 March 1690/1.
Bond 4 June 1691, administration to Sarah Hockley, intestate's widow.

1. Possibly Bushton, Cliffe Pypard.
2. Possibly Shaw, West Overton.

295 JOHN MUNDY
tailor [will] 25 April 1691 P1/M/297

In the Kitchen
One table, three joynt stooles, 6 chayers, 6 barrells, one cubboard, 4 Bibles with other books, a great and doggs and other iron things, one jack, one warmeing pan, brasse and pewter and other wooden thinges, one furnace and grate £8 17*s.*

In the Chamber over the Kitchen
One bed and bedsteed, one rugg, two blanketts, two bolsters, three pillows, curtins and vallions, four leather chairs, one chest, one table, four trunkes, one book sheilve, one lookeing glasse, three boxes, a cloosstoole, one payer of andiron, fireshoule and tonges, a silver cup and clock £9 9*s.* 6*d.*

In the Chamber at Stayerhead
One bed, one bolster, one payre of

blanketts, one coverled, one table and trunke £2.

In the Garrett
Wooden lumber £1.
In weareing apparell and lynen £7.
In wood and other lumber £2 10*s.*

Sub-total £30 16*s.* 6*d.*

One ground [the lease valued att *added in a different hand*] £50.

Total £80 16*s.* 6*d.*

Robert Gough and Edward Fribens, appraisors.

Buried St. Peter 28 April 1691 'John Munday'.
Will 8 April 1691; probate 8 December 1691 to executrix [Mary Mundy, testator's widow].

296 JOANE HUNT[1]

widow 19 September 1691[2] P1/H/538

Her wareing apparell £2 10*s.*
Her lining £2.
Monyes £1 15*s.* 6*d.*
Good debts 11*s.* 6*d.*
Bad debts £6 12*s.* 8*d.*

Total £13 9*s.* 8*d.*

John Reeves and John Hill, appraisors.

Buried St. Mary 20 September 1691
Bond 13 October 1691, administration to Charles Bligh of the City of London, principal creditor.

1. 'of St. Mareys Marlborough'.
2. There are two almost identical copies of this inventory.

297 PETER ANDREWS[1]

21 September 1691 P1/A/171

Wareing apparril and mony £1 10*s.*
To brass potts 8*s.*
To tenniments of lace hold £12.
To iorn potts 4*s.*
On chast and to coffors 5*s.*
To bedssteds 6*s.*
To beds £1.
Working tooles, roghel and wedgis and hathet and sawe 5*s.*
To ladders 1*s.* 6*d.*
To blanckets and a raggid rugg 5*s.*
To bedd matts 1*s.*
Thre pillos 4*s.*
Three repp hoocks 1*s.* 6*d.*
To coushings 1*s.*
Three chayors 1*s.* 6*d.*
On sept tosting iorn and gridiorn and thre candil sticks 2*s.*
To barrils and on hors 2*s.*
On pare of billos 4*d.*
On settil and coule or tubb 5*s.*
On tabel bord and frame 2*s.*
On cobert 2*s.* 6*d.*
On barriel 1*s.* 6*d.*
Linning 10*s.*
Wood 15*s.*
On peuter dish 9*d.*
On warmeing pann 2*s.*
Lumber 5*s.*

Total £18 16*s.* 7*d.* [*recte* £19 1*s.* 7*d.*]

John Bowsher and Mickel Pick, appraisors.

Buried St. Mary 17 September 1691.
Will 9 September 1691; probate 13 October 1691 to executrix [Mary Andrews, testator's widow].

1. 'of St marys in marlbrowh'.

298 JONE ALLIN
widow [will] 13 October 1691
P1/A/170

In the Outer Chamber
A bedstead, a feather bead and all things belonging to it £2 5*s.*
In the same roome a flock bead and all things belonging to it £1 15*s.*

In the Next Roome
A bedstead 10*s.* 6*d.*

In the above said Outer Chamber
Linen, warmeing pan, a chest and other lumber 18*s.* 8*d.*

In the Hall
4 pewter dishes and other small pewter 4*s.*
In the same roome 2 brass pots, 2 brass kitels, a brass pan, a brass skilett and candlestick £1 5*s.*
In the same roome a table board, frienpan, fire pan, tongs, andiers and spitt 8*s.*
3 barrels, 2 tubs and other lumber 6*s.* 8*d.*
In money in the house £4 10*s.*
Wood and lumber in the hovill 5*s.*
Her wareing apparell woolen and linen £4 10*s.*
Money on bond £123.

Total £139 17*s.* 10*d.*

John Blissett senior and Edward Browne, appraisors.

Burial not recorded.
Will 20 July 1691; probate 8 December 1691 to executor [George Webb of East Kennet, husbandman, testatrix's kinsman].

299 GABRILL MILLS[1]
15 October 1691 P1/M/296

His wareinge apparrell 3*s.*
One flocke bedd, one boulster and 2 pillows, 2 beddsteeds, one rugge, one blanckett, one sheet £1.
One brass pott, 3 kettills, 5 pewter platters, 3 pewter potts £1.
2 barrells, 2 civers, one tubb, 2 tabell boads, one payle 6*s.*
For wood £3 5*s.*
For old lomber 7*s.*
One old lease of a house 10*s.*

Total £6 11*s.*

Nathanuell Hone and John Elliott, appraisers.

Buried St. Mary 8 October 1691.
Bond 8 December 1691, administration to Joane Mills, intestate's widow.

1. 'of Marlborough St. Maryes'.

300 HENEREY COOLEY
?shoemaker [inventory goods] 29 October 1691 P1/C/412

The waring apareill £1 10*s.*

In the best Room
Too beds, on fethers and other flocks £2.
On fether boulster, too fether pelos 10*s.*
On trounck, on tabelbord, on boxe 6*s.*
Too chayers, on kofer, on koberd, too stools 5*s.*
Thre blanckets, on roug, on coferleid 10*s.*
Thre par of shets, 3 boulser casis 10*s.*
Thre par of peilobears 2*s.* 6*d.*, too tabel cloths 2*s.* 4*s.* 6*d.*

In the outer Room
Too beads and too boulsters and all that belong too them £2.
On chest and too cofers 8*s.*
On keitell pot, on forneis £1.
3 pots, 3 skeilets, on keitell £1.
On warming pan, too skeimers 4*s.*

8 peuter platers, 5 poringers, on flagoin, on tanckerd, too plats 18*s.*
Four candelsticks 1*s.* 6*d.*
On speit, on dreipinpan, on par of anders, on par doges, feirpnan and tongs 5*s.*
On tabelbord, on fourm, too chayers, on cooberd 10*s.*
5 barels, too toobs, too keifers £1.
The stanein of small ware £4.

Page total £17 2*s.*

For bends and uper leder £14.
26 par of shews £1 10*s.*
Two par of beack boots 10*s.*
Leumber things 2*s.*
Money in hous £13.
Depts despret £30.

Page total £59 2*s.*

Total £76 4*s.*

John Laburn and Edward Dangerfield, appraisors.

Buried St. Mary 18 October 1691 'Henry Culey the elder'.
Will [*blank*] 1691[1]; probate 8 December 1691 to executrix [Hanna Cully, testator's widow].

1. Holograph, signs 'Henry Cully'.

301 CHRISTOPHER BRATHWAITE

cutler 10 November 1691 P1/B/610

In the Chember over the Shop
1 fether bed and bedsteed, 1 rugg, 1 bowlster, 1 payr of blankets, 1 set of curtaints and valliants, 6 turky work chairs, 5 lether chairs, 2 chest of drawers, 2 table boards, 1 payr of doggs, 1 payr of fire pan and tongus, 2 trunks with other implements £9.

In the Garrat over the Chember
3 beds and bedsteeds, 4 ruggs, 1 coverleed, 3 payr of blankets, 3 bowlsters, 2 pillows, 1 table board, 1 trunk, 1 set of curtaints and vallaints with other implements £5 13*s.*

In the other Garrat
1 bed and bedsteed, 1 bowlster, 2 pillows, 1 rugg, 1 payr of blankeats, 1 set of [vallaints *deleted*] curtaints and vallaints, 1 press, 1 chest of drawers, 1 table board with other implements £4 10*s.*
[In linnen £3 *added*]

In the Hall
2 table boards, 6 joynstooles, 1 payr of firepan and tongus, 1 payr of andirons, 1 payr of doggs, 1 cast back with som small things £1 10*s.*
Pewter in the buttry £2.

In the Seller
1 brewing furnace, 1 ketle, 5 pots, 6 barrells, 1 meshing vessell, 2 kivors, 2 tubbs, 1 jack, 1 grate and back, 1 rack, 1 table board with other lumber £7.

In the Backside
Wood, cole and timber £30.

In the Working Shop
1 anvill, 3 visces withe other tooles £4.
In iron and steele, sceles and waights and other things £62.

In the Forestreet Shop
In trunks £3.
In muskets, pyks, bandileers and belts £27.
The lease of the house worth £70.
In mony and plate £20.
Wareing apparrell £10.
Debts good and bad £438.
For gindstons £7.

Total £703 13*s.* 6*d.* [*recte* £703 13*s.*]

John Horner and Joseph Webb, appraisors.

Buried St. Peter 5 October 1691.
Will 1 October 1691[1]; probate 8 Dec 1691 to executrix [Joane Brathwaite, testator's widow].

1. Endorsed 'wanting the testator's hand, who was surprised by sudden sleep'.

302 JOHN SLOPER
carpenter 16 November 1691 P1/S/560

In the Best Chamber
1 bed and bedsted, 1 rugg, 2 blankcoats, curtains and valliants, one bowlster, 2 pillows, 1 table board, 1 chest, 1 trunk, 1 box and other implements £3 10*s.*

In the Chamber over the Hall
1 bed and bedsteed, 1 coverleed, 1 bowlster, 1 blankcoat, 2 chairs, 3 joyn stooles, 1 trunk £1 12*s.*

In the Hale
1 table board, 4 stooles, [1 trunk *deleted*] 2 chairs, brass and pewter, 2 spits, 2 driping pans, 1 payr of doggs £2 12*s.*

In the Celler
4 barrells, 2 tubbs, 1 kiver, 1 powdring tubb, 1 lade payle 10*s.*
In linnen 10*s.* 6*d.*
Debts good and bad £16.
Wood and timber £10 5*s.*
Wareing apparrell £2 10*s.*
Working tooles £1.

Total £38 9*s.* 6*d.*

John Horner and Joseph Webb, appraisors.

Buried St. Mary 16 June 1691.
Bond 8 December 1691, administration to Jane Sloper, intestate's widow.

303 FRANCIS SMITH
tailor 16 November 1691 P1/S/561

In the Chamber over the Hall
1 bed and bedsteed, 1 rugg, 2 blank coats, curtains and valliants, 1 bowlster, 2 lether chairs, 4 flagg chairs, 2 joyn stooles, 2 table boards, 1 side cubbard, 1 wainscot chaire, 2 payr of doggs, fire pann and tongs and other implements £5.

In the Chamber over the Shop
2 bedsteeds and 2 beds, 2 bowlsters, 2 pillows, curtains and valliants, 2 ruggs, 4 blankcoats, 1 chest of drawers, 1 press, 1 table board, 1 chest, 1 coffer, 2 boxes with other implements £7.

In the Chamber over the Kiching
3 beds and bedsteeds, 6 blankcoats, 3 coverleeds, 3 bowlsters with other things £4.10*s.*

In the Hall
1 table board, 1 fourme, 8 chairs, 1 setle, 1 rack, 1 jack, 2 spits, 2 dripping pans, 1 grate, fire pan and tongs with other things £2.

In the Buttery
1 ketle, 3 pots, 1 boyler, 3 skillets £3 2*s.*
In pewter £2 7*s.*

In the Celler
9 vessells, 3 horses for beere with other things £5.

In the Brewhouse
1 furnace, 1 boyler, 1 meshfat, 3 coollers, 11 keevors and tubbs with other lumber £5 10*s.*
In linnen £2 5*s.*
In wood and lumber £5.
In wareing apparell and books £5.

Total £46 14*s.*

John Horner and Joseph Webb, appraisors.

Buried St. Mary 9 October 1691.
Will 6 October 1691; probate 8 December 1691 to executrix [Ann Smith, testator's widow].

304 RICHARD SMITH

labourer[1] 7 December 1691 P1/S/562

Monie at interest £136.

In the Chamber
One fether bed, a bolster and two pillows £1 10*s.*
One flock bed and too flock bolsters 13*s.* 4*d.*
Three fether bolsters 6*s.* 8*d.*
Three paire of sheetts 7*s.* 6*d.*
Two rugs, 2 paire of blanketts £1.
His apparell £3.
Three table clothes, one dozen of napkins 10*s.*
Three paire of pillow beares 5*s.*
Three bedsteeds 10*s.*
Two chests 10*s.*
Three boxes 4*s.*
More lumber in the chamber 10*s.*

In the Kitching
Brass and pewter there £2.
Other lumber goods there 10*s.*

In the Buttery
Lumber goods there £1.

In the Outhouse and Backside
Wood there £1.

Total £149 16*s.* 6*d.*

John Smith and John Bowsher, appraisors.

Buried St. Mary 18 November 1691.
Will 11 November 1691, probate 8 December 1691 to Joane Smith, testator's widow.

1. 'Husbandman' in burial register.

305 EDWARD TOWNSEND

carpenter 7 December 1691 P1/T/210

2 beds, 2 bedsteeds, 2 payr blanketts, 1 rug, 1 boulster, 3 pillows, 2 setts of curtain and vallens £5 12*s.*
1 pres, 2 boxes, 1 trunk, 1 chest of drawers, 1 cupbord, 4 table bords, 6 joynt stools, 2 coffers, 1 cradle, 1 cradle rug, 1 screen, 9 chayers, [1 looking glass *added*] £3 14*s.*
In pewter 1 basing ladell, 2 linon things £1 2*s.* 6*d.*
1 warming pan, 1 skillett, 1 basting ladell, 1 iron pott 10*s.*
In working tooles and lave [for turning *added*] 15*s.*
In timber £1.
A trencher rack, trencers, 4 pictures, glases and 6 bottle glases and other implements 7*s.*
2 payr andiors, 1 payr dogs, tongs, shovell, 1 payr billows, 1 barrill, 1 hogs head, 1 hors, 1 powdring tubb, 1 kiver, 1 tub, 1 buckett, 1 spitt, 3 candlestick, 1 grid iron, [1 fryin pan *added*] 19*s.* 6*d.*
In sheets and other lynon £1 2*s.* 6*d.*
His waring apparell [and books *added*] £2 15*s.*
In mony £4 15*s.*
In debts good and bad £5 6*s.* 7*d.*

Total £27 19*s.* 1*d.*

Noah Webb and Joseph Webb, appraisors.

Buried St. Mary 27 October 1691.
Will 20 October 1691; probate not recorded; inventory exhibited 8 December 1691.

306 SUSANAH HILL[1]

widow [burial register] 8 December 1691
P1/H/541

Her wareinge aparrell and monny in her purse £4 3*s.*
Leavft in wood £2 10*s.*
Two bedds and all that belonges to itt £2 10*s.*
Lomber goods £1.
One pigge £1 5*s.*
Monnyes dew one bond £10.

Total £21 8*s.*

Thomas Bury, appraisor.

Buried St. Mary 8 November 1691.
Bond 8 December 1691, administration to Stephen Hill, intestate's son.

1. 'of Marlebrough St. Maryes'.

307 HUGH HUTCHENS[1]

husbandman 8 December 1691
P1/H/540

A hows in which he lived £20.
His wareing aparill £1.
Thre bedsteeds and beds and what belongs thare unto £2.
His linning £1.
His bras and pewtur £1.
A chest and cofur and box and table bord and settell and other lumbering things 10*s.*
Muney or other wis bands for it £30.

Total £55 10*s.*

Robert Hill and Nicholas Rumsey, appraisers.

Buried St. Mary 18 November 1691, 'Hughe Huchings alias Forde'.
Will 14 [*lost*] 1688; probate 8 December 1691 to executrix [unnamed in will]; inventory exhibited 10 March 1691/2

1. 'who departed this life the sixteenth day of november 1691'.

308 JEREMIAH MATTHEWS

carpenter 9 December 1691[1] P1/M/295

His wearing aporill £5 10*s.*

The Bed Chamber
To flockbeds, one flock bolster, thre blankets £1 5*s.*
One browne and one read ruge £1 4*s.*
A bedsteed, curtins and valiones, mat and cord £1 6*s.*
One fether bed and to bolsters and 3 pilowes £3.
6 curtines and valiones 12*s.*
Bras kitoll, 3 sass pans, skilot and skimor £1.
4 pear of old fierpan and tonges, 10 cortin rodes 10*s.*
One peare of doges, brass heads 2*s.*
Mor an old bed sheet 3*s.*
Tining wear and to joren candellstick and one brass 2*s.* 4*d.*
Woden trenchers 6*d.*
Pictor freame and glass cobard, base violl and setoren 11*s.* 6*d.*
77 pownd of peuter at 6d ½ the lb. £2 0*s.* 5½*d.*

The Best Cheamber
9 old chayres 9*s.*

In Lining
7 sheetes 14*s.*
6 diapor napting and to tabell cloth 4*s.*
16 cors naptings and 4 teabell cloths 8*s.*
3 dozen and one cors towell 6*s.*
A feather bead 10*s.*

The Out Hows
Thre teabells and freames and 3 old tubes,

dog wheel 13*s.*
A cheste and 3 old lead payles and drapor 8*s.*
9 joynes stooles and napting prese and ot tube 9*s.* 6*d.*
Working tooles 5*s.*
The timber in the shambells 10*s.*
To old slikes 6*d.*

Total £21 18*s.* 9*d.* [*recte* £22 3*s.* 9½]

Roger Williams, Thomas Taylor and John Parsons, appraisors.

Buried St. Peter 19 November 1691.
Bond 8 December 1691, administration to Robert Cowsey and William Ragborne, creditors; inventory exhibited 8 December 1691; accounts submitted 9 April 1692.

1. Either this date or the date of the exhibition must be incorrect.

309 ELIXABATH MOORE

spinster [will] 2 February 1691/2
P1/M/298

With the bead and bedseted and all be longing therto £2.
A chest, a tronk and a boxs 7*s.*
A tabell bord and jent stoles and a forme 5*s.*
A coberd 2*s.*
3 cetes and 2 brase potes and bras pane and 2 skelets and wormen pane £2.
For pwaiter with a tening dreping pane and a friing pane 14*s.*
2 barrells and 3 cefers and 2 tobes 3*s.*
For ches and wheat 5*s.*
For a pasell of hard wood £1.
A jeark and 2 spetes 3*s.*
And for leomber goods 12*s.*
And for money and wering close £16 16*s.*

Total £24 1*s.* [*recte* £24 7*s.*]

John Stent and Andrew Cully, appraisors.

Buried St. Mary 1 February 1691/2.
Will 20 January 1691/2; probate 9 September 1692 to Mary Munday, testator's cousin.

310 WILLIAM MARTINE

parchment maker 17 February 1691/2
P1/M/299

His purse and apparell £2.
Fourteen dozen of harrows £6.
Twelve hundred of scrows £5 8*s.*
One hundred and twenty fouer pelts £1 10*s.*
Five glew trows 10*s.*
A ladder, two luggs, one beam and one old tubb 2*s.*
Five knives in their stocks or handles 8*s.*
Tallets, fern and hay 6*s.*
Two furnaces with the grates and dores £8.

In the Hall
Three bell brass pots, two brass skillets, one brass skimer, two paire of pott hookes, one spitt, one frying pan, one paire of andirons, one fire shovell and tongs, one paire of hangells, six pewter platters, one pewter flagon, one pewter candlestick and two brass kittles £1 16*s.*
One long table board and frame, two joynt chaires, one joynt fourme and one cupboard 10*s.*

In the Chamber
One fether bed, bolster and pillows, one rugg, one paire of blanketts with the bedsteed, cord, matt, curtaines and vallians £2.
Two chests, one box, one coffer 8*s.*

In the Buttery
Three barrills, one tunbole, one lade paile, one powdering tubb, one serch 10*s.*

In an Upper Room
Eight hundred of peces £2 10*s.*
Glew netts and lumber there 12*s.*

In the Clossett
The boys bed 5*s.*
Fifteen role and a halfe of parchment £11 15*s.* 6*d.*
A paire of beams, weights and scales with hatchett and forkes 5*s.*
In howses £8.

Total £52 15*s.* 6*d.*

Joseph Duffe and Edward Dickson, appraisors.

Buried St. Mary 16 February 1691/2 'William Martin'.
Will 12 June 1691; probate 5 April 1692 to Noah, Margery and Eglah Martine, testator's children.

311. [ELIZABETH KITE][1]
widow [will] 29 February 1691/2
P1/K/104

2 old bettels and 3 old bras vates £1 6*s.*
3 old platers, 2 vates, on bason, on salt all at 13 [?lb] at 6^{d} 6*s.* 6*d.*

In the Low Room
On tabell bord, on cobord, on form 2*s.* 6*d.*
Mor 2 toobes, on cever, 2 barels, on paile 5*s.* 6*d.*
On bed and bedsted with cord and mat, on roug, too blainkets, to bosters, on pelo with cortins and valenttes £1 16*s.*

In the Old Woomans Chamber
On cheast, on tabell bord, on cofer, on ioynt stoll 7*s.*
On trockel bedsted 2*s.*
Too par of shetes 4*s.*
Sub-total £4 9*s.* 6*d.*

The old womans warin clos 5*s.*
On skelet 1*s.* 6*d.*
[Mor for 2 tenementes £10. *added*]

[*Total omitted, by addition* £14 16*s.*]

William Picke and William Lester, appraisors.

Buried St. Peter 24 February 1691/2.
Will 20 February 1691/2; commission 8 March 1691/2, oath administered 12 April 1692 to Elizabeth Kinton; probate 26 April 1692 to Elizabeth Kinton, testator's daughter.

1. Name omitted, obtained from will.

312 THOMAS EDNE
?blacksmith [inventory goods] 3 March 1691/2
P1/E/127

His waring aparel and money in pors and detes oweing hem £4

In The Chambar
To bedes and the furniture thereto belonging £3.
And there to cheastes, on coffar, one box, one cobart, one chayer 13*s.* 6*d.*

In the Othare Chambar
One flock bed and bed stead 8*s.*

In the Hall
One tabel bord, one satel, to cobartes, three jint stoles £1.
Brass and pawtar £2 10*s.*
A pare off and irenes and othar iren goodes 12*s.*

In the Boutere
Three bareles and three toubes, to ceveres, one tounbouell 6*s.*

In the Shoup
An anveld, one payer off beleces and the othar toules £4 5*s.*
For the markat ware £2 5*s.*

Total £18 19*s.* 6*d.*

Richard Edne and Thomas Edne, appraisors.

Buried St. Mary 16 February 1691/2, 'Thomas Edney the elder'.
Bond 5 April 1692, administration to Martha Edney, intestate's widow.

313 ANNE LOVE[1]
widow [*undated*, c.1692] P1/L/218

In the Hows of Richard Martings
One scellit 1*s.*
One puter tankard and flagon, one bason and candallstick 5*s.*
One dreping pan 1*s.*
3 curten rodes [9*s. deleted*] 9*d.*
One diaper tabell cloth and one holand sheet and one callecoe sheet 8*s.* [6*d. added*]
One fuston wascote, 8 napkens and 4 cors towells 4*s.* 10*d.*
One box and sum od things 2*s.*

[*In the Hows of Richard Love* added]
3 pellows and one boulster, one bedsted, cord and matt, 1 brush 18*s.* 6*d.*
4 shefts, 23 peeces of small lining, one pare of sheets £1 2*s.*
One chest and waring clothes £1.
Other lumber good 10*s.*
[In monney £17. *added*]

Total [£5 1*s.* 10*d. deleted*; £22 1*s.* 10*d. deleted*] £21 12*s.* 7*d.* [*recte* £21 13*s.* 7*d.*]

George Ayliffe and Robert Chivers, appraisors.

Buried St. Mary 8 February 1691/2 'Luff'.
Will 5 February 1691/2; probate 5 April 1692 to Richard Love, testator's son.

1. 'Ann Luff' on will.

314 LUCY STAGG
widow 6 September 1692 P1/S/570

Her wearing apparell £1.
Six sheets and other linnen £1.
One bed, two blankets, one bolster, two pillows, one red rugg and one bedsteed £2 10*s.*
One hatt 2*s.* 6*d.*
Three coffers, one box, one trunk 9*s.*
Of pewter: seven dishes, three plates, three porringers and one fagon 16*s.*
One kitle, one pott, two skilletts, on iron pot 18*s.*
One cupboard, one table board and frame, three joynt stooles, three chaires 12*s.*
Two Bibles and two small bookes 6*s.*
Money in hand and debts £9 4*s.* 4*d.*
One paire of andirons, one paire of hangells, one paire of dogs, one spitt, one paire of billice, a fire shovell and tongs 3*s.*
One house £14.
One tubb, two barrills, one kiver, one powdering tubb with lumber 6*s.*

Total £31 6*s.* 10*d.*

Robert Brabant and Nathaniel Hone, appraisors.

Buried St. Mary 23 June 1692, 'Stegg'.
Will 11 August 1691, probate 9 September 1692 to Margaret Brabant, testatrix's kinswoman.

315 ROBERT FISHLOCK
7 February 1692/3 P1/F/198

In debts teen pounds £10
His wearing apparell foor pounds £4.
His workeing tooles forty shillings £2.
Lumber goods teen shillings 10*s.*

[*Total omitted, by addition* £16 10*s.*]

Thomas Keynton and Walter Hammond, appraisers.

Buried St. Mary 8 February 1692/3
Bond 14 June 1693, administration to Rebecca Fishlock, intestate's widow.

315A. [MARGARETT][1] FRANCIS
widow [*undated*, c.1693][2] P1/F/200

Rove comde oull ten lb. 5*s.* 6*d.*
Rell woll 5 score and 15 lb. £3 14*s.*
Four lb. and halfe of comde woll 6*s.* 9*d.*
Ten bundels of comd woll £6 10*s.*
Alaven lb. of yearne £1.
Chercole and fearne £1.
For the beeme and scealse and other things 10*s.*
The peeg £1 6*s.* 6*d.*
On remlet of searg 5*s.*
To bedse and what belong to it £1 10*s.*
On tronk, on box, on quaer 3*s.* 6*d.*
To toubs, to barels and a lanthorne 10*s.*
On pot and on spit, on platter 5*s.*
Some barly 7*s.* 6*d.*
A saddel and botes 5*s.*
Wareinge aparril £1.
In deets £4 2*s.*

[*Total* £18 18*s.* 9*d.* *deleted*]
Total £23 0*s.* 9*d.*

John Browne, Nicolas Haland and James Harnam, appraisors.

Buried Preshute, Wilts 23 September 1693.
Bond 15 December 1693; administration to William Young, intestate's brother.

1. Forename from bond.
2. Inventory 'of Marleburgh'; bond 'of Manton in the parish of Preshute'.

316 WILLIAM TEMPLE
husbandman 13 April 1693 P1/T/218

In the Chamber where he lodged
His weareing apparell £3.
1 feather bedd, 2 bolsters, blankets, sheets, rugge and furniture belonging £2 10*s.*
2 table cloathes and 1 dozen of napkins 6*s.*
7 paire of sheetes £2 5*s.*
10 pillowbeers and 6 old towells 6*s.*
2 mantles, 1 whittle and other small things 5*s.*
2 chests, 1 trunk, boxes and other lumber 10*s.*
1 looking glass 2*s.*

In the Outer Chamber
1 fether bedd, bolster, pillows, sheet, blanketts, rugg and other furniture £2.
1 tableboard and 4 joyned stooles and other lumber 10*s.*

In the Low Room
In brasse and pewter £3.
2 fire pans and tongs, andirons, spitt, dripping pans and other odd things 10*s.*
1 tableboard and 4 old chayres 2*s.* 6*d.*

In the Buttery
3 small barrells, tubbs and other lumber 10*s.*
In desperate debts [£7 *deleted*] £8.
The term of the lease of the house £10.

Total £33 16*s.* 6*d.*

Debts owing £8 per the testator[1]

John Richardson and Hugh Hankinson, appraisors.

Buried St. Peter 4 February 1692/3.
Will 29 January 1692/3; probate 5 May 1603 to Alice Temple, testator's widow.

1. Debtes owed by the deceased should not form part of the inventory.

317 WILLIAM SPACKMAN

?grocer [inventory goods] 26 April 1693
P1/S/582

In the Uper Chamber over the Shop
For weareing aparrell £2 10*s.*
1 flock bed, 2 blankets, 1 feather bolster, 3 feather pillows, 1 old green rug, curtains and vallians and bedstead, matt and cord, 5 sheets £2 10*s.*
3 leather chayers, 3 trunks, 1 box, 1 table bord, her part in the furnase, 3 paire of dowlace pelowbers, 3 ordinarye bowlster cases, 3 corse table clothes, 6 hand towels, 1 window curtane, 1 iron rod £1 10*s.*

In the Second Chamber
1 wanescaot bedstead, matt and cord, curtaines and valiens, 1 table board, 2 dozen and 8 drincking glases, 1 old sett of curtains, 1 old green carrpett £1 10*s.*

In the Lower Chamber over the Shop
1 feather bed, 1 pair of blancketts, 1 bedsted, matt and cord, 6 caen chaiers, 1 sett of drawers, 1 trunck, 1 tableboard, 2 cushions, 1 dresing box, 2 pictures, 1 looking glass, 1 paire of andirons, 1 pair dogs, 1 hanging shelfe, 2 calicoe curtains £4 10*s.*
2 dowlace table clothes, 8 dowlace knapkins, 1 diapper table clothe and 8 diaper knapkins, 3 damaske knapkins, 1 diapper cuberd clothe, 1 diapper towell, 3 holand pelowbers £2

In the Hall
1 table board, 1 litell round table, 1 joint stoole, 4 leather chaiers, 3 rush chaiers, 1 sckreene, 1 jack, 2 paier hangels, 1 iron bak, 1 paier of iron andirons, one paier of dogs, fier pann and tongs £2 6*s.*
1 chefing dish, 1 warmeing pann, 1 paire of candlesticks, 2 bras coks, 1 paire of belowes and books, 1 pewter salt, 1 picture £1
3 spits 3*s.*
51lb. pewter £1 9*s.* 9*d.*
2 skimers, 2 baesting ladels 2*s.*
2 latinge pans, 1 friingpan 2*s.* 6*d.*
32lb. wrought brass £1 12*s.*
1 trencher rack, 1 dozen trenchers 1*s.*
1 iron candlestick 3*d.*

[*In the Celler* added]
15 barrels and other lumber £1
3 gallons linill oyle 12*s.*
1 dozen hearth bisomes 10*d.*
½ bushell salt 1*s.* 10*d.*
3 [*measure omitted*] of pitch 9*s.*
1 parsell tobaco 4*s.*
2 bushels of sand 1*s.*
1 salt gardener 5*s.*
3 wooden horses, 1 forme 3*s.*
2 iron digers, 1 sledg 1*s.*
[*illegible line deleted*]

In the Shop
1 beeme and scales 6*s.*
4 ½cwt wayts: 2 lead, 2 iron £1 6*s.*
Wayts ¼cwt: 2 4lb laed, 1 7lb lead, 1lb laed, 2 bras lb, 1 bras ½lb, 2 brass ¼lb, 2 brass 2 ozs, 2 bras 1oz, 1 brass ½ oz, 1 brass dram 8*s.*
2 brass mortars 2:26 [*measure omitted*] and 1 pestle £1 7*s.*
3 persels of nayles 42lb 12*s.*
39lb corke 5*s.*
10lb alum 2*s.*
3lb whiteing 9*s.*
40lb London starch 10*s.*
8lb bw sugar 2s 6d, 4lb logwood 12d 3*s.* 6*d.*

2 rame ¼lb bw paper 4*s.*
40lb old Spanish 13*s.* 8*d.*
27lb hops and 26lb bw hops £1 15*s.*
14 linkes 2*s.* 4*d.*
6lb steele hemp 6*s.*
Rudle 1*s.*
15lb po blew 7*s.* 6*d.*
13lb gauls 6*s.* 6*d.*
18lb green copparis 1*s.* 6*d.*
9lb shott 1*s.*
12lb caraway seed 1*s.* 4*d.*
6lb beat ginger 1*s.* 6*d.*
3 parcels of tobaco and stems 3*s.*
3lb jamaco peper 5*s.*
3 dozen 1 coffee dishes 6*s.* 2*d.*
27lb glew 9*s.*
11 dozen canns £1 10*s.*
45 drincking glases 7*s.* 6*d.*
8 hour glases 2*s.* 8*d.*
8 white chamber potts 4*s.*
15: 2lb galypots 2*s.* 6*d.*
Small glases 2*s.* 8*d.*
3 dozen brushes 5*s.*
3lb ½ fine twine 2*s.* 6*d.*
7lb candls 2*s.* 4*d.*
10 dozen marline 3*s.* 6*d.*
Powder hornes, quils, leather buttons, brass curtaine rings, goeing strings 6*s.*
9 dozen ¼ balls 1*s.* 6*d.*
5 dozen bisomes, 1 dozen cards 1*s.* 8*d.*
Braided points and laces 11*s.*
8 ble lamblack 1*s.* 4*d.*
4lb brasile 3*s.*
Po lyquorish, sweet fennell seeds, ivorye, vardigrace, flower sulfer, white lead, arsnik, combs 5*s.*
9lb cutted thred 16*s.* 6*d.*
3 paquets of pins 3*s.*
25lb powder 3d paper 2*s.* 1*d.*
1lb ½ cutt bw thred 5*s.*
7 gros ordinary gimp buttons 6*s.* 6*d.*
Clapses and thred and combes 5*s.*
3lb sweet oyle 2*s.* 2*d.*
2lb brimstone 6*d.*
Buttons 7*d.*, pins 7*s.* 7*s.* 7*d.*
15000 2d nayles 15*s.*7*d.*
Combs and brushes 3*s.*
7000 4d L nayls 15*s.* 6*d.*
3lb ½ hemp 2*s.*
17 peces of inkell att 7d 9*s.* 11*d.*
32lb powder blew 16*s.*
21 dozen cards at 14d £1 4*s.*
6 dozen 4lb of bw and cutted threds £6 13*s.*
Inkels and tapes £1 5*s.*
12oz cloves 6*s.*
6oz mace 7*s.*
2oz ½ ordinary mace 1*s.* 3*d.*
1lb 3oz sinamon 7*s.* 6*d.*
3lb beat licquorish 1*s.*
3 rands thred, 1lb peper 2*s.* 8*d.*
2 dozen combes 3*s.*, for thred 3*s.* 6*s.*
3lb cutt bw thred N° 25 9*s.*
2lb cutt bw thred N° 16 4*s.*
½ lb cutt bw thred N° 26 1*s.* 7*d.*
2lb black thred 3*s.* 6*d.*
5 dozen of tinn and coppar boxes at 13½*d.* 5*s.* 7*d.*
1 dozen pins N° 11 6*s.* 2*d.*
½ dozen short whites 2*s.* 9*d.*
3000 cawkins 2*s.* 6*d.*
½ dozen L washballs 4*d.*
1½lb sealing wax 2*s.*
3 rands small thred 1*s.* 2*d.*
Whipcord, pins and tape 5*s.* 6*d.*
Testaments, psalters and hornbooks 11*s.*
Remnants of inkell 12*s.*
12 dozen and 10 skains thred at 2*s.* 2*d.* £1 6*s.*
2 dozen open tape and purle 5*s.*
3oz fine thred 1*s.* 4*d.*
1lb Coventree blew thred 2*s.* 8*d.*
½lb cutt bw thred N° 24 1*s.* 6*d.*
6oz thred 1*s.* 8*d.*
14 dozen thimbles 4*s.* 8*d.*
Pins and tape 3*s.*
Things on the sett of boxes 9*s.*
1lb 10oz case pepper 2*s.*
1lb aniseed 5*d.*
¾lb wormseed 2*s.* 3*d.*
1lb cutt ginger 9*d.*
3oz nutts 1*s.* 3*d.*
3lb grains 1*s.* 3*d.*
4lb fenicrik 1*s.* 3*d.*

Seuerall od things 2*s.*
Seuerall persells of thred £1
12lb red lead 2*s.*
Pipes 12d, binding thred 14*d.* 2*s.* 2*d.*
Remnants of tape 3*s.* 6*d.*
1 iron grate 6*s.*
4 pewter masures 3*s.*
5 paire of beames and scales 7*s.*
2 fier buckets 6*s.*
Draw boxes £1
Counters and shelues £1
48 boxes and barrels and tubbs 15*s.*
1 powdering tubb and wash tubbs 2*s.* 6*d.*
2 engins, boxes and press £4
Sub-total £71 2*s.* 9*d.* [*recte* £71 12*s.* 9*d.*]

1 bed and seuerall other things £2
In good debts £10
In bad debts £70

Total £153 2*s.* 9*d.* [*recte* £153 12*s.* 9*d.*]

Robert Butcher and Nathaniel Merriman, appraisors.

Buried St Peter 25 January 1692/3.
Bond 20 June 1693, administration to Catherine Spackman, intestate's widow.

318 JOHN STEVENS
24 May 1693 P1/S/580

In the Kitchin
One table, seaven chayres, two joyned stooles, one paire of iron doggs, one iron barr, one fire pan and tongs, one iron grate and fender, two paire of hangells, two gridirons, two spitts, a brass cheafing dish, five candlesticks, two dripping pans, one tin candlebox, three smoothing irons, two Bibles with other books £2 9*s.*

In the Shop
Two irons and four paire of sheers [*value included with the following item*]

In the Chamber over the Shop
One flockbed and bedsteed with cord and matt, one bolster, one coverled, two blankets, one table, three leather chayrs, two coffers, one paire of andirons, one iron back, one warming pan, one glass shelfe £3.

In the Inner Chamber
One featherbed and bedsteed with cord and matt, two feather pillows, one feather bolster, one rugg, two blankets, curtains and valence with iron rodds, one window curtaine and rodd, one chest, one table, one chest of drawers, one chayre, one looking glass, one glass case £5 5*s.*

In the back Chamber
One flock bed and bedsteed with cord and matt, one bolster, two blankets, two coverlids, one long table, two chayrs, one box £2.

In the Garret
One flockbed and bedsteed with cord and matt, one bolster, two blankets £1.

In the Buttery
One cupboard, one trencher rack, nine pewter platters, thirteen pewter plates, six porengers, one brass boyler, one keettle, two skillets, one frying pan, two tinn pans, one tinn cullender, one copper cup, one pewter cup, one dozen of glass bottles, one poudering tubb, one temser, one search £2 15*s.*

In the Cellar
Six barrells, one meashing tubb and four kivers £1.
In wareing apparell and linnen £9.
And all other lumber £1.

Total £27 9*s.* 6*d.*

Robert Gough and Thomas Hunt, appraisors.

[*endorsed*] 'Anna lately widdow of John Stevens now wife of Thomas Cann, tailor'.

Buried St. Peter 24 December 1692.
Commission 25 May 1693, oath administered to Ann Cann formerly Stevens, intestate's widow; bond 27 May 1693, administration to Ann wife of Thomas Cann.

319 THOMAS CHAMBERLAINE
shoemaker 20 June 1693 P1/C/433

His weareingr apparell £1 6*s.*
In moneys £6.

In the Hall and Buttery
One bed and bedsteed and things belonging £2.
Brass and pewter £3.
One truncke, 2 boxes, 1 chest, 1 cupbord, 2 barrells, 2 chayers, 1 tablebord and 2 stooles £2.
One jacke, fire tongs and other lumber £1 10*s.*
Linim £1 5*s.*

In an Outhouse
Dressers, lasts and other workeing tooles £4.

In the Shope
One vice and board and knife 10*s.*
Brewing vessells, one chest and one coffer £1 5*s.*

Total £22 16*s.*

Thomas Keynton and John Keynton, appraisors.

Buried St. Mary 14 June 1693.
Will 6 June 1693; probate 20 June 1693 to [unnamed].

320 EDWARD POWELL
woolcomber 20 June 1693 P1/P/391

In the Chamber
His wearing apparel 15*s.*
1 bed, 1 bolster, 2 pillows, 1 rugg, bedstead, matt and coard £1 10*s.*
1 chest of drawers 12*s.*
1 trunk, 4 chaires and a pair of bellows 7*s.* 6*d.*
6 old napkins and 2 pillow beers 5*s.*
1 pair of andirons with brassheads 4*s.*

In the Hall
1 brass kettle, 1 bellbrass pott, 1 little skellett and 1 pair little brass candlesticks 5*s.*
8 old pewter dishes, 23 plates, 1 flagon, 1 tankard, 1 salt and 2 little sawcers £1 5*s.*
1 dripping pan, 1 pasty pan, 1 candle box, 5 candlesticks, 1 skimer, 1 pepper box and 1 flower box 5*s.*
1 pair fire doggs, 1 pair tongs and 1 frying pan 2*s.*
1 old cupboard and 2 little tableboards 5*s.*
1 bacon rack 1*s.* 6*d.*
7 old chaires and 1 old settle 3s

In the Garrett

6 bundles of washt wooll att 12*s.* 6*d.* per bundle £3 15s
2 bundles of oily worsted att 14s £1 8*s.*
18 lb. ½ of pinyons at 5*d.* per lb 7*s.* 8½*d.*
11 lb.of fleece wooll at 6½*d.* 5*s.* 11½*d.*
36 lb.of short wooll at 4½*d.* 13*s.* 6*d.*
4 lb.of course locks at 2½*d.* 10*d.*
Rings, posts and comb pipe 6*s.*
Beam, scales and weights 5*s.*
1 paire of combs 3*s.* 6*d.*

In the Cellar

1 hogshead of beer and hogshead £1 10*s.* 6*d.*

2 barrels, 1 kilderkin, 2 little barrels 8*s.* 6*d.*
Debts desperate £2 10*s.*

Total £17 14*s.* 6*d.*

John Richardson, Samuell Fowler, Joseph Webb and John Reeves, appraisors.

Buried St. Mary 19 April 1693 'Edward Powell of St. Peters'.
Bond 20 June 1693, administration to Mary Powell, intestate's widow.

321 JOHN WILKES

carpenter 10 July 1693 P1/W/416

His weareinge aparrell and books £5.
His wood and tymber in the backside and backlane £60.
In his fore and backe shopps £7.
His workeinge tooles and small wares £8.

In the Kitchen
One table board, seaven [*blank*] chaires, one shelfe, one paire of bellowes, one warmeinge pan, one jacke, one paire of doggs, one paire of andirons, two paire of hangells, one racke, sixe candlestickes with other lumber there £2 10*s.*

In the Buttery
Two kettle potts, one brasse pott, one ketle, three skilletts with other lumber there £2.
His pewter of all sorts £1 10*s.*

In the Celler
One table board and frame, five barells with other lumber there £1.

In the Best Chamber
One bedd and bedsteed, one rugge, one paire of blankettes, one bolster, two pillow beers, nyne chaires, one presse bedd, on chest of drawers, one glasse shelfe, one lookinge glasse, one paire of doggs, one paire of andirons, one firepan and tongs, one paire of billows, one sett of curtaines and valence with other ymplementes there £10.

In the Chamber over the Foreshoppe
One bedd and bedsteed, one rugge, two blanketts, a sett of curtaines and valence, one chest of drawers, three chaires, two new frames, five glasse shelves, one table board and frame, one trunke, two boxes with other ymplementes there £7.

In the Out Chamber
One bedsteed, one coverledd and one blankett 15*s.*

In the Little Chamber
One truckle bedsteed, one bedd, two coverledds, one coffer and other lumber there £2 10*s.*

In the Garretts and Stayers
Two beddsteeds, three glasse shelves with other lumber there £3 14*s.*
In lynnen: eight paire of sheetes, twoe dozen of napkins, sixe table cloathes, sixe paire of pillow bers, one dozen of towells £4 10*s.*
The chattell lease of his house £50.
His plate £4.
In ready money in his house £3.
His brewinge vessell and furnace £2 10*s.*
His mare, bridle and sadle £2 10*s.*
In goodes and desparte debtes £120.

Total £297 9*s.*

Joseph Webb, Samuell Wilde and Robert Webb, appraisors.

Buried St. Peter 3 July 1693, 'John Weeks'.
Will 29 June 1693; probate not recorded; inventory exhibited 11 July 1693.

322 RICHARD OADUM
husbandman 15 September 1693
P1/O/53

His purse and apparel £1.
Money on a mortgage £15.
Upon bonds in desperate debts £90.

Total £106.

John Titcom and William Sheppre, appraisors.

Buried St. Peter 6 September 1693, 'Woodam'.
Will [nuncupative] 3 September 1693; probate 15 September [1693] to [unnamed].

323 JOHN BOWSHER
baker 21 November 1693 P1/B/638

In money and his apparell £15.
4 beds and that which doth belong £7.

In the Chamber
One chest of drawers, one press, one chest, one coffer, one table and frame £1 5s.

In the Kitching
Eight platters and other small pewter [three pots, one brass pan, one kittle *deleted*] 10s.
Three potts, one brass pan, one kittle, two skilletts, one brass frying pan, one warming pan, one ladle, one skimer £2.
One furnace and grate £1.
One jack, two spitts, one paire of andirons, one paire of dogs, two paire of pott hookes, fire pan and tongs with other small things 15s.
Three joynt stooles, one rack, one settle and one board 10s.
Three barrells, two kivers, three tubbs 10s.
One hog pigg £1 10s.
One stone for malting £1.
In wood and lumber £1.

At Mildenhall
Two cows £6.
Twenty six teggs £7.
One rick of hay £7 10s.
Six and twenty wathers £10 8s.
Forty five ewes £16 17s. 6d.
Five horses £14.
Two ropes and two cart lines 8s.
Nine paire of horses harness £1 10s.
Straw 15s.
Five piggs £1 7s. 6d.
Hurdles, rakes and prongs 15s.
Two ladders 2s. 6d.
One stone for malting and two trowes £1 10s.
One waggon £6.
Two dung potts, one cart, one rowler £3.
Two ploughs, harrows and cow racks £2.
One paire of wheeles 10s.
Eleven sacks 11s.
Two boards and a bedsteed 6s.
Page total £111 10s. 6d. [*recte* £112 10s. 6d.]

Two quarters and a halfe of wheat £6.
Twenty six quarters of otes £20.
Thirty five quarters of barly £43 15s.
Sixteen boards in the lower barne 10s.
One fan and scives with rudder 10s.
Plowing two acres of land and wheat to sow the same £2 5s.

Total £184 10s. 6d. [*recte* £185 10s. 6d.]

James Coster, Joseph Dufe and Jeremiah Fowller, appraisors.

Buried St. Mary 12 November 1693, 'the elder'.
Will 11 October 1693; probate 17 April 1694 to John and Margaret Bowsher, testator's son and daughter.

324 WALTER RANDOLL
glover 15 February 1693/4 P1/R/186

In the Upper Chamber
Two chests and a paire of iron dogs, old curtains and two bed steads 14*s.* 6*d.*

In the Side Roome
One bedstead 2*s.* 6*d.*

In the Stair passage in the Garrett
One old chest and one old cuppboard 5*s.*

In the Prison Chamber
One table, two flock beds, two bed steads 15*s.*

In the Hall Chamber
One joint stooll, one side board, two cushions, one chair, two bed steads, cords and matt, curtains and vallens and one rugg, one small flock bed £1 16*s.* 6*d.*

In the two Little Roomes
Two little boards 3*s.*

In the Fore Chamber
Two table boards, two long formes, four joint stooles, one chaire, a paire of iron dogs, one bedstead and a truckle bedstead, a paire of tongs, one old flock bed, one cover lid, one curtain £1 8*s.* 6*d.*

In the Kitching
One brass pan, four brass kettles, one boyler of brass, one bell metle pott, one bell mettle skillett, one bell metle little pot, tenn pewter platters, two pewter tanchards, two pewter wine measures, one table board, two long formes, one cubbord, three pewter flaggons, one pair of andirons, fire shovell and tongs, two spitts, one looking glass, a fender and pott hangings, a jack £3 8*s.*

In the Shop
Leather and gloves £2.

In the Celler
One furnace and a grate, three tubbs, three coolers, four barrels, two powdering tubbs £2 2*s.* 6*d.*

Total £12 15*s.* 6*d.*

William Benger and Thomas Fowler, appraisors.

Buried St. Mary 6 February 1693/4 'Wallter Randoll'.
Will 25 December 1693; commission 21 February 1693/4, oath administered 22 February 1693/4 to Edward Randoll; probate 28 Feb 1693/4 to Edward Randoll, testator's son.

325 WIDDO [Eleanor][1] **CLARK**
[*undated*, c.1693/4] P1/C/432

For har weringe aparrell both linien and woolen 10*s.*
One bedsted, matt and cord, one old fether bed, to bolsters, three pellos, to coverleds and one blanket and one parre of sheets £1 10*s.* 9*d.*
For one press, one tabbel bord, three stouls £1 7*s.* 6*d.*
For one old tob, one cever 5*s.* 6*d.*
For five platters and to plates, to brass ledells, to old kittells, to old skilets, one brass kanddell steak, one old flaggon 10*s.* 6*d.*
For one chare, tabbel bord 3*s.*
For one old brass warempann 1*s.*
For one cheast, one old cobbard 6*s.* 6*d.*
For one old jake [and one peat *deleted*] 1*s.*
[Total £4 15*s.* 9*d.* *deleted*]
For one firherth backe 2*s.*

Total £4 17*s.* 9*d.*

Samuel Fowler and Joef Maks, appraisors.

Buried St. Peter 26 October 1693.
Will 22 October 1675; probate 10 March 1693/4 to John Clarke, testator's son.

1. Forename from will.

326 MARY MILES
spinster 16 April 1694 P1/M/310

Her bed and beding there unto belonging £1 10*s.*
Her wearing apparell both linen and woollen £2 10*s.*
Good and bad debts £30.

Total £34.

Thomas Brunsdon and Thomas Bartlett, appraisors.

Buried St. Peter 30 October 1693.
Will 1 December 1692; probate 17 April 1694 to Thomas Hunt, testator's employer.

327 WIDOW [Jane][1] CHIFESE
[*undated*, c.1694] P1/C/435

In mony £1.
Waring aprell £1 10*s.*
Lening £1 10*s.*
Hiee bed and truckel bed and all be long to it £5.
Chest, trunk and cufer 10*s.*
A bed in the outer rum and all be long to [it *added*] £1.
A chust, a tabell bord and 2 trunks 10*s.*
The brad [?*recte* brass] £1 10*s.*
The puter £1.
The lumbr fesell 10*s.*
Tabel, forme, stoles, setell, cobard 10*s.*
The things boling to the fier plase 8*s.*

Total £14 18*s.*

The book, bainds and bills £30.

[*Total omitted, by addition* £44 18*s.*]

Phillip Chivers, John Blissett senior, Joseff Duff and Solomon Parke, appraisors.

Buried St. Mary 19 December 1693.
Will 7 December 1693; probate 17 April 1694 to Henry and Matilda Chivers, testator's son and daughter.

1. Forename from will.

328 WILLIAM SWINDON
cordwainer 12 June 1694 P1/S/586

In money and his wearing apparell £3 17*s.*

In the Kitching
Three small brass kittles, two small bellmetle pots, one small brass pot, one brass skillett, one skimer, fower pewter dishes, one pewter [porringer *added*], two pewter cupps, one barrill, one buckett, one tubb, one chaire and a paire of doggs 15*s.* 6*d.*

In the Chamber
One flock bed, two feather bolsters, three feather pillows, two coverlids, one blankett, one paire of sheets, two old coffers 12*s.*
One Bible and five old books 4*s.*

In the Outhouse
One haifer £1 10*s.*
In desprate debts £2 7*s.*

Total £9 5*s.* 6*d.*

Borrowed by the aforesaid William Swindon as followeth[1]
Of Simon Barnett to pay for a cow £1.

More of him to pay for meat for the cow 12*s.*

Due to my [*recte* his] daughter Barnett for tending her father and mother with washing and fire £1 2*s.*

Paid Dr Noys 1*s.*

Paid funerall expenses as followeth

For a sermon 10*s.*

For a coffin 8*s.*

For the bell and grave 4*s.*

For bread, butter, cheese and bear 10*s.* 3*d.*

For flanen and makeing up of the grave 1*s.*

For rosemary, rosewater, tobacco and pipes 7*d.*

Paid the women for laying of him out 1*s.*

Total £4 9*s.* 10*d.*

Thomas Fowler and Richard Edney, appraisors.

Buried St. Mary 17 May 1694, 'the elder'. No other documents extant; inventory exhibition undated.

1. Debts owed by the deceased, and administrator's expenses should not form part of the inventory.

329 NICHOLAS GREENEWAY

glover [will] 17 July 1694 P1/G/776

In the Ketchin

A table bord, 3 joynt stooles, 1 chest, 4 rushin chaires 15*s.*

10 pewter platters, 6 porringers, 2 pewter tanckards, 2 pewter plates, 1 brass warminpann, 3 brass potts, 1 copper cup, 1 spitt, a jack and line, 1 pair bellows, a fire pan and tongs, 2 iron dogs, 2 tinn drippinpans, 1 fryin pann, 4 steell plates and other lumber £1 10*s.*

In the Hall

A table bord, 3 rushin chaires, a iron coll grate, a pair of andiers, a pot hangins and crook 15*s.*

In the Chamber over the Kitchin

A table, 1 chest, 2 coffers, 1 cupbord, 1 bead stead, matt and cords, curtaines and vallens, 1 cover lid, 1 blanckett, 1 feather bed and bowlster £3.

In simstry ware in the same chamber with his warrin aparrell £20.

In the Chamber over the Hall

1 bed stead, 1 livery bedstead, 1 truck bed steed, matts and cords, 3 flock beds, 3 bowlsters, 2 ruggs, 2 blancketts, 6 deall boxes, 1 joint stooll £2 10*s.*

In the Buttery

4 barells, 3 tubbs, a meashin vate, 3 coolers £1 15*s.*

In the Out house

1 cow, 2 mares £6.

Wood, hay and lumber in the Backside £5.

The lease of the house £15.

In cash 5*s.*

In hopefull debts £3, in desperate debts 15*s.* £3 15*s.*

Total £59 15*s.*

Samuell Fowler, Thomas Fowler and John Greenoway, appraisors.

Buried St. Peter 9 July 1694 'Nicholas Grenaway'.

Will 6 July 1694; probate and inventory exhibition not recorded.

330 JOHN KEEBLE

innholder [will] 15 August 1694 P1/K/109

His wareing aparell and mony £7.

In the Crown
1 bed, curtains, valins with all other things in the said room £10.

In the Rose
1 bed, curtains, valins with all other things in the said room £5 5*s.*

In the Squerill
1 bed, curtains, valins with all other things in the said room £2 12*s.*

In the Bell
3 beds, curtains, valins with all other things in the said room £11 10*s.*

In the Greyhound
4 beds with all other things in the said room £5.

In the Flower de Luce
1 table, 2 bedsteads 16*s.*

In the Starr
Lumber goods £1.

In the Parlour
2 beds with all other things belonging to the said room £6.

In the Kitchin
Puter and brass with all other things in the said room £13.
The linin £5 10*s.*
A silver tankard £6.
Beare in the seller £5.
6 hogsheads and other barrell £3 12*s.*

Brewhouse
2 furnisses, mash fatt, civers, tubs and stands £13 10*s.*
4 piggs £2 10*s.*
The lease of a house £40.
8 pillows and other goods £1 8*s.*
Good debts £2 3*s.* 2*d.*
Hay, straw and corn £2 10*s.*
9 flagons, 2 pint pots, 3 cocks 15*s.* 6*d.*
1 litle table 2*s.* 6*d.*

[*Total omitted, by addition* £145 4*s.* 2*d.*]

[*Added in a different hand*] Jeremiah Fowle and Richard Smyth, appraisors.

Buried St. Peter 29 April 1694 'senior'
Will 13 February 1691/2; probate not recorded, will endorsed 'Anne Kebble executrix'.

331 ANN GLYDE
widow [will] 22 August 1695 P1/G/294

In the Garrat [*£1 5s. 6d. deleted*]
2 beds, 2 coverleeds, 1 bedsteed, 1 blaket, 2 chests, 2 coffers, 1 box 8*s.*
In linnen 14*s.*
In pewter £1 5*s.* 6*d.*
In pots and ketles and other brass £1 16*s.*

In the Chamber over the Hall
2 beds and bedsteed and vallians, 1 rugg, 2 blanketts £1 10*s.*
1 chest, 1 rownd table boord, 1 payr of doggs, 1 fire pan and tongs and one cubord 12*s.*

In the Celler
3 spits, 2 barrels 5*s.*
In cloats and books £1 10*s.*
In money [*£3 deleted*] £6.
1 dozen of botles 1*s.* 6*d.*

Total £14 2*s.*

Joseph Webb and Edward Fribbens, appraisors.

Buried St. Peter 8 June 1695 'Anna Glide widow'.
Will 11 November 1694; probate and inventory exhibition not recorded.

332 WILLIAM PETTY
button maker 18 September 1695
P1/P/400

His wearing apparrell £2
In ready moneys £23 8*s.*
One bed with its appurtenances and warming pann £2
One chest of drawers, one press, one table, twoe joyned stooles, one coffer, one box and pann £2
One [handkershiffe *deleted*] hanging shelf, one looking glass, two linse carpetts, one Bible and Testament, one fire greate, twoe iron doggs, one paire of billows, one tubb and one old piller 10*s.*

In the Garrett
One bedsteed, one feather bead and boulster with vallins and curtains, one rugg and two blancetts £1 5*s.*
One trucle bedsteed, one flock bed with one cover ledd, two blancketts, one little side board and two leather chaires 15*s.*

In the Hall
Three table boards, three joyned stooles, one bacon racke, one cubbard, one settle, two russia chaires £1
One jack with waitts, two spitts, one drippen pann, one fire pann and tongs and one pott hangers, two andirons, one fire pann, three smothings irons, one [iron *deleted*] gridirons, potts, hooks and fire forcks and two iron candle sticks 10*s.*
Seaven small pewtter platters, seaven plates, three porringers, one pewtter salt, one flagon, one pewtter tanckerd, two petwer candle sticks and three pewter chamber potts £1
Three brass kitles, three skilletts, one brass ladle, one skimer, one bastinge ladle, two kittle potts, one belmettle pott, one iron pott and one copper pott £1 10*s.*

In the Seller
Three tubbs, one dowe civer, one powderinge tubb, one buckett, wood, coale and other lumber £2 5*s.*
Due on two mortgages £215
Due for rent £2 5*s.*
Due att Michaelmas on bond £30
Desparate debts £15

Total £303 8*s.* [*recte* £300 8*s.*]

Samuell Fowler and Thomas Seymour, appraisors.

Buried St. Mary 13 September 1695 'Will Petty senior'.
Will 16 August 1695; probate and inventory exhibition not recorded.

333 RICHARD TASKER[1]
20 September 1695
P1/T/220

Due on bond and booke debts £21 5*s.*
Due in desperatt debts £1 18*s.*
His weareing apparrill £3 2*s.* 6*d.*

Total £25 5*s.* 6*d.* [*recte* £26 5*s.* 6*d.*]

Robert Webb and William Browne, appraisors.

Buried St. Peter 10 March 1694/5 'a stranger'.
Will 2 May 1694[2]; probate 22 May 1695 to Richard Edmonds, testator's cousin.

1. 'of Ogburn St Andrewes' [but see note 2].
2. Note appended: 'Memorandum This will of Richard Tasker was made whilst he lived at Ogborne in May 1694 but the Testator came afterwards to Marlborough where he lived and died and his will, at the request of his Executors, proved there'.

334 JOHN PARSONS
innkeeper [will] 3 December 1695
P1/P/414

His wearing apparell £5.

In the Back Chamber
One fether bed, 2 boulsters, 1 pillow, 2 rugs, 1 blankett, 1 bed steed, vallens and curtains, 1 truckell bed steed, 1 bed, 7 leather chayers, 1 payr of andirons, 1 payr dogs, fier pan and tongs, side cupbord and cloth, 1 window cloth, 1 looking glas, 1 hanging chilf, 1 round table board £7 7*s.*

In the Back Chamber Cald Eight
2 high bed steeds, 1 truckle bed steed, 2 fether beds, 2 fether bowlsters, 1 pillow, 1 flock bed, 1 flock bowlster, curtains and vallens, 3 rugs, 1 blankett, 2 table boards, 5 ruch chayers, 2 joynt stools £7 14*s.*

In The Chufle Board Room
1 bed steed, vallens and curtains, 1 fether bed, 1 bowlster, 2 pillows, 1 rug, 1 blanket, 1 chufell board, 9 joynt stools, 5 chayrs, 2 window curtains, 1 paire andirons, 1 payr dogs, fyre pan and tongs £6 19*s.*

In the Pres Room
1 bed steed, 1 fether bed, 1 bowlster, 1 pillow, 1 rug, 1 payr of blankets, 1 joynt stool £3.

In the Back Garrett
2 bed steeds, 1 fether bed, 1 flock bed, 1 bowlster, 1 pillow, 1 rug, 1 blankett, 1 side tabell, 1 trunk £3 6*s.*

In the Midle Garrett
2 bed steeds, 1 flock bed, 2 rugs, 1 pair blanckets, 1 joynt stool, 1 bowlster £1 10*s.*

In the next Garrett
1 bed steed, 1 fether bed, 1 bowlster, 1 pillow, 1 rug, 1 chest, 1 pres, tools and lumber £3 8*s.*

In the Back Room next Thomas Glyd
2 table bords, 1 forme, 3 joynt stools, 1 chayr, 4 flitches of backon, 1 payr of dogs, fyr pan and tongs £3 3*s.*

In the Passage
In lumber 8*s.*

In the Pantry
1 side bord, hanging chilf, 1 chayer 10*s.*

In the Litell Back Room
2 table bords, 4 chayers, 3 joynt stools, 1 payr dogs, fyr pan and tongs 18*s.*

In the Siller
In beer and ale £19.
In hogs heads and barrells £4.
One furnace, one mearch vate, one cooler and brewing vessells £5 10*s.*

In the Kitchen
In pewter dishes and plates, potingers, flagons and chamberpots £5 10*s.*
1 coper boyler, 4 bras pots, 2 kittles, 1 bras pan, 3 skillets, 2 basting ladells, 2 skimers, 7 bras candlesticks £4.
One jack, 4 spitts, 1 coal grate, 1 payr of andirons, fyre pan and tongs, 1 table £2 10*s.*
Board, 1 form, 4 chayrs, setle, rack and warming pan, 1 looking glas and other lumber £1.

In the Stable
In hay and talett stuf £1 14*s.*

In the Backside
In pigs £3 5*s.*
In coale £4.
In fagotts, hard wood and loos wood £10 10*s.*

In the Hous
15 payr of sheets, 3 dozen of napkins, 1 dozen of table clothes, 6 pillow cases, one dozen of towells £7.
1 silver tankert, 4 spoons, 4 tasters £6.
Mony in the hous £14 11*s.* 6*d.*
Debts good and bad £4.

Total £135 13*s.* 6*d.*

Joseph Webb and Noah Webb, appraisors.

Buried St. Mary 13 October 1695, 'the elder'.
Will 3 February 1691/2; probate 19 May 1696 to Margaret Parsons, testator's widow.

335 JOHN RUMSEY

basket maker 9 March 1695/6
P1/R/193

His appearll and mony in his pocket £4

The Chamber over the Hall
One feather bed, one feather boulster, 2 feather pillows, [pillows *deleted*], 2 blanchard, 1 shete, 1 green rudge and a bede steed, curtines and vallins £4.

The Chamber over the Entry
1 flocke bede, 2 boulsters, 2 pillowss, 1 blanket, 1 ruge, 1 bedstede and all the loumber in that rume £2.
The lumber in the Garret 15*s.*

The Chamber over the Shoop
The bede and whatt belongs to it and the lumber in the same roume £2.
In linnen and pewter £2.

Goods in the Hall
2 pots, 2 skillits, 1 kittell, 1 spite, hangels, tabell bord, stouls and all the rest in that rome £1 10*s.*

Household total £16 5*s.*

Goodes in the Shoope
1 iron mell, lumber in the shoope 12*s.*
3 berrells and bruing vessell 10*s.*
1 horse, 1 cowe, [1 calf *deleted*] 2 piggs £6.
Timber and fire woode £1.
Basket ware in the house £1 13*s.*
Bords £2.
And old house standing upon a willow bede which doe belong to Port Mill [which *deleted*] £2.
A horse mill [and *added*] house £2.

Shop total £15 15*s.*

Total £32.

Nathanuell Hone and Joseph Biss, appraisors.

Buried St. Mary 17 February 1695/6 'John Rumsey the elder'.
Will 14 January 1695/6; probate not recorded; inventory exhibited 19 May 1696.

336 JOHN BENDALL and JONE his wife

13 April 1696 P1/B/658

The wearing aparell £2.
2 beds and bedsteeds with what belong to them £2.
1 chest, 1 trunk, 1 coffer, 2 boxs 5*s.*
1 kittle, 2 potts, 1 skillet 10*s.*
5 pewter dishes, 2 plates, 2 poringers 8*s.*
2 barrells, 2 civers, 2 tubs 10*s.*
1 cupbord 3*s.*
1 skimer, 1 ladle, 1 fryinpan, 1 fierpan, 1 pair tongues, 1 spitt, 1 dripenpan and other lumber in the Low Room 15*s.*
Mony and rings £11.
6 forms 5*s.*
The house £5.

Total £22 16*s.*

Richard Martin and John Tannar, appraisors.

Buried (John) St. Mary 25 March 1696; (Jone) St. Mary 29 March 1696 'Jane Bendoll widow'.
Bond 19 May 1696, administration to Richard Edney and William Smith, guardians elected for John Bendall 'a minor, son', to administer 'the goods ... of John Bendall ... unadministered by Jone his widdow late alsoe deceased'.

337 RICHARD SUTTON senior
17 May 1696 P1/S/607

For boords in Workhouse 15*s.*
For shevels in the Butarey 2*s.* 6*d.*
For brass and peutar in the Hall £2 10*s.*
For all othar goods in the Hall £1.
For goods in the Sallar £1.
For 2 frook beads £1.
For 3 beadsteeds 15*s.*
For 2 boulstars and 2 covarleds and for a pare blanckuts and a pare sheets £1.
For all othar goods in that Chambar £1 10*s.*
For waring clothings and othar lumbar £1.

Total £10 12*s.* 6*d.*

Mr John Smith and Edward Jones, appraisors.

Buried St Mary 19 May 1696, 'the elder'.
Renunciation 19 May 1696 by Ann Sutton, intestate's widow, in favour of Edward Jones, carpenter of Marlborough, a principal creditor and intestate's son-in-law; bond 19 May 1696, administration to Edward Jones and Mary his wife, intestate's daughter.

338 THOMAS STONE
labourer 19 May 1696 P1/S/606

His wearing apparell £2.
1 flock bed, 2 pillows, 1 rug, 1 blankett and bedsteed £1 2*s.* 6*d.*
1 chest, 1 coffer, 1 trunk 6*s.* 8*d.*
2 pewter dishes, 2 potangers, 2 tankes, 1 iron pott, 2 kittles, 1 pott, 1 skillett, 1 warming pan £1 12*s.* 6*d.*
2 table bords, 2 joynt stools, 2 rush chayres, fyre pan and tongs, 1 par dogs, 1 spitt, 2 tubs, 1 kiver, 2 barrells and other lumber £1 2*s.*
His dwelling hows £7.
In mony and debts £4 10*s.*

Total £17 13*s.* 8*d.*

Noah Webb, William Sage and John Tanner, appraisors.

Buried St. Mary 11 May 1696 'Thomas Stone alias Belley'.
Bond 19 May 1696, administration to Thomas Chunn, bodicemaker of Marlborough and Edith his wife, intestate's daughter.

339 JOHN JONES
mason 4 June 1696 P1/IJ/124

In the Iner Camber
2 beds, 2 bedsteeds, 3 ruggs, 3 blankcoats, 2 bowlsters £3 10*s.*

In the Best Chamber
1 bed, 2 bedsteeds, 1 rugg, 3 blankcotts, 1 bowlster, 2 pillows, curtains and vallians, 1 chest, 1 chest of drawers, 2 trunks, 1 payer of andirons and other inplements £6 10*s.*

In the Kiching
1 jack, 5 brase candlsticks, 1 payr of andirons, 1 payr of doggs, 1 tongs, 2 fire

pans, 2 spits, 2 table boards, 6 flag chairs, 1 payr of firepan and tons, 1 skunc, 1 roster, 1 pewter candlstick, 1 payr of doggs with some smale implements £2.

In Buttry
2 table boards, 6 drinkvessells, 2 litle ketles, 2 skillets, 1 brass pot, 1 ladle, 1 skimer with some lumber £2 1*s.*

In the Brewhouse
1 furnace, 2 mashing fats, 4 kivers with some lumber £2 15*s.*
In pewter £2 7*s.*
In linnen: 4 payr of sheets, 6 pillowbeers, 2 table board cloats, 1 dozen of table-napkins £2 1*s.*
In working tooles 15*s.*
In wareing apparell £2.
Six silver spoons £2 8*s.*
In money £5.
In debts good and bad £15.
A horse, sadle and bridle £1 15*s.*

Total £38 2*s.*

Joseph Webb and Henry Tayler, appraisors.

Buried St. Mary 19 April 1696.
No other documents; inventory exhibited 27 October 1696.

340 RICHARD MARTINE
cooper 7 July 1696 P1/M/321

His purse and apparel £3 2*s.* 6*d.*
Monies in the house £30.

In his Chamber
One feather bed with its furniture £2 10*s.*
One chest, two paire of sheetes, one dozen of napkins with other linnen £1.
One press, one side cubboard, one little table board 9*s.* 6*d.*

In the Chamber over the Parlour
One bedsteed, one chest, one little table board with a small matter of beding 11*s.*

In the Chamber over the Wash House
Two beds of feathers and flocks, two bedsteeds with its furniture £1 10*s.*

In the Kitching
Six pewter dishes, fower pottinges, four brass potts, two kittles, one brass pann, three skilletts, one table board and frame, one jack, two spitts with a fire shovel, tongs and hangings £2 4*s.* 6*d.*

In the Parlour
One table board and frame, five joynt stooles, four chaires 10*s.*

In the Celler and Brew House
Five barrills, one hogshead, three stanns with brewing vessel 16*s.* 9*d.*

In the Workeing House
Tools there £1.
For hoops £17.

In the Garden, Backside and Worke Howses
Vessell timber £72 7*s.*
In timber abroud and att home, with the wear made upp now in the hosse and the two cellers in the Markett Place £125 17*s.*
Fire wood 10*s.*
Good debts £57 8*s.* 5½*d.*
For lumber £1 11*s.* 6*d.*
In desperat debts £5 17*s.* 3*d.*

Total £324 5*s.* 5½*d.*

Francis Raleigh and William Hoggett, appraisors.

Buried St. Mary 28 June 1696.
Will 11 October 1691, probate 27 October 1696 to Isaac Martine, testator's son.

341 ALSE SAMSON
widow[1] [*undated*, c.1696] P1/S/609

Money in tha hous £4 10*s.*
Waren aparill £3.
1 box and linen in it 15*s.*
1 box and linen in it 10*s.*
Old thinges 1*s.*
1 tankott, a plater and chamber pot 10*s.*
2 pans, 1 boull 8*d.*
3 gin stouls 2*s.*
2 chayers 6*d.*
1 fier shovl and a chafen dich, billes, hangles 2*s.*
1 father bad, 1 father boulstor, 2 pillos, 1 pare blankets, 1 cover lid and bad steed £2 10*s.*
1 flocx bad and boulstor, 2 blankots, 1 cover lid 12*s.*
2 pare of sheets, 2 bolstors cases, 2 pilos 10*s.*
1 hat and hat case 2*s.* 6*d.*
2 old kofers [and coferd *added*] 5*s.*
3 potes, 1 kitell, 1 skillott, 1 warmen pan £1 10*s.*
2 baralls, 2 kifers 8*s.*
Wood and lomber £1 10*s.*
Lucken glas 1*s.*
Money apon bond and yous £20 12*s.*
And in bad dates £3 2*s.* 6*d.*

Total £40 14*s.* 2*d.*

Joseph Duff and Joseph Biss, appraisors.

Buried St. Mary 4 August 1696.
Will 9 March 1695/6; probate [*undated*] to Joane Bayly, kinswoman, wife of Samuel Bayly, weaver; inventory exhibited 27 Oct 1696.

1. 'who deperted this Liff the first day of Agust In tha yare of our Lord 1696'.

342 RICHERD GILS and [ANNE *added*] his wife
8 September 1696 P1/G/301

In the Chamber naxt to tha Street
1 father bad, 2 boulstors, 1 pillo, 2 blankots, 1 rog, cortens and fallens, badsteed, mat and cord, corten rodes £3.
1 chust of draers, 1 tronk, 1 cofer and tabell bord and fram, 1 coverlid and 1 warmen pan £1 5*s.*

In tha Back Chamber
2 flock bades, 2 flock boulsters, 1 pare of blankets, 2 cover lides, 2 badsteedes, 2 mates and cordes, 1 peello, 1 lacken glas £2.

In tha Kichen
4 puter platers, 1 tanket, a jak, 2 spites, 1 kitell, 1 pott, 1 tabbell and fram, 5 stoules, 2 pare of hangells, 1 pare of angers, 1 pare of doges, tonges and fier pan, 1 skillet, 1 fornes, 2 barells, 1 fat, 2 kivers £2 19*s.*

Total £9 4*s.*

Joseph Duff, James Fowller and Joseph Biss, appraisors.

Burial (Richard) not recorded; (Anne) St. Mary 30 August 1696 'Ann Giles widow'.
Bond 27 October 1696, administration to Richard Clarke, son and principal creditor of Anne Giles, widow.

343 NATHANELLS HONE
fuller [will] 8 December 1696
P1/H/586

Waring apparrill and moniys in purse £6.

In the Best Chamber over the Hall
On fether bed, on flokbed, on bedsted, cortens and vallens, corten rods with

other beding belonging to the bed, on sid cubbered, on chest, 2 cofers, 4 boxes, on tronk, 2 pare of dogs [on *deleted*] £5.

In the Chamber over the Working Rum
On [flock *deleted*] fether bed, on bedsteed, 2 cofers and on tabbell bord £2 15*s.*
On brass pan, 4 brass pots, 3 skelletts, 2 brass candele stick, 3 cittels, [mor *added*] 3 pots, 1 saspan, 1 frying pan, 1 posnett, skellett, 1 iorn dripen pan, 1 peuter plate, 10 grate dishes, 11 small dishes, 8 sasers, 9 porengers, 2 salt selers, 1 cope, 2 tanketts, 1 bottell, 3 candels sticks, 1 flaggen, 1 basen and 1 peuter chamber pote £8.

In the Kichen
On jack, 3 spets, 2 tin dripenpans, on [cole *added*] grate, 3 pare hangels, a pare anders, 2 fier pans, 2 pare tongs, on forke, on grediorn, on pare billes, on rack, on settell, [the *altered to*] three tabbell bords, 6 joynt stools £4.
Thorty fower books £3.
1 bruing furness and grate, 2 mashen vats and 3 tubs, 8 kifers, 6 barrels for to hold beare, 1 powdering tub £5.
For wood and other lumber £2 10*s.*
7 quarters of cols £2.
For the shope goods and 1 end of hops £20.
6 pare shetts, 1 dozen napkins, 5 pare hollon pelo cases, 4 tabell cloths £3.
11 yards cloth 17*s.* 6*d.*

Total £62 2*s.* 6*d.*

Desperate debts £5.
The house £40.

John Gillmore and Thomas Glyde, appraisors.

Buried St. Mary 29 November 1696 'the elder'.
Will 18 November 1696; probate [*undated*] to Alice Hone, testator's widow.

344 RICHARD CLARKE
pinmaker [will] 14 February 1696/7
P1/C/454

Monnyes in the house £5.
Workinge tooles £3.
34 dosen of pins £10.
Orgell 9*s.*
2 rame of paper, pins and shrafe, [14 packetts *added*] £4 10*s.*

In the Best Chamber
A feather bedd, a flocke bedd, a seate of curtains,
2 beddsteeds, 6 pillows and 2 boulsters, 2 ruggs and 2 paire of blancketts and 2 payre of sheets £3.
4 paire of sheets, a boulster, a pillow and devrse tabell linnen £2.
A chest drawers, 2 trunckes, one chest, one coffer, one table bord and 4 chairs, one looking glass, a paire of andirones and other lomber £1 10*s.*

In the other Chamber
An old flocke bedd, a litell bedd, one sheete and lomber 10*s.*

In the Chitchin
9 dishes pewtter, 3 platts, 6 porringers and other pewtter in all thinges £1.
2 brass chittells, 2 skillettes, one warminge pann and pott, 2 litell candlestickes and skimers, a coll greate £2.
A tablebord, 4 joynt stooles, a jacke and 2 spitts £1 10*s.*
Two barrell and all other lomber £1.
Wood for the fire £1.
Debtes one the booke £7.
The house lase hould £20.

Total £64 3*s.*

Edward Jones and Andrew Cully, appraisors.

Buried St. Mary 21 January 1696/7.
Will 13 December 1696; probate 6 May 1697 to executrix [Margery Clarke, testator's widow].

345 THOMAS TRINDER[1]
tanner 10 March 1696/7 P1/T/232

His weareing apparrell £1.
In ready money £100.
In good debts £251.
In desperate debts £110.

In his Bedchamber
The bed, bolster, sheets, blanketts, ruggs, bedsteed, curtains, valens and appertenances £1.
The trundle bed and its appertenances 10s.
One chest and settle 6s. 8d.
A chest of drawers, cupboard, another chest, 3 leather chaires, two little boxes and old baskett chaire 15s.

In the Best Chamber
In table and other lynnen 8s. 6d.
A tableboard and frame 1s.

In the Kytchin
A tableboard and frame, 4 joint stooles, 3 chaires, 5 cushions, one cupboard 10s.
One bell mettle pott, one brass pott, two kettells, 2 skilletts and one warming pan 13s.
Five pewter dishes, 3 plates, 7 porringers, 2 tankards, 1 pott, 1 sawcer, 1 salt celler, 10 earthen dishes, 3 muggs and an hour glass 7s. 6d.
One copper cup, 2 basting ladles, 1 skimmer, 1 candlestick and 1 brass pott 3s. 9d.
2 spitts, 2 pothookes, 1 jack, [2 spitts *deleted*] beef forks, a tin dripping pan, fire pan, tongs, doggs, andirons, frying pan, 3 steele irons and steele box, 2 paire of hangells, 1 fender, one salt box, one Bible 8s. 6d.

In the Brewhouse
Fower kivers, one tunbowle, paile, strainer, old fornace and cole grate 7s. 6d.

In the Cellar
Two barrells, 1 old chaire and old lanthorne 4s. 6d.

In the Woodhouse
In hardwood, faggotts, hearth turf, tan and cole, 1 ladder, 1 crooke, 1 fender, 1 rake and lumber there and elsewhere 11s.

Total £468 6s. 11d.[2]

Francis Nalder and Robert Chi[v]ers, appraisors.

Buried St. Mary 1 March 1696/7, 'Thomas Trendell'.
Will 22 February 1696/7; probate not recorded; inventory exhibited 6 May 1697.

1. 'of the parish of St. Mary the Virgin in Marlebrough'.
2. Total in Roman numerals.

346. [Robert *overwritten with*] **PHILIP CHIVERS**[1]
10 April 1697 P1/C/453

His wereinge apperell and monnye in purss 10s.
Monnye in the house £1 1s. 6d.
One bedd, one boulster and pillow, one coverleed and one beddsteed with other thinges beloninge £1 2s.
One coffer, one chest, one bagg, one Bibell 7s. 6d.

In the Hall

Seaven pewtter dishes, one furnas, 2 brass potts, one ireon pott, 2 skittells, a dripinge pann and other thinges £1 6*s*.

2 barrell, 2 civres and other lomber goods 8*s*. 6*d*.

Total £4 16*s*. 6*d*. [*recte* £4 15*s*. 6*d*.]

Robert Chivers and Philip Marke junior, appraisors.

Burial not recorded.

Will 7 November 1696; probate not recorded; inventory exhibited 6 May 1697 by Margaret Chivers, testator's widow and executor.

1. 'Late of Marlborough St Petters'.

347 JONE GILLMORE

widow [burial register] 4 May 1697 P1/G/302

Her waring aparell £1 10*s*.

3 small gould rings and 1 silver spoone £1.

1 pare of dowlis sheets 7*s*. 6*d*.

3 holand sheets 15*s*.

3 table cloths 10*s*.

1 dozen of napkins and 3 towells 5*s*.

2 pare of pillow ceases 4*s*.

2 couberd clothes 1*s*. 6*d*.

1 small trunck and sarge carpett 5*s*.

2 Bibels and 2 English books 5*s*. 6*d*.

1 silver cupe 9 oz ½ £2 8*s*.

In redy money £1 19*s*. 2*d*.

9 lb½ of pewter 5*s*. 6*d*.

2 cushions and one roat 3*s*. 6*d*.

6 pesces of earthenware and looking glas 2*s*.

1 ould cheast 2*s*.

In desperet debts £2 5*s*.

Total £12 8*s*. 8*d*.

Samuell Fowler and Joseph Biss, appraisors.

Buried St. Mary 12 March 1696/7, 'Mrs.'.

Bond 6 May 1697, administration to Anne Withers, intestate's niece.

348 MICHOLL HUTCHINS

widow 5 May 1697 P1/H/589

2 fether beds, 2 bolsters, 1 bedsteed, curtins and valins and £2 5*s*.

1 chest, 1 coffer 6*s*.

Her wareing apparell 10*s*.

1 brass pott, 1 table bord, 1 barrell, 1 old cupbord and other lumber 10*s*.

A house £12.

Total £15 11*s*.

John Jacob and William Smith, appraisors.

Buried St. Mary 17 February 1696/7 'widow Huchings als Forde'.

Will 13 February 1692/3; bond 19 May 1696[1], administration to Richard and William Smith during the minority of Anne Smith, daughter of Richard, testator's niece and executrix; probate not recorded.

1. The year appears incorrect, probably 1697 was intended.

349 FRANCES NEWBY

widow [*undated*, c.1697] P1/N/113

The brasse and pewter and lattin weare 10*s*.

A little feather bed, boulster, boulster case and blankett £1 4*s*.

A feather bed and beding thereunto belonging £1 10*s*.

A warming pan, andirons and doggs [and bell brasse pott *added*] 15*s*.

A cupboard, lanthorn, cutting knkif and

other lumber 15*s.*
In money £3 4*s.*
In good and bad debts £52 3*s.* 6*d.*
In faggotts 8*s.*
The wearing apparell £3.

Total £63 9*s.* 6*d.*

Samuel Fowler and Thomas Hunt, appraisors.

Buried St. Peter 24 November 1696.
Will 3 March 1693/4; probate 17 May 1697 to Edward Garlike, testator's son-in-law.

350 ELIZABETH STEPHENS

widow 29 July 1697 P1/S/613

Her weareing apparrell £5.
In ready money £17 12*s.* 8*d.*
Two gold rings £1 6*s.*
In old silver 5*s.* 6*d.*
One feather bed, bedsteed, curtains, valens and all things thereto belongeing £5.
One arm chaire, one close stoole and pan, one fire pan, two paire of tongs, two little kittles, two stands for a trunck, 1 paire of steele plates, one brass candle stick and pewter bottle 10*s.*
One great Bible and severall other bookes 5*s.* 6*d.*
Seaven sheets, nine napkins, eight towells and two table cloaths, seaven pillow beares £2 3*s.*
In lumber 2*s.*

Total £32 4*s.* 8*d.*[1]

Henry Osmorn, John Stokes and Thomas Hunt, appraisors.

Buried St. Peter 28 July 1697.
Bond 31 July 1697, administration to Lewis Andley of London, lorimer, and Francis Bowshire of Marlborough, yeoman; commission 31 July 1697, oath administered to Lewis Andley, testator's son; inventory exhibited 4 August 1697.

1. Total in Roman numerals.

351 SAMUEL BAYLY

weaver 14 February 1697/8 P1/B/663

In the Roome over the Shop
His wearing apparell £2 10*s.*
One fether bed, one fether boulster, fower fether pillows, one rug, two blankets, curtains and vallance, one bedsteed, mat and cord with curtain rods £2 10*s.*
Five sheetes 12*s.* 6*d.*
One chest of drawers, nine leather chaires £1 5*s.*
One chest and five boxes 10*s.*
Two trunks, one chest, one coffer 5*s.*

In the Roome over the Hall
One flock bed, one boulster, two pillows, one rug, one blanket, one bedsteed, mat and cord £1.
One iron grate, andirons, fire shovell and tonges, one warming pan 12*s.*
Two paire of shares 5*s.*
One share board 1*s.*

In the Garrett
One flock bed and boulster, one rug and blankett £1.

In the Kitching
Brass of all sorts fifty lb. £2 5*s.*
[One iron pott 2*s.* 6*d.* *added*]
Pewter of all sorts: eighty eight lb. £2 11*s.* 4*d.*
One jack, one spitt, one paire of andirons, one paire of dogs, two paire of hangells, one fire shovell, one paire of tonges, one frying pan, five steele plates, one paire of billice £1.
One table board and frame, six joynt stooles, one cubboard, one looking glass, one glass case, eight bookes, one curtaine

and rod, four chaires, two boxes, two curtaine rods £1 5*s*.

In The Shop

Two loomes and harness, one warpping barr, two skarms, three tourns, two [*blank*], one beam and scales £2.

One rack and posts that the cloth is racked in £1.

In the Back Shopp

Two furnaces with grates and dores £8.

One hott press with all that belongs to it and a table board £3.

In the Buttery and the Backside

Fower tubbs, five kivers, one powdering tubb, one buckett, five barrells, two table boards, one cubboard, one stand, one pump and spouts £2 10*s*.

One horse with a halter and padd £3 12*s*. 6*d*.

In lumber 10*s*.

In the Weare house

Fower peeces of horse cloaths being one hundred and four yards at two shillings the yard £10 8*s*.

One peece of linsey, thirty yards at one shilling and six pence the yard £2 5*s*.

One peece of linsey, nineteen yards at one shilling the yard 19*s*.

Two peeces of linsey, fifety six yards at one shilling and three pence the yard £3 10*s*.

Thirteen bundles of linnen yarn at nine shillings a bundle £5 17*s*.

One peece of browne linsey, eight and twenty yards at one shilling and two pence the yard £1 12*s*. 8*d*.

Six yards of druggett at two shillings the yard 12*s*.

One hundred and seaventy four pound of wooll at five pence the pound £3 12*s*. 6*d*.

Two hundred and fifety pounds of woollen yarn at nine pence the pound £9 7*s*. 6*d*.

All the dyers stuffe £4 18*s*.

In debts £5.

Total £86 8*s*. 6*d*.

Joseph Duffe, Jeremiah Fowler and Joseph Biss, appraisors.

Buried St. Mary 10 February 1697/8.

Bond 21 May 1698, administration to Joane Bayley, intestate's widow; inventory exhibited 31 May 1698.

352 JAMES STEVENTON

innholder 14 March 1697/8 P1/S/614

In the Hall

A feather bed, wainscott bedsteed, rugg, two blanketts, one sett of curtains and valens, matt, cord, bolster and two pillows, one round table and three joint stooles £3.

In the Chamber over the Fox

A bedsteed, flock bed, bolster, spotted rugg, matt and cord £1.

In the Kytchin

An iron dripping pan, two frying panns, one gridiron, one fire pan and tonges, pair of doggs, clever, chaffindish, dresser board, store board 14*s*. 6*d*.

In the Celler

One shelfe, one pipe, one hogshead, one barrell of beere, one kilderkin and beere £5 17*s*.

More in the Kitchen

The cord, weights and lanthorne and one jack 10*s*.

Two hogsheads, two pipes, two kilderkins [three brass cocks *deleted*] £1.

Two halfe bushells, one gallon 3*s*.

Six basketts, seaven servers 8*s*. 4*d*.

Bowle and pins 1*s.*
Seaven sconces 3*s.*
Tallett and scaffold 15*s.*
Wood £5.
One cupboard 2*s.*
A hay reeke £12.
Three piggs £3 10*s.*
One box, two heaters 2*s.*
Seaven paire of sheetes £2 10*s.*
Nine napkins 3*s.*
Fower pillow cases 5*s.*
Six diaper napkins 3*s.*
Three table cloathes 7*s.* 6*d.*
The dung 10*s.*
A bag of feathers 10*s.*
His weareing apparrell £4 10*s.*
In good debts £8.
In bad debts £10 10*s.*
In lumber 4*s.*

Total £61 19*s.* 4*d.* [*recte* £61 18*s.* 4*d.*]

Abraham Hensley and William Smith, appraisors.

Buried St. Mary 13 March 1697/8.
Will 20 February 1697/8; renunciation 14 March 1697/8 by John Steventon (deceased died with debts more than his worth), in favour of William Wyatt or any other principal creditor; distress 15 March 1697/8, William Wyatt called at the Unicorn (late in the tenancy of the testator) to collect rent arrears, distrained on contents of the inn in leiu; bond [*day and month omitted*] 1698, administration to William Wyatt of Salisbury, brewer, and Joseph Duffe, gentleman, principal creditors; commission 29 March 1698, oath administered to William Wyatt and Joseph Duff.

353 THOMAS POPEJOY
maltster 16 May 1698 P1/P/417

His wareing apparrell £2.
Ready money in his house £3.

In his Chamber
One feather bed and bedstead and all that belonge to it £5.
One truckle bed stead and all that belonge to it £1.
One chest of drawers and one little table, six chayer stooles, two coffers, two boxes, one paire of andierons, one paire of iron dogs, one fire showle £2.
Two window curtains £1 5*s.*
Fower flitches of bacon, one bedstead £3 6*s.*

In the Hall
One table board, five joynt stooles 12*s.*
One jack, one dripping pan, one spitt, one cheffing dish, one warming pan, one paire of billowes, one fender, one iron grate, fire pann and tongues £1 10*s.*
One paire of iron dogs, one frying pann, three candle sticks, one cobart, two olde chaires, one iron backe 17*s.*
Three keettle potts, two skilletts, one other keettle, six pewter platters, five porringers, [one pewter pott *added*], one drestle board, five shelves in the shopp, three kivers, three tubbs, two searchiers, one temser, one olde bushell £3.
One malt mill and halfe a furnace £3.
[One pewter pot *deleted*]
Page total £26 10*s.*

One kive, one bushell, one peck, one gallon 6*s.* 8*d.*

In the Cellar
Five beere barrells, two hoxheads, one long kiver, one little powdering tubb, one other tubb £1.
One malt gardiner by the hall, one yoteing stone and the skilling over the head £1.
Two piggs £1.
One haire, one skreene 10*s.*

In leather 5*s.*
In malt £40.
In good debts £60.
In desparate debts £37 2*s.* 4*d.*
Page total £101 4*s.* [*recte* £141 4*s.*]

Total £127 14*s.*[1] [*recte* £167 14*s.*]

John Stone and Nathaniell Popioy, appraisors.

Buried St. Peter 29 April 1698 'Thomas Popjoy'.
Will 8 May 1693; probate 31 May 1698 to Marie Popjoy, testator's widow; bond 31 May 1698, administration to Mary Popjoy, 'the executors in the said will nominated neglecting to prove the same'.

1. Total in Roman numerals.

354 EDWARD DUCK

[*undated*, c.1698] P1/D/198

Two old bedsteds and one old bed with the furniture two it £1.
One old chest, som old linon and waring aparell 15*s.* 6*d.*
In old puter 10*s.* 2*d.*
In old brass 12*s.* 4*d.*
In old lumber 15*s.* 3*d.*

Total £3 13*s.* 3*d.*

Thomas Seymour and Isaac Martin, appraisors.

Buried St. Peter 28 June 1698 'Edward Dark'.
No other documents; inventory exhibition not recorded; inventory endorsed [in Latin] 'submitted by Ann Duck, daughter of the deceased'.

355 ELEZEBETH GARLICK[1]

widow [*undated*, c.1698] P1/G/313

Monnys in purse and waring close £20.
15 quarters malte £22.

In the Chamber over the Hall
1 flock bed, 1 feather bolster, 2 flock bolsters, cortings and vallings, 1 rug, 2 bedsteds and other things £5.

In the Malt Loft
1 chest, 1 hare and other lumber £1 10*s.*

In the Fore Chamber
Bed, bedsted and all be longing to itt £6.
1 tronk, 1 joynt stoole 8*s.*
3 pare of shets, 1 dozen napkins, tabbel cloths and other things £2 10*s.*

In the Garrard
Sum bords and other lumber 15*s.*

In the Hall
4 tabels, 7 lather chayers, 1 cobberd, anders and dogs, fier pan and tongs, 4 rushen chayers, a hanging shelf with corting and coring rod £3 3*s.*
1 clock £1 13*s.*

In the Batterry
15 peuter platters, 6 plats, 2 tancords, 1 warming pan, 1 frying pan, 1 cobbert, 1 puter flaging with other lumber £2 7*s.*

In the Kichen
6 joynt stools, 1 settell, 5 chayers, 1 jack, 1 speed, anderns and dogs, fierpan and tongs, 2 cobberds, 1 corting and rod with other lumber £2 15*s.*

In the Bru Howse
A malt mell, furness, bruing vessell and other lumber £5.
Page total £73 1*s.*

In the Malt House

3 brass pots, on yating ston, 1 skren, 2 kettels, 1 skellett with other lumber £2 10s.

In the Seller

5 barrels, powdering tub and 2 stands £1 10s.

In the Backsid

Faggots and hard wood with sum cols £7.

In depts exspected to be receved £19 15s.

In bad depts £9 14s.

A lace of the howse £20.

Page total £60 9s.

From the other sid £ 73 1s.

Total £133 10s.

Richard Edney and Thomas Glide, appraisors.

Buried St. Mary 16 September 1698.

Will 3 June 1698; probate and inventory exhibition not recorded.

1. 'desased the 13 Sep[r] 1698'.

356 JOHN ROBINSON

gardener [will] 20 January 1698/99 P1/R/202

His wering aparell boath lining and wolling £2 10s.

A bond of £20

Three yeares to come of the house £8.

Old silver that was in the house £1 0s. 6d.

Goods in the Roome

One fether bed and bed steed, one flocke bed and bedsteed, three bolsters, two blancotes [and rudge *added*] £4.

Three boxes and a coffer 4s.

The Chamber over the Kitching

One fether bed and bed steed with all the furniture there unto belonging £3 12s. 6d.

One chust and chayer 6s.

Hale

A tabell bord and four stools, a payer off andiorns, a payer of dogs, a fire pan and tongs, two spits, one frying pan, a payer of bellis, two payer of hangeils and a backe, a fire bucket £1 2s. 6d.

The Buttery

One dosen and eight pewter platters, one flagon, two pweter chamber pots, one tankerd, one pewter candell sticke £1 15s.

Fower kitells and three pots, one warneing pan, a bras chaffing dish, two paire of bras scales, a bras frying pan £2 0s. 6d.

One barrell and powdering tub, two civers, one forme, one paile, one bord 6s. 6d.

Hay and wood and lumber £1 4s. 8d.

[*in a different hand*] *Total* £46 2s. 2d.

John Horner and William Benger, appraisors.

Buried St. Mary 29 December 1698.

Will 19 March 1695/6; probate 19 May 1699 to Jone Bloxom, testator's daughter.

357 ALICE NOYES

spinster 3 April 1699 P1/N/116

The testators wearing apparell £12.

One feather bed, one bolster and rugg, two pillows, fower blancketts, two setts of curtaines and vallions, one high bedsteed with thappurtenances there un to belonginge £5 5s.

Three paire of sheetes £1 10s.

One dozen and halfe of napkins, three

dieper table cloathes and two paire of pillow cases £1 8*s*.
Two tables and two joynted stooles, two cubbardes, one trunck, two chests, seaven boxes, one stoole, one chaire and cushen, one brush and one table cloath £1 19*s*.
One fire shovell and tongues, one paire of dogges, one paire of iron andirons, one gridiron, one frying pan, one spitt, one kittle, one brass pott, one skillett, three pewter dishes with other pewter £1 18*s*.
Two looking glasses, fower barrells, two tubbs, one buckett, one powdringe tubb with other lumber £1.
In moneys in the house and debts due and owing unto the testator upon bond £200.

Total £225.

John Barnes and Robert Meggs, appraisors.

Buried St. Peter 18 February 1698/9
Will 30 August 1698; probate 24 April 1699 to Thomas Liddiard, testatrix's kinsman; inventory exhibited 19 May 1699.

358 SARAH JONES
spinster [will] [*day and month omitted*] 1699 P1/IJ/128

Har weareing apparell £2 10*s*.
One featherbeed, one boulster of feathers, one feather pillow, two rugs, three sheets, two blancots and the beedsteed £3 10*s*.
One paire of andirons, one paire of dogs, a firepan and tongs and a paire of billows 5*s*.
Books 2*s*. 6*d*.
Pewter 11 lb at 8*d*. a lb 7*s*. 4*d*.
Brass 10 lb at 8*d*. a lb 6s 8*d*.
A little trunk 2*s*.
Three chaiers and a joyne stoole 1*s*. 6*d*.
A little iron pott, a looking glass and fower forms 3*s*.
In money and debts £36 19*s*. 11*d*.
A chattell leace £7.

Total £51 7*s*. 11*d*.

John Gillmore and Richard Heall, appraisors.

Buried St. Mary 17 April 1699, 'the elder'.
Will 30 March 1699; probate 19 May 1699 to Elizabeth Jones, testator's cousin.

359 MARY HILL[1]
widow 2 November 1699 P3/H/786

8 score hides at £9 a score £72.
34 dozen of calf skins att 20*s*. a dozen £34.
Hornes, tayles and hair £2 5*s*.
One ½ hogshead and one tubb and al other implements [beloning in the hous *added*] 10*s*.

Total £108 15*s*.

Stephen Maberly, tanner, John Maberly and Giles Baily, appraisors.

'More of the goods in Marlbrough of the above said widdow Hills', 8 November 1699

In good debts due her £60 5*s*.
1 bedsteed, curtins and vallins, 2 feather beds, 2 feather boulsters, 4 pilloes, 2 coverlids, 1 rug, 4 blanketts £5 5*s*.
Books and wareing aparile £6.
Rings and plat £7 10*s*.
3 paire sheetts, 2 dozen napkins, 2 table cloths, 8 towels, 5 pilloe cases and other linen £2 8*s*.
1 chest draws, 4 boxes, 1 meall trough £1.
3 tubs, 1 barell, 1 kettle, 2 trunks, 2 coffers,

1 table boarde £1 15s.
3 potts, 1 kettle, 2 skelletts, 8 pewter dishes, 1 jack, 1 paire dogs, other brass and pewtter and iron £3.
All other lumber in the house 10s.
[£86 13s. *deleted*, £26 8s. *deleted*]
£67 13s. [*recte* £87 13s.]
£108 15s.

Total £176 8s. [*recte* £196 8s.]

[*Added in a different* hand] 1 dozen of plates 8s

Thomas Lewen and Nathaniell Merriman, appraisers.

Buried St. Mary 28 September 1699.
Will 7 September 1699; probate 9 November 1699 to Nicholas Rumsey, testator's father[2].

1. 'late of Westport' [a suburb of Malmesbury]; the first section appears to be goods appraised there.
2. This will was proved in the court of the Archdeaconry of Wiltshire.

360 THOMAS DANCE[1]

tiler 6 September 1700 P1/D/207

For wareing apparell and mony in purs £7.
For bras kitels and pots and other bras things £2.
For pewter £1 10s.
For 2 bedes and other beding £1 10s.
2 tabel bords 10s.
For 2 chests, 2 presses, 2 coberds, one cofer £1.
One bed sted 5s.
For linin 10s.
For three spets 5s.
For 4 barels, 3 civers and tubs 10s.
For tiles and cras and gutter tiles 10s.
For hurdls £1.
For 3 houses £15.
For fagets and other lumber £1 10s.

Total £32 10s.

William Miles and Nathaniel Hone, appraisors.

Buried St. Mary 26 August 1700 'Thomas Dance the elder'.
Will 12 June 1700; probate 19 September 1701 to William Dawnce and Jane Clarke, testator's son and daughter.

1. 'Daunce' on will.

361 JOSEPH DUFFE[1]

maltster [will] 10 January 1700/1
P1/D/201

His wareing aparrell £5.
Mony in the house £2 10s.

In the Kichen
4 brass pots, 2 kitels, 3 skilets, 1 warming pan, 2 brase pans with other lumber £2.
11 putter platers, 7 plats, 3 small dishes, 2 flagins, 2 basins and other lumber £1 10s.
3 jacks, 2 iorn tripin pans, 4 spits, 2 freyin pans, 2 pare of angers, 1 iorn back, 2 iorn dogs, 2 hangels, 1 grideion and other lumber £1.
2 joyntstouls, 1 table and chers and other lumber 5s.

In the Lettel Rume
1 table, 2 joyntstouls and other lumber 7s.

In the Buttreye
5 barrels and other lumber £1.

In the Grate Chamber
1 bede, 1 boulster, 2 pillos, 2 blankets, one ruge, cortens [and bedsted *added*] £2 10s.

One chest, 2 coffers and other lumber 8*s.*

In the Lettel Chamber
One bedsted 2*s.*

In the Garrot
One bede and other lumber 10*s.*
For plate £4.
7 pare of shets with napkins and other linen £1 10*s.*
Malt in the house £20.

In the Malt House
1 malt mill, 1 bushel, 1 skren, 1 peck, 1 gane, 1 hare cloth, 3 shouls, 1 kitell, one settel, one poudering tub, 6 sack with other lumber £2 3*s.*
For chese 10*s.*

In the Backside
For foules and bricks and coles 10*s.*
Two tables 5*s.*
1 coper, 5 keffers, 6 tubs, 2 buckets, 2 lading pals with lumber £1 18*s.*
One yeating stone 15*s.*
For fagetts £3 15*s.*
For cleft wood £3.
For luse timber and bords 10*s.*
For all other lumber in and abought the house and backside 5*s.*
Mony upon bond £37.
Depts desperat and others £40.

Total £133 3*s.*

Edward Dangerfield and Joseph Cosham, appraisors.

'This Goods here under mentioned ware disposed to his wife by thare marrag contract in the time of his Life by the Late decesed Joseph Duff':
One fether bede, tow down pillos, three fether pillos, tow boulsters, one flock the other fethers, fower blankets, one rugg, tow brass pots, tow kitels, one warming pann [*value omitted*].

Buried St. Mary 31 December 1700.
Will 26 October 1699; commission 22 January 1700/1, oath administered to Elizabeth Duffe, testator's daughter and Mary Coster als Duffe; probate 28 January 1700/1.

1. 'of Morlbrough in the Parrich of St Marys'.

362 THOMAS ENGLISH
labourer 8 January 1701/2 P1/E/149

His weareing apparell and 1 coffer £2 12*s.* 4*d.*
In ready money £40 4*s.* 5*d.*

Total £42 16*s.* 9*d.*

John Jacob and Robert Cooke junior, appraisors.

Buried St. Peter 24 December 1701.
Will 21 December 1701; probate 25 March 1702 to Anne Kible, testator's 'loving dame'.

362A. WILLIAM TREWMAN[1]
blacksmith 4 March 1700/1 P1/T/244

The testators weareing apparell £5 10*s.*
In pewter, wrought brass and cast brasse £4 13*s.* 4*d.*
One skymmer, one beasting ladle and other small thinges 3*s.* 4*d.*
One dripping pan 1*s.*
Andirons, firepan and tongues and hangells 7*s.*
One screw plate, one hand vice, hammers, tongues and fowerteene files 19*s.* 8*d.*
Three iron candlestickes, one anvell, one paire of bellowses, one peckhorne and in iron £4 12*s.* 3*d.*
One grindstone spindle and handle and

other small tooles 14*s.* 6*d.*

One cubbard, viseboard and box, two chaires, one barrell, one table board, two Bibles and one trunke £1 5*s.*

One chest of drawers, one dressing box, another little box and two pillows 17*s.*

Two large coffers and two chests and one table board £1 2*s.*

Two bell brasse potts, one silt and one spice morter £1 6*s.*

In debts due and oweing to the testator £1 10*s.*

Fower billhookes and in iron 7*s.* 6*d.*

In money 7*s.* 6*d.*

One chattell lease consisting of one messuage or tenement situate in Marlebrough aforesaid £5.

One bedsteed 8*s.*

In beeds, beddinge, lyninge and curtaines £5.

Total £33 14*s.* 1*d.* [*recte* £34 4*s.* 1*d.*]

William Bayley and Robart Alexsander, appraisors.

Buried Preshute, Wilts 26 January 1700/1, 'died at St. Margarets'.[2]

Will 18 June 1695; probate 19 September 1701 to [unnamed].

1. Will 'of Overton'; inventory 'of Marlbrough'.
2. A suburb of Marlborough, but in the parish of Preshute.

363 HENERY RUSS senior

23 March 1701/2 P1/R/208

His waring aparill and mony in purs £5.

To bonds, one of six pound and the other of five £11.

In the Best Chamber

One fether bed, one bolster, five pillows, one set of cortins, one rug, 2 blancots, three peare of sheets, 1 bed steed, one flock bolster, 1 bed matt and cord, 2 cortinrodes £7.

More in the same Chamber, one chest of drawers, one trunke, 1 little table, one coffer, 2 boxis, one loocking glass, 1 glass coberd, one pere of ainderes, a fier pan and tongs £2 10*s.*

In the Little Chamber

One flock bed, 1 rug, 1 bedsteed, mat and cord, 1 box £1.

In the Chamber over the Kiching

1 flock bed, 4 rugs, to blancotes, 1 fether bolster, one flock bolster, 2 bedsteedes, to mates, 2 cords, 1 litle table £2 16*s.*

In the Back Roome

One flock bedd, one flock bolster, 2 fether pillowes, one sett of cortins, 1 bed steed and cord, 1 mat, 1 rug, three blancotes, 1 sheete, three cortinrodes, 4 windo cortines, fower rodes, to table bordes, 5 chaiers, one gined form, 2 gined stools, 1 pere of dogs, a fier pan and tongs, a peare of billos, 8 frame pickteres £5 6*s.*

In the Hale

Fifteene pewter dishes, one dosen and a halfe of pewter plates, one tanckerd, six poringers, 2 pewter candellstickes, 1 pewter quarte, 3 pintes, 4 kittle brass pots, 1 smale bell brass pot, 2 bras scillotes, 2 pewter chember potes, one warming pan, one coper saspan, one table, 3 gined stooles, 7 chaieres, one settle, 1 cobard, one gack, 3 spites, 3 steele plates, one paty pan of tin, one tin colinder, one biffork and fower iren candellsticks, 2 fier pans, 1 peare of tonges, one pere of doges, one pere of hangils, one iren bar, one fender, 2 pere of billosis, one candell box, on glass cobard, to [to *repeated*] windo cortines and one rod, 4 erthen moges, 1 lanteren, one skimer, one baken rack, one trencher racke, one bastin ladel, one tining driping pan, one dosen of trencheres, halfe a dosen of sasers £7 12*s.* 6*d.*

In the Little Botery
To barilles, fower civeres, a meashinvate, 3 tubs, 1 boocket and a powdering toub, five hogshedes, 2 barills, a fornis, grate and dore £11 19*s.*
For wood and hay and other lumber £3 1*s.*

In the Little Rome
1 table, 1 chaier, 1 stoole 6*s.*
One hors £3 19*s.*
One mare 12*s.* 6*d.*
For hops 9*s.*
Nine dosen of glass bottles 13*s.* 6*d.*
In bad debts £5.

Total £68 4*s.* 6*d.*

John Fowler and Edward Cully, appraisors.
John Reeves and John Jones, witnesses.

Buried St. Mary 12 December 1701 'Henry Rus'.
Bond 25 March 1702, administration to Sarah Russ, intestate's widow.

364 SARAH HURLE
spinster [*undated*, c.1702] P1/H/622

Her wearing apparel £1 15*s.*
Two pair of sheets and other linnen 12*s.*
Two coverlids and two blanketts and two carpets 10*s.*
One flock bed and boulster and pillow thereto belonging 8*s.*
One bedsted and a chest 11*s.*
Six cushens 3*s.*
One silver spoon and a taster 5*s.*
All her pewter 15*s.*
Two brasse kettles 15*s.*
Three skillets and a small brass pott 5*s.*
A warming pan, a thriping pan and a spice morter 4*s.*
Two spitts, a paire of iron doggs 4*s.*
A tableboard and frame and two joyned stooles and one barrell [and other lumber *added*] 7*s.*
Her books 5*s.* 3*d.*
In ready mony and debts £10 14*s.*

Total £17 13*s.* 3*d.*

William Allen and Joseph Camm, appraisors.

Burial not recorded.
Will 24 February 1699/1700; probate 15 August 1702 to Elizabeth Allin and Mary Brooker, executrices.

365 THOMAS FOWLER
linendraper [*day and month omitted*] 1702 P1/F/223

In the Buttery
Three potts, two skilletts, one fryingpan and morter 18*s.* 6*d.*
One table, one dresser board, ioynt stooles and trenchers 14*s.*

In the Kitchen
Books £1 15*s.*
One jacke and ten little pictures 15*s.*
Two tables, one stoole and ten chaires £2 4*s.*
Fower brass candlesticks, two spitts, 3 iron barrs, one par of doggs, one fire pan and tonges, one kettle, glass shelf and glasses 14*s.* 6*d.*
One skreene, one curtain, one curtain rod and hangells 2*s.* 6*d.*

In the Roome over the Shop
One warmeing pan, a pair of andirons and tonges, a chest of drawers and table £2 8*s.*
Six cane chaires, two looking glasses £1 10*s.*

One shelf and glasses, pictures, one map and box 8*s.*
Three calicoe curtains, two rodds, one bed and furniture £4 1*s.*
One press bedsteed 10*s.*

In the Roome over the Kitchen
One par of andirons, five boxes 16*s.*
Six bushells of malt 13*s.* 6*d.*
Seaven sheetes and a tablecloath £1 10*s.*
One table cloath and napkins 7*s.*

In the Streete Garrett
Two coffers and a press 15*s.*
A bed and furniture £2.
Two bedsteeds, three par of beams and scales 5*s.*
Odd things in the chamber 10*s.*
Sixty pound weight of pewter £2.
In wood, coole, barrells and tubbs and standes £2 10*s.*
The deceaseds wearing apparell and money in purse £3.

In the Shopp
Lynnen cloath and wares, counters, boxes, shelves, two par of brass scales, weights and a temser £192 16*s.* 9*d.*
In good debts on the shopp booke £52 0*s.* 3*d.*
And severall badd debte lookt on as lost.

[*Total omitted; by addition* £275 4*s.*]

John Fowler senior and John Fowler junior, appraisors.

Buried St. Mary 20 September 1702
Bond and commission 17 December 1702, administration to Hannah Fowler, intestate's widow.

366 JOHN BARNES
gentleman 14 April 1704 P1/B/715

The furniture of a roome £17 13*s.*
Boock debts, money, plate and waring apparrell £300.

Total £317 13*s.*

William Bayley and Samuel Baylye, appraisors.

Buried St. Mary 20 February 1703/4.
Will 11 December 1703; probate 6 October 1704 to Elizabeth Barnes, testator's widow.

367 JOHN PARSONS
barber [will] 4 July 1704[1] P1/P/444

The goods in the Brewhouse
Furnace, brewing vessell etc. £5.

In the Kitchin
Brass and pewter £3.
1 jack, 1 grate, 2 spitts and other things in the kitchin £1 10*s.*
1 old gun 4*s.*

In the Parlour
1 table board, 6 old chairs 7*s.* 6*d.*

In the Celler
Beer and vessells £3 10*s.*

In the Shop
[*blank*]

In the New Room
1 feather bed and curtains etc £2 2*s.* 6*d.*

Kitchin Parlour
1 table, 4 old chairs 7*s.* 6*d.*

Best Chamber
1 bed, bedstead, 6 cane chairs and one table £3 18*s.*

In the Little Garret
1 flock bed and bedstead and rug and blanket 10*s.*

In the Great Garret
1 flock bed and bedstead 10*s.*

The Linnen
6 knapkins, 3 table cloathes, 5 pair of corse sheets, 3 pair of pillow beers £2.
Wood and coal 9*s.*

In the Shop
1 glass, 2 hoans, 12 razors, 12 old knapkins etc £1.
1 silver bason £3 10*s.*
Wearing aparrll £1.

Total £28 18*s.* 6*d.*

William Bayly and William Pik, appraisors.

Buried St. Peter 27 May 1704
Will 19 May 1704; probate [*undated*] to Elizabeth Parsons, testator's widow.

1. Heading states 'an Invatory of the Goods of Eliz. Parsons relict of John Parsons deceased'.

368 GEORGE AYLIFFE
cook 7 September 1704 P1/A/194

In the Outer Cellar
Two civers, one hogshead, two barrells, one poudering tubb, three drapers, one stand and two ferkins £1 10*s.* 6*d.*
Stone bottles and glasse bottles 6*s.*

In the other Cellar
Two butts, six hogsheads, two barrells and two tilters £1 16*s.*
One tun boule, one runlett, four stands and three brass cocks 12*s.*

In the Brewhouse
One maish vatt and stand, four civers, three tubbs, one underback, a buckett and hebitt and one bushell £2 0*s.* 6*d.*
Three coolers and spout £1.
One copper and one smalle furnis £7 10*s.*
Two potts, two kettles, two sawce panns, two skilletts and one stew pann £1 10*s.*
One hundred weight of pewter £2 10*s.*

In the Greyhound
Nine pair of sheets £1.
Table linen 5*s.*
One feather bed, two bolsters and three pillows £2.
One rugg, two blanketts, curtains and vallens 15*s.*
One press bedstead £1.
Two large old ovell tables 10*s.*
One table and frame 5*s.*
A chest of drawers 12*s.*
One chest 4*s.*
Three joynt stooles 3*s.*
Seaven rush chaires 5*s.*
One pair of bellowes 1*s.*

In the Lyon
One feather bed, blousters and pillowes £1 2*s.* 6*d.*
Two ruggs, two blanketts, curtains and vallens 15*s.*
One tester bedstead, matt and cord 7*s.*
Six rush chaires 3*s.*
One table board and frame 4*s.*

In the Sun
Two feather beds, 2 boulsters and 4 pillowes £3.
Two ruggs, two blanketts, curtains and vallens 15*s.*
Two high bedsteads, matts and cords 14*s.*
A shuffleboard table and frame 14*s.*
Four joynt stooles, five rush chaires 6*s.* 6*d.*
One ovell table and a pair of bellowes 1*s.* 4*d.*

In the Backside and Stable
Pooles, faggetts and billett and moores £2 2*s.*
Two piggs and one ston trough £1 3*s.*

Three prongs, 4 stooles and two hogg tubbs 4*s.*

In the Shopp
One table and frame and three pasty peeles 4*s.*
A hanging shelfe and four other shelfes [and two joynt *deleted*] 2*s.* 6*d.*
Two joynt stooles, two cuppboard and one glasse case 8*s.*
A neast of drawers, three boxes, bar and coster 4*s.* 6*d.*
Two fire bucketts and three tinn covers 2*s.* 6*d.*

In the Rainge
One hundred weight of iron 13*s.*
One spade, one iron oven lead 3*s.* 3*d.*
Four spitts £1.
Two iron peeles, a wyre ridder and garden rake 2*s.* 2*d.*
Two basting ladles and brasse slice 1*s.* 6*d.*
Column total £40 7*s.* 9*d.*

In the Parlour
One large iron frying pann 1*s.* 8*d.*
One pair of doggs and one dozen of iron candle sticks 2s 4*d.*
One greate fireshovell 1*s.*
Thirty pound of old iron 2*s.* 6*d.*
Five fireshovells, three par of tongs and one large tosting iron 6*s.*
Two tables and frames 6*s.*
A binn of corne 2*s.*
A screen and cloth 2*s.*
A salt tubb and bellowes 2*s.*

In the Kitchen
One table board, frame and rack 4*s.*
Six rush chairs 1*s.* 6*d.*
The grate, andirons and other lumber 16*s.* 6*d.*
Two jacks 10*s.*
One watering pott 6*d.*

In the Buttery
A punch bole and a par of ballence 2*s.* 6*d.*
One press cuppboard 2*s.*
One other cuppboard 1*s.*
The deceaseds wearing apparrell £3.

In the Bear
One feather bed and boulster £1.
Two ruggs, curtains and vallen 7*s.* 6*d.*
Two bedsteads 8*s.*
Three joynt stooles and three rush chaires 2s 6*d.*

In the Outer Garrett
One old feather bed, boulster and pillowes 10*s.*
Three old bedsteads, matts and cords 8*s.*
The partition of boards and other lumber 2*s.* 6*d.*

In the Garrett over the Sun
Two flock beds, one rugg, two blanketts and lumber 10*s.*
Three broken bedsteads 6*s.*
A dressing table 2*s.*
Three coffers and one joynt stoole 4*s.*
Column total £10 4*s.*

Total £50 11*s.* 9*d.*

Robert Parkes and Joseph Deane, appraisors.

Buried St. Peter 16 December 1703.
Renunciation 20 December 1703 by Sarah Ayliffe, intestate's widow, in favour of Thomas Ayliffe of Reading; bond 13 January 1703/4, administration to Thomas Ayliffe, intestate's son; inventory exhibited 7 November 1704.

369 JOHN SMITH[1]
tobacconist[2] 11 October 1704 P1/S/688

His wearing apparel and moneys in pocket £8.

In the Hall

One long table board, one round table, 4 join stools, one side cubbard, one pair of pot hangers 18*s.* 6*d.*

In the Kitchen

One coal grate, one table board and frame, 6 stools, one little table and frame, one settle and a cubbard, one bench and a rack, 3 spits and 3 brass candlesticks, a flower box and pepper box, one jack, weights and chain, 5 steel plates and a frying pan, jack, andirons, fender and bar £2 16*s.* 8*d.*

One pair of dogs and bellows and tongs, fire pan, chopping knife and cleaver, tobacco tongs and candle box and a grate for irons, 4 chairs, one Bible and some smal books, one forme, 5 pair of pot hangers, 31 pewter plates, a warming pan, one salt and a cup, one tin box £2 3*s.* 8*d.*

16 pewter dishes and 5 porengers and 2 pewter flagons, one chafing dish and an apple roster, 3 brass kettles, 2 boylers with covers, 3 cast brass pots, 2 pair of pot hooks, 2 pewter basons, 2 colanders, 2 tankerds and a pint pot, 2 brass skimmers and a ladle, 2 pudding pans, one wooden morter and pestle, 3 bowls and a bell mettle skellet, a sauce pan and a dripping pan £6 14*s.* 8*d.*

One iron toster and 2 gredirons, one little kettle pot, 2 chamber pots, one pewter candle stick, one trencher rack and trenchers 8*s.* 8*d.*

In the Hall Chamber

One oval table board, one chest of drawers, one pair of dogs, one leather chair, a bed stead, matt, cord and rods, a feather bed, bolster, curtains, vallance and a blanket £4 15*s.*

In the Chamber over the Kitchen

One table board and frame, a chest, 3 leather chairs, one stool box and pan, one trunk, one pair of bellows, 3 pair of tongs and a fire pan, 2 pair of andirons and a pair of dogs, one kettle, one brass pot and 2 skellets, blankets, 2 coffers and one old rug £2 15*s.* 6*d.*

One feather bed and a bedstead, one bolster, curtains, vallance, 2 pillows, one rug, one blanket, cord and matt, rods and a sheet £3 7*s.*

In the Chamber over the Buttery

One chest of drawers, 4 chairs, 2 stools and a form, a pair of andirons, one trunk, 12 diaper napkins, 6 hollandcloth napkins, 6 table cloths, a mantle, [12 *added*] pillow cases and 6 pair of sheets and a bolster case, 9 other napkins and 12 towels, a little trunk, one suit of sarge curtains and vallence, 2 pair of window curtains £7 15*s.* 2*d.*

In the Fore Garret

One chest of drawers, a side cubbard, one hanging shelf, one table board, a truckle bed stead, bed, bolster, cord, matt, rug and a blanket, one stooll and 2 chairs, 2 baskets, one silver tankerd and a colledg cupp £13 2*s.* 11*d.*

One feather bed, bolster, bed stead, matt, cord and 2 pillow cases, 2 cover lids, one blanket, curtains and vallance £3 10*s.*

In the Fore Garret next the George

One feather bed, bolster, pillow and case, one rug, blanket and bed stead, curtains and vallance £3 10*s.*

In the Shop

One pair of andirons, a counter, an old saddle and 3 join stools 13*s.*

In the Chamber over the Shop

6 turkey work'd chairs, one arm'd chair and one leather chair, one oval table board, one looking glass and a glass cubbard £2 10*s.*

In the Backward Garret
One chest, one truckle bed stead, cord and matt, 4 bolsters, 3 feather pillows and 2 flock pillows, 2 beds, one table board, one stool, 5 boxes, 3 flaskets, one coffer, one form, one old spit, one chamber pot, one drinking bowl and another spit £7 5*s.* 8*d.*

In the Cellar
2 hogsheads, one silt, one skimmer, 5 half hogsheads, one tun bowl and one jack £1 8*s.* 10*d.*

In the Brewhouse
26 tubs and coolers, 6 hogsheads, 3 butts, one press and 2 iron bars, one pail and a powdering tub, 2 leather bags, 2 coppers and 3 brass pans, one gallon pot and 2 quart pots, one pint pot, an half pint and a quarter of a pint, 2 hundredweights, one half hundred and 14 pound, one iron morter and pestle £15 3*s.* 4*d.*

In the Backside
2 old table boards and frams, one press, billets of wood, faggets and coals, one ladder and other lumber in and about the house £4 8*s.* 9*d.*

In the Shop at the 3 Tuns and Crown
9 tubs and a kiver, 22 boxes, one bowl, one dryer, one engine and press, one nest of boxes, 2 fire buckets, a furnace at Mr. Bartlets, 9 sacks, one pair of scales and weights with other lumber £5 4*s.*

At Bedwin
One bedstead, cord and matt, one table board and fram, 2 chairs, 4 stools, 2 [half *added*] hogsheads, one beam, scales and ½ hundredweight, 3 tubs and debts good and bad £23 7*s.* 6*d.* in all £25 11*s.* 6*d.*
2 acres of land in Port Field £8.
One rick of hay standing in Richard Marten's ground £6.

Goods in partnership with his executor the half of which appertain'd to him
Faggots in the garden £3.
Metheglin in the brewhouse £10.
26 rundels and metheglin drawn £2.
Debts at the shop and moneys received £45 4*s.* 9*d.*
The half of which is £30 2*s.* 4½*d.*
Tobacco £45 10*s.* 2*d.*
The half of which is £22 15*s.* 1*d.*
Wood, good debts and moneys received £42 6*s.* 6*d.*
Wood standing bought of Mr Jafferies £123 17*s.* 6*d.*
The half of which is £83 2*s.*
Doubtful debts £18 8*s.*

[*In a different hand*] *Total* £290 10*s.* 2½*d.* [*recte* £290 10*s.* 3½*d.*]

Noah Webb and Thomas Glide senior, appraisors.

Buried St. Peter 21 August 1704, 'senior'. Will 9 March 1698/9; probate 10 January 1704/5 to Samuel Smith, testator's son.

1. 'Mr.'.
2. 'tobacco cutter' on will.

370 THOMAS SPACKMAN
tailor 11 January 1704/5 P1/S/691

His purs and apparel £5.

In his Chamber
One fether bed with its furneture £2 5*s.*
One chest of drawers, 2 chests, one cofer, one stool, one box, 2 cheyers 18*s.*
Five sheets, one carpet and other linen 10*s.* 6*d.*
Two silver cups, 3 silver spoons and other od things £1 15*s.*

In the Kitchen
Eleven pewter platters, one flagon, one

chamber pott, six pleats with other things 19*s.* 6*d.*
Two brass kittels, three potts, one skelet, one brass pan, one candlestick, one chafendish £1 1*s.* 6*d.*
Two paier of andierns, two fier pans and tongs, two spits, one warmen pan with other things 9*s.*
One table bord, two stooles, one cuberd, one paire of drawers 10*s.*
In fier wood and other lumber goods 10*s.*
Three barels, one stand, two tubs, one tunboule 7*s.* 6*d.*
In depts £2 6*s.*

[*Total omitted, by addition* £16 12*s.*]

Isaac Martin and Francis Tedbury, appraisors.

Buried St. Mary 2 January 1704/5, 'the elder'.
Will 3 February 1700/1; probate 2 November 1705 to Jane Spackman, testator's widow.

371 ROBBART TANER[1]

mason [will] 19 May 1705 P1/T/250

His waring apparill and mony in purs £1.

In the Kitchin
[One old furnis and *added*] seven dishis of pewter and other lumber £2 10*s.*

In the Chamber over the Seler
One fether bedd, to bolsters and one pillow with all the partinancis there unto belonging £3 1*s.*

In the Garat
Sum lumber goods 4*s.* 6*d.*

In the Chamber over the Keitchin
One brass pann and one brass kittle with other lomber £5 4*s.*

[A chatall lease £6. *added*]

Total £17 12*s.* 6*d.* [*recte* £17 19*s.* 6*d.*]

William [Wo *deleted*] Orrem and John Reeves, appraisors.

Buried St. Mary 10 May 1705, 'the elder'.
Will 22 September 1703; probate 24 May 1705 to Sara Tanner, testator's daughter.

1. 'in the Parish of St. Marys in Marelborrough'.

372 NICHOLAS SNOW

apothecary 26 July 1705 P1/S/692

In the Kitchen and Buttery
Two table boards 15*s.*
Six ordinary chaires 4*s.* 6*d.*
A fire pan, tongs and poker, an iron fire grate and fender and 2 spitts [one ironjack *deleted*] 14*s.* 6*d.*
A pair of bellowus 6*d.*
Five pictures, a map and 3 prints 10*s.* 6*d.*
An iron jack and 2 iron doggs, 2 brass potts, 1 sauce pan, 1 warming pan, 1 fryingpan, 1 brass skillett and 4 brass ladles £1 6*s.* 9*d.*
2 dozen and 2 pewter plates, eleven pewter dishes, 1 pewter cheeseplate, 3 pewter candlesticks, four pewter porringers and four brass candlesticks £3 13*s.* 2*d.*
Other odd things 13*s.* 6*d.*

In the First Roome [?up] one pair of staires
A small table board and 1 chair 6*s.*
A small iron fire grate 3*s.*

In the Second Roome one pair of staires
A deale press, a trunk and a deale box 13*s.* 6*d.*
A truckle bed, bolster and two blanketts 16*s.*

In the Third Roome one pair of staires

A chest of drawers, a table board, dressing box and 6 cane chaires £3 9*s*.
A looking glass 6*s*.
2 pair of doggs, a fire pan and tongs 10*s*.
A bedsted, bedd, curtaines, valance and other things thereto belonging £7.
Window curtaines, rodds and other odd things £1 4*s*.

In the Garrett
A parcell of firewood and other lumber £2 12*s*.

In the Cellar
Six barrells £1 1*s*.
Two wooden horses 4*s*.
One still 15*s*.
Other odd things 5*s*. 6*d*.

In the Brewhouse
The brewing utensills 10*s*. 6*d*.
Four pair of sheets £2.
Eight pillow cases 4*s*.
Three table cloathes and 2 dozen of worne napkins 18*s*.
20 oz. and half of plate at 5*s*. per ounce £5 2*s*. 6*d*.
His wearing apparell £3.

Stephen Browne, brazier and Solomon Clarke, joiner, appraisors.

The goods in the shop £40.
Due on book to the deceased which are supposed good £50.
On book supposed desperate £47.

[*Total omitted, by addition*] £175 18*s*. 5*d*.

Edward Snow[1], appraisor of the shop goods.

Buried St. Peter 1 August 1704.
Commission 24 July 1705; bond 11 August 1705, administration to Anne Snow, intestate's widow.

1. 'brother of the deceased'.

373 ISAAC MARTIN
cooper 15 August 1705 P1/M/345

In the Inner Chamber
Four paire of sheets, eighteene napkins, two old flock bedds, one rugg, three blanketts, two bolsters, two small pillows, one chest, one press, one table board, one beddstead, six chairs, one pair of andirons, one pair of tongs, one prox £5.

In the Outer Chamber
Two old feather bedds, one rugg, two blanketts, two pillows, one bolster, one tableboard, one old chest, four chairs £3.

In the Kitchin
One dresser board, one duzen of plates, nine peauter dishes, two spitts, one fire shovell, one pair of tongs, one warming pan, one jack, one table board, four stools, six old chairs, three porringers, four candlesticks and some other odd things £2 18*s*.

In the Parlour
One table board, six chairs and other odd things £2.

In the Cellar
One vate, five barrells, one hogshead, ten tubbs and kivers £2.

In the Wash house
Three brass potts, three skilletts, one scimmer, one basting ladle, two tubbs, one furnace, two kittles £3 2*s*.
Ready money and cloaths £5.
Debts good and bad £99 0*s*. 7*d*.

In Mr Bayley's Cellar
Three mashing fates £2.
Thirteen barrells £2 10*s*.
Nine kivers £1 8*s*.
Thirteene tubbs £2 8*s*.

One tunbowle, one churn, two powdring tubbs and one well buckett 15*s.* 6*d.*
Six seed leps 8*s.*
Eighteen duzen bucketts £6 6*s.*
Ten duzen and halfe cheese vates £4 14*s.* 6*d.*
Eight prongs 6*s.*
One and thirty duzen of staves £4 15*s.*
Four duzen and halfe of forcks £1 7*s.*
Six duzen and halfe malt shovells £1.
One and twenty shovell trees 6*s.*
Three pair of fine bellows 7*s.* 6*d.*
Two gross and three duzen of trenchers 10*s.*
Three and thirty duzen of rackes £3 6*s.*
One duzen of sives 4*s.* 6*d.*
Twelve duzen and half of rubbers 19*s.* 6*d.*
Tenn duzen and five [of *added*] pecks and nine duzen of gallons £2 14*s.*
Two duzen and five of halfe bushells £1.
Four bushells 12*s.*
Six small bowles 1*s.* 6*d.*
Ten duzen and halfe of halfe gallons 14*s.*

In Mr Grinfeilds Cellar
Fourteens womens white chaires 8*s.* 6*d.*
Eight children's chairs [and six nurses chaires *added*] 6*s.*
Six low table white chairs 5*s.*
Two low armed white chairs 2*s.*
Page total £161 15*s.* 1*d.*

Eleaven black chaires 15*s.*
One child's table chair 1*s.*
Forty eight hand bucketts and pailes and five well bucketts £3 5*s.*
Thirty duzen of bowles and platters £3 16*s.*
Two duzen and two pair of bellows 18*s.*
Nine score and sixteen ladles 16*s.*
Thirteene mouse traps and three morters 5*s.*
Eight lanthornes 8*s.*
For all the bottles £2 7*s.*
Eight round mouse traps 2*s.* 8*d.*
Eight hundred and thirty dishes £2 1*s.* 3*d.*
Thirteen potlids and spring taps and spoons and small dishes 4*s.* 3*d.*
Five meale shovels and four pints 1*s.* 6*d.*
Seaventeene duzen of trenchers 9*s.* 6*d.*
Two cheese plates and one yoke 1*s.* 6*d.*
Two tubbs, one kive and tapps and spindles 16*s.*
Thirty eight tapp wadds and two tunning tunells 3*s.*
Sixteen rangers and twenty two milk strainers 8*s.* 6*d.*
Fourscore and ten skimingdishes 5*s.*
One duzen of basketts 1*s.* 6*d.*

In and about the Garden and Dwelling House
Four hundred and odd hambrough staves £8.
Eight hundred of dantsick staves £6.
Seaven hundred and a halfe of heading timber £3 15*s.*
Three hundred and ninety hundredweight civer timber 10*s.*
Sixty barrell staves 4*s.*
Two thousand small timber £2.
Three hundred barrell staves £1 4*s.*
Some odd timber 5*s.*
Some peeces of quarter board 5*s.*
One hundred thirty six hambro staves £2.
Small timber £1.
Nine planks £1 4*s.*
Four hundred and halfe of [ends of *added*] hambro staves £1 5*s.*
One lead furnace £1.
Eight quarter boards and odd ends £1 10*s.*
Six hundred of staves £1 4*s.*
Two thousand and nine hundred small staves £1.
One thousand three hundred and sixty small timber 15*s.*
Five hundred heading £1.
Eighteen hundred small timber £1 10*s.*
One thousand and sixty small heading £1.
Three hundred and five score small timber 6*s.*
Two hundred and five score tubb staves

9*s.*
Three hundred of paile timber 7*s.* 6*d.*
Two hundred thirty four firkin staves 10*s.*
Two hundred forty five duzen of hoops £10.
Seaventy nine duzen of rine hoops £2 10*s.*
One thousand two hundred and sixty smart hoggs 18*s.* 9*d.*
Paile bottoms £3.
Lapps and waggon hoops £1.
A parcell of old pailes £1.
Shoop tools and wood and timber £5.
Hoops in the chamber and other goods in the chamber £12 10*s.*
Timber in the streete £16 7*s.*

At the Devizes
Fourteen pails, 5 small civers and seaven tubbs £2.
Two churns, six barrells, one and twenty peece of bentware £1 10*s.*
Page total £111 4*s.* 11*d.*

Total £273.

John Blissett and Samuell Wild, appraisors.

Buried St. Mary 24 July 1705.
Will 16 July 1705; probate 16 August 1705 to William Hoggett, testator's brother-in-law, and Joseph Hockley.

373A. THOMAS JARRETT[1]
cordwainer [will] 27 December 1705 P1/IJ/139

His wearing apparell and money in his purse £5.
Three flock beds, two bedsteeds and all belonging to them £3 3*s.*
One cheast, three coffers, one box 10*s.*
Two table boards, one side table, four joynstoolls 10*s.*
One jack, one spit and andirons and other iron goods 10*s.*
Four kitles, five brass pots and two skilletts, aleven peuter platters, three tankets, six peuter poringers, two peuter candelsticks and other peuter £4 15*s.*
One warming pan, one brass spice morter and other brass things 3*s.* 6*d.*
A litle cabbinet and other things in the chamber 3*s.*
Seaven sheets, three table cloaths and other lining 10*s.* 6*d.*
One cheifing dish and four chairs and other things
5*s.*
Two buckets, two hangells 2*s.* 6*d.*
Two curtains 1*s.*
One frying pan 1*s.* 6*d.*
Good and bad debts upon bond and other securitys £122.
Four barells and wood and coall and other lumber about the house £2 6*s.*

Total £140 1*s.*

Edward Fribens and Francis Tedbury, appraisors.

Burial not recorded.
Will 15 January 1704/5; probate 17 December 1705 to Margaret Jarrett, testator's daughter; inventory exhibited 2 January 1705/6.

1. Will 'of Manton'; inventory 'of the parish of St Maryes in Marlbrough'.

374 RICHARD HAWKINS
yeoman [will] 13 July 1706 P1/H/640

His wearing apparrell and money in purse £1 10*s.*
A bedd, brass, pewter and other lumber £5.
A leasehold cottage for one life £5 10*s.*

[*Total omitted, by addition* £12]

Obadiah Burgess junior and Richard Kemm, appraisors.

Burial not recorded.
Will 7 June 1683; probate 24 July 1706 to 'Widow' Hawkins.

375 DOROTHY DISMORE[1]

widow [burial register] 24 January 1706/7 P1/D/223

In the Backside
Eleven dozen of harrows £2 15*s*.
Scrows £2.
Pelts £3 6*s*.
Parchment £3.
Wooll £4.
Cony skinns £4.
2 peices cloth and some blanketing £2 10*s*.
Knives 6*d*.

In the Room over the Kitchen
1 flock bed, 1 bolster, 2 pillows, 1 bedsteed, 2 blanketts, 1 rugg, 1 coffer, curtains and vallains £1.

The next Room
1 fether bed and bolster, 1 flock bed and bolster, 2 blanketts, 1 rugg, 1 bedsteed, curtains and vallains £1 5*s*.
1 press cupboard 12*s*. 6*d*.
1 pair of andiorns, 1 table, 1 carpett, 1 stool 5*s*.
9 sheets, 8 pillowbeers, 1 cupboard cloth, 6 bolster cases £1 10*s*.
Wareing apparell £4.
2 table cloths 5*s*.
3 pads of list 10*s*.

In the Kitchen
10 pewter dishes, 9 plates, 2 brass pots, 2 kitles, 2 skillets, 1 poringer, 1 tankard, 1 flagon, 1 jack, 1 spitt, 1 fire pan, 1 pair of tonges, 1 frying pan, 1 pair dogs, 1 pair andiorns £2.
One furniss 16*s*.
2 halfe hogsheads, one barell, 1 fatt, 1 boul and other brewing vessell and lumber 15*s*.
1 table, 2 stools, 5 chairs 5*s*.
Wood 5*s*.
Badd debts £20.

Total £54. [*recte* £54 8*s*.]

Nathaniel Hone and Edward Dixon, appraisors.

Buried St. Mary 21 January 1706/7.
Bond 24 July 1707, administration to Richard Dismore, intestate's son.

1. 'of the Parish of St Mary In Marlebrow … deceased the 19 Jan 1706'.

376 JOHN MORRICE[1]

carpenter 21 July 1707 P1/M/348

His wearing apparrell and money in purse £2.
Two bedds, bedsteeds and bedding thereunto belonging, one chest of drawers, two coffers with other lumber in the chamber £3.
Two tableboards and frames, four joynt stools, four pewter dishes, four rush chairs and other lumber in the kitchen £1 10*s*.
The brewing vessells and furnace in the brewhouse £2.
Four barrells, a frame and other lumber in the cellar 15*s*.
Timber and boards in and about the dwellinghouse £8.
All his working tooles £2.

Total £19 5*s*.

Edward Hancock and John Nalder, appraisors.

Buried St. Peter 10 July 1707, 'senior'.
Bond 24 July 1707, administration to Mary Morrice, intestate's widow.

1. 'of the parish of St. Peter and Paul thappostles in Marlebrough'.

377 WILLIAM SMITH
currier 10 November 1707 P1/S/701

In his Bed Chamber
One feather bed, one bolster, two pillows, one rug, one pair of blanketts, a tester bed steed, curtains and vallains £4 14*s.* 4*d.*
Wareing apparrell and books £1 18*s.*
A round table, chest of draws, trunck and lining £2 10*s.*
Two looking glasses and a spoon and other implements 7*s.* 6*d.*

In [an *added*] *other Chambers*
Two feather beds, two bolsters, three pillows, three bedsteeds, a rug and coverlid, 3 blanketts, curtains and vallains and other implements £5 19*s.* 8*d.*
One chest, box and coffer and close stoole and pan 13*s.*

In the Kitchen
One table board, 3 jont stooles and a rack, jack and cubbard, 9 chairs, a shilf and drawr 19*s.*
A iron grate, brass and pewter £8 17*s.*

In the Shop
Leather and working tools and other implements £30 4*s.*
Four barrells and brewing vessell £2.
A back house, furnace, tun and liden sink £1 10*s.*
Wood and cole and other lumber £1 10*s.*
In money and debts £30.
And desperate debts £10.

Total £101 2*s.* 6*d.*

Thomas Smith and Nathaniel Hone, appraisors.

Buried St. Mary 9 November 1707.
Bond 20 November 1707, administration to Ruth Smith, intestate's widow.

378 THOMAS GREENAWAY[1]
glover [will] [*undated*, c.1707] P1/G/339

The wereing apperrel £4.
Brass and puter £3.
Beds and beding £4.
All the lumber goods £2.
Linen £1.
[*Added in a different hand*] Money on bond and money in house £169.
The stock £5 13*s.*

Total £188 13*s.*

Richard Barrett and Joseph Greenaway, appraisers.

Buried St. Peter 7 December 1707, 'Mr'.
Will 9 September 1707; probate and inventory exhibition not recorded.

1. 'of the parish of St Peters'.

379 ANN KEEBLE[1]
widow [will] [*undated*, c.1707/8]
P1/K128

In the Flower de Luce
1 bed and bedsteed and other things 14*s.*

Greyhound
3 bedsteeds, 2 flock beds, 1 table and frame £1 5*s.*

Crown
1 fether bed, 1 rugg, bedsteed, curtains

and vallains, 2 tables, 4 joynt stools, 1 lookin glass, 2 bolsters, 1 fire pan and shovell £4 15*s.*

Rose
1 fether bed and bedsteed and other things belonging to the chamber £1 19*s.*

Squerell
1 bed, 1 bedsteed, 1 curtin and vallin, 1 table £1 11*s.*

Bell
2 beds, 3 bedsteeds, curtains and halfe vallains, 1 long table, 1 press, 1 cupboard, 6 pillows, 1 press and other lumber £6 3*s.*

Halfe Moon
1 little table 2*s.* 6*d.*

Warehouse
2 beds, 2 bedsteeds, 1 table and other lumber £2 10*s.*

Citchin
2 boylers, 1 iron pott, 1 jack, 1 settle, 1 pair andirons, 2 tables and 2 forms, 2 spitts, 2 dripen pans, 1 settle and other lumber, 27 puter platers, 3 dozen plates £7 10*s.*

Brewhouse
2 furniss, 1 mashfatt, 1 cooler, 1 tunn, 2 halfe hogsheads, 1 zilt and 5 quarter cole and 2 spouts £12.

Seller
1 bar, 3 hogs heads beare, 3 empty hogsheads, 3 stands, 1 powderin tub, 1 payle £7 6*s.*
5 piggs £2 10*s.*
Wood £2.
Hay and corn £1 10*s.*
In mony £3 7*s.* 6*d.*
Wearing apparell £1.
Lease of a house £50.
16 sheets and 3 dozen napkins £2.

Total £108 3*s.*

William Smith and William Blake, appraisors.

Buried St. Peter 6 January 1707/8 'Keble', [BT 'Kibble'].
Will 16 October 1702; commission 25 February 1707/8, oath administered 28 February 1707/8 to Thomas Seymour; probate 3 March 1707/8 to Thomas Seymour.

1. 'deceased 4 Jan 1707'.

380 JOHN HICHCOCK[1]
16 March 1707/8 P1/H/646

Waring aparell and money in purs 5*s.*
Bras and puther £1.
3 owele cheres 2*s.* 6*d.*
Bruing veshell 3*s.*
2 bedes and all belong to them £2.
A tronck and a coffar, a chest and box 10*s.*
A cow £2.
Wood and coll £1.
Money out one bad depts £10.

Total £17. 0*s.* 6*d.*

Richard Deare and Henry Tayler, appraisors.

Buried St. Peter 6 May 1707.
Will 18 April 1704; probate and inventory exhibition not recorded.

1. 'Leatt of Malbroughe Saint Peters'.

381 MARY DAVIS
spinster 17 April 1708 P1/D/227

In the Chamber
One feather bedd, two feather pillows, two blanketts, a rugg and bedsteed, two flockbeds, a bedsteed, a flock bolster, a blankett, coverlidd and old rug, two bed cords, two matts, one cupboard, one coffer, two boxes and the deceaseds wearing apparrell £5 10s.

In the Kitchen
A tableboard and frame, two joynt stools, one wainscott chair, four rush chairs, a brass warming pan, a brass skimer, one little brass pott, two kettles, a skillett, an iron pott, one spitt, a fire pan and tongs, a gridiron, a pair of doggs, two iron candlesticks, three smoothing irons, a frying pan, two pewter dishes, one flagon, one porringer, two barrells, a powdering tubb, two civers and two tubbs with faggotts and other lumber in the cellar £2 15s.
In ready money £38 18s. 6d.
In money due upon mortgage and bonds £95.

[*Total omitted, by addition* £142 3s. 6d.]

Obadiah Burgess and [?]Gd Doverdale, appraisors.

Buried St. Peter 15 April 1708.
Will 30 January 1707/8; probate 4 May 1708 to Edward Hancock.

382 THOMAS EDNEY
blacksmith 31 January 1708/9 P1/E/156

An anvill, bickern, two pair of vice, two sluggs, two hand hammers and naile stake £1 12s. 8d.
A cast anvill and cast box mould 4s. 8d.
Six pair of tongs, two prichers, one cleft, one stampt futter 2s. 6d.
A coaltrough, one paire of bellows, one bolster 13s.
One peice of new iron, three blocks and old iron horse shoes 9s. 8d.
Six files, shoeing tooles, baskett and holter 3s.
Two quarter of cole and two tubbs 17s. 6d.
Five and twenty pound of horse nailes 8s. 4d.
A bedd, bedsteed and bedding £1 10s.
A chest of drawers, a table, two chests and a trunk, three boxes and coffer 14s.
Wearing apparell £1.
Seaventeene stocklocks and tenn horse locks £1 4s. 2d.
Twenty nine gimbletts and nine firepan bitts 5s.
Five coffer locks, eighteene paire of jemmells 5s.
Three dozen and a halfe of rakes, four sneads and two sides of bacon £1 5s. 6d.
Two old bedsteeds, bedding and nine paire of patten rings 7s.
One feather bedd and bedding, two tables, five stooles, a cupboard, one jack, two spitts, two andirons, a paire of doggs, one bar and a hanging candlesticke £2 5s.
Twenty six pounds of pewter 13s.
Brass 16s.
Furnace and brewing vessell £1 12s.
A table, two dressers, three chayrs, a forme, hangells, doggs, barr, gridiron, one paire of bellows, bacon rack, bench, trenchards, eighty pounds of nailes, three piggs and lumber goods £3 7s. 4d.
Linnen 4s.
In debts £5 0s. 9d.

Total £25 0s. 1d.

Stephen Edney and William Burgss, appraisors.

Buried St. Peter 21 January 1708/9, 'senior'.
Bond 2 February 1708/9, administration to Margaret Edney, intestate's widow

383 JOHN GREENWAY[1]
glover [will] [*undated,* c. 1709][2]
P1/G/350

2 dozen mens sheep gloves at 4*s.* 6*d.* 9*s.*
1 dozen womens ditto 4*s.* 6*d.*
1 dozen childrens and short womens 4*s.* 6*d.*
2 dozen out-seamed gloves 6*s.*
20 pair of boyes breeches 10*s.*
4 pair of mens breeches 4*s.*
The standing and standing cloth and hamper 7*s.* 6*d.*
10 dozen of sheep skins at 3*s.* dozen £1 10*s.*
1 pair boots 2*s.*
[Five *deleted*] 3 dishes of pewter, 1 pewter flagon, 4 pewter plates 19*s.* 6*d.*
1 little furnes 18*s.*
2 kettles 8*s.*
1 bell brass pott 2*s.* 6*d.*
1 chest of drawers, 1 old chest, 1 small table board and 1 old cupboard 10*s.*
1 college cup £1 15*s.*
1 feather bed and bolster £1.
Wearing aparrel £1.
1 barrel, 2 joint stooles, 1 old chair 3*s.*
1 stake and with to rub skins on 6*d.*
1 plank in the shop 6*d.*
In moneys 1*s.* 6*d.*
1 parcell of leather shreds 5*s.*
Book debts supposed good £2.
Book debts supposed bad £1 19*s.*
Due for rent £6 13*s.*
Due on bond principall money (besides interest) but very desperate £60.

Total £80.

William Bayly and Anthony Greeneway, appraisors.

Buried St. Peter 30 March 1709.
Will 27 March 1709; probate 30 June 1709 to executor [William Smith 'of the Three Tuns in Marlebrough'].

1. 'Greeneway' on will.
2. 'deceased 27 mrch 1709'.

384 GEORGE DOBSON
chandler 25 April 1709 P1/D/233

The testators wearing apparrell and money in purse £2.
His household goods and shop goods £8 5*s.*
In debts on bond and other securityes £113 12*s.* 4*d.*
In book debts and otherways £26 3*s.* 2*d.*

Total £150 0*s.* 6*d.*

Alexander Allen and John Fowler junior, appraisors.

Buried St. Peter 21 April 1709.
Will 10 April 1709; probate 7 June 1709 to Obadiah Burges junior and Francis Holmes, executors.

385 EDWARD DANGERFIELD senior
baker 10 October 1709 P1/D/232

Wearing aparrell £1.
One bed and bedsted and other apurtenances belonging £3.
One trunck and linen £1.
One chest 3*s.*
Two chaires 2*s.*
Two silver bodkins 2*s.*
A litl hors £1.

Total £6 7*s.*

James Coller and John Pidding, appraisors.[1]

Buried St. Mary 21 May 1709.
Bond 12 October 1709, administration to Richard Dangerfield, intestate's son.

1. 'taken and signed (having on first her majestys dubll sixpeny stamp)'.

386 JOHN COPLAND

innholder [will] 29 Jan 1710/1

P1/C/520

His wearing apparrell £5.

In the Garratt over the Gatehouse
2 fether bedds with itts furniture, 2 tables and 5 chaires £6.

In the Garratt Called the Star
3 bedstedes and 2 bedds, 2 tables, 3 chaires and 2 iron doggs £3.

In the Garratt over the Best room
1 feather bed with itts furniture, 7 chairs, 2 chests, 2 pillows, 2 andirons, 1 brass fender etc £6.

In the Room over the Hall
2 fine feather bedds with itts furniture, 12 leather chaires, 2 brass andirons, a fire pan and tongs, 2 iron doggs, one table, 1 chest draws, 1 large looking glass and 1 stand etc £20.

In the Room over the Kitchen
One fine bedd with itts furniture, 2 tables, 12 chaires, one chest draws, a long looking glass, 2 brass andirons, 2 iron doggs and fire pan and tongs etc £13.

In the Room over the Gatehouse
3 fether bedds with itts furniture, one table, one side cubbord, one press bedsted and 6 old chaires £14.
The table linen with other linnin £20.

In the Great Parlour
One fine bedd with itts furniture, 3 tables, 6 chaires, 1 close stool box and pan, 2 iron dogg and firepan and tongs, 1 brass sconce, a large looking glass etc £14.

In the Room behind the Hall
One bed with itts furniture, 1 table, one trunk, 1 coffer £5.

In the Hall
One long table, 2 chests, 2 chaires, 2 andirons, 2 iron doggs and 1 pair tongs £1.

In the little Parlour
2 tables, 2 joint stools, 6 chaires, 1 clock, 1 sconce, 1 pair tongs and 1 pair iron doggs £3.

In the Kitchen
Thirty three pewter dishes and 2 pewter plates, 20 pewter porringers, 7 pewter chamber potts, 2 pewter bason, 16 pewter quarts and pint potts, 6 brass potts, 2 bell mettle ditto, 1 forness, 2 skilletts, 1 jack, 5 spitts, 1 frying pan, 1 larg grates, 4 fluthes bacon with tin ware, chaires and tables etc £23.

In the Celler
Fourteen hogsheads, ale and bear vessells, tubbs, kive stands etc £40.

In the Brew House
2 furnesses, 1 larg meash tubb, 2 coollers, 1 wash tubb with other tubb £9.

In the Back side
Wood and coales, eighteen piggs, three cowes and 2 calves £46.

In the Stable
Four horses with their harness, a shaire and harness, 1 plow and 3 harrows with wippences and riders etc £18 10s.
Hay in the tallett, corn in the barn, 1 malt mill, 1 stack hay in the ground, 1 dung cart, weelbarrow etc £27 10s.

[*Total omitted; by addition* £274]

John Nalder and John Fowler junior, appraisors.

Buried Aldbourne 24 January 1710/1.
Will 13 January 1710/1; probate 11 May 1711 to Naomi Copland, testator's widow.

387 ROBERT NEW
skinner[1] 11 May 1711 P1/N/134

His wareing aparill and mony in purse £1 5*s.*
In the bed and bed steed ine the best chamber £1 7*s.*
One bed steed 3*s.*
One cheest, barill, one coffer with other lumber 5*s.*
To tables, cubard 8*s.*
One warming pan, one pare of doggs, one scimer, one bras cittell, one skillett 7*s.*
One fire great, hangells, fire pan and tongues 2*s.*
All other lumber 2*s.* 6*d.*
One furnice £2.
The harowes and kniffes £1 10*s.*
Three troughes, four dusen of nettes 5*s.*
A bame and shalles 4*s.*
One hundred and quarter of glue £1 15*s.*

Total £9 13*s.* 6*d.*

William Dance, [*blank*] Pittnell and Walter Whitehart, appraisors.
John Reeve, witness.

Buried St. Mary 8 May 1711, 'the elder'.
Will 22 August 1704; probate 11 May 1711 to Robert New, testator's son.

1. Fellmonger on will.

388 WILLIAM ALDRIDGE
maltster 28 August 1711 P1/A/219

The deceased's wearing apparrell £4.
In household goods and shop goods £14.
In malt £56.
A malt mill £1.
In wood £30.
In book debts £101.

Total £206.

John Fowler and Thomas Lyppeatt, appraisors.

Buried St. Peter 13 August 1711.
Will 5 August 1711; probate 5 October 1711 to Elizabeth Aldridge, testator's widow.

389 WILLIAM TRIPPATT
waggoner 28 August 1711 P1/T/279

The deceseds wereing apparell £4.
In household goods £10 10*s.* 6*d.*
In fire wood and cole £1 10*s.*
In beds and beding £8.
In money and depts £11 7*s.* 3*d.*

Total £35 7*s.* 9*d.*

Joseph Greenaway and William Moxham, appraisors.

Buried St. Peter 27 August 1711, 'Trilbutt'.
Will 20 August 1711; probate 5 October 1711 to executrix [Sarah Trippat, testator's widow].

390 STEVEN DEREM[1]
hempdresser [will] 18 September 1711
P1/D/242

His waring aparel £2.
Two beds and beding £3.
The housel gads £2.
Hemp and flex £4.
A hous £2.

A hous in saint marys parish in marlbrogh 15*s.*
The infatarey of the goods 14*s.* 10*d.*

Total £29 10*s.* [*recte* £14 9*s.* 10*d.*]

John Brookes and William Ruff, appraisors.

Buried St. Mary 7 September 1711 'Stephen Durham'.
Will 26 November 1709; probate 5 October 1711 to Sarah Derham, testator's widow.

1. 'which departed this Lif december [*recte* September] 4'; 'Derham' on will.

391 ROBERT PARKES

innholder 10 March 1711/2 P1/P/511

His wearing apparell £5.
Ready money and plate £100.
In housing and corn [upon the corn *deleted*] upon the ground £54.
In debts [on bond *deleted*] abroad £20.
In old lead and linnen in the house £11.

In the Cellar
In strong and small beer and full and empty vessells £30.

In the Kitchen
Pewter, brass and other goods £7.

In the Parlour
Three quarters of malt, a table board and other lumber £6.

In the Milk-house
Two whitches and other odd old goods £1.

In the Low Room
A bed, bedstead [bed *added*] clothes with a table and chairs £4.

In the Room where Mrs Parkes lodgeth
A bed, bedstead and clothes £2 10*s.*

In the Room called the Half Moon
A bed, bedstead and bed-clothes, table and chaires £8.

In the Room called the Chequer
Two beds, bedsteads, bedcloathes and other lumber £4.

In the Room called the George
Two beds and bedsteads, tables, chaires and a press £12.

In the Room called the Sun
Two beds and bedsteads, a table and chaires £6.

In the Room called the Flower de Luce
A bed and bedstead and a table and chairs £3 10*s.*

In the Garret
A bed and old lumber and 8 chamber pots £2 10*s.*

In the House which Mr Edmonds dwells in
A bed, pewter and other things £4.
Hard-wood, faggots and coals £17.
A cow, calf and hogg £6.
Ten tun of hay £15.
Two furnaces and brewing vessells £12.

Total £330 10*s.*

Roger Williams, gentleman and Robert Croom, grocer, appraisors.

Buried St. Mary 24 January 1711/12, 'Mr.'
Will 21 September 1709; probate 26 June 1712 to Mary Parkes, testator's widow.

392 FRANCIS HANDCOCK

lime burner 24 June 1712 P1/H/686

In the Kitching
His weareing apparell £1.
48 lb. of pewter at 7*d.* a lb. £1 8*s.*
26 lb. of brass at 10*d.* £1 1*s.* 8*d.*
A jack, 2 spitts, a gridgiron and small things 10*s.*
A fire pan, tongs, 2 iron dogs and a frying pan 3*s.*
A table, 3 joyne stools, a cubbord, a dresser, 5 chaiers, a warming pan and other lumber 12*s.*

In the Iner Chamber
A little bed and bedsteed and all things there to belonging 15*s.*
A table, a coffer, a box and a chaier 4*s.*

In the Best Chamber
A bed, bedsteed, curtins and vallens and all things belonging £3 10*s.*
A chest, 2 boxes, 4 chaiers, a paire of sceals and some small things 8*s.*

[*In the Back Chamber* added]
A bed, bedsteed and all things belonging £1.
A settle, a box, an iron greate, a pair of andirons with other lumber 10*s.*

In the Buttery
4 tubs, 2 keevers, 1 barrell and lumber 10*s.*
A small furness and a greate and other lumber £1.
A horse, harness and cart £2 10*s.*
In debts 10*s.*

Total £15 11*s.* 8*d.*

John Gillmore, appraisor.

Buried St. Mary 18 April 1712 'the elder'.
Will 15 April 1712; probate 26 June 1712 to Ann Hancock, testator's widow.

393 WILLIAM FRY
pipemaker [*undated*, c.1712] P1/F/251

His waring apparril £4.

In the Chamber he lay in
One bed and furniture belonging £7 10*s.*
And one chest of drawrs, two chests, one coffer, one table bord, one looking glass, fire pan and tongs and two chairs and other small lumber with the linning £2 12*s.*

In the next Chamber
One bed and beding £1 10*s.*

In the Kitching
Two table bords and joint stools and all other lumber goods £1 14*s.*

In the next Room
Six chairs and other small lumber 10*s.*

In the next Room
All the brass and puter and other lumber £1 10*s.*

In the next Room that is a little Buttery
Three barrils and brewing vessel 13*s.*

In the Seller
All the working tooles and all the clay and pips made £23 10*s.*
Money that is dew from several hands £3.
For an old mare and all tacking belonging £2 10*s.*
The money that was in the house when he dy'd was £7.

Total £55 19*s.*

John Blissett, Ayliffe Blissett and Thomas Blackman, appraisors.

Buried St Mary 15 February 1711/2.
Will 7 February 1711/2; probate 26 June 1712 to Jane Fry, testator's widow.

394 CHRISTOPHER FREEMAN
maltster 3 October 1712 P1/F/254

His wearing apparel £3.
His dwelling house and malt house £160.

In the Kitchen
Two cupboards 4*s.*
Four joyn'd stools 1*s.* 6*d.*
A table and a settle 10*s.*
Four leather chairs and two stools 6*s.*
Two spitts, one dripping pan, one flesh fork, two iron candlesticks, one pair of dogs, one pair of tongs 5*s.* 6*d.*

In the Cellar
Weights and scales 3*s.*
Four barrels 10*s.*
One powdering tubb 1*s.* 6*d.*
A skimmer and ladle, tubs and kevers £1 2*s.* 10*d.*
Two skellets 3*s.* 6*d.*
A nest of boxes 3*s.*
A brass pan and kettle 18*s.* 4*d.*
A bell-brass pott and a morter and pestle 12*s.* 6*d.*

In the Hall
Two tables 8*s.* 6*d.*
One fire-pan and tongs and cupboard 4*s.* 6*d.*
One Bible 2*s.* 6*d.*

In the Pantry
One silver spoon 5*s.*
One dozen of pewter plates 6*s.*
Other pewter 12*s.* 10*d.*

In the Hall Chamber
One bed and boulster, one blanket and ruggs £1 19*s.*
One bedstead and rods and curtains and vallens 16*s.*
Three pillows 10*s.*
Six pair of sheets £1 10*s.*
Four pillow ties 6*s.*
Two table cloathes and twenty napkins 15*s.*
One trunk, one chest and four old boxes 14*s.*
One pair of doggs 2*s.* 6*d.*
In starch 10*s.*
Money in hand 10*s.*

In the Garret
One flock bed and boulster and one rugg 9*s.*
One bedstead and an old boulster and one old rugg 6*s.*
And some other lumber 5*s.*

Total £178 13*s.* 6*d.*

Robert Meggs and Joseph Greenaway, appraisors.

Burial not recorded.
Bond 9 October 1712, administration to Margaret Freeman, intestate's widow.

395 ALEXANDER ALDWORTH
maltster 11 December 1712 P1/A/221

In the Kitchen
One fire shovel, one pair of tongs and a pair andirons 4*s.*
A jack, 2 spits, a frying pan, a chaffing dish and gridiron 7*s.* 6*d.*
A teapot, candlebox, 2 steel plates, a frame and other lumber 2*s.* 6*d.*
A tableboard, frame and four old chairs 3*s.* 6*d.*
Ten pewter dishes and 13 plates £1 3*s.* 6*d.*
Three brass pots, 1 bell mettal pot, 2 skillets and a skimmer 16*s.*
Three brass candlesticks 2*s.* 6*d.*

In the Cellar
Five old tubbs, 5 kievers, tunn bowl, 2 pails and a buckett £1 2*s.*
A meshing vate, 6 barrels, 3 stands, a fire bucket and hand saw £1 6*s.* 6*d.*

Old boards, 2 spouts and a meshing tubb £1 15s. 6d.
Two tin pans, 3 dozen of glass bottles, a skreen, shovel and harecloth £1 0s. 10d.
Hard wood and faggotts £12.

In the Hall
Two pair of andirons, a fire shovel and a pair of tongs 4s. 6d.
A pair of cotterels, 2 tables and 4 joynt stools 17s.
Six chairs and a close stooll 8s. 6d.
A skreen and other lumber 3s. 4d.

In the Chamber
A bed, bedsteed and all things thereto belonging £3.
A chest of drawers and a looking glass 13s.
Six chairs, 2 boxes, 2 truncks and a glass shelve 9s. 6d.
A cupboard, 2 stools, a pair of andirons and a pair of doggs 7s.
A warming pan, 12 trenchards with some small earthenware 5s 6d.

In the Garrett
A bed steed, bed and things thereto belonging £1 10s.
Two old barrels and other lumber 2s. 6d.

In the Malthouse
Mault in the mault house and garners £15.
A mare £2 10s.
Linen 12s.

Wearing Apparell
Linen and woollen £3.
Debts upon book £31 11s. 9d.

Total £80 17s. 11d. [*recte* £80 18s. 11d.]

Edward Cully and Robert Miles, appraisors

Buried St. Peter 20 November 1712 'Alexander Alder'.

Will 17 November 1712; probate 17 April 1713 to Elinor Aldworth, testator's widow.

396 FRANCES HURLBUT
?carpenter [inventory goods] 15 June 1713 P1/H/689

Ann acount of what was in the Timber Yard
2 tun of ocken timber £4.
5 sid peses to the pit and od stuf thear £1 10s.

Ann acount of what timber about the Hous
In the passage and bord hous 470 ft of elm bord £2 10s. 6d.
In the bord hous 585 ft of ocken bord £3 10s.
For raftering stuf in the garden and other od stuf in the garden and baxide £7.
For 7 botams and lumber in Mr. Bengers shop £1.
For a peaire of drugs 6s.

Ann acount of the Housall Goods
In the Litel Shop
2 chests and od lumber 10s.

In the Litel Rome
2 small tables, 5 blach chairs 12s.

In the Hale
2 tabels, 4 lether chairs, 3 rush chairs, 2 joynt stols and od things £1.
In the hall chimney 1 paire of anders, 1 paire of dogs, 1 fiar pan and tongs, jack and spit 16s.
For books in that rome 10s.

In the Iner Chamber
1 fether bed, 1 flockbed, 1 flockbolster, 2 fether pillers, 1 bed stid and beding and curtin and valings and bed mat and cord £3.
In the same rome one chest of drars, 1

chest, 2 tabelbords, 3 joynt stols, 1 desck, 1 clos stole, 3 looking glases £1 10*s.*

In the Outer Chamber

3 flockbeds, 1 fether bolster, 1 flock pilow, 2 bedstids, curtins, valings and beding £3.
In the same rome 1 pres, 1 box, 1 owld chest, 1 joynt stole and in the chimney 1 cole great £1.
The lining at £1 10*s.*
Wearing aparell £1 10*s.*
Lumber in the garett 5*s.*

In the Ciching

1 furnest and grat £1.
1 still 5*s.*
9 pewter platers 18*s.*
7 pleats and too pewter poringers 4*s.* 6*d.*
Trenchers and glasbotels and earthenwear 2*s.* 6*d.*
The bras £1 10*s.*
2 cubbards, 1 chair, 1 tabelbord, 1 trencher rack 6*s.*

In the Seler

Thre barils, 1 stand and brewin vesel £1.
Thre jorn bars, 1 grinstone and all the worcking tools £1.
100 duzen of hurdels and stacks £10.
Du upon the book £15.

Ann acount what the teniments brings in yearly, taxes and repaiers and quit rents deducted

In the Marsh, 2 teniments dureing the life of his widow brings in 2 pounds a year £8.
In New Land Stret, 2 teniments dureing the life of his sun Frances brings in 2 pounds a year £16.
In Blowhorne Stret, 4 teniments dureing the life of his sun Frances and daughter Sarah Bailey brings in 2 pounds 10 shillings a year £20.

Total £110 5*s.* 6*d.*

Jonathan Austine and Joseph Hockly, appraisors.

Buried St. Mary 8 May 1713, 'senior'.
Bond 8 October 1713, administration to Susannah Hurlbutt, intestate's widow.

397 RICHARD EDNEY

gentleman 15 November 1713 P1/E/165

Wearing apparell £10.
In money and plate £28.

In the Hall

Two tableboards, settles, stools and other goods £3.

In the Chamber over the Hall

One bed and furniture thereto belonging, one table board, one chest of drawers, chairs and looking glass with other goods £7.

In the Chamber over the Shop

One bed and bedstead and furniture thereto belonging, one table board, boxes and other lumber, chest of drawers and several other things £4.

In the Garret over the Shop

One bed, bedstead and furniture thereto belonging, one table board, boxes and other lumber £2 15*s.*

In the Passage Garret

One press and other goods £1 5*s.*

In the Garret over the Best Chamber

Two bedsteads, 2 beds, curtains and other goods £2 15*s.*
Shop goods in the shop and garrett £66.
About 15 quarters of malt £18.
Laths, sneaths for sythes, rakes and prong stales £5.
Two grinding stones £1.

In the Backside
Wood and coals £6.

In the Cellar
Barrells, beer, two furnaces with other utensills for brewing £10.
One brown mare £4 10*s.*
Sheets, knapkins and other linen £5.
In brass and pewter £8.
The barley that grew upon 4 acres of land, now at St Margarets[1] £7.
One malt mill, skreen and shovells £2.
Page total £191 5*s.*

Debts standing on the book supposed to be good £137 9*s.*
[Bad or desperate debts £9 18*s. added*]
Lumber about the house £1.
Page total £138 9*s.* [*recte with added item* £148 7*s.*]
Brought from the other side £191 5*s.*

Total £329 14*s.*[*recte with added item* £339 12*s.*]

Roger Williams and Edward Garlick, appraisers.

Buried St. Mary 15 November 1713, 'Mr'.
Will 7 September 1713; probate 8 June 1714 to Sarah Edney, testator's widow.

1. A suburb of Marlborough, within the parish of Preshute.

398 EDWARD BELL senior
gentleman[1] 'on or about' 9 July 1714
P1/B/805

His wearing apparell £10.
In money and bills £52 8*s.* 9*d.*
In plate viz one tankerd, one poringer, one pepper box and five spoons £11 10*s.*

In the Brewhouse
1 copper, 1 boyler £4
4 brass pans £2
2 kettle potts and one brass cover, 3 kettles, 1 bell mettle pott, 1 bellmettle posnett, 2 brass skillets, 1 saucepan, 1 brass frying pan, 1 skummer, 2 brass ladles, 1 basting ladle, 1 lead cisterne £2.
1 marsh vate, 1 large wash tubb, 2 smaller tubbs, 1 long kiver, 2 kivers, 2 tubbs and 1 buckett £1 10*s.*
1 lade paile, 2 pasty plates, 2 fire bucketts, formes and other lumber 10*s.*
2 chamber pewter potts 2*s.*

In the Pantry
7 pewter dishes, 1 cheese plate, 1 py plate, 13 other plates, one old flagon, 2 wine measures, 1 brass morter, 1 iron dripping pan, 1 tea kettle, 1 search, 2 table boards, 1 safe, 1 dozen ½ of patty pans, 1 wood cheese plate, 3 earthen pans, 2 earthen potts, 1 joyn stool £2., 1 brass morter, 1 iron dripping pan, 1 tea kettle, 1 search, 2 table boards, 1 safe, 1 dozen ½ of patty pans, 1 wood cheese plate, 3 earthen pans, 2 earthen potts, 1 joyn stool £2.

In the Kitchen
1 jack, 5 spitts, 1 basting ladle, 2 pewter stands, 2 chopping knives, 4 brass candlesticks, 2 hand ditto, 1 cleaver, 1 brass morter and pestle, 1 plate chafing dish, 2 box iron grates, 1 brass flower and pepper box, 1 slip up candlestick, 1 tin flower and candlebox, 1 pair of doggs, firepan and tonges, 2 hangells, fender, iron barr, 4 iron scures, 1 pair of snuffers, 1 pair of bellows, 1 cheese toaster, 1 chaffing dish, 1 box iron, 4 other irons, 2 gridirons £2 4*s.*
1 dozen and ten plates and 13 dishes £3 6*s.*
2 warming pans 12*s.*
1 bacon rack, 2 rack andirons, 1 pewter baker and salt seller 6*s.*
1 settle, 2 table boards, 3 joyn stooles, 3 chairs, 2 window curtains and rod, the

covering belonging to the squabb, ½ dozen of knives and forkes £1 5s.

In the Little Parlour

1 pair of doggs, 1 pair of firepan and tonges, 1 pair of bellows, 1 brush, 2 [hand *added*] skreens, 1 dutch table and [some *added*] cheyney, 2 ovall table boards, 9 cane chaires, 1 armed ditto [and squab *added*] and 3 small pictures, [squabb *deleted*] window curtains and rodds £5 5s.

Glasses, earthen plates and [other implements *added*] 5s.

Column total £99 3s. 9d.

In the Great Parlour

2 pair of doggs, fire shovell and tongs, 12 leather chaires, 2 table boards and 3 pictures £2 4s.

In the Passage

1 clock [old *added*] and case £1 10s.

In the Great Parlour Chamber

1 pair of iron doggs, 1 pair of brass andirons, 1 brass fender, 1 pair of brass tonges and firepan, chimney hooks, one pair of bellows 15s.

6 chaires covered with serge 18s.

1 table board glass and stands £1 5s.

3 family pictures, 3 pair of window curtains and rodds 15s.

In the Little Parlour Chamber

One white fustian bed lined with callaco, one feather bed and boulster, 2 blanketts and white rug £7 10s.

[2 overwritten] 1 pair of chest of drawers, dressing box and 2 glasses, 1 table board, 1 pair of doggs, 3 black rush chaires, 1 easy chair, 1 close stool and pan, 2 pair of window curtains £4 15s.

In the Chamber over the Kitchen

1 serge bed lined with [white *added*] callaco, feather bed and bolster, 3 blanketts and green rugg £5.10s.

1 press bed with flock bed, 2 bolsters and one pillow, 4 feather pillows and one blankett £2.

1 chest and trunk, 1 black chaire 10s.

1 bed pan 3s.

1 grate 1s. 6d.

2 glass shelves 3s.

1 press for cloaths £1.

On the Stairs head

1 press for cloaths 10s.

In the Little Chamber

One truckle bedstead, one feather bed and boulster, 1 pair of blanketts and rugg £2 5s.

1 trunk, 1 wooden chair, 1 close stool box and pann, 1 curtaine, 1 box window [and *added*] curtains 10s.

In the Garrett over the Great Parlour

1 bedstead, feather bed, 1 blankett, 1 rugg, bolstor and 1 pillow £3.

1 truckle bedstead, 1 flock bed and bolster, 1 pillow, pair of blanketts and rugg £1 17s. 6d.

1 press for cloaths 8s.

1 table, 1 chest, 1 trunk and 1 box 15s.

In the Garrett over the Kitchen

1 truckle bedstead, flockbed and 2 flock boulsters, 2 feather pillows, [2 *overwritten*] 1 pair of blanketts, 2 coverlids £1 10s.

1 coale grate 12s.

1 chest, 1 churne, 1 skreen and some other lumber 10s.

Column total £40 17s.

In the Outward Cellar

1 kive, 4 [half *added*] hogsheads and 1 barrell, some glass, 2 iron racks, 2 horses £1 10s.

In the Inward Cellar

1 table board and 4 horses, 3 [half *added*]

hogsheads, bottle rack, powdering tubb and 2 little drappers £1 4*s.*
About 5 dozen of bottles 7*s.* 6*d.*

In Linnen
2 pair [and half *added*] of course sheets 18*s.*
2 pair [and half *added*] of sheets 14*s.*
3 pair of sheets £1.
1 pair of flaxen [sheets *implied*] 15*s.*
1 pair of new sheets 12*s.*
3 odd sheets £1.
1 large holland sheet 15*s.*
5 holland pillows bears 10*s.*
1 diaper table cloath and 10 napkins 10*s.*
2 diaper table cloaths and 3 napkins 6*s.*
5 table cloaths 5*s.*
2 towells 1*s.* 6*d.*

In the Woolloft over the Brewhouse
Wool £32.

In the Woolhouse
Wool £37 10*s.*
Beem, skales, weights and cords 10*s.*
One bushell, basketts and other lumber 3*s.*
Lumbs wooll and locks £1 2*s.* 8*d.*
3 rolls of parchment £3 15*s.*
7 packcloths £1.

In the Workhouse
10 dozen of frames £5.
11 pound of parchment 18*s.* 4*d.*
One little furnace and grate £1.
16 dozen of pelts £2 9*s.*
2 ladders, 1 wheelbarrow 12*s.*

Over the Workhouse
Short wool £4.
Skrowls of parchment £1.

In the Stable
1 bin, 3 old saddles 10*s.*

In the Backside
Wood and cole £7 10*s.*
Hey £8.
1 bay mare £4.

At the River
2 dozen short skins 8*s.*
Course cloath in the house £5.
Wool in the garrett £7.
[Waring apparell £10 *deleted*]
Books £2.
Settle in the garden 10*s.*
[*The next five lines and total added*]
In good debts and a small parcell of wooll £73 8*s.*
Due for rent and a chattell lease about £29.
Bad debts £26 4*s.*

Total £378 14*s.* 9*d.* [*recte with bad debts* £404 18s 9*d.*]

Thomas Bartlett and Nicholas Church, appraisors

Buried St. Peter 22 June 1714.
Will 29 September 1712; probate 13 July 1714 to Edward Bell, testator's son.

1. Parchment maker's goods in inventory.

399 JOHN JONES
tailor 11 October 1714 P1/IJ/152

His wearing apparell £1 10*s.*

In the Chamber over the Kitching
A cubbord, a table, a chest, 4 chaiers and 2 boxes 10*s.*
A bedsteed, mat and cord, curtins, vallens, 2 pillows and a boulster, allso a rug and a paire of blancots £1 4*s.*

In the Chamber over the Shoop
A feather beed, 2 rugs, a paire of blancots, a flock boulster, a bedsteed, curtins and vallens £1 10*s.*
A flock beed 3*s.*

A chest, 2 coffers, a cubberd and a box 8*s.*
A flascot, 6 paire of sheets and table lining £1 9*s.*

In the Kitching
8 pewter dishes, a flaggon and a tanket 12*s.*
4 potts, 2 kittels, 2 skillets, a warming pan and other small things £1 7*s.*
A table, 5 joyne stooles and 5 chaiers 6*s.*
A jack, 2 spitts, a driping pan, a pare of billess, andjrons and tongs and other small things 7*s.* 6*d.*

In the Shoop
A shoop belk and 2 geese 5*s.*

In the Seller
4 barrells, 2 horses, brewing vessell and other small things 12*s.*
A bucket and some wood 10*s.*
Money in the house eight pounds £8.
Debts two and twenty pounds £22.

Total £40 13*s.* 6*d.*

John Gillmore and Thomas Gillmore, appraisors.

Buried St. Mary 10 October 1714, 'clerk of the parish 30 yrs'.
Will 29 September 1714; probate 12 October 1714 to Elizabeth Jones, testator's daughter.

400 WILLIAM COSTER[1]
weaver [will] 28 March 1715 P1/C/560

Three coffers and one chest 8*s.*
One feather bedd, flock bedd and bedding £3.
Good debts upon bond and mortgage £40.
Bad debts on bond and bills £40.
Money in hand £200.
His wearing apparell, linnen and woollen £5.
Other linnen and woollen £5.
A bond for thirty pounds on Mr William Lawrence of Swindon, draper, given in the will of the testator unto his sister Jane and her daughter, Jane Banister £30.

[*Total omitted, by addition* £323 8*s.*]

John Bell and Richard Morris, appraisors.

Burial not recorded [St. Mary register not extant].
Will 2 November 1714; probate 3 June 1715 to executor [John Coster, testator's brother].

1. Will 'of Swindon', endorsed 'Marlbrough Ste. Marie'; inventory 'of Marlbrough'.

401 JANE SPACKMAN
widow 1 April 1715 P1/S/776

Her wearing apparell and 6 gold rings £4 9*s.*

Money in House
Ten guineas and an half £11 5*s.* 9*d.*
Two broad peices and an half at 23*s.* 6*d.* per peice £2 18*s.* 9*d.*
In silver £1 6*s.* 10*d.*
3 silver cups, 6 spoons and 3 pair of buttons £5 16*s.*

In the Garret
2 flockbeds, bedsteads and bolsters with the coverlids and blanketts £2.
Two coffers and two old boxes 3*s.*

In the Chamber
Two feather beds, 4 blanketts, one coverlid, one bedstead and curtains with two feather pillows and old lumber £5.
One chest of drawers 10*s.*

One old press *2s. 6d.*
Two old trunks and two old boxes *5s.*
Three chairs and two stools *5s.*
One pair of andirons with a firepan and tongs *3s.*
3 sheets, 2 pillowbeers and five napkins with other linnen *10s.*
Books *10s.*

In the Kitchen
One dresser, one cupboard and 5 old chairs *10s.*
8 pewter dishes, 3 plates, one platter, one poringer, 2 salts, 2 saucers, 2 pewter basons and 5 spoons *£1 10s.*
8 candlesticks, 2 spitts, two pair of dogs, one pair of tongs, one fire shovell and other lumber *10s.*
One warming pan, one frying pan, one large kettle, one small kettle, 2 bellmettle potts, 3 skilletts and one small boyler *£2.*

In the Kichen
Five pair of old sheets, one dozen of napkins *£1 10s.*
6 table cloaths *12s.*
4 barrells, 6 kivers, 3 tubbs and other lumber *£1.*
One iron grate *5s.*

Money lent out on Bill or
To Henry Turner *£5.*
To John Spackman *£5.*
More to John Spackman *£2 10s. 6d.*

Total £55 11s. 10d.

Joseph Barnard and Thomas Hancock, appraisors.

Buried St. Mary 26 December 1714.
Bond 25 May 1715, administration to Mary Tetbury, widow of Newbury, Berks, intestate's sister.

402 ROBERT BAYLY[1]
24 May 1715 P1/B/811

A bead and four small chairs and curtens *£1 5s.*
One trunk and coufer and small lumber *5s.*
One pare of dogs and fire pan and tongs *1s.*
Wearing cloths *10s.*
One old teabbel bord and bedsted *2s.*
Gras [?*recte* brass] *£1 10s.*
Five peuter small deshes and 4 pleats *5s.*
A warming pan and skemer and som small things *2s.*
A tabel bord and jack and a stool *4s.*
Five small old chairs, to pots and 3 letel barels *10s.*
To letel platers and trenchers and small things *2s.*
Mony in the house *£2 3s.*
Goody Strach a bad dept *£1 6s.*
Goodman Browne of Ruckly bad dept *15s.*
Mr Bell *2s.*

Total £9 2s.

Thomas Clark and William Glide, appraisors.

Burial not recorded [St. Mary register not extant].
Bond 3 Jun 1715, administration to Elizabeth Bayly, intestate's widow.

1. 'late of Marlborough St. Mary' [bond].

403. [Mary][1] BLACKMAN[2]
widow [*undated*, c.1715] P1/B/809

For the house and garden *£6.*
For bed and beding *12s.*
For brass *12s.*
Three cuberds and other lumber *2s.*

Total £7. 6s.

John Blissett and John Harris, appraisors

Burial not recorded [St. Mary register not extant]

Bond 3 June 1715, administration to Thomas Blackman, hellier, intestate's son.

1. Forename from bond.

2. 'in the Parrish of St. Marys'.

404 BENJAMIN NEW[1]

fellmonger [will] [*undated*, c. 1715] P1/N/146

Three bedstids and two beds and beding £1 10s.
One chest, two cofors, to boxes 5s.
His waring [cloath *altered to*] closes £1.
Brass and puter £1.
Two barrils, one tubb and civer 6s.
One furniss and grate £1 5s.
Eighty foure harrows and 4 knives £3 10s.
One hundred and fifty pelts £2 10s.
Five rowles of parchment 5s.
One horse £1.
One jack and spit and coberd 7s. 6d.
One table borde and three chairs 5s.
One long forme 6d.
Two tressells 1s.

Total £18.

Thomas Blackmore and William Simence, appraisors.

Burial not recorded [St. Mary register not extant].

Will [*undated*]; probate 3 June 1715 to executrix [testator's widow, unnamed in will].

1. 'of Marlborough in the Parrish of St. Mareys'.

405 JOHN TETCOMBE

cordwainer 3 June 1715 P1/T/294

One dwelling house that he dyed in £11.
One dwelling house late in the tenure of Thomas Clark (deceased) £6.
One table board 2s.
One cupboard 1s. 6d.

Total £17 3s. 6d.

Richard Martene and Walter Whitehart, appraisors.

Burial not recorded [St. Mary register not extant].

Bond 3 June 1715, administration to Thomas Coleman, carrier of Marlborough, principal creditor.

406 HENRY STENT[1]

4 July 1715 P1/S/780

In the Garrat

4 lether chaiers, a tabell bord and 2 joynt stoles and carpett 5s.

In the Parlor Chamber

Bead and bedsted and boustor and pellow and the hannings of the roome and cortins and valins £4.
A chest of drawes, a close stole, a lettell stoole and chair 8s.
2 pare of angiorns, fier pann and tongues 4s.
2 worken chairs, 2 joynt stoole, a looking glass 4s.
A tabell bord, a leather chaier, a trunk and frame 8s.
A pare of white curtins and 2 curtin rods 3s. 6d.
For waring aparill £1 10s.

In the Parler

5 leather chaiers, 2 tabellboards, 2 joynt stoles 9s.

4 peuter platers, 8 peuter plates and a puter basson 14*s.*
3 brass potts, a lettell brass ketell and a scllott, chafdish, a saucepan and warem pann £1.
A jack, 1 pare of angiorns and 1 pare of dogs, fierpann and tongue, 2 lettell spetts, 2 jorn chandesticks and chopp knife 6*s.*
Other lumber goods 1*s.* 6*d.*

In the Siller
2 barrills, 2 horses, 2 kivers, one mashing vate, 1 bucking tub, 5 lettell tubs, 1 buckcott, 1 fier buckcott 12*s.*
Part in the furness and other lumber goods £1 2*s.*

Total £11 7*s.*

Jonathan Austine and John Coster, appraisors.

Burial not recorded [St. Mary register not extant].
Bond 13 October 1715, administration to Mary Stent, intestate's daughter.

1. 'Mr.'

407 THOMAS KEATS

maltster 12 March 1715/6 P1/K/152

Wearing close and money in pockett £38.

In the Ciching
1 tabell, 3 joyntstools 6*s.*
6 chaiers 4*s.*
1 jack, 1 spit, 3 fiar pans, 3 tongs, 2 paier of andears and dogs 12*s.*
1 chefingdish, 1 frieingpan, 1 warming pan 3*s.*
2 small brass candell sticks, 2 ladels 1*s.* 6*d.*
Utensils in the ciching 1*s.* 6*d.*

In the Buttery
1 boyler, 1 brass pan, 2 scillets, 1 pott, 1 scimer, 2 cittels £1 10*s.*
12 pewter dishes, 10 pleats, 6 poringars and spoons £1 5*s.*

In the Ciching Chamber
1 fether bed, beding, curtins and vallings and 1 flockbed, beding and bed stids £3.
1 tabell, 1 chest, 2 trunks, 3 boxes, 1 cubard 12*s.*
4 chaiers, 1 glasshilf, 2 lookingglasses 3*s.* 6*d.*
The lining £2.

In the Littell Chamber
1 bed and beding and bedstid £1 5*s.*

In the Shop
4 bushils of wheate £1 1*s.*
4 bushels of pease 16*s.*
Utensils theare 6*s.*

In the Brewhouse
1 furness dore and frame and greate £1.
9 civers and tubs, 4 barrills, 1 vate £1.
1 bushel, 1 peck, 1 gallion and shovels 5*s.*
3 hundred ciching fagets and 6 hundred penney and od wood £5 10*s.*

In the Gardners
25 quarters of malt £28.
12 quarters of barly £9 12*s.*
The 2 tenniments at 50*s.* a year for 2 lives £20.
1 cow and haye £3 5*s.*
Depts good and bad £62 11*s.* 6*d.*

Total £182 10*s.*

Joseph Hockley, William Ruff and Joseph Cosham, appraisors.

Burial not recorded [St. Mary register not extant].
Bond 19 April 1716, administration to Sarah Keats, intestate's widow.

408 ABIGELL PAGGE[1]
widow [will] 6 April 1716 P1/P/532

Hur wearing aprell 5*s.*
One feather beed £1.
Tow feather boulsters 4*s.*
Tow feather pillows 2*s.*
Tow ruggs and blankatts 12*s.*
Tow sheets 1*s.*
One coffer 2*s.*
One beedsteed 5*s.*
Tow peutter dishis 2*s.*
Tow poots and tow skilatts 5*s.*
One chest 3*s.*
One kneadintrowe 2*s.*
Tow keefers and one tube 2*s.*
One halfe bushell and one boox 1*s.*
Skealls and beems 2*s.*
Som old lumber 1*s.*

Total £3 9*s.*

James Butt and Henry Bloxham, appraisors.

Burial not recorded [St. Mary register not extant].
Will 27 December 1710; probate 19 April 1716 to Ann Gately, testator's daughter.

1. 'Page' on will.

409 BENJAMIN BASSETT[1]
victualler 9 April 1716 P1/B/814

The goods in the kitchen 15*s.*
Wearing apparell and money in pockett £1 5*s.*

In the Chamber over the Kitchen
Two beds and bed steads and other things £2.

In the Chamber over the Cellar
4 beds 10*s.*

In the Back Chamber
1 bed and bedstead etc. 10*s.*

In the Back room below stairs
1 bed etc. £1.

In the Brew House
[1 furnace *added*] £1.
Brewing vessell and other lumber £1.

In the Pig Stye
2 pigs £1.

In the Buttery
The brass and pewter £1.

In the Cellar
The bear and vessells £1. 15*s.*

Total £12 5*s.*

[*In another hand*] The house given in the will did not belong to the deceased to dispose of.

Thomas Edney and John Morris, appraisors.

Buried St. Peter 27 March 1716.
Will 12 May 1708; probate 19 April 1716 to Martha Bassett, testator's widow.

1. 'late of the Parish of St Peter in the Town of Marlborough'.

410 LEONARD LEACH[1]
tailor 7 July 1716 P1/L/281[2]

One dwelling-house and garden in Ramsbury in Wiltes to which the said intestate was intitled for the residue of a certaine terme of yeares to come not yett expired £14 10*s.*[3]

James Simpkins and Jacob Savarey, appraisors.

Robert Ellet, witness.

Burial not recorded, see note 1.

Bond 7 July 1716, administration to Joseph Leach of Ramsbury, intestate's brother.

1. 'sometime of Marlbrough ... who dyed Intestate about three Yeares since in the Kingdom of Portugall ...'.
2. There are two almost identical copies of this inventory, the second omitting the signatures.
3. Roman numerals.

411 SIMON HAMLEN

26 April 1717 P1/H/737

Waring aparell and mony in purs £12.
For wood £7.
2 beds and 2 bedsteds and all the bed clos and pillos and boulsters £6.
In the same chamber to tabel bordes, one chest of drars and three chaires and a fier pan and tongs and a pare of dogs £1.
6 shetts and all other linen £2.
40 quarters of vots £26 2*s.* 6*d.*
260 quarters of malt £260.
5 quarters of barly £3.
The boock depts £120.
5 barels 12*s.* 6*d.*
1 pot, 1 skilet and a litel kitel 12*s.* 6*d.*
6 puter platers and 1 dozen of puter plats £2.
4 kifers, 1 mashing tub and all other bruing versel £1 10*s.*

In the Kichen
A tabell bord and a jack and 3 chaires 10*s.*

Total £442 7*s.* 6*d.*

William Dance and Joseph Lewis, appraisors.

Buried St. Peter 13 March 1716/7 'Hamlin'.

Bond 30 April 1717, administration to Elizabeth Hamlen, intestate's widow.

412 THOMAS BLANDY

maltster 19 September 1717 P1/B/841

Wearing apparrell and mony in his purse £20.

In the Parlour
A table board, six leather chairs, a cupboard, glass shelf and the furniture of the chimney £1 10*s.*

In the Kitchin
Two tables, 4 chairs and 4 joined stools 15*s.*
The furniture of the chimney 10*s.*
Eleven pewter dishes, 28 pewter plates, 3 tin pans, 1 tin cover, 2 spitts and other utensells £2 10*s.*

In the Buttery
Three bell-brass pots, 2 warming pans, 2 skilletts, 3 brass kettles, 2 chafing dishes, 2 brass skimmers, a frying pan and a box of knives £2 6*s.* 8*d.*

In the Brewhouse
A furnace and brewing vessell £4 10*s.*

In the Cellar
Eleven barrells and a kive £2 10*s.*

In the Parlour Chamber
A bed with its furniture, chest of drawers, a cabinet, side table, 7 cane chairs and the furniture of the chimney £10.

In the Kitchin Chamber
Books £2 10*s.*
A bed with its furniture, a deal chest, a chest of drawers, a side board, a table, 6 cane chairs, 3 other chairs and other small things £12.
In plate: a tankard, 12 spoons, a cup and 2

salts, all silver £10.
A suit of fustain curtains, sheets and table linnen £10.

In the Inner Garret
Nine boxes, a trunk and other lumber £1.

In the midle Garret
A chest, stools, chair and other lumber 10*s.*

In the outer Garret
A bed, a box, a press and chairs £2 10*s.*

In the Malthouse
A malt screen and other lumber £1 2*s.* 4*d.*
Wood and coals and other lumber £6.
Page total £90 3*s.* 2*d.*

A lease for the house he dwelt in, for 99 years determinable on 3 lives, 2 of the lives living £80.
A lease of land at Grafton for 99 years determinable on 3 lives, one life living £35.
Desperate debts £100.
Mony due on security £625.

Total £930 3*s.* 2*d.*

Richard Webb and Joseph Barnard, appraisors.

Burial not recorded [St. Mary register not extant].
Will 22 June 1713; probate 18 October 1717 to Elizabeth Blandy, testator's widow; inventory exhibited 10 April 1718.

413 STEPHEN PERRY
collarmaker 24 March 1717/8

P1/P/552

His wearing apparel £7.

In the Best Chamber
Two beds, one bolster, two pillows £2.
And one rug and three blankets 10*s.*
And four pair of sheets £2.
One bedstead 6*s.*
Two table clothes and fifteen napkins 12*s.* 6*d.*
One chest, one box and close stoolbox 12*s.*
One warming pan, fire pan and tongs and a pair of bellows and dogs 7*s.*
One chair and four small pictures 2*s.*
Three Bibles and two other old books 6*s.*
The window curtains and rod 2*s.* 6*d.*

In the Man's Room
One bed and bedstead, bolster and pillow and rug and two blankets 15*s.*
Two boxes 4*s.*

In the Garret
One bed and bedstead, bolster, pillow and rug and two blankets 15*s.*
And two sheets 7*s.* 6*d.*

In the Kitchen
One table, one form, two joynt stools, one settle 15*s.*
One side of bacon 15*s.*
Four chairs and a bacon rack 2*s.*
A jack and weight and spitt 10*s.*
A box iron and clamps and two candle sticks 6*s.*
One pair of bellows 3*s.*
One pair of andirons, one pair of dogs and fender, fire pan and tongs, chaffing dish and greediron and one pair of hangels 15*s.*

In the Buttery
Four pewter dishes, one dozen of pewter plates 12*s.* 6*d.*
Two brass stew pans with covers, one skillet, one frying pan and one sauce pan 12*s.*
Three brass potts, three brass ladles and a skimmer 15*s.*

One trencher rack and two dozen of trenchers 2*s.* 6*d.*
Three barrels and a tun bowl 15*s.*

In the Brewhouse
A furnace, two brass pans and two kettles £6.
Four tubbs, two kivers and a barrell horse £1 5*s.*
Three milk bucketts 3*s.*
One hundred of faggots 15*s.*

Shop Goods
Two dozen and one saddle trees 8*s.* 4*d.*
Four dozen and half of hames 18*s.*
Five horse collars and three pads 12*s.*
Fourteen bed cords 14*s.*
Ropes 8*s.*
Seven rands of thread 7*s.*
Flocks £1 10*s.*
Three boxes 2*s.*
Working tools 5*s.*
Horse skin leather 12*s.*
Two horse hides at Brookers[1] dressing 12*s.*
One hide and half of bull leather 15*s.*
Fourteen pair of pipes for horse harness £1 8*s.*
Half a dozen of belly bands, five cords and some fringe 5*s.*
Four bundles of whipcord 4*s.* 6*d.*
Other lumber 3*s.*
A cow and a calf £3 5*s.*
Hay 8*s.* 6*d.*
Nine hides now dressing £2 5*s.*
Book debts £30.

[*Total omitted, by addition* £75 7*s.* 10*d.*]

Robert Alexander and John Batt, appraisers.

Buried St. Peter 14 March 1717/8.
Inventory exhibited 13 September 1718, bond 17 September 1718, administration to Jeffery Perry, intestate's brother.

1. Brooker was presumably a leather dresser.

414 SARAH EDNEY[1]
widow 31 March 1718 P1/E/176

Her wearing apparrell £10.
5 sheets £1 5*s.*
3 pair of pillow cases 7*s.*
One blanket 8*s.*
Two sawce pans 4*s.*
One coffeepot 1*s.* 3*d.*
One chamberpot 2*s.*
One server, pewter 3*s.*
Half a dozen of earthen plates 1*s.*
One case knife and five forks 2*s.* 6*d.*
Two chairs 3*s.*
One copper pots 1*s.* 2*d.*
One chaffing dish 1*s.*
Malt in the house £65.
The dwelling house and shop in Kingsbury Street £80.
Good debts £55 0*s.* 5*d.*
[Bad or desperate debts £2 5*s.* 8*d. added*]

Total £212 19*s.* 4*d.* [*recte including added item* £215 5*s.*]

Thomas Clark and John Bridgman, appraisers.

Burial not recorded [St. Mary register not extant].
Will 27 February 1717/8; probate 23 April 1718 to Sarah Newby, testator's granddaughter.

1. 'relict of Richard Edney late of Marlebrough'.

415 JANE SLOPER
widow [will] [*undated* c.1718] P1/S/809

Total £16 9*s.*

Joseph Hockley and Henery Turner, appraisors.

Burial not recorded [St. Mary register not

extant].
Will 29 December 1714; probate 21 May 1718 to Elizabeth Rathband.

416 JOHN TOMBLYNS[1]

21 *May* 1718 P1/T/301

In the Kitching Chamber
One feather bed, 5 small pillows and 3 bolsters £2 5*s*.
1 old flock bed 7*s*. 6*d*.
1 old bedstead, curtains and rods £1 10*s*.
3 blanketts and rugg 14*s*.
6 black chairs 6*s*.
1 table board 2*s*.
1 chest of drawers and glass £2.
1 close stool box 2*s*.
4 pair of canvas sheets £1.
1 sheet of holland 10*s*.
2 diaper table cloths 8*s*.
1 dossen and half of napkins 9*s*.
1 dossen of napkins 4*s*.
Other linning 12*s*.
2 old boxes and trunk 3*s*.

In the Outward Garrett
1 cole grate 10*s*.
1 truckle bedstead 2*s*.
1 old chest 2*s*.

In the Other Garrett
1 old bed, bowlster and pillows 15*s*.
1 feather bed, bolster, rugg, 2 blanketts and bedstead £1 10*s*.

In the Kitching
6 old chairs 4*s*. 6*d*.
3 small chairs, 2 table boards 5*s*.
1 jack, frying pan, doggs and tonges, gridiron and other things £1 10*s*.
65 lbs. of pewter at 7*d*. £1 17*s*. 11*d*.
56 lbs. of old brass potts £1 12*s*. 8*d*.
3 steel plates 1*s*.
Cole 6*s*.
3 barrells, 2 tubbs 7*s*. 6*d*.
Some lumber in the celler 6*s*. 6*d*.

In the Pantry
Earthenware and lumber 5*s*.
Column total £20 7*s*. 7*d*.

In the Wood House
Some wood and lumber 14*s*.
Wearing apparell and money £1 10*s*.
In good and bad debts £3.
For leather whipps and other sadlery ware £3 10*s*.
Column total £8 14*s*.
On the other side £20 7*s*. 7*d*.

Total £29 1*s*. 7*d*.

Nicholas Church, John Fowler and John Kemm, appraisors.

Buried St. Peter 11 May 1718 'John Tomlins'.
Bond 21 May 1718, administration to Edward Sawyer, principal creditor.[2]

1. 'of Saint Peters in Marlbrough'.
2. Note on inventory, 'Joanna, relict, renunciat'.

417 JOHN FURNELL

cheesefactor 25 October 1718 P1/F/266

3 tenements in Silverles Street being a leasehold during the lifes of his 3 sons Abraham, Isaac and Jacob Furnell £40.
The testators wearing apparrell £1 4*s*.
One flock bed, 6 bolsters, 1 flock pillow and 2 feather pillows £1.
Two ruggs, one coverlid, 3 blankets, 4 curtains and vallings, 2 bedsteads 18*s*.
One old chest, 2 tableboards, 1 old fream for a table, 1 bucket, 4 old stooles 10*s*. 10*d*.
Six old chairs, 2 pictures, a pair of old bellows and a fire pan and tongs 5*s*. 8*d*.
Two boxes, one desk, 2 old horse locks and loggets, 3 cupboards and hencoops 8*s*. 6*d*.

One rack, 2 barrells, 1 old bushell, 1 gallon measure, 2 tubbs and some old timber 11s. 6*d.*
One spade and some old iron, 4 small weights, one iron back for a chimney 7*s.* 8*d.*
Three saddles and 2 bridles and stirrups, hay prongs and rakes and a watch bill 7*s.* 6*d.*
Some old sacks 2*s.*
Some books 12*s.*
One warming pan, one brass pott, one skillet, one sauce pan, one stew pan 10*s.*
One pewter flaggon, 1 pint, 1 half pint, 1 plate, 1 pewter chamber pot, 1 pewter scale 3*s.*
One beam, one ladle, one brass scale 2*s.* 6*d.*
One horse £1 10*s.*
Five dozen off calf reads 15*s.*
Debts due to him wich its hoped are good £4 17*s.* 6*d.*
One debt on bond supposed too bee lost £18.

Total £72 5*s.* 8*d.*

Walter Whitehart and William Page, appraisors.

Buried St. Peter 24 October 1718.
Will 8 October 1718; bond 29 October 1718, administration to Jacob Furnell of St. Martin in the Fields and Isaac Furnell of Marlborough, testator's sons, no executor being named.

417A. RUTH SMITH
[*undated*, c.1719] P1/S/1520

Wearing apparil and money in purse £9.
A fether bed, bolster and pillow and bed steed £2.
3 sheets, 2 bolster ceases, 3 pillow ceases and other linin 14*s.*
3 trunks, one box, one chest 10*s.*
Brass and pewter 10*s.*
Two cubberds and other lumber 6*s.*
Despret debts £4.
Total £17.

John Bowshier and John Jones, appraisors.

Burial not recorded [St Mary register not extant].
Will 18 August 1718; probate 23 September 1719 to [unnamed].

418 ALICE STOKES
widow 30 March 1719 P1/S/812

Her wearing apparell £10.
In cash £600.

In the Wood House
One quarter of coals 7*s.*
Fagots and other wood £4.
One stick of timber and other wood 4*s.*

In the Bakehouse
One furnace, 2 pots and 5 skillets £3.
Utensills belonging to the bakeing trade £2.
4 bushells of flower 18*s.*

In the Boulting Room
Weights, beam, scales, boulting mill, cloaths with measures and sieves £3.
4 quarters of meal and wheat £6.

In the Lofts over the Boulting-Room
One old bedstead 1*s.* 6*d.*
1 kettle, 1 brass pan, 1 table board and six dozen of bottles £1.
1 bolster, 2 pillows, 1 brass pot and other lumber £1.

In the Kitchen
2 spits, 2 dripping pans, 2 candle sticks, 1 pair of bellows, 1 fire pan, 1 pair of tonges, 6 chairs and 1 candle box 15*s.*

In the Cellar
5 barrells and brewing vessels £1 10*s*.

In the Paintry
Old pewter £1 10*s*.

In the Parlour
1 looking glass, 1 table, 6 leather chairs, 1 easy chair, 2 pair of dogs, 1 firepan and tongs and 3 picktures £5 10*s*.
1 Bible and other books £1.

In the Chamber over the Kitchen
1 table, 1 chest, 3 boxes, 1 pillow and 1 rug 10*s*.

In the Chamber over the Paintry
2 beds, curtains and valens, 3 bolsters, 2 pillows, 3 curtain rods, 1 rug, 3 blankets, 1 dressing box, 4 trunks and 1 close stool box £5 10*s*.
Page total £647 15*s*. 6*d*.

In the Chamber over the Parlour
2 beds, 2 blankets, 2 pillows, 1 cheast of drawers, 1 press, 3 chairs and 3 boxes £3 2*s*.
Linen in common use £5.
Paper 6*s*.
Houses £100.
Rent due £13.
Plate and rings £23 11*s*.
Book debts thought to be good £42.10*s*.
Desperate debts £12.
Money out at interest £1600.
Due for interest £62.
Page total £1861 9*s*.
Brought from the other side £647 15*s* 6*d*.

Total £2509 4*s*. 6*d*.

John Simmons and Jonathan Turner, appraisors.

Burial not recorded [St. Mary register not extant].

Will 18 October 1717; letter 13 March 1718/9 from Mountrich Hill, incumbent of St. Mary, refers to the 'will of a gentlewoman just died in my Parish' and the need for a quick probate as the executor needs to return to London; probate 30 March 1719 to Ephraim How, testator's brother-in-law.

419 WILLIAM HILL
butcher 22 September 1719 P1/H/753

Money in pocket 4*s*.
His wearing apparell £1.
One bed, one bolster and pillow, one rug, one blanket, one bedstead, curtains and valens £1.
Lumber in the lodging room 10*s*.

In the *K*itchen
Two table boards and one cupboard 6*s*.
3 leather chairs 4*s*. 6*d*.
Other old chairs 1*s*. 6*d*.
2 barrells and one little brass pot 6*s*.
Old iron 2*s*.
A leasehold estate in the Marsh ward in Marlebrough aforesaid, hold of the Chamber[1] there for two lives £38.
The crop of barley on two acres of ground in Portfield £6.

Total £47 14*s*.

Thomas Edney and John Brookes, appraisors.

Buried St. Peter 30 July 1719.
Bond 3 September 1719, administration to Joan Hill, intestate's widow..

1. Borough Council.

420 KATHERINE HILL
widow 28 September 1719 P1/H/752

In the Kitchin
2 brass pots, 1 skillett and other lumber 19*s.* 6*d.*

In the Little Room
1 table board, 2 chairs and other lumber 5*s.* 6*d.*

In the Cellar
One hogshead full of ale, 1 empty hogshead and barrells and other things £2.

In the Brew House
1 copper furnace and other things £4 11*s.* 8*d.*

In the Backroom
Three kevers, 1 table board and some hard wood etc 9*s.* 9*d.*

In the Bed Chamber
Two beds, bedsteads and other things £3 1*s.* 6*d.*

In the Back Chamber
Two beds etc £1 9*s.*
Wearing apparrell and two gold rings £2 9*s.*

Total £15 5*s.* 11*d.*

Joseph Westbury and Cristopher Bell, appraisors.

Burial not recorded [St. Mary register not extant].
Bond 23 September 1719, administration to Thomas Clark, Francis Gregory and Daniel Munday, Overseers of the Poor of the parish of St. Mary; inventory exhibited 14 March 1719/20.

421 FRANCIS BOWSHER
innholder [will] 9 December 1719
P1/B/853

In the Kitchen
13 great and small pewter dishes and 16 pewter plates weighing 61 lbs. and ½ £1 15*s.*
6 pewter quarts, 7 pewter pints and 2 half pints, a quarter and half quarter and a double flagon, a limbeck and a still, 6 porringers and 2 spoons and 5 chamber potts weighing 64½ lbs. £1 1s 4*d.*
2 brass panns, a boyler and kettle and a small kettle and skillett weighing 50 lbs. £1 16*s.*
Another boyler 18 lbs. ½ 11*s.*
A bell brass pott 12 lbs. 5*s.*
A chaffing dish, skimmer and basting ladle 2*s.*
3 spitts weighing 23 lbs. 5*s.* 6*d.*
A grate and fender and sliders ½ a cwt 11*s.*
2 cleavers, an iron peele, 4 steel plates, a gridiron, 1 pair of tongs and 2 pair of hangles and an andiron and fire pan 43 lbs. 7*s.* 6*d.*
A frying pan 1*s.* 6*d.*
A small cleaver 3*d.*
A choping knife and tosting iron 4*d.*
Hangels and spitt, staple and potthooks and old gridiron and 7 scures 4*s.*
2 iron dripping panns 21 lbs. 7*s.*
A jack and weights and a slideing candlestick 5*s.*
An iron mustard bowl 6[?d]
6 iron candlesticks 1*s.*
A candle box and an appleroster and a flower box and a petter box 1*s.* 6*d.*
A settle and bacon rack 8*s.*
2 cup boards and shelves 4*s.*
A table 2*s.* 6*d.*
A choping block and 2 wooden peels 1*s.*
A cupboard 2*s.*
A tin cover and pudding pan 6*d.*
A trencher racks and 4 dozen of trenchers 2*s.* 6*d.*
3 bucketts and a salt box 2*s.*
And 2 fire bucketts 2*s.*
3 quart earthen muggs and 7 pints 1*s.* 6*d.*
And 3 chaires 1*s.*

Some wainscott that belongs to the settle 2*s.*
Some old iron 38*d.* [?*recte* 38lb.] 6*s.* 4*d.*

In the Outer Cellar
A salt dish 2*s.* 6*d.*
A cheese press 1*s.*
2 or 3 old barrells and a kiver and 3 shelves 3*s.*
A cupboard 2*s.*
An oattub and form 1*s.* 6*d.*
A still bottom 2*s.* 6*d.*
4 old barrells and an horse and an iron hoop 6*s.*
Room total 18*s.* 6*d.*

In the Buttery in the Same Cellar
A powdering tub and cheese fatts and 5 shelves and other old lumber 7*s.*
Room total 7*s.*

In the Inner Cellar
Two barrells of ale N° 2 and N° 14 each about 36 gallons £2 10*s.*
7 empty barrells £1 4*s.*
And 2 hogsheads empty 8*s.*
A tunbowl 2*s.*
1 kive 5*s.*
4 tubs and 4 pailes 6*s.*
A powdering tub and a little barrell 2*s.*
A baskett and 2 dozen and ½ of bottles 3*s.*
A ½ cwt lead weight 5*s.*
An iron beam and old scales 2*s.*
3 stands 3*s.*
A cupboard and 3 shelves 2*s.* 6*d.*
2 barrells now full when empty valued at 7*s.*
Room total £5 19*s.* 6*d.*

In the Hall
One long table and frame 5*s.*
7 joint stools 5*s.*
A small square table and frame 1*s.* 6*d.*
2 chairs and a little cupboard 2*s.* 6*d.*
A shelf and 18 peices of earthern ware 3*s.*
A looking glass 1*s.*
1 dog, 1 fender and fire pann 1*s.*
Room total 19*s.*

In the Parlor
A table and frame and 3 stools 7*s.*
A wooden chair and cushion 1*s.* 6*d.*
Curtain and rod 6*d.*
Room total 9*s.*

In the Passage
A bushel and peck and gallon and quartern 4*s.*

In the Room over the Parlor
[One feather bed *deleted*] one sheet, 2 blanketts and coverlidd 12*s.*
Bedstead, cord and matt, curtains, vallens and rodds 10*s.*
A little ovall table 2*s.* 6*d.*
1 old coverlid 1*s.*
5 chairs and a stool and 2 cushions 2*s.*
2 andirons with brass heads and 2 dogs, fire pan and tongs 4*s.*
One window curtain and rod 4*s.*

In the Chamber over the Brewhouse
One coney furr bed and feather bolster 10*s.*
1 blanket and rug and counterpane 4*s.*
A coney furr bed and feather bolster and pillow 10*s.*
Bedstead, red curtains and vallens and matt, cord and curtain rod 14*s.*
A red rug and blanket and 2 old sheets 10*s.*
3 leather chairs, one stool and 1 other chair 3*s.* 9*d.*
An ovall table 5*s.*
A square table and 4 joint stools and window curtain rod 6*s.*
2 dogs, 2 andirons with brass heads and fire pann and tongs 4*s.* 6*d.*

In the Hall Chamber
One feather bed and 2 flock bolsters £1 15*s.*

1 blanket and 2 old coverlids 4*s.*
Bedstead, curtains and vallens, rod, matts and cords 10*s.*
A truckle bedstead, feather bed and 2 flock bolsters, 2 sacks and 3 old blanketts 15*s.*
A cupboard and frame 3*s.*
A large chest 5*s.*
A trunck 2*s.* 6*d.*
A close stool and pan 5*s.*
2 little chests and a coffer 6*d.*
2 deal boxes 1*s.* 6*d.*
3 chairs and 2 cushions 2*s.*
6 diaper napkins and a table cloth 4*s.*
9 sheets, a bolster case and 4 pilloecases 18*s.*
For earthen ware 1*s.* 6*d.*
An old Bible with brass clasps 4*s.*
3 old swords, a hanging shelf and a ragged stuff window curtain and rod 1*s.*
Room total £5 18s. 6d.

In the Passage
A tubb and an old saddle and a pillion 3*s.*

In the Garret over the Hall
A flock bed and flock bolster and 2 feather pillows 10*s.*
A rug and 2 blanketts 6*s.*
Bedstead, cord, matt, curtains, vallens and rod 7*s.*
3 coffers 3*s.*
2 boxes 1*s.* 6*d.*
An old arm chair and a low chair 1*s.*
A brass warming pan 2*s.*
2 pewter tankards and a salt sellar 18*s.*
A press 5*s.*
A table and 2 joint stools 2*s.* 6*d.*
7 old staiks 2*s.* 6*d.*
Room total £2 2s.

In the Back Garrett
A flock bed and one flock bolster, 2 bedsteads, matts, cords, curtains, rods and vallens 12*s.*

In the Passage
A meal whitch 3*s.*

In the Garret over the Parlor
A bed stead, curtains, vallens and rod and other lumber 5*s.*

In the Brewhouse
A furnace doore and grate £3 18*s.*
A cooler 2*s.* 6*d.*
9 kivers and 4 tubbs 13*s.*
A mash fatt and lead pail 7*s.*
2 wash tubbs, a horse and the boards that are fix'd for a coal penn 5*s.*
Room total £5 5s. 6d.

In the Tallett
About two hundred of faggotts 18*s.*
Two store pigs £3.

[*Total omitted, by addition £41 17s. 6d.*]

Joseph Deacin and Edmund Knight, appraisers.
Edmund Taylor and Francis Bowsher, administrators.

Burial not recorded [St. Mary register not extant].
Will 23 September 1717; probate 27 February 1719/20 to John Bowsher, testator's grandson; bond 27 February 1719/20, Francis Bowsher, testator's son and Edmund Taylor, testator's son-in-law to administer during the minority of the executor, presently about 5 years of age.

422 WILLIAM STAPLER[1]

25 January 1719/20 P1/S/848

Three joynt stools, one cupboard and a table 6*s.*
The pewter 9*s.*
One jack, 2 spitts, 2 old pans and 1 steelplate 3*s.*

2 rakes and 1 [*blank*] 8*d.*
1 settle, 1 foarm and old table 1*s.*
3 chairs, 1 looking glass 6*d.*
One furnace, one warming pan 8*s.*
Two pair of tongs, 2 pair of andirons 2*s.*
One pair of hangells and working tools 5*s.*
One candlestick and lumber 7*d.*
One little brass pott, 2 iron potts, one kettle 5*s.*
Three old barrells, 3 tubbs, 2 kevers etc 4*s.* 9*d.*
One bed, one bedstead, curtains etc £1.
Two boxes, 1 coffer 1*s.* 6*d.*

In the Little Chamber
One [old *added*] bed and bedstead 5*s.*
One bullock 10*s.*
One house and garden lease hold £7 10*s.*

Total £11 12*s.*

Thomas Pearce, senior and John Stapleton, appraisors.

Burial not recorded [St. Mary register not extant].
Will 10 January 1719/20; bond 2 December 1720, administration to Anne Stapler, testator's daughter, the executor having died before obtaining probate.

1. 'of Marlborough St. Maryes'.

423 JANATHAN AUSTIN[1]
shoemaker [will] 16 June 1720
P1/A/254

His waring aparill and money in hand £1.

In the Bestt Chamber
One bead and bead stead and whatt belonge to him £1 5*s.*
One tabell bord, one cheastt of drares, five chayers, to boxes, one cofer £1.
One litell silver cup, one soltt, to spoons £1 15*s.*
Lining and other lomber 15*s.*

In the Litell Chamber
One flock bead and bead stead, one pres and other lomber 12*s.* 6*d.*

In the Low Roome
One fornes £1 5*s.*
To bras pots, fife pewter dishes, 12 plats, to bras candell sickes £1.
One warming pane, one jack, to spits, one peare of hangells, to tabell bords, fouer joyne stools, three chayers and other lomber £1.

In the Shoop
Shoos and leather nott worked and lastes and other lomber £4.

In the Butery
Three barills and other lomber 5*s.*

In the Wood House
For wood 6*s.*
The booke deopts som desperatt when receve is £3.
The leas hould £2 10*s.*

Total £19 13*s.* 6*d.*

Francis Gregory and John Wellman, appraisors.

Burial not recorded [St. Mary register not extant].
Will 23 July 1717; probate 18 June 1720 to Anne Austine, testator's widow.

1. 'Latte of Stt maryes in marlborough'; 'Jonathan Austine' on will.

424 JOHN CLARKE *alias* WARREN
9 February 1720/1 P1/C/608

Wearing apparell and money in purse £1.

In the Chamber

Two flock beds, two flock bolsters, three pillows, two coverlids, one red rug, three bedsteads, four coffers, two chests, one table board, three boxes, one cupboard, one forme, curtains and rods £2 15*s.* 6*d.*

In the Lower Room

One grubing axe, one mattock, one iron barr, two tenant saws, a prong, two hand saws, a frying pan, a hatchet, two bill hooks, two hangels, a fire shovell, one pair of tongs, an iron back, four joynd stools, two chairs, one great table board, three tubbs, two kivers, one bucket, two little forms, an old cupboard, two barrells, one tun bowle, two wood bottles and a rack £1 16*s.* 6*d.*

Thirteen pewter dishes, three flaggons, three porringers, a salt sellar, a tin pan and tunnells, two warming pans, one skimer, one brass basting ladle, one brass kettle, two brass potts, two skilletts, one bell brass pot, a pig, wood and other lumber, three sheets, one bolster case, one table cloth, one knapkin and other linnen £4 1*s.* 6*d.*

A little iron pot 1*s.*

A well bucket and rope 5*s.*

Four boitles, four wedges, two andirons, a spade, two spits, two pair of tongs with all other lumber 4*s.* 6*d.*

[*Total omitted, by addition* £10 4*s.*]

Nathaniel Hone and William Blake, appraisers.

Buried St. Peter 20 July 1720.

Will 23 April 1720; probate 16 May 1721 to executrix [Anne Clarke alias Warren, testator's widow].

425 JOHN FOWLER junior linendraper 18 September 1722

P1/F/288

57 ells of washt dowlas at 16*d.* per ell £3 16*s.*

68 ells broad ditto at 2*s.* per ell £6 16*s.*

60 yards tow tuke at 14*d.* per yard £3 10*s.*

134 yards ½ ditto flax at 16*d.* per yard £8 19*s.* 4*d.*

12 yards ¾ narrow ditto at 10½*d.* 11*s.* 1¾*d.*

139½ yards best ditto ⅞ at 19*d.* £11 0*s.* 9½*d.*

11 yards ¼ Manchester ditto at 9*d.* 8*s.* 5½*d.*.

14 yards of blue striped barras at 8*d.* per yard 9*s.* 4*d.*

32 yards ½ ditto at 9*d.* £1 4*s.* 4½*d.*

22 yards ½ ditto at 11*d.* £1 0*s.* 7½*d.*

2 whole pieces at 27*s.* per piece £2 14*s.*

4 pieces of coarse barras at 16*s.* 6*d.* per piece £3 6*s.*

59 yards of sacking at 9*d.* £2 4*s.* 3*d.*

1 piece white all cotton fustin at 20*s.* £1.

2 pieces white hessens at 23*s.* per piece £2 6*s.*

Remnants 12 ells at 9*d.* per ell 9*s.*

Two pieces brown hessens at 18*s.* per piece £1 16*s.*

74 ells in remnants at 8*d.* per ell £2 9*s.* 4*d.*

169 ells ½ of rells at 7*d.* per ell £4 18*s.* 10½*d.*

46 yards ½ white narrow cheescloth at 7½*d.* £1 9*s.* 0¾*d.*

70 yards ditto at 6*d.* per yard £1 15*s.*

24 yards ditto at 5*d.* per yard 10*s.* 4*d.*

12 yards ¾ wide cheescloth at 9*d.* per yard 9*s.* 6¾*d.*

8 ells ditto at 7*s.* 6*d.* 7*s.* 6*d.*

15 ells ½ ell wide at 17*d.* per ell £1 1*s.* 11¼*d.*

29 ells ditto at 14*d.* £1 13*s.* 10*d.*

12 ells ¼ of hessens at 9*d.* per ell 9*s.* 2¼*d.*

63 yards of coloured fustin at 16*d.* yard £4 4*s.*

2 pieces cotton ribbd at £3 10*s.* £3 10*s.*

1 piece pillow at 18*s.* 18*s.*
15 yards black ditto at 18*d.* per yard £1 2*s.* 6*d.*
36 ells ¾ of barras in remnants at 7½*d.* £1 2*s.* 1¾*d.*
2 remnants of fustin 18 yards 18*s.* 18*s.*
20 yards of sarge at 16*d.* per yard £1 6*s.* 8*d.*
25 yards of white linsey at 16*d.* per yard £1 13*s.* 4*d.*
17 yards ½ of flannell at 11*d.* 16*s.* 0½*d.*
48 yards ditto welsh at 11*d.* £2 4*s.*
68 yards bed buckram at 9*d.* £2 11*s.*
61 ells ½ of fine check at 20*d.* per ell £5 2*s.* 6*d.*
30 ells ½ ditto at 20*d.* per ell £2 10*s.* 10*d.*
1 piece flowered fustin at 23[s.] £1 3*s.*
30 yards ditto at 16*d.* striped £2
30 yards ditto at 12*d.* per yard £1 10*s.*
2 pieces ditto at 40*s.* £2.
30 yards ditto at 18*d.* per yard £2 5*s.*
15 yards ditto at 16*d.* per yard £1.
2 yards striped fustin at 30*s.* £1 10*s.*
13 yards ¼ yellow canvas at 18*d.* per yard 19*s.* 10½*d.*
2 yards ditto at 2*s.* 4*d.* per yard 5*s.* 10*d.*
52 yards ¼ striped and flowered fustin in remnants at 15*d.* per yard £3 5*s.* 3¾*d.*
29 yards blue ditty at 18*d.* per yard £2 3*s.* 6*d.*
5 yards ¾ white callico at 20*d.* per yard 9*s.* 7*d.*
2 pieces of red striped holland of 38 yards at £1 14*s.* £1 14*s.*
50 check handkerchiefs at 10*d.* piece £2 1*s.* 8*d.*
34 yards of Irish sheeting at 14*d.* per yard £1 19*s.* 8*d.*
23 yards narrow hockaback at 12*d.* per yard £1 3*s.*
20 yards ½ broad at 2*s.* per yard £2 1*s.*
8 yards narrow scarlet tuke at 2*s.* 8*d.* £1 1*s.* 4*d.*
50 yards ½ striped holland and tuke at 14*d.* £2 18*s.* 11*d.*
8 pieces of striped holland at 17*s.* per piece £6 16*s.*
30 yards ¾ pillow fustin at 12*d.* per yard £1 10*s.* 9*d.*
3 yards ½ grogram at 16*d.* 4*s.* 8*d.*
8 yards of thicksett at 15*d.* 10*s.*
38 yards of grogram at 17*d.* £2 13*s.* 10*d.*
33 yards of yardwide blue at 12*d.* £1 13*s.*
2 pieces of 11 nail lockram at £2 10*s.* £2 10*s.*
3 pieces fustin at £3 15*s.* £3 15*s.*
1 piece thicksett at £1 7*s.* £1 7*s.*
371 yards buckram at 8d yard £12 13*s.* 4*d.*
Carried over £159 18*s.* 10½*d.* [*recte* £156 19*s.* 10½*d.*]

24 yards of buckram at 8*d.* 16*s.*
1 piece coarse ditto at 5*s.* 5*s.*
16 yards of thicksett fustin at 19*s.* 19*s.*
5 yards ditto at 6*s.* 6*s.*
3 remnants of woding at 7*s.* 7*s.*
A remnant of fustin at 4*s.* 4*s.*
2 remnants of Welsh flannell at 12*s.* 12*s.*
4 yards of patterbors at 6*d.* per yard 2*s.*
42 yards ½ blue ozen at 8*d.* £1 8*s.* 4*d.*
10 ells patterbors at 6*d.* 5*s.*
3 yards coloured fustin at 3*s.* 6*d.* 3*s.* 6*d.*
70 ells ⅛ yard wide Irish at 19*d.* £5 10*s.* 6*d.*
One flowered fustin coverlid at 21*s.* £1 1*s.*
60 yards yellow canvas at 11*d.* £2 15*s.*
29 yards ¼ yard wide canvas at 13*d.* £1 10*s.* 10½*d.*
38 yards ditto at 14*d.* £2 4*s.* 4*d.*
20 yards blue linsey at 20*s.* £1.
16 yards ditto striped at 12*d.* per yard 16*s.*
12 ells of rells at 8*d.* per ell 8*s.*
2 remnants narrow dowlas at 4*s.* 4*s.*
30 ells patterbors at 6*d.* per ell 15*s.*
42 yards ½ blue ozen at 7½*d.* £1 6*s.* 6¾*d.*
A remnant of washt dowlas at 4*s.* 4*s.*
2 pieces narrow dowlas at £2 10*s.* £2 10*s.*
43 yards blue ozen at 8*d.* £1 6*s.* 8*d.*
1 piece narrow dowlas at 23*s.* £1 3*s.*
10 ells of patterbors and remnant of dowlas at 8*s.* 8*s.*
3 remnants of dowlas at 2*s.* per remnant 6*s.*

17 yards of blue ozen in remnants at 10*s*. 10*s*.
2 pieces of lockram at 28*s*. per piece £2 16*s*.
1 piece ditto at 24*s*. £1 4*s*.
16 yards narrow blue at 6*d*. yard 8*s*.
84 ells lockram at 12*d*. ell £4 4*s*.
80 ells ditto at £3 15*s*. £3 15*s*.
100 ells of rusia in remnants of all sorts at £2 8*s*. £2 8*s*.
50 ells brown sprig linsey at 10*d*. per ell £2 1*s*. 8*d*.
45 ells ditto at 8½*d*. per ell £1 11*d*. 10½*d*.
1 piece dowlas at 37*s*. £1 17*s*.
2 pieces ditto at 26*s*. per piece £2 12*s*.
28 ells ditto at 16 per ell £1 17*s*. 4*d*.
4 ells ditto at 13½ per ell 4*s*. 6*d*.
16 ells rusia diaper at 7*d*. 9*s*.4*d*.
45 ells dowlas in remnants at 12*d*. £2 5*s*.
10 ells dowlas at 21[*d*.] per ell 17*s*. 6*d*.
20 ells canvas in remnants at 20*s*. £1.
23 yards coloured linsey at 9*d*. yard 17*s*. 3*d*.
111 ells of rells at 8*d*. per ell £3 14*s*.
2 pieces of linsey at £2 12*s*. £2 12*s*.
1 piece of flannell at 30*s*. £1 10*s*.
24 yards ditto at 13½ £1 7*s*.
3 pieces canvas no. 2:3:4 144 ells at 13*d*. £7 16*s*.
1 piece 42½ ditto at 12½ per ell £2 4*s*. 3½*d*.
45 yards of yellow fine at 22 per yard £4 2*s*.6*d*.
12¼ ells French lockram at 14*d*. per ell 14*s*. 3½*d*.
26½ ells of ditto dowlas at 2*s*. per ell £2 13*s*.
28 ells ditto at 2*s*. 3*d*. per ell £3 3*s*.
53 ells ditto at 21*d*. per ell £4 12*s*. 9*d*.
35 yards of grogram fustin at 16*d*. £2 6*s*. 8*d*.
29 yards of pillow coloured at 12d per yard £1 9*s*.
24 yards of boulter at 3*d*. per yard 6*s*.
27 ditto at 7*d*. 15*s*. 9*d*.
22 ditto at 9*d*. 16*s*. 6*d*.
31 ditto at 11*d*. £1 8*s*. 5*d*.
18 ditto at 12 18*s*.
24 yards linsey at 12*d*. £1 4*s*.
A piece of patterbors at 6*s*. 6*s*.
3 pieces narrow dowlas at £4 10*s*. £4 10*s*.
52 ells ⅞ dowlas at 2*s*. per ell £5 4*s*.
29 yards of yard wide Irish at 14 yd £1 13*s*. 10*d*.
Carried over £275 3*s*. 5¼*d*. [*recte* £272 2*s*. 1¼*d*.]

48 yards ½ yard ⅛ canvas at 16*d*. £3 4*s*. 8*d*.
45 yards of blue yard wide at 13*d*. £2 8*s*. 9*d*.
A piece of patterbors at 6*s*. 6*s*.
14 ells ½ of gulix holland at 5*s*. 9*d*. £4 3*s*. 3*d*.
1 whole piece ditto 21 ells at 4*s*. 6*d*. £4 14*s*. 6*d*.
8 ells bag holland at 6*s*. 9*d*. £2 14*s*.
32 ells broad garlix at 21*d*. per ell £2 16*s*.
6 ells ditto at 23*d*. 11*s*. 6*d*.
49 ells ½ of holland at 5*s*. £12 7*s*. 6*d*.
16 pound of thred at 2*s*. 6*d*. per lb £2.
5 papers of inkle at 8*s*. 8*s*.
A remnant of white fustin 8*s*. 8*s*.
15 ells of holland at 3*s*. 7*d*. £2 13*s*. 9*d*.
8 ells ½ ditto at 4*s*. 4*d*. £1 16*s*. 10*d*.
14 ells washt garlix at 22 £1 5*s*. 8*d*.
9 ells ghentish holland at 3*s*. 4*d*. £1 10*s*.
16 ells ¾ ditto at 4*s*. 6*d*. £3 15*s*. 4½*d*.
7 ells ditto at 3*s*. 4*d*. £1 3*s*. 4*d*.
20 ells washt garlix at 18*d*. £1 10*s*.
3 ells ⅞ dowlas at 5*s*. 5*s*.
10 ells ellwide garlix at 2*s*. £1.
A remnant of fine muslin at £3. £3.
2 yards muslin at 20*d*. 3*s*. 4*d*.
A remnant of holland 4*s*. 6*d*. 4*s*. 6*d*.
9 ells ⅞ garlix at 13*s*. 6*d*. 13*s*. 6*d*.
A remnant of cambrick 6*s*. 6*s*.
A remnant of holland 20*d*. 1*s*. 8*d*.
Lumber and odd things in the shop £5. £5.
4 hundredweight ½ tobacco at 13*d*. per lb £27 6*s*.
One cutting engine, two presses, a dryer and set of boxes etc £4.

In the Cellar
One hogshead of tobacco at £34. £34.
One and ¾ ditto at 53 £53.
40 lbs. of goose feathers at 12*d.* per lb £2.
40 lbs. ditto hen at 16*s.* 16*s.*
Weights and scales and lumber in the feather room 10*s.*

Household Goods
In the Street Garrett
2 beds, a rug, 3 blanketts, 2 boulsters, 3 pillows, a press bedstead, 2 old chairs, an old cupboard, trunk, coal grate and close stoole £7 10*s.*
7 pair of sheets, a fustin quilt and napkins £3 3*s.*

In the Back Garrett
Bed and bed stead, blanketts and rug, an old press, 6 old boxes £1 15*s.*

In the Best Chamber
A bed, bedstead, curtains and vallions, a truckle bedstead, an easy chair, 5 old chairs, a chest of drawers, looking glass, table and window curtains, books in the closett and odd things £7 7*s.*

In the Street Chamber
A bed, bedstead, curtains, quilt and vallions, chest of drawers, looking glass, table, scrutore, 5 chairs, window curtains and other odd things £8 8*s.*

In the Back Chamber
2 tables, 7 chairs, a chest, pictures, looking glass, bellows, 2 pair of hand irons, window curtains, etc £2 10*s.*
Carried over £487 19*s.* 6¾*d.* [*recte* £484 18*s.* 2¾*d.*]

In the Kitchin
A table, chairs, jack, chimney back, fire pans and tongs, dogs and odd things £1 10*s.*

In the Buttery
Dressers, tables and other lumber 12*s.*

In the Cellar
Barrells, civers, safe, horses, tunboul, tubbs etc £1 15*s.*

In the Malthouse
A plate on the kiln, a lead cistern, table board, large pair of [tongs *deleted*] dogs, spitt, iron back, screen and malt mill, pair of tongs, beam and scales and old bedstead £8
18 quarters of malt at 18*s.* a quarter £16 4*s.*
Wood in the backside £21.
Two coolers in the washouse at 20*s.* £1.
Seven acres of barley in straw £14
Wheat £4
Brass and pewter at: £12 4*s.* 3*d.*
Cash in hand £3.
Debts good and bad £169 3*s.* 0½*d.*
Two tenements in the Marsh £34.
A tenement in Frigins Lane £6.
Wearing apparell £2 2*s.*
Rings and plate £3.

Total £785 19*s.* 10½*d.* [*recte* £782 8*s.* 6¼*d.*]

Richard Webb and William Hawkes appraisors.

Buried St. Peter 7 September 1722.
Bond 19 March 1722/3, administration to Mary Fowler, intestate's widow.

426 GRACE ROYCE
widow 5 July 1723[1] P1/R/286

In the Kitchen
One iron grate, fender and doggs, firepan, tongs and spitt, pott hooks, small poaker and toasting iron, a pair of bellows, two cloaths irons and frame, a jack and leaden weight, three brass candlesticks,

a brass pestle and mortar, flower box, clock and case, one skreen, two oval table boards and frames, four rush chairs and cushions, a corner cupboard and tea table, two window curtains and vallens, a looking glass, one dozen of great and small pictures, a brass warming pan, five earthen basins, six coffee dishes, three muggs and a lanthorne £5 9*s.* 6*d.*

In the Pantry
Two pewter dishes, one dozen of plates, two small brass pots, five barrells and frame £1.

In the Best Chamber
One feather bed, bedsteed, curtains, vallens, bolster, pillows, a pair of blanketts, quilt and counterpane, two joynt stools, four chairs, a chest of drawers, two trunks, a close stoole, picture and two sconces £17 18*s.*

In the Inner Chamber
One featherbedd, bedsteed, bolster and pillow, curtains and vallens, a pair of blanketts and a quilt, seven sheetes and a box £1 5*s.*

In the Washhouse
One washing tubb and mashing tubb 4*s.*

In the Woodhouse
Five quarters of coale £1 10*s.*
The deceaseds wearing apparrell and money in purse £3.

[*Total omitted, by addition* £30 6*s.* 6*d.*]

Richard Sloper and William Major, appraisors.

Burial not recorded [St. Mary register not extant].
Will 19 July 1723; probate 27 August 1723 to executor [Richard Amer, testator's brother].

1. This does not agree with the date of the will; perhaps August was intended.

427 JOHN SMITH
butcher 12 August 1723 P1/S/874

His books and wareing apparell £2.
18 diaper napkins, 2 paire of pillowbears, 1 diaper tabelcloth, 2 pair of sheets £1 7*s.*

In the Garretts
1 flockbed and bed stid, rug, bolster, blankets, mat and curtins and 2 coffers and truckle bed and bed stid and bolster £1 19*s.*

In the Chamber
[Fethr *added*] bed sid, bolster and pillows, rug, blankets, mat, curtins and rod £3 10*s.* 6*d.*
In the same chamber 6 chairs, a paire of drawers, a desk, looking glas, fiar shovel, tongs and andiars £1 1*s.*

In the Kitchin
A fiar shovel, tongs, andiars, billows, jack, frying [?pan] gridiorn, spit, warming pan, bras candlesticks, peper box and flower box, 2 boylers, 2 skilletts and a sawcepan £1 16*s.* 6*d.*
In the kitchin 1 cupboard, 6 chairs, 2 tabelboards, 3 joyntstools and other lumber 11*s.* 6*d.*
In the same 1 duzen plats, 10 dishes, 1 pye plate and bason, 6 porringers, 1 silfur cup, 2 spoons £3 5*s.* 6*d.*

In the Celler
5 barrils, 7 kivers, 5 tubs, othr lumber £1 8*s.*
In the sellar 1 furnace and a grate £1 10*s.*

[*Total omitteed, by addition* £18 9*s.*]

Richard Webb and Joseph Hockley, appraisors.

Burial not recorded [St. Mary register not extant].
Bond 23 August 1723, administration to Mary Smith, intestate's widow.

428 CLEMENT RAYNOLDS
brazier 26 March 1724 P1/R/291

In the Parlour
Three tables, 6 chairs, a looking glass, window curtains and some books, a jack, 2 spitts, shovell, tongs and doggs, fender, gridiron, toaster, frying pan, warming pan, 2 chaffing dishes, 3 irons for clothes, knives, forks and tea pott £4 6*s.* 2*d.*

In the Kitchen
Two tables, the pewter: 63 lb with three chamber potts and other coarse pewter, the brass: one pan, two bucketts, a skimmer, 3 ladles, an egg slice, 8 candlesticks, tea kettle and a little furnace, the cast metal: 3 skilletts, a mortar and slice, 18 dozen of bottles, a tubb and rack £5 1*s.* 4*d.*

In the Cellars
7 barrells, a safe, a tubb, 3 boxes and an iron grate £1 17*s.*

In the Brewhouse
2 furnaces and brewing vessells whereof the tenant in part of the house has the use for 4 years £5.

In the Dining Room
A table, 6 cane chairs, window curtains, 2 pictures and his wearing apparell £3 10*s.*

In the Back Chamber
The bedsted, curtains, quilt and 3 blanketts, a dressing table and box, a looking glass and press, andirons, bellows and fender, 3 china basons and 2 sawcers [and hangings *added*] £6 17*s.* 6*d.*

In the Fore Garret
A feather bed, 3 bolsters, 2 pillows and curtains, a chest of drawers, looking glass, little cabinett, 2 trunks and a box £3 11*s.* 6*d.*

In the Back Garrett
Two bedds, one bolster, one pillow, bedsted, curtains, a coverlett and 2 blanketts, 6 chairs and 2 trunks £3 12*s.* 4*d.*

In the other Garrett
2 bedsteds, a flock bed and bolster, a rugg and blankett, a chest and old side saddle, pilleon, tilts and virginals £1 13*s.*
Ten sheets, two pillow cases, 5 table cloths, 12 napkins and small linnen all old £2.
A silver tankard, cup, 2 tasters, 7 spoons and old silver £7 12*s.*
Two dwelling houses with gardens for the remainder of a term of 100 years as from 28 September 1653 subject to 20s per annum chief rent and a annuity of £9 per annum to Mrs Anne Orton for her life [and 2 years arrearage thereof *added*] £82.
In money at his decease £3 3*s.*
In debts supposed good £21 17*s.* 3*d.*
In dangerous debts £3 8*s.* 11½*d.*

Goods in the Shop and Workshop
1 ray kettle weight 15 lbs. at 17*d.* a lb. £1 2*s.* 3*d.*
22 skilletts weight 24¾ lbs. at 21*d.* the lb. £2 3*s.* 2*d.*
11 brass sawce pans weight 10¼ lbs. at 20*d.* the lb. 17*s.* 1*d.*
8 copper sawce pans weight 11 lbs. at 22*d.* the lb. £1 0*s.* 2*d.*
19 iron potts, 5 iron kettles, 4 cwt. 10 qtr. at 16*d.* lb. £3 15*s.* 8*d.*
5 furnaces weight 1 cwt. 0 qtr. 26½ lbs. at 15*d.* lb. £11 4*s.* 5*d.*
35 kettles wired 3 cwt. 3 qtr. 9 lbs. at 13*d.* lb. £22 17*s.* 5*d.*
11 boylers weight 1 cwt. 1 qtr. 6 lbs. at 12*d.*

lb. £7 6*s.*
Ten round potts with iron ears 2 qtr. 1½ lbs. at 12*d.* per lb. £2 17*s.* 6*d.*
3 round potts with brass ears 0 cwt. 1 qtr. 0 lb. at 15*d.* per lb. £1 15*s.*
6 chaffing dishes 17*s.* 11*d.*
2 rough morters, one bell skillett 11*s.*
36 sheets of tinn (6 large) 14*s.* 6*d.*
Three fire shovell bitts 2*s.* 5*d.*
One brass pan at 16*d.* lb. 14*s.* 8*d.*
23 copper drinking potts weights 19¼ lbs. at 2*s.* lb. £1 18*s.* 6*d.*
11 tea kettles £3 10*s.* 11*d.*
16 pair of brass candlesticks £2 6*s.* 4*d.*
14 brass frying pans weight 37¾ lbs. at 20*d.* lb. £2 19*s.* 5*d.*
14 iron frying pans at 5*d.* lb. £1 10*s.* 5*d.*
3 bright warming pans at 2*s.* 4*d.* lb. £1 2*s.* 4*d.*
Page total £226 17*s.* 1½*d.*

Two bright chaffing dishes 10*s.*
Four chocolate potts £1 1*s.* 6*d.*
Two coffee potts, one tea pott 6*s.*
Two nursing candlesticks 3*s.*
Three bright morters 9*s.* 6*d.*
Three brass tinder boxes 3*s.* 8*d.*
Four brass pestles 4 lbs 14 ozs 5*s.* 3*d.*
Two brass candleboxes 7*s.*
Six pair of doggs with brass £1 0*s.* 5*d.*
Two pair of plaine 4*s.*
Four pair of firepan and tongs with brass topps 8*s.*
Nine pair of plaine 7*s.*
Six iron chaffing dishes and 3 grid irons 10*s.*
One dozen and five pair of pattens att 1*s.* a pair 17*s.*
Four pair at ten pence a pair 3*s.* 4*d.*
Seaven pair at nine pence a pair 5*s.* 3*d.*
Six pair at eight pence a pair 4*s.*
Five pair of cloggs at ten pence a pair 4*s.* 2*d.*
Five pair of cloggs at six pence a pair 2*s.* 6*d.*
Four pair of leather cloggs 7*s.* 8*d.*
Eighteen iron candlesticks at 8*d.* a peice 12*s.*
One and twenty iron candlesticks at five pence a peece 8*s.* 9*d.*
One and twenty iron candlesticks at three shillings per dozen 5*s.* 3*d.*
Two iron candlesticks, one at eight pence, one at five pence half penny 1*s.* 1½*d.*
Seaven warming panns £1 17*s.* 8*d.*
Nineteen long brooms £1 9*s.* 7*d.*
Seaven long scrubbers 7*s.* 11*d.*
Nineteen small brooms 7*s.* 6*d.*
Seaven and forty small brushes 13*s.* 9*d.*
Five brushes 4*s.* 2*d.*
One hundred and two pounds of sadware at ten pence a lb. £4 14*s.*
Fourteen dozen and one plate £7 15*s.* 6*d.*
One cheese plate 3*s.* 10*d.*
One cheese plate, two stands, two masereens 9*s.* 10*d.*
Four warming pans weight 5 lbs. at 2*s.* 2*d.* lb. 10*s.* 10*d.*
Eight handles for candlesticks and curtain rings 2*s.* 6*d.*
Six hard porringers 4*s.* 6*d.*
Six hard mettal butter dishes 7*s.* 8*d.*
One pair of salvers 3*s.* 3*d.*
Seaven lb. of graine tin 6*s.* 4*d.*
Fifty lanthorn horns 4*s.* 6*d.*
Five hard mettall chamber potts 16*s.* 1*d.*
Fifteen lbs. ½ poringers at 11*d.* a lb. 14*s.* 2*d.*
Twenty lb. and a quarter of pints and quarts at 10*d.* lb. 16*s.* 10*d.*
Five hard pints, one hard quart, one hard tankard 14*s.* 9*d.*
Thirty two lb. of wine measures at 9*d.* a lb. £1 4*s.*
Thirty one lb. of stool pans at 12*d.* lb. £1 11*s.*
One and twenty lb. of basons at 12*d.* lb., 1 barbers bason £1 4*s.*
Forty two lb. of chamber potts at 9*d.* lb. £1 11*s.* 6*d.*
Five wood handles for warming pans 2*s.* 6*d.*
One and thirty lb. of Alborne bells at 13*d.*

lb. £1 13*s.* 7*d.*
One sett of weights 4*s.* 6*d.*
Shelves, chests, one glass case and other things £4 10*s.* 3*d.*
Brass pott weight 22 lbs. ½ at 6*d.* lb. 11*s.* 8*d.*
Ten pewter funnells 8*s.* 4*d.*
Page total £45 12s. 5½d.

One brass stew pann and cover 5 lbs. ¾ at 20*d.* lb. 9*s.* 9*d.*
Two brass tosters 5*s.* 7*d.*
Scales weight 4 lbs. ½ at 20*d.* lb. 7*s.* 6*d.*
Seaven water potts 12*s.* 11*d.*
One and twenty lanthorns £1 7*s.* 8*d.*
Fifteene dripping panns 14*s.* 4*d.*
Seaven pasty panns 9*s.*
Seaven round pudding pans 5*s.* 11*d.*
Four cullenders 5*s.* 11*d.*
Six candle-boxes 5*s.* 6*d.*
Three dust shovells and two cake hoops 4*s.* 9*d.*
Nine tinn kettles 8*s.* 9*d.*
Eight tinn covers 6*s.* 8*d.*
One tea kettle, one stue pan 3*s.* 6*d.*
Fifteen tin funnells 4*s.* 5*d.*
Two dozen and eight tin dishes 6*s.* 11*d.*
Three and twenty tinn potts 4*s.* 11½*d.*
Twelve common tinn cannisters 3*s.* 6*d.*
Twelve tin sawce panns 4*s.* 1½*d.*
Three tobacco boxes and five pudding potts 4*s.* 2½*d.*
Two apple roasters and tin citchins 6*s.* 2*d.*
Nine tinn coffee potts 4*s.* 10*d.*
Eleaven flower boxes and pepper boxes 2*s.* 6*d.*
Six dozen and seaven patty panns 19*s.* 0½*d.*
Three tinder boxes, two spitting potts, two oyl potts 2*s.* 10*d.*
Six skimming dishes and seaven Christmas boxes 3*s.* 4½*d.*
Seaven snuff cannisters 1*s.* 3*d.*
Four tinn candlesticks, two fish plates and other tinn goods 5*s.*
Six bread graters and thirteene fine cannisters 7*s.* 10*d.*
Four sinder shovells and a nursing candlestick 3*s.* 5*d.*
Three flower boxes, three pepper boxes, two candlesticks 2*s.* 6½
Twelve coffee potts bright and five cupps and three papdishes 13*s.* 1½*d.*
Three chocolate mills, four egg slices and ten for poaching eggs 3*s.* 7½*d.*
One stand, twenty biskett panns and three punch strainers 5*s.* 2*d.*
One dark lanthorne, one toy lanthorne, two basters 2*s.* 5*d.*
Four bright candleboxes, one lanthorne with a glass 8*s.* 3*d.*
Twelve brass flower boxes and four pepper boxes 10*s.* 4*d.*
One gallon coffee pott, four casters, two brass egg slices 6*s.* 3*d.*
Seaven brass ladles and six brass slices 11*s.* 2*d.*
2 brass snuffers and boxes, two bright chaffing dishes 7*s.* 6*d.*
Two pewter tea potts and two hussys 5*s.* 8*d.*
Six fire dishes, two sconces, one hand candlestick 5*s.* 4*d.*
Eighteen pair of scales £1 11*s.* 7*d.*
Eight box irons £1 7*s.* 1*d.*
Thirteen pair of kitchen bellows £1 10*s.* 9*d.*
Five pair of chamber bellows 13*s.* 10*d.*
Eleaven lock cocks £4.
Ten drilled cocks 16*s.* 8*d.*
Ten small cocks, 8 of the next, 9 of the next £1 17*s.* 7*d.*
Ten hogshead cocks 15*s.*
Forty small weights 5*s.*
Nineteen brass weights 8*s.* 10*d.*
Two pair of brass holders 3*s.*
Eight pewter dram dishes 1*s.*
Eight larding pinns 1*s.* 6*d.*
Fourteen clock pinns 3*s.* 6*d.*
Nine savealls 3*s.* 3*d.*
Nine pair of snuffers 2*s.*
Six brass nobbs, 6 nutmegg graters 1*s.* 10*d.*
Three jagging irons, 2 steels, four savalls, 2

graters 1s. 8d.
One standish, 2 dram dishes, one pair of nipple shells 2s. 6d.
Ten screw tapps 2s. 11d.
Seaven pair of brass snuffers 4s. 1d.
One pair of fire shovell and tongs 3s. 6d.
Nineteen skimmers and handles 15s. 4d.
Page total £26 15s. 4d.

Eight ladles and handles 5s. 3d.
Two pair of brass heads for doggs 2s.
Seaven and twenty skillett frames weight 49 lbs. ½ at 6d. lb. £1 4s. 9d.
One pewter sawce pan 1s. 7d.
Common spoons seaven dozen 8s. 2d.
Ockelme spoons 10s. 6d.
Six brass ladles 3s. 4d.
Three breakfast basons hard 3s. 6d.
Four suck bottles 4s. 4d.
Five pewter surringes 2s. 6d.
Two and twenty lb. of Wigon ware £1 2s.
A parcell of odd things 8s. 9d.
Three brass sconces 9s. 6d.
Four iron steels 7 lbs. at 6d. lb. 3s. 9d.
Twenty nine pounds of yellow brass at 9d. lb. £1 0s. 9d.
Trifle metall 9 lbs. ¾ at 6d. lb. 5s.
Three latin bells at 10d. lb. 2s. 2d.
Fifteen lb. and half of lay at 5d. lb. 6s. 6d.
One load peck at 12 lbs. and one still 14½ lbs. 9s. 3d.
Platter mettall £2 5s. 6d.
Twenty five lb. of lead 2s. 1d.
One small beame and scales 3s. 6d.
One large beame and scales 14s. 1d.
Copper shruff weight 5 lbs. ¼ 5s. 6d.
One lymbick, 3 pair of iron doggs and brass and other things £1 7s. 5d.
Kettle potts and frying panns, hand candlesticks and frying panns £5 11s. 3d.
Weights of lead 2 cwt. at 14s. per hundred £1 8s.
A parcell of small things 3s. 6d.
One stow, one pair of steps to drawers 11s.
To a parcell of rotten stone, 1 spitt, a parcell of beams, one old tea kettle, one old boyler £1 1s. 9d.
Thatch plate, new copper and yellow brass 17s. 9d.
Copper shruff, copper rails, copper tacks, 3 sheets tin £1.
One chaffing dish, one pottlead 1s. 6d.
New wyre 22 lbs. at 8d. lb. 14s. 8d.
Brass shruff 43 lbs. ½ at 9d. lb. £1 10s. 5d.
Plate brass weight 77 lbs. at 10d. lb. £3 6s. 3d.
A wheel and things belonging to it £1 11s.
One grindstone and trough and iron 2s. 6d.
One pair of bellowes 10s.
Realing barrs 7s. 6d.
Seaven and thirty hammers £1 10s. 6d.
Working tools weight 3 cwt. 1 qtr. 15 lbs. at 4d. lb. £6 6s. 4d.
One vice weight fourteen lb. 3s. 6d.
One frying pan, handles, wire and bailes 13s.
Lead 38 lbs. at 1d. lb. 3s. 2d.
One dozen of sawce pan handles 3s.
A parcell of old iron 9s.
A parcell of things in the workhouse 5s.
Anvill, blocks and other things 15s.
Three skimmer handles and grate for a chaffing dish 3s. 6d.
Ten basketts and one tubb 5s.
Six pair of brass candlesticks, four pair of doggheads, 14 ozs boreax soder 1 cwt. 3 qtr. £1 15s. 7d.
Four pair of small doggheads 5s. 6d.
Page total £44 6s. 4d.

Total £343 11s. 10d.

John Brown and George Raynolds, appraisors.

Buried St. Peter 23 March 1723/4.
Commission 6 July 1724, oath administered 9 July 1724 to Mary Reynolds; bond 9 July 1724, administration to Mary

Raynolds, intestate's widow; inventory exhibited 8 December 1724.

429 JANE COLLY
widow 17 August 1724 P1/C/633

Her wearing apparell £1.

In the Inner Chamber
Two beds, bedsteds and all things thereto belonging with one table £1.

In the Chamber over the Kitchen
One bed and bedsteed and all things thereto belonging 10*s.*

In the Chamber over the Shop
One bed and a table 12*s.*

In the Backhouse
One bed and bedstead etc 12*s.*

In the Inner Room below Stairs
One bed and bedsted and all things thereto belonging, one chest of drawers and one chest 15*s.*

In the Kitchen
Two dozen and two plates, four platters, one bason and one porringer 17*s.*
Two bellmettle potts and 1 brass pott, 1 little kettle and 2 warming pans, one brass skimmer and 1 flower box 15*s.*
One table board, 8 chairs etc 12*s.*

In the 2 rooms over the Cellar
Lumber 2*s.*

In the Hovill
500 of chamber faggots £2 5*s.*

In the Brew House
One furnace and case and grate, one brass kettle and three keevers £2 2*s.*

In the Cellar
Twenty gallons of drink 10*s.*
Nine barrells, 3 stands, one kive and horses for the barrells etc to stand on £1 19*s.*

Total £13 11*s.*

Thomas Edney and Francis Homes, appraisors.

Buried St. Peter 2 August 1724.
Bond 8 December 1724, administration to Joseph Colly, intestate's son.

430 WILLIAM LEACOCK
barber 29 October 1724 P1/L/325

In the Shop
The pole, windows and window shetters, the door, hones, rasours and rasour cases and sheaves, the working table, vices and frame sticks, cards, brushes, blocks and stands, chairs, curling pipes and threads, basins, pots and a little furnace, a bench, dresser board and drawers, a powder trow, shelves, boxes and pins, a looking glass, candlestick, a map, pictures and combs, a linnen press, an earthen pot, a morter, a real, powder tuffs, an inkhorn, a goose oyl and powder, washballs, weights and scales, wiggs and hair £27 9*s.*

In the Kitchin
One clock and weights, three table boards, one joynt stool and board, one jack and weights and chain, one rack, four crooks, fourteen chairs, two joynt stools, one glass shelf and glasses, a cole box, one tin candle box, eight iron candle sticks, seven brass ones, one tin tinder box, one pair of bellows, one coal grate and fend iron, one pair of iron andiers, one spit, one fire pan and tongs, one poker, one brass fire pan, one gridiron £6 18*s.* 6*d.*

In the Buttery
Eighty seven lbs. and an half of pewter, two boylers, two skillets, one brass pan, one bellmettle pot, two skimmers, two basting ladles, two sauce pans, one dripping pan, a pudding pan, a dresser board, a cupboard and cheese board, table board, trenchers and trencher rack and other odd things £2 2*s.*

In the Brewhouse
A furnace with its appurtenances, one iron pot and stow, three tubs and a mash vate, one wooden horse, two pails, a frying pan, an horse for cloaths, one stool and a bowl £2 1*s.* 6*d.*

In the Wood House and Stable
Wood and a partition, a rack and manger, a cieling and a tallet £3 10*s.*

In the Cellar
Nine barrels, four horses, six civers, one cive, cole, powdering tub, bottles and bottle rack, one spade, cole rake, prong and rudder, two barrel stoopers, one furnace lid, tun bowl and two brass cocks £5 3*s.* 6*d.*

In the Chamber
One bed and bed stead, curtains and vallings, one quilt, one bolster, two pillows, one coverlid, two blankets, one chest of drawers, a press and close stool and stool pan, three trunks, one box, one easy chair, seven other chairs, one looking glass, five pictures, a pair of dogs, fire pan and tongs, five lbs. of candles and coffee dishes £8 13*s.* 6*d.*

In the Little Chamber
The bed and bed stead, curtains, one cover lid, two blankets and bed mat, one chest, two chairs, one bolster £3 4*s.* 3*d.*

In the Best Chamber
The bed and bed stead, curtains and vallings, one bolster, two pillows, two quilts, one counter pin, one coverlid, one chest of drawers, two looking glasses, two window curtains, one table, ten chairs, two pair of dogs, fire pan and tongs, one pair of bellows, one Bible and other books, three picktures, and in the closet one little table, one warming pan, two brushes and some other odd things £16 16*s.*

In the Garrets
Two beds, two bed steads, two mats, two cords, one coverlid, two bolsters, five blankets, one curtain, one deal box, one chair, one table board, one chest, one sack, a saddle, a side saddle, one pillion, a chamber pot, one pewter bed pan and pot, two box irons, two clamps, a great, one screen, a deal box, on civer, a temzer and search, one horse, one barrel, one wooden trough, box and lanthorn £5 12*s.* 3*d.*

Plate
One silver tankard, six spoons, one paire of salts and two tea spoons £10 2*s.*
His wearing apparel [*value omitted*]
The linnen at £6.
In cash £13 18*s.*
Upon bill £5.
Book debts £22 9*s.* 6*d.*
Bad debts £89.

[*Total omitted, by addition* £228]

Thomas Bartlett and Richard Andarray, appraisors.

Buried St. Peter 16 October 1724.
Inventory exhibited 8 November 1724; bond 8 December 1724, administration to Mary Leacock, intestate's widow.

431 EDWARD BARNARD
13 May 1726 P1/B/923

His wearing apparel and books £2.

In the Kitchin

One table, 3 joynt stools, 6 rush chairs, dresser, bacon rack, benches and shelves, a jack and 2 spits, shovel, tongs and bellows, grate and andirons, 2 boxes to iron clothes and heaters, dripping pan, frying pan, 8 iron candlesticks, tin wares and small things £3 11*s.* 6*d.*

The pewter: ten dishes, 28 plates, 10 potts, 6 chamber potts, 4 spoons £2 13*s.*

The brass: 3 potts, a skillet, saucepan and 2 candlesticks 16*s.*

In the Parlour

2 tables, 8 chairs, dogs and bellows, window curtains and pictures 18*s.*

In the Long Room

Two tables, a form, benches and a chest £1.

In the Brewhouse

A little furnace, 2 tubbs, 5 kevers, a pail, bucket and ladepail, the well bucket and chain and small things £1 19*s.*

In the Cellar

3 tubbs and a cupboard, 20 barrels with the stands, about 6 hogsheads of beer and ale, some brandy and cider £16.

About 8 dozen of bottles with glasses, cups, panns and earth wares 16*s.*

In the Best Chamber

A bedsted with curtains and window curtains, a feather bed, bolster and 2 pillows, 3 blankets, a quilt, 2 tables, 6 chairs, 2 stools, pictures, lookinglass, dogs, shovel and tongs £6 8*s.*

In the Back Chamber

Bedsted and curtains, feather bed, bolster and 2 pillows, 3 blankets and a rugg, a press bed, close-stool, lookinglass, doggs, 2 chairs and 2 stools £3 14*s.*

In the Inner Chamber

A bedsted, bed, bolster and 2 pillows, a press, drawers, a chest and trunk £1 15*s.*

In the Garrets

3 bedsteds, a flock bed, 2 blankets and a rugg £1 2*s.*

Page total £42 12*s.* 6*d.*

In the Parlour Chamber

Two bedsteds with curtains, 2 beds, 2 bolsters, 4 pillows part feathers part flock, 3 blankets, 2 ruggs, a table, 3 chairs, 3 stools and doggs £6 2*s.*

In the Back Chamber

2 bedsteds, 2 flock beds, 2 bolsters, rugg, coverlet and 2 chairs £2 1*s.*

The linnen: 8 pair of sheets, 4 pair of pillowcases, 4 table clothes, a dozen of napkins and small linnen £4 2*s.*

Some cole, luggs, hardwood and fagots £3 10*s.*

About 25 hundred of hay, a sack of oates, some beans, 2 old horsecloths and halters £2 8*s.*

A wheelbarrow, handbarrow, prongs and small things abroad 10*s.*

Four little silver spoons £1 2*s.*

Money in the house and good credits £30.

Total £92 7*s.* 6*d.*

Thomas Brunsdon and Francis Skull, appraisors.

Buried St. Peter 22 December 1725.

Bond 14 May 1726, administration to Susanna Barnard, testator's widow.

432 ELIZABETH MANN

spinster [will] 13 May 1726 P1/M/461

An old bed, bolster, 3 pillows, a pair of

old sheets, 3 blankets and a rugg £1 13*s.*
A table and two cupboards 7*s.*
A chest 3*s.*
A trunck and stand 2*s.* 6*d.*
A frying pan 2s 3*d.*
A deal box 1*s.*
Pewter 1*s.* 10*d.*
A skillet 1*s.* 2*d.*
A pair of dogs 1*s.*
Her waring apparrel £1.
Part of a joynt stool and a candlestick 6*d.*

Subtotal £3 13*s.* 3*d.*

A debt due from Benjamin Merriman of Newbury £16.

Total £19 13*s.* 3*d.*

Richard Webb and Mary Smith, appraisors.

Burial not recorded [St. Mary register not extant].
Will 3 January 1725/6, probate 14 May 1726 to Mary Furnell, testator's kinswoman.

433 JOHN TARRENT

31 October 1726[1] P1/T/341

In the Chamber
Table bords and forms and od things 16*s.*
3 chears, 1 joynt stole 2*s.*
8 pewter dishes, 1 duzen plats 12*s.*
2 boylers, 1 small pot, 1 scillett 14*s.*
Barrills and brewing vesell 18*s.*

In the Iner Chamber
1 bed, bed stid and beding [and curtings *added*] £2 10*s.*
Bed lining and tabell ling and window curtings £1 10*s.*
1 chest of drars, 2 tablebords £1 10*s.*
5 chears, 1 close stole 6*s.*
1 warming pan, 1 looking glass 8*s.*
For od things 2*s.*

In the Garrett
1 bed and beding and bed stid £1.
For a chest and od things 4*s.*

Total £10 12*s.*

Thomas Arman and Joseph Hockly, appraisors.

Burial not recorded [St. Mary register not extant].
Bond 31 October 1726, administration to Mary Tarrent, intestate's widow.

1. A second copy of this inventory exists, giving summary details only.

434 THOMAS GILMORE senior

27 February 1727/8 P1/G/452

In the Outer Chamber
1 chest of drawers, bed and waring apparrell etc £1 11*s.*

In the Inner Chamber
Hops and lumber £2 13*s.* 4*d.*

In the Kitchinn
Two platters, one table and other lumber 7*s.* 6*d.*

Inn the Room within the Kitchinn
A pot, frying pan etc 2*s.* 8*d.*

Inn the Out Buttery
Lumber 7*s.* 6*d.*

Inn the Stable
A horse etc £4 1*s.*

Total £9 3*s.*

Thomas Coleman and Nicholas Rumsey, appraisors.

Burial not recorded [St. Mary register not extant].
Bond 28 February 1727/8, administration to Mary Gilmore, intestate's widow.

435 JONATHAN TANNER
yeoman 4 May 1732 P1/T/368

His wearing apparell [and lumber *added*] £1.
Due on bond £20.

Total £21.

John Bridgeman and Edward Bridgeman, appraisers.

Burial not recorded [St. Mary register not extant].
Renunciation 4 May 1732 by Elizabeth Tanner, intestate's widow, in favour of Susanna Bridgeman, only child of intestate, and wife of Thomas, gentleman of Marlborough; bond 5 May 1732, administration to Susanna Bridgeman.

436 NATHANIEL WILKINS
whitesmith 10 October 1733 P1/W/685

His wearing apparell and money in purse £12.

In the First Chamber
Beds and beding £7 10*s.*
Chest of drawers £1 10*s.*
Seven chairs £1 2*s.*
A table and glass and bellows 15*s.*

In the Next Chamber
Beds and beding £5.
Seven chairs, 2 chests and a press 19*s.*
A table, a box and cushions 4*s.*

In the Little Chamber
Bed and beding £1 1*s.* 6*d.*

In the Garrett
Two beds £1 10*s.*
Linnen £5 13*s.*

In the Kitchen
A clock and watch £7.
Dresser board and chairs 12*s.*
A table and stools 8*s.*
A little table, settle, a coutch, a cupboard and rack 17*s.* 6*d.*
A jack and spit £1 10*s.*
Books, curtain and rod £2 4*s.*
Candlesticks 11*s.*
Copper potts and flower boxes 10*s.*
Coal grate, fireshovel and tongs, boxirons, bellows, a brush and a glass £1 8*s.* 6*d.*

In the Cellar
Six barrells and brewing vessells £2 11*s.*
Coals £5.
Three brass potts £1 13*s.* 6*d.*

In the Little Room
Table, chairs and corner shelf 18*s.* 6*d.*
Stove, grate, doggs and fender 8*s.*
Pictures and glass 16*s.*
Pewter £2 6*s.*
A cupboard 5*s.*
The effects [in the shop *added*] £54 2*s.* 10*d.*
Book debts £117 19*s.* 10*d.*

[*Total omitted, by addition* £238 6*s.* 8*d.*]

J. Blisselt and Nathaniel Merriman, appraisors.

Burial not recorded [St. Mary register not extant].
Bond 11 October 1733, administration to Elizabeth Wilkins, intestate's widow.

437 FRANCIS HURLBATT[1]
carpenter 1 and 4 February 1733 /4 P1/H/922

[*These four items have been deleted, and inserted into other parts of the inventory*
His wearing apparell £1 10s.
Money in the house £70.
A house in Herd Street held by lease under Mrs Crabb £10.
House in the Green held under Lord Bruce £20.]

His stock in timber and so forth
In the Street
105 deal planks £10 10s.
Slab stuff 11s. 6d.
Six ladder poles 9s.
Forty two foot and a halfe of deal timber £2 2s. 6d.
560 foot of raftering at 9s. the hundred £2 10s. 4½d.
And 3 deal pieces 9 foot 6s.

In Thomas Hurlbats shop
19 short deals 15s. 10d.
Odd stuff and working bench 7s.

In Francis Hurlbats shop
72 foot elm board 9s.
17 deal planks £1 14s.
53 deal quarters £2 13s.
Odd stuff 9s.
Odd board 9s.
Spanish oak plank 3s.
Working bench 2s. 6d.
Seven bundles of laths 9s.
897 foot of raftering at 9s. the hundred £4 0s. 7d.
12 coffin sides 6s.
And 2 sides 1s.
25 coffin tops £1 5s.
Sub-total £29 13s. 3½d.

And 2 ditto 2s.
1 deal pole 1s. 6d.
Pair of drugs 3s.
2 ladders 5s.
Wheelbarrow 3s.
Working tools 3s.
Odd slab stuff £1 10s.

In the Lower Shop
101½ foot of raftering 16s. 9d.
Eleaven deal planks £1 2s.
400 foot of oak board £3.
69 foot of elm board 8s. 7½d.
15 deal quarters 15s.
2 coffin sides 1s.
2 coffin tops 2s.

In the Shop in Herd Street
27 foot of raftering 2s. 4d.
Slab stuff 15s.
Two deal planks 4s.
[*Added in a different hand* Given by the will to executor and his brother Francis they paying for all timber due att testators death]
Sub-total £42 4s. 6½d.

His Stock in Household Goods
In the Chamber over the Kitchen
2 barrells 1s. 6d.
An old brass cock 6d.
4 leather chairs 5s.
An elbow chair 1s.
2 cane chairs 1s. 3d.
11 pictures 13s
1 feather bed, rug and blankett, curtains and bedstead £1 15s.
1 chest of drawers 10s.

In Elizabeth Hurlbatts Chamber
1 chest of drawers 1s. 6d.
1 flock bed, bolster, feather pillow and case, 2 quilts, a sheet and blankett 15s. 6d.
A low stool 2d.
Sub-*total* £4 14s. 5d.

A bedstead and sacking 3s.
Curtains, vallens, window curtain and tester 2s. 6d.

In Thomas Hurlbatts Chamber
A flock bed, 2 flock bolsters, bolster case, sheet, 2 blanketts, 2 ruggs, bedstead, matt, cord and stool 14s.

In a Cupboard over the Stairs
Lumber 6*d.*

In the Cellar
2 hogsheads, 1 halfe hogshead, 1 little barrell, tun bowl, tub and spout 7*s.*

In the Brewhouse or Lower Shop
A brass boyler 5*s.*
A lanthorn 4*d.*
3 tubbs 3*s.*
2 buckets 6*d.*
A brass pott and kettle 8*s.*
Frying pan 2*s.*
Cooler and kiver 6*s.*
Lumber 1*s.*
A spitt 6*d.*

In the Kitchin
2 sheets 5*s.*
4 pillow cases 2*s.*
4 pictures 3*d.*
A warming pan 1*s.*
2 brushes 8*d.*
7 peuter dishes and eight peuter plates 18*s.*
1 peuter tankard and 1 peuter pint 1*s.*
6 earthen plates 1*s.*
1 earthen dish 3*d.*
3 small earthen dishes 3*d.*
1 brass chaffendish 2*s.* 6*d.*
12 brass candlesticks 10*s.*
Pezzle and morter 2*s.*
Sub-*total* £9 11*s.* 8*d.*

2 pepper boxes and a flower box 1*s.*
Brass ladle 6*d.*
Tin candlestick 3*d.*
Jack 3*s.*
Candlebox 1*s.*
Iron grate, firepan, tongs and gridiron 3*s.*
Pair of bellows 3*d.*
A small glass 3*d.*
An oval table 5*s.*
Small table or stool 1*s.*
1 brass kettle 6*d.*
1 great chair and 4 small chairs 2*s.* 6*d.*
Coal box, brush and fender 1*s.*

In the Well House
3 brass potts and 2 kettles 15*s.*
3 peuter porringers 1*s.* 6*d.*
1 peuter strainer 1*s.*
1 coffer pott 1*s.*
Powdring tub and earthen ware 9*d.*
[*In another hand*] *Total household goods* £11 16*s.* 2*d.*

A house in Hurd Street held by lease under Mrs Crabb given to the widow for her life then to Mary Morecock the younger £10.
House in the Green held under Lord Bruce for the life of the executor and his brother Francis, given by the will to the widow for life and the remainder to the executor and his brother Francis £20.

Note the household [goods *implied*] are given to the widow for her widowhood then to executor, his brother Francis, his sister Elizabeth Hulbatt and Sarah wife of Jonothan Hancock equally between them.

Cash in the house, bills of business done and due to the testator att his death
[*reverts to first hand*]
Mr Brathwaites bill £21 10*s.* 5*d.*
Mr Baylys bill £20 18*s.*
Mr Tribes bill £5 19*s.* 6*d.*
William Whittakers bill £3 8*s.*
Thomas Bridgmans bill £1 16*s.*
Mr Bowshers bill £5 4*s.* 1*d.*
Madam Fletchers bill £5 18*s.* ...d.
Mr Martins bill £2 8*s.* 7*d.*
Mr Collings's bill £2 11*s.* 7*d.*
Thomas Hutchens's bill 17*s.* 8*d.*
Mr Burgess's bill £4 2*s.*
Mr Megs's bill £13 9*s.*
Madam Itchener's bill £82 12*s.*
Mr Savery's bill £2 2*s.* 6*d.*
Mr Blissetts bill £2 5*s.*

Thomas Morecock's bill £6 8s. 6d.
Mr Jones's bill £11 5s.
Joseph Hess bill 9s. 6d.
Mr Dances bill £2 6s. 9d.
Mr Churches bill £41 15s.
Mr Nights bill 8s. 10d.
Mr Savages bill 15s.
Mr Dangerfields bill the joyner 4s. 6d.
Mrs Crabbs bill £2.
[*reverts to second hand*]
Cash in the house £70.
Wearing apparel £1 10s.
Total (cash and bills) £312 5s. 11d.

Rent due from Thomas Higham £3 13s.
Ditto William Whiteare 8s.
Due from Jonathan Hancock as [rent *deleted*] mony lent £2 0s. 2d.
Ditto nine lent ditto £5.

Total £323 7s. 1d.

[*Appraisors' names omitted*]

Debts received and ballanced with several people
Received of Thomas Higham in full £3 13s.
Ditto William Whiteare 8s.
Ditto Thomas Bridgeman [ballance of account *added*] 15s. 6d.
Ditto Mr Savery in full £2 2s. 6d.
Ditto Mr Blissett ballance 11s. 6d.
Ditto Mr Brathwayte ballance £6.
Ditto Mr Burgess ballance £2.
Ditto Mrs Fletcher in full £5 18s.
Ditto Joseph Eyles in full 9s. 6d.
Ditto Mr Martin ballance 9s.
Ditto Mr Dangerfiels in full 4s. 6d.
Ditto Mrs Itchiner in part £20.

24 Apr. Cash received (*Total*) £42 11s. 6d.
Cash and wearing apparel £71 10s.

Executor (*Total*) £114 1s. 6d.
(*Less*) Credit £38 8s. 11d.
Total £75 12s 7d.

Debts paid by Executors[2]
Paid Mr Bowshire ballance 3s. 4d.
Paid for paper to write bill 8d.
Ditto Mr Tribe ballance 7s. 6d.
Ditto Thomas Morecock ballance 7s. 6d.
Ditto Richard Collins ballance £1 11s. 8d.
Ditto Mr Savage ballance £4 18s.
Funerall expenses £4 17s. 1d.
Paid paper for the inventory 8d.
A book to keep accounts 1s. 6d.
Coppying the inventory 2s. 6d.
Proveing the will £3 15s. 6d.
Paid appraseing the effects 10s.
Money paid in book £19 18s. 6d.

Total (*of debts*) £38 8s. 11d.

Burial not recorded [St. Mary register not extant].
Will 7 September 1733; probate 11 February 1733/4 to Thomas Hulbatt, testator's son.

1. 'the elder, late of the Green in the parish of St. Mary'
2. Debts owed by the testator, and executors' expenses, should not form part of the inventory.

438 MARY WYATT
widow [will] 27 May 1735 P1/W/693

In the Best Room
A bed, boulster, blankett and rug, curtins and valins and bed steed 15s.
Four chairs and chestt off drawrs 7s. 6d.
Thre sheets, thre napkins and four pillows 5s. 6d.
And window curtins 6d.

The Under Chamber
One bed and bedsted, blankett and rugg 9s.
A chestt and other lumber 1s.

The Third Room
Lumber 1*s.*

In the Kittchin
A table 1*s.* 6*d.*
A warming [pan *added*] and jack 3*s.*
Two spitts, seven ir candlesticks 3*s.*
A iron greatt, crane in the chimney 7*s.* 6*d.*
A pair of bellows, six chairs 3*s.*
Nine dishes, ten platts, one porringer £1.
Other lumber 2*s.* 6*d.*

In the Celler
Five barrells, other lumber 10*s.*

In the Brew House
A brass pott, saws pan, scillett, frying pan 9*s.* 6*d.*
A pair off iron dogs 1*s.* 6*d.*
A brass furnice and boyler £2 10*s.*
Other lumber 2*s.* 6*d.*

With Outt Door
Buckett and rope 1*s.* 6*d.*
A large boyler 10*s.*
Two piggs alive £3.

In the Outt House
Ropes and other lumber 2*s.* 6*d.*

Total £11 7*s.* 6*d.*
Weiring apparell £1 10*s.*

George Baily and John Hopkins, appraisors.

Burial not recorded [St. Mary register not extant].
Will 12 October 1734; probate 8 July 1735 to Susannah Wyatt, testator's daughter.

439 THOMAS ARMON
?carpenter [inventory goods] [*undated* c. 1736] P1/A/316

In the Citching
A dale tabel board 6*s.*
6 chaires 3*s.*
A warming pan and 2 spits 6*s.*
A gunn 6*s.*
In the chimny: a pair of doggs, a pair of andires, 2 pair of hangells, fire pan and tongs 5*s.*
Candle sticks 4*s.* 6*d.*
A jack and wait 6*s.*
A pair of billows and cup board 2*s.*
7 pictures 1*s.* 2*d.*
1 dozen of plates in the pantry 6*s.*
5 dishes 15 lb. 8*s.* 9*d.*
2 skillets, a saspun and skimer [and ladle *added*] 4*s.*
A frying pan and cullinder 3*s.*
A boyler 10*s.*
Od things in the pantry 1*s.* 6*d.*
5 barrels and horses and other od things in the celler £1 10*s.*

In the Chamber
A press £1.
A pair of drawers 6*s.*
6 leather chairs 15*s.*
A close stool 3*s.*
A bed, curtins and vallings, 2 blankets and quitt £3.

In the Other Chamber
A bed, bedstead, 2 blankets and rugg £2.

In the Garret
One bed, 2 blankets and other things £1.
A pair of drawers and other things £1.
A large looking glass 10*s.*
A ovil table board 8*s.*
90 feet of elme 11*s.* 9*d.*
Oak boards 13*s.* 1*d.*
Coffin boards 5*s.*
Bedstead stuff 5*s.* 6*d.*
4 beanches and leafes £1 5*s.*
Deal boards, the level and other lumber 5*s.*
A vise 5*s.*
The working tools £1 10*s.*

Od timber 10*s.*

Total £20 15*s.* 3*d.*

Francis Holmes and John Simmons, appraisors.

Buried St. Peter 27 August 1736.
Renunciation 23 September 1736 by Elizabeth Arman, intestate's widow; bond 16 October 1736, administration to Elizabeth Warne of Chippenham, principal creditor.

440 JOSEPH BLAKE[1]

25 November 1737 P1/B/1071

Wearing apparell £5.
A bed, bedcloathes, curtains and vallens £3.
Linning £2.
Pewter £1. 10*s.*
Brass £2.
Furness, door and grate £1 10*s.*
Brewing vessell and a mash tubb £1 1*s.*
5 barrells £1 1*s.*
6 chairs 15*s.*
A cupboard 5*s.*
2 tables and 2 stools 15*s.*
A chest and 2 boxes £1.
A jack 5*s.*
A larham £1.
A pair of andirons and doggs 5*s.*
2 fire shovells, 2 pair of doggs and a spitt 10*s.*
Money in purse £10.
Wood and coals £5.
Birch £3.
The house £30.

Total £69 17*s.*

William Dance and Thomas Dance, appraisors.

Burial not recorded [St. Mary register not extant].
Bond 25 November 1737, administration to Sarah Church and Mary King, intestate's sisters.

1. 'of the parish of St Peters'.

441 WILLIAM FLOWER

baker 26 February 1739/40 P1/F/353

Wearing apparell and money in house £120.
Bills, bonds and book debts deemed to be good £198 12*s.* 9*d.*
Bill and book debts deemed to be bad £4 6*s.* 8*d.*

Stock in Trade
Seven sacks of wheat at 18*s.* the sack £6 6*s.*
Two hundred of kitchen faggotts at 17*s.* the hundred £1 14*s.*
Thirty one bushels of flower at 5*s.* the bushel £7 15*s.*
One flower trough 6*s.*
One moulding board and peels etc 3*s.*

In the Wellhouse
Lumber 5*s.*

In the Shop
A table and other household goods £1.

In the Bakehouse
A table and two joint stools 2*s.*

In the Buttery
Brass £1.

In the Little Chamber or Best Room
A chest of drawers 7*s.* 6*d.*
A chest, trunk and chair 10*s.*
Pewter and earthen ware 12*s.*
A feather bed, bedstead and furniture and a brass boyler £2.

In the next Chamber
A feather bed, bedstead and other things £2 10*s*.

At the Stairhead and in the Garrett
Lumber 10*s*.

In the New Room
A table etc 2*s*.

In the New Garrett
Lumber 7*s*.
A silver watch £2 2*s*.
Table and bed linnen £1.

Total £347 4*s*. 3*d*.

Thomas Crips and Edward Reeves, appraisers.

Burial not recorded [St. Mary register not extant].
Will 7 February 1739/40; probate 4 March 1739/40 to William Jackson, executor.

442 ROBERT TUCK[1]

?spoonmaker [inventory goods] [*undated*, c.1744] P1/T/426

Three feather beds and bedstedes £ 4 10*s*.
9 large chests 15*s*.
Coffer, box and 4 chairs 10*s*.
4 pair of andiers 6*s*.
Pewter and working tools used in spoonmaking £2 10*s*.
Brass kittels, pots, pewter dishes and plates, household goods £2 10*s*.
A silver cup £2 10*s*.
Fire pang and tongs and candelsticks 4*s*.
Barrils and brewing vesels 10*s*.
Warming pang and frying pang 5*s*.

Total £14 10*s*.

John Swinden, appraisor.
William Whitaker, witness

Buried St. Mary 22 December 1743.
Bond 4 September 1744, administration to Ursley Tuck, intestate's widow.

1 'of the Parish of S[t] Marys the virgin in Marlborough'.

443 ELEANOR DRURY[1]

widow 2 May 1745 P1/D/354

Wearing apparel and money in house £40.
Two feather beds, bedding and furniture thereto belonging £8.
A clock £2.
Four gold rings £3.
Four silver spoons and a pair of tea tongs £1 10*s*.
Brass and pewter £2.
A chest of drawers and a looking glass £1 10*s*.
Debts supposed to be good £120.

Total £178.

Thomas Rudman and Thomas Bridgeman, appraisors.

Buried Ludgershall 31 March 1745.
Will 13 April 1742; probate 27 May 1745 to Thomas Rudman and William Stevens, executors.

1. 'of Marlebrough, Relict and Administratrix of Nicholas Drury late of Ludgershal in the said County of Wilts yeoman'.

444 JOHN MORRIS

?carpenter [inventory goods] 13 May 1746 P1/M/585

Wareing apparil and money in pockett £1.

In the Kitchen
Eight pewter dishes 16*s.*
Fourteen pewter plates, three old pewter pints 8*s.* 6*d.*
Three small spitts and a jack 6*s.* 6*d.*
Four brass candle sticks and two pepper boxes 1*s.* 6*d.*
One flatt candlestick and two small brass ladles 1*s.*
A driping pan and brass tinder box and skimer 1*s.* 9*d.*
A candle box and two iron candle sticks 6*d.*
A warming pan 1*s.* 6*d.*
Two old fire shovels and two pair of tongs 1*s.* 4*d.*
Two fire doggs, two hand irons and three steeling irons 2*s.*
Two hangells, one pair of bellows and two small crooks 2*s.*
Two little round tables, four chairs and two joynt stools 7*s.* 6*d.*
An old brass frying pan and a small bacon rack 2*s.* 6*d.*

In the Parlour
Two round tables and one sqare one, six cane chairs 14*s.* 6*d.*

In the Room over the Kitchen
One flock bed, two blankets, one bolster, two pillows, a bed quilt and bed stead, a sett of old curtains and vallands £1 10*s.* 4*d.*
A small sqare table, two chests of draws, two oak chests £1 15*s.*
Six small chairs and two arm chairs 5*s.* 6*d.*
A pair of fire doggs with brass heads, thirteen small pictures 2*s.* 6*d.*
A earthen punch bowl 1*s.*

In the Room over the Parlour
Tirty seven bushels of malt £4 12*s.* 6*d.*

In the South Garrat
One bed, two blanketts, one sheet, one quilt, a bolster and case £1 1*s.*
One flock bed, one bolster, one blanket, one sheet, two old cover lids, a sacken bottom bedstead £1 1*s.*
One old bed more and six common chairs, three window curtains 19*s.*

In the Middle Garratt
Three chairs and one cofar 2*s.* 6*d.*

In the North Garatt
One old bed, an old coal grate and old jack, about two hundred weight of other old iron £1 18*s.* 8*d.*
Page total £17 6*s.* 1*d.* [*recte* £17 5*s.* 7*d.*]

In the Uper Malt Floor
Thirteen tressells 3*s.* 3*d.*
Fifty seven crooked slabbs 19*s.*
Six oaken boards measured 30 foot 5*s.*
Eight slabbs more 2*s.* 8*d.*
Forty two elming boards measures 312 foot, two inch deals 29 foot £2 0*s.* 7½*d.*
A eleven inch deals 110 foot, ten half inch deals 100 foot £1 1*s.* 9*d.*
Three half inch elme 36 foot, a frame saw 10*s.* 6*d.*

In the Lower Malt Floor
Two inch oak boards 18 foot 3*s.*
Four two inch and half elme slabbs 32 foot 8*s.*
Twenty three oak boards 106 foot, one wainscott board 5 foot 17*s.* 6*d.*
One ovell civer, one tubb, three small skivers 7*s.* 3*d.*
The sides of an old bed head, an old cofar without a led and a broad ronged ladder and a couch frame and posts 10*s.*

In the Mill House
One malt mill and bend 12*s.*
One bushell, one peck and one half peck 5*s.*

In the Kiln House
A screen, an iron grate and a iron door and a fire dogg £1 1*s.* 6*d.*

One malt shovel, one seeve and six sacks 8*s.* 6*d.*

In the Brew House
One old copper, a grate, a door and a cover £1 5*s.*
A small mash tun and a wooden horse 7*s.*
Two small brass boilers, one pott, one kettle 15*s.*
One pair of druggs, fifteen slabbs, 80 old hurdles £1 6*s.* 8*d.*
One cord of billett wood, three two inch deal planks £1 6*s.*
Four inch deals, three inch and half deals, one two inch plank 5*s.* 4*d.*
Seven piecs of elme quartered sixty six foot 5*s.* 6*d.*
A working bench, three saws and other tools £1 2*s.* 6*d.*

In the Stable
Five bushells of coal 5*s.*
Sixteen bushells of coaked coal and a hoggs tubb 18*s.*
Seven crooked oak boards 33 foot 4*s.*

In the Backside and Garden
Two hundred three quarters of kitchen faggotts £2 15*s.*
Two cord of billett wood and a wheel barrow £2 4*s.*
One grinding stone and a wood boytle 2*s.*
Two iron bars, a ladle and a spade 4*s.*
Page total £23 0*s* 6½*d.*

In the Celler
Five barrells, three tubbs and a tun bowl 17*s.*
A spout, a lade pail and a buckett 1*s.* 6*d.*

In the Room over the Porch
One box and tools and about 63 lb. of nails £1 15*s.* 9*d.*
About 5000 brads and 34 pair of joynts £1 2*s.* 10*d.*
One dozen and half of large coffin handles 9*s.*
Two dozen of small ones 6*s.*

In the Clossetts
Six sheets, six napkins, one table cloath and two pillow cases 12*s.*

In the Malt Grainerys
33 quarter of malt £33.
Page total £38 4*s.* 1*d.*

1st collunn £17 6*s.* 1*d.* [*recte* £17 5*s.* 7*d.*]
2nd collumn £23 0 6½*d.*
Fire wood in the Backside etc £2 9*s.*

Total £80 19*s.* 8½*d.* [*recte* £80 19*s.* 2½d]

Thomas Grose and John Hopkins, appraisors.

Buried St. Peter 7 May 1746.
Bond 1 December 1749, administration to Jane Morris, intestate's widow.

445 STEPHEN WILLOUGHBY
vintner 14 October 1746 P1/W/797

Money in the buro etc £12 7*s.* 7¼*d.*
Debts £50.
Wearing apparell £14 8*s.* 6*d.*
Plate: a gold ring and a silver watch £14 8*s.* 9*d.*

Coffee Room
Iron grate, crane, 2 checks, iron fender, ditto back, a poker and 4 small iron hooks 10*s.*
A small brass jack and weight £1 1*s.*
Eleven maps and prints 5*s.*
Four tin and two wood tobacco dishes 9*d.*
A looking glass 13*s.*
A dial clock £2 5*s.*
Window curtains and rods 4*s.* 6*d.*
Three small claw tables 10*s.*
Wainscotting and four boxs £1 10*s.*

Two oak tables or long drinking boards 6*s.*
A weather glass 1*s.*
The bar, draws and two cubberts £1 10*s.*
Curiosities 5*s.*
Sign and a lamp 12*s.*
In the bar a small box with tobacco and a box with pipes 3*s.* 6*d.*
Carried over £101 1*s.* 7¼*d.*

In the Passage
A turn up bed head 4*s.*
A flock bed and boister 4*s.*
Two old blanketts 3*s.* 6*d.*
One coarse sheet and a pillow case 2*s.*
Four chairs, a pair of bellows and a lantron 2*s.* 6*d.*
A warming pan and two fire pans 6*s.*
Five tin coffee pots and two tin canisters 1*s.* 6*d.*
Two earth chamber pots 6*d.*
Twenty one earth mugs 2*s.*
Four mahogany tea boards 3*s.*
A clease brush and a tin shovell 1*s.*
A tin candle box and three tin quarts 1*s.* 4*d.*
A paddle and 2 iron candle sticks 7*d.*
Five earth tea pots 1*s.*
A window curtain and rod 1*s.*
Shelves 1*s.*
Four print 8*d.*
Eight pair of iron snuffers, 2 tin extinguishers 1*s.*
Carried forward £102 18*s.* 2¼*d.*

In the Kitchen
A iron grate, two cheecks and two hooks 6*s.* 6*d.*
Two pair of tongs, a pooker, a trippett and an heater 2*s.* 6*d.*
Two gridd irons and one hook 1*s.*
A draw up jack, weight, chain and 3 spitts 11*s.* 6*d.*
An iron ballance to put on the spitt 2*s.* 6*d.*
A dozen iron candle sticks, two pair stake tongs 3*s.* 6*d.*
A cleaver and 2 chopping knifes 1*s.* 6*d.*
A pair of ballances and weight 1*s.* 8*d.*
One box iron, 5 heaters and 2 iron stand 4*s.* 6*d.*
Three wood candle sticks and an chaffing dish 3*s.* 3*d.*
Two frying pans 5*s.*
A tin fish plate, 3 tin dripping pans 1*s.* 6*d.*
A fire screen, a pair of bellows and a small mortar and pestle 8*s.* 6*d.*
A chaffing dish, an tin oven and 4 tin drippers 1*s.* 6*d.*
Three tin dish covers, ditto collinder and a gratter 2*s.* 6*d.*
Six straw matts, wood dishes and a laddle 2*s.* 10*d.*
A table, 2 stools and 2 pair of steeps 6*s.*
A dresser and shelves, a long board to iron clease on 6*s.*
Two screens to hang clease on and five chairs 5*s.* 6*d.*
Seven Delf dishes and 8 plates, a dozen of earth pots 5*s.*
Two brass boilers, one ditto pot, 5 sauce pan, one stew pan and a brass laddle [and pepper box *added*] £1 17*s.*
A tin fish pan, a large spoon, 4 window curtains 2*s.* 6*d.*
Tea kettle and lamp, 5 earth potts and a wood salt box 6*s.* 3*d.*
Trencher rack, 11 trenchers and safe 4*s.*
Cheese, 3 brushes and a buckett 8*s.* 11*d.*
A tin floor box, ditto slice and a toasting fork 8*d.*
Carried over £110 0*s.* 3¼*d.*

In the Parlour
An oak oval table 9*s.*
Six rush chairs 3*s.*
Four brass candle sticks 2*s.* 6*d.*
A copper stew pan, cover ditto, a little pot ditto, a patty pan and a brass plate 9*s.*
Six oval pewter dishes, ditto two strainers, one dozen hard mettal plates and 16 other plates £1 15*s.*
Six small tin dripping pans, ditto 3 plate

covers 2*s.* 9*d.*
Three large earth potts 1*s.* 6*d.*
A dozen stammpers and basketts 3*s.*
A tin watering pott and two small sives 10*d.*
Corks and fire wood 15*s.*
A dozen quart bottles of Bristol water 3*s.*
Four window curtains 1*s.*
A cask of tamarinds £1 2*s.*
Nine small pewter dishes 15*s.*
Carried forward £116 2*s.* 10¼*d.*

Doctor's Room
A larum clock 15*s.*
A folding bed stead, canvas curtain and rod 9*s.*
Two chairs and a lantren 3*s.*
A small feather bed, 3 pillows and a mattras £1 6*s.*
A quilt and 2 blanketts 10*s.*
Canes, walking sticks and 2 whipps 11*s.*
A square oake table with a draw 8*s.*
A gun, a dozen brushes, wood punch laddles 10*s.* 6*d.*
Watch strings and keys 4*s.* 6*d.*
Three snuff boxes and a spie glass 1*s.* 3*d.*
Steel nippers, ditto tooth drawers and cork screws 3*s.*
A fishing real and a sand dish 3*s.*
A mohawk and a pair of plyers 1*s.*
Two dozen of tooth brushes and a smelling bottle [and case *added*] 3*s.*
A brass pen, a pen case and 3 pencils 1*s.*
A pair of scissors and odd buckles 1*s.*
Window curtains and a lantern 1*s.* 6*d.*
Daffy elixer, British oile etc 10*s.*
A hanger, bridle, saddle and a belt 7*s.* 6*d.*
Carried over £122 12*s.* 1¼*d.*

In the Port a Bello
A press bed stead £1 1*s.*
A pair of draws 8*s.*
A deal cubbert 3*s.*
An oake oval table 10*s.*
Nine chairs 4*s.* 6*d.*
A stove grate and a pair of iron dogs 9*s.* 6*d.*
A fire pan, pooker and iron trippett 2*s.*
A close stool and an earth pan 3*s.*
Tooth drawers, hand vice etc 5*s.*
A vice board, vice and a prickett 3*s.*
A nail box and odd screws 2*s.*
A lead candle stick and a brush 4*d.*
A small dial and an iron laddle 1*s.*
Lumber 2*s.*
Carried forward £126 6*s.* 5¼*d.*

Mr Smith Rooms
A bedstead with harrowteen curtains £1 1*s.*
A stove grate, fender, fire pan, a pair of tongs and pooker 10*s.*
A pair of bellow, a brush, a picture and window screen 3*s.*
Three rush chairs and a small table 4*s.*
A spring tinder box, candle stick, a pair of snuffers, extinguisher, a bason and a chamber pot 2*s.*
A close press, an canvas tent and mackey £3 5*s.*
Two fire busketts and two sives 3*s.*
A bottle rack and bottles £1.
A pair of vice, a binch, a form and a hold fast 4*s.*
A turning frame and tools £2.
A measuring wheel and gun powder 9*s.*
A brass furnish and grate £1 1*s.*
A wire sieve, a fire pan, a brass skimer and a dripping pan 2*s.* 6*d.*
Coals and faggots, bottles and lumber £1 7*s.*

In the Yard and Garden
A dial plate, settles, sparrows, garden potts, binches, a wheel barrow and fruit trees 17*s.* 6*d.*
Empty casks, two bottle racks and bottles £2 7*s.*

In the Necessary House
A cubbert, 10 prints and iron barr 3*s.* 6*d.*

In the Stable
An old horse £1 10*s.*

Carried over £142 15s. 11¼d.

The Billard Room
Billard table, sticks and balls £8 8s.
A square deal table and one dozen tin candle sticks 3s.
Binches, window curtains 3s.
A small iron grate, ditto fender, blower, fire pan, tongs and pooker 4s.
Six chairs and three stools 3s.
A pair of bellows and a brush 1s.
Candles, lead bulletts and lumber £2 13s. 2d.

The Maids Room
A folding bed stead 4s.
A flock bed, one pillow, two blanketts and a rugg 11s.
A hammock, a swing glass and six chairs 8s. 6d.
Eleven small wood bottles 6s.
Two iron dogs and a pair of tongs 1s.
Camomile flowers 15s.
Carried forward £156 16s. 7¼d.

The Vernon
A grate, blower, fender, tongs, a fire pan and a pooker 5s. 6d.
A mahogony table 18s.
A mahogony tea table, ditto stand, tea kettle and lamp £1 3s.
Four mahogony hand boards, ditto cheese, ditto two bottle stands and a tobacco dish 8s. 6d.
A buro and square deal table £4 13s.
Six chairs, a tea chest 6s. 6d.
A dozen knifes, ditto forks and case 15s.
A back gamon table and a draught board £1 1s.
A looking glass and a pair of brass arms £1 3s.
Three pictures, 3 prints and a corner cubbert 10s. 6d.
Two china dishes, ditto 3 punch boiles £1 8s.
Two dozen china plates 16s.
China sausers, ditto tea and coffee dishes 11s.
China slopp basons 2s. 6d.
Earthren ware: slopp basons, cups, tea potts and a sugar dish 4s.
A glass cup 6d.
Delf ware: a boile, coffee cupps, strainers, cream pots and 2 small dishes 1s. 4d.
Carried over £171 3s. 11¼d.

The Vernon continued
Three Delf punch boiles, ditto 2 plates, six tea potts and 3 chambers potts 5s.
Two reading glasses, 5 ditto daunters, 2 ditto candlesticks 8s.
Four water glasses, 7 ditto cups, 6 ditto salts, 14 ditto half pints 6s.
Ten dozen drinking glasses £1.
A tobacco dish, a ratt cage and 8 bell 5s.
Ten sheets, ditto 4 check £2 5s.
Five dammask table cloaths, ditto one dozen and ½ napkins £1 9s.
Five Russia table cloaths, ditto 17 napkins 13s.
Twenty small hand cloaths, 4 small pillow cases 6s.
Sixteen knifes, ditto forks, 14 pen knifes 15s.
Old knifes, 2 rasors and mettle buttons 2s. 6d.
Two black silk hatt bands 5s.
Three boxes, a rasor strapp and a pair of scale etc 3s.
A nest of open boxes 2s.
Rules and an old quadrant, six yards of check cloath 12s.
Bookes £1.
Syrup of red poppies 8s.
Usquebah, arrack, rum, cistren water £1 18s.
Lancetts and a pair of shirt bottons 2s.
Two tin quarts and a half pint 1s.
Carried forward £183 9s. 5¼d.

Cellars and Clossetts
Two hundred and ten gallons of strong beer £7.
Cyder 5 dozen £1.

Bristol water 6*s.*
Port wine in cask: 10 gallons at 4*s.* per gallon £2.
Port wine in bottles: at 4*s.* per gallon £12.
White wine in cask: 10 gallons at 4*s.* per gallon £2.
Made wine: 30 gallons £3.
Madera wine: 2 dozen at 4*s.* per gallon £1 4*s.*
124 gallons of British spirits at 2*s.* per gallon £11 8*s.*
Rasbury brandy, ditto cherry, wormwood water and British gin in bottles £1 10*s.*
Foreign brandy in cask and bottles at 7*s.* per gallon £2 16*s.*
Rum in casks: 42 gallons at 7*s.* per gallon £14 14*s.*
Spirits of wine 3*s.* 9*d.*
Vinegar and cask 8*s.*
Brass cocks 7*s.*
Tobacco and a box £2 2*s.*
Casks in the cellars £1 18*s.*
Horses and lumber £1 18*s.*

Total £245 1*s.* 2¼*d.* [*recte* £249 4*s.* 2¼d]

Edward Farmer and Samuell Deavin, appraisors.

Buried St. Peter 15 August 1746.
Commission 16 October 1746; bond 17 October 1746, administration to John Lane, innholder, principal creditor; inventory exhibited 30 June 1747.

446 WILLIAM SERLE[1]
13 February 1746/7 P1/S/1152

In the Fore Garret No 1
A red large bed and bedstead with rods £1 10*s.*
1 feather bed, bolster and pillows £1 12*s.*
1 close-stool and pewter pan 4*s.* 6*d.*
1 pair of dogs 2*s.*
1 Windsor chair 4*s.*
3 blankets and 1 old coverlid 3*s.* 6*d.*
1 press bedstead 7*s.* 6*d.*
1 small feather bed and bolster £1 2*s.* 6*d.*
1 small ditto flock 5*s.*
Room total £5 11*s.*

In the Back Garret No 2
Two housings and a pair of bras stirrups 7*s.* 6*d.*
1 old musket and a mourning sword 5*s.*
A bundle of walking sticks 2*s.*
7 boxes and a trunk 5*s.*
1 bolster 4*s.* 6*d.*
1 pillow, cushions and a chaise cushion 9*s.* 6*d.*
2 sash locks and a basket of lumber 4*s.*
A box of roots, coffee mill and tinder box 5*s.*
A box with odd things 5*s.*
2 boxes full of bottles 5*s.* 6*d.*
2 pocket books and 3 pair of slippers 10*s.*
1 pocket book and a small box 3*s.*
Silk and velvet 18*s.*
1 pair of shoes and a window curtain 2*s.* 6*d.*
Surgeon's instruments £1 10*s.*
A box of brushes 2*s.*
1 box with lumber 1*s.*
French plate £1 1*s.*
Room total £7 0*s.* 6*d.*

The Back Chamber No 3
2 pair of pistols £1 10*s.*
2 pair of tongs, 2 firepans, a fender, brush and 1 pair of bellows 7*s.*
A coal grate 2*s.* 6*d.*
A tea kettle 2*s.*
3 chairs 5*s.*
1 brass tea chest 2*s.* 6*d.*
A tea board 3*s.*
1 china sugardish and stand 2*s.* 6*d.*
1 tea pot, 4 dishes and saucers 5*s.*
Part room total £2 19*s.* 6*d.*

Other odd china 4*s.*
Broken china and 2 Delf bowls 5*s.*
3 drinking glasses 1*s.*
2 glasses and a table £1 3*s.*

A hanger and belt £1 7*s.*
An old cubbard 3*s.* 6*d.*
2 walking canes 4*s.*
5 pictures 5*s.*
Part room total £3 12*s.* 6*d.*

The Street Chamber No 4
1 low chest of drawers 7*s.* 6*d.*
A desk and book case 10*s.*
1 stove grate 7*s.*
1 mahogany table 12*s.*
7 glasses 1*s.* 6*d.*
1 white quilt 17*s.*
2 blankets 4*s.*
Old stockins and old wastcoats 2*s.*
12 old towels and a bucking cloth 3*s.* 6*d.*
5 table cloths 4*s.* 6*d.*
4 odd things 1*s.*
1 pair of sheets and 1 old ditto 14*s.*
3 pair of sheets 16*s.*
2 bolsters cases 3*s.*
1 table cloth and 6 napkins 5*s.*
7 damask napkins and cloth 4*s.* 6*d.*
6 pillow cases and toilight 2*s.* 6*d.*
Room total £6 15*s.*

Linnen
1 large huckerback table cloth and 1 small ditto 3*s.* 9*d.*
4 napkins and 2 towells 3*s.*
3 foul shirts, old 3*s.*
4 long cravats 4*s.*
4 pillow cases 2*s.*
12 shirts foul and clean, very good at 8*s.* a piece £4 16*s.*
3 old shirts 5*s.*
12 neck stocks, good 10*s.*
9 ordinary ditto 3*s.*
8 long cravats 7*s.*
6 caps 1*s.* 6*d.*
7 handkercheifs 4*s.* 6*d.*
2 pair of shoes and slippers 4*s.*
3 hats 9*s.*
Linen total £7 15s 9*d.*

Wearing Apparel
4 white wastcoats 8*s.*
5 pair of old breeches 14*s.*
Old stockins 9*s.*
5 wastcoats 17*s.*
A gown and green bannian 12*s.*
6 coats £4.
2 great coats 18*s.*
1 cap and leather hood 1*s.* 6*d.*
4 wigs 18*s.*

In a Long Box
2 peices of cloth, 3 wastcoats, 3 breeches, 1 silk night-gown and 4 coats £10.
Apparel total £18 17*s.* 6*d.*

18 ounces of old silver at 4*s.* 6*d.* £4 1*s.*
A watch £2.
A gold ring 4*s.*
In the book-case 5*s.*
Razors, knives, sizers and box 7*s.* 6*d.*
Section total £7 [*recte* £6 17*s.* 6*d.*]

In the Pantry and Back Room
A tea kettle, lamp and stand 7*s.*
1 pair of brass candle sticks 2*s.*
1 small drinking pot and coffee pot 1*s.* 6*d.*
A hand candlestick 1*s.* 3*d.*
1 brass ladle and skimmer 1*s.* 6*d.*
Knives and forks with a box 2*s.*
1 candle box 8*d.*
6 Delf plates 2*s.*
3 Delf dishes 1*s.* 6*d.*
2 fruit china dishes 1*s.* 6*d.*
5 pickle pots 2*s.* 6*d.*
1 cheese plate 6*d.*
1 nest of drawers with odd things in it 10*s.*
A larrum 16*s.*
1 old table basket and boots 4*s.*
Earthen ware and china 3*s.* 6*d.*
1 warming pan and brass bason 3*s.*
1 chopping knife and trivet 1*s.* 6*d.*
1 jack, a bell and 2 whips 7*s.*
A box and odd things and scales 2*s.* 6*d.*
25 glasses and 1 cruet 5*s.*
A box with cards, 4 packs 2*s.* 6*d.*
1 spit 1*s.*

Room total £3 19s. 11*d.*

In the Celler
1 saddle and bridle 6s.
1 dozen of bottles, odd ones 1s.
Earthen ware 1s.
1 pot and stewpan 7s. 6*d.*
1 tobacco pot with some in it 1s. 6*d.*
1 small ferkin, jar, and tobacco bowl 3s. 6*d.*
1 shovel and saw 2s.
Room total £1 2s. 6*d.*

In The Kitchen
6 leather chairs 8s.
1 square table 4s.
1 joint stool and tub 2s.
1 fire shovel, tongs, poker, 1 trivet and gridiron 4s. 6*d.*
1 small jack 2s. 6*d.*
5 candlesticks 1s. 3*d.*
In the cupboard brass things and tin ditto 4s.
39 lbs. ½ of pewter at 7*d.* £1 2s. 9*d.*
Lumber 1s. 6*d.*
The cubboards 10s.
1 window curtain, 1 stooper and lumber 1s. 6*d.*
1 kettle and skillet 2s.
Room total £3 4s.

In Mr Neat's House
1 oaken press 10s.
3 cubboards 5s.
Goods belonging to the stable, barrels and lumber £2 1s. 6*d.*
Omitted 2 pr of stockins and a silver grater 5s.
Section total £3 1s. 6*d.*

Money in pocket £1 8s. 6*d.*
The study of books comes to £19 5s. 1*d.*
Valued and appraised by me Walter Gillmore Bookseller in Marlborough
A Catalogue of which Books is ready to be produced when required.[2] (*signed*) James Serle and Mary Serle

[*Total omitted, by addition* £91 10s. 9*d.*]

[*Note in another hand*] In desperate debts due from several persons as by the deceased's books appears, which the party exhibitant protests against charging himself with or with any part there of more than such as shall be recovered nor untill the same shall be so recovered £179 4s. 3*d.*

Mr John Rogers and Mr Henry Hill, appraisors.

Buried St. Peter 12 February 1746/7, 'Dr. William Sirel'.
Will 10 March 1737/8; renunciation 4 June 1747 by Edward Greenfield of Marlborough in favour of Rev. James Serle of Froxfield; renunciation 18 June 1747 by Edward Greenfield of New Sarum (late of Lockeridge); bond 20 July 1747, administration to James Serle, testator's brother[3].

1. 'Doctor of physic' on renunciation; Serle was a student of Merton College, Oxford, and was awarded the degree of Doctor of Common Laws in 1724.
2. This catalogue is not extant.
3. Incumbent of Froxfield.

447 JANE JEFFARISS[1]

widow [burial register] 28 May 1747
P1/IJ/217

One lease hold paddock and little garden £6.
Wearing apparrell and money in pockett £2 10s.
Gold rings £2.

Total £10 10s.

Benjamin Bassett and William Smith, appraisors.

Buried St. Mary 20 May 1747 'Widow Jafferies'.
Will 1 May 1747; probate 1 June 1747 to Robert Jefferies, testator's son.

1. 'late of the parrish of the Virgin Mary in Marlbrough'.

448 FRANCIS GREGORY

cutler 6,10 and 11 May 1748 P1/G/580

In the Kitchen
One oval table 10*s.* 6*d.*
Five chairs 3*s.* 4*d.*
One jack, lyne and weight 6*s.*
One pair of andirons 2*s.* 6*d.*
One pair of doggs 1*s.*
One pair of tongs 8*d.*
Two fire panns 1*s.*
One pair of bellows 1*s.* 6*d.*
Two spitts 3*s.*
Two brass candlesticks 3*s.*
Two iron candlesticks 8*d.*
Two brass pepper boxes 6*d.*
One brass flower box 4*d.*
One brass tinder box 6*d.*
One brass sconce 6*d.*
One tin candle box 4*d.*
One corner cubbard 2*s.*
One chaffing dish 2*s.*
One grid iron 6*d.*
One bacon rack 2*s.* 6*d.*
One fire curtain and rod 3*s.* 6*d.*
One pair of hangells 1*s.*
One looking glass 1*s.*
Three Oxford almanacks 1*s.*
Two other pictures 4*d.*
One gun 1*s.*
One heater 2*d.*
One fire brush 1*d.*
One pair of snuffers 2*d.*
One long iron candlestick 8*d.*
One box iron, one stand and two clamps 2*s.* 6*d.*
One iron fender 2*d.*
One salt box 6*d.*

In the Pantry
One tea table 2*s.*
One other table 2*s.* 6*d.*
One warming pann 2*s.* 6*d.*
Nine pewter dishes, twenty three pewter plates, two pewter poringers and one pewter bason £1 16*s.* 8*d.*
One tin cullender and two tin cupps 10*d.*
One tin tunnell and two tin dripping panns 1*s.* 6*d.*
One tin coffee pott 2*d.*
Two brass boylers and two brass lidds 14*s.* 3*d.*
Two brass skyllets and one brass kettle 5*s.* 6*d.*
Two brass sauce panns 1*s.* 6*d.*
One brass pott ledd 1*s.*
Two brass cocks 2*s.*
Half a dozen of tin patty panns 6*d.*
Five iron candlesticks 1*s.*
One lantern 6*d.*
One flower tubb 2*d.*
One earthen pan 4*d.* and one cubbard 2*s.* 2*s.* 4*d.*
One ratt trapp 3*d.*, one wooden platter and one pye board 8*d.* 11*d.*
A small quantity of earthen ware 1*s.* and one iron pott and grate 2*s.* 3*s.*
One frying pan 2*s.* and one brass skymer and ladle 1*s.* 2*d.* 3*s.* 2*d.*

In the Cellar
One furnace and grate £1.10*s.* and one mashing tubb 4*s.* £1 14*s.*
One great washing tubb 4*s.* and one little ditto 2*s.* 6*s.*
One long kiver 2*s.* 6*d.* and three other tubbs 4*s.* 6*s.* 6*d.*
Five round kivers 6*s.* and one tun bowle 1*s.* 6*d.* 7*s.* 6*d.*
Two lead pails and three bowles 2s 6*d.* and seven barrells 17*s.* 6*d.* £1.
One cooler 4*s.* and two wooden horses and two stools 3*s.* 6*d.* 7*s.* 6*d.*
One stirrer 2*d.*, one cubbard 1*s.*, one spout 2*s.*, two bucketts 2*s.* 5*s.* 2*d.*
One tea kettle 2*s.*

Page total £11 5s. 1d.

In the Inner Garrett

One feather bed, bedsteed, curtains, vallens, two feather pillows and one bolster £2 5s.

Two blanketts and one coverlid 7s. 6d. two chairs 2s. 9s. 6d.

One coffer and two boxes 1s. 6d., one grate and one heater 5s. 6s. 6d.

In the Outer Garrett

One feather bedd, one pillow and one flock bolster £1 4s.

Three blanketts and one rugg 4s., one bedsteed 4s. 8s.

Two little chests 4s., one flasket and one basket 1s. 6d. 5s. 6d.

Two hampers and two locks 1s. 6d.

Two pictures 6d.

Three dozen and a half of quart glass bottles 3s. 6d.

One dozen of pint dittos 6d.

In the Best Chamber

One feather bedd, one bolster and 2 pillows £2.

One bedsteed, curtains, vallens and window curtains £2.

Three blanketts 8s., one quilt 8s. and one chest of drawers 10s. £1 6s.

One dressing table and one glass 11s., six chairs and one cushion 3s. 14s.

One close stool 2s., four pictures 1s. and two chamber potts and one box 1s. 4s.

In the Little Room

One table 5s., one chest of drawers 6s. and three chairs 1s. 6d. 12s. 6d.

One cloathes press 10s., two ironing boards 3s. and three pictures 1s. 14s.

Two brass andirons, one fire shovell and one pair of tongs 4s. and two tea boards 1s. 6d. 5s. 6d.

One corner shelf 8d. and one cubbard 2s. 2s. 8d.

Two chairs 8d. and one baskett 4d. 1s.

Lynnen in and about the House

Four pair of sheetts 12s.

Four table cloathes 3s.

Three pair of pillow bears 2s.

Six short towells 1s., five long towells 1s. 3d. 2s. 3d.

One bowlster case 4d., one dyapper table cloath and four napkins 3s. 3s. 4d.

One hockerback table cloath and six dyapper napkins 7s.

One holland sheett and one pillow bear 5s.

Wearing Apparel

One coat, one wastcoat and one pair of breeches 15s.

One great coat 7s.

One grey coat 7s. and one old coat 4s. 11s.

One pair of breeches and two wastcoats 3s. 6d., one wigg 2s. 5s. 6d.

One hatt 3s. and one pair of new breeches 6s. 9s.

One pair of bootts and two pair of shoes 4s. and two pair of stockings 3s. 7s.

Four shirts 10s. and four neck cloaths 2s. 12s.

In the Shop and other places in and about the House

One dozen of knives and one dozen of forks with buckshorn handles 12s.

One dozen of knives and one dozen of forks, buckshorn norths 7s.

Half a dozen of ivory knives and half a dozen of forks 10s.

Half a dozen of stagghorn knives and half a dozen of forks 6s.

Half a dozen of coco handle knives and forks 3s.

Half a dozen of blackhorn handle knives and forks 2s.

Half a dozen of buck ruffhorn handle knives and forks 5s.

Three dozen and a half of box knives 15s. 9d.

Five knives and two forks 2s. 4d.

Six cookes knives and one fork 7*s.* 6*d.*
Fifteen buckshorn butcher knives 7*s.* 6*d.*
Half a dozen of pruning knives 4*s.*
Three large butchers knives 2*s.*
Seven knives and three forkes 4*s.*
One dozen and a half of shoemakers knives 6*s.*
One dozen and a half of smaller ditto 4*s.* 6*d.*
Three pair of shears 5*s.*
Two pair of ditto 2*s.* 8*d.*
One pair of ditto 2*s.* 2*d.*
Four box irons 6*s.*
Three stands 6*d.*
Four steels 5*s.*
One ditto 1*s.*
Two dozen and a half of mouse traps 4*s.* 2*d.*
Two dozen of knives and two dozen of forks 7*s.* 6*d.*
Eight knives and forks 5s 4*d.*
One dozen of knives and one dozen of forks 6*s.*
Three pair of small taylors shears 1*s.* 10*d.*
A quantity of common sisars 2*s.* 9*d.*
Three cheese irons 1*s.*
Two punches and two compasses 10*d.*
Page total £25 15*s.* 7*d.*

A quantity of ink horns 3*s.* 6*d.*
A quantity of tacks and blades 6*s.* 6*d.*
Nine hones 13*s.*
A quantity of fork blades 1*s.* 8*d.*
Three dozen of horn combes 4*s.*
A quantity of snuff boxes 2*s.*
A quantity of tobacco boxes 7*s.* 6*d.*
Four pair of nut crackers 8*d.*
A quantity of brass fleam cases 3*s.* 4*d.*
Nine oyster knives 2*s.* 3*d.*
Three dozen and a half of clasp knives 9*s.* 4*d.*
A quantity of clasp knives of several sorts 8*s.* 7*d.*
A quantity of clasp buckshorn handle knives 17*s.*
One dozen and three snuffers 3*s.* 6*d.*
A quantity of lance cases 3*s.* 9*d.*
One dozen of twesers 1*s.* 6*d.*
Three dozen and three ivory knives and forks £1 15*s.* 6*d.*
One dozen of fleams 15*s.*
Eight lances 8*s.*
Eight pen knives 5*s.* 6*d.*
Ten pair of tind spurs 5*s.*
Fourteen pair of steel spurs 10*s.*
Seventeen pair of sisars 6*s.* 4*d.*
A quantity of corke screws 3*s.* 8*d.*
A quantity of seals and key rings 1*s.* 2*d.*
One pair of sisars and two razors 1*s.* 6*d.*
One dozen of pen knives 12*s.*
Eight other pen knives 6*s.*
Razor sceals 1*s.* 6*d.*
Eight pair of buckells 4*s.* 1½*d.*
Four west bond ditto 1*s.* 8*d.*
One dozen of ditto 4*s.* 6*d.*
A quantity of buckells of several sorts £1 2*s.* 1*d.*
A quantity of mourning buckells and buttons 16*s.* 3*d.*
A quantity of sleave buttons and girdle buckells 4*s.* 8*d.*
A quantity of aul hafts 1*s.* 4*d.*
A quantity of spur rowells 4*s.*
A quantity of calves tails 4*d.*
Two canes 6*s.*
Two dozen and four of razors £2 2*s.*
Three dozen and two pair of sisars £2 7*s.* 6*d.*
A quantity of cases and sheaths of all sorts 16*s.* 4*d.*
A quantity of blades £2 8*s.* 2*d.*
A quantity of files 2*s.* 2*d.*
Nine dozen of buckshorn hafts 9*s.*
A quantity of small hafts 5*s.*
A buff belt 1*s.*
Six dozen of ivory combes £1 11*s.*
Nine other ivory combes 6*s.* 1*d.*
One dozen and a half of spectacles 3*s.*
Nine pen knife blades 2*s.* 3*d.*
Six old hones 6*s.* 6*d.*
Four sawes 6*s.*
One wheel 5*s.*
One pair of billows 7*s.* 6*d.*
One grind stone 7*s.*

A quantity of stones and gleazers 10*s.* 6*d.*
One dozen of ripping hooks 10*s.*
One counter with drawers £4.
One vice board 1*s.*
Glass windows [not belonging to the house *added*] 16*s.*
And one fire buckett 8*d.*
Page total £27 11*s.* 10½*d.*
Other side £25 15*s.* 7*d.*
First side £11 5*s.* 1*d.*
Sub total £64 12*s.* 6½*d.*

Three pair of vices 14*s.*, one anvil £1 1*s.*
Beckiron and hammers 6*s.* and one cane 3*s.*
Sub total £2 4*s.*

Total £66 16*s.* 6½*d.*

Sold by the said Executrix Since the Testators Death
Three pruning knives 3*s.* 6*d.*
Two knives and forks 3*s.* 6*d.*
Three pair of buckells 1*s.* 10*d.*
One snuff box 8*d.*
Various shoemakers things 1*s.* 2*d.*
A butchers knife 6*d.*
Two pair of sisars 1*s.*
A quantity of buttons 1*s.* 1*d.*
One razor 8*d.*
One screw 8*d.*
One ink horn 2*d.*
One knife 5*d.*
Two pair of buckells 1*s.* 4*d.*
One knife and fork 1*s.*
One pen knife 5*d.*
One inkhorn 3*d.*
One knife 4*d.*
One cheeseiron 6*d.*
One pair of buckells 6*d.*
One pair of sisars 6*d.*
One pair of flames 2*s.*
One pair of buckells 6*d.*
One pair of buckells 10*d.*
Four new blades 2*s.*
One new blade 6*d.*
One knife 6*d.*
One pair of buckells 6*d.*
Two tobacco boxes 2*s.* 6*d.*
One pair of buckells 4*d.*
One new blade 6*d.*
One knife 3*d.*
One knife and fork 1*s.*
One pair of buckells 6*d.*
One combe 1½*d.*
One pair of buckells 9*d.*
One knife 1*s.* 6*d.*
One knife and fork 7*d.*
One cheeseiron 8*d.*
One cane 3*s.*
One stock buckell 6*d.*
One knife 3*d.*
One pair of sisars 1*s.* 6*d.*
Page total £2 0*s.* 3½*d.*
On the other side £66 16 6½*d.*

Total £68 16*s.* 10*d.*

William Jackson[1], John Chivers[1] and Richard Smith[2], appraisors.

Buried St. Mary 30 March 1748, 'Mr.'.
Will 20 November 1747; probate 23 May 1748 to Sarah Gregory, testator's daughter.

1. 'as to the househoold goods'.
2. 'as to the goods and tools of the trade of a cutler'.

449 THOMAS KENDALL[1]

vintner 17 April 1749 P1/K/226

In the Seler
The beer and cask and the horses in the seler and gin, rum and brandy £36 8*s.* 10*d.*

In the Fore Room
2 tables, 5 chayers, one forme, two window curtens and rods 16*s.*

In the Back Parlour
Two tables, 7 chayers, one looking glass,

six prints, one peer of brass dogs, one small bell £1 4s. 6d.

In the Brew House
One brewing copper and grate, one mesh tubb, 2 coolers and 2 pails, one hopp strayner, one boull, 5 tubbs, one old cask, one cole box, one lead pipe £8 3s.

In the Skulery
One small copper and grate £1 16s.

In the Pantry
Two tables, one iron frying pan, 2 saspans, 2 buckets, one skymer and earthen ware 12s. 6d.

In the First Chamber
One flock bed and bolster, 2 blankets, one bed stide, on chayer and a small end of hops £2 8s. 6d.
Page total £51 9s. 4d.

In the Second Chamber
Two feather beds, 4 blankets, on bedstide and 3 pair of sheets and other linning £3 19s.

In the Garrat
One flock bed and bolster, 2 ruggs and 2 bedstids £1 1s.

In the Kitchen
9 pweter dishes, 24 pweter plates, one plate rack, 11 trenchers, one pweter basson, 3 ditto pints, one ditto quart, 2 quarterns ditto, 2 ditto half, one ditto half pint, 7 ditto spoons, one tin driping pan, one tin cullinder, one warming pan, one jack, 6 spits, 13 iorn candelsticks, 2 fier shovels, one pair of tongs, one beasting leadell, one pair of billows, one brass candelstick, 2 brass peper boxs, one flower box, one iorn grate and fender, one heater and one pair of hanging dogs, one gridiorn, 3 flatt iorn, 6 earth quarts, 7 ditto pints and 2 half pints, one beacking rack, one hammer, one hatchet, one spead, on shovel, 2 pair of window curtins, 2 settels, 2 tables, one tin quart, one tin kittell, 1 brass bowller, 3 benches and a dresser and shivels and the spitt, bracketts and shelves, 2 chayers and salt box, 2 small matts, one tea kittel and trivet £6 14s. 6d.
Page total £11 14s. 6d.
Brought forward £63 3s. 10d.

In the Yard etc
4 piggs, 8 hardells and 6 hand of faggots, chamber £8.

Total £71 3s.10d.

Edward Turner and William Whitaker, appraisors.

Burial not recorded.
Bond 8 May 1749, administration to Elizabeth Kendall, intestate's widow.

1. 'att the Phenix in Marlbrough'.

450 WILLIAM CLIFFORD
shopkeeper 2 May 1749 P1/C/834

In the Best Chamber
Wearing apparrell £7 5s.
One feather bed, bedsteed, 2 pillows, curtains and vallens, 4 blanketts, a rugg and quilt and bolster £8.
One looking glass 11s.
A close stool 7s. 6d.
7 chairs 18s.
A chest of drawers and 1 table 12s.
4 pictures 4s.

In the Little Chamber
One flock bed, 2 blanketts, 1 rugg and bedsteed £2 10s.
2 chairs 1s. 8d.

In the Two Garretts
Lumber £2.

In the Kitchen
Brass 19*s.*
Jack and iron things in the chimney 9*s.*
7 chairs 7*s.*
3 tables, 1 cupboard 7*s.*
A skreen 5*s.*
Pewter 18*s.*
Books 12*s.*

In the Brewhouse
Potts, kettles and a furnace £4.
Barrells and brewing vessells £1 10*s.*

In the Backside
Wood and coale £1 10*s.*

In the Shop
Boxes, weights and scales £1 10*s.*
Six sides of bacon £4 10*s.*
3 hundred of cheese £4 4*s.*
Gingerbread and sugar plumbs £10.
Sope and candles 18*s.*
Inkle, thread, pins and laces £1 10*s.*
Paper, carraways, salt and tobacco £2.
Sugar, figgs and bissoms £1.

In the Room for Spiritous Liquors
Spiritous liquors £6 10*s.*
Shop debts £8.

Total £73 8*s.* 2*d.*

John Rumsey and William Sutton, appraisors.

Buried St. Mary 26 February 1748.
Bond dated 9 May 1749, administration to Hester Clifford, intestate's widow.

451 MARY GILLMORE
widow [*undated*, c.1751] P1/G/594

1741 December 24[1] A mortgage from Richard Smith of his house in Kingsbury Street carrying interest from 24 December 1748 at £4 10*s.* per cent £100.
1742/3 February 1 A mortgage from Richard Phelps of a farm at Avebury on which about a years interest at £4 10*s.* per cent was due at the death of the testatrix £400.
1746/7 January 31 A bond from Benjamin Merryman carrying interest of £5 per cent from 31 January 1749/50 £100.
1746 July 12 A note from the Rev. Mr Harris carrying interest at £5 per cent from 12 July 1750 £30.
1747/8 February 20 A bond from Charles Garrard Esquire and Thomas Garrard Gentleman carrying interest at £5 per cent from 20 February 1748/9 £100.
1748 April 27 A mortgage from Edward Buckerfield of lands at Chisledon and interest at £5 per cent £50.

Caish in the house £100.
More caish £10.
A bond from Frances Gillmore and Mary Gillmore dated 5 June 1744 interest for £250 being legacys left them by the will of John Gillmore deceased which were paid to them by the testatrix in her lifetime[*amount omitted*]
Rent received of Mr Dangerfield for the ground 18*s.* 6*d.*
1751 October 12 Two years rent of ten acres in Portfield received of John Gillmore £16.

Two silver tankards, one porringer, one waiter, four salts, ten large spoons, six small spoons and tea tongs, a silver girdle buckle, eight gold rings and a little pair of gold earings, a china basin, sugar dish and five tea dishes and saucers [*amount omitted*].

[*Added in another hand*] There were divers household goods and other particulars in the dwelling house of the testatrix at her death of which the said executrix can give no particular account [thereof, the said *deleted*], [for that *added*] Joseph Gillmore the party promoting this suit did a few days after the death of the said testatrix forcibly turn the said executrix out of the said testatrix's dwellinghouse and the possession thereof and of the said goods and other particulars and took possession thereof himself, by means whereof the said goods and other particulars never came to the hands or possession of the exhibitant since the same were taken out of her custody as aforesaid.

[*Total omitted*]

Elizabeth Fowler, executrix [*appraisors' names omitted*].

Buried St.Mary 21 November 1750 'in the church, widow of Mr. John'.

Will 27 April 1744; commission 7 January 1750/1, oath sworn 14 January 1750/1 by Elizabeth Fowler; probate 16 January 1750/1 to Elizabeth Fowler, testatrix's niece; accounts submitted and inventory exhibited 12 December 1754.

1. The dates of many of the items appear to be those of investments made during the lifetime of the deceased.

452 THOMAS GOATLEY[1]

yeoman 14 February 1758 P1/G/634

No 1. Chamber over the Kitchen

One bedstead, feather bed, one bolster and two old pillows £2 2*s.*

Green harrateen curtains, vallens and rod 8*s.*

One pair of blanketts 4*s.*

One green quilt 4*s.* 6*d.*

One little bedstead, feather bed and bolster 8*s.*

Red curtains, vallens and rod 3*s.* 6*d.*

Two blanketts and one quilt 4*s.*

Two white window curtains and rod 1*s.* 3*d.*

Part of an old broken chest of drawers 1*s.* 6*d.*

Six pair of dowlas sheets, three bolster cases, four pillow cases, two table cloths, six napkins and six towells £1 10*s.* 6*d.*

One coffer and one deal box 3*s.*

One old armd chair 2*s.*

One pair of brass headed doggs 3*s.*

One fire pan and tongs 1*s.* 6*d.*

One little looking glass 2*s.* 6*d.*

Wearing apparel and an old silver watch £3.

No 2. Chamber over the Parlour

One bedstead, feather bed, bolster and 2 blanketts 13*s.* 6*d.*

One green rugg 1*s.* 6*d.*

Old green curtains, vallens and rod 4*s.* 6*d.*

One bedstead, feather bed and bolster £1 10*s.*

A pair of blanketts 3*s.*

One old white quilt 7*s.*

Old white fustain curtains, vallens and rod 10*s.*

Two white window curtains and rod 1*s.*

Six painted withy rush bottom'd chairs 4*s.*

One chest 2*s.* 6*d.*

Firepan, tongs and iron dogs with brass heads 3*s.* 6*d.*

One cloaths brush 6*d.*

One long and one short handle brush 9*d.*

No 3. In the Closet over the Passage

One old bedstead and clothes flaskett 1*s.* 6*d.*

No 4. In the Soldiers Room in the Chamber over the Stable

Three old bedsteads and three old beds, one dust, and beding £1 10*s.* 6*d.*

Four earthen chamber potts 6*d.*

No 5. In the Kitchen
Nine pewter dishes 51lb. at 8*d.* per lb. £1 14*s.*
One dozen and a half of plates 8*s.* 6*d.*
One pewter quart, half pint and 2 quarterns wine measure 2*s.* 6*d.*
One pewter quart and 2 pints beer measure 2*s.* 3*d.*
One old brass warming pan 3*s.*
One jack 10*s.* 6*d.*
Two spits and a tin driping pan 2*s.*
One copper tea kittle 4*s.*
Two pair of brass candlesticks 2*s.* 6*d.*
One quart and one pint copper 2*s.* 6*d.*
Seven iron candlesticks 1*s.* 2*d.*
One copper coffee pott 3*s.* 6*d.*
One old brass hand candlestick 6*d.*
One brass pepper box 4*d.*
One brass ladle 6*d.*
One tin dridging box 2*d.*
One brass pot lid 6*d.*
Two box irons, two stands and 4 heaters 5*s.*
One bell brass morter and iron pestle 2*s.*
Nine ash split bottomd chairs 10*s.*
One table 2*s.*
One joint stool 3*s.*
One grate, one crane, 2 crooks and 1 gridiron 18*s.*
Fire pan, tongs, poker and a tripet 2*s.* 6*d.*
A pair of bellows and brush 1*s.* 3*d.*
Four stone quarts and 6 stone pints 2*s.* 4*d.*
Four stone half pints 6*d.*
Six drinking glasses 1*s.*
Two Delf punch bowles, 6 Delf plates and a punch ladle 2*s.* 9*d.*
Six china tea dishes and 6 saucers, a slop bason and a Delf tea pott 4*s.*
Nine knives and forks 3*s.*
One bacon rack 1*s.* 6*d.*
A child's iron swing 1*s.*

No 6. In the Passage
One cupboard 1*s.* 6*d.*
One spring bell 1*s.*

No 7. Fore Parlour
One oak oval table 8*s.*
One tea table 5*s.*
Twelve withy twig'd bottom'd chairs 6*s.*
One grate, fire pan and tongs 4*s.*
A pair of bellows and brush 1*s.* 2*d.*
One corner cupboard 2*s.* 6*d.*
Six old prints 6*d.*
One looking glass 2*s.* 6*d.*
Green window curtains and rod 2*s.* 6*d.*
Carried forward £23 6*s.* 5*d.* [*recte* £23 5*s.* 11*d.*]

No 8 Back parlour
One old chest 2*s.*
Two old joint stools 2*s.*
Three old withy chairs 1*s.*
An old tea table 1*s.* 6*d.*
A pair of iron doggs 6*d.*

No 9. Brewhouse
One copper furnace and grate £5 5*s.*
One maish tubb and horse £1 10*s.*
One underback £1 4*s.*
Four coolers £1 10*s.*
Two stirrers, a hop strainer and huckmuck 2*s.*
One large and one small pail 2*s.* 6*d.*
One tun and one handle bowle 2*s.*
One long and 1 short cover 9*s.*
One long tubb and 2 water spouts 5*s.*
One large water tubb and horse 3*s.* 6*d.*
Two water bucketts 2*s.* 6*d.*
Two old washing tubbs 2*s.*

No 10. Ale Cellar
Eleven pipes £6.
Seven hogsheads £2 16*s.*
One gin vessell 2*s.*
Five wooden horses and stands 5*s.* 6*d.*
Six hundred gallons of ale at 9*d.* per gallon £22 10*s.*
Ten gallons of gin 3*s.* 6*d.* per gallon £1 15*s.*
Three gallons of rum at 8*s.* per gallon £1 4*s.*
Three gallons of brandy at 8*s.* per gallon

£1 4s.
One large stone jarr 1s. 6d.
Four brass cocks 5s.

No 11. Small Beer Cellar
One hogshead and 3 half hogsheads 12s.
One stand 1s.
Thirty gallons small beer at 1½d. per gallon 3s. 9d.
Two well bucketts 3s.
One powdering tubb 1s. 4d.
One large copper boyler £1 5s.
One small brass boyler 3s.
Two little brass kittles 4s.
One brass skillet 6d.
One sauce pan 1s. 2d.
Two brass skimmers and basting ladle 1s. 3d.
One copper chaffing dish with iron frame 2s.
Four wooden workers 1s.
Twelve wooden trenchers 8d.
One wooden tray and choping knife 1s.
A rolling pin 2d.
One cleaver 4d.

No 12. Woodhouse
One ladder 1s.
Weights and scales 7s. 6d.
Two old hatchetts and 2 billhooks 2s.
One bytle and 3 iron wedges 1s. 6d.
One malliard and chisle 4d.
One hand saw and whip saw 3s.
Two boryers 4d.
Chips and lumber 10s.

No 13. Stable
Two prongs 8d.
One shovel 1s.
One spade 1s.
One small iron rake 9d.

No 14. In the Backside
Fifteen hundred of chamber faggotts at 8s. per hundred £6.
Five hundred of kitchen faggotts and baffins at 16s. per hundred £4.
Ten hundred of luggs and hard wood at 10d. per hundred 8s. 4d.
Skittle pins and two bowles 3s. 6d.
Carried forward £85 16s. [*recte* £85 13s. 4d.]

No 15. In the Garden
A wooden fatting trough 1s. 6d.
One stone trough 1s. 6d.
One piggs scoop 1s.
One piggs buckett 9d.
One grinding stone 2s. 6d.
Total goods £86 3s. 3d. [*recte* £86 0s. 7d.]

An account of cash in house, notes of hand, book and other debts due at the decease of the late Thomas Goatley (being good)
Cash in house £24 6s. 3½d.
Mr William Pearce £2 15s. 9d.
Mr Joseph Rix 5s.
Mr John Pearce £1 8s. 6½d.
Mr John Wentworth 12s.
Mr Thomas Cheeseman 19s. 6d.
Mr Jeremiah Harris 8s. 2d.
Mr Ruddle 5s.
Total good debts £31 0s. 3d.

Book debts etc being desperate, not recoverable, standing out and due at the time of the late Thomas Goatley's decease
1755 April 20 William Major £1 4s. 1d.
1756 March 4 Thomas Kenn £2 2s. 6d.
1756 June 22 Roger Andrews 17s. 2d.
1757 June 18 Richard Mills 1s. 6d.
1757 June 21 Stephen Perkins and Son 11s.
1757 Sept 2 Mr. Deane 3s. 2d.
1757 Dec 15 John Marten a note of hand £1 0s. 10½d.
Total bad debts £6 0s. 3½d.

James Harper and John White, appraisors.

Buried St. Mary 7 February 1758.
Bond 1 June 1762, administration to Sarah

Goatley, intestate's widow; accounts submitted 23 February 1763 by Sarah Goatley.

1. 'late of Saint Martins in the parish of Saint Mary the Virgin in Marlborough'.

453 HARRY ROSE

gentleman 22 September 1766

P1/R/434

One bedstead and curtains £1 1*s.*
One feather bed, two pillows, one flock bolster £1 16*s.*
Two old blanketts and one quilt 7*s.*
One bed quilt 8*s.*
One pair of best blanketts 8*s.* 6*d.*
One pair of sheets 4*s.*
One old flock bed, two pillows and one rug 5*s.*
One press bedstead 6*s.*
One old desk 8*s.*
One old stand desk 1*s.* 6*d.*
Twenty old pictures 2*s.*
Seven small glass prints 1*s.*
Two small corner shelves 4*d.*
One shelve for chiney 1*s.*
One warming pan 3*s.* 6*d.*
One brass fire pan and tongs and two hooks 3*s.* 6*d.*
Three old brass candlesticks 10*d.*
One brass flour box and pepper box 6*d.*
One old cubbord 10*d.*
Three old sheets 7*s.* 6*d.*
One damask tablecloth and two napkins and two hockaback ditto 5*s.* 6*d.*
One bolster case 10*d.*
Six ash chairs 7*s.*
Five old ditto 1*s.* 8*d.*
One stool and pan 3*s.* 6*d.*
One tea kettle 2*s.*
One corner cubbord 2*s.*
One tea table 3*s.* 6*d.*
One swing glass 3*s.*
One small pier ditto 7*s.*
Five old knives and forks 1*s.*
An old parcell of earthen ware 1*s.*
One fire pan and tongs, one pair of dogs and fender 2*s.*
One stool 1*s.*
One old table 9*d.*
One old pair of billows 6*d.*
One pewter dish and six plates 3*s.* 6*d.*
One tub and buckett 4*s.* 6*d.*
One spring lock 1*s.* 3*d.*
One small ditto 9*d.*
One ditto 8*d.*
One old trunk 1*s.* 6*d.*
Two old boxes 1*s.* 6*d.*
One glass 3*s.* 6*d.*
Page total £9 5*s.* 5*d.*

One old box 2*s.*
Two small ditto 6*d.*
One old safe 6*d.*
One copper frying pan 1*s.* 10*d.*
One small brass boiler 2*s.* 6*d.*
One small ditto 3*s.*
One small kettle, one sauce pan and one skimmer 1*s.* 6*d.*
Old bricks and tiles 5*s.*
One old wheelbarrow 4*s.* 6*d.*
Faggots 7*s.*
Five pannell doors 11*s.*
A small quantity of books £2 2*s.*
Three old [silver tea *added*] spoons and one small pair of [tongs *deleted*] silver tongs 5*s.*
One well buckett and rope 7*s.*
One ladder 4*s.*
Hooks, hangings and old iron 5*s.*
The wearing apparel of the said deceased £1 1*s.*
Page total £6 3*s.* 4*d.*

Total £15 8*s.* 9*d.*

And the said Mary Rose the widow and executrix doth hereby declare that no other goods, chattles, rights or credits which were of the said deceased, have at any time since his decease come to the hands, possession or knowledge of the said Mary Rose, the widow and executrix, other than those mentioned and specifyed in the above written inventory.

And the said Mary Rose, the widow and executrix, doth hereby further declare that she doth not in any sort charge herself with any other goods, chattles or effects of the said deceased, any further or otherwise than as the same actually have or shall come to her hands and be by her received.

[*signed*] Mary Rose

Feb 9th 1767 Mary Rose was duly sworn to the truth of this Inventory before me, T. Frome, surrogate

Henry Shepherd and William Perrin, appraisors.

Buried St. Mary 24 August 1766 'Henry Rose'.

Will 10 June 1766; probate 9 February 1767 to Mary Rose, executrix [testator's widow]; accounts presented 9 February 1767 by Mary Rose.

454 HESTER CLIFFORD[1]

widow 10 January 1775 P1/C/984

One feather bed, boulster and two pillows £2 7*s.*
Three blancketts and one quilt 12*s.*
One bedstead and two curtains 6*s.* 6*d.*
Two pair of sheets 11*s.*
Four pillow cases 1*s.* 6*d.*
One light colour'd cloak 5*s.*
One camblet cloak 4*s.*
One black silk cloak 4*s.*
One pair stays 2*s.*
One camblet gown 3*s.* 6*d.*
One stuff gown 3*s.* 6*d.*
One linen gown 4*s.*
One black gown 4*s.* 6*d.*
One plack peticoat 4*s.*
Two under peticoats 2*s.* 6*d.*
One under waistcoat 6*d.*
Nine old shifts 10*s.* 6*d.*
One napkin 6*d.*
Fourteen plain capps 3*s.*
Four pair of cuffs 6*d.*
One pair of small ruffles 3*d.*
Two aprons 2*s.* 6*d.*
Sub-total £6 12*s.* 9*d.*

Four colour'd aprons 3*s.*
Two old white handkerchiefs 3*d.*
One black handkerchief 2*s.*
Four cotton handkerchiefs 3*s.* 6*d.*
One pillow case 6*d.*
Two pair pockets 6*d.*
Seven old hoods 1*s.* 3*d.*
One cane, one fann, one pair sissars, one snuff box and a pair of spectacles 9*d.*
One pair of Bristol stone buttons 1*s.* 6*d.*
One silver tea spoon 8*d.*
One gold ring 4*s.*
One large gold ring (B. Clifford) 12*s.*
Two pair shoes, a pair pattings, a pair clogs, a pair steel buckles and a pair of gloves 2*s.* 9*d.*
A Common Prayer book 1*s.* 6*d.*
One coffer 3*s.* 6*d.*
One watch £1 5*s.*
Sub-total £3 2*s.* 8*d.*

Total £9 15*s.* 5*d.*[2]

William Perrin and Thomas Perrin, appraisers.

Buried St. Mary 2 March 1774.

Bond 1 March 1774[3], administration to William Clifford, intestate's son; accounts submitted 10 January 1775 by William Clifford.

1. 'of St. Martins in the parish of St. Mary the Virgin'.
2. '[goods] that came into the hands of William Clifford her Eldest Son and Heir at Law'.
3. Includes instruction to produce an inventory before 31 May 1775.

GLOSSARY

It is hoped that the following will provide both a glossary and an index for the Probate Inventories of Marlborough. Every attempt has been made to make this as comprehensive a list as possible, with cross-references for the many variations in spelling. Alternative spellings follow the standard spelling of a word, except where these are adjacent to the standard.

Inevitably, there are, despite rigorous searching, a few words which have not yielded their meanings. These are indicated and the WRS would be delighted to hear from any readers who can throw light on such words.

4 in a row a paper of pins inserted in rows of four 232

aburtonences appurtenances 188
acar acre 32
acre 82, 104
addes adze 72
afterleaze herbage remaining after the hay harvest 30
ainder andiron 277, 363, **aindiorne** 153, **aindoran** 191A
aish wood of the ash tree 294, **aishe** 160
aker acre 73, 180
aksys axes 10
alaven eleven 315A
Alborne bell one made at Aldbourne 428
ale 7, 261, 334, 420, 421, 431, 452
ale and bear vessells 386
ale bowle vessel in which ale is served 7
ale cup 56
alembic gourd-shaped distilling vessel *see also* **hot still, lembicke, limbeck, limbeecke, limbick, limbicke, lymbick**
alequart container holding one quart of ale 18
ale tubbe cask for ale 7
aleven eleven 373A
alleblade possibly the business end of an awl 115
allome alum 242
allumminge treating with alum 31
alum mordant used in dyeing 317
alypynte alepint: container holding one pint of ale 18
andear andiron 118, 407, **andeer** 45, **andeier** 188, **andeir** 285, **ander** 58, 157, 283, 300, 343, 355, 396, **andere** 138, 157, **andern** 355
andfeld anvil 38
andian andiron 211, **andiar** 427, **andiare** 66, **andiarne** 153, **andier** *passim* **andierne** 207, 370, **andieron** 140, 353, **andior** 304, **andiorn** 168, 253, 266, 356, 375, **andiorne** 38, 42, **andiran** 145, **andire** 32, 40, 100, 108, 109, 110, 113, 123, 129, 177, 439, **andirene** 312
andiron support for a spit, used in pairs *passim*, *see also* **ainder, aindiorne, aindoran, aneyen, anger, aunder, aynder, fire dogg, hand iron, hanging dog**
andirone andiron 122, 258, **andjrons** 244, 399, **andorion** 235, **andyarn** 25, **andye** 143, **andyer** 6, 63, 67, 135, 141, 154, 164, 180, 187, 190, **andyere** 37, **andyron** 4, 18, 28, 112A
andirons with brass heads 320, 421
ane one 45
aneyen andiron 62
anfilde anvil 220
anger andiron 46, 128, 131, 146, 342, 361, **angger angiorn** 406, **angr** 209
aniseed 317
annuitie annuity 175
annuity 184, 226
anveld anvil 312, **anvell** 25, 146, 362A
anvil 182, 448, **anvill** 40, 169, 301, 382, 428, *see also* **andfeld, anfilde**
apareill apparel 300, **aparel** 149, 294, 312, 390, **aparell** 13, 63, 71, 127, 196, 215, 218, 230, 238, 280, 289, 330, 336, 347, 354, 356, 380, 396, 411, **aparile** 359, **aparill** 231, 276, 307, 341, 363, 370, 387, 406, 423, **aparle** 95A, **aparrel** 383, **aparrell** 258, 265, 317, 325, 329, 360, **aparrill** 191A, 240, **aparrll** 367, **apearreall** 70
apece apiece 156
aperell apparel 188

apern apron 51, **aperne** 96
apleroster apple roaster 150
aporill apparel 308
apparel clothing 182, 275, 320, 322, 340, 369, 370, 394, 413, 430, **apparell** *passim* **apparil** 417A, 444, **apparill** 168, 279, **apparrel** 52, 432, **apparrele** 125, **apparrell** *passim* **apparril** 264, 297, 333, 393, **apparrill** 343, **appearll** 335, **apperell** 346, **apperil** 278, **apperle** 135, **apperrel** 378, **apperrell** **apprell** 38, **aprell** 327, **aparle** 95A, *see also* **apareill, aperell, barell, parell, parill, parrell,** and compounds beginning **wearing,** and variants
apparell of wollen and lynnen 31
appern apron 54, **apperne** 97
appertenances appurtenances 237, 345
apple roaster iron utensil for roasting apples over an open fire 428, **appleroster** 369, 421
appurtemses appurtenances 256
appurtenances everything pertaining to an article 84, 94, 102, 116, 142, 158, 162, 194, 197, 261, 263, 269, 332, 357, 430, **appurtenennces** **appurtinances** 271, **appurtnances** 293, **appurtnes** 293
aprell apparel 408
apron 16, 29, 46, 243, 454, barber's 113
apsyn aspen wood 105
apurtenances appurtenances 200, 385, **apurtinances** 132, 200
aqua vita strong spirits taken as a drink 11, 87, 180, **aquavite** 45
arbor trelliswork to train plants over 45
arm support 445
arm chaire large chair with arms 350, 421, 444, **armd chair** 369, 452, **armed chair** 373, 398
armes for pykes *possibly* the iron spikes fitted to pikes 40.
arrack the fermented juice of the date 445
arras superior type of tapestry or carpet, originating at Arras in Flanders
arreare arrears 226, **arrere** 184,
arres arras 27, *see also* **orres**
arsnik arsenic 317
ash wood from the ash tree 452, 453
ashes ingredient for glass 249
auger 52, 180, **augur** 11
aul haft handle of an awl 448
aunder andiron 50, **aynder** 10
ax axe 1, 11
axe 33, 50, 52, 113, 203, 253
axe axle 154
axis axles 294
axx axe 180, **axxe** 37

back back board 16, 72
back back plate 250, 294, 301, 318, 361, 424
back for a chimney 417, **chimney back** 425
back board board placed behind a bench to exclude draughts
backboorde back board 22,
backbowrde 27
backe back board 18, 41
backe back plate 125, 200, 259, 353, 356
backebord back board 18, **backe borde** 5
backe ketchin *possibly* bakehouse 159
backen bacon 174, 283, 293, 294
backgammon table 445
backon bacon 334
back plate large flat piece of iron or steel fixed to the masonry behind the fire to protect the chimney wall 111
backreeg *possibly* a pedlar's pack, or type of back pack 81
bacon 26, 50, 86, 97, 125, 134, 154, 155, 191, 204, 227, 237, 353, 382, 386, **bacone** 167
bacon rack 320, 413, 421, 431, 444, 448, 452, **bacon racke** 177, 213, 248, 332
bad bed (mattress) 278, 341, 342
badd bed (mattress) 264
badsteed bedstead 341, 342
baere beer 215
baesting ladel basting ladle 317
baffin bavin: bundle of untrimmed brushwood 452
bag 7, 85, 150, 352, 369, **bage**47, 70, 151, 293, **bagg** 40, 212, 224, 227, 346, **bagge** 102
baican bacon 259
baile bail: metal handle of e.g. a bucket, a kettle 428
baind bond (debt) 327
bak back board 111, fire back 317
baken bacon 188
baken rack bacon rack 382, 363, 398
baker small portable oven 261, 269, 398
bakon bacon 158, 273
ball billiard ball 445
ballance balance 445
ballance to put on the spitt 445
ballands balance 45
ballence balance 368
bame and shalles beam and scales 387
band pair of strips of white fabric, worn round the neck, with the ends hanging down in front 28, 97, 151, 161, 112A, bond: money 48,

50, 136, 229, 243, 261, 269, 307, hat band 96, 234 unspecified 71
bande band: clothing 20, 21, bond: money 97, 188
bandileer bandoleer: shoulder belt with cartridge loope 301
bandoro bandora: plucked stringed instrument in the base register 50
bane pan 267
bannian banian: man's morning gown, Indian in origin 446
bar piece of metal, usually iron, fixed across a fire, *passim, see also* **parr**
bar serving table 445
barall barrel 174, 202, 341
barber's bason basin used for shaving 428
barber's block head-shaped piece of wood to support a wig 430
bare bar (metal) 108, 174 (husbandry implement)
barel barrel 56, 88, 137, 173, 180, 218, 230, 294, 300, 311, 315A, 360, 370, 402, 411, **barele** 157, 312, **barell** *passim*
barell apparell 88
barelle barrel 15, 38, 47, 113, 200
barely barley 170
baril barrel 284, 396, **barill** 235, 276, 363, 387, 423, **barille** 170
barke tree bark used in tanning leather 34, 35, 44, 65, 72, 236
barke bark 34, 35, 44, 72, 236
barke hewer bark cutting tool 65
barke mill bark mill 34, 35, 43, **barke mile** 65
bark mill device for shredding bark for the tanning industry 72
barle barrel 6
barley 13, 34, 35, 37, 68, 73, 143, 274, 289, 397, 419, **barly** 31, 32, 83, 109, 168, 220, 315A, 323, 407, 411, **barlye** 66
barley in straw barley straw 425
barr bar (fire) *passim* (tool) 424
barr lead for glassworking 177
barras canvas or hessian fabric 425
barre bar (fire) 11, 31, 34, 35, 43, 72, 97, 111
barrealle barrel 70
barrel liquid measure of 2 kilderkins *passim* **barrele** 40, 147, **barrell** *passim* **barrelle** 4, 6, 29, 38, 52, 72, 83, 100, 108, 224, **barriel** 297, **barril** 220, 264, 272, 278, 297, 393, 404, 427, 442, **barrill** 129, 131, 160, 279, 286, 292, 304, 310, 314, 328, 340, 406, 407, 433, **barrille** 93
barrell horse support for barrels 413
barrell stave section of wood to make up the side of a barrel 373
barrel stooper 430
barrowe pigge castrated boar 250
base *possibly* unshaped wheel nave 294
basen basin 19, 28, 27, 55, 95A, 112A, 343
base violl bass viol: large stringed instrument played with a curved bow 308
basin 9, 361, 430, 451
basing basting 305
baskat basket 111
basket 11, 18, 51, 71, 369, 448
basket chaire one made of woven willow work 248, **baskett chair** 168, 345
baskett basket 37, 108, 140, 170, 352, 373, 382, 398, 421, 428, 445, 448, **baskette** 119
basketware products of a basketmaker 335
bason basin *passim* **basonn** 190, **basson** 4, 154, 222, 261, 269, 406
bason leadle basin ladle 216
basson basin 6, 449
bast basting 237, 263, **basten** 186, **basteing** 261, 269, **bastin** 93, 363
basteinge sticke a baster 125
baster type of metal spoon for pouring fat over meat while cooking 428
basting 40, 83, 86, 120, 145, 146, 185, 247, 248, 253, 260, 305, 334, 345, 368, 373, **bastinge** 45, 125, 127, 129, 159A, 172, 245, 259, 292, 332, 398, 421, 424, 430, 452, *see also* **baesting, basing, bast, basten, basteing, bastin, beasting, bosting**
basyn basin 18
batelle bottle 38
bauster case bolster case 88
bay light reddish brown colour, used of horses 176, 398
baye *not known* 9
beack *possibly* black 300
beacking rack bacon rack or baking rack 449
bead bed (mattress) *passim* **beade** 70, 131
beaden bedding 283
beadstead bedstead 131, 329, 423, **beadsted** 137, 170, 229, 283, **beadsteead** 39, **beadsteed** 37, 54, 290, 337
beam calibrated support for scales 310, 320, 369, 417, 418, 421, unspecified 428
beam and scales weighing apparatus 180, 249, 365, 425, **beame and scales** 28, 33, 72, 108, 119, 317, 351, 428, **beame and skales** 11, 16, 18, 35
beame support for a hide while removing the

hair before tanning 34, 43
beam knife long, heavy, curved knife, used by tanners for removing hair from skins **beame knives** 72, **beame knyves** 34, 43
beams, pair of weighing beam 15, 38, 121, 241, 310, unspecified 35
beanch bench 439
beans 205, 431, **beanes** beans 125, 190
bear beer 147, 328, 409, **beare** 45, 47, 100, 145, 153, 157, 167, 190, 222, 237, 261, 287, 330, 343, 379
bearly barley 121
beason basin 95A
beast farm animal 30
beasted bedstead 64
beasting ladle basting ladle 362A, **beasting leadell** 449
beat ginger bruised ginger 317
beating herdle after dyeing, the wool is cleaned by placing it on a hurdle & beating it with willow rods to remove remains of dye-stuffs 22, **beatinge hurdell** 16
beat liquorish bruised liquorice 317
beckhorn anvil with points at both ends 146
beck iron beckhorn 448
bed bedstead 330, 332,
bed mattress *passim, see also* **bad, badd, bead, bedd, bedde, bede, bedse, beed, beede**
bed case mattress cover 172
bedcloathes bed clothes 391, 440, **bed clos** 411
bedclothes 391, **bed cloths** 156
bed cord cords woven across the bed frame to support the mattress 28, 122, 127, 413
bedd bed: mattress *passim*
bedd bedstead 21
bedd coard bed cord 40
bedde bed: mattress 2, 4, 11, 18, 19, 35, 47, 73, 99, 108, 125
bedding all that pertains to a bed 55, 128, 148, 178, 183, 213, 244, 376, 382, 400, 443, **beddinge** 14, 166, 208, 362A, *see also* **beaden, beding, bedinge, bedstead stuff, bedding, beeding**
bedd matt bed mat 78, 105, 125, 297
beddstead bedstead 244, 373, **beddsteed** 40, 45, 78, 105, 116, 162, 225, 242, 299, 321, 344, 346
beddsteed corded bedstead laced with bed cords 40
bede bed: bedstead 335, mattress 6, 13, 47, 67, 97, 103, 138, 157, 188, 277, 312, 335, 361, 380
bedesteed bedstead 335
bed for children (bedstead) 92
bed for servants (bedstead) 92
bedhead the board at the head of the bedstead 444
beding bedding 193, 270, 326, 340, 343, 348, 360, 377, 389, 390, 393, 396, 403, 404, 407, 433, 436, 452, **bedinge** 214, 241
bed lining bed linen 433
bed mat cloth covering the bed cords to stop the bed (mattress) from chaffing on them 430, **bed matt** 125, 127, 222, 294, *see also* **bedd matt, mate, matt, matte**
bed pan almost certainly a warming pan 251, 285, 398, **bed pan and pot** *peossibly* a warming pan and a chamber pot (here both made of pewter) 430
bed quilt 453
bedse beds (bedstead or mattress) 315A
bedseted bedstead 309, **bedssted** 297, **bedssteed** 185, **bedstad** 157
bed staves boards laid across the bedstead to support the mattress 95A
bedstead the framework of the bed *passim, see also* **badsteed, beadsted, beasted, bed, bedd, bedstead, beddsteed, bede, bedesteed, bedse, bedseted, bedssted, bedssteed, bedstad, bedsteade, bedsted, bedstedd, bedstead, bedsteed, bedsteede, bedsteet, bedsteeted, bedsteid, bedstid, bedstide, beedsted, beedsteed, beedsteede, besteed**
bedsteade bedstead 4, 5, 9, 28
bedstead stuff bedding 439
bedsted bedstead *passim*
bedsted corded bedstead with cords woven across the frame to support the bed (mattress) 47
bedstedd bedstead 207, 239, **bedstede** 2, 6, 8, 13, 17, 18, 27, 45, 85, 104, 125, 157, 168, 277, 335, 386, 442, **bedsteed** *passim*
bed steed corded *see* bedsted corded
bedsteede bedstead 6, 11, 18, 21, 27, 35, 100, 111, 120, 200, 235, **bedsteet** 235, **bedsteeted** 235, **bedsteid** 22, **bedstid** 253, 284, 396, 404, 407, 427, 433, 449, **bedstide** 449
bedtick fabric bag to hold the mattress filling 249
beear beer 285
beed bedstead 362A, mattress 33, 69, 116, 139, 141, 143, 191, 239, 240, 261, 269, 358, 399, 408

beedding bedding 163
beede bed: mattress 191A
beeding bedding 167
beedsted bedstead **beedsteed** 66, 163, 167, 178, 191, 191A, 261, 269, 358, 408, **beedsteede** 41
beefe pricker beef pricker: large cooking fork 61, 153, 237 **beif pricker** 180
beeff hooke hook to hang a joint of meat in the chimney 222
beef fork flesh fork 345
beem beam 294, 398, 408, **beeme**
beem and scales beam and scales 317, **beeme and scealse** 315A, **beeme and scales** 104
beer 7, 235, 320, 334, 367, 391, 397, 431, 445, 449, **beere** 140, 250, 274, 352, 353
beere barrell 35
beere horse support for a barrel 80
beer measure 452
bees 71, 108
beetle heavy wooden hammer used for driving wedges, crushing, beating or flattening *see also* **bettle, betel, bettelle, bittle, boitle, boytle, buetle, bytell, bytle.**
beleces bellows 312
bell 428, 445, 446, 449
bell bell metal 194
bellaces bellows 155
bell brass bell metal 250, 260, 265, 310, 320, 363, 383, 394, 412, 421, 424, 452, **bell brasse** 194, 348, 362A
bellett billet wood 127
bellis bellows 212, 356, **bellissis** 261, 269, **bellos** 25, **bellose** 294
bell metal alloy of copper and tin, using more tin than in bronze, 185, **bell metle** 324, 328, **bell mettal** 395, **bell mettle**324, 345, 369, 386, 398, 401, 429, 430 *see also* **bell, bell brass, bell brasse, belmettle**
bellowcase pillowcase 143
bellowes 17, 37, 39, 40, 42, 101, 105, 127, 146, 150, 153, 321, 368, **bellowses** 362A, **bellowus** 372, **bellusses** 66
bellows *passim, see also* **beleces, bellaces, bellis, bellisis, bellos, bellose, bellowes, bellowses, bellowus, bellusses, belose, belowes, beluses, billes, billess, billice, billis, billos, billosis, billows, billowes, billoweses, billowse, billus, billows, bles, blower, byllowes, byllows**
bell skillett one made of bell metal 428
bellyband band which passes round the belly of a horse in harness, to check the movement of the shafts 413
belmettle bell metal 332
belose bellows 229, **belowes** 317
belt 445, 446
belt for ammunition 301, **belte** 40, sword [belt] 151
beluses bellows 196
bench *passim, see also* **benche, bentch, bince, binch, bine, bynches**
benche 3, 9, 15, 18, 21, 27, 31, 39, 56, 153, 287
bend *possibly* a bent pipe used in malting 444
bend part of the butt (*q.v.*), used for the soles of shoes and boots 300, **benn** 187, 201
bentch bench 39
bentware bent wood 373
berrell barrel 335
besteed bedstead 145, 171
bettel beetle 101, 311, **bettelle** 123
Bibel Bible 154, 347, **Bibell** 174, 346, **Bibiel** 284
Bible *passim*
Bible and Testament Bible of the New and Old Testaments 332
Bible with brass clasps 421
bickern beckhorn 382, **bickforme** 38, **bickhorne** 146, **bikern** 182
biffork beef fork 363
bilhooke billhook 11
bilis probably bills, as in billhooks 38
bill bill hook 6, 8, 18, 22, 61, 100, 101, written order to pay a sum on a given date 121, 140, 159A, 222, 254, 327, 398, 400, 430, 441
billes bellows 341, 343, **billess** 399
billett billet wood 140, 153, 368
billet wood thick pieces of wood cut into suitable lengths for use as fuel 444, **billets of wood** 369
billhook tool for lopping and pruning hedges and trees 424, 452, **billhooke** 33, 177, 362A
billiard table 445
billice bellows 265, 314, 351, **billis** 55, **billos** 297, 363, **billosis** 363
billows bellows 111, 125, 159, 180, 211, 223, 224, 227, 304, 321, 332, 358, 427, 439, 448, **billowes** *passim* **billoweses** 287, **billowse** 153, **billus** 220, **bilows** 202
bin 398, **binn** 368
bince bench 104, **binch** 7, 54, 95A, 111, 125, 153, 220, 235, 445, **bine** 153
binding thred twine used to bind sheaves of corn 317
birch wood of the birch tree 440

biscake biscuit 265
biscake mould biscuit mould 265
biskett pann 428
bisome besom: broom made of twigs 317, **bissom** 450
bittle beetle 33
black bill military weapon used by the infantry, usually painted black or brown 15, **blackebill** 18
blackthorn *prunus spinoza*, used for cutlery handles 448
black work embroidery in black thread on white fabric 20
black wole black wool 64
blade shaft of a cart 154 **blad** 294
blades knife blades 448
blainkcett blanket 125, **blainkcette** 125, **blainkecotte** 125, **blainket** 311, **blainkett** 205, 266, **blaket** 331, **blancett** 332, **blanchard** 335, **blanckerd** 245, **blancket** 27, 47, 102, 129, 130, 143, 147, 157, 160, 202, 248, 264, 297, 300, **blanckete** 27, 47, **blanckett** *passim* **blanckette** 13, 29, 68, 78, 83, 97, 119, 122, 277, **blanckitt** 259, **blanckkette** 39, **blanckoate** 28, **blanckut** 337, **blancot** 61, 358, 363, 399, **blancote** 356, **blancott** 121, **blancotte** 121, **blankat** 10, 63, 229, **blankatt** 408, **blankcett** 171, **blankcoat** 302, 303, 339, **blankcott** 339, **blanke** 239
blanket *passim* **blankete** 3, 8, 33, 32, 36, 45, 69, 71, 73, 106, 111, 123, 129, 138, 235
blanketing undyed woollen broadcloth with raised nap 375
blankett blanket *passim* **blankette** *passim* **blankit** 92, **blankitt** 269, **blankot** 284, 341, 342, **blanquett** 56, **blaynket** 54
bles bellows 285
blew blue 140, 229, 243
blind horse 137
ble *possibly* bundle 317
block piece of wood used in fastening a heel to a shoe 120
block large piece of wood used for hammering on 382, 428, **blocke** 38
blocke fuel, *possibly* peat blocks 220
blocke square cut timber 140
blood dish *possibly* cooking dish for animal blood 150
blower bellows 229, 445
blue, wrought with embroidered with blue silk or thread 150
boale bowl 12
board shoemaker's table 319
board *passim* **boarde** *passim, see also* **boearde, boord, boorde, bord, borde, bourd, bowrd, bowrde**
board cloth cloth for a table or sideboard 128, 270, **board cloathe** 186
board to cutt tobacco on 265
board to iron closae on ironing board 445
bocet bucket 157, **bockett** 253, **bockut** 66
bodice, payre corset with fastenings at front and back 96
bodken bodkin 229
bodkin thick blunt needle 385
boearde board 70
boile bowl 445
boiler large kettle 444, 445, 453
boileing skillett small pan for heating liquid 146
boister bolster 164, 233, 445, **bojlster** 111
boitle beetle 424
boke book 50
boldster bolster 21
bole bowl 52, 127, **boll** 100, **bolle** 71
bollstar bolster 126, 290, **bollster** 17, 127, **bolstare** 126
bolster *passim, see also* **bauster, boister, bojlster, boldster, bollstar, bolster, bolstare, bolstere, bolstor, boster, boulstar, boulster, boulstor, bouster, boustor, bowelster, bowlester, bowllester, bowlster, boyste, boyster, boystor, bwster**
bolster case 146, 172, 212, 248, 254, 263, 289, 369, 375, 421, 424, 437, 444, 446, 452, 453, **bolster cease** 417A
bolstere bolster 175, **bolstor** 235
bolstors case bolster case 341
bolting seiving, usually flour 82
bond written agreement to pay a debt *passim*
bond of principall money 224
bonde band (clothing) 93
bonde bond (debt) 108
bone animal bone used for jewellery 45
bone lace lace made of linen thread using bone bobbins 253
boock book 248
boock debt book debt 366, **boock dept** 411, **booke dept** 293
boocket bucket 363
book account book 327, 372
book reading book *passim*
book case 446
book debt money owed to a craftsman or

retailer, recorded in the shop book 230, 243, 383, 384, 388, 413, 418, 430, 436, 441, 452, **booke debt** 333
booke reading book *passim* tradesman's account book 104, 153, 154, 201, 222, 230, 233, 238
book sheilve book shelf 295
boole bowl 73, **booll** 130
boolock bullock 285
boord board 52, 82, 337, **boorde** 31, 111
boots 201, 242, 300, 383, 446, **bootes** 17, 28, 105, 165, 187, **bootts** 448
boox box 95A, 408, **booxe** 167
bord board *passim* **borde** 5, 6, 10, 11, 33, 35, 55, 56, 113, 121, 125, 150, 206
bordcloth 33, 38, 54, 198, **bord clothe** 98
borded made of boards 62
borde to lay clothes uppon 33
boreax soder borax solder 428
borrenger porringer 180
boryer auger 10, 452
bosas bosses: decorative finials 202
boster bolster 233, 311
bosting basting 196
botam bottom: thin plank sawn across the full width of the tree 396
bote boot 315A
botel bottle 396, **botell** 55, 167, **botle** 180, 229, 331, **bottel** 11, 97, **bottelis** bottles 131, **bottell** 235, 249, 343, **bottelle** 18, 108, **bottl** 52
bottle *passim*
bottle glases *possibly* drinking glasses 305
bottle rack 398, 430, 445
bottle stand 445
bottll bottle 253
bottom base of an article *passim*
botton button 445
boul bowl 375, **boule** 42, 131, 198,
boule tipet with silver silver edged bowl 168
boull bowl 341, 449
boullok bullock 215
boulstar bolster 202, 337, **boulster** *passim*
boulster case 42, 119, 140, 158, 294, 348, **boulster casis** 300
boulstor bolster 341, 342
boulter open-weave fabric used for making fine sieves 425
boulting bolting 105, 418, **boultnge** 63
bourd board 47
bouster bolster 143, 164, **boustor** 406
bow 72
bowderinge powdering 245
bowelster bolster 54
bowl 101, 137, 368, 369, 430, **bowle** *passim, see also* **boale, boile, bole, boll, bolle, boole, booll, boul, boule, boull, bowll, boyle**
bowle ball for skittles 452
bowle to drinke in 87
bowlester bolster 24
bowll bowl 229
bowller boiler 449
bowllester bolster 277, **bowlster** *passim*
bowlster case bolster case 317, 448
bowrd, **bowrde** board *passim*
bowstrings spare strings for a long longbow 81
box *passim*
box and pann commode 332
boxe box 24, 38, 82, 84, 107, 300
box iron smoothing iron with a cavity for hot iron billets 398, 413, 428, 430, 436, 448, 452, **box to iron clothes** 431
boxis boxes 9, 261, 264, 363, **boxses** 121, 205, **boxsis** 269
box knives *possibly* knives to be made into boxed sets 448
box mould container for a sand mould, used in casting 382
box of drawers chest of drawers 212, 254
box of knives 412
boxs boxes 309
box with pipes a case of pipes for smoking , probably for public use in the tavern 445
box with tobacco a box containing tobacco for public consumption in the tavern 445
boyes breeches 383
boyle bowl 241
boyler boiler *passim*
boys bed bedstead for an apprentice 310
boyste bolster 201, **boyster** 154, 173, 180, 187, 190, 195, 198, 201, 230, 233, 239, 241, 245
boysters case bolster case 241, **boysters casse** 245
boystor bolster 267
boystor case bolster case 267
boytle beetle 38, 108, 444
bracelette bracelet 29
brackett shelf support 449
brad small headless nail 444
braided point plaited point 317
brake break 1, 83, 125, 127, 160
brandier brandiron 47, 61, 121
brandiron stand by the fire for a kettle 6, 13, 34, 35

brandy 431, 449, 452
bras made of brass *passim* **brase** *passim* **brasen** 7, 11, 17, 27, 70, 104, 126, 143, 158, 194, **brash** 56, 157
brasile herb basil 317
braslet bracelet 45
brass made of brass *passim* **brasse** *passim* **brassen** 13, 167, **brasst** 52, **brazen** 17, 29, 194
breaches breeches 17, **brechis** 161
bread 125, 328, **bred** 111
bread grater implement for making breadcrumbs, similar to a cheese grater 73, 428
break kneading trough *see also* **brake**
breakfast basin *possibly* a porringer 428
breeches 20, 28, 61, 255, 446, 448, **bretchies** 3
bresh brush 229
bretches breeches 248
breweing brewing 167, **brewin** 396
brewing 34, 133, 141, 148, 216, 229, 248, 250, 301, 319, 340, 372, 393, 418, 433, 442, 449, 450, **brewinge** 32, 153, 236, 321
briches breeches 151
brick 361, 453
bridel bridle 283
bridle 31, 82, 176, 186, 237, 265, 321, 339, 417, 445, 446
bright (metal) burnished metal 428
brimstone 317
brinche cup in which a person's health is drunk *see also* **brnche**
brish brush 52
Bristol stone rock-crystal mined from limestone beds at Clifton, Bristol 454
Bristol water medicinal water taken from the warm springs at Clifton, Bristol 445
britches breeches 185, 243
British gin 445
British oile [not known] 445
British spirits alcoholic drink distilled in Britain 445
brnche *possibly* brinche 16
broach the rod of a spit 24, 61, 82, 110, **broache** 27, 28, 29, 68, 171
broade list wide strip of fabric 61
broad peice broad piece: gold coin of 20 shillings value, minted during the reign of Charles II 401
broch broach 45, 85, 101, 103, 126, **broche** *passim* **brochies** broaches 4, 9
brode grater bread grater 77
broiler iron plate on which meat was cooked over the fire *see also* **bryler**
broken golde fragments of metal to be melted down for future use 71
broken silver fragments of metal to be melted down for future use 45, 71
brooch broach 43, **brooche** 33
brooke woolle broken wool: pieces of wool detached from the fleece 119
broom 428
brouche broach 47
brown bill *see* black bill 2
brown hops *possibly* dried hops, as opposed to fresh ones 317
brown paper 317
brown sugar 317
brsse brass 147
brubboule brewing bowl 5
brueinge brewing 141, 147, **bruen** 270, **bruing** 118, 145, 192, 193, 235, 335, 343, 355, 380, 411, **bruinge** 194, 223
brush *passim* **brushe** 11, 31, 40, 47
brwing brewing 191
brydell bridle 54
bryler broiler 174
brytchies breeches 21
buchet bucket 95A
buchil bushel 3
buckat bucket 111, **buckcott** 406
buckell buckle 243, 448
bucket 1, 8, 19, 24, 45, 52, 73, 82, 150, 202, 361, 374A, 399, 417, 424, 431, 437, 449, **buckete** 2, 111, **buckett** *passim* **buckette** 1, 105, **buckkett** 37
bucking steeping, boiling or bleaching cloth and clothes 406
bucking cloth used to cover the tub during bucking 446
buckiram buckram 24
buckle 445, 454
buckram coarse linen or cotton cloth, stiffened with gum 425
buck ruffhorn staghorn 448
buckshorn deer horn used for cutlery handles 448
buckshorn norths cutlery handles made of roe antler, or of buckthorn wood 448
buckskin skin of the male deer 31
buetle beetle 80
buff belt leather belt 448
bukat bucket 57
bullett bullet 445
bull hide 31, 186

bull leather leather from the hide of a bull 413
bullock 20, 34, 422, **bullocke** 5, **bullucke** 220
bundel bundle 315A
bundle 351
burding peece birding piece: small gun for shooting birds 27, 50, **burdinge pece** 50
buro bureau 445
bushe *possibly* a measuring standard made of wood, cf. bushel 83
busheal bushel 70
bushel measure of capacity, usually of four pecks, but with regional variations. Where the term is used on its own, it refers to a wooden container which measures this quantity 125, 182, 265, 317, 361, 407, 421, 441, **bushele** 66, **bushell** *passim* **bushelle** 83, **bushil** 407, **bushill** 6, 7, 21, **bushll** 174
butcher knives large, strong-bladed knives, typically used to cut up meat 448
butel bottle 202
buter deshe butter dish 157
buter dishe butter dish 168, 229
butes boots 151
butres butteris: tool used by a farrier for paring horses' feet 283
butrie buttery 56
butt the thickest part of a hide *see also* **bend**
butt vessel holding two hogsheads 368, 369
butter 50, 96, 328
butter churn mechanical device for turning milk cream into butter 1
butter dish 97, 112A, 125, 140, 147, 180, 185, 221, 428, **butter dishe** 29
butterey buttery 47
buttery room where provisions are kept *passim*
button 317, 401, 448, 454
buttry buttery *passim*
bw *possibly* brown: unbleached 317
bwster bolster 229
Byble Bible 27, 40
byllowes bellows 6, 31, **byllows** 63, **byllys** 10
bynches benches 95A
bynn bin 32
byshill bushel 33
bytell beetle 52, **bytle** 452
bytte bit: the mouthpiece of a bridle 9

cabberd cupboard 154
cabbinet cabinet 374A
cabidgplants cabbage plants 197
cabinet cupboard or case with shelves or drawers for storage or display 412, **cabinett** 428
caen cane 317
caine chain 95A
caish cash 451
cake hoop thin blade for turning oatcakes during cooking 428
calderen cauldron 27
caldron cauldron 8, 11, 13, 18
calf 185, 215, 335, 391, 413, **calfe** 11, 34, 100, 261, 269
calfe skene calfskin 277
calf read *possibly* a sieve for rennet 417
calf skin calf leather 359, *see also* **calf skynne, calfe skene, calfes skin, callfe skin, calveskyn, calves skin, caulfe skinn**
calf skynne 31, **calfes skin** 65
calico cloth, printed on one side, originally from Calicut, India *see also* **calicoe, callaco, callecoe, calico, callowque, caulyco**
calicoe 317, 365, **callaco** 398, **callecoe** 313
caliver a light musket *see also* **calyver, colliver**
calkin part of a horseshoe, turned up and sharpened, to prevent slipping; so here *possibly* a small stud attached to a horseshoe for the same purpose, *see also* **cawkin**
callfe skine calf skin 44, **calveskyn** 31, **calves skin** 186
callico calico 212, 425, **callowque** 269
calthrone cauldron 65
calves young cattle 386
calves leather 248
calves tails a design of cutlery handles, *cf.* the modern rat-tail 448
calyver caliver 15
camber pote chamber pot 111
camblet camlet 454
cambrick cambric: fine white linen, originally from Cambrai, Flanders 425
camlet rich fabric made from various combinations of fibres 243
camomile flowers dried flowers of *anthemis nobilis*, steeped to make a tonic 445
can vessel, not necessarily of metal, for holding liquids 140, **cann** 317
candalstick candlestick 202, **candallstick** 313, **candele stick** 343
candell box candle box 363
candelle candle 100
candelle sticke candlestick 188, **candell sicke** 423, **candell steke** 157, **candell stick** 47, 131, 290, 308, 363, 407, **candellsticke** 45, 55, 168, 356, **candellstik** 235

candell stike 95A
candels stick 343, **candelsteck** 88, **candelstek candelsteke** 191A, **candelstick** 205, 211, 300, 374A, 442, 449, **candelsticke** 2, 6, 8, 11, 13, 16, 18, 100, 101, 220, 259, *see also* **kanddell steak, kandlestick, kandll sticke**
candel stike 93, **candesticke** 27, **candilstick** 297, **candilsticke** 4, 7, 14, **candillsticke** 3, **candill stycke** 3, 5
candl candle 317
candle 430, 445, 450
candle box store for candles 318, 320, 369, 395, 398, 418, 421, 428, 430, 437, 444, 445, 446, 448
candle pott container for candles 181
candlesick candlestick 201, **candlesteke** 112A
candlestick *passim* **candlesticke** *passim* **candlestik** 67, 111, 160, **candlestyk** 10, **candlestyke candlllstike** 196, 229, **candlstick** 40, 339, **candlsticke** 52, 129, **candlstike** 229, **candoll stik** 276, *see also* **canstecke, canstek, chandestick, condillstik**
candlestick against the wall *possibly* sconce 287
candmus canvas 95A
cane walking stick 243, 445, 448, 454
cane woven reeds, used in chairmaking 365, 367, 372, 398, 412, 428, 437, 444
canfos canvas 126
canister 445
canne can: vessel, not necessarily of metal, for holding liquids 19
canmas canvas 38, 224, **canmus** 95A
cannister canister 428
cannvase canvas 66
canopy tester 32
canstecke candlestick 70, **canstek** 126
canvas coarse unbleached hempen or flaxen cloth *passim*, *see also* **candmus, canfos, canmas, canmus, cannvase, canvass, canvasse, canvis, cavnas, chanvas**
canvass 54, **canvasse** 56, **canvis** 71, 168, 248, 261, 269
cap 20, 446, **capp** 454
cape 151
caraway seed the seeds of *Carum carvi* used for flavouring 317, *see also* **carraway**
card rake *possibly* curd rake, or agitator, used in the dairy 108
cards *possibly* playing cards 430
cards implements for combing wool or flax before spinning, used in pairs 16, 51, 317, **cardes** 28, 278
cards, box with *possibly* playing cards, but impossible to tell 446
careg carriage: the wheeled framework which supports the body of a vehicle 294
carpentars toollse carpenters' tools 137
carpert carpet 114
carpet piece of fabric used to cover a bed or table 122, 123, 124, 125, 128, 129, 27, 71, 114, 123, 202, 364, 370, **carpete** 123, 174, **carpett** *passim* **carpette** 13, 219, 226, **carpit** 168, 194, 247, **carpitt** 153, 200, 227
carpet cloth carpet **carpett cloth** 125, **carpitcloth** 202
carraway caraway450
carrpett carpet 317, 347
cart 207, 259, 273, 323, 392, **carte** 259
cart line rope for binding loads on wagons 323
cart wheele 323
case container 317, 429, container for cutlery 140, 274, 448, pillow or bolster covering 105
case closed container 113
case knife 414, **case of kniffes** 140
casement a vertically hinged window 80
case of boxis nest of boxes 9
cash 329, 418, 430, **cash in hand** 425, **cash in house** 452
cashen cushion 111, **cashin** 111
cask barrel 445, 449
casselty desperate 156
cassis cases 261
cast made of cast metal 32, 164, 217, 249, 274, 294, 301, 362A, 369, 382
cast cask 190
caster small vessel with a perforated lid for sprinkling sugar 428
casting frame glaziers' tool 249
cast lead glazier's material 177
cauldron large vessel for heating liquids over the fire 9, 21, **cauldrone** 78 *see also* **calderen, caldron, calthrone**
caulf calf 215
caulfe skinn calf skin 9
caulyco calico 54
cavnas canvas 174
cawberd cupboard 1
cawkin calkin 317
ceever kiver **cefer** 309, **ceffer** 88, **ceover** 159
ceiling the wooden lining of the ceiling or walls of a room 430
cete kettle 309, **cetele** 283, **cetell** 218, **cettel**

88, **cettle** 64
cevear kiver 157, **cever** 40, 69, 311, 312, 325
chafdish chaffing dish 406, **chafen** (dish) 27, 83, 174, 229, 283, 341, 370, **chafeing** 46, **chafene** 126, **chafing** 111, 123, 398, 412, **chafinge** 31, 87
chafe chaff: bed filling 137
chafer chaffer 113, 125, **chaferne** 32
chaff husks of grain remaining after threshing, used as a bed filling 204, 230, 267, 274, **chaffe** 222, 265
chaffeing (dish) chaffing dish 248, **chaffen** 37, 437, **chaffin** 64, 113, 131, 220, 237, 352, **chaffine** 3
chaffer small portable brazier containing hot charcoal, placed under a chaffing dish 27
chaffing dish container for food to be placed on a chaffer 9, 16, 39, 92, 102, 128, 150, 356, 395, 398, 413, 414, 421, 428, 445, 448, 452, *see also* **chafdish, chafen, chafeing, chafene, chafing, chafinge, chaffeing, chaffen, chaffin, chaffine, chaffinge, chaffinn, chafin, chafing, chafinge, chafinn, chafyn, chaving, cheffen, cheffine, cheffing, chefing, cheifing**
chaffinge (dish) 13, 45, 47, 52, 97, 127, **chaffinn** 4, **chafin** 19, 38, 113, 153, 263, **chafing** 18, 22, 29, 40, 50, 100, 121, 133, 288, 369, **chafinge** 6, 31, 87, 125, **chafinn** 4, **chafyn** 11, **chaving** 65
chaier chair 17, 34, 78, 103, 218, 277, 278, 317, 358, 363, 392, 399, 406, 407, **chaiere** 188
chain for a jack 445, for a well bucket 283, 431, **chaine** for a jack 181, 250, 369, 430, for a well bucket 6, 8, 11, 16, 29, 47, 61, 177 *see also* **caine, chayne, cheyne, leyne**
chaior chair 126, 290
chair, chaire *passim, see also* **chaier, chaiere, chaior, chare, chayor, chayer, chayor, chayr, chayre, cheer, cheayer, cheier, cheir, cheire, cher, chere, cheye, cheyer, cheyre**
chairstool stool with a back, **chairstoole** 27, *see also* **chayer stoole, chayre stoole, cheirstoole**
chaise cushion *possibly* a cushion for a carriage 446
chambar pot chamber pot 202
chamber bellows bellows used on the fire in a bedroom 428
chamber faggot bundle of wood for bed chamber fire 428, 452
chamber pot receptacle for urine, used in a bed chamber 61, 71, 160, 168, 182, 185, 229, 334, 341, 356, 369, 391, 414, 417, 430, 431, 445, **chamber pote** 123, 157, 174, 343, **chamber pott** *passim* **chamber potte** 4, 6, 18, 27, 31, 45, 100, 113, 115, 125, **chambor pot** 276, **chambor pote** 235, **chambr pot** 196 *see also* **camber pote, chambar pot, chember pot**
chandestick candlestick 406
chanvas canvas 47
charcoal partially burnt wood used as fuel, *see also* **chercole**
charcole charcoal 40
chardger charger 24
chare chair 4, 5, 261, 325
charger large plate or flat dish 31, 34, 194, 265
chast chest 264, 278, 297
chatall lease 371, **chatell** 167, 236, **chatle** 210, **chattell** 110, 289, 292, 398, **chattle** 142, 216, 223, 227, **chattll** 261
chatel lase for life 264
chattel lease contract for the conveyance of property for rental *passim*
chattell leace chattel lease 358, **chattell lease** 62, 362A, 116
chattells in leases 263
chattle lease house 269
chaving (dish) chafing (dish) 65, 80
chayar chair 229
chayer chair *passim*
chayer stool chairstool 353
chayffin (dish) chafing (dish) 5
chayne chain 33, 57, 72, for a well bucket 1, 2, 9, 18, 31, 63, 72, 103, 150, 155, 176, 183
chayor chair 264, 297, **chayr** 137, 251, 273, 318, 334, **chayre** *passim*
chayre stoole chair stool 28, 111
cheafeing (dish) chaffing (dish) 212, **cheaffen** 147, **cheaffinge** 95A **cheafing** 318
chear chair 433, **cheayer** 95A
cheast chest 54, 61, 118, 137, 311, 325, 347, 374A, **cheaste** 312
cheast of drawers 418, **cheastt of drares** 423
check cheek: iron plate placed inside a grate to reduce its width 445, **cheeck** 445
check cloath 445
cheese 15, 18, 61, 86, 123, 125, 134, 177, 204, 263, 328, 445, 450 *see also* **cheess, ches, chese**
cheese board 430, 445
cheesecloth thin, loosely-woven cloth for wrapping cheeses 425
cheese fatt cheese vat 421

cheese iron tool for extracting a morsel of cheese for tasting 448
cheese plate plate on which to stand a cheese 372, 373, 398, 446
cheese press screw press for consolidating curd in cheesemaking 421, **cheese presse** 159A *see also* **chespres**
cheese rack a shelf for the storage of cheeses 22, 31, **cheese racke** 18, 24, 68
cheese stool *possibly* a frame used in the making of cheese 91
cheese toaster implement for toasting cheese, *perhaps* as in Welsh rarebit 398
cheese vat vessel in which curd is placed to be turned into cheese
cheese vate cheese vat 373
cheess cheese 294
cheest chest 272, 387
cheet sheet 192
cheffen (dish) chaffing (dish) 129, **cheffine** 249, **cheffing** 159, 353, **chefing** 202, 251, 253, 317, 407
cheier chair 45, 100, **cheir** 52, **cheire** 83, 100
cheifing 374A
cheirstoole chairstool 27
chelfe shelf 6
chember pote chamber pot 363
cher chair 361, **chere** 380
chercole charcoal 315A
cherry brandy 445
ches cheese 309, **chese** 129, 154, 190, 361
chese fat cheese vat 129
chesell chisel 257
chese racke cheese rack 6
chespres cheese press
chesse chest 130
chessel chisel 10, 180
chest, cheste large storage box *passim, see also* **chast, cheast, cheest, chesse, chestt, chiste, chute, chust**
chest for a bed *possibly* a chest to stand at the foot of a bed 274
chest of drares chest of drawers 277, **chest of drars** 396, 411, 433
chest of drawers *passim* **chest draws** 359, 386, **chest of draws** 377, 444, **chest of drawes** 406, **chest of drawrs** 393
chestt chest 284, 438
chestt off drawrs chest of drawers 438
cheye chair 239, **cheyer** 154, 159, 164, 173, 180, 187, 190, 198, 201, 229, 233, 236, 241, 245, 294, 370
cheyere frame framed chair 159
cheyne chain for a well bucket 86, 110
cheyney china 398
cheyre chair 108, 110, 113
chicell chisel 24
chiching kitchen 95A
childbed linene special bedlinen or linen clothing, often elaborately worked, for receiving visitors after the birth of a child 71, **childbed lynnen** 177, **childbed woollen** special woollen clothing 177
childrens chair 373
childrens gloves 383
children shoes 201, **childrens shoes** 187
childs chayer 249, **childs chayre** 177
childs swing 452
childs table chair a child's chair with table attached 373
chimney hook pot hook 398
china 428, 445, 446, 451, 452, 453 *see also* **cheyney, chyner**
chips small pieces of wood 452
chisel carpenter's tool *see also* chesell, chessel, chicell, chisell, chisle
chisell chisel 146, **chisle** 452
chiste a shift; or a frilled shirt 3
chiste chest 70
chitle kettle 38, **chittell** 344
chiver kiver 252
chock choker: neckerchief worn high round the throat 54
chocolate mill instrument for grinding chololate to a powder, to prepare the beverage 428
chocolate pott vessel for preparing hot chocolate 428
chopen bord chopping board 38, **choppinge boorde** 24, 31
choping block butcher's block 421
choping knife chopping knife 421, 452, **choping knyff** 10, **chopinge knyfes** 7, **choppeing knife** 46
chopping 369, 398, 445, 446, **chopen** 283
chopping board wooden board for cutting up food 45 *see also* **chopen bord, choppinge boorde**
chopping knife 11, 52, **chopping knives** 100, **chopping knyffe** 17, **choppinge knyfe** 37, **chopinge knyves** 33, 127, **choppinge knyves** 31, **chopp knife** 406
Christmas box earthenware container used by servants to collect gratuities at Christmas

428
chufell board shuffle board 334
church Bibell large Bible used on a lectern 47
churn 373, **churne** 398
chushen cushion 111, **chushione** 226
chust chest 283, 327, 356
chust of draers chest of drawers 342
chyner china 140
chyve kive 40
ciching faget kitchen faggot 407
cider 431
cieling ceiling 430
cistern water tank 425, **cisterne** 398
cistren water *possibly* water taken from a cistern, i.e. rainwater, as opposed to well water 445
citchin kitchen 428
cittel, cittell kettle 95A, 343, 387, 407
cittern wire-stringed instrument played with a plectrum *see also* **setoren, sythern**
cive kive 95A, 147, 168, 188, 234, 430
civer kiver 95A, 174, 242, 299, 330, 332, 336, 356, 360, 363, 368, 373, 381, 404, 407, 425, 430
civerled coverlet 146, **civerlid** 38, 191A
civer timber timber for making a kiver 373
civre kiver 292, 346
clamp 413, 430, 448
clanser raying sieve 38, **clanseve** 45
clapse clasp 317
clasp knives 448
claw table one with feet shaped as claws 445
clay white earth from which pipes are made 393
cleaver broad-bladed knife or axe for cutting meat into joints 122, 250, 369, 398, 421, 445, 452 *see also* **clever, clevor**
cleffte cleft 45
cleft wood cut up for fuel 28, 382, *see also* **clift**
cleft wood 102, 125, 127, 160, 179, 241, 289, 361, **clift wood** 206
clensieve raying sieve **clenseave** 28, **clenseeve** 8, 18, **clenseve** 6, **clensyve** 31, **clensingsive** 17
clever cleaver 11, 18, 123, 125, 174, 202, 352, **clevor** 147
clevyemantle clavel beam: mantlepiece 80
clift cleft 78
clippers, pair glazier's tool 177
cloaathes apparell 185
cloak 454, **cloake** 12, 17, 115, 118
closse brush clothes brush 445
closse press clothes cupboard 445
cloat cloth 339
cloath bolting cloth for sieveing flour 418
cloath cloth 223, 365, apparel 398, 404
cloathe cloth 263
cloathes press clothes cupboard 448
cloaths apparell 373, **cloathes** 73, 118, 165, 180, 186, 217, **cloats** 331
cloaths brush 452
cloaths iron pressing iron 426
clock 295, 355, 386, 398, 426, 430, 436, 443, ***see also*** **clocke, cloke, clokk**
clock case 398, 426
clocke 39, 146
clock pinn *possibly* a cloak pin 428
clogs 454, **cloggs** 428
cloke cloak 3, 4, 5, 6, 20, 28, 125, 165
cloke cloak *or* clock, most likely the latter 75
clokk clock 50
cloose stoole commode 289, **cloosstoole** 295
clos clothes (apparel) 311, **close** 235, 257, 283, 284, 309, 355, 404, 407
close piece of ground hedged about for pasturage 1, 24, 31, 34
close coate close-fitting outer garment 160
close stole close stool 56, 251, 406, 433
close stool commode 425, 426, 431, 439, 448, 450, **close stoole** 27, 111, 123, 153, 192, 219, 250, **close stooll** 395, **closstall** 202, **clos stole** 396, *see also* **close stoole, cloosstoole, cloose stoole**
close stool and pan 398, 421, 445, 446, **close stoole and pan** 171, 212, 226, 274, 350, 377, **close stool and stool pan** 430
close stool box 413, 416, 418, **close stool box and pan** 386, **close stool box and pann** 398, *see also* **stool and pan, stool box and pan, stool pan**
cloth piece of fabric 29, 68, 96, 343, 375, 446
cloth fabric to make clothing 241, 243
cloth piece of fabric used as a covering 45, 368
cloth woven fabric 121, 158, 199
cloth saddle cloth 159
clothar tablecloth 126, **clother** apparel 277
cloth chair upholstereed chair 150
clothe apparel 157, **clothes** 58, 92, 103, 138, 146, 156, 159, 160, 170, 202, 220, 291, 313, **clothings** 337, **cloths** clothes 137, 402
clothes apparel *see also* **cloaathes, cloaths,**

cloathes, cloats, clos, close, clother, clothe, cloths, clothings
clothes flasket 452
cloves dried flower buds of *Eugenia aromatica*, used as spice 317
coach carriage 205 *see also* **cotch**
coachepoole coachpole: one fixed to the front of the coach, onto which the horses are harnessed 154
coaffer coffer 118
coaked coal coke 444
coal pit-coal or charcoal 367, 369, 391, 397, 412, 418, 436, 440, 444, 445, **coale** 426, 450, **coall** 374A, *see also* **col, cole, coll, colle, coole, seacole**
coal box for storing coal 437
coale coal 183, 190, 332, 334, 386
coale irons fire irons 171
coal grate container for burning coal in the hearth 334, 369, 425, 430, 436, 444, 446, **coale grate** 398
coal penn container for coal 421
coal rake implement for raking coals or embers in the hearth, **coalrake** 127, *see also* **colerake, collrake, colrake**
coaltrough *perhaps* a coal scuttle 382
coard bed cord 129, 158, 165, 185, 249, 287, 320, **coarde** 71
coat 161, 185, 241, 255, 265, 446, 448, **coate** 12, 17, 28, 118, 120, 151, 165
cobard cupboard 13, 70, 193, 290, 327, 363 **cobarde** 70, **cobart** 118, 312, 353, **cobbard** 325, **cobbart** 261, **cobberd** 101, 355, **cobbert** 355, **cobbord** 259, **cobeard** 145
cobbard cloth cupboard cloth: cloth to cover a cupboard 248, **cobberd cloathe** 79, 164, **cobbord cloth** 261, **couberd cloth** 347, **cubard cloth cubbard cloth** 147, 168, **cubbart cloth** 269, **cubberd cloth** 125, 160, 245, **cubbert cloath** 153, **cubbert cloth cubbord clothe cuberd cloth** 202, **cuberd clothe** 317, **cupboard cloath** 250, **cupboard cloth** 212, 375, **cupboard clothe** 212, **cupbord cloth** 16, 31
cobercloth cupboard cloth
coberd cupboard 50, 57, 63, 67, 174, 285, 309, 360, 404, **coberde** 66, **cobert** 145, 264, 278, 297, **cobord** 196, 209, 311, **cobrde** 283
cock haystack 185, **cocke** 78, tap 290, 330, 352, 368, 430, 437, 445, 448, 452
coco cocobolo wood, an imported hardwood 448
cofar coffer 290, 444
cofarled coverlet 126
cofer coffer *passim*
coferd *possibly* cover 341
coferled coverlet 63, **coferleid** 300
coffar coffer 312, 380, **coffare** 126,
coffeare 70
coffee dish cup without handles for drinking coffee, 317, 426, 430, 445
coffee mill implement for grinding coffee beans 446
coffee pot tall, conical vessel, usually made of metal, for brewing coffee 414, 428, 445, 446, 448, 452 *see also* **coffer pott**
coffer strong box, usually with a curved lid, in which money and valuables were kept *passim* **coffere** 37, 39, 54, 138, *see also* **coaffer, cofar, cofer, coffar, coffare, coffeare, coffir, coffor, cofor, cofur, coffer, coufer, cufer, kofer, koffer**
coffer lock lock for coffer 382
coffer pott coffee pot 437
coffin board usually elm boards, used for making coffins 439
coffin handle coffin furniture 444, **coffin side** 437, **coffin top** 437
coffir coffer 292, **coffor** 27, 297, **cofor** 137, 404, 423, **cofur** 307
cok cock: tap 317, **coke** male bird 6, tap 125
cokloft cock loft 38, 188
col coal 343, 355
colander perforated vesse4l to strain off liquid in cooking 369
cold still may come from stillage, a frame for keeping things off the floor while draining, drying, etc., *possibly* even a cooling rack 265
cold trow blacksmith's trough for cooling metal 169
cole coal 45, 148, 153, 181, 197, 223, 263, 301, 345, 361, 377, 379, 382, 389, 398, 415, 416, 431
cole box coal box 430, 449
cole grate coal grate 263, 343, 345, 416, **cole great** coal grate 396
colendar colander **colender** 64, 123, 229
colerake coal rake 11, 16, 18, 35, 430
coletrough coal trough 182
colinder colander 363
coll coal 380
collar holster halter for securing a horse in its stall 237
colle coal 220, 285
college cup type of drinking vessel 383,

colledg cupp 369
coll grate coal grate 329, **coll greate** 344
collender colander 100
coller horse collar 186
collering stone a colouring stone 177
collinder colander 445
colliver caliver 27
collrake coal rake 34, **colrake**
colt young horse 30, 72, 194, **colte** 32
comb hair comb 317, 430, **combe** 448
combes, pair woolcomber's tool 22
comb pipe another word for a 'diz', an instrument used for smoothing or regulating fibres in the woollen industry 320
combs, pair woolcomber's tools 320
comd woll combed wool 315A, **comde oull** 315A, **comde woll** 315A
commode chair or cupboard concealing a chamber pot
common chair simple, joined chair 444
Common Prayer book 454
common sisars scissors 448
compasses a pair of compasses for drawing 146, 448
condillstik candlestick 253
coney rabbit
coney furr rabbit fur used to stuff a mattress 421
cony skinn rabbit skin 375
coobe coop
cooberd cupboard 300, **seid cooberd** side cupboard 285
cookes knives 448
cooffer coffer 104
coole coal 365
coole cowle 4
cooler large cask or tub for cooling malt liquor or milk 294, 324, 329, 334, 368, 369, 379, 421, 425, 437, 448, 449, 452
cooll cool
cooller cooler 303, 386
coome comb 220
coop cup 229
coopery pertaining to the making of barrels etc.
coopery timber 282
coopery ware 282
coord bed cord 111, **coorde** 111
cooshen cushion 27, 247, **cooshenn** 143
coot coat 243
cooting knife cutting knife 191
coow cow 285
cope cup 343
cope church vestment 45
coper copper (water vessel) 361
coper made from copper 269, 334, 363
copery stufe coopery stuff: vessels made by a cooper 50, **coperye stufe** 63
coppar made of copper 317
copper made from copper 45, 168, 249, 261, 273, 274, 318, 329, 332, 345, 414, 420, 428, 436, 445, 452, 453, quantity of metal 428
copper large vessel for heating water 368, 369, 398, 444, 449
coppery coopery 57
coppie boocke copy book: exercise book in which copies were written or printed for pupils to imitate 146
cord bed cord *passim* for beam and scales 398, line connecting the jack to the spit measure of 128 cubic feet of timber 444, unspecified 413
corde bed cord 38, 111, 150, 157, 164, rope 6, 121, **corede** bed cord 111
coring rod curtain rod: window 355, **corten rode** bed 342, **cortin rode** window, **curten rode** unspecified 313, **cortinrod** 363, **curtain rod** bed 351, 418, **curtain rod** window 365, **curtaine rod** bed 351, **curtin rod** window 406
corks for bottles 445, **corke** 317
corkscrew 445, 448
corn 273, 330, 379, 386, 391, **corne** 61, 129, 152, 168, 192, 259, 368
corner cubbord 453
corner cupboard 426, 445, 448, 452
corner shelf 436, 453
corpete carpet 235
corse leg wole coarse leg wool; *possibly* the rougher wool from a sheep's legs 64
corslette corselet: piece of body-armour 40
cortain curtain (bed) **cortaine** 235, **corten** 342, 343, 361, **cortene** 157, **cortin** 196, 218, 311, 363, 406, **corting** 193, 355
cort cubard court cupboard: open cupboard for displaying plate 276
corting curtain (window) 355
corvet cravat; could possibly be corset, but unlikely 151
coshen cushion 229, **coshene** 229
coster coaster: *possibly* a small tray or mat for a bottle or glass 368
cotch coach 294
cotchpol coach pole 294

cotch stock coach stock 294
cotch wheel coach wheel 294
cote coat 21, 243
cotterel adjustable hook for hanging a pot over a fire 395, **cotterell** 25, 45, 61, **cotterill** 140, *see also* **kotrel**
cotton thick woollen fabric, similar to frieze (*q.v.*) 61, 454
coubbert cupboard 27, **couberd** 95A, 253, **couberde** 38, **coubord** 235
couch sofa 226
couch frame the framework of a couch or sofa 444
coufer coffer 402
couffolett coverlet 205
coule cowle *passim* **coulle** 47
counter shop board 247, 317, 365, 369, **counter with drawers** 448
counterpane coverlet 421, 426, **counterpin** 430
coup cup 168
courd bed cord 119
course of handels handles fitted with teazles for nap-raising 26
course wooll coarse wool 31, **course woollen cloth** 61
courtain curtain (bed) 174
coushing cushion 297
coutch couch 436
couverled coverlet 88, **covarled** 337
coval glase *possibly* a cheval mirror, i.e. a long mirror 229
covell cowle 46, **covelle** 8
Coventree blew thred blue embroidery thread originally from Coventry 317
cover cowle 200, 261, 269, 276, 368, 452
cover lid: boiler 369, copper 444, cup 229, pan 413, 445, plate 445, unspecified 95A, 251, 398, 412, 421, 428
covering bed cover 47, 54, 56, 111, 145, 244, 275, 289, cushion cover 398, **coveringe** bed cover 58, 69, 100, 122, 267, **coverng** 145
coverle coverlet 233
coverlead coverlet 39, 41, 42, 118, 232, **coverleade** 112A, **coverled** *passim* **coverledd** 15, 34, 68, 177, 321, 332, **coverledde** 2, 11, 18, 46, 97, **coverlede** 19, 24, 67, 110, 111, 278, **coverleed** 192, 269, 301, 302, 303, 331, 346, **coverleedde** 119
coverlet unquilted covering, sometimes made from patchwork, placed on top of the bedclothes 27, 102, 129, 230, 431 *see also* **civerled, civerlid, cofarled, coferled, coferleid, couffolett, couverled, covarled, coverle, coverlead, coverleade, coverled, coverledd, coverledde, coverlede, coverleed, coverleedde, coverlete, coverlet, coverlette, coverlid, coverlid, coverlidde, coverlide, coverlit, coverlite, coverlyd, coverlydd, coveurled, cuferlid, cufferled, cyverled, keiverled, keverled, keverlet, keverlyd, keverlyde, kiferled, kifferled, kiverlid, kiverlide, kyforlead, kyverlede, kyverlet**
coverlete 27, 33, 73, 121, **coverlett** 13, 17, 22, 32, 35, 98, 106, 120, 171, 250, 260, 272, 428, **coverlette** 8, 17, 31, 35, 83, 98, 103, 108, 113, 121, 144, **coverlid** *passim* **coverlidd** 29, 43, 78, 122, 125, 381, 421, **coverlidde** 29, 224, **coverlide** 40, 79, **coverlit** 33, **coverlite** 33, **coverlyd** 10, **coverlydd** 9
covers bed coverings *see* **cuvers**
coveurled 95A
covl cowle 51, **covld** 64, **covle** 180, 218
cow *passim*
cowbbert cupboard 27
cowe cow 6, 32, 34, 132, 172, 225, 250, 283, 335, 386
cowell cowle 127, **cowl** 160
cowhouse 193
cowle cask in which malt liquor etc. is placed to cool *passim*, *see also* **coole, coule, coulle, covell, covelle, cover, covl, covld, covle, cowell, cowl, kowl, kowle**
cow rack manger 323
cowshinge cushion 47
coyne *not known* 97
cra *not known* 360
crabbe crab apple 14
crab mill device for crushing crab apples
crackmill wheele probably a machine for cracking wheat 127
cradell cradle 73, 220
cradle 8, 11, 86, 103, 106, 120, 146, 304
cradle rugg covering for a cradle 254, 305
crane chimney crane: ratchet mechanism, fixed in the chimney, from which pots were suspended 445, 452
crane in the chimney 438
crap darnel: a grain usually fed to poultry 193
crashion cushion 50
crasse *not known* 33
crasse cloathes cross cloths 112A
crate frame in which a glazier carries glass 177

cravat necktie 446, **cravatt** 243
cream pot vessel for cream 445
credits money and investments owed to the deceased 431
crisping iron barbers' tool for making hair wave 80
cristall glasse high quality glass containing a high proportion of lead 146
crock shallow vessel, made from earthenwaren or metal 42, **crooke** 52
croke crook 88
crook pot hook 329, 430, 444, 452, **crooke** 150, 227, 267, 345
crosclothe cross cloth 97
crosebowe lathe early lathe 24
cross cloth linen cloth worn across the forehead
cruet small table container for salt, pepper, oil or vinegar 446
crupper strap passing round a horse's tail 9
cruse small vessel of earthenware or wood 8, 16, 144
cubard cupboard 6, 61, 103, 121, 137, 294, 387, 407, **cubbard** *passim* **cubbarde** 7, 357, **cubberd** *passim*
cubberd cushion cupboard cushion: one used to decorate the top of a cupboard 125
cubberd cloth cupboard cloth 45, 100
cubberde cupboard 10, 40, 122
cubberd in the wale wall cupboard 111
cubberd table *possibly* a bureau 194
cubbered cupboard **cubbert** 45, 84, 85, 96, 119, 131, 241, 245, 445, **cubboard** 14, 21, 128, 186, 225, 295, 351, 446, **cubboord** 252, **cubbor** 93, **cubbord** 22, 26, 52, 55, 72, 73, 105, 123, 140, 146, 147, 168, 179, 205, 240, 324, 392, 399, 453, **cubborde** 3, 4, 9, 15, **cuberd** 6, 112A, 165, 170, 188, 202, 219, 273, 370, 403
cubbord clothe cupboard cloth 123, **cuberd cloth** 111
cubert cupboard 95A, 132, 135, 201, **cublerd** 141, **cuboard** 129, **cubord** 331, **cuburd** 127
cufer coffer 327
cuferlid coverlet 276, **cufferled** 153
cuffes, pair of 151, **cuffs, pair of** 454
culberd ***possibly*** andiron 217
cullender colander 31, 261, 263, 269, 318, 428, 448, **cullinder** 439, 449
cunny skin coney skin: rabbit skin 80
cup 127, 186, 294, 295, 318, 329, 345, 369, 370, 401, 412, 423, 427, 431, 442, 445 *see also* **coop, cope, coup, cupe, cupp, cuppe**
cupbard cupboard **cupbert**
cupboard recess or piece of furniture with shelves and doors *passim, see also* **cabberd, cawberd, cobard, cobarde, cobart, cobbard, cobbart, cobberd, cobbert, cobbord, cobeard, coberd, coberde, cobert, cobord, cobrde, cooberd, coubbert, couberd, couberde, coubord, cowbbert, cubard, cubbard, cubbarde, cubberd, cubberde, cubberd, cubbered, cubbert, cubboard, cubboord, cubbor, cubbord, cubborde, cuberd, cubert, cublerd, cuboard, cubord, cuburd, culberd, cupbard, cupbert, cupboord, cupbord, cupboard, cupboarde, cupboard, cuppord, koberd**
cupboard cloth 114
cupboarde 258, **cupboord** 120, **cupbord** 16, 31, 34, 35, 56, 68, 82, 99, 150, 304, 319, 329, 334, 336, 348
cup dish drinking dish 140
cupe cup 188, 347, **cupp** 24, 61, 78, 83, 102, 177, 200, 212, 217, 221, 254, 328, 428, 448
cupp with a cover 29
cuppboard cupboard 324, 368, **cuppord** 25
cuppe cup 2, 6, 11, 18, 21, 31, 213
curiosities collection of miscellaneous objects of interst 445
curling pipe barber's crimping implement 430
currall coral for jewellery 45
currall branches branching pieces of coral 45
curtain bed *passim* window 150, 289, 365, 398, 421, unspecified 45, 374A, 424, *see also* **curtaine, curtaines, curtainn, curtaint, curtane, curtayn, curtayne, curten, curteyne, curtin, curtine, curtings, curttens, curtyn, cutin**
curtaine bed *passim* window 125, 146, 147, 153, 226, 250, 287, 318, 351, unspecified 398, **curtaines for one bed** 4, **curtainn** window 317, **curtaint** bed 301 **curtane** bed 175
curtaine ring ring through several of which a pole is threaded to suspend a curtain 317
curtayn curtain: bed, window 111, **curtayne** bed 15, 111, unspecified
curtayne rode curtain rod: bed 71, **curtayn rodd** bed 111
curten curtain: bed 27, 31, 168, 249, 402, window 31, unspecified 61
curten rod unspecified 61
curteyne curtain: bed 32, 100, 123, 140, 171, window unspecified
curteyne rod curtain rod: bed 100, **curteyne**

diapor 308, **diapper** 317
dich dish 341
dicker ten of an item, usually used for hides and skins 34, 35
dieper diaper 194, 357
diger digger: some sort of spade 317
diper diaper 28, 125
dippin dripping 158
dises dishes 277
dish, dishe *passim, see also* **dech, deses, deshes, dich, dises, diss, disshe, dishese, disheses, dishis, disses, dyche, dyshe**
dish cover 445
dishese dishes 229, **disheses** 229, **dishis** 202, 261, 371, 408, **disses** 245
diss 256, **disshe** 8, 18, 51, 220
ditty dimity: strong cotton cloth, woven with raised stripes and fancy figures 425
doare door 40
dobbell double 51
doblett doublet 17
doe skin skin of female deer **doe skyn** 31
dog fire dog *passim* **doge** 123, 129, 130, 141, 147, 157, 160, 170, 193, 229, 283, 300, 308, 342, 363
doge *not known* 111
dogg fire dog *passim* **dogge** 27, 45, 78, 102, 123, 144, 146, 153, 177, 212, 216, 219, 221, 223, 249, 266, 287, 357, **doggue** 223
dog wheel jack wheel turned by a dog 308
dooble salt double salt 31
dooeskin doe skin 243
dooge fire dog 112A
door 430, *see also* **doare, doore, dore**
doore 17, 54
doosen dozen 220
dore door 45, 95A, 104, 150, 157, 158, 310
dore locke door lock 220
dornix mixed linen/woollen fabric, originally from Dornix/Tournai, Flanders 27, *see also* **danix**
dosen dozen 6, 27, 37, 45, 126, 205, 220, 261, 277, 283, 356, 363, **doshen** 39, **doson** 118, 137, **dossen** 15, 16, 27, 40, 47, 61, 97, 120, 125, 167, 192, 416
doubell barel vessel holding twice the capacity of a normal barrel 285
double flagon vessel holding twice the capacity of a normal flagon 260, 421, **duble flaggon** 269
double salt *possibly* a double salt cruet 102, *see also* **dooble salt, dubble salt**
doublet close-fitting male body garment 120, *see also* **doblett, dublet, dublete, dublett, dublette**
dough bread mix *see also* **dow, dowe**
dough trendle tub for mixing dough 200
doulace dowlas 185, 194, **doule** 194, **doulis** 158, **doullas** 205
douzen dozen 232
dow dough 11, 259, **dowe** 61, 102, 332
dowlace dowlas 317
dowlas coarse linen, originally from Daoulas, Brittany 113, 125, 159A, 243, 249, 425, 452, *see also* **doulace, doule, dowlace, dowlis**
dowle dowel: wooden peg or rod 34
dowlis dowlas 158, 250, 347
downe down: soft feather filling for pillows, bolsters and (later) beds 123
dowsan dozen 9, **dowsand** 4, 14
dowson 95A, **dowzin** 232
dowtrogh dough trough 82
dozen twelve, *see also* **deson, dezen, doosen, dosen, doshen, doson, dossen, douzen, dowsan, dowsand, dusen, dussen, duzen**
draer drawer 188
drafte *possibly* a spokeshave 10
draftshave *possibly* a spokeshave-type of instrument, used for dehairing a skin 65
dram one sixteenth of an ounce 317
dram dish container for a portion of cordial or liquor 428
draper small tub with a handle on one side formed by a hole in a stave taller than the others 261, 368, **drapor** 308, **drapper** 398, *see also* **dropper**
draught board for the game of draughts 445
draw drawer 445
draw boxes nest of boxes 317
draweing block device for drawing out wire 232
drawer sliding box within a larger piece of furniture 146, 213, 428, 431, *see also* **draer, draw, drawr**
drawers male undergarment for the lower body 20
drawr drawer 377
draw up jack type of jack worked by a chain and weights 445
dredging box flour sprinkler 261, 269, *see also* **dridging box**
dreipin dripping 300
drench vate container in which skins are steeped 158

drepen dripping 283, 290, **dreping** 127, 309, 313, **dreppenes** 126, **dreppinge** 85
dressed leather prepared and finished leather 31
dresser sideboard used particularly to display plate 32, 111, 153, 382, 392, 401, 425, 431, 445, 449
dresser tool with a hammer at one end and a pick at the other 319
dresser board table for dressing meat and other food 191A, 352, 365, 373, 430, 436, **dresser bord** 31, **dresser bowrd** 27
dresser board and drawers dressing table 430
dresing box dressing box 317
dressing board dresser board 147, 261, 269
dressing box one to hold toiletries 362A, 372, 398, 418, 428
dressing table 223, 368, 428, 448
drestle board dressing board 353
dridging box dredging box 452
drilled cock screwed tap 428
drincking dishe drinking dish 42
drincking glase drinking glass 317
drink alcoholic beverages 429
drinkeinge dish 80
drinking board 445
drinking bowl 369 **drinking bowle** 52
drinking cup 18, 61
drinking dish shallow cup 108, *see also* **drincking dishe, drinkeinge dish, drinking pot, drinking pott**
drinkinge boule 158
drinkinge clothe napkin used to wipe the chin when drinking 53, **drinckinge clothe** 31
drinking glass 445, 446, 452
drinking pot drinking dish 276, **drinking pot** 446, **drinking pott** 105, 428,
drinkvessell drinking dish 339
dripeinge dripping 292, **dripen** 188, 196, 294, 336, 343, 379, **dripin** 176, **driping** 83, 86, 145, 148, 160, 191A, 194, 197, 202, 211, 216, 235, 251, 261, 269, 302, 363, 399, 444, 449, 452, **dripinge** 4, 13, 121, 159A, 206, 221, 346, **dripings** 174, **drippeing** 200, **drippen** 27, 129, 267, 332
dripper dripping pan 445
drippin dripping 147, 164, 177, 186, 213, 329
dripping (pan) dish placed under a spit to catch drips from the meat *passim, see also* **dippin, dreipin, dripeinge, dripen, dripin, driping, dripinge, dripings drippeing, drippen, dripper, drippin, drippinge, drypen, dryping, drypinge**
drippinge 6, 15, 29, 31, 45, 47, 56, 119, 125, 143, 153, 181, 259
dropper draper 194
druckett drugget 223
drug, pair of *possibly* a pair of cross-cut saws 437, **drugg, pair of** 444
drugget coarse woollen or mixed fibre fabric **druggett** 351
drum *possibly* musical instrument 50
drum cussion flat, circular cushion 164
dry beanes 234
dryer drier 369, 425
drye tubb container for dry goods 24
dry fate vat for dry goods 144, **drye fate** 27
drypen dripping 67, **dryping** 10, **drypinge** 57
dry tubb wooden container for dry goods 31
dry vatte vat for dry goods 6
dubble salt double salt 45
dublet doublet 3, 5, 20, 28, 185, **dublete** 4, **dublett** 61, **dublette** 21, 125
dugpot dungpot 207
dung 352 *see also* **dunng**
dung cart dung pot 386
dungpot cart with a falling door in the base, for spreading dung on the fields, *see also* **dugpot**
dungpot blad dungpot shaft 294
dungpott dungpot 105, 273, 323, **dunge pott** 259
dunng dung 261, 269
dusen dozen 174, 387, **dussen** 2, 8, 10, 11, 18, 19, 71, 139
dust chaff used as a bed filling 177, 179, 452
dust shovell fire shovell 428
dutch table a tripod table, with a top that tips up, so that it can be stored against a wall 398
duzen dozen 127, 129, 160, 168, 202, 270, 373, 427, 433
dyaper diaper 31, 34, **dyapper** 448
dyche dish 3, **dyshe** 4, 5, 7, 9, 33, 188
dye fate vat used for dyeing 98
dyers stuffe materials used for dyeing 351

earing earring 451
earling yearling 34
earnest *possibly* oast hair 125
earth made of earthenware 33, 445, 445, *see also* **eorth**
earthen earthenware *passim* **earthern** 71, 177
earthenware clay pottery 105, 347, 395, 396, 416, 421, 437, 441, 446, 448, 449, 453 *see also*

earthen, earthern, earthenweare, earthren ware, earth ware, erthen
earthenweare 147, **earthren ware** 445, **earth ware** 431
earth plow plough 32
east hair oast hair **east haire** 24, **east heare** 8, 10, **east heore** 127, **easts haire** 265
east plate oast plate 247
easy chair armchair, not always upholstered 398, 418, 425, 430
effects in the shop all goods 436
egg slice implement for slicing hard boiled eggs 428
eighteene eighteen 212, 373, 382
elbow chair armchair 437
eleaven eleven 122, 269, 373, 428
ell linear measure of 45 inches 425, **elle** 29
elm wood of the elm tree 294, 437, 444, **elme** 108, 294, 439, **elmin** 206, **elming** 105, 444
elm bord elm board 396
emtey empty 235, **emtie** 157
end of hops *possibly* a measure; or hops still attached to the stalk 343, 449
engin engine 317
engine device used for cutting tobacco
engine and press cutter and press for tobacco 369
English book 347, **English booke** *possibly* books written in English as opposed to Latin or French 212, 223
enstcoop hen coop 64
entery entry 47
eoirn *probably* iron 257
eorth earthen 235, **erthen** 363
estate realty 148, 177
est heare oast hair
estplate oast plate
eure ewer 45
ewe female sheep 6 , 323
ewer pitcher with a wide spout 123
exspencis expenses 261, **expens** 264
extinguisher candle snuffer 445
eyren iron 95A

faate vat 69
faather feather 215
face cloth 103
facket faggot 158
fag *not known, but possibly* faggot 91
fagat faggot 215, 229, **faget** 360
faget pile pile of faggots 157
fagett faggot 127, 361, **fagget** 369, **faggete** 1, **faggett** 368, **faggod** 241
faggot bundle of twigs and small branches bound together for use as firewood 102, 179, 219, 252, 355, 369, 413, 445, **faggott** 140, 237, 288, 345, 421, 453, **faggotte** 78, 125, **fagot** 418, 431, **fagott** 180, 334, **fagotte** 83
faggot wood 140, 145, 160, **faggott wood** 224, 274, 289
fagon flagon 314
fallens valence 342
falling band band: clothing 61
family picture family portrait 398
fan device for winnowing grain after threshing 323, **fann** 40, 454, *see also* **vann**
farnituer furniture (bed) 215
fat vat 87, 285, 339, 342, 375, **fate** 6, 24, 29, 31, 34, 35, 50, 63, 68, 72, 102, 181
fatch vetch 32
father feather 165, 196, 229, 278, 341, 342
fatt vat 33, 289, **fatte** 10, 40
fatting trough feeding trough for fattening pigs 452
fearne fern for firing 315A
feather filling for beds, bolsters and pillows *passim, see also* **faather, father, feathere, feether, feothor, feth, fethar, fether, fetherd, fethr, feyther, vether**
feathere 39
feele bedsted field bedstead 71
feether feather 45
feier pane fire pan 277, **feirpnn** 300
felie felloe 294
felloe curved timber section of the outer rim of a wheel, *see also* **velle, vellye**
felt cloth made by rolling and pressing 4
fender metal frame placed in front of a fire to stop coals from rolling away from the hearth *passim* **fendor** 160, 241, 324
fend iron fender 430
fenicrik fenugreek: the aromatic seeds of *Trigonella foenum-graecum* 317
fennell seed the aromatic seeds of *Foeniculum vulgare* 317
feothor feather 235
ferken firkin 50, **ferkin** 368, 446
ferme form: a simple seating bench 5
fern bedding for animals 310, **ferne** 100
fesell vessel 327
fetch in grasse vetch in the field 171
feth feather 218, **fethar** 126, 202, **fether** *passim* **fetherd** 108, **fethr** 427
fetters, pair D-shaped shackles for tethering a

flascot flasket 399, **flaskat**
flaske container for gunpowder 40
flasket long shallow basket with a handle at each end 18, 45, 71, 95A, 140, 202, 369, 448, **flaskett** 21, 29, 34, 40, 78, 92, 103, 108, 119, 170, 181, 212, 263, **flasscot**
flat iorn smoothing iron 449
flax the blue-flowered plant *Linum usitassimum* cultivated for its fibres and seed 263, **flaxe** 3
flax fabric woven from flax 425
flaxen made from flax 45, 150, 164, 194, 398, **flaxson** 125
fleam knife used in bleeding animals, or for incising the gums 448.
fleam case case for a fleam knife 448
fleche flitch 66
fleece wooll wool shorn from a living animal 320, **fleese** 263
fleme fleshehooke flesh fork 18
flesh fork long metal implement with hooks at the end for retrieving meat from a large cooking pot 247, 394
flesh hocke flesh fork 6, **flesh hoock** 248, **flesh hooke** 17, 31, 33, 40, 43, 56, 68, 102, 125, 170, **flesh houck** 45, **fleshoke** 10, **fleshooke** 11, 22, 29
fletch flitch 154
flex flax 390
flexen made of flax 31, **flexin** 239, **flexon** 168
flice woole fleece wool 119
flitch side of bacon, cured and salted 26, 86, 97, 134, 204, 227, 237, 259, 294, 334, 353 *see also* **fleche, fletch, fluthe**
flock coarse tufts and refuse of wool, used as stuffing for pillows, bolsters and beds *passim*, *see also* **frook, vlocke**
flocke *passim* **flocx** 341, **flok** 111, 196, 343, **floke** 6, 174, **flook** 215, **floocke, flooke** 95A
floor box flour box 445
flour box box for the storage of flour 453
floure cuppe flour cup: *possibly* a measuring cup 18
floure pott flour pot 4, 5, **floure potte** 5
flower flour 125, 127, 418, 441
flower box flour box 320, 369, 398, 421, 426, 427, 428, 429, 436, 437
448, 449
flowerpote flour pot *or* flower pot 16, 229
flower sulfer flowers of sulphur: the purest form of the element 317
flower trough flour trough 441
flower tub flour container 448
flowre cup flour cup 19, **flowre cuppe** 19
fluthe flitch 386
foarm form 422, **foarme** 155, 167
folding bedstead a collapsible item 445
foor four 315
foorem form 235, **foorme** 102, 271
foornituer furniture (bed) 215
foot (feet) twelve inches *see also* **foote, fote**
foote feet (measure) 105
forceinge shears implement for clipping the upper layer of the fleece 31
forchel futchell: part of the undercarriage of a coach or wagon 294
foreign brandy imported brandy 445
forem form 202, **foreme** 235
forge house blacksmiths' workplace 40
fork garden implement 45, **forke** 203
fork table cutlery 194, 261, 398, 414, 428, 446, 448, 452, 453
fork flesh fork 269, table fork 445
fork blades the prongs of table forks, set separately into handles 448
forke flesh fork 263, 343
forke husbandry tool 45, 373
forke implement used in parchment making 310
forke part of a lock 220
forks and case set of table forks 445
forles *not known* 168
form a seating bench 17, 174, 285, 336, 369, 413, 421, 433, *see also* **foarm, foarme, foorem, foome, forem, foreme, forme, formm, forne, fourm, fourme, fowrme, fuorme, furme, furom, furrm**
forme form *passim*, **formm** 17
fornace furnace 6, 16, 31, 123, 148, 263, 274, 345, **fornes** 157, 215, 423, **forness** 386
forne form 241
forneis furnace 285, 300, **fornes** 253, 342, **forness** 292, **fornis** 235, 363
fornituer furniture (room) 215
fosser small chest for holding valubles, usually covered with leather and strengthened with iron bands, and with a lock 37
fote feet (measure) 45
foule *possibly* fowl, but with bricks & coles 361
4 in a row a paper of pins inserted in rows of four 232
foure four 8, 32, 52, 59, 61, 99, 108, 109, 111, 123, 170, 187, 188, 190, 233, *see also* **fower,**

originally from Fostat, Egypt 68, 263, 398, 412, 425, **fustin** 61, 425, **fustine** 51, 243, **fuston** 313
fyer fire, *see also* compound names beginning **fiar, fier, fire, fyer, fyre**
fyerpan fire pan 32, **fyerpann** 135, 187
fyer pan fire pan 43, **fyer pann** 143, 154, 164, 173, **fyer panne** 14, 31, 90
fyer shovell fire shovel 15, 31
fyer tonges fire tongs 16
fyfe five
fyfteene fifteen 121
fyle file 25
fyre fire 42, 84 *see also* compound names beginning **fiar, fier, fire, fyer, fyre**
fyre buckett fire bucket 113
fyre pan firepan 5, 50, **fyre pann** 113, **fyrepanne** 97, 109
fyre sheovill fire shovel 4, **fyre shovell** 140, **fyre shovill** 3, **fyre shovl** 273, **fyre shovle** 10, 63
fyve five 3, 5, 6, 11, 13, 15, 16, 27, 29, 55, 68, 72, 123

gack jack (fire) 363
gads goods 390
galland gallon 21, **gallen** 174, **gallion** 407
gallipot small glazed earthenware pot, especially used by apothecaries for ointments *see also* **gallypott, galypot**
gallon container to hold one gallon 11, 18, 52, 127, 272, 352, 353, 369, 373, 421, 429, 445, *see also* **galland, gallen, gallion, gallone, gallon, gallon measure**
gallone gallon 42, **galon** 31, **gallon measure** 417,
gallypott gallipot 254, **galypot** 317
gane gawn: vessel with a long handle to reach to the bottom of deep brewing vesels 101, 361
gardener garner 37
garden of plants 234
garden palle garden pail, one for use in a garden 47, **gardenn pale** 45
garden rake 368, **gardening rake** 28
gardine garden
gardner garner 84, 121, 143, **gardnere**
gardner board marker board for use in the garden 91
gardyer garner 10
garlix linen fabric, originally from Görlitz, Silesia 425, *see also* **gulix**
garner storage box or storehouse for grain etc. 31, 68, 133, 395, *see also* **gardener, gardner, gardnere, gardyer, geardner, gerner, graner**
garnished currall worked coral for jewellery 45
garter band for holding up stockings 28, 97
gartering narrow, woven fabric used as garters 61
gaul gall: an excresence growing on trees, used to make ink or tannin 317
geardner garner 95A
geere machinery for a well 111
geese tailors' goose: smoothing iron 399
gelding castrated male horse 78, 263, 273, **geldinge** 45, 144
gene joined 126, **gente** 126
gerner garner 168
get jet 45
gilt gilded 27, 108, **gilt silver** 159A, *see also* **guilt**
gimblett gimlet 382
gimlet threaded boring tool **gimlut** 220
gimp button button covered with gimp: a twisted thread with a wire running through 317
gin joined 188, 196, 341, **gine** 111, 207, **gined** 363, **gines** 218
gin alcoholic liquor 449, 452
gindstone grindstone 301
gingerbread 450
ginniel jemmel 220
ginte *not known* 220
gin vessell container for gin 452
girdle waistband 60, 61, 96, *see also* **gyrdell**
girdle buckell 448, 451
glas made of glass 396
glase, blew blue glass, *possibly* a vase 229
glase drinking glass 305, 317
glass drinking glass 102, 365, 430, 431, 446, glazier's stock in trade 211, *possibly* looking glass 436, 437, 446, 448, made of glass 363, 395, 445, 448, unspecified 45, 47, 71, 367, 398, 416, 453 *see also* compound names beginning **glass, glasse**
glass case open-fronted cupboard for displaying glass and other fragile items 318, 351, 428, **glasse case** 368
glass cobard glass cupboard 308, **glass coberd** 363, **glass cubbard** 369 **glass cuboard** 129, **glass cubbord** 248
glass cupboard case to store glasses, or case with a glass front 164

glasse drinking glass 61, 125, 140, glazier's stock 92, glassware made of glass 194, 249, unspecified 15, 27, window glass 177
glasse diall watch face 146
glasse of the wyndowes glass window 13
glasse shelfe glass shelf 321, **glasshilf** 407
glass print a painting on glass *or* a framed, glazed print 453
glass shelf shelf on which to store or display glasses, or a shelf made of glass 365, 398, 412, 430, **glass shelfe** 318, **glass shelve** 395
glass window not belonging to the howse moveable window separately appraised 448, **glasse wyndowe** 3, 4
gleazer an emery wheel 448
gleme used with 'imbry', so some sort of polishing material 40
glew glue 225, 310, 317
glew furnace *possibly* a small device for heating up glue to be applied to the surface of parchment 225
glew nett a mesh for sieving glue for parchment; *see also* nette 225, 310
glew trow glue trough 310
glofes gloves 161, **gloufes** 151
gloss glass 235
glovers beamel *possibly* a wooden last or shape for glove-making 64
gloves 28, 36, 105, 141, 243, 248, 324, 454
glue 387, *see also* **glew**
glue peece strip of hide for boiling down to make glue 31
glyve *not known* 6
goblet drinking vessel with a foot and a stem 27, **goblett** 29
goddard drinking cup or goblet 227
goeing string *not known* 317
gold article made of gold 59A, 68, 97, 175, 213, 226, 229, 231, 239, 350, 401, 420, 443, 445, 446, 447, 451, 454, **golde** 29, *see also* **gould**
goldware 164
goodes goods 312, 321
goods articles in general 114, 236, 287, 330, 335, 373, 390, 391, 397, 409
goods in the shop 372, **goods in the shopp** 201, 242, 250
goorgete gorget 54
goose feathers 425
goose oyl goose oil for dressing hair 430
gorget an article of clothing for women, covering the neck and breast, *see* **goorgete**
gouge goudge 257
gould gold 243, 347
gould ware readie made goldware made for sale, not to order 45
goun gown 51, **gound** 278
gown loose flowing garment, dress 12, 446, 454, **gownd** 120, **gowne** 6, 16, 37, 54, 96
goynt joined 247
grace grease 294
grain 317
graine tin container for grain 428
graner garner 40
grat fire grate 396
grate fire grate *passim*
grate coate great coat 160
grate door fire grate door 444, **grate dore** 363
grater wooden storage crate, suspended from the ceiling 40, 127
grater grating implement 428, 446
grater for bread an implement for making breadcrumbs 29, 111, 428
gratt grate 277
gratter grater: grating implement 445
gray grey 119, 243, **graye**
great grate 158, 294, 295, 430, **greate** 153, 178, 248, 392, 407, **greatt** 438
great Bible usually applied to Coverdale's Bible of 1535 or revisions of it, such as Cranmer's of 1540 129, 147, 198, 350
great coat large, heavy overcoat 446, 448
greate Bible great Bible 45
great leather *possibly* uncut hides 248
gredian gridiron 185, **gredier** 47, 241, **grediorn** 343, **gredirn** 290, **grediron** 32, 33, 38, 56, 108, 157, 292, 369, **gredyarn** 25, **greediron** 413
green copparis proto-sulphate of iron, used in dyeing 317
greidiron gridiron 265, **griddier** 98, 121, 125, **griddiron** 445, **grideion** 361, **grideron** 164, 190, 198, **grideyrn** 95A, **gridgiron** 392, **gridiorn** 174, 229, 297, 427, 449, **gridioron** 6, **gridiorun** 13, **gridire** 11, **gridireon** 153
grene green 95A
gridiron metal grid placed on or near the fire for roasting and toasting *passim, see also* **gruddier, grydiron, gryfyer, grydyre, grydyron gridjorne** gridiron 191A, **gridyer** 61, **gridyron** 27, 52
grinding stone grindstone 397, 444, 452, **grindinge stone** 15, 119, **grindston** 38
grindstone stone used for sharpening and polishing 35, 120, 169, 176, 182, 274, 293, 428,

448, **grindstoon** 191, **grineing stone** 146, **grinestone** 198, **grin stone** 396, *see also* **gindstone, gryndstone, grynestone**
grindstone spindle the axle through the middle of a revolving grindstone 362A, **grinsstone spindel** 220
griste grist: corn ready to be ground 85, 227
grogram grosgrain: coarse silky taffeta, usually stiffened with gum 425
grooneing chair childbirth chair 170
gros gross 317
gross 144 of an article 373
grubing axe grub axe: instrument for rooting up large plants especially weeds 424
gruddier gridiron 28, **grydiron** 2, **grydyer** 63, **grydyre** 3, **grydyron** 9
gryndstone grindstone 10, 40, 43, **grynestone** 135, 154
guge jug 66
guilt gilded 45
guinea coin originally struck in 1663 with a nominal value of 20s., but valued at 21s. from 1717 onwards 401
gulix garlix 425
gun 222, 367, 445, 448, **gunn** 439
gunpowder 445
gutter 153
gutter tile *possibly* a V-shaped tile, used in the valley between two roofs 360
gynd joined 165, **gyned** 160
gyrdell girdle worn round the waist 2
gyrse girth: saddle band passing under the body of the horse 9

hachet hatchet 38, 82, 257, **hachete** 38, **hachett** 115
hackney mare animal of middling size and quality, used for riding 132
haft handle, especially a knife or small tool 448, *see also* **aul haft**
haie hay 15
haifer heifer 328
hair animal hair 359, *see also* **haire, hare, hayr, heare, heere**
hair human hair used for wig making 430
haircloth stiff wiry cloth with a linen or cotton warp and horsehair weft used to hold malt in the kiln
haire hair sieve 101, 353, **hair seive**
halberd long handled weapon, combining a spear and a battleaxe, *see also* **holberte**
halbertt halberd 265,
hale hall *passim*
half *passim* **halfe** *passim* **halffe**
halfe a backe small back board 6
halfe a hundred a half hundredweight 12, **halfe a wayte** 10
halfe heded bedsteed bedstead with short corner posts and no tester 159A
half sleve sleeve of half the usual length 151
half vallains *possibly* an unusually short valance, or one which did not extend all round the bed 379
hall the main living room of a house *passim, see also* **hale, haulle, hawlle**
halter restraint for a horse 186, 351, 431, *see also* **collar holster, holter, houlter**
hamborough timber imported from Hamburg 373, **hambro** 373
hame crooked wooden support on which to form a horse collar 105, 413
hamer hammer 10, 146, 257, 283
hammer 17, 20, 220, 362A, 428, 448, 449, *see also* **hember**
hammock 445
hammper hamper 445
hamper large covered basket, often used as a packing case 8, 48, 383, 448, **hampier** 234
handbarrow *possibly* a small wheelbarrow 431
handbasket a small basket carried in the hand or over the arm 11, 52, 82
hand basket 64 **hand baskettes** 31
hand board tea-tray 445
hand buckett *possibly* wooden bucket for milking 73
hand candlestick 398, 428, 446, 452
handcarcher handkerchief 151, **handcerchev** 243
hand cloath *possibly* a hand towel or a flannel 445, *see also* **hand towel**
hand cuffe detachable cuff frills 112
hander pot hanger 267
hand hammer blacksmith's tool 182, 382
handkercheif handkerchief 446, **handkercheiffe** 96
handkerchief 425, 454, **handkershiffe** 332, *see also* **handcarcher, handcerchev**
hand iron andiron 261, 269, 425, 444
handle grindstone handle 362A, knife handle 310, pan or pot handle 428, tucker's handle 85, winding handle for a well 108, 177
handle bowle bowl with a long handle, used in brewing 452
handle brush *possibly* brushes for carpets or

hangings 452
hand of faggots quantity of cut wood 449
hand saw 108, 395, 424, 452, **handsawe** 37, 52, 180
hand towel 27
hand vice small, moveable vice which can be fixed to a bench 362A, 445, **hand vise** 146
hangeil pot hanger 356, **hangel** 85, 99, 125, 154, 160, 191, 294, 317, 335, 343, 361, 413, 421, 424, **hangele** 112A, 138, 283,
hangeinge bason hanging basin: a suspended basin 80
hangell *passim* pot hanger **hangelle** 83, 110, 224, 225
hanger *possibly* for hanging a bridle from, or hanging items from a saddle 445, loop or strap on a belt from which a sword was hung 446, pot hanger 98, 104, 118, 120, 122, 133, 150, 190, 245
hanggel pot hanger **hangil** 363, **hangill** 43, 139, 286, **hangille** 222
hangin cubberd hanging cupboard: one fixed to a wall, not part of an item of furniture 111, **hanging cubberd** 185, **hanging cuberd** 170
hanging pot hanger 102, 146, 170, 171, 186, 202, 265, 324, 340, 453, **hanginge** 227, 237, **hangin** 329
hanging fabric wall covering 428
hanging candlesticke one suspended from a stand or a bracket 382
hanging chilf hanging shelf 334
hanging dog andiron 449
hanging shelf one fixed to the wall, often used for books 294, 332, 355, 369, 421, **hanging shelfe** 274, 317, 368, **hanginge shelfe** 223
hangl pot hanger 209, **hangle** 82, 111, 144, 180, 185, 187, 197, 201, 241, 256, 341, **hangler** 159
haninge pot hanger 33
hannings decorative wall hangings 406, *see also* **painted wall hangings**
hardell hurdle 449
hard mettal *possibly* made of iron 428, 445
hard wood 215, 252, 274, 309, 334, 355, 391, 395, 420, 452
hare hair cloth 355
hare cloth oast hair 361, 395
harness straps for attaching a horse to a cart, plough etc. 259, 273, 386, 392, **harnesse** 32, **harnis** 160, 171, **harniss** 207, *see also* **horse harness**
harness frame with loops of twine through which the warp threads on a loom pass 351
harowe harrow (parchment making) 277, 387
harowe to make parchment
harrateen harrowteen 452
harrow an implement used in parchment making, *but whose precise_definition is not known* 225, 310, 375, 404, **harrowe** 118
harrow implement for raking ploughed ground 32, 259, 323, 386
harrowteen linen cloth used for making curtains 445
hat 20, 28, 197, 257, 341, 446, *see also* **hate, hatt, hatte**
hat brush 212
hat case 341
hatch *possibly* hatchet 64
hatchat hatchet *passim*
hatchet a light, short-handled axe 1, 2, 8, 18, 19, 424, 449, **hatchett** 16, 22, 33, 52, 115, 254, 310, 452, **hatchette** 37, **hatshett** 180, *see also* **hachet, hachete, hachett**
hate hat 51, 151
hathet hatchet 253, 297
hatt hat 4, 16, 21, 96, 97, 120, 243, 314, 448
hatt band 445
hatte hat 54, 103, 105
haulle hall 41, 47, **hawlle** 47
have half 104
hay *passim*, **haye** 31, 45, 61, 153, 167, 407, *see also* **haie, heay, hey**
hay prong hay fork 417
hayr animal hair:stuffing for a bed 40
hay reeke rick 352
headging bill hedging bill 37
heading timber for the head of a cask 373
heading block tool for making the head on a pin 232
head of a skimmer the business end of a skimmer 22
head stall part of a bridle or halter fitting behind the horse's ears 9
heare for a neast oast hair 45
heare lyne hare line: *possibly* a snare for catching hares, or a rope made of hair 45
hearth bisome hearth brush 317
hearth turf 345
heater billet of metal to heat a box iron 352, 431, 445, 452, food heater 448, 449
heay hay 261
hebitt *not known* 368
hed head: knob on the end of a fire dog 249
hedging bill tool for stopping up gaps in

hedges using bunches of severed twigs 2, *see also* **headging bill**
hedg mounding the boundary of a property defined by a bank with a hedge growing on it 64
hed peese head piece: head armour, helmet 27
heel shoe heel
heele heel 187, 201
heel maker maker of shoe heels 120
heepe heap 104
heere hair 9
helevling bord weavers' equipment: helve is the hammer part of a tilt hammer 33
hember hammer 38
hempe hemp: fibre of the plant *cannabis sativa*, used for making cord 245
hen 6, **hene** 47
hen cobe hen coop 13, **hencoobe** 31, **hen coop** 417, **hencubb** 72, **hene coobe** 47
hen feather 425
henn cubb hen coop 45
herthe heath (furze) used as bedding for animals 100
hessens hessian: strong coarse cloth made from a mixture of hemp and jute 425
heth brush hearth brush *or* one made of heath (furze) 212
hewe ewe 5
hewed cleft cut cleft 45
hewer heavy cutting tool 34
hey hay 18, 154, 185, 190, 245, 274, 398
heyfer bullock year-old beef animal 91
hide animal skin, raw or dressed 34, 236, 359, 413, **hidde** 44, *see also* **hyde**
hie bedstead high bedstead 153, 191, **hiee bedstead** 127
hiee bed high bedstead: 327, **highbedd** 84
high (bedstead): standing bedstead, as distinct from a truckle bedstead 111, 129, 144, 145, 179, 196, 224, 282, 334, 356, 368, **highe** 196, **hihgh** 111, **hye** 153
high candlestick candle stand: tall branched candle holder standing on a spread foot 140
hingell pot hanger 191A, **hingl** 168
hoabe hob: hobend 173
hoan hone 367
hob flat metal surface for heating a pan over a fire, *see also* **hoabe**
hobend flat-topped sidepiece for a fire, on which small pots can be set 11
hockaback huckaback 425, 453
hocke flesh hook 38
hockerback huckaback 448
hog male pig 160, **hogg** 26, 391, **hogge** 148, 181, **hog pigg** 323
hogge of bacon *possibly* hock of bcon 153
hoggesheade hogshead 56, **hoggshead** 153, 270, **hoghead** 145, *see also* **hooges head**
hogg tubb swill container 368, **hoggs tubb** 444
hogshead large cask of varying capacity, depending on the contents *passim* **hogshed** 100, 147, 363, **hogshedde** 31, *see also* **hoxhead**
hogshead cock tap for hogshead 428
hogtrow feeding trough for swine 11
holand holland 68, 124, 168, 313, 317, 347
holberte halberd: long-handled weapon, combining a spear and a battleaxe 27
holder of unspecified use 428
hold fast bench hook 445
holen holland 174, 202 **hollan** 159A, 164, 173
holland fine quality linen fabric, originally from the Low Countries 29, 31, 52, 56, 71, 92, 125, 150, 158, 159A, 185, 194, 243, 250, 398, 416, 425, 448, **hollands** 24, **hollane** 126, **hollen** 239, **hollin** 239, **hollon** 269, 343, **hollond** 172, 205, **hollandcloth** 369, *see also* **howlland shettes**
holter halter 382
hone whetstone 10, 430, 448
honey bag *possibly* a bag for straining honey to rid it of wax 265
honiger *possibly* a dish into which honey is decanted 248
hood item of clothing for the head 446, 454
hooges head hogshead 167
hook pot hook 332, 445, 453, **hooke**
hoop circle of flattened metal used for binding the staves of a barrel 340, 373, 421
hoorse horse: support 47
hope hoop 6
hopes hops 293
hops 265, 317, 363, 434
hop strainer *possibly* a sieve for straining wort 452, **hopp strayner** 449
horn animal horn used for combs, handles etc. 448
hornbook small printed alphabet, mounted on a board, covered with a sheet of transparent horn 317
horne horn of an animal 359
hors horse: animal 197, 283, 363, support 160,

196, 297, 305, unspecified 385
horse animal 15, 30, 31, 56, 82, 186, 205, 207, 245, 294, 323, 335, 339, 351, 386, 392, 434, 445, support for barrels etc. *passim* unspecified 232, 404, 417, *see also* **hoorse**
horsebeast horse (animal) 26, 61, 83, 171
horse bell bell attached to the harness of plough horses 146
horse coome horse comb 220
horse cloath horsecloth 351
horsecloth cloth to cover a horse after exercise or in winter 431
horse collar the collar worn by heavy horses, to which the long reins are attached 413
horse for beere support for a beer barrel 303
horse for cloathes frame on which to hang or dry clothes 430
horse for the barrelles to stand in 224, **- stand on** 428
horse harness the reins and straps used on heavy horses or carriage horses 323
horse hide leather made from horse skin 186, 413
horselock hobble or shackle to prevent a horse from straying 382, 417, **horselocke** 2
horse mill one worked by a horse 335
horse naile nail for attaching horseshoes 382
horse shoe 274, 382
horse skin leather horse hide 413
hors meatt food for a horse 176
horss beast horse 259
horsse horse, could be either a stand for clothes, or an animal 37
hose close-fitting breeches 4, 5, 120, 125, 241, **hosen** alternative plural of hose 60
hose cloth cloth from which hose were made 28
hot press smoothing iron 351
hot still alembic 265
houer glass hour glass 202
houlter halter 38
hounss hound: forecarriage of a waggon 294
hour glase hour glass 317, *see also* **hower glass**
hour glass reversible glass device containing sand, which times an hour 345
household goods 238, 384, 388, 389, 442, **housel gads** 390, *see also* **howshold goods**
housing horse-covering attached to a saddle or pannier 446
hovel raised storage for crops 95A, **hovell** 37, 47, 121, **hovelle** 72, **hovell house** 28
howckes hooks 95A
howelle *possibly* 'hovel', a shed where the parchment maker's equipment was kept or where parchment was hung to dry 277
hower glass hour glass 248
howlland shettes Holland sheets 95A
howshold goods household goods 152
hoxhead hogshead 353
huckaback stout linen fabric with a rough surface, *see also* **hockaback, hockerback**
huckerback huckaback 446
huckmuck strainer made of peeled osiers for filtering beer from the mash tub 452
hudrith hundred 10
hundered hundred 277
hundred hundredweight 86, 182, 431, 450
hundredweight eight stones, or 112 lbs., 368, 369, 444
hunger hyde hides in the process of tanning are known as hungry hides 9, 31
hurdel 26, 73, 396, **hurdele** 40, **hurdell** 16, 290, **hurdelle** 72, **hurdl** 360
hurdle rectangular frame with horizontal bars for fencing sheep in temporary pens 6, 83, 120, 127, 323, 444, *see also* **hardel**
hurst *possibly* here means a hearse, being in conjunction with a carriage 294
hussy a tea caddy; or a hastener (portable tin oven); or a huswif 428
hutch witch 83
hyde hide: leather 201

iern made of iron 174
imbry *possibly* the same as emery, a material for polishing or fine-grinding 40
implements fire irons 339, *see also* **implements, inplemts**
implements about the fyre 84
implements goods in general 18, 109, 192, 266, 273, 301, 302, 303, 305, 359, 377, 398, tools of a trade 125
implements of worke 227
implyments tools of a trade 248
ingrediens bed furniture 158, **ingrediente** ingredient(s) 236, **ingredyence** 154, **ingredyents** 154
ink horn small portable horn container for ink 448 **inkhorn** 430
inkle inferior grade of linen tape 425, 450, **inkel** 317, **inkell** 317
inner bound , pales of the pales of wood, fencing the premises 72
inplements fire irons 339, **inplemts** 154

instruments kitchen tools 123
iorn made of iron 361
iorn made of iron 264, 297, 343, 361, 449, quantity of iron 278
ioyne joined 34, 121, 125, 140, **ioyned** 8, 18, 22, 29, 31, 34, 35, 43, 78, 82, 85, 87, 133, 162, 177, 181, 183, 213, **ioynt** 224, 311, 365
ir made of iron 438, **ire** 111, 137, **iren** 10, 125, 312, 363, **ireon** 153, 346
ireyeare ironware 163
irne made of iron 50, quantity of iron 40, stock of 220
iron made of iron *passim* , *see also* **eiorn, eyren, iern, iorn, ir, ire, iren, ireon, irne, irone, irron , jerone, joren, jorn, jorne, joron, jron, yeieren, yeren, yorn, yoron, yre, yreion, yron**
iron quantity of iron 17, 38, 84, 159A, 362A
irone made of iron 33, 178, 259
iron for clothes smoothing iron 428
iron goods 374A
ironing board 448
irons fire irons 233, 240, smoothing irons 398
iron stuffe fire irons 109
iron to set before the fire fire iron 73
iron unmaid iron unmade into articles 25
ironware goods made of iron 55, *see also* **yreware**
ironwork made of iron 194
irron made of iron 56
iuge jug 56, **iugg** 43
ivory 448, **ivorye** 317

jack (fire) mechanism for turning a spit in front of a fire *passim, see also* **gack, jacke, jak, jake, jeark, jhack, jock, draw up jack**
jack large jug of waxed leather, tarred on the outside; sometimes difficult to distinguish from the jack above, but probably in 369, 377
jacke fire jack *passim*
jacke and weights 241
jacke padded jacket worn by foot soldiers 6
jacke line jack line 153
jack line cord connecting the jack to the jack wheel, *see also* **jacke line, line, lyne**
jack wheel part of the mechanism of a fire jack , *see also* **jack whell, dog wheel**
jack whell jack wheel 146
jak fire jack 342, **jake** 104, 222, 325
jagging iron staff with a prong for lifting root vegetables 428
jamaco peper allspice 317
jar 446, **jarr** 452
jeark fire jack 309
jemmell hinge consisting of an eye and a hook 382, *see also* **ginniel**
jened joined 95A
jent joined 309
jerkin close-fitting jacket, often made of leather 28, *see also* **jurkin, jurkyn**
jerone iron 36
jeyn joined 285
jhack fire jack 202
jhoyn 202, **jhoynt** joined 202
jine joined 111, **jint** 312
jirkin jerkin 4
jock fire jack 196, 235
jogg jug 101
join joined 157, 169, 185, 194, 197, 369, 374A, **joind** 127, **joine** 6, 128, 157, 158, 185
joined article made by a joiner, secured by mortice and tenon joints, rather than nailed or pegged *passim, see also* **gene, gente, gin, gine, gined, gines, goynt, gynd, gyned, ioyne, ioyned, ioynt, jened, jent, jeyn, jhoyn, jhoynt, jine, jint, join, joind, joine, joint, jont, joyen, joyn, joynd, joyne, joined, joynde, joynes, joynn, joynt, jointed, yeined, yuine**
joint 237, 262, 263, 274, 317, 324, 329, 345, 352, 383, 386, 393, 421, 446, 452, **jont** 377
joist supporting timber in a floor or roof, *see also* **joyce, joyste**
joren iron 308, **jorn** 253, 396, 406, **jorne** 191A, 253, **joron** 235
joule *possibly* a generous amount 45
joyce joist 106
joyen joined 283 **joyn** 159, 180, 229, 272, 279, 301, 302, 303, 398, **joynd** 38, 129, 394, 424, **joyne** *passim* **joyned** *passim* **joynde** 95A
joyned work joined work
joynes joined 308, **joynn** 285, **joynt** *passim* **joynted** 219, 221, 249, 284, 287, 357
joynt jointer: metal plate fixed to two pieces of wood to reinforce the joint 444
joynter long plane used by a carpenter or cooper, for dressing the edges of a board for jointing 180
joyste joist 121
jron iron 150, 181
judge jug 73
jug deep vessel for holding liquids, *see also* **guge, iuge, iugg, jogg, judge, juge, jugg,**

kneading trough large vessel in which dough is mixed, usually made of wood, *see also* **neading**
kneadintrow kneading trough 408
knif knife 257
knife 18, 127, 147, 174, 202, 227, 283, 319, 448, **knifes** 445, **kniffe** 96, **kniffes** 387, **knkif** 349
knitting needles 80
knives 165, 233, 274, , 398, 446, 448, 452, 453
knives (used in parchment making) half-moon knives used for scraping skins 64, 277, 310, 375, 404
knives and forks with a box canteen of cutlery 446
knyfe knife 45, **knyff knyffe knyves** 33, 40, 122
knyfe blades knife blades, to be fitted into handles 40
koberd cupboard 300
kofer coffer 291, 300, 341, **koffer** 48, 125
kotrel cotterel 174
kowl cowle 251, **kowle** 111
kyever kiver 67, **kyfer** 10
kyffe kive 10
kyfforre kiver 37, **kyfore** 39
kyforlead coverlet 37
kytle kettle 13, 50, **kyttell** 16, **kyttle** 6, 10, 37, 39, 42, 67, 110,
kyve kive 11, 31, 72, 119
kyver kiver 2, 8, 11, 19, 29, 31, 34, 35, 43, 46, 73, 78, 119, 120, 177, 224
kyverlede coverlet 37, **kyverlet** 6

lace cord used to bind or fasten 61, 317, 450 bobbin lace 112A, 176,
lace lease 355
lace hold leasehold 297
lacken glas looking glass 342
lad lead 253, **lade** 263, 283, 302, 310, 398, 431, **lading** 361
ladder *passim, see also* **lader, leaddeare**
ladder pole the long side of a ladder 437
laddl ladle 196
laddle ladle 237, 445, **ladel** 126, 172, 211, 317, 363, 407, **ladele** 147, 292, **ladell** 8, 18, 52, 78, 157, 168, 200, 276, 305, 334
lader ladder 6, 38, 95A
ladill ladle 93
lading made of lead 202, 361, **ladinge** 241
ladle long handled spoon with a cup-shaped bowl at the end *passim, see also* **laddl, laddle, ladel, ladele, ladell, ladill, leadell, leadall, leadle, ledell, loedelle**
ladle spoon ladle 113
laed made of lead 317, **laid**
lambe lamb 32, *see also* **lome**
lambes woole lambswool 119, 263 **lambswooll,** *see also* **lumbswooll**
lamblack lampblack, a pigment made from soot 317
lamp 445, **lamp and stand** 446
lance surgeon's knife 448
lance case case in which lances or lancets are kept 448
lancet small lance: surgical knife 445
lanteren lantern 363
lantern lamp with transparent case protecting a candle flame 445, 448, **lanterne** 8, 11, 19, 33, 72, **lanthorne** 34, 37, 52, 59, 79, 140, 150, 219, 241, 260, 315A, 345, 352, 373, 426, 430, **lantorne** 92, **lantern** 64, 445, **lantron** 445
lanthorne horn thin strips of animal horn used instead of glass in a lantern 428,
lanthorne with a glass 428
lapp *not known* 373
larding pinn large pin used to pierce meat to inset lumps of fat 428
larham clock alarm clock 440, **larrum** 146, 446, **larum** 146, **larum clock** 445
lase lease 104, 215, 264
lase hold leasehold 344
lases laces for shoes
last *possibly* similar to a cobbler's last 61
last foot-shaped mould on which to make or mend shoes 187, 201, 319 **laste** 115, 423
latan latten 174, **laten** 229
latchet *possibly* a door latch 52
lath thin strip of wood to support plaster on a wall 397, 437, **lathes** 123
lathe machine for shaping wood or metal, *see also* **lave**
lather made of leather 229, 355
latin latten 428, **latinge** 317
latten metal similar to brass, often hammered into thin sheets 7, 154, 173, 177, 241, **lattin** 260, **lattinge** 259
lattin weare latten ware 349
lave lathe 146, 305
lay lye 428
leacies leases 5
lead made of lead 11, 16, 24, 177, 211, 308, 317, 373, 391, 398, 421, 425, 445, 448, 449, quantity of metal 11, 16, 428, *see also* **lad, lade, lading, ladinge, laed, laid, leade, leaden, led, lid,**

lidden, liden
leaddeare ladder 70
leade lead 249
leadell ladle 449 **leadall** 95A
leaden made of lead 22, 31, 119, 153, 426
leades leaded lights for a window 54
leadging lidging 37
leadle ladle 216
leafe windowe window leaf 81
leas lease 247
lease contract for the conveyance of real property for a number of years *passim* **lease for yeares** fixed temr lease 31, *see also* **lace, lace hold, lase, leas**
lease for lives one to last during the lifetimes of (usually three) named persons 216, 224
leases laces for shoes 15, 132, **leasses** 8
leather made of leather *passim* pieces of leather 15, 34, 35, 60, 72, 103, 115, 158, 248, 324, 353, 377, 386, 423, *see also* **lather, leder, lether, letheren, letherne, lethren, leyther**
leather in the pitts hides being processed 31
leatherne made from leather 34, 249, **leathring** 247
leather shreds leather offcuts 383
leaves for a window window leaves 80
leavft left 306
led lead, quantity, or made of, 2, quantity of lead 92
led lid 444
ledell ladle 325
leder leather 300
ledging lidging 61
ledgs leggings 201, **ledgt, paire** 187
leell *possibly* lisle, a fine cotton for stockings 33
lefere bedstead livery bedstead 126
lefery bedsted 174
legacy 268
leineing household linen 285
lembicke alembic 97
lenen linen: unspecified 229
lennen household linen 270
lening linen: unspecified 327
lente *not known* 38
leomber goods lumber goods 309
lether pieces of leather 64, 141, made of leather 45, 52, 108, 150, 248, 301, 303, 396, 406, **letheren** made of leather 151, **letherne** made of leather 201, **lethren** made of leather 187
lethers stirrup leathers on a saddle 220, 293
lett 137
lettis lattice: structure made of laths used as a screen, as in windows 11
leumber things lumber 300
level instrument for ensuring an item is horizontal 439
levere livery: bedstead 157, **levery** 50, 66, 95A, 157, **leverye** 3, table board 4
leyne chain for a well bucket 38
leyther leather 9
licker tubb one to hold dye liquor 98
licquorish liquorice 317
lid made of lead 247, **lidden** 77, **liden** 377
lidd lid for a boiler 448
lidging steeping ashes in water to produce lye 11, **lidginge** 15, *see also* **leadging, ledging, lodging, lydgeinge, lydginge**
limbeecke alembic 27
limbeck alembic 421, **limbick** 194
limber shaft of cart or wagon 294
lime quicklime used in tanning 44
lime coob in husbandry, lime coop: cart made of close boards to carry anything which would fall through open boarding 64
lime pite pit in which tanners dress skins with lime to remove hair 65
line jack line 329
line in common use 418
lineings undergarments, usually for the lower body 248
linen clothing and household goods made from linen fabric 92
linen bed 170, 188, 219, 359, 370, 411, household 298, 361, 397, clothing 298, 326, 395, 454, unspecified 229, 286, 293, 341, 378, 385, 395
linen cupboard 92
linene linen clothing 71
linen turn spinning wheel for flax, *see also* **linnen turne, linnen wheel, lynen tourne, lynninge tourne, lynning turne, lynnen whele, lynnen whele**
ling linen 432
linges, couple of may be washing lines 133
linien linen clothing 325
linige linen: bed 239
linill oyle *possibly* linseed oil 317
linim linen, unspecified 319, 360, **linin** bed 330, 417A, **linine** bed 145, 160, clothing 62
lining *possibly* wooden panelling 266
lining made of linen 146, 235, bed linen 167, 235, 374A, 407, linen clothing 107, 151, 163, 185, 191, 296, 313, 356, household linen 377, unspecified 396

lininge bed linen 99, 104, 178
lininges, pair undergarments 161
linkes chain links; or pitch and tow torches 317
linne cloth 61
linnen linen: bed and household *passim* clothing 103, 400, cloth 223, unspecified 258, 303, 318, 382, 386, 391, 400, *see also* **leineing, lenen, lennen, lening, linene, ling, linien, linige, linim, linin, linine, lining, lininge, linnen, linne, linnin, linnine, linning, linninge, linon, lynen, lynen, lyninge, lynnen, lynninge, lynon**
linnen press linen cupboard 430
linnen turne linen turn 19, **lynen tourne** 31, **lynninge turne** 7, **linnen wheele** 40
linnen yarn spun flax thread 351
linnin linen: clothing 279, **linnine** household 73, clothing 58, unspecified 247, 257, 268, **linnine** 58
linning linen: bed 207, 240, 449, household 297, 416, clothing 51, 307, unspecified 393, 440
linninge made of linen 51
linon linen: clothing 251, unspecified 305, 354
linse linsey 253, 332
linsey inferior fabric of wool mixed with linen or flax, used for clothes and furnishings by the poor 351, 425
list strips or bands of cloth
liste list 74
liverie livery: bedstead 29, 69, food storage 27
liverie board livery cupboard 45, 83, **liverie bowrde** 27
livery food storage and presentation for retainers
livery bedstead: one intended for servants' use *passim*, *see also* **lefere, lefery, liverie, lyverie, lyvery**
livery cupboard: a cupboard in which food rations for retainers were stored 32, 81, 125, 129, 147, 287, *see also* **lyvery**
liverye livery bedstead 59
liverye boord livery cupboard 80, **liverye boorde** 24, **livery bord** 123
livery table for presentation of food rations 108
living stoor pige living store pig 235
load peck *not known* 428
lock cock part of the workings of a lock 428
locken glase looking glass 229
lockeram lockram 31, 52, 174, **lockerom** 95A, **lockerum** 54, 249
lockram coarse linen cloth, originally from Locranon in Brittany 425, **lockrom** 125, **lockrum** 69, **locrum** 71, 102
locks lamblocks: first shearing from lambs 398
lock stock stock lock 220
lode load 14
lodging lidging 28
lodgings all that pertains to a bedstead 15
loedelle ladle 235
loft, lofte attic, or room over a stable, *passim*
logg log 127
logget heavy block of wood tied to a horse's leg to prevent it from straying 417
logwood heartwood of the American tree *haematoxylon campechianum* used in dyeing 317
loimber lumber 235
loke stok stock lock 10
loking glase looking glass 196
lombare lumber 126
lombe loom 101
lomber lumber 61, 72, 193, 235, 242, 259, 285, 292, 299, 341, 344, 371, 423, **lomberd** 25, **lomber goods** 306, 346, **lombres** 157, **lomber things** 285
lome watchmaker's tool 146, loom 33, 101, lamb 6
London starch made in London, not Holland, where it originated 317
loocking glass looking glass 248, 363
lood load 42, **loode** 33
looking glase looking glass 231, **looking glasse** 212, 223, 295, **looking glassis** 261, 269, **lookeinge glass** 180, 227, 241, 256, **lookeinglasse** 113, **looking glas** 334, 427, **looking glase** 396, **lookin glass** 379, **looking glass** *passim*, **looking glasse** 28, 219, 223, 249, 287, **lookinge glas** 233, 347, **lookinge glasse** 29, 31, 80, 194, 321, *see also* **glass, lacken glas, locken glase, loking glase, loocking glass, louching glas**
loom weaving apparatus , *see also* **lombe, lome, loome**
loome loom 33, 351
loome work lase woven lace 61, **loome worke** 61
loose bedsteade *possibly* a truckle 24
loos wood loose wood 334
loucking glas looking glass 341
loumber lumber 235, 335, **lounbe** 235, **lounber** 235

lousse woule loose wool: broken wool 47
low bell small bell 265
lug long stick or pole 176
luge lug: chopped wood for firing 120, **lugg** 80, 153, 158, 310, 431, 452, **lugge** 18, 31, 45, 78, 105, 125, 140
lugs dowells for pinning felloes together 154
lumbar lumber 94, 104, 145, 202, 227, 253, 288, 289
lumbe lumber 157, 188, **lumbear** 70
lumber articles of low value *passim, see also* **leomber, loimber, lombare, lomber, loumber, lounbe, lounber, lumbar**
lumber for the glew trade 225
lumber good miscellanwous articles of low value 313, **lumber goodes** 162, 167, **lumber goods** *passim* **lumbery goods** 284
lumber goods in his shop 214
lumberment lumber 66, **lumbering things** 279, 307, **lumber stuff** 77, lumber stuffe 90, **lumber things** 287, **lumbor** 276, **lumbr** 209, 327, **lumbur** 279, **luombear** 70
lumbswooll lambs wool 398
luse timber loose timber 361
lydgeinge lidging 14, **lydginge** 16
lye alkaline solution made from wood ash, used for washing fabrics and clothes, *see also* **lay**
lymber limber 154
lymbick alembic 428
lyme lime 31, 34
lyne line 2, 113, long rein, 171, jack line 448,
lyneed get lined jet 45
lynen bed linen 221, 223, household linen 295, table linen 244, unspecified 244
lynen tourne linen turn 31
lyninge bed linen 154, 175, 187, 201, 230, 362A, linen clothing 81, 173, 239, table linen 141
lynnen bed linen 213, 227, 237, 274, 321, household linen 32, 56, 123, 287, linen clothing 31, 60, 159A, 214, 263, thread and fabric made from flax 11, 365, unspecified 109
lynnen whele linen turn 45
lynninge bed linen 236, household linen 84, **lynon** 305
lynninge tourne linen turn 7
lyquorish liquorice, the black root of *Glycyrrhiza glabra* 317
lyverie livery: cupboard 32
lyverie livery: bedstead 106, **lyvery** 31, 73, 120, 140
mace dried outer covering of the nutmeg 317
mackey *not known* 445
madera wine madeira 445
made ware goods made to sell, not to order 61, 158
made wine *possibly* homemade wine 445
mahogany 445, 446
maishing mashing 272, *see also* compound names beginning **mashe, mesh, mashen, meash, mease, meshing, mesing**
maish tubb mashtub 452
maishvatt mashing vat 368
male linine men's undergarments and/or shirts 62
male pillion a pillion saddle designed to be ridden astride 237, **male pyllyon** 9, *see also* **mayle pillion**
malliard mallet 452
mallt malt 266, **malt** *passim*, **malte** 13, 79, 130, 191, 355
malt barley which has been steeped, germinated and dried, for use in brewing, *see also* **mault, maulte, maut, moealte, molt, moule, moult** and compound names beginning with these
maltemell malt mill 38
malte querne malt quern 127, *see also* **quern**
malte seave malt sieve 127
malt gardiner malt garner 353, *see also* **garner**
malt green and dry green malt is from hops immediately after harvesting. Dry malt is used later; hops do not last long green and must be dried for further use 241
malting wetting and heating barley to make malt 323, **maltinge** 13
malt mill *passim*, **malt mell** 355
malt screen malt sieve 412
malt seeve malt sieve 11, 16, 18, 68, **maltseeve** 1, **maltseve** 174
malt shovel a wooden shovel used for turning the germinating barley 444, **malt shovell** 373, *see also* **molt shovel, shoul, shovel, shovel, shovle**
maltsive malt sieve 24
malt skreene malt sieve 159A
manger rack for animal fodder 31, 47, 64, 82, 153, 430, **mangere** 66, **maninger** 27, **manger** 27, *see also* **maynger**
mantle loose sleeveless garment, open at the front 263 316, 369
mantle laced with silver 263
map 365, 372, 430, 445

marble stone boulder found in glacial clay, used as a grindstone 146
mare 30, 72, 81, 82, 111, 125, 151, 193, 194, 273, 274, 321, 329, 363, 393, 395, 397, 398
markat ware marketware 312
marketware articles made to sell at the market 169, 182
markin ire marking iron 91
marking iron branding iron for animals; or *possibly* a stake for marking out ground in the garden
marline thin line made of two strands of thread 317
marshment *recte* parchment 64
marsh vate mashing vat 398
maserd mazer 28
masereen pie plate 428
masheing fat mashing vat 285
mashen vat mashing vat 343
mash fatt mashing vat 330, 379, 421, **meshfatt** 56
mashing fat mashing vat 339, **mashing fate** 373
mashing tub/vat vessel in which to mix malted barley with hot water to produce the wort 411, 426, **mashing tubb** 448, *see also* compound names beginning **maish, mashe, mesh, mashen, meash, mease, meshing, mesing**
mashing vat *see* mashing tub **mashing vate** 406
mash tubb mashing tub 440
mash tun mashing tub 444
mash vate mashing vat 261, 263, 269, 430
masure measuring vessel 317
mat cloth covering the bed cords to stop the bed (mattress) from chafing on them 38, 111, 150, 157, 158, 185, 194, 202, 235, 281, 290, 294, 308, 311, 351, 363, 399, 427, 430, covering for a bench 28, *see also* **mate, matt, matte**
matarels materials 159
materials goods, *see also* **matterialls**
mate bed mat 111, 123, 157
mathoocke mattock 174, **mathooke** 64
matt bed mat *passim* **matte** 39, 47, 12, 123, 144
matt bench cover 28
matt table cover 445, 449
mattake mattock 10
matted made of matted straw or rushes 129, 140, 159A, 225
matterialls goods 223
mattock kind of pickaxe with one end of the blade arched and flattened at right angles to the handle 28, 75, 203, 424, **mattocke** 2, 34, *see also* **mathooocke, mathooke, mattake**
mattras mattress 445, **mattris** 40
mattress the bed proper, stuffed with chaff, straw, flock or feathers
mault malt *passim* **maulte** 15, *see also* compound names beginning **malt, maulte, molt, moule, moult**
maulte myle malt mill 10, **maulte myll** 5, **mault mill** 121, 177, 181, 289, **mault mille** 131, **mault myll** 5, 6
mault gardner malt garner 47
mault querne hand mill for malt 47
mault seeve malt sieve 21, 31, 46, **mault sieve** 34, **mault seve** 40, 45, 79, **mault sive** 17
mault stone trough for wetting barley to make malt 84
maut seeve malt sieve 80
mayle pillion male pillion 77
maynger manger 111
mazar cupp tipped and fotid with silver mazer: silver-mounted wooden drinking cup 12
mazer a broad-based cup or drinking bowl , *see also* **maserd**
meal ground grain 111, 4418, 421, **meale** 80, 125, 144, 155, 212, 373, **meall** 160, 279, 359, *see also* **meele seve**
mealtrow meal trough 294
mearch vate mashing vat 334
measeinge mashing 190, 195, 245
meashfate mashing vat 294
meashin mashing 329, 262, **meashing** 11, 181, 224, 237, 318, **meashinge** 24, 47, *see also* compound names beginning **maish, mashe, mesh, mashen, mease, meshing, mesing**
meash tubb mashing tub 386
measinge mashing 143, **meassinge** 222
measure vessel constructed to contain a standard measure 11, 241, 265, 418, *see also* **masure, meser**
measuring wheel device for measuring out gunpowder for a firearm 445
meat victuals of any sort **meate** 89, 111
meat for a cow fodder 328
medly medley: fabric woven with coloured wools 16, 96, **medlie cloth** made from coloured wools or mixed fibres 119, **medly cloth** 28, 83, **medly wool** coloured wools 119
meele seve meal sieve 21

mell large hammer 335
mell mill 335, 355
melting kittle pot to melt solder 177
melting pann glazier's tool 177
mens breeches 383
mens sheep gloves gloves of sheepskin 383
mens shooes 187, 210
meser measuring vessel 229
meshfat mashing vat 303, **meshfatt** 56
meshing mashing 183, 301, 395, **mesing** 6, *see also* compound names beginning **maish, mashe, mesh, mashen, meash, mease**
mesh tubb mashing tub 449
messuage dwelling house with its outbuildings and land 362A, **message** 192
metal button 445
metheglin fermented liquor made from honey and water 100, 369
mettle metal 232, 324, 445
middle woole middle grade wool 119, **middle wooll** 31
milch cow cow in milk 69
milk bucket 413
milk strainer strainer for sieving out impurities in milk 373
mill apparatus for grinding 232, 418, *see also* **mell, myll**
millstone shaped and dressed stone used in a mill for grinding corn 105
milter *not known* 216
mincing chopping food finely 18, 174, **minsing** 93, 147, 202, **minsinge** 29, 95A, *see also* **mincing, mynceing, mynsing**
minsing knife one for finely chopping food 93
mittins mittens: fingerless gloves 248
moealte malt 70
moge mug 363
mohawk *not known* 445
moiety half, *see also* **moyety**
molt malt 28, *see also* compound names beginning **malt, mault, maulte, moule, moult**
molt mill malt mill 235
moltseave malt sieve 28
molt shovel malt shovel 28
mondes mounts: mounting blocks 80
money *passim, see also* **mouny, muney, munney**
money at interest 177, **money at intrest** 213, **money att intrest** 218, **money out at interest** 418
moneyes money 343, **money** 313, **monny** 160, 220, 242, 257, 306, 355, **monnye** 346, 259, 344
money in hand 314, 423
money upon yous [use] : lent out at interest 341
monnyes dew one bond money due upon bond 306
mony money *passim* **money** 57, 107, 134, **monyes** 207, 296, **monys** 191A,
moore peat used as fuel 368
morgage mortgage 239
mortar vessel of hard material, in which ingredients are pounded with a pestle 254, 260, 317, 426, 428, 445, *see also* **morter**
morter mortar *passim*
morte snagg *not known* 52
mortgage 228, 322, 332, 381, 400
mould glass cutting pattern 177
moulding board on which dough or pastry is kneaded and shaped 83, 160, 441, **mouldinge boarde** 125
mouldinge bord 127
mouleseve malt sieve 38
moulseve malt sieve 66
moult malt 50, **moulte** 10, 37, *see also* compound names beginning **malt, malte, molt, moule**
moulte seve malt sieve 37
moulting howse malting house 37
moult myll malt mill 67
mounters *possibly* the flaps on a hat, which let down on each side, to be fastened under the chin 151
mouny money 88
mourning buckell decorated buckle worn at time of mourning 448
mourning sword special sword kept for times of mourning 446
mousetrap 373, 448
moveables 154
movement working parts of a watch 146
moyety moiety 210
mugg drinking mug 345, 421, 426, 445, see also **moge**
muney, money 307, **munney** 279
musket an infantryman's light gun, often supported ion the shoulder 127,
muskette 40, **muskey** 294, 301, 446
muslin fine, delicately woven cotton fabric 425
mustard bowl bowl for grinding mustard seeds 421

musterd pote mustard pot 229
myll mill 137
myll to grinde crabbes mill to grind crab apples 14
myncing mincing 11, **mynceing** 123, **mynsing** 122

nag small riding horse 160, 176, 185, **nagg** 76, 274, **nagge** 32, 35
nail 444, **naile** 382, see also, **nayl, nayle, neyle**
nail box 445
nailing hammer 182
nail stake small anvil used by a smith 382
napken napkin 27, 126, 127, 313, **napkene** 66
napkin passim **napkine** 39, 59, 93, 95A, 129, 157, **napkinge** 47, **napkin** 18, **nappin** 283, **naptikin** 174, **naptkein** 285, **naptkin** 28, 91, 185, 194, 235, **naptin** 261, **napting** 308, **naptting** 269 see also **knapkin, napken, natkene,** and variants of **table napkin**
napkin wrought with blue 150,
napting prese cupboard for napkins 308
natkene napkin 54
nayl nail 317, **nayle** 15, 317
neading kneading 147
nealing annealing: process of heating and beating metal
neast heare oast hair 143, **neast haire** 31, 83, 95A, **neasthayre** 28, 84
neast heare skreene oast hair screen 241
neast lought oast loft 95A
neast of boxes nest of boxes 247
neast of drawers nest chest of drawers 368
neast plate oast plate: support for an oast hair 83
neck cloath kerchief worn about the neck, usually by men 448, **neckclothe** 97
neck stock close-fitting neck-cloth 446
nessasaryes household articles 167, **nessesaryes** 167
nest of boxes cupboard with a door, behind which are a number of small drawers 369, 394, **nest of drawers** 446
nest of open boxes 445
nett packaging material 13, hair net 113, **nette** hair net 80, for straining glue in parchment making 387
network openwork embroidery 31
neyle nail 55
nightcap 243
nightgown 446
nineteene nineteen 172
nipper small pair of pliers 445
nipple shell hollow, shell-shaped device used to protect a nipple 428
nobb knob 428
noble coin with a value of 6s 8d 118
note of hand promissory note 452
nurle knurle: milling tool 220
nurses chair nursing chair: low chair used for nursing infants 373
nursing candlestick candlestick accompanying the above 428
nutcracker 448
nutmeg grater implement for grating hard spices 428
nutt nut 317
nyne nine 39, 53, 123, 143, 198, 261, 269, 287, 321
nyneteene nineteen 121

oak 437, 439, 445, 452, **oake** 294, 445, **oaken** 444, 446
oaken bord oak board 294, **ocken bord** 396, *see also* **ocken timber, oken**
oast hair coarse open fabric made of horse hair, used for drying hops or malt over a kiln *see* **earnest, east hair, east haire, east heare, east heore, easts haire, est heare, hair cloth, hair for a neast, nęast heare, neast haire, neasthayre, ost heare, ost haire**
oast plate *possibly* the frame on which the oast hair was fixed, *see also* **east plate, est plate, plate for east hair, plate on the kiln**
oaten dust oat chaff 158
oates oats 32, 125, 274, 431
oatinge yoting 101
oatmeale oatmeal: meal made from ground oats 78
oats 190, see also **otes**
oattub *possibly* the vessels in which oats were ground 421
ob. Obolus: half a penny 150
obligation written agreement to pay a debt on the due date 106, 227
occamy alloy of tin with copper and zinc, resembling silver; a corruption of 'alchemy'
ockelme occamy 428
ocken timber oak timber 396
odden wooden 51
oilestone oil stone: fine-grained whetstone, oiled in use 146
oily worsted unwashed worsted fibres 320
oken oak 206

omtey empty 235
ond *possibly* one in this case 95A
open tape openwork or netted tape 317
ordneorey ordinary 235
orgell *not known* 344, **orgyle** 232
orig *possibly* orange 95A
orres arras 27
ossett laome loom for weaving osset: a kind of worsted 33
ost heare oast hair 64, **ost haire** 133
ot to: two 308
otemeale measure oatmeal measure 18
otes oats 323
oute howses that ar movable sheds, *possibly* on wheels or on staddle stones 63
outseamed gloves gloves with seams on the outside 383
oval dish 445
oval table 437, 445, 448, 452, **oval table** 421, **ovell table** 368
oval table board 369, 398, 426
ovell civer oval kiver 444
ovil table board oval table board 439
oven portable metal container, placed in front of the fire, to keep food warm 445
oven lead *possibly* a cauldron for boiling meat 368
oven peel 147, *see* **peel**
owele old 380
Oxford almanack one of a series of broadsheets, published by OUP since 1674, 448
oyle oil 272
oyl pott 428
oynions onions 100
oyntement 283
oyster knives 448
ozen ozenbrig: coarse linen cloth, originally from Osnabruck, Westphalia 425

pack *possibly* of playing cards 446
pack binch *possibly* a bench for storing horse packs 111
pack cloth laid on the back of a horse, under the pack saddle, to prevent chaffing 398
packet 344
packing packing paper 232
pack sadle pack saddle: support for packs carried by a horse 61
packthread twine used for tying up a pack 13
pad piece of cloth placed under a saddle, to protect the horse's back from chaffing 413, **pad of list** one made of list. 375, **padd** 186, 265, 351, *see also* **pade**
paddel paddle, unspecified 180
paddle spade-like implement for cleaning the earth from a plough 77
paddle spade-like implement for stirring the mash 445
pade pad 95A
paier pair 33, 47
pail bucket 369, 373, 395, 421, 430, 431, 444, 448, 449, 452, **paile** *passim* **paill** 202, 290, **paille** 47, *see also* **pal, pale**
paile bottom pail bottom 373
paile timber for making a wooden pail 373
paint pint 229
painted chair 452
painted cloath painted cloth 17
painted cloth canvas cloth painted with floral or geometric patterns, used as a substitute for tapestry bed or wall hangings 52, 125, **painted clothe** 2, 7, 11, 27, 45, 56, 61, *see also* **hannings**
painted tester painted bed board 80
pair *passim* **paire** pair *passim* **pairen** 115, *see also* **paier, pare, payer, pear, peare, peer, peere, peir, peire, per, pere**
pair of drawers small chest of drawers 439, **pair of draws** 445, **paire of drawers** 370, 427
pal pail 361, **pale** 3, 17
pale thin strip of wood, particularly used for fencing 28, 31, 40, 45, 56, 58, 61, 72, 82, 92, 105, 121 **palle** 37
pan *passim* **pane** 4, 6, 54, 88, 115, 127, 188, 235, 277, 309, *see also* **pang, pann, panne, penn**
pancake slice implement for lifting pancakes from the pan 28
panel pannel 283
pang pan 442, **pann** *passim* **panne** *passim*
pannell kind of saddle, particularly a wooden saddle for donkeys 186, 193, 232
pannell door one made of panels, rather than in one piece 453
pap dish pap pan: one for keeping food warm 428
paper 232, 344, 418, 450
pappron dish for keeping food or drink warm 22
paquet packet 317
parcel assemblage of goods 150, 317, **parcele** 40, **parcell** 155, 180, 186, 200, 227, 234, 258, 263, 372, 373, 383, 398, 428, 453, *see also*

parsell, pasel, pasell, percel, persel, persell
parchment 118, 310, 375, 398, 404, **parchmente** 277, *see also* **marshment**
pare pair *passim*
pareing knives paring knives 248
parell apparell 44, **parill** 174, 209
paril post *not known* 294
parr bar 10
parrell apparell 45, 46, 193
parse book of grammatical exercises 146
parsell parcel 146, 211, 229, 317
parte part 106
parte tree type of saddle tree, but precise type not known 9
particion of boards partition made of boards 214, **partition of boards** 368
partinancis appurtenances 371
partition 430
partlat partlet: women's neckerchief, collar or ruff 51, **partlete** 54, **partlett partlette** 16, **partlotte**
pasel parcel 283, **pasell** 309
pastern horse shackle 9
pastie peile pasty peele 127
pasty pan 260, 320, **pasty pann** 428, *see also* **patty pan**
pasty peele oven peel for pasties 368
pasty plate dish on which pasties are cooked 398
patten wooden sole mounted on an iron ring, to raise the foot above muddy ground 428, *see also* **patting**
patten ring 382
patterbors a patterned fabric 425
patticot petticoat 51
patting patten 454
patty pan 398, 428, 445, **patty pann** 448, **paty pan** 363, *see also* **pasty pan**
pautor pewter 215, **pauyter** 88, **pawtar** 312, **pawter** 95A
payer pair 33, 38, 51, 54, 97
payl pail **payle** *passim*
payll 196, **paylle** 37
paynted cloathe painted cloth 5, **paynted clothe** 4, 5, 6, 9, 13, 40, 96, **paynted clote** 63
paynted testurne painted tester 6
peale (oven) peel 73
pear pair 294, **peare** 10, 26, 55, 72, 73, 106, 118, 123, 126, 139, 168, 186, 191A, 248, 277, 308, 363, 423
pearll pearl for jewellery 45
pease peas 32, 407
peasse piece 70
peat *not known* 325
peauter pewter 373, **peawter**
pece piece 10, 17, 38, 45, 50, 85, 106, 131, 135, 174, 253, 310, 317
peck dry measure of capacity of two gallons 16, 21, 31, 33, 61, 68, 127, 289, 353, 361, 373, 407, 421, 444, **pecke** 6, 11, 18, 29, 37, 46, 85, 164, 168
peckhorn beckhorn 362A
peece piece *passim*
peece firing piece: gun 40
peece of gold gold guinea 170
peeg pig 315A
peel long-handled implement with a broad, flat end, to place bread etc. in the oven and retrieve it after baking, often made of iron, **oven peel** 147, **iron peele** 421, 441, **peele** 11, 18, 127, 368, 421
peele oven peel 16
peello pillow 342
peer pair 449, **peere** 91, 111
peese piece 25
peg pig 70, **pege** 283
pegg small tapered block of wood to close the ventilation hole in a barrel 190
peg trow pig trough 283
peice piece 247, 375, 382
peile oven peel 127
peilobear pillow case 300
peinted clothe painted cloth 27
peir pair 27, **peire** 27, 96
pekestafe pikestaff 66
pelebare pillowbear **peliber** 174
pelew pillow 229, **pella** 126
pellacase pillowcase 126
pello pillow 174, 300, 325, **pellou** 88, **pellow** 51, 118, 264, 313, 406, **pellowe** 47, 54, 137, 138, 143, **pelo** 311
pelobear pillowbear 157, **pelobere**
pelocase pillowcase 343
pelose pillows 157
pelow pillow 202, 291
pelowbeare pillowbear 54, **pelowber** 317
pelt undressed skin of sheep and other small animals 310, 375, 398, 404, **pellte** 277, **pelte** 31, 118
pen and case 445
pencer pincer 283
pencil 445
pen knife 445, 448
pen knife blade 448

penn pan 292
penner pinner 54
penney *possibly* penny faggots 407
pennywayte one twentieth of a Troy ounce 45
pentess board one used to make a penthouse: the shelter over a door or window 45
peore pewter 21
peper pepper 317
peper box pepper box 427, 449
pepper 317, *see also* **peper, petter**
pepper box box for storing peppercorns 320, 369, 398, 428, 437, 444, 445, 452, *see also* **petter box**
pepurbol pepper bowl: *possibly* one in which peppercorns were ground 229
per pair 50, 63, 67, 69, 110, 113, 141, 143, 154, 233, 248
percel parcel 294
perch centre pole connecting the fore and hind carriages in a four-wheeled wagon 294
pere pair 111
perlowe pillow 66
persel parcel 317, **persell** 317
pesce piece 347, **pese**
pesell pestle 259
peses pieces 396, **pesis** 264
pesse piece 93
pessell pestle 56, 73, 180, **pestell** 2
pestle club-shaped implement for grounding substances in a mortar 16, 34, 40, 83, 87, 123, 254, 260, 317, 369, 394, 398, 426, 428, 445, 452
peticoat petticoat 454, **peticote** 6, **pettecoate** 120
petter pepper 421
petter box pepper box 421
petticoat underskirt, the front panel of which was intended to be seen through the front opening of the skirt, and was therefore often decorated, *see also* **patticot, petticoat, peticote, pettecoate**
petticoate petticoat 96, **petticot** 51, **petticote** 16, **pettycoat** 278, **pettycoate** 60
petycoote petticoat 54
peutar pewter 337, **peuter** *passim* **peutter** 408
pew long bench with a back 40
pewtar pewter 52, 202
pewter alloy of tin and lead *passim* **pewtter** 205, 259, 292, 332, 344, 346, 359, **pewtur** 307, *see also* **pautor, pauyter, pawtar, pawter, peauter, peawter, peore, peutar, peuter, peutter, pewtar, poter, pouter, powter, powther, putar, puter, puther, puttar, putter, pwaiter, pewter, pwetr**
peytear pewter 70
pezzle pestle 437
pibble pebble 177
pick pickaxe 79
pickle pot 446
pickter picture **pickture** 418, 430, **picter** 164, **pictor** 308
pickt wolle picked wool, which has been sorted and graded 51
pictor freame picture frame 308
picture *passim*
picture board painted tester 111
pidg pig 170, **pidge** 215
pier glass large mirror, often set between two windows 453
pig 172, 179, 191, 258, 285, 334, 409, 424, **pige** 6, 157, 193, **pigg** 82, 154, 155, 181, 182, 194, 197, 222, 323, 330, 335, 352, 353, 368, 379, 382, 386, 438, 449, **pigge** 15, 32, 72, 78, 83, 84, 100, 123, 144, 152, 153, 183, 250, 252, 287, 306
piggs buckett 452
piggs scoop scoop for pig feed 452
pigtrough 191 **pigtrow** 82
pike *not known*, but *possibly* a poker or stirrer 11
pike hay fork 28
pikestaff shaft of a pike, *see also* **pekestafe**
pill pile or measurement of wood [pilling = wood shavings] 160
pillabeare pillow case 173, **pillaber** 58, **pill case** 267
pille pile *or* pill 215
pilleon pillion 428
piller pillow 332, 396
pilliber pillow case 83
pillin pillion 232, **pilling** 200
pillion light saddle used mainly by women riding sidesaddle, or a pad attached to a saddle to enable a second person to ride 226, 237, 421, 430, *see also* **male pillion, male pyllyon, mayle pillion, pilleon, pyllyon,**
pillo pillow 290, 297, 341, 342, 361, 411
pillobeare pillow case 62, 129, 176, 169
pillo case pillow case 120, 198, 239, 241
pilloe pillow 97, 129, 160, 164, 165, 230, 359
pilloe bear pillow case 160, **pilloe case** 359, 421, **pillopere** 6, **pillou bere** 56
pillow transverse timber positioned between

the bolster and body of a cart to provide clearance for the wheels 154, **pilo** 294
pillow head cushion on a bed *passim*, *see also* **peello, pelew, pella, pello, pelloa, pellow, pellowe, pelo, pelose, pelow, perlowe, piller, pillo, pilloe, pillowe, pilo, pillow, pilowe, pyllo, pillow, pyllowe**
pillow kind of plain fustian 425
pillow bar pillow case 137,
pillowbear pillowcase 2, 398, 427, 448, **pillowbeare** 31, 127, 129, 140, 159, 171, 176, 204, 269, 289, 304, 350, **pillowbee** 11, 18, 111, 185, 194, **pillowbeer** 17, 40, 159A, 249, 316, 320, 321, 339, 367, 375, 401, **pillowbeere** 24, 39, 92, 122, 248,
pillowber 13, 16, 45, 61, 68, 97, 100, 121, 123, 321, **pillowbere** 179, **pillowberr** 8
pillowcase *passim* **pillow cass** 294, **pillow casse** 130, 205, 245, **pillow cease** 347, 417A, *see also* **bellowcase, peilobear, pellacase, pelobear, pelobere, pelocase, pill case, pillabeare, pillaber, pilliber, pillo case, pillobeare, pilloe bear, pilloe case, pillopere, pillou bere, pillow bar, pillow cloth, pillow tie, pillow tiese, pillow tye, pillow tye, pilow cloth, pyllowbeere pyllowe beare, pyllowebe**
pillowe pillow *passim*
pillowe case 98, 153, 158
pillowe tye pillow case 46, **pillow tie** 394, **pillow tiese** 71, **pillow tye** 87, 119, 147
pilo pillow 341
pilow pillow 253, 396
pilow cloth pillow case 202
pilowe pillow 308
pin liquid measure of 4½ gallons, usually of beer 352; pointed wire fastener 232, 317, 344, 430, 450
pincers 8, 17, 146, *see also* **pynsers, spincer**
pinion refuse wool from the fleece *see also* **pinyon**
pin mettle pin metal: tinned or plated brass for pinmaking 232
pinne pin: fastener 61
pinner narrow piece of cloth round the neck of a woman's gown, *see also* **pynner**
pinninge timber pine 227
pint container holding one pint 42, 140, 154, 202, 241, 256, 260, 369, 373, 386, 417, 421, 428, 437, 444, 445, 448, 449, **pinte** 27, 47, 125, 200, 363
pinyon pinion 320
pip tobacco pipe 393
pipe tube for conveying liquid 449
pipe liquid measure of 2 hogsheads 1, 265, 352, 452
pipe metal or wooden fitment on a horse collar through which the reins pass 186, 413
pipe tobacco pipe 328, *see also* **pip**
pipe metallic trimming for garments 317
pistale pistol 40
pistol 294, 446, **pistole pistoll** 100, **pistoule** 45
pitch black, resinous substance obtained from tar 317
pitchforke long-handled, two-pronged fork for lifting hay etc. 39
plack black 454
plaine wood smoothing plane 180, **plainer** *possibly* a plane 52
plaink plank 125, **plainke** 235, **planck** 45, **plancke** 105, 180
plank 28, 61, 82, 111, 373, 383, 437, 444, **planke** 1, 4, 11, 17, 40, 72, 82, 146, 168, 206, 233, *see also* **table planckt**
plat plate: backplate 174, 211, 229
plat backplate 253, 294
plat plate: food dish 233, 300, 355, 361, 411, 423, 427, 433, precious metal 359
plate food dish 126, 186, 194, 200, 248, 250, 256, 261, 263, 269, 314, 318, 320, 325, 329, 332, 334
plate backplate *passim*
plate goods made of precious metal 125, 175, 192, 194, 236, 289, 301, 321, 361, 366, 372, 391, 397, 398
plate tinplate *passim*
plate brass *possibly* platter metal 428
plate for a chimmney back 159A, 111, **plate ... to sett behind the fire** 29
plate for east hair oast hair plate **plate on the kiln** 425
plater platter 38, 168, 218, 283, 285, 300, 311, 341, 342, 361, 379, 396, 402, 406, 411
plate rack wooden rack for drying or storing plates 449
platt plate: food 253, 292, 344, 438
plattar platter 126
platter large flat dish *passim* **plattere** 39
platter metal pot metal: an alloy of copper with 10% tin 428
platter to stand before the fyre large dish for warming food in front of an open fire 42
playeinge table marked out for backgammon

and other games 59
playne covering unadorned bed cover 111
pleat back plate 95A
pleat plate (food) 294, 370, 396, 402, 407, **pleate** 95A, 235, 285, **pleatte** 235
pliers 146
plocke block of sawn wood 42
plough 273, 323
plow plough 259, 386
plow horse one trained for ploughing 32
plyers, pair of pliers 445
po *possibly* powder 317
poaker poker 426
pocke hooke pot hook 241
pocket pouch attached to a garment, but hanging loose 232, 284, 335, 369, 407, 419, 444, 446, 447, **pockett** 232, 407, 409, 444, 447, 454
pocket book small notebook 446
point lace or tie for closing a garment or shoe 317
poker 372, 430, 445, 446, 452, *see also* **poaker, pooker**
pole *possibly* measure or weight of pewter 9
pole *possibly* curtain rail 114
pole long slender lengths of wood 179, 437
pole advertising sign outside a barber's shop 430
pompe pump 194
pooch pouch hanging from a girdle 96
pooker poker 445
poole pole 125, 368
pooll pole (of pewter) 47
poot pot 10, 47, 127, 159, 290, 408, **poote** 37, **poott** 95A
poote hock pot hook **poothock** 229, **poothoocke** 37, **pootwhocke** 47
poothangell pot hanger 47, **poothanger** 37
porcenett posnet 17
porcion portion 184
poredgdishe porringer 71
porengar porringer 202, **porenge** 267, **porenger** 173, 233, 241, 248, 294, 318, 343, 369, **poringar** 407
poringer porringer *passim* **porrenger** 140, 198, 245, 261, 268, 269
porridg dish 17, 45, porringer **porridge dish** 29, 34, 125
porringer small metal or pottery bowl for soft foods such as soups, stews, and puddings *passim* **porringger** 146, *see also* **potanger, potenger, potinger, pottenger, pottinge, pottinger, pottynger, purridge dyshe, borrenger, breakfast basin, poredgdishe, porengar**
pors purse 312
porsenett posnet 16
porshon portion 149
porsnett posnet 15, 26, 127, 222, **porsnette** 100
portall portal: wooden-framed screen attached to the inside of a door to keep out the cold 105, 150, **porthall** 41, **port holl** 104
portmantle case or trunk for carrying clothes when travelling 237
port wine 445
posenett posnet, **posnat** 10, 50, 130
posnet small cooking vessel with a handle and three feet 1, 4, 27, 28, 145, 174, 265, 291, **posnete** 47, **posnett** 22, 43, 68, 83, 87, 108, 119, 125, 164, 168, 170, 180, 221, 269, 343, 398, **posnette** 11, 18, 31, 34, 35, **posnitt** 261, **posset** 3, **possnet** 71, 129, 141, 200, 201, **possnett** 187, *see also* **porcenett, porsenett, porsnett, porsnette, posenett, posnat, postnett, postnette**
post wooden upright 121, 159A, 169, 444, **poste** 18, 40
post *see* rack and post
post the draught post, or centre pole, which joined the two axles of a wagon 154
post post to which wool was attached for wool combing 320
postnett posnet 103, **postnette** 13, 98, 121
pot cooking pot *passim, see also* **poot, poote, poott, pote, pott, potte**
potanger porringer 338
pote pot 55, 56, 70, 111, 157, 174, 188, 235, 283, 309, 341
pote hangil pot hanger 202
poteinge stick pot stick: one for stirring broth, porridge etc. 45
potenger porringer 168
poter pewter 284
pothange pot hanger 58, **pothangeinge** 46, **pothangel** 6, 24, 88, 253, **pothangelle** 38
pot hanger piece of chain or ironwork, attached to the chimney breast, on which pothooks were hung 2, 8, 11, 17, 18, 19, 27, 369, **pot hangill** 176, 179, **pot hanging** 159A, **pot hanginge** 73, **pot hangins** 55, **pothangle** 3, 52, 120, 158, **pothangelle**, *see also* **hander, hangeil, hangel, hangele, hangell, hangelle, hanger, hanggel, hangil, hangill, hangille, hanging, hanginge (pot), hangin, hangl,**

hangle, hangler, haninge, hingell, hingl, poothangell, poothanger, pote hangil, pothange, pott hanginge
pothock pothook 63, 67, 88, 126, 211, **pothocke** 38, 112A, **pothok** 10, **pothoke** 2, 6, 174, 180, **pothoock** 248, **pothoocke** 58
pot hook implement to hang pots over the fire, attached to the pothanger at the back of the chimney 147, 155, 159A, 169, 185, 247, 286, **pot hooke** *passim, see also* **potthocke, pott hook, pott hooke, chimney hook, crook, hook, hooke, pocke hooke, poote hook, poothock, poothoocke, pootwhocke**
potick pot hook 202
potinger porringer 10, 67, 273, 334
potkittle kettlepot 158, **pott kettle** 217
potled pot lid **potlid** 373, 452, **pottlead** 428
pott pot *passim*
pottage porridge or broth
pottage dish dish for holding pottage 102
pott bras pot brass: metal alloy from which cooking pots were made 58, **pott brasse** 45
potte pot *passim*
pottenger porringer 6, 7, 19, 22, 28, 29, 31, 39, 54, 56, 78, 83, 85, 98, 116, 127, 176, 292
potthange pothanger **pott hangel** 32, **pott hangell** 61, 68, 78, 216, 221, **potthangelle** 15, 123, **pott hanger** 16, 22, 26, 31, 34, 35, 39, 40, 42, 84, 92, 113, 332, **potthangere pott hanging** 127, **pott hanginge** 72, 106, **pott hangle** 4, 5, 7, 9, 14, 21, 100, 121, **potthanngell** 13
pott hanginge pot hanger 106
potthocke pot hook 13, 38, 45, 146, **pott hook** 33, 221, **pott hooke** *passim*
pottinge porringer 340, **pottinger** *passim*
pottled pot lid 38, **pottledd** 177, 448
pottynger porringer 2
poudering powdering 171, 290, 318, 361, 368, **pouderinge** 92, 198, **poudringe** 6, 38, 40, **pouldring** 174, **pouldringe**
poultry 127, 137
pouncing jerone pouncing iron: implement for smoothing the nap of a cloth 36
pounde pound weight 199, *see also* **pownd**
pounde pound sterling 188, *see also* **pownde**
poustar bolster 10
pouter pewter 38
powder hair powder 430
powder powdering 288
powder 3d paper powder paper: paper impregnated with salts, used as a substitute for gunpowder 317
powder blew washing blue 317
powdered salted 96
powder horn flask of horn for gunpowder 317
powderin powdering 379
powdering salting meat for preservation 102, 168, 260, 310, 314, 317, 324, 343, 351, 353, 355, 356, 363, 369, 394, 398, 421, 430, 452, **powderinge** 7, 154, 155, 194, 241, 332, *see also* **powder, powderin, powdring, powdringe, puddringe, puldrynge, bowderinge**
powder lyquorish powdered liquorice root 317
powder trow container for hair powder 430
powder tuff *possibly* powder puff: ball made of small tufts of wool 430
powdring powdering *passim* **powdringe** 21, 26, 29, 103, 125, 164, 357
powlster bolster 140
pownd pound weight 308
pownde pound sterling 200
powter pewter 66, **powther** 193
pres press 305, 334, 396, 423, **prese** 235
press cupboard with shelves *passim*, **presse** *passim, see also* **prest**
press device to consolidate malt 265, 369
press bed press bedstead 398, 431
press bedstead one which folds into a cupboard when not in use 365, 368, 386, 425, 445, 446, 453, **prest** 287
press cupboard shelved cupboard, often used for storing clothes 368, 375
presse bedd press bedstead 321
presse cloth cloth to cover a press 27
press for clothes tall cupboard with shelves 398
pressing ire smoothing iron 19, **pressing iron** 17, **pressinge iron** 89
prest press: cupboard 233
pricher prichel: instrument for punching nails in horseshoes 382
pricher pricker: large fork 145
prickett candlestick with a spike on which to impale the candle 445
principall money capital at interest 383
print framed printed illustration 372, 445, 449, 452
prong hay fork 18, 19, 61, 323, 368, 373, 424, 430, 431, 452, **pronge** 38, 45, 72, 127, 203, 283

pronge *not known* but some sort of weaver's tool on a chain 33
prongstafe prong stave 220
prong stale *possibly* prong stave 397
prong stave handle of a hay fork
provision perishable food 204
prox *not known* 373
pruning knives 448
psalter book of psalms 317
pudding pan 369, 421, 428, 430
pudding pott 428
puddringe powdering 6, **puldrynge** 14
pump for drawing up water 144, 147, 232, 351, *see also* **pompe**
punch metal tool for making holes or impressions 448
punch a drink of wine or spirits, mixed with fruit juices and spices
punch boile punchbowl 445, **punch bole** 368
punch bowl large bowl for holding punch 444, 452
punch laddle punch ladle 445
punch ladle deep, long-handled spoon for ladling out punch 452
punch strainer small sieve for straining punch 428
purle tape garment trim with a looped stitch at the edge 317
purridge dyshe porringer 7
purs purse 360, 363, 370, 371, 380, 411
purse *passim* **purss** 205, 259, 346
putar pewter 126, 137, **puter** 138, 157, 160, 218, 313, 327, 330, 342, 354, 355, 377, 379, 393, 404, 406, 411, **puther** 380, **puttar** 126, **putter** 261, 277, 361
puttine *not known* 220
pwaiter pewter 309, **pweter** 95A, 356, 449, **pwetr** 130
pye board one on which pies were made or baked 448
pyge pig 63, **pygg**
pyke pike: long-handled infantry weapon 40, **pyk** 301; pickaxe 11, 28, 45, 80
pyle pile 39
pyllo pillow 10, **pyllow** 50, 63, 67
pyllowbe pillowcase 67, **pyllowe beare** 4, **pyllowbeere** 7
pyllowe pillow 4, 6, 7, 14, 177
pyllyon pillion 9
pynner pinner 96
pynsers pincers: pliers 10
pynt pint 40, **pynte** 5, 6, 11
py plate pie plate 398, **pye plate** 427

qarter quarter 294
quadrant instrument for taking angular measurements 445
quaer *possibly* pocket-book; the word is derived from quire 315A
quare *recte* square 27
quare table bourd square table board 27
quart liquid measure of two pints *passim*
quart bottle bottle containing two pints 448
quarte 125, 363
quarte quarter: weight 45
quarter weight of 28lb. *passim*
quarter of a pint 369, 421, of a yard 96
quarter tree trunk cut into quarters 159A, 206, 437
quarter board piece of timber cut radially from the heart to the bark of a tree 373
quartere weight of 28lb.
quartered tree trunk cut into quarters 444
quartern quarter of a pint 449, 452
quartern vessel holding a quart 261, 269
quarterne quarter of an ounce 45
quartern pin one of the smallest sizes, *possibly* a size 4 232
quartter weight of 28lb. 191, **quatter** 130, **queartеare** 70
quelt quilt 6
queren quern: hand mill 13, **querne** 11, 15, 16, 18, 31, 108
quilt *passim* **quilte** 15, 27, 57, lightly padded covering for a bed, *see also* **bed quilt, quelt, quitt, quylte**
quisshion cushion 17
quitt quilt 439, **quylte** 4

rack openwork shelf *passim, see also* **rak, rake, recke**
rack andiron adjustable andiron 398
rack and posts tucker's rack and post to which wool is attached for combing 351
racke rack 29, 32, 85, 119, 123, 125, 147, 153, 154, 177, 188, 213, 222, 248, 321, 373
racke with cordes rack suspended from the ceiling 6
raftering timber for rafters 396, 437
ragg rag 177, 232
ragged stuff made of rag 421, **raggid** 297
raiing seve raying sieve 127
rail 428, **raile** 8, *see also* **rayle**
rak rack 111, 290, **rake** 422

rake husbandry tool, 45, 203, 323, 345, 382, 397, 417, 452, *see also* **rike**
rame ream: 20 quires of paper 317
rand *possibly* skein 317, 413
ranger chimney rack 373
raper rapier 151
rapier light, narrow sword 24, **rapyer** 40
rasbury brandy raspberry brandy 445
rasor razor 445, **rasour** 430
rasor strapp *possibly* razor strop 445
rasour case one for razors 430
rath frame fixed to the side of a cart to increase its capacity 294
rath stane rave stave: longitudinal side boards on a cart, giving additional support for the wheels 294
ratt cage rat trap 445
ratt trapp 448
raw hide undressed animal skin 293
raying seave raying sieve 28, **raying seif, raying seve** 37, 95A, **rayinge seve** 45
raying sieve fine-meshed sieve for riddling and cleansing corn, *see also*, **clanser, clanseve, clensieve, clenseave, clenseeve, clenseve, clensyve, clensingsive, klenser, raiing seve, raynsyve, renseve, renseeve**
ray kettle *possibly* made of copper, which heated more quickly than iron 428
rayle rail 40, 114
rayne rein: hand-strap of a horse's bridle 9
raynsyve raying sieve 16
razor 261, 367, 446, 448, *see also* **rasor, rasour**
razor sceals scales, (protectors) with no blades; the cutler would assemble his own razors 448
readie ready (money) 61
reading glass large magnifying glass 445
readle riddle 82
ready (money) *passim*, *see also* **reddey, reddie, redie, redy**
real *possibly* a reel of tape or thread 430
realing barr *not known* 428
ream 20 quires of paper 232
recke in the chimney chimney rack: metal framework from which pots were suspended over the fire 27
recke rack for animal feed 27
reddey ready (money) 280, **reddie** 121, **redie** 13, **redy** 87, 347
red lead oxide of lead, used as a pigment 317
reek hay rick 202
reele reel 8, 11, 16, 18, 22, 33, 40, 85, 108, **reell** 65, *see also* **real, rell**
reephooke riphook 8
rell reel 278
rells may mean reels, or it may be a fabric 425
rell woll *possibly* reeled wool, i.e. wound on a reel or spool 315A
remlet remnant 315A
remnant 35, 61, 317, **remnante** 119
renseve raying sieve 7, **renseeve** 11, 18
repp hoock riphook 297
resh made of woven rushes 229, 254
rick haystack 323, 369, *see also* **reek**
ridder coarse oblong sieve for winnowing corn 368
rider piece of wood with which a pair of field harrows are connected 386
riding coate long coat, usually deeply divided in the tail 151
rike rake 259
rine hoop *possibly* riven lengths, or wood with the rind or bark still on 373
ring for drawing and straightening wire in pinmaking 232; finger ornament *passim*, *see also* **rynge**; to hang a curtain 428; used by a woolcomber to draw wool through into a reasonably sized sliver for spinning 320
ringe *not known* 220, 293
ringe finger ornament 29, 45, 122, 208, 229
riphook reap hook: small scythe with a serrated edged blade **ripe hook** 203, **ripping hook** 448, *see also* **reephooke, repp hoock**
roalingpin rolling pin 38
roaster iron implement for roasting apples or small pieces of food over an open fire, *see also* **roster**
roat *not known* 347
rod for bed curtain 95A, 111, 150, 153, 194, 222, 369, 394, 416, 427, 445, 446, 452, for window curtain 111, 123, 153, 250, 317, 351, 355, 398, 436, 445, 449, for unspecified curtain 421, 424
rodd rod: bed curtain 318, 421; window curtain 31, 287, 372, 398; unspecified curtain 365, **rodde** 31, 111, window curtain 226, 318, **rode** bed curtain 111, window curtain 363
rodd rod: stick cut from a living tree 78
rode sadle riding saddle 61, 200
rog rug 342, **roge** 235
roghel *possibly* a woodworking tool 297
role roll 310
roller implement to smooth the ground after ploughing, *see also* **rowler, voler**

ronnd stand round stand for a barrel 33
roog rug 235
roope rope 33
roots *possibly* cheroots, small cigars 446
rope *passim*, *see also* **roope**
rosemary the fragrant shrubby herb *Rosemarinus officinalis* 328
rosewater water perfumed with roses 328
roster roaster 154, 339
rosting roasting 194
rotten stone powdered stone used for polishing metal 428
roug rug 300, 311, **rouge** 47, 54, 147, **rougge** 174
round tabel bord
round table 11, 102, 120, 154, 186, 194, 200, 272, 317, 352, 369, 377, 444, **round table board** 108, 334, **round table borde** 10, **rounde table bord** 108
rousett russet coloured 21
rove sliver of wool or cotton, drawn out and slightly twisted 315A
rowle roll of parchment 404
rowler roller 323
rowll roll 277
rownd table 7, **rownd table boord** 331
rubber coarse file or whetstone 373
ruch rush 334
rudder instrument for stirring malt in the mash tub323, 430
rudg rug 170, **rudge** 137, 170, 335, 356
rudle *possibly* reddle: red ochre used for marking sheep 317
ruffe outstanding frill on neck or sleeve of garment 96
ruffles gathered frills at cuffs 454
rug covering for a bed or table *passim* **ruge** 69, 71, 104, 127, 138, 146, 153, 157, 160, 168, 229, 277, 290, 308, 335, 361, **rugg** *passim* **rugge** *passim*, *see also* **rog, roge, roog, roug, rouge, rudg, rudge**
rule ruler, straight edge 445
rum 445, 449, 452
rundel runlet: cask or barrel of varying capacity 369, **rundlet** 182, **rundlett** 265, **runlett** 368
rush made of woven rushes, often used in chairmaking 249, 273, 274, 294, 317, 338, 368, 376, 381, 396, 398, 426, 445, 452, **rushen** 153, 174, 177, 212, 355, **rushin** 329, **rush bottomd** 452, *see also* **resh**
rusia coarse linen fabric 425, **russia** 445
russia a very durable type of leather, originally from Russia, used for upholstering chairs 332
russet reddish-brown colour 35, **russett** 119, *see also* **rousett**
rynge finger ring 46

sacepan saucepan 261, 269
sacer saucer 28, 38, 173, 198, 211, 248
sack container made of coarse fabric 28, 31, 40, 83, 84, 108, 265, 323, 361, 417, 421, 430, 431, 441, 444, **sacke** 2, 8, 129, 146, 155, 220, 259, 369, *see also* **sax**
sacken bottom bedstead one where the bed (mattress) is supported on sack-cloth 444
sacking sack-cloth: a coarse hempen fabric 425, 437
saddel saddle 315A, **saddell** 15, 54, 193
saddle 31, 45, 82, 176, 186, 369, 398, 417, 421, 430, 445, 446, *see also* **side, saddle, sid sadle, side sadle, side sadle, pack sadle, pannell, pillion** (and variants), **male pillion** (and variants), **rode sadle**
saddletree wooden framework of a saddle 413, *see also* **dennis tree, parte tree, tree**
saddil saddle 9, **sadel** 283, **sadell** 253, **sadle** 232, 237, 265, 321, 339
sad irne sad iron: smoothing iron 220
sadlery ware 416
sadware heavy metalware used for firebacks, large pots and chargers 428
safe ventilated cupboard for meat 29, 32, 111, 159A, 171, 241, 398, 425, 428, 445, 453, *see also* **save**
safe container for the safe-keeping of valuables 44
safgard safeguard: outer skirt worn by women to protect their clothes while riding 54
saich search 196
sale goods made to sell, not to order 61
sale salt cellar 243, **sallt** 127
salt condiment 78, 317, 450, *see also* **sealt**
salt box wooden box for storing cooking salt 61, 106, 248, 421, 445, 448, 449, **salt boxxe** 111, *see also* **salte box, salte boxe**
saltcellar vessel holding salt for table use 78, **saltceller** 1, 2, 8, 11, 18, 19, 29, 345, *see also* **sale, salt, salte, salte sellr, salte siller, salt seler, salt sellar, salt seller, satsellere, selt, sout, solt, soltsellar, soult, soulte**
salt dish salt cellar 421
salte salt cellar 3, 5, 26, 27, 31, 34, 37, 39, 111, 125
salte box salt box 38, **salte boxe** 40

salte sellr salt cellar 253, **salte siller** 79
salt gardener salt garner 317
saltinge preserving meat in salt 259
salting tub vessel in which meat is salted down, *see also* **selt, selt trow**
salt seler salt cellar 196, 343, **salt sellar** 421, 424, **salt seller** 13, 16, 17, 21, 22, 28, 40, 42, 56, 61, 85, 200, 256, 267, 292, 398
salt tubb *possibly* **salting tub** 368
salver tray of gold, silver or brass, for presenting letters or drinks 428
samestery ware haberdashery 165, **sempstry** 176
sand ingredient for glass 249, grocer's stock 317
sand dish *possibly* a spittoon 445
sarch search 52, 111, **sarche** 160
sarge serge 194, 223, 243, 347, 369, 425
sasar saucer 290, **saser** 10, 85, 107, 146, 196, 253, 267, 285, 343, 363, **saserdish** 54, **sasere** 157
sash lock lock for securing sash windows 446
sasore saucer 235
saspan saucepan 343, 363, 449, **saspane** 235, **saspun** 439, **sasspan** 308
satel settle 312
satsellere salt cellar
sauce dishe saucer 29
saucepan small pan in which sauces were prepared 369, 372, 398, 406, 413, 417, 430, 431, 445, 448, 452, 453, **saucepann** 217, *see also* **sacepan, saspan, saspane, saspun, sasspan, sawcepan, sawce pann, sawspan**
saucer shallow dish in which sauces were served 7, 22, 56, 127, 158, 176, 186, 401, 445, 446, 452, *see also* **sacer, sasar, saser, saserdish, sasere, sasore, sausar, sauser, sawcer, sawessere, sawser, tea dish and saucer**
sault saltcellar 46, 146, 223, **saulte** 7, 47, **sault seller** 6
sausar saucer 202, **sauser** 46, 71
savall saveall 428
save safe 18, 83
saveall device set into a candlestick to allow the candle to burn to the end 428
savttine seventeen 253
saw 257, 444, 446, 448, **sawe** 5, 10, 24, 297, *see also* **curveing sawe, drug, frame saw, hand saw, hand sawe, tenant sawe, tenon saw, whip saw, za**
sawcepan saucepan 414, 428, **sawce pann** 368, 428
sawcer saucer *passim* **sawessere** 39, **sawser** 4, 5, 26, 34, 35, 45, 55, 67, 8, 95A, 98, 102, 103, 106, 112A, 190, 205, 294
sawspan saucepan 438
sax sacks 70
scaberde scabbard: the sheath of a sword 40
scaffold wooden platform for a rick, raised on staddle stones 352
scales *passim, see also* **sceals, sceles, skales, skeales, skelles,** *see also* variants of **beam and scales**
scarme batton for consolidating the weft in weaving 33
sceals scales 168, 392, **sceles** 301
scellat skillet 126, **scellet** 157, **scellit** 313
scemler skimmer 68, **scemmer** 126
scilleate skillet 70, **scillet** 95A, 211, 407, 433, 438, **scillot** 363
scimer skimmer 146, 211, 260, 387, 407, **scimmer** 373, 95A
scissors 445, *see also* **common sisars, sisars, sissars, sissers, sizers**
scive sieve 323
sckreene screen 317
scllott skillet 406
sconce bracket candlestick 123, 352, 386, 426, 428, 448, *see also* **skunc**
scoope scoop 33, 35
score debt due 83, twenty 2, 31, 102, 111, 294, 359
score board board on which debts are written up 140
scottis tree a type of saddle tree, but *not known* exactly what type 9
scowrer scourer: implement to clean out the barrel of a gun 222
scrach brush one made of fine wire, used for cleaning metal articles 146
screen (large sieve) 143, 265, 368, 425, [with room furniture] 305, (unspecified) 430, **screene** 269, **screne** 168, 174, **malt screen** 412, *see also* **sckreene, skren, skreen, skreene, skrine, skryne, skyrne**
screen to hang closae on airer 445
screw fixing screw 445, 448
screwe screw: for attaching skins to a frame in parchment making 118
screwplate steel plate with screw holes of different sizes 362A
screw tapp for making threads on a screw 428
scroll finished length of parchment
scrow scroll or screw, both used by parchment

makers 310, 375, *see also* **skrowe**
scrubber *possibly* long-handled coarse brush 428
scrutore escritoire: writing desk 425
scull armoured headpiece 6
scure skewer 398, 421
scutchion shield with a coat of arms; may also be ornamented brass plate round a keyhole 72
scutle scuttle 71
scuttle large open basket for carrying corn, vegetables etc., *see also* **skuttle**
scythe implement with long, curved blade with a long handle, used for mowing/reaping, *see also* **riphook, sithe, sythe**
seacole coal brought by sea, usually from north-east England 40, *see also* **coal**
seal piece of embossed metal for pressing into hot wax 448
sealing wax 317
seall ring signet ring 151
sealt salt 229
seamstry haberdashery, *see also* **sempstry ware, simestrie ware, simstry ware**
search type of sieve 28, 35, 144, 155, 177, 248, 318, 398, 430, **searchier** 353, **searsh** 45, *see also* **saich, sarch, sarche, serch, serche**
searg serge 315A
seate of curtains set of curtains 344
seave sieve 38
seave seven 140, **seaven** *passim*
seaventeene seventeen 373, 382
securatie security 226
security written evidence of a debt 210, 412, **securitys** 374A, **securityes** 384
seedlep seedlip 373
seedlip box or basket in which a sower carries his seed
seeds 234
seeve sieve 18, 21, 31, 39, 68, 177, 444, **seive** 50
selfar silver 126
selt salting tub 233
selt saltcellar 174, 180
selt trow trough for salting meat 283
sempstry ware seamstry 176
sept set 297
serch search 24, 33, 38, 40, 102, 127, 310, **serche** 8, 18, 19
serge hard-wearing woollen fabric 398, *see also* **searg, sarge**
server salver 352, 414
servise boke book containing the Book of Common Prayer, with proper lessons and psalms etc. 50
set *see also* **sept, sett, sute**
setall settle: bench 202, 245, **setell** for barrels 290, bench 188, 285, 327, **setle** bench 147, 171, 230, 270, 272, 303, 334, unspecified 140, 180, **setll** unspecified 196
setle chayre one with a storage compartment under the seat 147
set of boxes nest of boxes 425, **sett of boxes** 159, 317
setoren cittern 308
sett set 153, 217, 222, 247, 253, 305, 352, 363
settel settle: for barrels 361, bench 449, unspecified 229, **settele** for barrels 52, **settell** bench 225, 253, 307, 343, 355, unspecified 143, **settil** for barrels 297
settl set of shelves on a cupboard 64
settle high-backed wooden bench *passim* stand: for barrels and vats 11, 18, 111, for table 11, unspecified 398, *see also* **satel, setall, setell, setle, setll**
sett of drawers chest of drawers 226, 273, 317
sett rug *not known* 125, 192
seve sieve 33, 40
seventeene seventeen 111
severall several 214, 227, 229
shaire ploughshare 386
shambles small building where animals were slaughtered 30
shamy soft supple leather, originally that made from the skin of a chamois 151, 243
shareboard shearboard 351
shares shears for cloth 351
shave *possibly* a draw knife 34
shearboard board on which cloth was laid for the nap to be sheared, **shearebord** 85, *see also* **shareboard, sherbord**
sheares shears: tailor's large scissors 4
sheares shears: tucker's implement for shearing the nap of cloth 26, 85, 119,
sheare waights weights used to increase the pressure of tuckers' shears 85
shears unspecified 257, 448 leather dresser's 31, tailor's 448, shearman's 263, *see also* **fordeinge shears, shares, sheares, sheeres, sheers, taylors' shears**
sheat sheet 10, 57, 88, 131, **sheate** 38, 118
sheathes for knyves 40, **sheaths of all sorts** 448
sheaves sheaths: razor protectors 430
sheep 30, 172, 192, **sheepe** 2, 3, 127, 204, 263

sheep skin 383, **sheepe skyn**
sheeres shears 11, 17, 248, **sheers**, 318
sheet *passim* **sheete** *passim, see also* **cheet, sheat, sheate, sheet, sheette, shet, shete, shett, shette**
sheeting an Irish fabric for sheets 425
sheett sheet 104, 146, 160, 168, 180, 191A, 198, 205, 304, 359, 448, **sheette** 33, 115
sheft shift 313
shelf 17, 111, 157, 365, 421, **shelfe** 4, 27, 40, 72, 102, 111, 187, 321, 352, 368, **shelfes** 22, 72, **shelue** 317, **shelve** 125, 453, **shelves** *passim* **shelvfes** 37, *see also* **chelfe, shilf, shilfe, shylfe, tack, tacke**
shelves shelves 95A
sheooes shoes 3
sheovill shovel 4
shepe sheep 6
sherbord shearboard 26
sheres large scissors 61, **shers** 65
sherte shirt 5, 21
sherth sheath for a knife 96
shet sheet 50, 67, 126, 154, 157, 196, 284, 291, 300, 355, 361, **shete** 5, 13, 47, 137, 174, 311, 335
shetlock crosspiece at the back of a wagon into which the tailboard is fixed 294
shett sheet 231, 261, 343, 411, **shette** 34, 95A, 277
shevel shovel 269, 337, **shevell** 191**shevill** 261; *it is possible that in some instances this means shelf*
shewes shoes 15, 21, **shews** 300
shift woman's undergarment 454, *see also* **chiste, sheft**
shilf shelf 377, **shilfe** 95A
shillinge shilling (twelve pennies) 55, 227
ship sheep 191A
shipp skine sheep skin 118
shirt 28, 120, 446, 448, **shirte** 20, 105, 119, **shirtt** 161
shivel shovel 449
shoe horne 28, **shohorne** 19, **shooing horne** 96
shoeing tooles farrier's tools 382
shoemakers' knives 448, **shoemakers' things** 448
shoes 20, 28, 96, 105, 201, 446, 448, 454, *see also* **sheooes, shewes, shews, shoos, shous, showes, shue,** *also* **women's shoes, children's shoes**
shooe leather 60
shooes 4, 151, 172
shoop belk *not known* 399
shoop tools shop tools 373, **shop tooles** 220
shoos shoes 243, 423
shoote *possibly* a tube or funnel for liquid 34, 35
shop board serving counter 158, **shopbord** 61, **shope bord** 4, **shoppboard** 249, **shoppe board** 89, **shoop board** 64
shop book tradesman's account book 169, 172, **shop booke** 138, 282, **shope boocke** 146, **shopp booke** 186, 187, 236, 365, **shoppe booke** 242
shopbrd shopboard 284
shop debt trading debt 450
shop goods 388, 394, 397, **shope goods** 343, **shopp goods** 186
shop linnen towels for shaving, etc. 80
shopp shop *passim*
shopp instruments barber's tools 113
shop toules shop tools 293
short white (pins) made of white metal as opposed to brass 317
short wool short staple, probably from Down sheep 398, **short wooll** 320
shott shot for firearms 317
shouffall boord shuffleboard 235
shoul malt shovel 361
shoultree shovel tree 220
shous shoes 51
shovel fire shovel 431, husbandry tool 182, 452, malt shovel 395, 407
shovel *see also* **shivel, shevel, shevell, shevill, shoul, shovle, showel, showle, shufell**
shovell fire shovel 305, 379, 428, husbandry tool 34, malt shovel 289, 397, unspecified 8, 445, stable 31
shovell tree handle of a shovel 373, *see also* **shoultree**
shovle shovel 38, malt shovel 174
showel shovel 283, **showle** 155
showes *possibly* horseshoes 38,
shrafe shruff 344
shreedes shreds: shredded fabric used as a stuffing for beds, pillows and bolsters 19
shruff metal waste 428
shue shoe 165
shufell shovel 174
shuffleboard table marked out for the game of shuffleboard 368
shurt shirt 243, **shurte** 151
shute suit of clothes 165, set of bed hangings

248
shutlock shetlock 154
shylfe shelf 18
sicer scissor 40
sidbord sideboard 100, 253, **sidborde** 188, **sid cobberd** 174, **sid cobord** 229, **sid cubberd** 141, **sid cubbered** 343, **sid cubbord** 173 **sid cubberd cloth** 173, **side cupbord cloth** 334
side bedstead one with two posts, one each at the head and foot, the side without posts being pushed against the wall 294
side bentch under the wyndow a bench kept along the wall beneath the window 37
sideboard dresser or serving table 41, 108, 145, 148, 192, 213, 244, 248, 332, 412, **side boarde** 111, **side boord** 128, 130, **sidebord** 106, 109, 126, 153, 160, 171, 273, 334, **sideborde** 123, **side cubbard** 100, 266, 303, 369, **side cubberd** 111, 164, 171, 180, 187, 201, **side cubbert** 153, 239, **side cubboard** 340, **side cubbord** 123, 248, 386, **side cupboard** 159A, 217, **side cupbord** 265, 334
side cupboard with a drawer 212
side of bacon 413, 450
sider cider 222
side saddle saddle for ladies to ride with both feet on the same side of the horse 428, 430, **sid sadle** 159, *see also* **syde sadle**
side tabell side table 334
side table 125, 127, 145, 248, 412, **sid table** 140
sieve 92, 418, 445, *see also* **scive, seave, seeve, sieve, seve, sive, syffe, syve**
sifter 146
sign shop sign 445
signe in the streete inn sign 111
silfur silver 427
silk made of silk 445, 446, 454, **silke** 97, 263
silke lase silk lace 61
sillver made of silver 71
silt trough for salting meat 155, 159A, 168, 204, 362A, 369, **silte** 206, *see also* **selt trow, zilt**
silver made of silver *passim, see also* **selfar, silfur, silver, sivelliur, sylver, white plate, white silver**
silver guilt silver gilt: silver covered with gold leaf 29, 31
silverware 164
simestrie ware seamstry: haberdashery 253, **simstry ware** 329
sinamon cinnamon 317
sinder shovell fire shovel 428
singel single 54, **singell** 51
sink 377
sisars scissors 448, **sissars** 454, **sissers** 80, 261
sithe scythe 22, 52
sive sieve 24, 61, 373, 445
sivelliur made of silver 235
sixe six 15, 29, 31, 32, 40, 59, 100, 108, 119, 123, 127, 167, 321
sixte six 130
sixteene sixteen 41, 71, 184, 245, 287
sizers scissors 446
skaffould scaffold 37
skain skein 317
skales scales 11, 15, 22, 144, 398
skarm scarme 351
skeales scales 170
skealles and beame beam and scales 38, **skealls and beem** 408
skeilet skillet 285, 300, **skelat** 196, 229, **skeimer** skimmer 300
skelet skillet 71, 101, 283, 291, 294, 309, 311, 370, **skelete** 188
skelles scales 277
skellet skillet 51, 127, 128, 129, 171, 202, 369, 394, **skellett** 159, 248, 250, 320, 343, 355, 359, **skellot** 264, **skellute** 66
skemer skimmer 47, 283, 402, **skemor** 196
skene skein 277
skilatt skillet 408, **skilet** 99, 170, 174, 325, 361, 411, **skilett** 97, 298, **skillat** 112A, 130, **skillate** 38, 69, **skillatt** 290, **skillatte** 125
skillet cooking utensil with three or four feet and a handle, used for boiling and stewing *passim* **skillete** 7, 55, 56, 123, **skillett** *passim* **skillette** 8, 31, 32, 40, 78, 83, 100, 113, 121, 344, *see also* **bell skillet, boileing skillet, scellat, scellet, scellit, scilleate, skillet, scillot, scllott, skeilet, skelat, skelet, skellet, skellett, skellot, skellute**
skillett frame *possibly* a frame from which to hang skillets 428
skilling *possibly* the ceiling 353
skillit skillet 168, 245, **skillitt** 261, 269, 335, **skillitte** 11, 145, **skilot** 308, **skilote** 235, **skillott** 341
skimar skimmer 202, **skimber** 33, **skimer** skimmer *passim*
skimer ladle skimmer 249
skimingdish skimmer 373, **skimming dish** 428
skimmer shallow cooking ladle for skimming the surface of liquids *passim* **skimor** skimmer 276, 308, *see also* **scemler, scemmer, scimer, scimmer, skeimer, skemer, skemor, skimar,**

skimber, skimmer, skmmer, skummer, skymer, skimmer, skymner
skin leather made from animal skin, lighter than hide 61, 398, **skine** 118, **skinn** 236
skitle skillet 201, **skittell** 346, **sklet** 218
skittle pin 452
skiver kive *or* kiver 444
skmmer skimmer 267
skoore score: twenty 41, **skore** 188
skren screen 355, 361, 450, **skreen** 395, 397, 398, 426, **skreene** 133, 164, 259, 289, 353, 365, **skrine** 27
skrowe *possibly* scroll; also screw, used by parchment makers 277
skrowl scroll of parchment 398
skryne screen 31
skummer skimmer 398
skunc sconce 339
skuttle scuttle 34
skylett skillet **skyllate** 67, **skyllet** 6, 9, 448, **skyllete** 4, 34, **skyllett** 5, 15, 16, 17, 21, 37, 39, 42, 234, **skyllette** 68
skymer skimmer 8, 10, 18, 31, 37, 177, 448, 449, **skymmer** 7, 11, 15, 19, 26, 34, 42, 78, 106, 108, 122, 362A, **skymner** 154
skyrne screen 5
slabbs large pieces of timber 444, **slab stuff** 437, **slab timber** 206
slates roof covering 123
sleave button sleeve button 448
sledg sledge 317
sledge large heavy hammer 38, 40, 182, 220, **sledgis** sledges 25
sleekstone smooth stone used for polishing
sleeve ironing board for sleeves
sleeve detachable part of the garment 19, 243
slekston sleekstone 51
slice spatula with a handle, for turning food in a frying pan 147, 159A, 368, 428, 445
slider bar over grate along which trivets & grillers could be slid 421
sliding candlestick one with a ratchet or screw mechanism to raise the candle as it burns down 421
slike sleekstone 308
slikstone sleekstone 85
slippers 446
slip-up candlestick sliding candlestick 398
slop basin utensil for tea leaves 452, **slopp bason** 445
slugg heavy piece of crude metal 382
slyce slice 10
small beer weak beer for everyday drinking 452
small leather probably cut hides 248
small ware small goods made for sale, not to order 45, 300
smart hogg in coopery, a hog is a machine for reducing wood to chips 373
smaule waires small ware 21
smelling bottle and case 445
smock man's loose shirt 62
smocke smock: loose chemise worn by women 16, 46, 96, 97, **smoke** 51, 54
smoothing iron device which is heated, with which to press clothes 318, 381, **smothing** 202, **smothings** 332, *see also* **box iron, flat iorn, geese, hot press, iron for clothes, pressing iron, sad irne, yron**
snafer snuffer 229
snead shaft of a scythe 52, 382 **sneath** 397
sneud *not known* 220
sneed *not known* 37
snoffers snuffers 95A
snuff box small, personal container for snuff 445, 448, 454
snuff canister *possibly* a larger storage tin for snuff 428
snuffer small hollow metal cone on a handle for extinguishing candle flames 398, 428, 445, 448
snuffle snaffle: simple bridle-bit without curb 9
snyppers snippers: clippers 6
soard sword 45
soder solder 211, 249
solder fusible alloy used to join less fusible metals, *see also* **boreax soder, souder**
sole base of a shoe
sollt salt cellar 423, **solt** 126, **soltsellar** 290
soonne spoon 157
sope soap 450
sord sword 294
sorrell bright chestnut colour, used of horses 76
souder solder 177
soudering iron soldering iron 177, **sowdring** 249
soue sow 70
soule sole: in this instance, *possibly* soles for shoes 293
soult salt cellar 10, 168, **soutte**
sow female pig 11, 222, **sowe** sow 6, 39, 127, 250

soword sword 6
spad spade 174
spade *passim*
Spanish *possibly* Spanish iron 317
Spanish oak timber from Spanish oak trees; it is not known if this was a specific species 437
sparrows in cages, or dead ones hung up in the yard 445
spead spade 203, 449
speal spill or splinter; a lath or little board of wood or stone 294
speciallty specialty 128, **specialtie** 87, 125
specialty sealed contract 189, 198, **specialtye** 96
spectacles 448, **pair of** 454
speed spade 355
speet spit 290, **speit** 300
spencer, pair dispensers: pair of decanters 61
spendell for a well spindle, or tumbril, (the turning drum) of a well 47
spet spit 137, 283, 343, 360, **spete** 309, **spett** 277, 406
spice morter spice mortar: vessel in which spices are groud 7, 13, 27, 29, 31, 56, 73, 78, 88, 98, 103, 108, 113, 131, 158, 362A, 364, 374A, **spise mortar** 126, *see also* **spycemorter**
spie glass spyglass 445
spincer pincers 24, 38
spindle 373
spininge whele spinning wheel
spinning torne spinning wheel 33, **spininge turne**
spirits of wine pure alcohol 445
spiritous liquor 450
spit *passim* **spite** 27, 157, 167, 174, 191A, 197, 335, 342, 363, **spitt** *passim* **spitte** 40, 123, 145, 146, 274
spitting pott spittoon 428
spittoon pot or dish filled with sand for spitting into, *see also* **sand dish**
spleeten woven from split twigs 31, 83, 159A, **splet spleten** 78, **splitten** 87, **split bottomd** 452
spoke rod radiating from the hub to the rim of a wheel 255, 294
spone spoon 2, 6, 8, 11, 13, 16, 18, 38, 45, 126, 205, 229, 239, **sponne** 7, 39, 42, 95A
spooke spoke 154
spoome spoon 111
spoon *passim* **spoone** *passim* **spoune** 47
spout 351, 368, 379, 395, 437, 444, 448
spring bell one on the end of a spring, activated by a string from the bell-pull 452
spring lock lock in which the bolt shoots automatically by means of a spring 453
spring tap *not known* 373
spring tinder box *possibly* a tinder box with a spring catch 445
spullingtorn a wheel for filling weavers' bobbins 33
spur rowell the spiked revolving disc at the end of a spur 448
spurs 237, 243, 448
spycemorter spice mortar 4
squab cushion 398, **squabb** 398
square bourd square table board 27
square tabelle square table 47
square table 29, 32, 421, 445, 446, **sqare table** 444
square table bord 31, **square table bourd** 27, **square table bowrde** 27
stable *passim*
stable plancke wood for building a stable 45
stack stake 396
stack hay stack 31
stack hay 386
staddle stone short, tapering stone with mushroom-shaped top, on top of a number of which storage buildings are stood to prevent rats from entering, *see also* **stavell**
staff stick or handle; may also be stave 47
stager set of openwork shelves 34, 35
stagghorn deer antler used for knife handles 448
staik stake 421
staine stand 125
stake small anvil146
stake wooden post, *see also* **stack, staik**
stake tongs *possibly* tongs for hot wood 445
stake to rub skins on glover's apparatus 383
stalle stall: beehive 108
stampt futter futter: a metal plate in ship or boat building, but here stamped with holes or pattern 382
stan stand 104, 265
stand support: for a barrel *passim* for a cupboard 173, for a table 194, 235, 445, for a smoothing iron 452, for a trunk 350, 432, for a wig block 430, unspecified223, 226, 241, 249, 386, 398, 428, 445, 448, 452, *see also* **stonde**
stand desk desk with writing surface at standing rather than sitting height 453

stande stand (barrel) 72
standerd frame to support a table board 31
standing barrel support 100, 176, 248, support for a hamper 383
standing[e] (bedstead) one with corner posts and a tester, standing out into the room *passim* 4, 16, 29, 31, 38, 103, 125, 129, 141, 143, 147, 164, 173, 187, 239, **staning** 157, **staninge** 125
standing cloth *possibly* storage or packaging for gloves 383
standing cupboard a freestanding cupboard, not one attached to a wall 142
standinge furnished *possibly* the tanning vats or pits 72
standinge stuff for the market *possibly* pieces of wood to make a market stall 84
standing high bedstead 147
standing stoole device to support a child learning to walk 120, 146
standing stuff *possibly* the crops in the fields 15
standing table solid table, not boards and trestles 200
standish stand containing an inkwell 428
stand to sett beere one support for a barrel 39
stanein stand (unspecified) 300
stanlle stand: barrel 7, **stann** 340
stanninge glass standing mirror 234
stannin stuf stand (barrel) 220
staple an iron loop, pointed at both ends, knocked into the wall to hold suspended things, cf. the modern staple 421
starch 394
state estate 1, 172
stave section of wood making up the sides of a barrel 373
stavell staddlestone 259
stayer stair 95A
stayned cloth stained (painted) cloth: bed 47, wall 42
stays, pair of corsets 454
steabell stable 47
steane earthenware vessel with two handles or ears, used for storing liquids or butter 212
steel made of steel *passim* **steele** 45, 120, 146, 150, 211, 245, 250, 274, 292, 301, 345, 350, 351, 363, **steell** 329, *see also* **stele, stell, still**
steel sharpener for knives and other blades 428
steele hemp similar to wire wool, for polishing or cleaning 317
steeling iron sharpening steel 216, 444
steeps stepladder 445
stekins stockings 21, **stockins**
stele made of steel 82, 85, 95A, 170, 225 **stell** 95A, 174
stem handle of a tool or implement 317
steps to drawers, pair of 428
stew pan 413, 417, 445, 446, **stew pann** 368, 428
stew cover lid for a stew pan 250
stick billiard cue 445
stick of timber *possibly* stack: 108 cubic feet 418
still distilling aparatus 31, 113, 159, 170, 200, 372, 396, 421, 428
still steel 144, 253
still bottom 421
stirrer long-handled stick for stirring, used in brewing; *possibly* the same as a paddle 448, 452
stirrupp leather strap attaching the stirrup to the saddle 237, *see also* **lethers, sturryp leyther**
stirrups shaped irons for the rider's feet 417, 446
stoal stool 118
stoare pige store pig 69
stoccards stockcards 85
stock beehive 71
stock block or table on which meat was cut up 45 **stocke** 153
stock neck cloth 446
stock trade goods 378
stock handle for a knife 310
stock piece of timber shaped to form the sides of a barrel or vat 282
stock hub of a wheel 255, **stockes for wheeles** 154, *see also* **wagon stocks**
stock buckell buckle for fastening the stock or neck-cloth 448
stockcards large cards fastened to a support 119
stockens stockings 243, **stockins** 446, **stockings** hose 448, **stockinges** 96, 105, **stokinges** 151, **stokings** 161, *see also* **stekins, stockins, stokins**
stock lock lock enclosed in a wooden casing, often fitted to an outside door 382
stocks cooper's tools; or stocks of wood 282
stokins stockings 20, 28, 61
stol stool 137, 196, 396, **stole** *passim*, **stoll** 50,

126, 174, 207, 290, 311, **stolle** 38, 39, 42, 104, 125, 138, 188, 267, 277
stomager stomacher: ornamental covering for the chest worn by women 96
ston stone trough 355, **ston trough** 368
stonde stand (barrel) 253
stone trough or other container cut from stone *passim, see also* **stoune stone** made of stoneware 18, 29, 52, 97, 368
stone precious stone for jewellery 45, 104,
stone ring one set with a precious stone 151
stoneware impermeable ceramic ware, partly vitrified
stoning stoneware 11
stool *passim* **stoole** *passim* **stooll** 160, 163, 279, 369, 324, 329, 374A, **stoolle** 104, 167, *see also* **stoal, stol, stole, stoll, stole, stooulle, stoul, stoule, stowells, stowle**
stool and pan commode 453, **stool box and pan** 369
stool pan one for a close stool 428
stooper wedge used for tilting a barrel 446
stooulle stool 47, **stoul** 168, 325, 335, 341, 342
stopping stick shoemaker's tool for filling crevices 115
store board dresser for, *possibly*, food 352
store pig animal acquired for fattening
store pigg 237, 269, 273, 274, 421, **store pigge** 73
stoule stool 146
stoune (trough) 70
stove closed device for burning fuel for cooking or heating 436
stove grate grate containing a stove, rather than an open hearth 445, 446
stow wooden windlass over a shaft 428; a stove 430
stowells stools 95A, **stowle** 37
strae straw (bed) 93
strainer 269, 345, 437, 445, *see also* **strayner**
strap part of horse tackle 9
straugh straw: bed filling 47
straw animal bedding or fodder 83, 323, 330, filling for a bed (mattress) 37, 40, 56, 71, 125, 229, **strawe** mattress 87, 102, 111
strayner strainer 254, 261
strech *possibly* a strike: a stick for levelling off the top of a measure 64, 95A
street dore street door 206
stringe of flaskes row of small containers for gunpowder 40
striped cloth woven in stripes 212
stue pan stewpan 428
stuf stuff: hay, straw, etc. stored in the tallet 334
stufe in the garden *possibly* goods or produce for sale 104
stuff goods in general 56, **stuffe** 32, 84
stuff any woven fabric, more specifically worsted 454 **stuffe** 151
stuffes bedclothing 41
stuffe to make turfes *see* turfes 72
sturryp stirrup 9
sturryp leyther stirrup leather 9
sucinge pygg sucking pig 50
suck bottle baby's feeding bottle 269, 428
sucking pig new-born or very young animal
sugar 450
sugar dish dish in which sugar is served 445, 451, **sugar dish and stand** 446
sugarplumb small round sweetmeat made from boiled sugar and flavourings 450
sulling plough tackle 283
sumer summer tree: the part of a wagon which supports the body 294
surgeon's instruments 446
surringe syringe 428
sussingle surcingle: girth for a horse, especially a large one to secure a pack 9, **sussingle strap** 9
sut suit of clothing 151
sute *possibly* set 29
swatchell a shred or patch 248
sweet oyle oil used in woolcombing 317
swepe sweepings of a goldsmith's floor, of value for recovering gold dust 45
swift *possibly* swist, a variation of kist or chest 80
swine pigs 137
swing glass pivoted mirror 445, 453
sword 15, 72, 113, 421, **sworde** 40, *see also* **soard, sord, soword**
sword hilte sword handle 40
syde cupboard 87
syde sadle side saddle 27, 200
syffe sieve 10
sylver silver 27, 46
syrup of red poppies extract from poppies used to colour medicines 445
sythe scythe 397
sythern cittern 50
syve sieve 37
syxe six 95A

tabbel bord tableboard 325

tabbel cloth table cloth 355, **tabelcloth** 283, 300, **tabelclothe** 202, 212, **tabell cloes tabell cloth** 308, 313, 343, **tabell clothe** 174, 285, **tabilcloothe tablcloth** 40, **table cloath** 24, 448, **table cloth** *passim* **table clothe** *passim* **tabele clothar** 126, **teabell cloth** 208
tabbell table 342
tabel table 284, 285, 327, 355, 396
tabelboard table board 427, 439, **tabel boord** 202, **tabelbord** 157, 191, 202, 278, 283, 297, 300, 360, 396, **tabelborde** 188, 411
tabel cloth tablecloth 427
tabell table 174, 285, 407
tabell boad 299, **tabell board** 167, 205, 242, 259, 406, **tabell boarde** 73, **tabell bord** 55, 157, 168, 174, 191A, 193, 253, 290, 292, 327, 335, 342, 343, 406, 411, 423, **tabell borde** 47, 157, 188, 311, **tabilborde**
tabell cloath table cloth 205, **tabell cloth** 47
tabell lenen 277, **tabell ling** table linen 433
tabellnacken table napkin 51
table *passim, see also* **tabbell, tabel, tabell, tabll, teabell, teobell, teobelle** and compounds beginning with these
table and other lynnen 345
table basket *possibly* a basket used to contain bread or other food on the table 446
tableboard flat board supported on trestles or a frame to form a table *passim* **table boarde** 14, 41, 54, 200, 258, 359, **table boord** 16, 22, 24, 105, 114, 128, 132, 145, 265, **table boorde** 24, 27, 111, **tablebord** *passim* **tableborde** 3, 4, 6, 10, 13, 29, 50, 67, 83, 125, 404, **table bourd** 27, **table bowrd** 27, **table bowrde** 27, **teabeall boearde** 70,
table board cloat tablecloth 339, **table board cloth** 192, **table borde clothe** 4
table board plank 158
[table] boorde *passim, see also* **tabll bord, teabeall boearde, teabel bord**
table borde with a cuberd in may be a table with a drawer underneath 6
table chair *possibly* the type with a back which hinges on the arms, to tip over to become a table top 373
table cloath 183, 185, 190, 211, 245, 263, 357, 263, 365, 372, 398, **table cloathe** *passim*
table linen 260, 368, 386, **table lining** 399, **table linnen** 344, 412, **table linning** 200
table napkin 11, 16, 24, 31, 45, 158, 159A, 339, **table naptking** 13, **table napkyn** 18
table planckt *possibly* a single board forming a table 102
table with drawers 226
tabll table 174
tabll bord table board 196, 229
tack shelf 31, 111, **tacke** 46, **take** 66
tack, tackle fittings for a horse *passim,* **tacklen**193, **tacking** 393
tacks knife blanks 448
tacks small nails 294, 428
taffety taffeta: silk fabric of various grades and finishes 61
taiper taper 196
talett tallet 334, **tallat** 206
tallet hay loft, often free-standing 45, 111, 147, 310, 430, **tallett** 68, 153, 352, 386, **tallette** 11, 125, **tallute** 66
tallow skillett pan used for melting animal fat for candle-making146
tamarind fruit of the Indian date tree 445
tan tree bark used for fuel 345
tanchard tankard 324, **tanckard** 186, 329, **tanckerd** 300, 332, 363, **tancord** 355
tange *possibly* a fork used in cheesemaking 6
tankard *passim* **tanke** 338, **tankerd** 185, 200, 219, 221, 223, 229, 241, 272, 277, 287, 294, 356, 369, 398, **tankerde** 33, **tankert** 334, **tanket** 342, 374A, 399, **tankett** 245, 343, **tankord** 261, 269, **tankott** 341
tanned hyde dressed animal skin 237
tanners toulls tanner's tools 44
tanvat large vessel in which hides are steeped during tanning 65
tape 317
taper wick coated with wax for conveying flame *see also* **taiper**
tapp tap 373
tapp wads *possibly* washers or wadding to make the bungs on barrels watertight 373
tapstry tapestry 40
taster shallow cup for tasting wines 334, 364, 428
tayle animal tail 359
taylers' sleeve board for pressing sleeves 19
taylors' shears cutting out scissors 448
teabeall boearde table board 70, **teabbel bord** 402
teabell table 308
tea board tea table 445, 446, 448
tea chest chest in which tea was transported or stored 445, 446
tea dish wide, shallow teacup 445, 452, **tea dish and saucer** 451

tea kettle vessel in which water was boiled for tea 398, 428, 445, 446, 448, 453, **tea kittel** 449, **tea kittle** 452
teapot 395, 445, 446, **teapott** 428, 445, 452
teaspoon 430, 453, 454
teaster tester 71
tea table 426, 445, 448, 452, 453
tea tongs *possibly* the same as sugar tongs, or they may have been used for measuring out tea, though a spoon was the more likely implement for this 443, 451
teen ten 315
teg young sheep of either sex
tegg teg 323, **tegge** 5
tember timber 294
temser fine-meshed sieve 42, 66, 68, 102, 127, 143, 144, 196, 248, 254, 318, 353, 365, **temsor** 160, **temzer** 430
tenant sawe tenon saw 108, 424, **tennant sawe** 79, **tenent saw** 64, **tennt saw** 180
tening tin 309
tenn ten 125, 144, 159A, 245, 324, **tenne** 8, 16, 27, 32, 71, 100, 123
tenon saw thin saw for cutting tenons
tent *not known* 445
teobell table 235, **teobelle** 235
terese terse: cask of 42 gallons 235
testament the New Testament 146, 317
tester canopy over a bed 18, 21, 24, 29, 98, 121, 437, *see also* **teaster**
tester bedstead 157, 158, 211, 266, 368, 377
testor tester 16
thappurtenances the appurtenances 31
thatch plate *not known* 428
ther three 118, **there** 54
therty thirty 247
thicksett stout twilled cotton cloth 425
thimble 317
thinges for gotene articles omitted by the appraisors 70
thirdendale pot holding three pints, *see also* **thyrdendeale**
thirdendeale thirdendale 18
thirteene thirteen 61, 373, 428
thirtie thirty 80 **thirtye** 41, *see also* **thorty, thourty, tirty**
thole stand for a vat 11
thonges tongs 193
thorty thirty 343, **thourty** 149
thoule thole 40
thre three *passim, see also* **ther, there**
thread 413, 430, 450, **thred** 80, 317, 425, **thredd** thread 113
threeping dripping 146
threescore sixty 111, 223
thriping drippiing 364
thrum waste yarn after weaving, used as a coarse filling 111, **thrumbe** 80
thyrdendeale thirdendale 18
tile roofing material 360
tilt tilter 158, 234, 248, 428, **tilte** 100, 176
tilter block of wood for keeping a barrel at an angle 368
timber *passim, see also* **tember, tymber,** *see also* **wod, wode, wodde, wodes, wood, woodd, woode,**
timber bord timber cut into planks 131
timber in the street 373
tin made of tin *passim* **tind** 448, **tining** 216, 235, 308, 363, **tininge** 127, 153, **tinn** 317, 318, 329, 428, **tinneing** 200, **tinnen** 267, *see also* **tening, tynn, tynnen**
tinder box 428, 430, 444, 445, 446, 448
tinn, sheets of 428
tinware kitchen utensils made of tin 386, 431, *see also* **tynne**
tirty thirty 444
to two *passim*
toaster device or utensil for toasting food 428, *see also* **toster**
toasting fork 445
toasting iron 194, 426, **toasting iroon** 127, *see also* **tosting iorn, tosting ire, tosting iron, tosting yre, tostinge irone, tosting yron**
tob tub 325, **tobe** 70, 220, 283, 309
tobacco 328, 369, 425, 445, 446, 450, **tobaco** 191, 317
tobacco bowl dish in which tobacco served 446
tobacco box storage for tobacco 428, 445, 448
tobacco dish for serving tobacco 445
tobacco pot any one of the three above 446
tobacco tongs *possibly* fine tongs for handling tobacco, to prevent the fingers becoming tainted with the smell 369
tod weight of 28lb, often used in weighing wool **tod stone** 18
toe two 168
toerne turn 147
toilight a) Toilette - a type of green cloth used by tailors to protect garments in delivery b) Toilinet – fabric of cotton & silk with wool filling, used for men's waistcoats, usually brightly-coloured 446

tolls tools 50, **tolles** 38
ton tun 38
tone *possibly* tun 157
tonge fire tongs 32, **tonges** *passim* **tongs** *passim* **tongue** 190, **tongues** *passim* **tongus** 301, **tonngs** 261, 269, **tons** 339, **tons** *possibly* sugar tongs 126, **tonuges** 95A, *see also* **tounges, toungs**
too two 38, 101, 129, 130, 132, 160, 191, 191A, 193, 218, 240, 285, 293, 300, 304, 311, 396
toob tub 300, **toobe** 285, 311
tooe two 93
tooles tools 18, 105, 119, 169, 177, 180, 182, 198, 227, 230, 232, 249, 255, 301, 362A
tools 334, 340, 444, 445, *see also* **tolls, tolles, toules, toulls, twoles**
tooth bush 445
tooth drawer dentist's instrument 445
torne turn 51, 68, 113, 278
torne whelle spinning wheel 95A
toster toasting iron 369, 428
tosting iorn toasting iron 229, 297, **tosting ire** 111, **tosting iron** 11, 18, 19, 29, 102, 108, 170, 368, 421, **tosting yre** 61, **tostinge irone** 38, **tosting yron** 100
toth picke tooth pick 229
toub tub 315A, 363, **toube** 312
touch box box containing priming powder for a gun or musket *see also* **tutch boxe**
toueell towel 45
toules tools 312, **toules, working** 131,
toulls 44
tounbouell tunbowl 312
tounges tongs 25, 196, 259, **toungs** 145, 174
tourne turn 28, 351
tow two 51, 54, 55, 71, 118, 129, 205, 292, 408, **towe** 167
towel 111, 143, 150, 202, 211, 359, 369, 446, **towell** *passim* **towelle** 100, *see also* **toueell**
towell wrough with black work towel embroidered in blackwork, a form of embroidery using only black thread 22
toy lanthorne *possibly* a child's small lantern 428
trammell *possibly* a triple drag-net for fish 80
tray 45, 127, 248, 452, **traye** 31, **treay** 95A
tree saddletree 9, 413
tree three 37
treen wood ware 2, 11, 22, 33, **treene** 7, 34, 41, 61, 127, *see also* **trene, trining ware, trinnen ware**
trencer trencher 305, **trenchard** 234, 382, 395, **trencharde** 43
trencher wooden dish *passim*, *see also* **trencer, trenchard, trencharde, trenckers, trentcher, trinchar, trincher**
trenchere 24, **trenchr** 17
trencher rack a shelf for storing trenchers 274, 305, 317, 318, 369, 396, 413, 421, 430, 445, **trencher racke** 363
trenchild trendle 9
trenckers trenchers 95A
trendle tub for making dough 61, *see also* **dough trendle, trenchild, trenhill, trenynge vessel**
trene treen 33, 38
trenhill trendle 6, 9
trentcher trencher 37
trenynge vessell trendle 84
tres trees (for timber) 10, fruit 445
tresle trestle 56, **tressel** 2, 8, 52, 102, **tressell** 21, 37, 41, 45, 52, 176, 404, 444, **tresselle** 8, 31, **tressle** 34, 40, 102, 105, 125
trestle hinged support for a tableboard, used in pairs
trevett trivet 29
trewell trowel 11, 20, 33
trey tray 11, 18
trier drier 146
triffet trivet 147
trifle metall *possibly* cheap pewter 428
triminge cloth placed round the shoulders when cutting hair 113
trinchar trencher 290, **trincher** 222
trining ware treenware 266, **trinnen ware** 103
tripet trivet 452
triping dripping 361
trippat trivet 158, **trippett** 445
trivet iron grid for supporting pans placed close to the fire 129, 446, 449, *see also* **trevett, triffet, tripet, tryvett**
trockel truckle 311, **trockellbed** 235, 285, **trockle** 103, **trokell** 73, 157
trogh trough 82
tronck trunk 193, 285, 380, **tronk** 290, 309, 315A, 342, 343, 355, **tronke** 40
trouckle truckle 27
trough large shallow wooden or stone vessel for mixing, or for filling with animal food 54, 108, 182, 289, 368, 428, 430, 452, **troughe** 41, 387, *see also* **trogh, trow, trowe**
trounck trunk 300
trow trough 1, 105, 147, 259, 279
trowckle truckle 27

trowe trough 38, 120, 125, 127, 153, 154, 225, 323
trowsers trousers 243
troy waite troy weight: system of weights used for fine metal, originallyy from Troyes, France 146
truck truckle 329
truckel truckle 45, 327, **truckell**, 16, 39, 47, 145, 191, 334
truckle (bedstead) low bedstead on casters, stored beneath a high or standing bed *passim* **trucle** 125, 332, *see also* **trockel, trockellbed, trockle, trokell, trouckle, trowckle, truck, trundell, trundle, trundle bed, underbed**
trumpery articles of little value 55,
trunck trunk *passim* **truncke** 29, 45, 58, 147, 248, 259, 274, 277, 284, 319, 344
trundell truckle 172, 191A, 253, 274, 282, **trundle** 140, 147, 153, 179, 185, 194, 224, 226, 248, 263, **trundle bed** 345
trunk heavy chest, sometimes covered with leather *passim* **trunke** *passim, see also* **trounck, trunck, truncke**
tryvett trivet 5
tub *passim* **tubb** *passim* **tubbe** *passim, see also* **tob, tobe, toob, toobe, toub, toube**
tubb to waish glasses vessel in which to wash drinking glasses140
tubb stave individual curved wooden section of a tub or vat 373
tube tub 4, 6, 38, 40, 54, 168, 170, 174, 191, 252, 408
tucker's handle handle fitted with teasels 119, *see also* course of handles
tucker's rack used in finishing cloth 26
tuke canvas fabric 119, 425
tumbrill two-wheeled cart constructed so that the body tilts backwards to empty the load 155, part of the well gear 111, 177
tun vessel holding 252 gallons 1, 377, 452, *see also* **ton, tune, tunn**
tun ton weight 294, 391, 396
tunboale tundish 17, **tunbole** 310, **tunboll** 82, **tunborale** 95A
tunboul 425, **tunboule** 289, 368, 370, **tunbowl** 369, 413, 421, 430, 437, 444, **tunbowle** 24, 31, 40, 102, 241, 249, 345, 373, 424, 448, **tunbowlle** *see also*, **tunnbole, tunn bowl, tunnbowle, tunning bowle, tounbouell**
tundish shallow wooden vessel with a hole in the bottom, used as a funnel in brewing and dairying 56, 146, **tun dishe** 31
tune tun: vessel 47, 52, 112A, weight 294
tunell funnel 222, **tunelle** 38
tungs tongs 290
tunn tun 379
tunn ton weight 154
tunnbole tundish 261, 269, **tunn bowl** 395, **tunnbowle** 187
tunnell funnel 34, 424, 448, **tunell** 216, **tunelle** 38
tunning racking fermented ale 373
tunning bowle tundish 11
tunning tunell tunning funnel 373
tunrelles well workings 95A, *see also* **tumbrill**
tuo two 56, 135, 168
turfes, stuff to make: cakes for firing, made by tanners from the refuse of oak bark 72
turkeywork pile knotted onto canvas in imitation of Turkey rugs,
turkey work'd 369, **turkywork** 301
turky cussion turkeywork cushion 239
turn spinning wheel **turne** 2, 3, 4, 10, 18, 22, 34, 35, 46, *see also* **toerne, torne, torne whelle, tourne, turnne, tworne**
turne for lynnen spinning wheel for flax 11
turne for woollen spinning wheel for wool 11
turneing lave turning lathe 146
turneing toules turning tools 146
turnes *recte* **turves** 65
turning frame *possibly* a frame for a lathe 445
turnne turn 37
turn up bed head one belonging to a bed which could fold away into a cupboard 445
turprit *not known* 220
tutch boxe touchbox 40
tw two 52, 125, 164, 173, 239, 243, **twe** 52
twelfe twelve 292, *see also* **twlve**
twentie 21, 119, 153, **twentye** 119
twesers tweezers 448
twigd bottomd with a base of wickerwork 452
twigg wickerwork 140
twine 317
twist *possibly* garden twine 91
twlve twelve 261
two *passim* **twoe** 92, 153, 157, 227, 263, 321, 332, **twoo** *passim, see also* **to, toe, too, tooe, tow, towe, tuo, tw, twe**
twoles tools 180
tworne turn 16
tymber timber 10, 12, 15, 30, 50, 84, 154, 199, 321

tyn made of tin 154, 159, 177
tynne tin ware 128
tynnen made of tin 31, 144

underback broad low tub into which the wort runs from the mash tub 368, 452
underbed truckle 95A
under peticoat garment worn beneath the visible petticoat 454
under wistcoat sleeveless jacket worn under sleeved waistcoat 454
unthreshed barley 34
uper leder leather for making shoe uppers 300, **upper lether** 201, **upper leather hide** 187
upstand stand for barrel 6, 14, 16, 28, 34, 35, 38, 61, **upstande** 5, 11, **upstond** 79
useing file fine file used in watchmaking 146
usquebah whisky 445
utensell utensil 412
utensil 407, **utensill** 227, 372, 397, 418

valence short curtain round the canopy of a bed 32, 100, 123, 145, 318, 321, 372, **valenes** 157, **valens** 150, 224, 252, 263, 274, 289, 294, 352, 418, 419, **valenttes** 311, **valianc** 171, **valians** 196, **valiauntes** 125, **valiens** 294, 317, **valierne** 140, **valines** 235, **valings** 396, **valins** 212, 330, 348, 406, 438, **valiones** 308, **valions** 194, **vallains** 232, 375, 377, 379, **vallaints** 301, **vallands** 248, 444, **vallans** 266, **vallayne** 111, **vallen** 368, **vallence** 179, 369, **vallens** *passim* **valliance** 272, **vallense** 247, **vallians** 249, 250, 260, 310, 317, **valliants** 301, 302, 303, **vallience** 147, **valliens** 147, 192, 205, 253, **vallin** 379, **vallings** 239, 355, 407, 417, 430, 439, **vallins** 111, 164, 175, 211, 231, 245, 289, 332, 335, 359, **vallions** 186, 194, 222, 295, 357, 425, *see also* **fallens**
vann winnowing fan 15
vardigrace verdigris, used as a medicine 317
varsall vessel 229
vat large container **vate** *passim, see also* **fate, fat, fate, fatt, fatte, vatt, vatte, veate**
vatt 13, 222, **vatte** 37
vattestocke stock (barrel) 72, **vatt stocke** 80
vayle *possibly* curtain; could be rayle (rail) 114
veate vat 47
velle felloe: part of a wheel rim 154, **vellye** 255
velvet 446
ver fir *possibly* pine 177
verges verjuice: crab-apple juice, used as vinegar 6, **vergies** 5
versel vessel 411, **vesel** 396, 442, **vesell** 193, 215, 433, **veshell** 380
vessel large container for liquids 33, 118, 145, 191, 195, 236, 270, 340, 393, 418, **vessell** 15, 32, 41, **vesselle** 32, 100, 133, 141, **vessill** 235, *see also* **varsall, wessell**
vessel timber wood to make woodden containers 340
vetch fodder plant related to peas and beans, *see also* **fatch, fetch**
vether feather 88
viall glase small, thin glass bottle 229
vice an instrument with clamping jaws 38, 92, 169, 177, 182, 211, 319, 382, 428, 430, 445, 448, *see also* **vise, visces, visese, vyse**
vice board mounting for a vice 445, 448, *see also* **viseboard**
vile file 146
viles for springs files used in the making of watch springs 146
vinegar 445
violl, base viol: stringed instrument, held vertically on the knees or between the legs 308
virginals keyed instrument of the harpsichord family 428, **virginalls** 200
vise vice 40, 439, **visces** vices 301, **visese** 146
viseboard vice board 362A
vlocke flock 88
voler *recte* roller: horse equipment 220
vots oats 411
voyder basket or tray used to clear the table of food scraps 140
vyse vice 25

wach bell watchbill 66
wadden wooden 85
waggon wagon 259, 273, 323
waggon hoop *possibly* the hoped framework of a covered wagon 373
wagin blade wagon shaft 154
wagin poole wagon pole 154
wagon four wheeled vehicle for heavy loads 171
wagon pole shaft fitted to the forecarriage of a wagon and attached to the collars of the draught animals 294
wagon stock hub of a wagonwheel 294, *see also* **stock**
waight weight 301, **waighte** 59, 79, 80, 119, 121

waight hundredweight 119
wainescit wainscot 125, **wainescoot** 135, **wainescote** 6, 47, **wainescott** 41, 195, **waineskot** 27
wainscot superior quality oak, imported from northern Europe, often used for panelling 140, 206, 303, **wainscote, wainscot, wainescotte** 29, 31, 95A, 123, 352, 381, 421, 444, **wainscotting** 445, **wainskot** 27, **wainskott** 15, *see also* **wanescaot, wanesecoate, wanscot, wanscott, wanscutt, wanskott, waynescot, waynscot, waynscott, wenscot, wenscote, wenscott, wenskott, weynscot, windscott, winescote, wine scott**
waires wares 21
waiskot waistcoat 151
waistcoat originally a long, thin jacket, with or without sleeves, worn under an outer jacket, the early versions having long fronts and short backs, *see also* **under wistcoat, wascoot, wascote, wascott, wascotte, wastcoat, wastcoate, wastcot, wastcote**
waiste bole waste bowl 140
wait weight 101, 247, jack weight 439, **waite[s]** 64, 103, 153 **troy waites** 146,
waiter *possibly* a 'dumb waiter' or serving table 451
waitt jack weight 332
walking cane 446
walking stick 445, 446
wall candlestick sconce 80
walnut table table of walnut wood 64
wanescaot wainscot 317, **wanesecoate** 115
wanscot wainscot 253, **wanscott** 61, 121, **wanscutt** 287, **wanskott** 85
ware wares 219, 230, 238
wareing (apparel) wearing *passim* **wareinge** 45, 135, 189, 242, 259, 299, 306, 315A, **waren** 341, **warin** 218, 311, **waring** *passim* **waringe** 50, 56, 136, 145, 279, 283, **warrin** 329
warem pan warming pan 325, **warem** 406, **waring pan** warming pan 145, 229, **waringe** 267, **waringe pan** warming pan 154
wares goods made for sale, not to order 61, 178, 237, 245, 321, 365, *see also* **waires, ware, wear, weares**
warmeing warming 171, 212, 213, 224, 232, 248, 262, 278, 281, 295, 297, 298, 317, **warmeinge** 125, 159A, 187, 190, 200, 201, 233, 239, 321, **warmen** 168, 188, 283, 341, 342, 370, **warmene** 126, **warmige** 47, **warmin** 174, 218, 329
warming (pan) container of hot coals used for warming a bed *passim* **warminge** 31, 85, 87, 92, 123, 127, 130, 140, 143, 169, 172, 194, 205, 237, 242, 247, 259, 344, 365, **warmninge** 164, **warmynge** 97, **warneing** 356, **warning** 196, **warninge** 47, *see also* **woreming, wormen, worming**
warming pan 407, 421, 429, 444, **warming pane** 423, **warming pang** 442, **warming pann** 428
warpinge barr frame used to prepare the warp for weaving 33, **warpping barr** 351
wascoot waistcoat 243, **wascote** 313, **wascott** 125, 161, **wascotte** 60
washball soap 317, 430
washe bowle 253, **washinge bowle** 24
washe tubb wash tub 6, **washing tubb** 426, **washtubb** 82, 317, 386, 398, 421, **wasshing tubb** 452
washinge vessel for washing clothes 267
washinge bason basin for personal washing 80
washing stock bench on which wet cloth or clothing was laid to be beaten to release the dirt 33, 40
washt wooll washed wool 320
washvat wash tub 82
wastcoat waistcoat 278, 446, 448, **wastcoate** 96, 97, **wastcot** 51, **wastcote** 20, 51
watch small timepiece worn about the body 114, 146, 436, 441, 445, 446, 452, 454
watchbill weapon similar to a halberd 417, **watch bille** 79
watch string *possibly* a watch chain, or ribbons looped to a watch with seals attached 146, 445
wate weight 22
water buckett 452
water glass *possibly* a tumbler 445
watering pot small water container, in some cases maybe a watering can 445, **water pott** 428, **waterpotte** 113, **watering pott** 368
water shoote construction for directing water over hides to clean them 43
water spout *possibly* a pipe carrying water from the copper to the mashing vats 452
water tubb vat or barrel containg water 452
wather wether: castrated ram 323
watle over the head rod laid on roof timbers to support the thatch 64
wattell hurdle 64

way beame weigh beam 22
wayght jack weight 202
wayght stone weight, usually of iron, used with a beam and scales 28
waynescot wainscot 102, 150, **waynscot** 45, 54, 111, **waynscott** 40, 84, 109
wayt weight 294, **wayte** 15, 45
wayte hundredweight 121, metal weights for scales 317
wear wares 308, 340, **weares** 148
weareing wearing *passim* **weareinge** *passim* **wearing** (apparel) clothing *passim* **wearinge** *passim* **wearring** 40, **wearringe** 70
weareing lynine linen clothing 81, **wearing linene** 71, **wearing lynnen** 29
wearing (apparel) clothing 452, *see also* **wareing, wareinge, waren, warin, waring, waringe, warrin, wearing, wereing, wereinge, wering, weringe, werring, whearinge**
wearing apparell 374A, **wearing apparill** 417A, **wearing apparrell** 112A, 446, **weareing apparell** 362A, **weareinge apparell** 159A, *see also* **weiring apparell**
weather glass barometer 445
weavers loome weaver's loom 60
wedge 2, 6, 13, 28, 52, 108, 113, 203, 424, 452, **wedgge** 37, **wedgis** wedges 297, **wege** 24, 50, 63, 253, **wegge** 33, **wegis** wedges 10
weelbarrow wheelbarrow 386
weight balance weight 445, 450, 452, clock weight 430, hundredweight 8, 68, 83, 368, jack weight 250, 352, 369, 413, 421, 430, 445, 448, *see also* **waight, waighte, wait, waitt, wate, wayght, wayt, wayte, weyte**
weights for scales 2, 68, 108, 127, 194, 250, 310, 320, 365, 369, 394, 398, 418, 421, 425, 428, 430
weiring apparell clothing 438
welbucket well bucket 6, 11, 18, 61, 86, **welbuckett** 26, **welbukut well bocket** 38, 283, **well bokat** 63, **well buckat**
well bucket 2, 45, 47, 176, 424, 431, **well buckett** 9, 16, 29, 72, 92, 100, 103, 110, 155, 177, 183, 249, 373, 452, 453
well throck windlass over a well 40
Welsh flannel very fine flannel 425
wenscot wainscot 64, **wenscote** 221, **wenscott** 127, **wenskott** 37
weoring wearing (apparel) 235, **wereing** 146, 378, 389, **wereinge** 172, **wering** 209, 309, 356, **weringe** 325, **werring** 38
weshinge washing 3, 38, 216
wessell vessel 88
west bond buckell type of buckle for fastening the neck band or stock 448
weynscot wainscot 18
weyte weight 38
whate wheat 160
wheareinge wearing 239
wheat 31, 32, 37, 68, 102, 128, 182, 309, 323, 418, 425, 441, **wheate** 83, 104, 125, 134, 144, 171, 183, 224, 259, 274, 407, **wheatt** 176, *see also* **whate, wheete**
wheel *possibly* the wheel which turned the pinmaker's mills 232, *possibly* a wheel used by a brazier for polishing 428
wheele 25, 37, 105, **whelle** 37
wheelbarrow 398, 431, 437, 444, 445, 453, **whelebarrow** 198, *see also* **weelbarrow**
wheete wheat 174
which witch 27, 174, **whiche** 63
whicker wicker 34
whipcord thick, twill-woven fabric 317, 413
whip horse whip 446, **whipp** 237, 416, 445
whip saw frame saw with a narrow blade 452
whitch witch 144, 391
white bone polished bone for jewellery 455,
white lead compound of lead oxide, used as a paint 317
whitening crushed chalk, used to whiten floors or walls 317
whit erthen white earthen: made of white china clay 229
white plate plain or gilded silver 45
white silver silver 45
white wine 445
whittle blanket 316
whollinge woollen (clothing) 239
wicker made of woven willows 17, *see also* **whicker**
wier wire 146, 153
wig hairpiece 446, **wigg** 430, 448
Wigon ware Wigan ware *not known* 428
willey large deep basket with two handles 34, *see also* **willowe**
willow basket 28,
willowe willey 29, 79
willows *possibly* osiers for basket-making 72
wimble gimlet 146
windo cortine window curtain 363, *see also* **wyndowe curten**
window removable window frame 430, *see also* **wyndowe**

window cloth window curtain 334
window curtain 334, 353, 369, 398, 413, 421, 425, 426, 428, 430, 431, 437, 444, 445, 446, 448, 452, **window curtane** 317, 372, **window curten** 449, **window curteyne** 123, **window curtin** 153, 212, 438, 449, **window curting** 433
window curtain rod 413
windowe curteyne 123
window leades leaded lights forming a window 54
window leaf removeable window including both glass and frame, *see also* **leafe windowe**
window leafe window leaf 105,
window leafes 439, *see also* **leaves for a window**
window screen lattice-work in a frame to fit a window opening 445
window shetter shutters 430, **windscott** wainscot 95A
Windsor chair wooden dining chair with semicircular back supported by upright rods 446
wine *see also* **white wine, made wine**
wine measure 324, 398, 428, 452, *see also* **wynequarte**
wine potte container for wine 100, *see also* **wyne pote**
winescote wainscot 104, **wine scott** 104
winning sheet winnowing sheet: cloth on which the threshed grain was placed to be fanned to blow away the chaff 28, **winnow sheete** 83, **winniwinge sheete** 127, **winoe sheete** 129, **winowing shete** 79, **winuing shet** 66
wippence whippence: the forecarriage of a plough or harrow 386
wire 232, 428, 445, *see also* **wier, wyer, wyre**
wishtub wash tub 66
witch bin made of planks of split wood, *see also* **hutch, which, whiche, whitch**
withes, iron *not known* 31
withy cut branch of a willow tree 452
wod timber 25, 69, 157, 207, 235, 278, **wode** 70, **wodde** 93
wodden wooden 17, 24, 116, 150, 201, **woden** 95A, 188, 207, 308
wodes timber 229
woding fabric coloured with woad 425
wod pile wood pile 206
woemans shoes women's shoes 201, **woemens shoes** 187, 201
wole wool **woll** 16, **wolle** 118, made of wool 33
wollen woollen clothing 31, 58, 103
wollene turne woollen turn 52
wolling woollen 356
womens white chairs chairs painted or upholstered in white, *possibly* specifically for the use of women in their chambers 373
womens sheep gloves sheepskin gloves 383
won one 138, 157, **wone** 138, 157
wood timber *passim* made of wood 33, 52, 398, 424, 428, 445
woodd timber 12, 31, 109, 292
woodden, made of wood 11, 19, 31, 40, 72, 86, 100, 105, 108, 122, 123, 177, 194
woode made of wood 3, timber 33, 111, 118, stock of ?firewood 5, 37, 283
wooden made of wood *passim, see also* **odden, wadden, wodden, woden**
wooden ware treen 170
wood for the fire 344
woodpile stacked wood 28, 29, 45, **wood pille** 47, **woode pyle** wood pile 10
woodwax dyer's greenweed: *genista tinctoria* 98
wool 398, **woole** 189, *see also* **wole, woll, wolle, wooll, woule, woull**
woolen made of wool (clothing) 107, 185, 298, 325, 400, (unspecified) 400,
wooll wool 8, 21, 68, 99, 121, 127, 156, 172, 204, 241, 277, 283, 351, 375, 398
wooll baskette basket for carrying wool 31
woollen clothing 103, 159A, 173, 247, 268, 279, 326, 395, **woolling** 191, 257 *see also* **woolen, woollen, wolling**
woollen cloth 35, 61, 96, 119
woollen tourne spinning wheel for wool **woollen turne** 7, 19, *see also* **wollene turne**
woollen yarn spun woollen thread 351
wooll felles sheepskins with the wool still on 31
woorkinge tooles working tools 9
woosted worsted 223, 243
worcking tools 396, **worckinge tolles** 38
woreming warming 235
worke cussion worked cushion 164
worked tapestry, embroidery, turkey work etc.
workeing board work bench 177, 272
worken worked 406
worker heavy stirring implement used in brewing 452
working beame a support for skins when

defleshing or dehairing 72
working bench 437, 444
working knives knives for defleshing, etc. in parchment making 277
working stuffe tools 73
working table work bench 430
working tools used in spoonmaking 442
working tooles belonginge to his tread (trade) 235
working tooles for a hatt maker 197
work tooles 263, **workeing tooles** 105, 162, 245, 272, 315, 319, **workeinge tooles** 148, 321, **working tooles** 40, 152, 165, 211, 297, 302, 305, 308, 339, 376, 393, **working tools** 294, 377, 413, 422, 428, 437, 439, **workinge tolls** 50, **workinge tooles** 15, 103, 116, 120, 132, 135, 154, 164, 282, 344, *see also* **woorkinge tooles, worcking tools, worckinge tolles**
worme long coiled tube connected to the head of a still, in which the vapour condenses 159, 265
wormen warming 309, **worming** 276
wormseed plant used as a worming medicine 317
wormwood water cordial of the medicinal plant *artemisia absinthium* 445
worsted long-stapled wool and the fabric made from it 16, *see also* **oily worsted, woosted**
woule wool 47
woull wool 95A
wraper *not known* 171
writen written 54, **wryten** 55
wrought metal in a malleable form, produced by puddling and hammering 317, 362A
wyer made of wire 198, 216
wylls wheels 137
wyndowe window 3, 4, 13
wyndowe curten window curtain 31
wyne pote wine pot 123
wynequarte quart measure of wine 18
wyre made of wire 368, quantity of wire 428

yallow yellow 248
yard linear measure of three feet *passim* **yarde** 119, 121, *see also* **yeard, yerd**
yard stick one yard long for measuring cloth 61
yarne yarn 119, 123, 263
yarning made of linen yarn 243
yating yoting 355
yeard yard 61
yeare year *passim*
yearling a year-old animal, *see also* **earling**
yearn yarn 95A, **yearne** 45, 83, 315A
yeating yoting 361, **yeatinge** 259
yeieren made of iron 88
yeined joined 3
yellow brass a paler shade of the alloy, formed by varying the proportion of zinc to copper 428
yeoting yoting 68, **yeotinge** 47, **yeoutinge** 45
yerd yard 96
yeren iron 95A
yett gilt: young female pig 50
yewe ewe 32
yewer ewer 27, 100, 111, 125
ymbrodered embroidered 32
ymplements implements: kitchen 108, chamber 116, weaver's tools 33, **ymplementes** barber's tools113, miscellaneous objects 26, 321
yoateing yoting 143, 289, **yoateinge** 241, **yoating** 102, 108, 130, 262, **yoatinge** 164
yoke wooden shoulder-piece for carrying a pair of pails 373
yore ewer 64
yorn iron bar 253
yoron made of iron 6
yoteing yoting 32, 353
yoting steeping barley before malting 8, 11, 15, 34, 50, 100, 133, **yotinge** 16, **yotting, youtteane** 70, *see also* **yating, yeating, yeatinge, yeoting, yeotinge, yeoutinge, yoateing, yoateinge, yoating, yoatinge**
youghting stones *possibly* stones on which to stand the yoting vat 95A
youre ewer 95A
yre made of iron **yreion** 130
yreware ironware 103
yron iron 129, made of iron 28, 52, 83, 121
yron smoothing iron 4, 61
yuine joined 253

za saw 253
zilt silt 379

BIBLIOGRAPHY TO GLOSSARY

Alcock, N.W., *People at Home: Living in a Warwickshire Village 1500-1800* (Phillimore, 1993)
Arnold, James, *The Shell Book of Country Crafts* (John Baker, 1968)
Aspin, Chis, *The Woollen Industry* (Shire Publications Ltd., 1982)
Bailey, Jocelyn, *The Village Blacksmith* (Shire Publications Ltd., 1989)
Bailey, Jocelyn, *The Village Wheelwright* (Shire Publications Ltd., 1994)
Baily, N., *An Universal Etymological English Dictionary* (1770)
Bristow, J., *The Local Historian's Glossary and Vade Mecum* (Nottingham, 1994)
Britten, James, *Old Agricultural & Farming Words Gleaned from Agricultural Books* (English Dialect Society, 1880)
Byrde, Penelope, *The Male Image: Men's Fashion in England 1300-1970* (Batsford, 1979)
Carew Hunt, P., *Cheesemaking* (Wiltshire Folklore Society, Information Sheet No.1)
Chapman, C.R., *How Heavy, How Much and How Long?* (Lockin Publishing, 1995)
Dartnell, G.E. and Goddard, E.H., *A Glossary of Words used in the County of Wiltshire* (1893)
Halliwell, J.O., *A Dictionary of Archaic and Provincial Words* (1904)
Havinden, M.A., *Household and Farm Inventories in Oxfordshire* (Oxford, 1965)
Hoad, T.F. (ed.), *The Concise Oxford Dictionary of English Etymology* (OUP, 1986)
Hurley, Beryl (ed.), *The Book of Trades or Library of Useful Arts 1811, vols. 1 &2* (Wiltshire Family History Society, n.d.)
Lawrie, J., *Wiltshire Saddlery* (Wiltshire Folk Life Society Information Sheet 3)
Millbank Publications and the National Committee for the 900th Anniversary of the Domesday Book, *Domesday: 900 Years of England's Norman Heritage* (Millbank Publications, 1986)
Milward, R., *A Glossary of Household, Farming and Trade Terms from Probate Inventories* (Chesterfield, 1982)
Moore, J.S., *Clifton and Westbury Probate Inventories 1609-1761* (Bristol, 1981)
Moore, J.S., *The Goods and Chattels of our Forefathers: Frampton Cotterell and District Probate Inventories* (1976)
Needham, S., *A Glossary for East Yorkshire and North Lincolnshire Probate Inventories* (Hull, 1984)
Ogilvie, J., *The Comprehensive English Dictionary* (1864)
Reed, M., *Buckinghamshire Probate Inventories 1661-1714*, Buckinghamshire Record Society Vol. 24 (1988)
Reed, M., *The Ipswich Probate Inventories 1583-1631* (Woodbridge, Suffolk, 1981)
Roberts, E. and Parker, K., *Southampton Probate Inventories 1447-1575* (Southampton, 1992)
Roberts, Hugh, *Downhearth to Bar Grate* (Wiltshire Folk Life Society, 1981)
Seymour, John, *The Forgotten Arts & Crafts* (Dorling Kindersley, 2001)
Skeat, Walter, *The Book of Husbandry by Master Fitzherbert* (English Dialect Society, 1882)
Smith, Ken, *The Blacksmith* (Wiltshire Folk Life Society Information Sheet No.4)
Titcombe, L.J., *The Wheelwright* (Wiltshire Folk Life Society Information Sheet 2)
Wright, J., *The English Dialect Dictionary* (Oxford, 1898)
Wyatt, P. and Staines, R. (eds.), *Uffculme, A Peculiar Parish* (Uffculme Archive Group, 1997)
Yarwood, D., *The English Home* (Batsford, 1969)

INTERNET SITES

www.dedas.com/parchment/uk/recipe.html
www.guildofmodelwheelwrights.org/newsite03/techniques/terms1.html
www.princetonimaging.com/library/mechanical-dictionary/subjects/index.html

OTHER SOURCES

Bath Museum of Costume (Elly Summers, Museum Assistant)
Mr Kenneth Rogers (Wiltshire Record Society)
Royal Pharmaceutical Society of Great Britain (Briony Hudson, Keeper of the Museum Collections)
The Company of Blacksmiths (Clerk)
The Company of Cutlers (Clerk)
The Company of Horners (Len Smith, Clerk)
The Geffrye Museum (Dr Kathy Haslam, Assistant Curator)
The Goldsmiths Company (David Beasley, Librarian)
V & A Museum: furniture, textiles and fashion dept. (Lucy Wood, Senior Curator, and Susan North)

INDEX OF TESTATORS' OCCUPATIONS

INDEX OF PERSONS AND PLACES

All places are in Wiltshire, unless otherwise stated.. M = Marlborough.
Testators' names in bold type. Abbreviations of forenames have been modernised, where possible.
Numbers refer to inventory numbers.

WILTSHIRE RECORD SOCIETY

(AS AT JANUARY 2007)

PRIVATE MEMBERS

ADAMS, MS S, 23 Rockcliffe Avenue, Bathwick, Bath BA2 6QP
ANDERSON, MR D M, 6 Keepers Mews, Munster Road, Teddington, Middlesex TW11 9NB
BADENI, COUNTESS JUNE, Garden Cottage, Norton, Malmesbury SN16 0JX
BAINBRIDGE, DR V, 45 Parklands, Trowbirdge BA14 8NR
BAINES, MRS B M, 32 Tybenham Road, Merton Park, London SW19 3LA
BANKS, MR B H, 16 Velley Hill, Gastard, Corsham, SN13 9PU
BARNETT, MR B A, 22 Martin's Close, Chippenham, SN15 3NB
BATHE, MR G, Byeley in Densome, Woodgreen, Fordingbridge, Hants SP6 2QU
BAYLIFFE, MR B G, 3 Green Street, Brockworth, Glos GL3 4LT
BENNETT, DR N, Hawthorn House, Main Street, Nocton, Lincoln LN4 2BH
BERRETT, MR A M, 10 Primrose Hill Road, London NW3 3AD
BERRY, MR C, 17 Fore Street, Hayle, Cornwall TR27 4DX
BISHOP, MRS S M, Innox Bungalow, Market Place, Colerne, Chippenham SN14 8AY
BLAKE, MR P A, 18 Rosevine Road, London SW20 8RB
BOX, MR S D, 73 Silverdale Road, Earley, Reading RG6 2NF
BRAND, DR P A, 155 Kennington Road, London SE11 6SF
BRITTON, MR D J, Overbrook House, The High Road, Ashton Keynes, Swindon SN6 6NL
BROWN, MR D A, 36 Empire Road, Salisbury SP2 9DF
BROWN, MR G R, 6 Canbury Close, Amesbury, SalisburySP4 7QF
BROWNING, MR E, 58 Stratton Road, Swindon SN1 2PR
BRYANT, MRS D, 1 St John's Ct, Devizes SN10 1BJ
BRYSON, DR A, 125 Walkley Crescent, Sheffield, S6 5BA
BURGESS, MR I D, 29 Brackley Avenue, Fair Oak, Eastleigh, Hants SO5 7FL
BURGESS, MR J M, Tolcarne, Wartha Mill, Porkellis, Helston, Cornwall TR13 0HX
BURNETT-BROWN, MISS J M, Lacock Abbey,

Lacock, Chippenham SN15 2LG
CARR, PROF D R, Dept. of History, 140 7th Ave South, St Petersburg, Florida 33701 USA
CARRIER, MR S, 9 Highfield Road, Bradford on Avon BA15 1AS
CARTER, DR B J, JP PHD BSC FSG, 11 Woodspring Court, Grovelands Avenue, Swindon SN1 4EH
CAWTHORNE, MRS N, 45 London Road, Camberley, Surrey GU15 3UG
CHALMERS, MR D, Bay House West, Bay House, Ilminster, Somerset TA19 0AT
CHANDLER, DR J H, Jupe's School, The Street, East Knoyle, Salisbury SP3 6AJ
CHARD, MR I, 35 Thingwall Park, Fishponds, Bristol BS16 2AJ
CHURCH, MR T S, Mannering House, Bethersden, Ashford, Kent TN26 3DJ
CLARK, MR G A, Highlands, 51a Brook Drive, Corsham SN13 9AX
CLARK, MRS V, 29 The Green, Marlborough SN8 1AW
COBERN, MISS A M, 4 Manton Close, Manton, Marlborough SN8 4HJ
COLCOMB, MR D M, 38 Roundway Park, Devizes SN10 2EO
COLEMAN, MISS J, Swn-y-Coed, Abergwili, Carmarthenshire SA32 7EP
COLES, MR H, Ebony House, 23 Lords Hill, Coleford, Glos GL16 8BG
COLLINS, MR A T, 36 Wasdale Close, Horndean, Waterlooville PO8 0DU
CONGLETON, LORD, West End Farm, Ebbesbourne Wake, Salisbury SP5 5JW
COOMBES-LEWIS, MR R J, 45 Oakwood Park Road, Southgate, London N14 6QP
COOPER, MR S, 12 Victory Row, Wootton Bassett, Swindon SN4 7BE
COULSTOCK, MISS P H, 15 Pennington Crescent, West Moors, Wimborne, Dorset BH22 0JH
COVEY, MR R V, Lower Hunts Mill, Wootton Bassett, Swindon SN4 7QL
COWAN, COL M, 24 Lower Street, Harnham, Salisbury SP3 8EY
CROOK, MR P H, Bradavon, 45 The Dales, Cottingham, E Yorks HU16 5JS
CROUCH, MR J W, 25 Biddesden Lane, Ludgershall, Andover SP11 5PJ
CROWLEY, DR D A, Hambleton House, Duke Street, Hadleigh IP7 5DP
CUNNINGTON, MS J, 1177 Yonge Street, #214, Toronto, Ont. M4T 2Y4, Canada
D'ARCY, MR J N, The Old Vicarage, Edington, Westbury
DAVIES, MRS A M, 283 Longstone Road, Iver Heath, Bucks SL0 0RN
DAVIS, MR L F, 16 Methuen Way, Corsham, SN13 0EA
DIBBEN, MR A A, 18 Clare Road, Lewes, East Sussex BN7 1PN
DYSON, MRS L, 1 Dauntsey Ct, Duck St, West Lavington, Devizes SN10 4LR
EDE, DR M E, 12 Springfield Place, Lansdown, Bath BA1 5RA
EDWARDS, MR P C, 33 Longcroft Road, Devizes SN10 3AT
ELLIOTT, DR J, South Barn, Old Standlynch Farm, Downton, Salisbury SP5 3QR
ELRINGTON, PROF C R, 34 Lloyd Baker Street, London WC1X 9AB
FIRMAGER, MRS G M, 72b High Street, Semington, Trowbridge BA14 6JR
FLOWER-ELLIS, DR J G, Swedish Univ of Agric Sciences, PO Box 7072 S-750 07, Uppsala, Sweden 1972
FORBES, MISS K G, Bury House, Codford, Warminster
FOSTER, MR R E, 129 Lower Road, Lower Bemerton, Salisbury, SP2 9NJ
FOWLER, MRS C, 10 Ullswater Road, Wimborne, Dorset, BH21 1QT
FOX, MS B, 7 Crespigny Road, Hendon, London NW4 3DT
FOY, MR J D, 28 Penn Lea Road, Bath BA1 3RA
FROST, MR B C, Red Tiles, Cadley, Collingbourne Ducis, Marlborough SN8 3EA
GALE, MRS J, 169 Spit Road, Mosman, NSW 2088, Australia
GALLAGHER, MR A, MBE, Manor Cottage, Lower Street, Harnham, Salisbury SP2 8EY
GHEY, MR J G, 18 Bassett Row, Bassett, Southampton SO1 7FS
GIBBS, MRS E, Home Farm, Barrow Gurney, Bristol BS48 3RW
GODDARD, MR R E H, Sinton Meadow, Stokes Lane, Leigh Sinton, Malvern, Worcs WR13 5DY
GOODBODY, MR E A, Stockmans, Rectory Hill, Amersham, Bucks
GOSLING, REV DR J, 1 Wiley Terrace, Wilton, Salisbury SP2 0HN
GOUGH, MISS P M, 39 Whitford Road,

Bromsgrove, Worcs B61 7ED

GOULD, MR L K, 263 Rosemount, Pasadena, California 91103 USA

GRIFFIN, D, C J, School of Geography, University of Southampton, Highfield, Southampton, SO17 1BJ

GRUBER VON ARNI, COL E E, 11 Park Lane, Swindon SN1 5HG

HAMILTON, CAPTAIN R, Amberley, Amesbury Road, Cholderton, Salisbury, SP4 0ER

HARDEN, MRS J O, The Croft, Tisbury Road, Fovant, Salisbury SP3 5JU

HARE, DR J N, 7 Owens Road, Winchester, Hants SO22 6RU

HARTE, DR N, St Aldhelm's Cottage, 5 Stokes Road, Corsham SN13 9AA

HATCHWELL, MR R C, Cleeve House, Rodbourne Bottom, Malmesbury SN16 0EZ

HAYWARD, MISS J E, Pleasant Cottage, Crockerton, Warminster BA12 8AJ

HEATON, MR R J, 16 St Bernard's Crescent, Harlow Road, High Wycombe HP11 1BL

HELMHOLZ, PROF R W, Law School, 1111 East 60th Street, Chicago, Illinois 60637 USA

HERRON, MRS Pamela M, 25 Anvil Crescent, Broadstone, Dorset BH18 9DY

HICKMAN, MR M R, 184 Surrenden Road, Brighton BN1 6NN

HICKS, MR I, 74 Newhurst Park, Hilperton, Trowbridge BA14 7QW

HICKS, PROF M A, King Alfred's College, Winchester SO22 4NR

HILLMAN, MR R B, 18 Carnarvon Close, Chippenham SN14 0PN

HINTON, MR A E, Glenside Cottage, Glendene Avenue, East Horsley, Surrey KT24 5AY

HOBBS, MR S, 63 West End, Westbury BA13 3JQ

HOLLEY, MR R J, 120 London Road, Calne SN11 0AH

HORNBY, MISS E, 70 Archers Court, Castle Street, Salisbury SP1 3WE

HORTON, MR P.R.G, OBE, Hedge End, West Grimstead, Salisbury SP5 3RF

HOWELLS, Jane, 7 St Mark's Rd, Salisbury SP1 3AY

HUGHES, MR R G, 6 Castle Court, St John's Street, Devizes, SN10 1DQ

HUMPHRIES, MR A G, Rustics, Blacksmith's Lane, Harmston, Lincoln LN5 9SW

HUNT, MS S, 24 High Street, Bradninch, Devon EX5 4QL

HUNT-GRUBBE, MR & MRS R, Eastwell, Potterne, Devizes, Wilts, SN10 5QG

INGRAM, DR M J, Brasenose College, Oxford OX1 4AJ

JAMES, MR & MRS C, 20 The Willows, Yate, Bristol, BS37 5XL

JEACOCK, MR D, 16 Church Street, Wootton Bassett, Swindon

JELLICOE, RT HON EARL, Tidcombe Manor, Tidcombe, Marlborough SN8 3SL

JOHNSTON, MRS J M, Greystone House, 3 Trowbridge Road, Bradford on Avon BA15 1EE

KENT, MR T A, Rose Cottage, Isington, Alton, Hants GU34 4PN

KITE, MR P J, 13 Chestnut Avenue, Farnham GU9 8UL

KNEEBONE, MR W J R, Rose Cottage, Barbican Hill, Looe PL13 1BB

KNOWLES, MRS V A, New Woodland Cottage, Stanton St Bernard, Marlborough SN8 4LP

KUNIKATA, MR K, Dept of Economics, 1-4-12, Kojirakawa-machi, Yamagata-shi 990, Japan

LANSDOWNE, MARQUIS OF, Bowood House, Calne SN11 0LZ

LAURENCE, MISS A, 1a Morreys Avenue, Oxford OX1 4ST

LAURENCE, MR G F, Apt 312, The Hawthorns, 18-21 Elton Road, Clevedon BS21 7EH

LAWES, MR G, 48 Windsor Avenue, Leighton Buzzard LU7 1AP

LEE, MR J, 245 Fortfield Road, Whitchurch, Bristol, BS14 9QT

LODGE, MR O R W, Southridge House, Hindon, Salisbury SP3 6ER

LOWE, MRS P, Sunnymead, Old Storridge, Alfrick, Worcs WR6 5HT

LUSH, DR G J, 5 Braeside Court, West Moors, Ferndown, Dorset BH22 0JS

LYONS, MAJ GEN A, CBE, Stoke Farm House, Beechingstoke, Pewsey SN9 6HQ

MARSH, REV R, 67 Hythe Crescent, Seaford, East Sussex BN25 3TZ

MARSHMAN, MR M J, 13 Regents Place, Bradford on Avon BA15 1ED

MARTIN, MS J, 21 Ashfield Road, Chippenham SN15 1QQ

MASLEN, MR A, 8 Alder Walk, Frome, Som BA11 2SN

MATHEWS, MR R, P O Box R72, Royal Exchange, NSW 2000, Australia

Matthews, Canon W A, Holy Trinity Vicarage, 18a Woolley St, Bradford on Avon BA15 1AF
Mattingly, Mr N, 7 St Maragret's Street, Bradford on Avon, BA15 1DA
Moles, Mrs M I, 40 Wyke Road, Trowbridge BA14 7NP
Montague, Mr M D, 115 Stuarts Road, Katoomba, NSW 2780, Australia
Moody, Mr R F, Fair Orchard, South Widcombe, East Harptree, Bristol BS40 6BL
Morioka, Prof K 3-12, 4-chome, Sanno, Ota-ku, Tokyo, Japan
Morland, Mrs N, 33 Shaftesbury Road, Wilton, Salisbury SP2 0DU
Moulton, Dr A E, The Hall, Bradford on Avon BA15
Murray, Ms J, Beechcroft, Haxton, Salisbury, SP4 9PT
Napper, Mr L R, 9 The Railway Terrace, Kemble, Cirencester GL7 6AU
Newbury, Mr C Coles, 6 Leighton Green, Westbury BA13 3PN
Newman, Mrs R, Tanglewood, Laverstock Park, Salisbury SP1 1QJ
Nicolson, Mr A, Sissinghurst Castle, Cranbrook, Kent TN17 2AB
Nokes, Mr P M A, Wards Farm, Ditcheat, Shepton Mallet, Somerset BA4 6PR
O'Donnell, Miss S J, 42 Wessington Park, Calne SN11 0AU
Ogbourne, Mr J M V, Dale View, Redmire, Leyburn, N Yorks DL8 4EH
Ogburn, Mr D A, 110 Libby Lane, Galena, Missouri 65656, USA
Ogburn, Senior Judge R W, 303 West Hahn's Peak Avenue, Pueblo West, Colorado, 81007, USA
Osborne, Col R, Unwins House, 15 Waterbeach Road, Landbeach, Cambridge CB4 4EA
Parker, Dr P F, 45 Chitterne Road, Codford St Mary, Warminster BA12 0PG
Patience, Mr D C, 29 Priory Gardens, Stamford, Lincs PE9 2EG
Perry, Mr W A, Noads House, Tilshead, Salisbury SP3 4RY
Potter, Mrs J, 6 Round Chimneys, Glanvilles Wootton, Sherborne DT9 5QQ
Powell, Mrs N, 4 Verwood Drive, Bitton, Bristol BS15 6JP
Radnor, Earl of, Longford Castle, Salisbury SP5 4EF
Raybould, Miss F, 20 Radnor Road, Salisbury SP1 3PL
Rogers, Mr K H, Silverthorne House, East Town, West Ashton, Trowbridge BA14 6BE
Rooke, Miss S F, The Old Rectory, Little Langford, Salisbury SP3 4NU
Saunt, Mrs B A, The Retreat, Corton, Warminster, BA12 0SL
Sheldrake, Mr, B, The Coach House, 4 Palmer Row, Weston super Mare, BS23 1RY
Shewring, Mr P, 73 Woodland Road, Beddau, Pontypridd, Mid-Glamorgan CF38 2SE
Sims-Neighbour, Mr A K, 2 Hesketh Crescent, Swindon SN3 1RY
Singer, Mr J, 49 Bradwall Road, Sandbach, Cheshire CW11 1GH
Slocombe, Mr I, 11 Belcombe Place, Bradford on Avon BA15 1NA
Smith, Dr C, 102 Calton Road, Linden, Gloucester GL1 5DY
Smith, Mr P J, 6 Nuthatch, Longfield, Kent DA3 7NS
Sneyd, Mr R H, Court Farm House, 22 Court Lane, Bratton, Westbury BA13 4RR
Sopp, Mr G A, 70 Steve Place, Sequim, Washington 98382-9547, USA
Spaeth, Dr D A, School of History and Archaeology, 1 University Gardens, University of Glasgow G12 8QQ
Stevenage, Mr M R, 49 Centre Drive, Epping, Essex CM16 4JF
Suter, Mrs C, 16 Swindon Road, Highworth, Swindon, SN6 7SL
Sweeting, Mrs L, 1 Cooks Close, Creech St Michael, Taunton, TA3 5EA
Sykes, Mrs M, Conock Manor, Conock, Devizes SN10 3QQ
Tatton-Brown, Mr T, Fisherton Mill House, Mill Road, Salisbury, SP2 7RZ
Taylor, Mr C C, 11 High Street, Pampisford, Cambridge CB2 4ES
Thompson, Mr & Mrs J B, 1 Bedwyn Common, Great Bedwyn, Marlborough SN8 3HZ
Thomson, Mrs S M, Home Close, High St, Codford, Warminster BA12 0NB
Tighe, Mr M F, Strath Colin, Pettridge Lane, Mere, Warminster BA12 6DG
Tsushima, Mrs J, Malmaison, Church Street,

Great Bedwyn, Marlborough SN8 3PE
VINE, MR R E, 4 Stickleback Road, Calne, SN11 9RB
WAITE, MR R E, 18a Lower Road, Chinnor, Oxford OX9 4DT
WALKER, MR J K, 36 Southern Avenue, West Moors, Dorset, BH22 0BL, 1990
WARNEFORD, MR F E, New Inn Farm, West End Lane, Henfield, West Sussex BN5 9RF
WARREN, MR P, 6 The Meadows, Milford Hill Road, Salisbury SP1 2RT
WILTSHIRE, MR J, Cold Kitchen Cottage, Kingston Deverill, Warminster BA12 7HE
WILTSHIRE, MRS P E, 23 Little Parks, Holt, Trowbridge BA14 6QR
WOODWARD, A S, 28-840 Cahill Drive West, Ottawa, Ontario K1V 9K5, Canada
WORDSWORTH, MRS G, Quince Cottage, Longbridge Deverill, Warminster BA12 7DS
WRIGHT, MR D P, Haileybury, Hertford SG13 7NU
YOUNGER, MR C, The Old Chapel, Burbage, Marlborough SN8 3AA

UNITED KINGDOM INSTITUTIONS

Aberystwyth
  National Library of Wales
  University College of Wales
Bath. Reference Library
Birmingham
  Central Library
  University Library
Brighton. University of Sussex Library
Bristol
  University of Bristol Library
  University of the West of England
Cambridge. University Library
Cheltenham. Bristol and Gloucestershire Archaeological Society
Chippenham. Chippenham Museum & Heritage Centre
Coventry. University of Warwick Library
Devizes
  Wiltshire Archaeological & N.H. Soc.
  Wiltshire Family History Society
Durham. University Library
Edinburgh
  National Library of Scotland
  University Library
Exeter. University Library
Glasgow. University Library
Leeds. University Library
Leicester. University Library
Liverpool. University Library
London
  British Library
  College of Arms
  Guildhall Library
  Inner Temple Library
  Institute of Historical Research
  London Library
  Public Record Office
  Royal Historical Society
  Society of Antiquaries
  Society of Genealogists
  University of London Library
Manchester. John Rylands Library
Marlborough
  Memorial Library, Marlborough College
  Merchant's House Trust
  Savernake Estate Office
Norwich. University of East Anglia Library
Nottingham. University Library
Oxford
  Bodleian Library
  Exeter College Library
Poole. Bournemouth University Library
Reading
  Central Library
  University Library
St Andrews. University Library
Salisbury
  Bourne Valley Historical Society
  Cathedral Library
  Salisbury and South Wilts Museum
Sheffield. University Library
Southampton. University Library
Swansea. University College Library
Swindon
  English Heritage
  Swindon Borough Council
Taunton. Somerset Archaeological and Natural History Society
Trowbridge
  Wiltshire Libraries & Heritage
  Wiltshire and Swindon Record Office
Wetherby. British Library Document Supply Centre
York. University Library

INSTITUTIONS OVERSEAS

AUSTRALIA

Adelaide. Barr Smith Library, Adelaide University
Crawley. Reid Library, University of Western Australia
Melbourne
 Baillieu Library, University of Melbourne
 Victoria State Library

CANADA

Halifax, Killam Library, Dalhousie University
London, Ont. D.B.Weldon Library, Univ-ersity of Western Ontario
Ottawa, Ont. Carleton University Library
Toronto, Ont
 Pontifical Inst of Medieval Studies
 University of Toronto Library
Victoria, B.C. McPherson Library, University of Victoria

EIRE

Dublin. Trinity College Library

GERMANY

Gottingen. University Library

JAPAN

Osaka. Institute of Economic History, Kansai University
Sendai. Institute of Economic History, Tohoku University
Tokyo. Waseda University Library

NEW ZEALAND

Wellington. National Library of New Zealand

UNITED STATES OF AMERICA

Ann Arbor, Mich. Hatcher Library, University of Michigan
Athens, Ga. University of Georgia Libraries
Atlanta, Ga. The Robert W Woodruff Library, Emory University
Baltimore, Md. Milton S. Eisenhower Library, Johns Hopkins University
Binghampton, NY, Glenn Bartle Library, State University of New York
Bloomington, Ind. Indiana University Library
Boston, Mass. New England Historic and Genealogical Society
Boulder, Colo. University of Colorado Library
Cambridge, Mass.
 Harvard College Library
 Harvard Law School Library
Charlottesville, Va. Alderman Library, University of Virginia
Chicago.
 Newberry Library
 University of Chicago Library
Dallas, Texas. Public Library
Davis, Calif. University Library
East Lansing, Mich. Michigan State University Library
Eugene, Ore. University of Oregon Library
Evanston, Ill. United Libraries, Garrett/Evangelical, Seabury
Fort Wayne, Ind. Allen County Public Library
Houston, Texas. M.D. Anderson Library, University of Houston
Iowa City, Iowa. University of Iowa Libraries
Ithaca, NY. Cornell University Library
Las Cruces, N.M. New Mexico State University Library
Los Angeles.
 Public Library
 Young Research Library, University of California
Minneapolis, Minn. Wilson Library, University of Minnesota
New Haven, Conn. Yale University Library
New York.
 Columbia University of the City of New York
 Public Library
Notre Dame, Ind. Memorial Library, University of Notre Dame
Piscataway, N.J. Rutgers University Libraries
Princeton, N.J. Princeton University Libraries
Salt Lake City, Utah. Family History Library
San Marino, Calif. Henry E. Huntington Library
Santa Barbara, Calif. University of California Library
South Hadley, Mass. Williston Memorial Library, Mount Holyoke College
Stanford, Calif. Green Library, Stanford University
Tucson, Ariz. University of Arizona Library
Urbana, Ill. University of Illinois Library
Washington. The Folger Shakespeare Library
Winston-Salem, N.C. Z.Smith Reynolds Library, Wake Forest University

LIST OF PUBLICATIONS

The Wiltshire Record Society was founded in 1937, as the Records Branch of the Wiltshire Archaeological and Natural History Society, to promote the publication of the documentary sources for the history of Wiltshire. The annual subscription is £15 for private and institutional members. In return, a member receives a volume each year. Prospective members should apply to the Hon. Secretary, c/o Wiltshire and Swindon History Centre, Cocklebury Road, Chippenham SN15 3QN. Many more members are needed.

The following volumes have been published. Price to members £15, and to non-members £20, postage extra. Most volumes up to 51 are still available from the Wiltshire and Swindon History Centre, Cocklebury Road, Chippenham SN15 3QN. Volumes 52-9 are available from Hobnob Press, PO Box 1838, East Knoyle, Salisbury SP3 6FA.

1. *Abstracts of feet of fines relating to Wiltshire for the reigns of Edward I and Edward II*, ed. R.B. Pugh, 1939
2. *Accounts of the parliamentary garrisons of Great Chalfield and Malmesbury, 1645-1646*, ed. J.H.P. Pafford, 1940
3. *Calendar of Antrobus deeds before 1625*, ed. R.B. Pugh, 1947
4. *Wiltshire county records: minutes of proceedings in sessions, 1563 and 1574 to 1592*, ed. H.C. Johnson, 1949
5. *List of Wiltshire boroughs records earlier in date than 1836*, ed. M.G. Rathbone, 1951
6. *The Trowbridge woollen industry as illustrated by the stock books of John and Thomas Clark, 1804-1824*, ed. R.P. Beckinsale, 1951
7. *Guild stewards' book of the borough of Calne, 1561-1688*, ed. A.W. Mabbs, 1953
8. *Andrews' and Dury's map of Wiltshire, 1773: a reduced facsimile*, ed. Elizabeth Crittall, 1952
9. *Surveys of the manors of Philip, earl of Pembroke and Montgomery, 1631-2*, ed. E. Kerridge, 1953
10. *Two sixteenth century taxations lists, 1545 and 1576*, ed. G.D. Ramsay, 1954
11. *Wiltshire quarter sessions and assizes, 1736*, ed. J.P.M. Fowle, 1955
12. *Collectanea*, ed. N.J. Williams, 1956
13. *Progress notes of Warden Woodward for the Wiltshire estates of New College, Oxford, 1659-1675*, ed. R.L. Rickard, 1957
14. *Accounts and surveys of the Wiltshire lands of Adam de Stratton*, ed. M.W. Farr, 1959
15. *Tradesmen in early-Stuart Wiltshire: a miscellany*, ed. N.J. Williams, 1960
16. *Crown pleas of the Wiltshire eyre, 1249*, ed. C.A.F. Meekings, 1961
17. *Wiltshire apprentices and their masters, 1710-1760*, ed. Christabel Dale, 1961
18. *Hemingby's register*, ed. Helena M. Chew, 1963
19. *Documents illustrating the Wiltshire textile trades in the eighteenth century*, ed. Julia de L. Mann, 1964
20. *The diary of Thomas Naish*, ed. Doreen Slatter, 1965

21-2. *The rolls of Highworth hundred, 1275-1287*, 2 parts, ed. Brenda Farr, 1966, 1968

23. *The earl of Hertford's lieutenancy papers, 1603-1612*, ed. W.P.D. Murphy, 1969
24. *Court rolls of the Wiltshire manors of Adam de Stratton*, ed. R.B. Pugh, 1970
25. *Abstracts of Wiltshire inclosure awards and agreements*, ed. R.E. Sandell, 1971
26. *Civil pleas of the Wiltshire eyre, 1249*, ed. M.T. Clanchy, 1971
27. *Wiltshire returns to the bishop's visitation queries, 1783*, ed. Mary Ransome, 1972
28. *Wiltshire extents for debts, Edward I - Elizabeth I*, ed. Angela Conyers, 1973
29. *Abstracts of feet of fines relating to Wiltshire for the reign of Edward III*, ed. C.R. Elrington, 1974
30. *Abstracts of Wiltshire tithe apportionments*, ed. R.E. Sandell, 1975
31. *Poverty in early-Stuart Salisbury*, ed. Paul Slack, 1975
32. *The subscription book of Bishops Tounson and Davenant, 1620-40*, ed. B. Williams, 1977

33. *Wiltshire gaol delivery and trailbaston trials, 1275-1306*, ed. R.B. Pugh, 1978
34. *Lacock abbey charters*, ed. K.H. Rogers, 1979
35. *The cartulary of Bradenstoke priory*, ed. Vera C.M. London, 1979
36. *Wiltshire coroners' bills, 1752-1796*, ed. R.F. Hunnisett, 1981
37. *The justicing notebook of William Hunt, 1744-1749*, ed. Elizabeth Crittall, 1982
38. *Two Elizabethan women: correspondence of Joan and Maria Thynne, 1575-1611*, ed. Alison D. Wall, 1983
39. *The register of John Chandler, dean of Salisbury, 1404-17*, ed. T.C.B. Timmins, 1984
40. *Wiltshire dissenters' meeting house certificates and registrations, 1689-1852*, ed. J.H. Chandler, 1985
41. *Abstracts of feet of fines relating to Wiltshire, 1377-1509*, ed. J.L. Kirby, 1986
42. *The Edington cartulary*, ed. Janet H. Stevenson, 1987
43. *The commonplace book of Sir Edward Bayntun of Bromham*, ed. Jane Freeman, 1988
44. *The diaries of Jeffery Whitaker, schoolmaster of Bratton, 1739-1741*, ed. Marjorie Reeves and Jean Morrison, 1989
45. *The Wiltshire tax list of 1332*, ed. D.A. Crowley, 1989
46. *Calendar of Bradford-on-Avon settlement examinations and removal orders, 1725-98*, ed. Phyllis Hembry, 1990
47. *Early trade directories of Wiltshire*, ed. K.H. Rogers and indexed by J.H. Chandler, 1992
48. *Star chamber suits of John and Thomas Warneford*, ed. F.E. Warneford, 1993
49. *The Hungerford cartulary: a calendar of the earl of Radnor's cartulary of the Hungerford family*, ed. J.L. Kirby, 1994
50. *The Letters of John Peniston, Salisbury architect, Catholic, and Yeomanry Officer, 1823-1830*, ed. M. Cowan, 1996
51. *The Apprentice Registers of the Wiltshire Society, 1817- 1922*, ed. H. R. Henly, 1997
52. *Printed Maps of Wiltshire 1787–1844: a selection of topographical, road and canal maps in facsimile*, ed. John Chandler, 1998
53. *Monumental Inscriptions of Wiltshire: an edition, in facsimile, of* Monumental Inscriptions in the County of Wilton, *by Sir Thomas Phillipps*, ed. Peter Sherlock, 2000
54. *The First General Entry Book of the City of Salisbury, 1387-1452*, ed. David R. Carr, 2001
55. *Devizes Division income tax assessments, 1842-1860*, ed. Robert Colley, 2002
56. *Wiltshire Glebe Terriers, 1588-1827*, ed. Steven Hobbs, 2003
57. *Wiltshire Farming in the Seventeenth Century*, ed. Joseph Bettey, 2005
58. *Early Motor Vehicle Registration in Wiltshire, 1903-1914*, ed. Ian Hicks, 2006

VOLUMES IN PREPARATION

Wiltshire papist returns and estate enrolments, 1705-87, edited by J.A. Williams; *The Diary of William Henry Tucker*, edited by Helen Rogers; *Crown pleas of the Wiltshire eyre, 1268*, edited by Brenda Farr; *The Hungerford cartulary, vol.2: the Hobhouse cartulary*, edited by J.L. Kirby and C.R. Elrington; *The Parish registers of Thomas Crockford, 1613-29*, edited by C.C. Newbury; *Wiltshire rural industry organiser surveys and reports, c. 1938 - c. 1957*, edited by John d'Arcy; *William Small's Notebook*, edited by Jane Howells and Ruth Newman; *Gleanings from Wiltshire parish registers*, edited by Steven Hobbs; *Brinkworth and Charlton court rolls*, edited by D.A. Crowley. The volumes will not necessarily appear in this order.

A leaflet giving full details may be obtained from the Hon. Secretary, c/o Wiltshire and Swindon History Centre, Cocklebury Road, Chippenham SN15 3QN. Details may also be found on the Society's website: www.wiltshirerecordsociety.co.uk.